Small Business Management
An Entrepreneur's Guide to Success

William L. Megginson
University of Georgia

Mary Jane Byrd
University of Mobile

Charles R. Scott
University of Alabama

Leon C. Megginson
University of Mobile

IRWIN

Burr Ridge, Illinois
Boston, Massachusetts
Sydney, Australia

Dedicated to our spouses—
Peggy, Jerry, Addie, and Joclaire

© *RICHARD D. IRWIN, INC., 1994*

Senior sponsoring editor: *Craig Beytien*
Marketing manager: *Kurt Messersmith*
Project editor: *Gladys True*
Production manager: *Ann Cassady*
Art coordinator: *Heather Burbridge*
Cover designer: *Crispin Prebys*
Cover illustrator: *Dan Garrow*
Compositor: *Carlisle Communications, Ltd.*
Typeface: *10.5/12 Times Roman*
Printer: *R.R. Donnelley & Sons Company*

Library of Congress Cataloging-in-Publication Data

Small business management : an entrepreneur's guide to success /
   William L. Megginson—[et al.].
      p.   cm.
    ISBN 0-256-14094-4
    1. Small business—Management.   2. Small business—Management—
   Case studies.   I. Megginson, William L.
   HD62.7.S5943   1994
   658.02'2 — dc20   93–6704

Printed in the United States of America
1 2 3 4 5 6 7 8 9 0 DOC 0 9 8 7 6 5 4 3

Most people seek a sense of meaning, identity, creativity, independence, and achievement in their work and in their lives. One of the best ways to achieve this goal is to become the owner or manager of a small business. Managing such a business, however, is a complex, challenging, rewarding, and sometimes frustrating occupation. Success requires knowledge, desire, and hard work on your part, plus a certain amount of luck.

TO THE INSTRUCTOR

This text takes a practical, down-to-earth approach to planning, organizing, and managing a small business. While based on current research, theory, and practice, the material is presented from a "how-to" perspective, with many practical examples and applications from the business world.

The material explores the role of small business and its growing importance. It also discusses the reasons for and against owning such firms and stresses up-to-date thinking in preparing, starting, organizing, and operating a small business. It explains how to achieve optimum benefits from the limited resources available to small firms and how to plan for growth and succession.

Organization of the Book

Part I, The Challenge of Owning and Managing a Small Business, explains the important role of small business, the characteristics of small business owners, reasons why you should or should not own a small business, some current opportunities and challenges in small business, and the legal forms you can choose for your business.

Part II, Planning for and Organizing a Business, discusses how to become the owner of a small business, how to do strategic and operational planning, the growing opportunities in franchising, how to prepare and present a winning business plan, and obtaining the right financing for your business.

Part III, Marketing Goods and Services, discusses how to develop marketing strategies for producing a product; selling and distributing it; and doing international marketing, marketing research, and other related activities.

Part IV, Organizing and Managing the Business, tells how to recruit, select, train, compensate, motivate, and maintain favorable relationships with employees—and their union, when one is involved.

Part V, Operating the Business, deals with such operating factors as locating and laying out facilities, purchasing and maintaining inventory, and assuring quality control.

Part VI, Financial Planning and Control, explains how to plan for profit, how to budget and control operations, how to deal with taxes, and how to use the computer and management information systems to do these things more effectively.

Part VII, Providing Present and Future Security for the Business, tells how to use insurance and crime prevention for better risk management, how to deal with laws, social responsibility, and business ethics; and how to plan for the future—including estate planning.

Aids to Learning

Each chapter begins with relevant, thought-provoking quotations and Learning Objectives that define what should be learned from the chapter. These are then coordinated with the chapter summary. A Profile, which describes how an actual business or business owner operates, is related to the subject of the chapter. The text—written for the TV generation—provides ample visuals such as photos, tables, figures, charts, checklists, and cartoons, along with real-life examples that illustrate the concepts being discussed. Each chapter also includes a box entitled "Using Technology to Succeed," which explains how to use technology to improve your operations.

Important words or phrases that are defined in the chapter are boldfaced in the text for easy recognition and then defined in the margin. End-of-chapter features are a summary—called "What You Should Have Learned"—which is coordinated by number with the Learning Objectives to help you review the text material; questions to test mastery of the chapter; and a case for you to analyze.

We hope this material will stimulate your interest in small business. We also hope you will identify with the individuals profiled in the text and cases and through them and their experiences learn to be a better owner or manager of a small firm.

Cases to illustrate the material have been selected for each chapter.

Features of the Text

The strengths of this text include simple, clear, and concise conversational writing style, numerous visuals, and the use of applications to reinforce the basic concepts being presented. The prevailing topics of interest to small business owners, such as franchising, computers, taxes and government regulations, estate planning, ethics and social responsibility, preparing and presenting a meaningful business plan, international business, risk management, and—of course—how to plan for and make a profit, have been included in sufficient depth to be meaningful to you and your students. We have included Learning Objectives, a Profile, and a box on Using Technology to Succeed in each chapter, along with a summary, questions, and a real-world case. Some chapters have appendixes to help explain or expand on the text material.

Each chapter begins with philosophical, thought-provoking quotations to pique students' interest in the main thoughts being presented in the chapter. These quotes are followed by behavioral Learning Objectives that prepare readers for what they should learn from the chapter. These objectives are coordinated—by number—with the chapter summary. The learning objectives are followed by a Profile, which is the biography of some person who is or has been involved in small business, or a case involving actual business situations and events in small firms. This Profile provides the tone for the chapter and focuses students' attention on the main thoughts being presented as they read the balance of the material.

Each chapter contains many types of visuals, including photographs, figures, tables, and—where appropriate—cartoons. Examples, illustrations, and real-life vignettes are set off from the body of the text to help students apply the material they are learning to actual small business situations. The most important words and/or phrases defined in the text are boldfaced for easy recognition and the definitions are then repeated in the margin. Footnotes are used to give authority to, and cite the sources of, the material used so that readers can get further information if desired. They are grouped at the end of the book, however, to prevent "clutter" on the text page.

Several end-of-chapter features aid learning. Chapter summaries, called "What You Should Have Learned," are coordinated with the Learning Objectives to provide a basis for better review of the material. Short-answer and discussion-type review questions can be used for student assignments, class discussion, or quizzes. Finally, a case is provided to help students analyze the text material from the point of view of real-world situations.

Important Current Issues Facing Small Business People

We have included topics about which small business owners and managers tend to be concerned. These include an entire chapter on taxes and their payment, business laws, social responsibility, and managerial ethics. Also, topics such as marketing, particularly international marketing; developing and presenting the business plan; and use of computers have been included. Next, the discussions of location and purchasing with an orientation toward retailing and services is included. The expanding roles of small businesses, franchising, women, minorities, and sources of financing are covered from a practical, applications-oriented point of view. Finally, the functional areas are covered from a small business perspective. These features make this an excellent, up-to-date teaching tool, relevant to today's changing environment.

An innovative feature is the *Workbook for Developing a Successful Business Plan,* which provides a hands-on guide for use in developing an actual business plan. This is in addition to the Sample Business Plan, which is an appendix to Chapter 8.

ACKNOWLEDGMENTS

Our thanks go to those who contributed cases, profiles, and examples to the text. Our recognition is shown by the sources at the end of each. Thanks are also due for the many contributions made by teachers, entrepreneurs, managers, professional people, and members of the North American Case Research Association. Our special thanks go to Dr. Walter H. Hollingsworth, of the University of Mobile, and to Dr. Charles E. Scott, Loyola College in Maryland, for their expert contributions to the management information systems and computer areas. We also appreciate the research and writing contributions of Jay and Ragan Megginson.

Comments and contributions from colleagues around the country and the following reviewers were most helpful.
Paul J. Londrigan, *Charles Mott Community College*
Barry Ashmen, *Bucks County Community College*
William Motz, *Lansing Community College*
Kathy Daruty, *Los Angeles Pierce College*

It pleases us greatly to give a resounding vote of thanks and praise to our spouses, Peggy Megginson, Jerry Byrd, Addie Scott, and Joclaire Megginson. Their support, suggestions, and patience have lightened our task. Also, thanks go to J. B. Locke, Rob Sims, Lisa Aplin, Sherron Boone, Karla Blake, Melissa Moody, Lori Patrick, and Jonathan Austin, for the assistance they gave us in preparing the text materials, obtaining permissions, and providing other meaningful assistance.

Gayle M. Ross made a tremendous contribution by preparing the excellent *Instructor's Manual.* It should materially assist teachers in presenting the text material.

We have no adequate way of expressing our sincere appreciation to Suzanne S. Barnhill. This text would not have been possible without her help in editing, correcting, revising, typing, and proofreading. Her contributions have been of inestimable value in making the production of this book possible.

We would also like to thank our colleagues and friends at Richard D. Irwin, Inc., for their assistance in bringing about this first edition: Gladys True, Project Editor; Laurie Entringer, Designer; Crispin Prebys, Cover Designer; Ann Cassady, Production Manager; and our editor Craig S. Beytien.

Finally, we would like to thank President Mike Magnoli and Dean Audrey Eubanks, of the University of Mobile, and the J. L. Bedsole Foundation for their generous support. Without it, we could not have completed this important work.

If we can be of assistance to you in developing your course, please contact any one of us.

William L. Megginson
Mary Jane Byrd
Charles R. Scott
Leon C. Megginson

PART I

THE CHALLENGE OF OWNING AND MANAGING A SMALL BUSINESS

1 The Dynamic Role of Small Business   *2*

2 Why Own or Manage a Small Business?   *20*

3 Opportunities and Challenges in Small Business   *40*

4 Legal Forms of Ownership   *56*

PART II

PLANNING FOR AND ORGANIZING A BUSINESS

5 How to Become a Small Business Owner   *76*

6 Strategic and Operational Planning   *96*

7 Growing Opportunities in Franchising   *116*

8 Preparing and Presenting the Business Plan   *136*

9 Obtaining the Right Financing for Your Business   *166*

PART III

MARKETING GOODS AND SERVICES

10 Developing Marketing Strategies   *188*

11 Marketing the Product   *214*

12 Other Marketing Activities   *236*

PART IV

ORGANIZING AND MANAGING THE BUSINESS

13 Managing Human Resources in Small Firms   *256*

14 Leading and Motivating Employees   *278*

15 Maintaining Good Relationships with Employees   *298*

PART V

OPERATING THE BUSINESS

16 Locating and Laying Out Operating Facilities   *320*

17 Purchasing, Inventory, and Quality Control   *340*

PART VI

FINANCIAL PLANNING AND CONTROL

18 Planning for Profits   *362*

19 Budgeting and Controlling Operations   *384*

20 Taxes and Their Treatment   *404*

21 Using Computers and Management Information Systems   *424*

PART VII

PROVIDING PRESENT AND FUTURE SECURITY FOR THE BUSINESS

22 Risk Management, Insurance, and Crime Prevention   *448*

23 Business-Government Relations and Business Ethics   *470*

24 Planning for the Future   *490*

WORKBOOK FOR DEVELOPING A SUCCESSFUL BUSINESS PLAN   *511*

Endnotes   *535*

Index   *548*

CONTENTS

PART I

THE CHALLENGE OF OWNING AND MANAGING A SMALL BUSINESS

1 The Dynamic Role of Small Business 2

Profile: Michael Dell, Dell Computers: Young Entrepreneur in a Hurry 3

It's an Interesting Time to Be Studying Small Business 4
  The Number of Small Businesses Is Growing Rapidly 4
  Small Firms Generate Most New Employment 4
  The Public Favors Small Business 5
  Increasing Interest at Colleges and Universities 6
  Trend toward Self-Employment 6
  Small Business Is Attractive to All Ages 6
  Using Technology to Succeed: The Whiz Kids Strike It Rich 8
Defining Small Business—No Easy Task 8
  What Is Small? 9
  Distinguishing Small Businesses from Entrepreneurial Ventures 9
  Size, Sales, and Employment 11
Some Unique Contributions of Small Businesses 11
  Encourage Innovation and Flexibility 12
  Maintain Close Relationships with Customers and Community 14
  Keep Larger Firms Competitive 14
  Provide Employees with Comprehensive Learning Experiences 14
  Develop Risk Takers 14
  Generate Employment 15
Some Problems Facing Small Businesses 15
  Inadequate Financing 15
  Inadequate Management 16
  Burdensome Government Regulations and Paperwork 16

Case: Sue Thinks of Going into Business 18

2 Why Own or Manage a Small Business? 20

Profile: Judy Jones' Try J. Advertising Agency 21

Why People Start Small Businesses 22
  To Satisfy Personal Objectives 22
  To Achieve Business Objectives 25
  Need to Mesh Objectives 26
Characteristics of Successful Small Business Owners 26
  Desire Independence 27
  Have a Strong Sense of Initiative 27
  Are Motivated by Personal and Family Considerations 28
  Expect Quick and Concrete Results 29
  Are Able to React Quickly 29
  Are Dedicated to Their Business 29
  Enter Business as Much by Chance as by Design 29
Doing an Introspective Personal Analysis 29
  Analyzing Your Values 30
  Analyzing Your Mental Abilities 30
  Analyzing Your Attitudes 30
What Leads to Success in Managing a Small Business? 31
  Serving an Adequate and Well-Defined Market 32
  Acquiring Sufficient Capital 32
  Recruiting and Using Human Resources Effectively 33
  Obtaining and Using Accurate Information 33
  Coping with Government Regulations 33
  Using Technology to Succeed: Using Electronic Scanners to Study the Market 34
  Both the Owner and Employees Having Expertise in the Field 34
  Managing Time Effectively 35

Case: Victor K. Kiam II: How to Succeed as an Entrepreneur 38

3 Opportunities and Challenges in Small Business 40

Profile: Sherri Hill: Dressing the World's Most Beautiful Women 41

Where Are the Opportunities? 42
  What Are the Fastest-Growing Industries? 42
  Using Technology to Succeed: Technology Lets Taxis Trade Cash for Credit 44

Factors Affecting the Future of an Industry or a
  Business   *44*
Some Practical Ideas for Small Businesses   *44*
Growing Opportunities for Women and Minorities in
Small Business   *46*
For Women   *46*
For Minorities   *47*
Areas of Concern for Small Business Owners   *51*
Poorly Planned Growth   *51*
Threat of Failure   *52*

Case: Shanghai Restaurant   54

4   Legal Forms of Ownership   56

Profile: Bloomin' Lollipops, Inc.   57

Selecting the Right Legal Form   *58*
Factors to Consider   *58*
Relative Importance of Each Form   *58*
Why Form a Proprietorship?   *60*
Why Form a Partnership?   *60*
How a Partnership Operates   *61*
Using Technology to Succeed: How to Form a
  Limited Partnership   *63*
Types of Partnerships   *63*
Rights of Partners   *63*
Why Form a Corporation?   *64*
How to Form a Corporation   *64*
How a Corporation Is Governed   *66*
The S Corporation   *66*
Using Technology to Succeed: It's Legal   *67*
Other Forms of Business   *68*
The Limited-Liability Company (LLC)   *68*
The Trust   *68*
The Cooperative   *68*
The Joint Venture   *69*

*Case: Henry E. Kloss: Proprietor, Partner, and
Corporate Owner   72*

———————— PART II ————————

**PLANNING FOR AND ORGANIZING
A BUSINESS**

**5   How to Become a Small Business
Owner   76**

*Profile: Jerry and Mona Samuel: Combining
Old-Fashioned Newsstand and Modern
Gift Shop   77*

How to Go into Business for Yourself   *78*
Using Technology to Succeed: Computerized
  Business Start-Ups   *79*
How to Start a Business   *79*
Steps in Starting a Business   *79*
Identifying a Needed Product   *80*
How to Decide on a Product   *81*
Choosing the Business to Enter   *82*
Studying the Market for the Product   *84*
Methods of Obtaining Information about the
  Market   *84*
Method Used to Study the Market   *84*
Deciding Whether to Start a New Business, Buy an
Existing One, or Buy a Franchise   *86*
To Start a New Business?   *86*
To Buy an Existing Business?   *87*
To Buy a Franchise?   *91*

Case: Tips for Buying an Existing Business   95

6   Strategic and Operational Planning   96

*Profile: Space Services Inc.: Ushering In the U.S.
Commercial Space Industry   97*

The Role of Planning   *98*
Why Small Businesses Need to Plan   *99*
Why Small Businesses Neglect Planning   *99*
Types of Planning   *99*
The Role of Strategic Planning   *100*
Mission and Objectives   *101*
Using Technology to Succeed: What's Your
  Competition Up To?   *103*
Strategies   *103*
The Role of Operational Planning   *104*
Setting Up Policies, Methods, Procedures, and
  Budgets   *105*
Planning to Operate the Business   *105*
The Role of Financial Planning   *109*
Estimating Income and Expenses   *109*
Estimating Initial Investment   *110*
Locating Sources of Funds   *112*

*Case: ArtWatches: Turning a College Thesis into a $4
Million Business   115*

7   Growing Opportunities in Franchising   116

*Profile: Porterfield Wilson: From Shining Shoes to
Importing Foreign Cars   117*

Extent of Franchising   *118*

What Is Franchising? *119*
   Definition *119*
   Types of Franchising Systems *120*
Why Franchising Is Growing in Importance *120*
   Recent Rapid Growth *121*
   Causes of Rapid Growth *122*
How to Tell Whether a Franchise Is Right
  for You *122*
   Look at the Opportunities *123*
   See What the Franchise Can Do for You *123*
   Investigate the Franchise *123*
   Study the Franchise Offering Circular *125*
   Check with Existing Franchisees *125*
   Obtain Professional Advice *126*
   Know Your Legal and Ethical Rights *126*
The Future of Franchising *127*
   Expected Areas of Growth *127*
   Using Technology to Succeed: Careers USA, Inc.:
    Taking the High-Tech Road *128*
   International Franchising *129*
   Minority Ownership of Franchises *132*
Turning Your Dream into a Reality *132*

Case: *Ray Kroc: Father of Franchising* *134*

**8 Preparing and Presenting the Business
Plan** *136*

Profile: *Jim Busby: Preparing and Using a ''Living
Business Plan''* *137*

Purposes of the Business Plan *138*
Preparing the Plan *140*
   Who Should Prepare the Plan? *140*
   Developing Action Steps *141*
Components of the Plan *141*
   Cover Sheet *141*
   Executive Summary *142*
   Table of Contents *143*
   History of the (Proposed) Business *143*
   Description of the Business *144*
   Definition of the Market *144*
   Description of the Product(s) *144*
   Management Structure *145*
   Objectives and Goals *145*
   Financial Data *145*
   Appendixes *146*
Presenting the Plan *146*
   Writing the Plan *146*
   The Written/Oral Presentation *147*
Implementing the Plan *147*

   Using Technology to Succeed: 20/20
    Hindsight *148*
Sample Business Plan *148*

Case: *Using Computer Software to Prepare a Business
Plan* *150*

Appendix: *A Sample Business Plan: Bradley's Sporting
Goods* *151*

**9 Obtaining the Right Financing for Your
Business** *166*

Profile: *Roy Morgan: Pioneer in Air Medical
Transport Services* *167*

Estimating Financial Needs *168*
   Principles to Follow *168*
   Using Cash Budgets *169*
Reasons for Using Equity and Debt Financing *169*
   Role of Equity Financing *170*
   Role of Debt Financing *170*
Types of Debt and Equity Securities *170*
   Equity Securities *171*
   Debt Securities *172*
Sources of Equity Financing *172*
   Self *172*
   Small Business Investment Companies
    (SBICs) *173*
   Venture Capitalists *173*
   Angel Capitalists *175*
   Other Sources *175*
Sources of Debt Financing *177*
   Trade Credit *177*
   Commercial and Other Financial
    Institutions *177*
   Small Business Administration (SBA) *178*
   Using Technology to Succeed: SBA Goes On-Line
    179
   Small Business Investment Companies
    (SBICs) *180*
   Economic Development Administration
    (EDA) *180*
What Lenders Look For *180*

Case: *Short of Cash? Try Bartering* *184*

—————————————— PART III ——————————————

MARKETING GOODS AND SERVICES

10 Developing Marketing Strategies *188*

Profile: *Byrd Surveying: Marketing a Service* 189

The Marketing Concept *190*
  Determining Customers' Needs *190*
  Meeting Customers' Needs *191*
  Implementing the Marketing Concept *192*
  Seeking a Competitive Edge *193*
Developing a Marketing Strategy *194*
  Setting Objectives *194*
  Choosing Target Markets *194*
  Developing an Effective Marketing Mix *197*
The Product Life Cycle *197*
  Stages of the Product Life Cycle *197*
  Using Technology to Succeed: Your Personal
    Robot *199*
  Need for a Wide Product Mix *199*
Packaging *200*
How to Price Your Product *200*
  Establishing Pricing Policies *200*
  How Prices Are Set by Small Businesses *202*
  Other Aspects of Pricing *204*
Strategy for Marketing Services *205*
  Nature of Service Businesses *205*
  How Services Differ *206*
  Developing Service Marketing Strategies *207*
Implementing Your Marketing Strategy *208*
  The Introductory Stage *208*
  The Growth Stage *209*

Case: *Finding a Special Niche* 212

11 Marketing the Product *214*

Profile: *Mel Farr: Sales Superstar* 215

Choosing a Distribution Channel *216*
  Distribution Channels for Consumer Goods *216*
  Distribution Channels for Industrial
    Goods *216*
  Factors to Consider in Choosing a Distribution
    Channel *217*
Selling through Intermediaries *219*
  Brokers *219*
  Agents *219*
  Wholesalers *219*
  Retailers *219*
  Using Technology to Succeed: Interac Corporation:
    "Your Order, Please?" *221*
Selling with Your Own Sales Force *221*
  Need for Personal Selling *222*
  Steps in the Creative Selling Process *223*
  Attributes of a Creative Salesperson *226*

Advertising *226*
  Types of Advertising *226*
  Developing the Advertising Program *227*
  Setting the Budget *227*
  Selecting Advertising Media *228*
  Developing the Message *230*
  When and How to Use an Advertising
    Agency *230*
  Measuring the Results of Advertising *230*
Merchandising, Sales Promotion, and Publicity *231*
  Merchandising *231*
  Sales Promotion *231*
  Publicity *231*
Considering Ethnic Differences *232*

Case: *Taking Your Store to Your Customers* 235

12 Other Marketing Activities *236*

Profile: *Clark Copy International Corporation's China
Experience* 237

Opportunities for Small Firms in International
  Operations *238*
  Importing by Small Firms *238*
  Exporting by Small Firms *238*
Marketing Research *243*
  How Does Marketing Research Fit into
    Marketing? *243*
  How to Do Marketing Research *244*
  Using Technology to Succeed: Marketing Research
    via Television *245*
  Using Computerized Databases *246*
Distribution *246*
  Storing *247*
  Order Processing *247*
  Transportation *247*
Credit Management *248*
  Methods of Payment *249*
  Setting Credit Policies *250*
  Carrying Out Credit Policies *250*

Case: *To Open or Not to Open?* 254

───────────── PART IV ─────────────

ORGANIZING AND MANAGING THE BUSINESS

13 Managing Human Resources in Small
Firms *256*

Profile: *Compu-Screen Systems, Inc.: Providing
Effective Preemployment Screening* 257

Planning for Personnel Needs *258*
    Determining Types of Employees Needed *258*
    Developing Sources of Personnel *260*
Recruiting and Selecting Employees *264*
    Methods of Recruiting Employees *264*
    Method of Selecting the Right Person for
      the Job *264*
    Orienting the New Employee *268*
Training and Developing Employees *268*
    Need for Training and Development *269*
    Ways of Training Nonmanagerial
      Employees *269*
    Outside Help with Training *270*
Selecting and Developing Managers *270*
    Selecting Managers *270*
    Using Technology to Succeed: Micro Support
      Resource Corporation: Training People to Call
      Back *271*
    Developing Managers *271*
Complying with Equal Employment Opportunity
  (EEO) Laws *271*
    Enforcing EEO Laws *272*
    Terminating Employees *274*

*Case: Supreme Plumbing and Heating Company:
Where Are the Workers?* *277*

14 Leading and Motivating Employees *278*

*Profile: Murry Evans: Developing Winning
Teams* *279*

Good Human Relations Is Needed in Small
  Firms *280*
Exercising Effective Leadership *280*
Communicating with Employees and Others *281*
    What Happens When You Communicate? *281*
    Barriers to Effective Communication *282*
    How to Improve Communication *282*
Motivating Employees *282*
    What Is Motivation? *283*
    Why Motivate Employees? *284*
    How to Motivate Employees *285*
    Some Practical Ways to Improve
      Motivation *286*
    Does Money Motivate? *287*
    Motivation Is More Than Mere Technique *287*
Appraising Employees' Performance *287*
Compensating Employees *288*
    Legal Influences *288*
    Setting Rates of Pay *289*
    Using Money to Motivate *289*

    Compensating Managerial and Professional
      Personnel *291*
    Employee Benefits *291*
    Using Technology to Succeed: Computer
      Specialists, Inc.: Flexible Spending
      Accounts *295*
Need for an Integrated Approach *295*

Case: Personnel Policies Help Intermatic Grow *297*

15 Maintaining Good Relationships with
Employees *298*

*Profile: Mary H. Partridge and Michael Levy: ''His
and Hers'' Businesses* *299*

Setting Up the Organizational Structure *300*
    Some Basic Organizational Concepts *300*
    Some Organizational Problems in Small
      Firms *301*
    Some Ways of Organizing a Small Business *302*
    Preparing an Organization Chart *303*
Protecting Employees' Health and Safety *304*
    Factors Influencing Workers' Health
      and Safety *305*
    The Occupational Safety and Health Act *306*
    Environmental Protection *307*
Counseling Troubled Employees *307*
    Using Technology to Succeed: Combining Idealism
      with Opportunism *308*
    Areas Needing Counseling *308*
    Dealing with Employee Complaints *310*
Imposing Discipline *311*
    Encouraging Self-Discipline *311*
    How to Discipline Employees *311*
Dealing with Unions *312*
    Laws Governing Union-Management
      Relations *312*
    What Happens When the Union Enters *313*
    Negotiating the Agreement *314*
    Living with the Agreement *315*

Case: The Case of Sam Sawyer *317*

——————— PART V ———————

OPERATING THE BUSINESS

16 Locating and Laying Out Operating
Facilities *320*

*Profile: Teague Brothers: Cleaning Persian
Carpets* *321*

Developing Operating Systems   *322*
    What Are Operating Systems?   *322*
    How Operating Systems Work   *323*
    How to Begin Operations   *324*
Choosing the Right Location   *324*
    Why Choosing the Right Location Is So
       Important   *324*
    Some Important Factors Affecting Location
       Choice   *325*
Locating Retail Stores   *327*
    Types of Stores   *327*
    Types of Locations   *328*
Locating Manufacturing Plants   *330*
    Using Technology to Succeed: Autodesk, Inc.
       Designers Get into Their Designs   *331*
Planning Physical Facilities   *331*
    Determine Product to Be Produced   *332*
    Identify Operations and Activities to Be
       Performed   *332*
    Determine Space Requirements   *332*
    Decide on the Best Layout   *332*
    Implement Your Plans   *336*
How to Improve Operations   *336*
    State the Problem   *336*
    Collect and Record Information   *336*
    Develop and Analyze Alternatives   *336*
    Select, Install, and Follow Up on New
       Methods   *337*
Setting and Using Performance Standards   *337*

Case: *Manufacturing Smart Phones   539*

17 Purchasing, Inventory, and Quality
Control   *340*

Profile: *Anders Book Stores: Dealing with Hundreds
of Suppliers   341*

The Importance of Purchasing   *342*
    What Purchasing Involves   *342*
    Why Purchasing Is So Important   *343*
Making Someone Responsible for Purchasing   *343*
Selecting the Right Supplier(s)   *344*
    Types of Suppliers   *344*
    Use Few or Many Suppliers?   *344*
    Investigating Potential Suppliers   *345*
    Evaluating Supplier Performance   *346*
Establishing an Effective Purchasing Procedure   *346*
    Requisitioning Goods or Services   *346*
    Making and Placing the Purchase Order   *348*
    Receiving the Items   *349*

Using Computers to Aid Purchasing and Inventory
    Control   *349*
Controlling Inventory   *349*
    Types of Inventory   *351*
    Costs of Carrying Inventory   *351*
    Determining When to Place an Order   *351*
    Determining How Much to Order   *351*
Operations Planning and Control   *352*
    Handling Variations in Demand   *352*
    Scheduling Operations   *352*
    Controlling Operations   *353*
    Using Technology to Succeed: Instant Travel
       Scheduling   *354*
Quality and Its Control   *354*
    What Is Quality?   *354*
    Improving and Controlling Quality   *355*

Case: *To Make, Buy, or Lease?   359*

———————————— PART VI ————————————

FINANCIAL PLANNING AND CONTROL

18 Planning for Profits   *362*

Profile: *Checkers Drive-In Restaurants   363*

Need for Profit Planning   *364*
How a Business's Financial Position Changes   *364*
    Using Technology to Succeed: Gaining Power over
       Your Money   *365*
    Tracing Changes in a Company's Financial
       Position   *365*
    Importance of Accounting   *365*
What Is the Financial Structure of a Business?   *367*
    Assets   *367*
    Liabilities   *368*
    Owners' Equity   *369*
Profit-Making Activities of a Business   *370*
    Revenue and Expenses   *370*
    Profit   *371*
How to Plan for Profit   *371*
    Need for Profit Planning   *371*
    Steps in Profit Planning   *372*
    Need for Realism in Profit Planning   *372*
Profit Planning Applied in a Typical Small Business   *372*
    Step 1: Establish the Profit Goal   *373*
    Step 2: Determine the Planned Sales
       Volume   *373*
    Step 3: Estimate Expenses for Planned Sales
       Volume   *376*

Step 4: Determine the Estimated Profit   *376*
Step 5: Compare Estimated Profit with Profit Goal   *376*
Step 6: List Possible Alternatives to Improve Profits   *376*
Step 7: Determine How Expenses Vary with Changes in Sales Volume   *377*
Step 8: Determine How Profits Vary with Changes in Sales Volume   *377*
Step 9: Analyze Alternatives from a Profit Standpoint   *378*
Step 10: Select and Implement the Plan   *379*

Case: *What Is Profit?*   *382*

19 Budgeting and Controlling Operations   *384*

Profile: *M & I Ford: "We Don't Have a Budget"*   *385*

What Is Involved in Control?   *386*
  The Role of Control   *386*
  Steps in Control   *386*
  Setting Performance Standards   *387*
Characteristics of Effective Control Systems   *387*
  Timely   *387*
  Cost-Effective   *387*
  Accurate   *388*
  Quantifiable and Measurable   *388*
  Indicative of Cause-and-Effect Relationships— When Possible   *388*
  The Responsibility of One Individual   *388*
  Acceptable to Those Involved with Them   *388*
Using Budgets to Communicate Standards   *388*
  Types of Budgets   *389*
  Preparing the Operating Budget   *389*
  Preparing the Cash Flow Budget   *390*
  Using Technology to Succeed: The Check Is in the Computer   *392*
Using Budgetary Control   *393*
  Controlling Credit, Collections, and Accounts Receivable   *393*
  Other Types of Budgetary Control   *394*
  Using Audits to Control the Budget   *394*
Obtaining and Using Performance Information   *395*
  Obtaining the Information   *395*
  Comparing Actual Performance with Standards   *395*
  Determining Causes of Poor Performance   *396*
Evaluating the Firm's Financial Condition   *396*
  Comparing Your Company's Current and Past Performance   *397*

Comparing Your Company with Similar Companies   *397*
Some Important Ratios and Their Meanings   *397*
  Are Profits Satisfactory?   *397*
  Are Assets Productive?   *398*
  Can the Business Pay Its Debts?   *399*
  How Good Are the Business's Assets?   *399*
  Is Your Equity in the Business Satisfactory?   *400*
  Ratios Are Interrelated   *400*

Case: *How to Deal with Cash Flow Problems*   *403*

20 Taxes and Their Treatment   *404*

Profile: *Jack Bares: Estate Planning to Minimize Taxes*   *405*

The U.S. Tax System   *406*
  Who Pays the Taxes?   *406*
  How Taxes Affect Small Businesses   *406*
  Get Professional Help!   *408*
  Types of Taxes   *408*
Taxes Imposed on the Business Itself   *408*
  Taxes and Fees Paid to Operate the Business   *408*
  Excise and Intangible Property Taxes   *409*
  State and Local Sales and Use Taxes   *409*
  Federal, State, and Local Income Taxes   *410*
  Treatment of Federal Corporate Income Taxes   *411*
Employment-Related Taxes   *413*
  Income Tax Withholding   *413*
  Social Security/Medicare Taxes   *414*
  Unemployment Compensation Insurance   *414*
  Using Technology to Succeed: Magnetic Media Reporting   *415*
  Workers' Compensation   *415*
Personal Taxes Paid by Owners Themselves   *415*
  Taxes on Amounts Withdrawn from the Business   *415*
  Taxes on Amounts Received from Sale of the Business   *416*
Estate Planning to Minimize Taxes   *417*
  Estate Planning Issues   *417*
  Estate Planning Techniques   *417*
Record Keeping and Tax Reporting   *418*
  Maintaining Tax Records   *419*
  Reporting Your Taxes   *419*

Case: *How to Reduce Your Business Tax Burdens*   *422*

21 Using Computers and Management Information Systems 424

Profile: The Maine Line Company: Obtaining and Using Accurate Information 425

Importance of Information 426
Elements of a Management Information
    System (MIS) 426
        What Information Is Needed? 428
        Timing of Information Flow(s) 429
        Choosing an MIS 429
The Role of Computers in Small Business 429
        The Development of Computers for Small
            Businesses 430
        Strengths and Weaknesses of Computers for Small
            Firms 433
        Manual versus Computer MIS 434
        Computers Require Added Security 436
        Choosing Software, Hardware, and Employee
            Training 436
The Accounting System as an MIS 436
        Using Technology to Succeed: The Hawthorne
            Hotel: 19th-Century Hotel, 20th-Century
            Technology 437
        Sales 438
        Cash Income and Outgo 439
        Accounts Receivable 439
        Accounts Payable 439
        Inventory 440
        Expenses 441
        Financial Statements 442

Case: Herman Valentine: Customizing Computers for Military Use 444

Appendix: Some Frequently Used Computer Terms 446

——————— PART VII ———————

PROVIDING PRESENT AND FUTURE
SECURITY FOR THE BUSINESS

22 Risk Management, Insurance, and Crime Prevention 448

Profile: Business Risks International Inc.: Corporate Protection 449

Risk and Its Management 450
        Types of Risk 450
        Ways of Coping with Risk 451

Using Insurance to Minimize Loss Due to Risk 451
        Types of Insurance Coverage 452
        Guides to Selecting an Insurer 452
        Noninsurance Methods for Dealing with
            Risk 457
Crime Prevention to Protect Assets 458
        Armed Robbery 458
        Theft 460
        White-Collar Crime 463
        Document Security 464
        Using Technology to Succeed: Kroy Sign Systems:
            Watch That Sign—It May Be Watching You 465
Safeguarding Employees with Preventive
    Measures 465

Case: Beware of ''Softlifting'' 468

23 Business-Government Relations and Business Ethics 470

Profile: Georgio Cherubini: SCORE Scores a Hit! 471

Understanding the Legal Environment 472
Some Basic Business Laws 472
        The Uniform Commercial Code (UCC) 472
        Contracts 473
        Sales 475
        Warranties 475
        Product Liability 475
        Property 476
        Patents, Copyrights, and Trademarks 476
        Agency 477
        Negotiable Instruments 477
        Torts 477
        Bankruptcy 478
Government Help for Small Businesses 478
        Small Business Administration (SBA) 478
        U.S. Department of Commerce 479
        Other Government Agencies 479
Handling Government Regulations and
    Paperwork 479
        Using Technology to Succeed: The Commerce
            Department Reports by Computer 480
        Dealing with Regulatory Agencies 481
        How Small Firms Can Cope with
            Regulations 482
Choosing and Using a Lawyer 482
        Choosing the Lawyer 482
        Maintaining Relationships with Your
            Attorney 483

Socially and Ethically Responsible Behavior   *484*
    Social Responsibility   *484*
    Business Ethics   *485*

Case: *The Grounded Charter Boat Service*   *489*

24 Planning for the Future   *490*

Profile: *Keeping the Business in the Family*   *491*

Role of Family-Owned Businesses   *492*
    The Family and the Business   *492*
    Family Interactions   *493*
    Family Limitations   *495*
    Family Resources   *496*
    Preparing the Next Generation   *496*
Preparing for Management Succession   *498*
    Why Succession Is a Problem   *498*
    An Overlooked Problem   *500*
Plan Ahead!   *500*

Sudden Departure   *500*
Planned Departure   *501*
Selling to Family Member(s)   *501*
Selling to Outsiders   *501*
Using Technology to Succeed: Let Your Computer
    Value Your Business   *504*
Making the Transition Easier   *504*
The Moment of Truth   *505*
Tax and Estate Planning   *505*
    Tax Planning   *505*
    Estate Planning   *505*

Case: *The Son-in-Law*   *508*

WORKBOOK FOR DEVELOPING A SUCCESS-
    FUL BUSINESS PLAN   *511*

Endnotes   *535*

Index   *548*

I

THE CHALLENGE OF OWNING AND MANAGING A SMALL BUSINESS

Small business is everywhere! When you think of "business," you may think of large corporations—Fortune 500 companies—but if you look around you, where you work and live, you will realize that the great majority of businesses are small. Small businesses are not only numerically significant but also important as employers, as providers of needed (and often unique) goods and services, and as sources of satisfaction to their owners.

For these reasons (and many more), there is hardly anyone who has not at some time been tempted to start a business. Part I of this text is designed to show what is involved in owning or managing a small business. The material covered should help you decide whether pursuing a career in small business is the right course of action for you.

The dynamic and challenging role of small business is covered in Chapter 1. Chapter 2 then discusses reasons for starting a small business, along with some characteristics of successful small business owners. Chapter 3 explores some opportunities in small firms, especially for women and minorities. Finally, the more popular forms of ownership for small business are presented in Chapter 4.

1

The Dynamic Role
of Small Business

There is an entrepreneurial revolution sweeping this country, and it's a great time for all of small business.—June Nichols, Southeast administrator, Small Business Administration

Small businesses may still fail in prodigious numbers, but the small business owner is clearly a winner—an American folk hero, a source of jobs and growth, a role model, a cultural icon. . . . The entrepreneur has been transformed during the 1980s into a courageous taker of risks.—Bernard Wysocki, Jr., small business editor, *The Wall Street Journal.*

LEARNING OBJECTIVES

After studying the material in this chapter, you will be able to:

1. Explain why now is an interesting time to study small business.

2. Define the term *small business.*

3. List the unique contributions of small businesses.

4. Describe the limitations of small businesses.

MICHAEL DELL, DELL COMPUTERS: YOUNG ENTREPRENEUR IN A HURRY

The computer industry is known for its wonder-kids—people who at an early age make huge strides and profits in the profession. You have probably heard of two of the most famous prodigies of the computer age, Bill Gates and Steve Jobs. This trend in the computer industry has continued with the meteoric rise of Michael Dell, CEO of Dell Computer Corporation (DCC).

In 1984, at age 19, Dell began selling computer parts by mail from his dorm room at the University of Texas in Austin. By the end of his freshman year, he was shipping $80,000 worth of merchandise a month. After dropping out of school, Dell created PC's Limited and ran ads in a computer magazine. The results were phenomenal: first year, $6 million in revenue; second year, $33 million; and third year, $69 million.

After hiring a team of veteran executives to help ensure stability, Dell soon expanded his enterprise, making IBM-PC clones. In 1984, he invested $1,000 in DCC. It is now worth $890 million and is ranked 70th on *Fortune*'s "Fortune Fast 100." Dell is projected to be the youngest entrepreneur ever to reach the Fortune 500, beating out Steve Jobs by a year.

Dell's success resulted from two factors. First, DCC is known throughout the industry for making quality products

Source: "Dell Sizes Up Competition in Price War," *USA Today*. August 6, 1992, p. 4B. Tim Dillon, USA TODAY.

and having excellent customer support systems. In 1991, J. D. Power, in its first-ever customer satisfaction survey, ranked DCC first—ahead of IBM, Apple, Hewlett-Packard, and archrival Compaq. Second, Dell computers are inexpensive, often costing hundreds and even thousands of dollars less than comparable units. Dell keeps prices low by selling through mail order, a computer marketing technique he pioneered, eliminating costly middlemen.

The past eight years have been explosive for Dell; however, the computer industry is currently suffering from a glut of companies, resulting in a vicious price war. DCC has already dropped its prices by 20 percent, and Compaq has slashed its prices up to 56 percent. In the middle of this industry ruckus, DCC recently unveiled its new Gemini series, which includes a powerful 486 PC selling for $1,300. Sticking to the basics that have brought him success, Dell says he is ready for a fight with the competition: "They've come into our ring to play our game, and we think we know the game much better than they do." Dell introduced a new line of 18 personal computers in December 1992.

DCC's revenues for 1993 are expected to approach $2 billion, up 122 percent from 1992.

Sources: Various, including "Dell Sizes Up Competition in Price War," *USA Today*, August 6, 1992, p. 4B; Catherine Arnst, "This Is Not a Fun Business to Be in Right Now," *Business Week,* July 6, 1992, pp. 68–69; Alan Deutschman, "America's Fastest," *Fortune,* October 7, 1991, pp. 46–58; Jim Bartimo, "J. D. Power Rates Computers," *The Wall Street Journal,* May 9, 1991, p. B1; Tom Richman, "The Entrepreneur of the Year," *Inc.,* January 1990, pp. 42–43; and "Powerful PCs," *USA Today,* December 2, 1992, p. 1B.

Why start a book about small business with a profile of Michael Dell, who is the youngest entrepreneur to be worth $1 billion? While he is no longer a *small* business-man, he was when he started selling computer parts at age 19. Despite encountering many initial difficulties, he soon hit his stride, and Dell Computer Corporation took off. This is true of most large firms: Almost all were once small businesses!

IT'S AN INTERESTING TIME TO BE STUDYING SMALL BUSINESS

This is an interesting, challenging, and rewarding time to be studying small business. Owning and operating such a firm is one of the best ways to fulfill the American Dream. More than 4 out of 10 Americans believe this is one of the best paths to riches in the United States.[1] Every year, around three quarters of a million people in the United States turn this dream of owning a business into a reality, and many of these dreams become true success stories.

The following are some of the reasons for the increased interest in small business:

1. The number of small businesses is growing rapidly.
2. Small firms generate most new employment.
3. The public favors small business.
4. There is increasing interest in small business at colleges and universities.
5. There is a growing trend toward self-employment.
6. Small business is attractive to people of all ages.

The Number of Small Businesses Is Growing Rapidly

The development of small businesses in the United States is truly an amazing story. As an economic power, U.S. small businesses rank third in the world, behind only the U.S. economy as a whole and the Japanese economy.[2] If small business is this important, how many small firms are there in the United States? The estimates vary from a low of about 13 million[3] to the U.S. Treasury Department's estimate of 19.8 million.[4] The U.S. Small Business Administration (SBA) estimates that there are around 20 million small companies, and that is the figure we will use through-out this text.[5]

More important than the total number of small businesses, though, is the fact that the number of such firms is growing by about 700,000 to 1 million every year.[6] Also significant is the fact that nine new firms are organized for every one that fails, and during a typical year, these businesses generate nearly half of our gross national product (GNP).[7]

Small Firms Generate Most New Employment

In addition to the many other benefits, small businesses contribute greatly to employment, especially in the creation of new jobs. According to R. Wendell

Moore, an official of the SBA, businesses with fewer than 500 employees, representing slightly over half of all private employment, produce the most new jobs. In fact, from 1988 to 1990, during a period of economic contraction, small businesses created 3,107,000 net new jobs, while firms with over 500 employees lost some 501,000 employees, and from 1988 through 1991, *small companies "added all net new jobs in the United States."*[8] According to Kemper Financial Services, employment by the 500 largest U.S. companies fell from 14 million (20.1 percent of U.S. employment) in 1971 to 12 million (10.9 percent) in 1991.[9] Recent Bureau of Labor Statistics figures indicate that around 71 percent of future employment in the fastest-growing industries (such as medical care, business services, and the environment) will likely come from small business firms.

Robert L. Bartley, editor of *The Wall Street Journal*, calls the 1980s the heyday of "an expanding, entrepreneurial economy."[10] Some of the new names that exploded on the business landscape during that time were Microsoft, Lotus, Apple, Sun MicroSystems, Liz Claiborne, and McCaw Cellular.

Finally, small businesses are a particularly good source of jobs for older workers. According to a study for the SBA, businesses with fewer than 25 employees account for more than two-thirds of new hiring of workers age 65 and over.[11]

The Public Favors Small Business

Generally, small business owners and managers believe in the free enterprise system, with its emphasis on individual freedom, risk taking, initiative, thrift, frugality, and hard work. A poll of 2,000 adults by the Roper Organization found that, for these and other reasons, people have a much higher opinion of small firms than of large. It found that 93 percent of the public viewed small companies favorably, while only 71 percent viewed large corporations that way.[12] Also, the public evidently believes that small business should continue to be healthy and to flourish. According to a survey by Comprehensive Accounting Corporation, a nationwide accounting franchise specializing in small business, while 77 percent of those surveyed knew of the high failure rate of small firms, 53 percent of them would still like to own one.[13]

Another indication of interest in small business and entrepreneurship is the large number of magazines and journals aimed at that market. These include older publications, such as *Black Enterprise, Entrepreneur, Inc.,* and *Hispanic Business,* as well as many new ones. Some of these journals are targeted for specific markets. *Family Business* targets family-owned businesses; *Entrepreneurial Woman* aims at female business owners; and *Your Company,* sent free by American Express to the million or more holders of its small-business corporate card, targets small firms. Other journals include *Journal of Small Business Management, Small Business Journal, New Business Opportunities,* and *Business Week Newsletter for Family-Owned Businesses.*

Interest Increasing at Colleges and Universities

Another indication of the growing favor of small business is its acceptance as part of the mission of many colleges and universities, where small business management is now an academically respected discipline. Virtually unheard of 20 years ago, courses of study in entrepreneurship were offered at 417 colleges in 1992.[14]

Community colleges, especially, are now offering courses for small business owners. One study found that 90 percent of community colleges offer such courses, while 75 percent of public community colleges also provide training courses. This activity is "one of the fastest-growing areas in the community college field," according to a spokesman for the American Association of Community and Junior Colleges.[15] Many colleges and universities are now offering specialized business courses, such as programs in family business, franchising, and international operations. Finally, many students are now starting businesses to finance their own education.

For example, Mark Frank went to Washington University at St. Louis to study accounting and finance. He noticed that many students bought items such as computers, VCRs, and microwave ovens at the beginning of the year, then had to cart them home during summer break. He started renting the basement of his house on campus to store the items for other students. With his profits, he bought 100 microwave ovens for about $90 each and rented them to students for $95 per year. After two years, he had earned an $18,000 profit from his basement operations.[16]

According to a long-running survey by the Higher Education Research Institute at the University of California at Los Angeles, America's students are still attracted to the entrepreneurial life. As shown in Figure 1–1, 42 percent of college freshmen in 1991 said succeeding in their own business was essential or very important to them. While this figure was less than the 52 percent in 1985, it was still at about the same level as in the 1970s.

Trend toward Self-Employment

The growth rate for self-employment is greater than the growth rate of the general work force. Small business grew rapidly in the mid-to-late 1980s as investors became more willing to assume the risk of starting or revitalizing small businesses. Many of these were middle-aged executives from large corporations who were eager to put their management skills to work in reviving smaller companies in aging industries.[17]

Small Business Is Attractive to All Ages

Entrepreneurship knows no age limits! From the very young to the very old, people are starting new businesses at a rapid rate. Particularly heartening is the large

Figure 1–1   Tomorrow's Entrepreneurs

Share of college freshmen who say succeeding in their own business is essential or very important

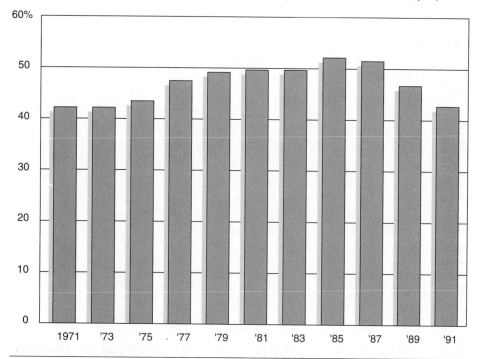

Source: Higher Education Institute, UCLA, as reported in *The Wall Street Journal,* April 6, 1992, p. B2. Adapted by permission of THE WALL STREET JOURNAL, © 1992 Dow Jones & Company, Inc. All Rights Reserved Worldwide.

number of teenagers and other young people who are starting small businesses, as the following example shows.

Howard Stubbs is known as "Mr. Hot Dog" in the South Bronx, an area known for its drug dealers, rubble-strewn lots, and burned-out buildings. As a 15-year-old student at Jane Addams Vocational High School, Stubbs borrowed $800 from friends and relatives to buy an umbrella-topped hot dog cart. Two years later, he grossed $10,000! He buys hot dogs—with all the trimmings—for 33 cents and sells them for $1; soda costs 20 cents and sells for 75 cents. Stubbs works at his stand on weekends, school holidays, and during the summer; he also sells candy at school and gives haircuts to his friends—for $5.[18]

Many student organizations are being formed on college campuses to encourage entrepreneurship. For example, the Association of Collegiate Entrepreneurs (ACE), founded in 1983 at Wichita State University, now has hundreds of chapters

USING TECHNOLOGY TO SUCCEED

THE WHIZ KIDS STRIKE IT RICH

In 1972, at age 26, with a master's degree in aeronautical engineering from Stanford University, Sandra Kurtzig quit her job at General Electric to raise a family. In addition to caring for her two sons, she started developing computer programs in the bedroom of her apartment. She founded ASK Computer Systems to develop and market programs to help manufacturers keep track of inventory and work in progress. She and her company became so successful that she was referred to as the most successful woman entrepreneur in Silicon Valley.

She left ASK in 1985 to spend more time with her two sons. But when the company ran into trouble in 1989—slackening demand hurt earnings—the directors asked her to come back and help revive the firm, which she did.

* * *

William Gates was only 19 when he dropped his undergraduate work at Harvard to found Microsoft in 1975. After producing best-selling business software for companies such as IBM® and Apple®, as well as developing the popular computer game *Flight Simulator*, Gates was worth $313 million when he went public in 1986. His outstanding talents have led him to extraordinary wealth and fame.

Sources: Kevin Anderson, ''Whiz Kids Reap Riches from Offers,'' *USA Today,* February 5, 1986, p. 2B; Andrew Pollack, ''ASK Computer Founder Severs Her Last Ties,'' *The New York Times,* February 22, 1989, p. C4; Stratford P. Sherman, ''How to Beat the Japanese,'' *Fortune,* April 10, 1989, p. 145; and ''Founder Acquires 490,000 ASK Shares,'' *USA Today,* November 20, 1989, p. 6B.

throughout the world.[19] ACE found in one study that a third of all new companies are started by people under 30, many of whom made their fortunes in computers or high-tech industries (see Using Technology to Succeed). Other organizations include the University Entrepreneurial Association (UEA) and Students in Free Enterprise (SIFE).

A word of caution is needed at this point. If you start a business, you must realize that you can't just ''turn it off and on'' like a light switch. That is, you can't take time off whenever you want to. If your business is to succeed, you can't shut down for holidays or vacations or when things aren't going well.

Older people are also involved in forming new companies. For example, a study by the National Federation of Independent Business found that most owners of small firms are in their 40s and 50s.[20] Also, 40 percent of those who form new businesses each year already have some management experience, and one-fourth of them have managed or owned a business before.

DEFINING SMALL BUSINESS—NO EASY TASK

Now that we've seen how much interest there is in small business, what *is* a small business? There is no simple definition, but let's look at some definitions that are frequently used.

Table 1–1   Classification of Businesses by Size, according to the SBA

Under 20 employees	Very small
20–99	Small
100–499	Medium
500 or more	Large

Source: Small Business Administration.

What Is Small?

What is a small business? At first, this question appears easy to answer. Many firms that you patronize—such as independent neighborhood grocery stores, fast-food restaurants, barbershops or beauty salons, dry cleaners, campus record shops, and the veterinarian—are examples of small businesses. However, even with 8,500 employees, American Motors was once considered a small business: The SBA deemed it eligible for a small business loan. Why? Because American Motors *was* small compared to its mammoth competitors—General Motors, Ford, and Chrysler, which bought it in 1987.

Qualitative factors are also important in describing small businesses. The Committee for Economic Development says that a small business has at least two of the following features:[21]

1. Management is independent, since the manager usually owns the firm.

2. Capital is supplied and ownership is held by an individual or a few individuals.

3. The area of operations is primarily local, although the market isn't necessarily local.

4. The firm is small in comparison with the largest competitors in its industry.

Perhaps the best definition of small business is the one used by Congress in the Small Business Act of 1953, which states that a small business is one that is independently owned and operated and is not dominant in its field of operation.[22] We'll use that definition in this text, unless otherwise indicated.

As will be shown in Chapter 9, the SBA, for loan purposes, uses different size criteria by industries. But, in general, it uses the size classification shown in Table 1–1.

Distinguishing Small Businesses from Entrepreneurial Ventures

We also need to distinguish between small businesses and entrepreneurial ventures. A **small business** (or mom-and-pop operation) is any business that is independently owned and operated, is not dominant in its field, and does not engage in many new or innovative practices. It may never grow large, and the owners may not want it to, as they usually prefer a more relaxed and less aggressive approach

A **small business** is independently owned and operated, is not dominant in its field, and doesn't engage in new or innovative practices.

to running the business. In other words, they manage the business in a normal way, expecting normal sales, profits, and growth.

In an **entrepreneurial venture**, the principal objectives of the owner are profitability and growth.

On the other hand, **an entrepreneurial venture** is one in which the principal objectives of the entrepreneur are profitability and growth. Thus, the business is characterized by innovative strategic practices and/or products. The entrepreneurs and their financial backers are usually seeking rapid growth, immediate—and high—profits, and a quick sellout with—possibly—large capital gains, as the following example illustrates.

In 1989, a Sharon, Massachusetts, firm introduced a new, technologically advanced "multipliance" called the MicroFridge. It's a compact combination of a 500-watt microwave oven; a 2.9-cubic-foot refrigerator; and a real zero-degree, 0.7-cubic-foot freezer—with a $429 price tag. It is targeted at college students, office workers, and hotel guests.

MicroFridge is manufactured by Sanyo E&E Corporation with final assembly in San Diego, California. Financing has been provided by the founders and private investors. MicroFridge's cofounder, Robert Bennett, is a classic example of an entrepreneur, for his primary objectives are high profit and rapid growth. Using an innovative idea and an aggressive marketing plan, he hopes to dominate the field.[23]

Photo courtesy of MicroFridge, Inc.

A **small business owner** establishes a business primarily to further personal goals, including making a profit.

It is not easy to distinguish between a small business owner and an entrepreneur, for the distinction hinges on their intentions. In general, **a small business owner** establishes a business for the principal purpose of furthering personal goals, which may include making a profit. Thus, the owner may perceive the business as being an extension of his or her personality, which is interwoven with family needs and desires.

The goals of an **entrepreneur** include growth, achieved through innovation and strategic management.

On the other hand, the **entrepreneur** starts and manages a business for many reasons, including achievement, profit, and growth. Such a person is characterized principally by innovative behavior and will employ strategic management practices in the business.

Of course, the owner's intentions sometimes change, and what started out as a small business becomes an entrepreneurial venture, as the following example shows.

Texas Long Distance, a small Dallas business, was started by Bill Wiese, 65, a retired executive; his wife, Chleo; his son Roger; and his nephew John. The company began by using long-distance lines leased from discounters (such as Sprint) and secondhand switching equipment to find the cheapest route for each call. Bill Wiese said the objective of Texas Long Distance was to have a good time and—hopefully—make some money at it.

But the business became an entrepreneurial venture in 1989 when it evolved into a full-service long-distance company with new switching equipment, more lines, and over 800 customers. With offices in Austin and Houston, as well as Dallas, the firm employed 25 to 26 people, including Scott Wiese, another of Bill's sons. The name was changed to Digital Network Inc., to reflect its new mission.[24]

Size, Sales, and Employment

The Internal Revenue Service classifies 96 percent of American businesses as small.* Yet small businesses generate only 12 percent of the total receipts each year, while the 4 percent of firms that are classified as large generate 88 percent of all revenues.[25]

Still, as has been shown, one of the greatest advantages of small businesses is their ability to create new jobs. Figure 1–2 shows that small businesses† account for 81 percent of employees in all U.S. businesses.

As you can see from Figure 1–3, small firms are more prevalent in agriculture, contract construction, and wholesale and retail trade, where they provide over 90 percent of all employment. Yet they generate the largest number of actual jobs in services (18,975,000 employees), retail trade (17,821,000), and manufacturing (11,917,000). These figures show how important small firms are in generating employment opportunities.

SOME UNIQUE CONTRIBUTIONS OF SMALL BUSINESSES

As indicated throughout this chapter, small firms differ from their larger competitors. Let's look at some of the major contributions made by small businesses that set them apart from larger firms.

Smaller firms tend to:

1. Encourage innovation and flexibility.

2. Maintain close relationships with customers and the community.

3. Keep larger firms competitive.

---

*The definition of small is based on the amount of annual revenue—$1 million or less.
†Those having fewer than 500 employees.

Figure 1–2   Percent Distribution of Business Establishments and Employees by Size of Employer

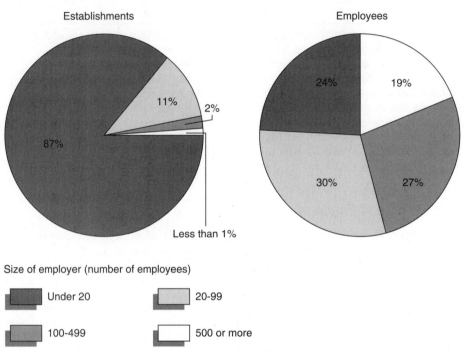

Size of employer (number of employees)

- Under 20
- 20-99
- 100-499
- 500 or more

Source: U.S. Bureau of the Census, *Statistical Abstract of the United States, 1991,* 111th ed. (Washington, D.C.: U.S. Government Printing Office, 1991), Table 873, p. 532.

4. Provide employees with comprehensive learning experiences.

5. Develop risk takers.

6. Generate employment.

Encourage Innovation and Flexibility

Smaller businesses are often sources of new ideas, materials, processes, and services that larger firms may be unable or reluctant to provide. Big companies are usually committed by their investment in personnel and facilities to producing large quantities of product(s) over extended periods of time in order to benefit from economies of scale. Hence, they may not be as flexible as smaller ones. If a small firm is to be successful, then, it must devote its efforts to developing and marketing innovative products and services.

These demands for innovation have forced smaller firms to be able to quickly switch operations in the face of changing market conditions and to adapt quickly to changing demands within their field and capacity. They can even change fields.

Figure 1–3   Percent Distribution of Employees in Large and Small Firms in Selected Industries

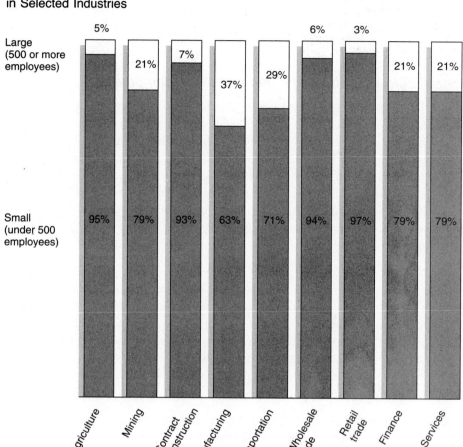

Source: U.S. Bureau of the Census, *Statistical Abstract of the United States, 1991,* 111th ed. (Washington, D.C.: U.S. Government Printing Office, 1991), Table 873, p. 532.

In small businesses, experiments can be conducted, innovations initiated, and new operations started or expanded. As mentioned earlier, many of today's products originated in small businesses. This trend is especially true in the computer field, where initial developments have been carried on in small companies.

For example, it is no coincidence that IBM didn't produce the first electronic computer, as it already owned 97 percent of the then popular punched-card equipment, which the computer would make obsolete. Instead, the Univac was conceived and produced by Univac Corporation, a small firm formed by John Mauchly and J. Presper Eckert. Although they were design experts, they lacked production and marketing skills, so they sold out to Remington Rand, which controlled the remaining 3 percent of the punched-card business. So the first giant computers at organizations such as the U.S. Census Bureau and General Electric's Appliance Park plant in Kentucky were Univacs. Nonetheless, IBM's marketing expertise overcame Remington's production expertise, and IBM soon dominated the computer industry.

Maintain Close Relationships with Customers and Community

Small, local businesses usually have an intimate knowledge of their communities and are usually in close touch with their customers, suppliers, and others in the area. They can do a more individualized job than big firms can, thereby attracting customers on the basis of specialty products, quality, and personal services rather than solely on the basis of price resulting from mass production and mass marketing. While competitive prices and a reputation for honesty are important, an atmosphere of friendliness makes people feel good about patronizing the business and encourages them to continue shopping there.

Keep Larger Firms Competitive

Smaller companies have become a controlling factor in the American economy by keeping the bigger concerns on their toes. With the introduction of new products and services, small businesses encourage competition—if not in price, at least in design and efficiency. As indicated earlier, this is what happened in California's Silicon Valley, where the personal computer was developed.

Provide Employees with Comprehensive Learning Experiences

A small business provides employees with a variety of learning experiences not open to individuals holding more specialized jobs in larger companies. Along with performing a greater variety of functions, small business employees also have more freedom to make decisions. This freedom and the variety of activities and functions can lend zest and interest to employees' work experience, so that small businesses train people to become better leaders and managers and to develop their talents and energies more effectively.

Develop Risk Takers

Small businesses provide one of the basic American freedoms—risk taking, with its consequent rewards and punishments. Small business owners have relative freedom to enter or leave a business at will, to start small and grow big, to expand or contract, and to succeed or fail. This freedom is the basis of our free-enterprise system. Yet founding a business in an uncertain environment is risky. Much planning and study must be done before start-up. Even then, unforeseen changes can occur, so owners must see the need for change, make the right decisions, and make the changes.

Generate Employment

As repeatedly emphasized throughout this chapter, small businesses generate employment by creating job opportunities. A 1992 study by the commissioner and former commissioner of the Bureau of Labor Statistics found that 20 million such jobs were created during the 1980s.[26] Many of these were meaningful, high-paying positions. Small firms also serve as a training ground for employees who then go on to larger businesses as experienced workers. With their more comprehensive learning experience, their emphasis on risk taking, and their exposure to innovation and flexibility, these people become valued employees of the larger companies.

SOME PROBLEMS FACING SMALL BUSINESSES

Just as small companies make some unique contributions, there are special problems that affect them more than larger businesses. These problems can result in limited profitability and growth, the decision to voluntarily close the business, or financial failure.

According to Bruce Phillips, chief economist for the SBA, start-up firms don't fail as often as some people think. He found that 4 out of 10 new businesses survive at least the first six years.[27] He also found that *the vast majority of businesses that close do so for voluntary reasons,* such as the desire to enter a more profitable business, legal changes, and disenchantment, or a family's decision to end the business after the owner's death.

Why do new businesses fail? A Minota Corporation survey of 703 businesses with fewer than 500 employees found that the main reasons are (1) lack of capital (48 percent), (2) no business knowledge (23 percent), (3) poor management (19 percent), (4) inadequate planning (15 percent), and (5) inexperience (15 percent). As you can see, the last four reasons can be summarized as *inadequate management.*[28]

Inadequate Financing

Notice in the list above that inadequate financing is the primary cause of new business failure. *It cannot be stressed enough that the shortage of capital is the greatest problem facing small business owners.* Without adequate funds, one is unable to acquire and maintain facilities, hire and reward capable employees, produce and market a product, or do the other things necessary to run a successful business. In fact, two small business consultants concluded that most start-up businesses fail because of undercapitalization.[29] A later study for the SBA, done by CERA Economics Consultants, Inc., found the same results.[30]

Inadequate Management

Inadequate management, in the forms of limited business knowledge, poor management, inadequate planning, and inexperience, is the second problem facing small firms. Many owners tend to rely on one-person management and seem reluctant to vary from this managerial pattern. They tend to guard their position very jealously and may not select qualified employees, or may fail to give them enough authority and responsibility to manage adequately. Most small businesses are started because someone is good at a specific activity or trade, not because of managerial skill.

Managers of small firms must be generalists rather than specialists. Because they must make their own decisions and then live with those choices, managers are faced with a dilemma. Because the business's resources are limited, it can't afford to make costly mistakes; yet because the organization is so small, the owner can't afford to pay for managerial assistance to prevent bad decisions.

Burdensome Government Regulations and Paperwork

If you want to upset small business managers, just mention government regulations and paperwork. That is one of their least favorite subjects—and with good reason. At one time, smaller firms were exempt from many federal regulations and even some state and local ones. Now, small firms are subject to many of the same regulations as their larger competitors. These regulations are often complex and contradictory, which explains why small business managers find it so difficult to comply with governmental requirements. While most businesspeople do not purposely evade the issues or disobey the law, they are often just unaware of the regulations and requirements.

But, as will be shown in Chapter 23, small businesses often benefit from many of these regulations.

WHAT YOU SHOULD HAVE LEARNED

1. This is a challenging and rewarding time to be studying small business because the field is popular and is expected to continue growing in employment and productivity. The public attitude toward small business is favorable, and self-employment is so popular that around 750,000 people each year—young and old—start their own businesses.

2. Defining *small business* is difficult because the definition of smallness varies widely. In general, a small business is independently owned and operated and is not dominant in its field of operation. It is difficult to draw a clear distinction between a small business and an entrepreneurial venture, as this depends on the intentions of the owners. If they start a small business and want it to stay small, it is a small business. If, on the other hand, they start small but

plan to grow big, it is an entrepreneurial venture. Although 96 percent of U.S. businesses are small, they generate only 12 percent of the total receipts each year. Also, firms with fewer than 500 employees account for 81 percent of existing jobs.

3.   Small firms differ from large ones in many ways, but the unique advantages of small firms include *(a)* flexibility and room for innovation; *(b)* the ability to maintain close relationships with customers and the community; *(c)* the competition they provide, which forces larger companies to remain competitive; *(d)* the opportunity they give employees to gain experience in many areas; *(e)* the challenge and freedom they offer to risk takers; and *(f)* the employment opportunities they generate.

4.   Some of the problems that plague small companies more than larger ones— and place limitations on their development—are *(a)* inadequate financing, *(b)* inadequate management (especially as the firm grows), and *(c)* burdensome government regulations and paperwork.

QUESTIONS FOR DISCUSSION

1. Do you agree that this is an interesting time to be studying small business? Why are you doing so?

2. All of us have personal experiences with small business—as an owner, an employee, a friend, or a relative of an owner, or in other relationships. Explain one or more such experience(s) you have recently had.

3. What comes to your mind when you think of a small business? How does your concept differ from the definition given in this chapter?

4. Distinguish between a small business and an entrepreneurial venture. If you were to start your own business, which would you wish it to be? Why?

5. How do you explain the growing interest young people have in small business? Relate this to your personal small business experience.

6. What are the unique contributions of small businesses? Give examples of each from your own experience owning or working in a small business or from small businesses that you patronize.

7. What are some of the problems facing small businesses? Again, give examples from your experience.

SUE THINKS OF GOING INTO BUSINESS

Sue Ley had been a truck driver for a local oil company for about four years. Before that, she had worked as a forklift truck operator in the same company. In a recent interview, she said, "I was getting fed up with this type of work. I like working with people and thought I'd like to get into selling. One day a friend in personnel, when I indicated interest in getting into marketing, called my attention to the company's education program, which pays tuition for employees taking college courses. So I applied for it and was accepted."

Sue, whom the interviewers found to be a woman of above-average intelligence, personality, and drive, enrolled in the marketing program at the local university. She completed her marketing coursework and graduated in three years with a business administration degree. She had continued driving the truck while working on her degree.

When she approached her employer about the possibility of transferring to the marketing department, she was told that it would be "four or five years" before there would be an opening for her.

A short time after that, Sue's uncle suggested that she go into business for herself. The uncle, who had taken over Sue's grandfather's steel oil drum cleaning business about 200 miles away, advised her that she could make around $100,000 per year ($300,000 by the third year) if she started and ran a business of this sort. He offered to help her form a business and get it started.

Sue, who had been married and had two grown children, said, "I could not see any future with the oil company in marketing, and I did not want to drive trucks the rest of my life. I had saved $25,000 that I could put into the business. Why not?"

QUESTIONS

1. What do you see as Sue's alternatives?
2. What are Sue's qualifications for going into business for herself?
3. What are Sue's deficiencies?
4. What do you think of Sue's uncle's profit predictions?
5. What do you recommend that Sue do?

Source: Prepared by William M. Spain, Service Corps of Retired Executives (SCORE), and Charles R. Scott, University of Alabama.

2

Why Own or Manage a Small Business?

Entrepreneurship isn't an event, it's a career. True entrepreneurs do it over and over again whether they succeed or fail. — Charles W. Hofer, professor of management, University of Georgia

Guts, brains, and determination—key ingredients of the American entrepreneurial spirit—[have] sustained this nation through good times and bad, and launched it on an economic journey unlike any ever witnessed in history. — John Sloan, Jr. president and CEO, National Federation of Independent Business

LEARNING OBJECTIVES

After studying the material in this chapter, you will be able to:

1. Explain why people start small businesses.

2. Describe the characteristics of successful small business owners.

3. Assess how qualified you are to be a small business owner.

4. Explain the requirements for success in small business.

JUDY JONES'S TRY J. ADVERTISING AGENCY

Judith Anne Jones's advertising agency, Try J. Advertising, of Carlsbad, California, sells service! It specializes in automobile dealerships such as Toyota Carlsbad, and Lexus Carlsbad. When asked what started her in business, Jones gave the following answer:

I was attracted to creative writing by my father, Scott W. Irwin, who was an announcer, copywriter, advertising manager, and manager of a radio station in Baton Rouge, Louisiana. My mother's career, library work, also influenced my career, as her dedication to her field set an example to me and gave me the opportunity to go to college. I studied advertising in the School of Journalism at Louisiana State University, including taking extra courses during summers to achieve a certificate of specialization in public relations.

After graduating in 1976, I became a field reporter for the *Louisiana Contractor Magazine,* which led to my first pair of work boots and hard hat. After three years, I transferred to the *San Diego Contractor Magazine.* My stay there was brief, as I had to sell ads in Los Angeles two weeks out of every month. Its smog and crowded freeways energized me to start my own business in Carlsbad.

After being marketing director for Wendy's Old-Fashioned Hamburgers' San Diego County Region, I joined the Ad Group,

Source: Correspondence and communication with Judith Anne Jones.

Judy Jones
Photo courtesy of Judy Jones.

an advertising agency, as the account executive for one of its main accounts, the San Diego Toyota Dealers' Advertising Association. One of the dealers appreciated my work so much he offered me a position at his store, Toyota Carlsbad, from which I started my own ad agency in 1981.

Try J. Advertising, Inc., was incorporated with Judy Jones as president and equal shareholder with Louis V. Jones, president of Toyota Carlsbad. The two later married, and Judy bought out his interest. In addition to Ms. Jones, the agency's staff consists of an account executive, who works four days a week; a computer technician, who develops graphic cuts; and a bookkeeper who works as an independent contractor.

Jones and her people (1) provide for clients' printing needs by acting as their agent; (2) prepare items such as business cards, letterheads, and stationery; (3) prepare and distribute newsletters to clients' employees and customers; (4) write and print direct mail pieces; (5) produce training videos; (6) write and produce radio, newspaper, and television ads; and (7) plan special events, such as grand openings and new model introductions.

Table 2–1   Why People Start Small Businesses

Reason	Percent Answering
To be own boss, with more control over their work and lives	38
For the money	24
The opportunity presented itself	21
Took over family business	10
Wanted to be an entrepreneur	7

Source: 1991 MasterCard BusinessCard Small Business Survey poll of 405 owners of businesses with 100 or fewer employees, as reported in "Poll: Most Like Being Own Boss," *USA Today,* May 6, 1991, p. 18. Copyright 1991, USA TODAY. Reprinted with permission.

Now that you've seen the dynamic role played by small business, it's time to see what is needed to succeed in owning such a business. Also, it's time for you to determine whether you have the qualities needed to succeed in small business.

WHY PEOPLE START SMALL BUSINESSES

Owning a small business provides an excellent opportunity to satisfy personal objectives while achieving the firm's business objectives. Probably in no other occupation or profession is this as true. But there are almost as many different reasons for starting small businesses as there are small business owners.

To Satisfy Personal Objectives

Small business owners have the potential to fulfill many personal goals. In fact, owning a small business tends to satisfy most of our work goals. According to a survey for the magazine *Working Woman,* these goals are to (1) do a good job, (2) be challenged, (3) improve ourselves, (4) attain financial security, (5) be independent, and (6) show our abilities.[1] How these personal objectives are achieved depends on the knowledge, skills, and personal traits owners bring to the business.

The objectives of owners of small businesses differ from those of managers of larger firms.[2] Managers of large firms tend to seek security, place, power, prestige, high income, and benefits. By contrast, the primary objectives of small business owners are to:

1. Achieve independence.

2. Obtain additional income.

3. Help their families.

4. Provide products not available elsewhere.

In summary, as shown in Table 2–1, small business owners tend to be achievement oriented, as opposed to managers of large firms, who tend to be power and prestige oriented.

Figure 2–1   Which Road to Take?

To Achieve Independence

While all of the above objectives may lead someone to own a small business, the owner's primary motive is usually independence (see Figure 2–1), that is, freedom from interference or control by superiors. Small businesspeople tend to want autonomy to exercise their initiative and ambition; this freedom often results in innovations and leads to greater flexibility, which is one of the virtues of small businesses. People who operate small firms know they are running a risk when they strike out on their own, but they hope to realize their goal of independence. In essence, owning your own business provides a feeling of satisfaction that may be missing if you manage a firm someone else has built.

To Obtain Additional Income

Many people start a business in order to obtain needed income. This need varies with different people. For example, a retired person may want to earn just enough to supplement Social Security payments and possibly provide a few luxuries; that person may be content with a business that provides a small supplement to retirement income, as the example on the following page illustrates.

On the other hand, owning a business can provide the opportunity to make a great deal of money and to take advantage of certain tax benefits.* In fact, you are 10 times more likely to become a millionaire by owning your own business than by working for someone else. America's typical millionaire is a small business entrepreneur, a 57-year-old man who works six days a week, "has mud on his

*You should consult your lawyers and tax accountants, though, to make sure you stay on the right side of tax laws, which have been modified to remove many of these benefits!

Margaret Williamson began sewing when she was 10. She learned much from her mother and from home economics classes in high school. In the mid-1930s, she was employed by a government works program, the WPA, and later she sewed for her family, making all her daughter's school clothes.

In the 1960s, Mrs. Williamson began making and selling handicrafts to boost her Social Security income. The Alabama Cooperative Extension Service advised her on marketing her crafts, with instructions on how to participate in craft shows and how to make effective displays. This training gave her the opportunity to participate in many local craft shows and school bazaars, and she has displayed items in local beauty shops and schools.

Photo courtesy of Barbara Smith, Mobile College.

shoes, drives a second-hand car, and has been married to the same woman for 32 years."[3] Yet not all small business owners and managers make a lot of money.

At times, a person may start a small business in order to survive after being unable to find employment elsewhere or being discharged from a larger firm. Small businesses are often founded by athletes, whose bodies are a wasting asset and who must retire early. For example, Roger Staubach, former quarterback for the Dallas Cowboys, is the owner of a multimillion-dollar real estate business.[4]

To Help Their Families

Small business owners are probably motivated as much by personal and family considerations as by the desire for profit. Students may return home to operate the family business so their parents can retire or take life easier. They may form a business to help their family financially or take over the firm upon the death of a parent.

To Provide Products Not Available Elsewhere

The saying "Necessity is the mother of invention" applies to the beginning of many firms. In fact, most American economic development has resulted from innovations born in small firms. Relative to the number of people employed, small firms produce two-and-a-half times as many new ideas and products as large firms.[5] The first air conditioner, airplane, automobile, instant camera, jet engine, helicopter, office copier, heart pacemaker, foam fire extinguisher, quick-frozen foods, sliced and wrapped bread, vacuum tube, zipper, and safety razor—not to mention the first giant computer, as well as many other breakthroughs—either resulted from the creativity found in small companies or led to the creation of a new business.

To Achieve Business Objectives

One of the most important functions the business owner must perform is setting **objectives**, which are the ends toward which all the activities of the company will be aimed. Essentially, objectives determine the character of the firm, for they give the business its direction and provide standards by which to measure individual performance.

Objectives are the goals toward which the activities of the business are directed.

Among the objectives that are important to a business are (1) service, (2) profit, (3) social, and (4) growth. These objectives tend to be interrelated. For example, the service objective must be achieved in order to attain the profit objective. Yet profits must be made if the business is to continue to reach its social and service objectives. Growth depends on attaining both profit *and* social objectives, which are not necessarily incompatible.

Service Objective

In general, the objective of a business is to serve customers by producing and selling goods or services (or the satisfactions associated with them) at a cost that will ensure a fair price to the consumer and adequate profits for the owners. Thus, a person who aspires to operate a small business *must set service as the primary objective—but seek profit as a natural consequence*. The pragmatic test for a small firm is this: If the firm ceases to give service, it will go out of business; if profits do not result, the owners will cease operations.

Profit Objective

We expect a private business to receive a profit from its operations because profit is acceptable in a free-enterprise economy and is considered to be in the public interest. Simply stated, the **profit motive** is entering a business to make a profit, which is the reward for taking risks. Profits are needed to create new jobs, acquire new facilities, and develop new products. Profits are not self-generating, however; they result from satisfying the customers' demand for a product. Goods or services must therefore be produced at a low enough cost to permit the firm to make a profit while charging customers a price they are willing and able to pay.

The **profit motive** is expecting to make a profit as the reward for taking the risk of starting and running the business.

Profits, then, are the reward for accepting business risks and performing an economic service. They are needed to assure the continuity of a business.

Social Objective

As discussed further in Chapter 23, successful small businesses must have **social objectives**, which means helping all groups in the community, including customers, employees, suppliers, the government, and the community itself. Even small

Social objectives are goals regarding assisting groups in the community and protecting the environment.

firms have a social responsibility. Owners occupy a trusteeship position and should act to protect the interests of all parties as well as to make a profit. Profit and social objectives are not necessarily incompatible.

Another important social contribution of the small organization is the opportunity to provide employees with a sense of belonging, identity, and esprit de corps.

Growth Objective

Owners of small firms should be concerned with growth and should select a growth objective, which will depend on answers to questions such as the following:

1. Will I be satisfied for my business to remain small?
2. Do I want it to grow and challenge larger firms?
3. Do I seek relative stability or mere survival?
4. Do I seek a profit that is only "satisfactory," considering my effort and investment, or do I seek to maximize profits?

Need to Mesh Objectives

Personal and business objectives can be integrated in small business. For example, a survey of 97 small owner-managed firms in the San Antonio area revealed a close connection between profitability, customer satisfaction, manager satisfaction, and nonfinancial rewards.[6] It also indicated increased chances of success when the objectives of the business—service at a profit—are meshed with owner's personal objectives. The results of the study indicate that small firms can achieve both personal and business objectives.

For example, Addie Lindstrom had what she calls a "cushy" job as office manager for a giant forest products firm, but she wanted to do something different. So, after 22 years with the company, she borrowed $50,000, took a travel agent's training course, rented an office in the building where she worked, and opened her own travel agency. After working at the forest products firm from 6:00 A.M. to 10:00 A.M., she'd go down the hall to her agency and work until midnight.

After an auto crash that nearly killed her, Addie ran the agency from her hospital bed, specializing in services for disabled tourists. Two years later, having hired 10 new employees, Addie returned to her business—by then in the $2 million–plus range.[7]

✳ CHARACTERISTICS OF SUCCESSFUL SMALL BUSINESS OWNERS

The abilities and personal characteristics of the owner(s) exert a powerful influence on the success of a small company. Also, the methods and procedures adopted in such a firm should be designed not only to offset any personal deficiencies the owner may have but also to build on his or her strengths.

What characterizes owners of successful small companies? A set of characteristics for small business entrepreneurs developed by Victor Kiam (found in the case at the end of the chapter) includes willingness to make sacrifices, decisiveness, self-confidence, ability to recognize and capitalize on opportunities, and confidence in the venture.

Another set of characteristics was suggested by the 2,740 readers of *Venture* magazine who responded to the following questions: "What type of person becomes an entrepreneur, and what psychological factors influence their future in business—and in life?"[8] The results showed that most of these entrepreneurs were firstborn children who had a positive relationship with their fathers. Over 36 percent had held jobs before they were 15 years old, and 23 percent started their first business before they turned 20. Typically, these entrepreneurs were dedicated to their business, had a strong sense of enterprise, and were usually hard at work by 7:30 A.M. Ninety-five percent had completed high school, 64 percent had graduated from college, and 30 percent held a postgraduate degree.

From these and many other sources, we conclude that the characteristics of successful owners of small businesses are that they:

1. Desire independence.
2. Have a strong sense of initiative.
3. Are motivated by personal and family considerations.
4. Expect quick and concrete results.
5. Are able to react quickly.
6. Are dedicated to their business.
7. Enter business as much by chance as by design.

Desire Independence

As shown earlier in the chapter, those people who start small businesses seek independence and want to be free of outside control. They enjoy the freedom that comes from "doing their own thing" and making their own decisions—for better or for worse, as the example on the next page illustrates.

Have a Strong Sense of Initiative

Owners of small businesses have a strong sense of initiative that gives them a desire to use their ideas, abilities, and aspirations to the greatest degree possible. They are able to conceive, plan, and carry to a successful conclusion ideas for a new product. This is not always true in a larger organization.

Another aspect of initiative usually seen in small business owners is their willingness to work long, hard hours to reach their goals. They tend to be capable, ambitious, persevering individuals.

Jean McMillen, owner of Mystery Bookshop
Photo by Rick Dugan.

After spending 20 years working for others, Jean McMillen wanted to do something new, different, and interesting. So, after three years of careful planning, much traveling, and looking at other shops, she and Ronald, her husband, opened Mystery Bookshop in Bethesda, Maryland.

Devoted to a full range of services geared to mystery lovers, the shop caters to both young and old. It has 1,000 offerings for young readers, including "everything ever written about Nancy Drew." For older readers, there is a comfortable spot to rest and read. It is furnished to recreate the atmosphere of an English country-house mystery.

The store provides a variety and depth of services (over 12,000 volumes, games, and murder mystery house parties) that other stores can't, which gives McMillen the sense of achievement and independence she sought.[9]

Are Motivated by Personal and Family Considerations

As shown earlier, small business owners are often motivated as much by personal and family considerations as by the profit motive. They start and operate their businesses to help their parents, children, and other family members. As will be discussed in Chapter 24, there now seems to be a trend toward children helping their parents—financially and otherwise—to start small firms. This trend builds on the past practice of parents helping their children, as the following classic example shows.

John H. Johnson, one of the nation's leading black entrepreneurs, founded Johnson Publishing Company, which owns *Ebony* and *Jet* magazines, radio stations, and a cosmetic firm. When asked what was the key to his success, Johnson answered, "My mother . . . made so many sacrifices. . . . She even let me mortgage her furniture [for $600] . . . to start my business. . . . I couldn't let her down."[10] Now he's one of the nation's 400 richest individuals, and his daughter, Linda Johnson Rice, heads the company. She says, "I was exposed to the company at an early age. While other kids played after school, I'd come work in my dad's office."[11]

Another interesting trend is the shift toward more couples doing business together, as several of our previous examples have shown. Also, the SBA found that the number of joint proprietorship tax returns filed by wives and husbands jumped over 60 percent from 1980 to 1986, while the increase for all proprietorships was only 38 percent.[12]

Expect Quick and Concrete Results

Small business owners expect quick and concrete results from their investment of time and capital. Instead of engaging in the long-range planning that is common in large businesses, they seek a quick return on their capital. And they become impatient and discouraged when these results are slow in coming.

Are Able to React Quickly

Small businesses have an advantage over larger firms in that they can react more quickly to changes taking place both inside and outside the company. For example, one characteristic of a small business is its vulnerability to technological and environmental changes. Because the business is small, such changes have a great effect on its operations and profitability. A small business owner must therefore have the ability to react quickly.

Are Dedicated to Their Business

Small business owners tend to be fiercely dedicated to their company. With so much of their time, energy, money, and emotions invested in it, they want to ensure that nothing harms their ''baby.'' Consequently, they have a zeal, devotion, and ardor often missing in managers of big companies.

Enter Business as Much by Chance as by Design

An interesting characteristic of many small business owners is that they get into business as much by chance as by design. These are the owners who quite frequently ask for assistance in the form of management training and development. This type of individual differs sharply from those who attend college with the ambition to become professional managers and who gear their programs toward that end.

For example, Thurman Scheumack, while recovering from a broken neck, turned to the centuries-old craft of broom making as part of his therapy. He did such an admirable job of making the brooms that he was soon selling them to neighbors and others in Mountain View, Arkansas. Now he, his wife, and their five employees produce about 20,000 brooms each year.

While most of their output is of the standard kitchen model, the brooms Scheumack most enjoys making are those decorated with hand-carved faces on their handles. These are sold in galleries and gift shops throughout the country and at tourist attractions such as Colonial Williamsburg, Disneyland, and Disney World at prices ranging from $18 to $50.[13]

DOING AN INTROSPECTIVE PERSONAL ANALYSIS

Now that you have seen some of the characteristics of successful small business owners, do you think you have enough of those characteristics to be successful?

The following personal evaluation will help you decide this important question. No one of these items is more important than any other; rather, you need to determine whether the combination of qualities you have will help you succeed as a small business owner.

Analyzing Your Values

In order to manage your firm effectively, you need a set of basic principles to serve as guidelines for managerial decision making. The more important questions you need to ask are the following: What are your true motives? What real objectives do you seek? What relative weights do you give to service, profit, and social responsibilities? What type of interpersonal relations do you want to establish with employees and customers?

Everyone has a philosophy, whether conscious or unconscious, and that philosophy depends on personal values—that is, a conviction of what is right or wrong, desirable or undesirable. Your personal philosophy will more than likely become your management philosophy. Your business objectives and resulting policies and procedures will be based on that philosophy. In the business world, the greatest esteem seems to be granted to those people viewed as builders—that is, the ones who create a product and a company to produce it.

Analyzing Your Mental Abilities

Next, you should analyze your mental abilities to determine the type of business that will satisfy your objectives. Ask questions such as these: Can I see my choice of a business in its entirety—physically and economically? Can I see things logically, objectively, and in perspective? Can I generate ideas about new methods and products? Can I interpret and translate ideas into realistic activities? Can I accurately interpret the feelings, wants, and needs of others?

Remember, *you don't have to have all these abilities to be a successful small business owner*. But an analysis of them can help you understand what you can do if you try. It helps determine how you can move toward succeeding in business.

Analyzing Your Attitudes

Another way to determine whether you should become a small business owner is to analyze your attitudes. Ask questions such as these: Am I willing to accept responsibility? Am I mentally and emotionally stable? Am I committed to the idea of operating a small business? Am I willing to take risks? Can I tolerate irregular hours? Am I self-disciplined? Self-confident? Let us again emphasize that you will not—and need not—have all the necessary attitudes, but you should be able to develop as many of them as feasible.

Figure 2–2   Test Your Potential as an Entrepreneur

Do you have what it takes to be a success in your own business? Below is a list of 20 personality traits. Consider each carefully—and then score yourself by placing a check under the appropriate number with 0 being the lowest and 7 being the highest. Tally your score and find out what kind of entrepreneur you would make, using the key below.

	0	1	2	3	4	5	6	7
I have the ability to communicate.	—	—	—	—	—	—	—	—
I have the ability to motivate others.	—	—	—	—	—	—	—	—
I have the ability to organize.	—	—	—	—	—	—	—	—
I can accept responsibility.	—	—	—	—	—	—	—	—
I can easily adapt to change.	—	—	—	—	—	—	—	—
I have decision-making capability.	—	—	—	—	—	—	—	—
I have drive and energy.	—	—	—	—	—	—	—	—
I am in good health.	—	—	—	—	—	—	—	—
I have good human relations skills.	—	—	—	—	—	—	—	—
I have initiative.	—	—	—	—	—	—	—	—
I am interested in people.	—	—	—	—	—	—	—	—
I have good judgment.	—	—	—	—	—	—	—	—
I am open-minded and receptive to new ideas.	—	—	—	—	—	—	—	—
I have planning ability.	—	—	—	—	—	—	—	—
I am persistent.	—	—	—	—	—	—	—	—
I am resourceful.	—	—	—	—	—	—	—	—
I am self-confident.	—	—	—	—	—	—	—	—
I am a self-starter.	—	—	—	—	—	—	—	—
I am a good listener.	—	—	—	—	—	—	—	—
I am willing to be a risk taker.	—	—	—	—	—	—	—	—

Key:

110–140	Very strong
85–109	Strong
55–84	Fair
54 or below	Weak

Prepared by Sherron Boone and Lisa Aplin, of Mobile College.

If your answers to the questions in this section were yes, or if you feel that you can make them yes in the near future, you may have the qualities that would make an entrepreneurial venture a satisfying and rewarding activity. The self-test in Figure 2–2 should help you decide whether you have these qualities.

In addition, Jerry White, Director of the Caruth's Institute of Owner-Managed Business at Southern Methodist University, thinks you should have stamina, self-motivation, and self-confidence and be a calculated risk taker.[14]

WHAT LEADS TO SUCCESS IN MANAGING A SMALL BUSINESS?

Although it is difficult to determine precisely what leads to success in managing a small business, the following are some important factors:

✳ 1. Serving an adequate and well-defined market for the product.

✳ 2. Acquiring sufficient capital.

✳ 3. Recruiting and using human resources effectively.

   4. Obtaining and using accurate information.

   5. Coping with government regulations effectively.

   6. Both the owner and the employees having expertise in the field.

   7. Managing time effectively.

Serving an Adequate and Well-Defined Market

As shown in Part II of this book, there must be an adequate demand for your product. One of the greatest assets you can have is the ability to detect a market for something before others do and then devise a way of satisfying the market. A company providing venture capital to small business entrepreneurs found that 90 percent of the 2 million U.S. millionaires owned their own firms. The primary reason for this was that larger firms rejected the new—and often superior—ideas of employees, who then went out and started their own companies.[15]

It also helps if you can find a market that is not being satisfied and design a unique product for it, as happened in the following example.

Photo courtesy of Snugli, Inc.

When Ann and Michael Moore were in the Peace Corps in West Africa, they noticed how peaceful the native children were. The mothers carried their children in pouches on their chest or back, held in place by straps over the shoulders and tied around the waist. The mother could go about her work with her hands free, and the child was comforted by the closeness of its mother. The Moores started making the same kind of cloth pouch when they returned home. Over $4.5 million worth of Snuglis had been sold worldwide when they sold Snugli, Inc., to the Huffy Corporation in 1985.[16]

Acquiring Sufficient Capital

As shown in Chapter 1, a major problem for small business owners is obtaining sufficient capital—at a reasonable price—to acquire the resources needed to start and operate a business. Owners who become successful have been able to obtain needed funds, either from their own resources or from others. They are willing to delay satisfying the desire for profit or dividends now, in the long-run interest of the business.

Although lack of investment capital is a problem for small firms, even worse is a shortage of working capital. In fact, probably *the biggest crisis for a small business is a lack of cash,* as will be discussed in Chapter 19.

Recruiting and Using Human Resources Effectively

The effective recruitment and use of human resources are especially important to owners of small businesses, who have a closer and more personal association with their employees than do managers of larger businesses. Workers in a small firm can be a good source of information and ideas, and their productivity should increase if you allow them to share ideas with you, especially if you recognize and reward their contributions.

Obtaining and Using Accurate Information

You need to stay informed of financial and marketing conditions affecting your business (see Using Technology to Succeed). You must analyze and evaluate information and develop plans to maintain or improve your position. The "information explosion" of the 1980s has not been accompanied by an increased ability to interpret and use all the data available. Instead, information's increased complexity sometimes overwhelms small business owners. There are limits to the amount and types of information owners can absorb and use in their operations.

Coping with Government Regulations

As discussed in Chapters 1 and 23, the days when small businesses were exempt from governmental regulation in areas such as equal employment opportunity, occupational safety and health, and environmental protection have passed. Instead, the cost in time and money to comply with the regulations is of major concern to small business owners, whose responses are varied and often negative. Not only must small business owners be able to handle red tape effectively, but it is especially important that they become involved in governmental activities.

What can small business owners do about government regulation? Possible responses include the following:

- Learn as much as possible about the regulations, especially if they can be helpful to you. You will find throughout this text descriptions of many laws, regulations, and agencies—including the SBA—available to help smaller firms.

- Challenge detrimental or harmful laws, either alone—perhaps appearing before a legislative small business committee—or by joining organizations such as the National Federation of Independent Business.

====== USING TECHNOLOGY TO SUCCEED ======

USING ELECTRONIC SCANNERS TO STUDY THE MARKET

More than half of the supermarkets in the United States now use electronic scanners, which essentially are computerized checkout machines that read the bar codes on merchandise labels. Originally used to speed the checkout process, these electronic scanners are now being connected to central computers to do market research as well. The computers gather, record, and analyze valuable information essential for speedy and effective managerial decisions. Analysts predict that profit margins, which average only about 0.5 to 1.5 percent, could very well double in the near future.

Hannaford Brothers, the Maine-based owner of Shop-n-Save stores, offers an example of how well the new system works. Such data as shipping expenses, warehouse handling requirements, bulk displays, energy needs of various stores, and the amount of time canned corn stays on the shelf before being bought are sent to Shop-n-Save's headquarters. This information is processed into "Plan-a-Grams," which give managers a detailed shelf-by-shelf description of where to put stock to increase profit.

Expected future developments include electronic shelves that give nutrition and cost information about products at the press of a button. This innovation could be operative by the time this book is published.

Sources: Correspondence with Hannaford Brothers; and S. Weinstein, "A Conversation with Hannaford's James Moody," *Progressive Grocer,* April 1988, pp. 119–20.

- Become involved in the legal-political system, either by electing representatives who will help change the laws or by running for office yourself.
- Find a better legal environment, if possible, even if it means moving to a different city, county, or state.
- Learn to live with the laws and regulations.

Both the Owner and Employees Having Expertise in the Field

If you are to succeed in a business of your own, ambition, desire, drive, capital, judgment, and a competitive spirit are not enough. In addition, you'll need technical and managerial know-how and expertise to perform the activities necessary to run the business. Some types of business, such as general retail establishments, may need only general skills. But the more technical and complex the business is, the greater the need for specialized skills, which can be acquired only through education, training, and experience, as the following example shows.

In 1989, Honeybee Robotics won a $1.5 million contract to operate a joint venture with Ford Aerospace to produce the "hands" for a robot that Martin Marietta was to build for NASA. The robot was the most sophisticated space robot ever planned.

While Honeybee was too small to get one of the major contracts with NASA on its own, it had the specialized expertise to design and build sophisticated computer-driven robot systems, particularly robotic arms and effectors, or "hands." Honeybee had made such camera-guided robot arms to pick up vials from conveyor belts and place them symmetrically in rows, accurate to within 1/1,000 of an inch. This technical expertise and experience was the reason Honeybee got the contract, according to the company's president.[17]

Managing Time Effectively

The effective use of time is especially important to small business owners because of the many and varied duties that only they can perform. While managers of large firms can delegate activities to others, freeing time for other uses, small business owners are limited in their ability—or willingness—to do so. They often prefer to do things themselves rather than delegate authority to others. Another problem is the long hours worked by new business owners. As you can see from Figure 2–3, over half (53 percent) of such owners spend 60 hours or more per week working at their business, according to a study by the National Federation of Independent Business. And over three-fourths of them spend 50 or more hours per week on the job.

Where do these long hours go? A survey of people who had owned their businesses between three and four-and-a-half years found that most of their time is devoted to selling and production.[18] Dealing with employees and suppliers, keeping records, and arranging financial matters are also great consumers of time.

Figure 2–3   Hours per Week Worked by New Business Owners

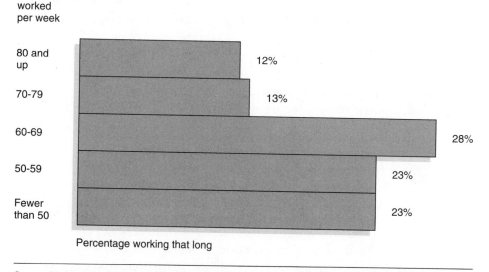

Hours worked per week

80 and up	12%
70-79	13%
60-69	28%
50-59	23%
Fewer than 50	23%

Percentage working that long

Source: National Federation of Independent Business, as reported in Mark Robichaux, "Business First, Family Second," *The Wall Street Journal,* May 12, 1989, p. B1. Adapted with permission of THE WALL STREET JOURNAL, © 1989 Dow Jones & Company, Inc. All Rights Reserved Worldwide.

While there is no magic formula for effective time management, the following are some specific methods for saving your time.

- Organizing the work, including delegating to subordinates as many duties as feasible.

- Selecting a competent person to sort out unimportant mail, screen incoming calls, and keep a schedule of appointments and activities.

- Using electronic equipment for letters and memos.

- Adhering to appointment and business conference times.

- Preparing an agenda for meetings, confining discussion to the items on the agenda, and making follow-up assignments to specific subordinates.

WHAT YOU SHOULD HAVE LEARNED

1. People start businesses for many personal and business reasons. While income is an important consideration, the primary personal reason is to achieve independence. The need to exercise initiative and creativity leads entrepreneurs to take the risk involved in striking out on their own. Many small business owners are also motivated by family considerations, such as taking over a family business to permit parents to retire or starting a family business to have more time with their families. Also, some people start businesses chiefly to provide a product or service not readily available elsewhere. Finally, some entrepreneurs start businesses in order to achieve business objectives such as providing services to their customers; making a profit; providing social benefits to society; and growing into large, profitable organizations.

2. The characteristics most typical of the more successful business owners are that they (a) desire independence, (b) have a strong sense of enterprise, (c) tend to be motivated by personal and family considerations, (d) expect quick and concrete results, (e) are able to react quickly to change, (f) are dedicated to their business, and (g) often enter business as much by chance as by design.

3. If you are interested in becoming an entrepreneur, you should carefully examine your values, mental abilities, and attitudes in order to see if you have the characteristics required for success. Your ability to think logically, generate new ideas, translate these ideas into a useful product, do effective planning, and relate to the feelings and needs of customers and employees is also important. Your success in any business depends on your level of aspiration, willingness to accept responsibility, ability to handle setbacks and disappointments, commitment to the business, willingness to take risks, ability to live with an irregular schedule, self-discipline, and self-confidence.

4. The most prevalent factors leading to success in managing a small business are *(a)* serving an adequate and well-defined market, *(b)* acquiring sufficient capital, *(c)* recruiting and using human resources effectively, *(d)* obtaining and using accurate information, *(e)* coping effectively with government regulations, *(f)* having expertise in one's chosen field, and *(g)* managing time effectively. In essence, it is sticking to the basics that leads to success rather than using gimmicks or catering to fads.

QUESTIONS FOR DISCUSSION

1. Discuss the four personal objectives that people seek when starting a new business.

2. Explain the four business objectives small business owners try to achieve.

3. Explain the interrelationship between the *service* and *profit* objectives.

4. Are the social objectives really that important to small business owners? Explain your answer.

5. What are some of the characteristics found in successful small business owners? Evaluate the importance of each of these.

6. How did you make out with the self-test in Figure 2–2? Do you think the results accurately reflect your potential? Explain.

7. What factors lead to success in owning a small business?

VICTOR K. KIAM II: HOW TO SUCCEED AS AN ENTREPRENEUR

In a famous TV commercial, Victor Kiam says, "I was a dedicated blade shaver until my wife bought me this Remington Microscreen shaver. . . . I was so impressed with it, I bought the company." Whether or not that was the reason for his purchase of Remington Products, Inc., Kiam did pick up the firm from Sperry Corporation in 1979 for a "mere" $25 million, most of which was provided by Sperry and various banks. Since then, sales have increased many-fold. Market share has more than doubled, and profits have skyrocketed. Since 1988, Kiam has been the majority owner of the New England Patriots.

Victor K. Kiam II, President, Remington Products, Inc.
Photo courtesy of Remington Products, Inc.

After acquiring an M.B.A. degree from Harvard in 1951, and after 18 years of selling foundation garments for Playtex and toothpaste for Lever Brothers, Kiam bought an interest in the Benrus Corporation, where he sold watches and jewelry for another 11 years. These 29 years of experience, not to mention his years as CEO at Remington, demonstrate that he fits the profile of a successful entrepreneur—a profile Kiam developed in his best-selling book *Going for It! How to Succeed as an Entrepreneur*.

In the book, Kiam says a person has "the right stuff" if he or she can answer the following questions affirmatively:

- Am I willing to sacrifice?
- Am I decisive?
- Do I have self-confidence?
- Can I recognize an opportunity when it presents itself and capitalize on it?
- Do I have confidence in my proposed venture?
- Am I willing to lead by example?

In his book *Live to Win*, Kiam explains how you can figure your "Personal Balance Sheet" and your "Intangible Balance Sheet."

Kiam's success has been based on the guiding principles he has followed since 1935, when he became an entrepreneur at the age of eight. That summer, when people stepped off the streetcar named *Desire* near where he lived in New Orleans, they looked as if they would drop if they didn't have something cold to drink. Victor's grandfather staked him to $5 to buy 100 bottles of Coca-Cola to sell to the suffering passengers. The young entrepreneur set his price at 10 cents, a 100 percent markup, expecting to make a substantial profit. Sales zoomed, and his supply of drinks was soon sold out. He and his grandfather were both shocked when Victor learned he had only $4 to show for his efforts. Since this new venture was launched during the Depression, most of the customers couldn't pay the 10 cents; being soft-hearted, Victor couldn't turn them away. While this business was a financial disaster, it did build much goodwill for him and taught him some valuable business lessons.

QUESTIONS

1. What business and personal needs might Victor Kiam have been attempting to satisfy when he decided to risk millions on Remington Products, Inc.?

2. How, and to what degree, has Kiam's background and personal business experience

helped him build Remington Products into the profitable company that it is?

3. Consider some of the risks and obstacles Kiam had taken and overcome in 1979 just before he bought Remington Products. Would you have been willing to take a multimillion-dollar chance? Why or why not?

4. Assume that you are now CEO of Remington Products, a multimillion-dollar company. What

would you do to increase the company's market share, profitability, and competitive advantage?

5. What personal and entrepreneurial qualities might Kiam possess that have helped him achieve his success? Which of these would you classify as the most important?

Sources: Based on Victor Kiam, *Going for It! How to Succeed as an Entrepreneur* (New York: William Morrow, 1986) and *Live to Win* (New York: Harper & Row, 1989); Dave Nelson, ''Patriots' Cleanup Man,'' *The New York Times*, November 14, 1988, p. 21; and correspondence with Remington Products.

3

Opportunities and Challenges in Small Business

A wise man will make more opportunities than he finds. —Francis Bacon

The role of small and midsized firms . . . has never been more important to America's future. —Tom Peters, co-author of *In Search of Excellence*

LEARNING OBJECTIVES

After studying the material in this chapter, you will be able to:

1. Discuss some of the currently promising opportunities for small business.

2. Present some practical ideas for small business opportunities.

3. Explain some of the growing opportunities in small business for women and minorities.

4. Discuss some areas of concern for small business owners, especially the problem of poorly planned growth, and the prospect for failure.

SHERRI HILL: DRESSING THE WORLD'S MOST BEAUTIFUL WOMEN

Sherri Hill believes in taking advantage of opportunities when they knock! Opportunity knocked for her in 1985, when a contestant in the Miss Oklahoma pageant bought a dress from Sherri's family-run shop in Norman, Oklahoma.

Wanting to "watch our dress," she and her partners attended the pageant. She was disturbed during the show to see another contestant wearing the same design as theirs. While their client was understanding about the duplication, the partners were upset.

Seeing the problem caused by more than one contestant's wearing the same design, Sherri decided to capitalize on the situation by custom-designing and selling dresses on a registration basis. When a customer buys a "Temptations by Sherri Hill"

Vonda Vass (left) and Sherri Hill show gowns worn by 1988 Miss USA contestants and a cocktail dress (held by Mrs. Hill) worn by 1989 contestants.

Source: Mobile (Alabama) Press Register, February 28, 1989, pp. 1B + 3B. Photograph by Jay Ferchaud, © 1989, Mobile (Alabama) Press Register. All rights reserved.

dress costing anywhere from $1,500 to $6,000, the design is registered to that person on a computer system so that no other contestant can purchase the same dress.

Soon after her dresses were seen by the Miss Oklahoma and Miss USA pageant directors, she became the exclusive designer of gowns for the Miss Universe, Miss USA, and Miss Teen USA winners. At the 1988 Miss America contest, 48 women wore her gowns—which were all of different design! At the 1989 Miss USA pageant, seven finalists were gowned by Mrs. Hill, as was Courtney Gibbs, the 1988 Miss USA, who was also present.

As you can see, what was an embarrassing moment at the time proved to be the knock that opened the door to a successful enterprise.

Source: Cathy Jumper, "Oklahoma Woman Designer of Gowns for Beauty Pageants," Mobile (Alabama) Register, February 28, 1989, pp. 1-B and 3-B.

Figure 3–1   Where the New Jobs Will Be: These Industries Are Expected to Produce the Most New Jobs by the Year 2000

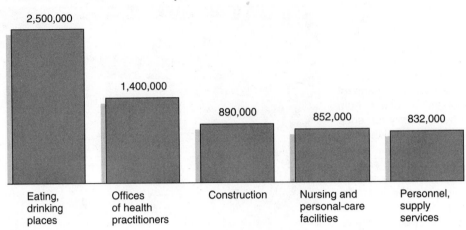

Source: U.S. Department of Labor, Bureau of Labor Statistics.

In Chapter 1, we described the dynamic role of small business, and in Chapter 2, we explained why you might want to own and manage such a business. In this chapter, as the Profile indicates, we discuss some of the opportunities available in small business, suggest areas for innovation by small business, explain some of the growing opportunities for women and minorities, and discuss some areas of concern for small business owners, especially the problem of poorly planned growth and the possibility of failure.

WHERE ARE THE OPPORTUNITIES?

You can explore the opportunities to become a small business owner in many ways. First, study industry groupings or categories to see what types of small businesses are growing. Second, study the factors affecting the future of industries and businesses. Third, study some innovative ideas that entrepreneurs are turning into successful businesses. From all this information, you can see where opportunities exist for a new business.

What Are the Fastest-Growing Industries?

According to the Bureau of Labor Statistics, no industry is growing faster than services, and this trend is expected to continue at least into the 21st century. This trend is evident in both the number of new businesses being created and, as Figure 3–1 shows, the number of new jobs being created. Most of the growing industries are dominated by small private companies. According to the SBA's Office of Advocacy, only construction and personnel/supply services tend to be dominated by larger businesses.

Figure 3–2   1990s Rage: Service

The hottest small businesses in the 1990s will be service firms such as accountants,
lawyers, architects, and computer consultants. In this case, a small business is defined
as having fewer than 100 employees.

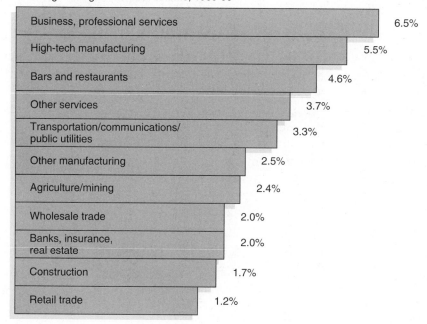

Percentage change in number of firms, 1989-99

Industry

Industry	Percentage
Business, professional services	6.5%
High-tech manufacturing	5.5%
Bars and restaurants	4.6%
Other services	3.7%
Transportation/communications/public utilities	3.3%
Other manufacturing	2.5%
Agriculture/mining	2.4%
Wholesale trade	2.0%
Banks, insurance, real estate	2.0%
Construction	1.7%
Retail trade	1.2%

Source: Cognetics, Inc., as reported in *USA Today,* May 8, 1989, p. 1E. Copyright 1989, USA TODAY.
Adapted with permission.

A similar picture emerges when we look at the number of *new firms expected to
be established* during the 1990s. For example, as shown in Figure 3–2, services
tend to dominate this group. Notice that 7 of the 11 industries shown are in the
service-performing areas.

We may have led you to believe up to this point that small businesses are
being formed primarily by daring young entrepreneurs who use their college
degrees to turn brilliant ideas into glamorous high-tech firms. But these firms
are only the most visible ones. Instead, most small firms are just that: small,
limited in scope, and involving long hours of hard work to perform everyday
activities needed by the general public. For example, the SBA has found from
its data that the 10 small-business-dominated industries with the lowest failure
rates have tended to be businesses of this kind.[1] These stable industries—such
as funeral services; fuel and ice dealers; laundry, cleaning, and repair services;
and drugstores—offer the public a service that is needed regularly by a large
segment of the population.

USING TECHNOLOGY TO SUCCEED

TECHNOLOGY LETS TAXIS TRADE CASH FOR CREDIT

For years, taxicab companies have been trying to find a way to accept credit cards. The drawback has been to find a feasible way to check to see if cards have been stolen or if the owner has overused the credit limit. Also, cab drivers have been reluctant to fork over part of their fee to credit-card companies, instead of accepting the cash customers are in the habit of paying.

All that is now changing, as taxis are finally going plastic! In late 1992, over 600 of New York City's 12,000 cabs were equipped with machines connected to their meters that read the magnetic strip on American Express cards. The cab driver punches in tips and tolls, and a receipt, in duplicate, pops out. The driver still must check against a list of lost or stolen cards, but that is expected to change soon. By the end of 1993, cab companies will be able to obtain credit-card authorization by sending a signal to the dispatcher, who electronically checks the card number and then notifies the driver if everything is OK.

MasterCard International plans to test the system in Montreal and other major cities by 1994. It will also experiment with pizza deliverers, plumbers, and other workers on wheels to get them to use the system.

One drawback is that most of the 171,000 cabs in the United States are driven by independent contractors who are reluctant to pay the usual 3 to 5 percent of the amount charged as a discount fee to the credit-card companies. However, this is changing, as drivers say people who use cards generally leave fatter tips that more than offset the discount fee.

Source: Dell Jones, "Technology Lets Taxis Trade Cash for Credit," *USA Today,* November 1992, p. 6B. © 1992, USA TODAY. Adapted with permission.

Factors Affecting the Future of an Industry or a Business

Many changes are now occurring that will affect the future of an industry or business (see Using Technology to Succeed), and small business owners should study them intently in order to adjust to them. These changes can cause slow-growing industries to speed up or fast-growing ones to slow down. And a change that provides an opportunity for one industry or business may pose a threat to others. For example, aging of the population may increase the need for retirement facilities but hurt industries supplying baby needs.

Figure 3–3 shows some selected examples of factors that affect various industries and businesses. These factors will be discussed more fully in Chapters 5, 6, and 8.

Some Practical Ideas for Small Businesses

As shown in Chapter 1, entrepreneurs tend to be innovative and to develop new ideas. What are some of the innovative ideas currently being developed that should

Figure 3–3 Examples of Factors Affecting Industry and Business Trends

1. *Economics*—gross national product (GNP), interest rates, inflation rates, stages of the business cycle, employment levels, size and characteristics of business firms and not-for-profit organizations, and opportunities in foreign markets.

2. *Technology*—artificial intelligence, thinking machines, laser beams, new energy sources, amount of spending for research and development, and issuance of patents and their protection.

3. *Lifestyle*—career expectations, consumer activism, health concerns, desire to upgrade education and climb the socioeconomic ladder, and need for psychological services.

4. *Political-legal*—antitrust regulations, environmental protection laws, foreign trade regulations, tax changes, immigration laws, child-care legislation, and the attitude of governments and society toward the particular type of industry and business.

5. *Demographics*—population growth rate, age and regional shifts, ethnic moves and life expectancy, number and distribution of firms within the industry, and size and character of markets.

lead to the big businesses of tomorrow? These new types of business provide opportunities for those wanting to become small business owners.

One way to do this is to see which small businesses are growing most rapidly. *American Business Information* used a unique approach to determine the business categories that grew the most rapidly during a recent year. It surveyed Yellow Pages listings and found the following increases: (1) facsimile communication equipment, 119 percent; (2) money order services, 48 percent; (3) exercise and physical fitness, 43 percent; (4) bed and breakfast accommodations, 40 percent; and (5) collectibles, 37 percent.[2]

Some other innovative ideas for small businesses are specialized shopping, especially for dual-career families and shut-ins; desktop publishing; on-site auto tune-ups and cleaning at clients' homes; helping small businesses and other organizations computerize their activities; low-power TV stations for specially targeted audiences; presorting mail by ZIP codes for businesses sending out large mailings; at-home pet grooming; the use of fax machines for mass mailings and franchising fax vending machines; exotic family tours; utilization review firms to review hospital costs for employers, point out unnecessary treatments, and suggest cheaper alternatives; biotechnology; and specialized delivery services.

For example, Cuisine Express provides fast, effective delivery of meals from seven gourmet restaurants in Maryland to customers in the Bethesda, Chevy Chase, Glen Echo, and Somerset areas. Customers choose the restaurant and meal they desire and place an order with Cuisine Express's operator. The operator orders the meal from the restaurant, and a driver picks it up, delivers it, and collects payment by Visa, MasterCard, or personal check.

David Gumpert, author of *How to **Really** Create a Successful Business Plan*, looked at emerging trends and problems, talked to those in the know, and came up with the following ventures that seemed to be headed for success in the 1990s:[3]

1. Catering.
2. Computer and office machine repair.
3. Day care.
4. Educational services and products.
5. Career counseling.
6. Financial planning.
7. Home health care.
8. Printing, copying, and mailing.
9. Marketing, promotion, and public relations.
10. Senior fitness and recreation.

GROWING OPPORTUNITIES FOR WOMEN AND MINORITIES IN SMALL BUSINESS

Small firms provide excellent opportunities for women and minorities to gain economic independence. The opportunities for women, blacks, Hispanics, and Asians are increasing in number and frequency, as will be shown by several examples in this chapter.

For Women

The 1980s have been called the "decade of women entrepreneurs."[4] Women are now starting new businesses at twice the rate of men. In 1972, women owned only 5 percent of all businesses; in 1992, they owned one-third.[5] This is an increase of 184 percent from the 1.9 million owned in 1977. Moreover, women founded 70 percent of all new firms in 1991.[6] According to the SBA, women are expected to own half of the nation's small businesses by the year 2000.[7]

In 1992, women-owned firms employed 11 million people—and that number is increasing rapidly—while Fortune 500 firms, employing only 12 million, were regularly announcing reductions.[8] The change in women-owned businesses is occurring faster in the nontraditional industries such as transportation, construction, manufacturing, mining, and agriculture—as well as services, trade, and finance. However, 6 out of 10 women owners are still in public relations, marketing, data processing, business service/personnel, finance, and retailing.[9]

A poll of National Association of Women Business Owners members found that these owners are not the mythical women who inherited the family—or their spouse's—business. Instead, 90 percent of them either started the business for themselves, bought a business, or bought a franchise—primarily to prove that they could succeed, to earn more money, or to control their work schedule. The surveyed women entrepreneurs were highly educated—only 5 percent of those responding had a high school education or less—and over half (57 percent) worked over 50 hours per week.[10]

Opportunities for women entrepreneurs are growing all across the nation, as are the organizations to help women found their own businesses. These include the Women's Economic Development Corporation in Minneapolis, Minnesota; the Women's Business Development Center in Chicago; the Midwest Women's Business Owners Development Joint Ventures in Detroit; and the American Women's Economic Development Corporation (AWED) in New York. Also, Young Women's Christian Association groups around the country have been helping for years.

Yet there are many problems still facing women entrepreneurs, including getting a loan, dealing with male employees and clients, getting moral support in the industry, and dealing with female employees and clients.[11] In order to overcome some of these problems, the Women's Business Ownership Act, passed in late 1988, extended antidiscrimination laws to include commercial and personal credit for women.

For Minorities

Small business ownership also provides growing opportunities for minorities, that is, for blacks, Hispanics, and Asians. Small business has traditionally owed a great deal to immigrants, who have been responsible for much of the surge in new firms. A flood of immigrants poured into the United States around the turn of the century, and many of our great companies were started by the newcomers.

Now, the situation is quite similar, as 8.7 million people moved to the United States in the 1980s.[12] Nearly half of these were from Mexico, the Caribbean, and Central and South America; and over a third were from Asia. These promising entrepreneurs, with their bilingual skills, family ties, and knowledge of how things are done in other countries, can contribute—especially to the growing Asian and Latin American markets. But the influence of immigrants is also felt at home. For example, the computer industry today is highly dependent on microprocessor chips made by Intel, which was founded by Andrew Grove, a Hungarian immigrant.

Blacks

There are many good opportunities for blacks in small business. Small firms hire about 10.5 times as many blacks as do large firms. The number of black-owned businesses increased 38 percent, to 424,165, from 1982 to 1987,[13] as compared to 14 percent growth in the number of all U.S. companies.[14] Yet according to Barbara Lindsey, founder of the Los Angeles Black Enterprise Expo, while blacks make up 12 percent of the U.S. population, they account for only 3 percent of its business owners.[15] But some of those owners do quite well, according to *Black Enterprise* magazine, which found that its 100 largest black-owned companies grew 10.2 percent in revenues, as compared to 7.6 percent for the Fortune 500.[16]

Yet most black-owned businesses are small. While they account for 3 percent of all U.S. companies, they employ only 1.1 percent of U.S. workers. In fact, 87 percent of black-owned companies consist of only the owner.

The role of black entrepreneurs is rapidly changing. Once engaged primarily in mom-and-pop businesses such as barbershops, cleaners, and grocery stores, they are now moving into such fields as electronics, advertising, real estate development, insurance, health care, computers, and automobile dealerships. (See the case at the end of Chapter 21, and the Profiles for Chapter 7, ''Porterfield Wilson: From Shining Shoes to Importing Foreign Cars,'' and Chapter 11, ''Mel Farr: Sales Superstar,'' for outstanding examples.)

Big companies are also helping blacks start small businesses. They do it through creating joint ventures, lending their personnel to help start—or advise—the business, providing low-cost facilities, and providing an assured market, as the following example illustrates.

As part of its minority supplier program, McDonald's asked George Johnson and David Moore to start a business making croutons for the new line of salads it planned to introduce. Johnson and Moore, managers at a brewing company, had never run a business, knew nothing about baking, and had only one client—McDonald's. They invested $100,000 each and, with such an assured market, persuaded a Chicago bank to lend them $1.6 million. Also, a McDonald's bun and English muffin supplier bought a Chicago pork-processing plant and leased it back to their company, Quality Croutons, Inc. Sales for the first year exceeded $4 million, including sales to McDonald's, United Airlines, Kraft Foods, and Pizza Hut.[17]

Hispanics

According to the SBA's 1987 census of minority businesses, the number of businesses owned by Hispanics grew 80.5 percent between 1982 and 1987, to 422,373 firms (see Figure 3–4). This growth was nearly five times as great as that for all U.S. firms—including minority firms.

Hispanic businesses are particularly booming in the food area. This field was previously dominated by mom-and-pop grocers, but supermarkets are now invading the field because of the Hispanic view of shopping as an eagerly awaited social event.

The Hispanic market represents one of the fastest-growing groups of customers in the country. According to the U.S. Census Bureau, the Hispanic population

Figure 3–4   Hispanic-Owned Businesses Are Growing Rapidly

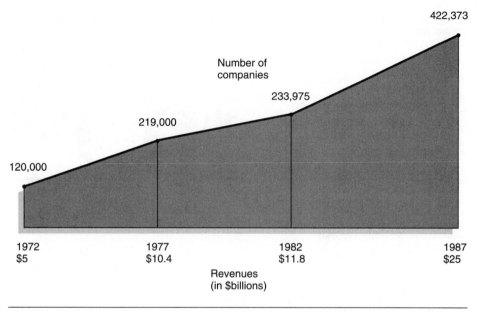

Source: U.S. Hispanic Chamber of Commerce, as reported in *USA Today,* November 2, 1984, p. 3B; and Dorothy J. Gaites, "Short-Term Despair, Long-Term Promise," *The Wall Street Journal,* April 3, 1992, p. R4.

grew 53 percent from 1980 to 1990, over five times the overall U.S. growth rate.[18] Entrepreneurs are trying to cash in on this market, as the following example illustrates.

After two years—and $2.5 million—spent researching the market, Vons Companies started Tianguis, a Southern California supermarket chain. The store's shelves are stocked with Spanish items, including handmade tortillas, and mariachi singers stroll the aisles. Hispanics are driving from as far as 65 miles away to shop in the stores because they like the products, the music, and the fact that "everyone speaks Spanish."[19]

Asians

The recent flood of Asian refugees entering the United States has resulted in a wave of small mom-and-pop businesses; according to the U.S. Census Bureau, there are now 57 Asian-owned firms in the United States per 1,000 Asians, compared to 21 Hispanic-owned firms and 15 black-owned ones.[20] This growth in business ownership partially results from the 105 percent increase in the U.S. Asian population during the 1980s. This increase was twice as high as that of Hispanics, almost 9 times as high as that of blacks, and 25 times as high as that of whites. Asians now account for 42 percent of U.S. immigrants.[21]

Figure 3–5   Asians Benefit from Networking

Recently arrived Asian immigrants establishing U.S. business enterprises gain support from cultural networks.

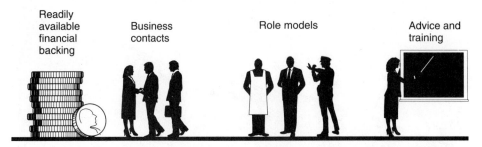

Source: U.S. Department of Commerce, as reported in Robert Lewis, ''Asian Immigrants Find Large Profits in Small Stores,'' *Mobile* (Alabama) *Press Register,* March 5, 1989, p. G-1. Adapted with permission of Newhouse Graphics.

A key factor in Asians' success is their tradition of self-employment. Also, they are motivated to open their own businesses because language and cultural barriers prevent them from obtaining ordinary wage or salary jobs. Hence Asians— especially Koreans—go into business for themselves, even if it means setting up a street stand or opening a store in a poor, run-down neighborhood. Also, as shown in Figure 3–5 and in the following example, Asian immigrants receive considerable support from cultural networks when they try to set up a small business.

Dae Song, 36, arrived in Baltimore from Korea with $400, which he soon lost. Unable to speak or understand English, and not knowing what to do, he moved in with an aunt and started working in the family's drycleaning business in a Washington suburb. After learning the business, he opened his own shop with help from a Korean support group. Each of the 30 members of the group contributed $1,000 to Dae Song as a loan. Eventually, each of them will have access to the full $30,000 to finance his own business.[22]

Cultural factors alone do not explain the outstanding success of Asian entrepreneurs. Instead, a study of small businesses in California—the state with the highest concentration of Asian businesses—found several important differences between businesses owned by Asians and those owned by non-Asians. While only 69 percent of non-Asians had a business plan when they started their company, 84 percent of Asians did. Also, Asians were more prone to use outside attorneys and accountants to assist them, and to use personal computers. According to a spokesman for Pacific Bell Directory, which sponsored the study, Asian businesspeople are prospering not because they are Asians but because they understand the key ingredients of running a successful business.[23]

AREAS OF CONCERN FOR SMALL BUSINESS OWNERS

So far, we have indicated that opportunities abound for anyone with a good idea, the courage to take a chance and try something new, and some money to invest. That's what small business is all about. But, as shown in Chapter 1, the success of smaller firms tends to be limited by factors such as inadequate management, shortages of capital, government regulation and paperwork, and lack of proper record keeping. Two other concerns are (1) poorly planned growth that is too slow or too fast and (2) the danger of failure.

Poorly Planned Growth

Poorly planned growth appears to be a built-in obstacle facing many small businesses. For example, if the owners are incapable, inefficient, or lacking in initiative, their businesses may flounder and eventually fail. If the owners are only mediocre, their businesses remain small. However, if the owners are efficient and capable and their organizations succeed and grow, they risk losing the very things they seek from their companies.

Loss of Independence or Control

With growth, owners must please more people, including employees, customers, and the public. There are also new problems, such as hiring and rewarding managers and supervising other people — exercising the very authority they may resent in others.

Many otherwise creative entrepreneurs are poor managers. They are able to generate ideas and found the business but are unable to manage it on a day-to-day basis. If the firm becomes large enough to require outside capital for future success and growth, the owner may lose control over the company, as the following example shows.

Two design geniuses, Steven Jobs, 21, and Steve Wozniak, 19, founded Apple Computer in 1976 with capital obtained by selling Jobs's Volkswagen microbus and Wozniak's Hewlett-Packard scientific calculator. They managed its growth until 1980, when they sold stock in it to the public. Although Jobs and Wozniak were worth $165 million and $88 million, respectively, they could not manage the day-to-day operations, so they hired John Sculley away from PepsiCo in 1983 to manage the floundering firm.

But both men were unhappy when Apple grew so big that they lost control. In 1985, after a dispute with Sculley, Wozniak sold his Apple stock and founded another company, Cloud 9. And when Jobs was ousted as chairman by the directors representing the outside stockholders, he sold all but one share of his stock and also formed a new company, NeXT, Inc.

Figure 3–6   Stages in the Development of a Small Business

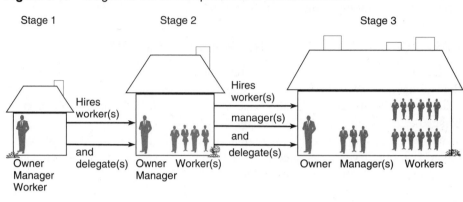

Typical Growth Pattern

Historically, the ownership and management of small businesses have tended to follow a growth pattern similar to that shown in Figure 3–6. During stage 1, owners manage the business and do all the work. In stage 2, the owners still manage their companies but hire employees to help with routine and/or management activities. In stage 3, the owners hire managers to run the firms. Thus, the business takes on the form, the characteristics, and many of the problems of a big business.

The length of service of professional managers (as opposed to owner-managers) in small businesses tends to be relatively short; they move from one company to another as they progress upward in rank and earnings. Often, owners must give managers a financial interest in the business in order to hold them.

Threat of Failure

A **discontinuance** is a voluntary decision to terminate a business.

A **failure** results from inability to succeed in running a business.

Formal failures are failures ending in court with loss to creditors.

In **personal (informal) failures**, the owner who cannot succeed voluntarily terminates the business.

As shown in Chapter 1, the threat of failure and discontinuance is a reality for many small businesses. A **discontinuance** is a voluntary decision to quit. A discontinuance may result from any of several factors, including health, changes in family situation, and the apparent advantages of working for someone else.

A **failure** results from inability to make a go of the business; things just don't work out as planned. There are two types of failure: (1) **formal failures**, which end up in court with some kind of loss to the creditors, and (2) **personal (informal) failures**, where the owner cannot make it financially and so voluntarily calls it quits. Personal failures are far more numerous than formal ones. People put their money, time, and effort into a business only to see losses wipe out the investment. Creditors usually do not suffer, as the owners tend to absorb the losses. The owners are the ones who pack up, close the door, and say, ''That's it!''

WHAT YOU SHOULD HAVE LEARNED

1. There are many opportunities for prospective small business owners, especially in business and professional services, high-tech manufacturing, bars and restaurants, and other services. The best opportunities are in small firms, limited in scope, that involve long, hard hours working to satisfy basic human needs.

2. Some practical suggestions for future small firms are specialized shopping, desktop publishing, helping organizations computerize their activities, applications of fax machines, utilization review firms to help employers reduce their health-care costs, and specialized delivery services.

3. Opportunities in small business abound for women and minorities. Women are starting new businesses at a rapid rate. They now own one-third and are expected to own half of all small firms by the year 2000. Women owning small firms tend to be well educated, capable, and committed owners.

   While black entrepreneurs are progressing in small business, their firms tend to be smaller and less profitable than other firms. The Hispanic market is growing fast and expects to provide many opportunities in the future, especially in mom-and-pop food stores. Cultural networks, along with shrewd business practices—such as having a business plan, hiring professional consultants, and using computers—are aiding the flood of Asian entrepreneurs.

4. Unplanned growth and failure are of particular concern to small business owners. While poorly planned growth can be a real problem, failure to grow can mean the death of a business.

   Another problem is failure and/or discontinuance. Some businesses discontinue for health, family, or other personal reasons, while others fail. Although relatively few of these are formal failures, personal failures resulting from unprofitability or general discouragement can be just as devastating for small business owners.

QUESTIONS FOR DISCUSSION

1. Name the fastest-growing small businesses, as indicated by the number of jobs. Explain their growth.

2. As far as new firms are concerned, what are the fastest-growing industries during the 1990s?

3. Name some practical ideas for small businesses during the 1990s.

4. Evaluate the opportunities in small business for women, blacks, Hispanics, and Asians.

5. How does success cause problems for some small businesses? Can you give examples from your experience or suggest ways to avoid the problems of growth?

SHANGHAI RESTAURANT

Mai and Bob Gu are a perfect example of the adage, "Hard work pays off." Married for five years, the couple has gone from working in the kitchens of other people's restaurants to owning and operating a successful small restaurant, opened in Mobile, Alabama, in 1988. Their first establishment was a modestly sized operation, serving only takeout Chinese and South Vietnamese cuisine. Mai was the sole cook for the business, coming in at 9 A.M. and working hard until at least 10 at night, six days a week.

Mai Gu (upper right) and one of their daughters greet two of their favorite customers.
Photo courtesy of Leon C. Megginson

1975. For several years, she worked in the kitchen for the owner of a successful Hunan restaurant. Although working behind the scenes, she was learning all she could about the operations. Then Bob Gu, who had moved to Mobile from China, entered the picture. It wasn't long before the two were married—and starting their own business.

Business was very good, so the Gus decided to expand their operations. They moved to a larger building where they were able to include dining space and table service. Since their opening day, the Gus say, business has been steady.

The Gus also own a small Oriental market located adjacent to the restaurant. It offers everything from special Oriental teas and spices to hand-carved clocks. According to Mai, the market doesn't attract very much business on its own, but occasionally draws a curious restaurant customer.

The Gus used personal experience in the restaurant industry and a sharp business sense to successfully launch their own enterprise. Mai and Bob both held various jobs in restaurants long before they met in early 1988. Mai has always loved to cook, and she used her culinary skills to find work in Oriental restaurants, first in Los Angeles, California, then in Mobile.

In 1972, Mai divorced her South Vietnamese husband "to find my fortune in America." She knew that she wanted to cook, so she looked for work in the restaurant field. Not satisfied with the job prospects that Los Angeles offered, she moved to Mobile in

Bob is the planner; Mai is the implementer. Bob takes care of the "paper" end of the business, managing the books and ordering supplies and equipment, while Mai runs things in the kitchen and on the restaurant floor. Greeting customers with genuine graciousness when they enter the front door, cooking Oriental dishes with an expertise that comes only from years of hands-on culinary experience, and taking time out to chat with the regulars, Mai and Bob are the perfect hosts. It is quite obvious that they enjoy what they are doing.

Although they own a house in Mobile, Bob and Mai live in an apartment above the market in order to save money. They supplement their income by renting their house to carefully screened tenants. The Gus say the benefits of having additional funds for restaurant and market supplies outweigh any possible inconveniences of living above their business.

Employees of the restaurant, from the kitchen help to the waitresses, are family members lending a hand to make the operation a success. Mai seems especially proud of the fact that all of her children work for her in one way or another. This family involvement adds another dimension to the dining experience for the customer; customers see the same friendly faces each time they visit the restaurant, eventually making them feel almost as if they were eating a meal at home.

Hoping to attract new customers, Mai and Bob obtained a liquor license for the restaurant. They also advertised in the local newspaper in an effort to increase revenues. At present, the Gus say they have no plans to expand or move their operation.

QUESTIONS

1. What is your opinion of the Shanghai Restaurant? Would you choose to patronize the establishment? Why or why not?

2. Assume that the Gus have hired you as a consultant. Make at least three specific recommendations that would improve business and streamline operations.

3. What factors might affect the future of this small business? Discuss.

4. Speculate as to the future success or failure of this small business. Discuss.

Source: Prepared by Ragan Workman Megginson, with the Alabama Radio Network.

4

Legal Forms of Ownership

Good order is the foundation of all good things. —Edmund Burke

To me, going public [incorporating] would be like selling my soul.
—Carlton Cadwell, manufacturer

LEARNING OBJECTIVES

After studying the material in this chapter, you will be able to:
 1. Name the legal forms of ownership a small business can have.

 2. Explain the reasons for and against forming a proprietorship.

 3. Explain the reasons for and against forming a partnership.

 4. Explain the reasons for and against forming a corporation.

 5. Discuss some other legal forms a business can take.

BLOOMIN' LOLLIPOPS, INC.

In 1989, Dot and Jiggs Martin, along with their married daughters, Michele Statkewicz and Renee Thompson, started a small business, Bloomin' Lollipops, Inc., in order to supplement their retirement income and provide future income for their children—and grandchildren, one of whom works in the business. The business specializes in making chocolate flowers, hard candy lollipops, candy animals, a caramel-chocolate-pecan-dipped gourmet apple "drizzled" with white chocolate, and eight varieties of gourmet popcorn. These are arranged in gift baskets, mugs, vases, and other containers. Their unique arrangements are not only sold in the store but are also delivered within a 15-mile radius and shipped nationwide and overseas. The business is advertised on local radio and TV and in local upscale magazines.

The owners did extensive

The Martin Family of Bloomin' Lollipops
Source: Mobile Press Register photographs, February 8, 1990, p. 4–B. © 1990. All rights reserved.

aspects of the ones they liked. Although each person has a job specialty—making candy, arranging the lollipops creatively in containers, or delivering the candy bouquets—each one has learned every phase of the enterprise and helps in all activities as demand dictates.

The Martins also studied what form of ownership would be best for them to use. They wanted to form an S corporation but for technical reasons decided on a C-corporation. All the stock is held by the family. The Martins hold 50 percent of the stock (25 percent each), Michelle 30 percent, and Renee 20 percent. There is a "buy-out" clause in the charter, which permits the other stockholders to buy the stock of anyone leaving the business.

The business has grown so rapidly that the stockholders have opened a satellite location and are considering franchising—selling rights for

research for about six months before opening their store. They worked closely together on all aspects of organizing, promoting, opening, and operating the business. The family members searched for and tried many recipes for candy, then developed their own by combining the best an entire city to a single franchisee. Even with the normal "growing pains," the owners are not only doing an outstanding job of running the business but also enjoying social interaction with each other and with other family relations.

Source: Conversations with the owners, and various newspaper and magazine articles.

The Profile illustrates an important decision small business owners face, namely, what legal form to use. The Martin family chose the corporate form because it best fit their needs at the time. They'll probably change as needs dictate.

SELECTING THE RIGHT LEGAL FORM

Going into business for yourself and being your own boss is a dream that can become either a pleasant reality or a nightmare. Though it may be satisfying to give the orders, run the show, and receive the income, other factors must be considered when choosing the legal form to use. Income tax considerations, the amount of free time available, responsibility for others, and family wishes—as well as the amount of available funds—must also be considered in choosing a proprietorship, partnership, corporation, or other legal form for the business.

Factors to Consider

When choosing the proper legal form for your business, you should ask several basic questions. For example, to what extent is your family able to endure the physical, psychological, and emotional strains associated with running the business? Second, how easy is it to start, operate, and transfer to others your interest in the company? Third, to what extent are you and your family willing to accept the financial risks involved, including being responsible for not only your own losses and debts but also those of other people? Finally, how much information about yourself, your family, and your economic status are you willing to make public? For example, if you choose the corporate form, information about the business—including profits and/or losses—may have to be made public knowledge.

Of course, the choice of legal form does not have to be final. Instead, the usual progression is to start as a proprietorship or partnership and then move into a corporation.

Relative Importance of Each Form

As you can see from Figure 4–1, the proprietorship is by far the most popular form of business in the United States. Around 71 percent of all businesses are proprietorships, while only 20 percent are corporations, and 9 percent are partnerships. Notice in Table 4–1 that the proprietorship is most popular in all industries. Finance, insurance, and real estate use the partnership more frequently than do the other industries, and the corporation is the norm in manufacturing.

While the proprietorship is the most popular form, it accounts for only a small share of total revenues. As Figure 4–1 shows, proprietorships generate only around 6 percent of all revenues, while corporations account for 90 percent, and partnerships provide around 4 percent.

Figure 4–1   Relative Position of U.S. Proprietorships, Partnerships, and Corporations

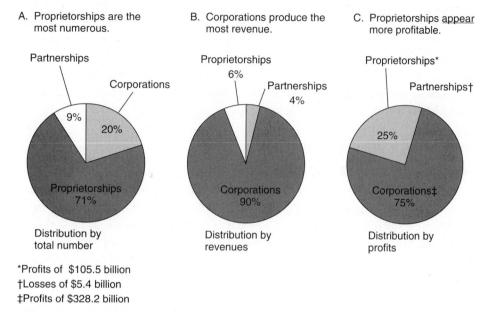

A. Proprietorships are the most numerous.

Partnerships

Corporations

9%

20%

Proprietorships
71%

Distribution by
total number

B. Corporations produce the most revenue.

Proprietorships
6%

Partnerships
4%

Corporations
90%

Distribution by
revenues

C. Proprietorships appear more profitable.

Proprietorships*

Partnerships†

25%

Corporations‡
75%

Distribution by
profits

*Profits of $105.5 billion
†Losses of $5.4 billion
‡Profits of $328.2 billion

Source: U.S. Department of Commerce, *Statistical Abstract of the United States, 1991* (Washington, D.C.: Government Printing Office, 1991), Table 861, p. 525.

Table 4–1   Comparison of Proprietorships, Partnerships, and Corporations in Selected Industries

Industry	Percentage of Firms in the Industry			Percentage of Industry's Business Receipts		
	Proprie-torships	Partner-ships	Corpora-tions	Proprie-torships	Partner-ships	Corpo-rations
Services	81	4	15	20	13	67
Trade	67	5	28	8	2	90
Construction	79	3	18	16	5	79
Finance, insurance, real estate	48	32	20	2	7	91
Manufacturing	52	5	43	*	1	99

*Less than 1 percent
Source: Statistical Abstract of the United States, 1991 (Washington, D.C.: Government Printing Office, 1991), Table 861, p. 525.

Table 4–1 shows that corporations dominate the business receipts in all areas. However, proprietorships account for significant revenues in services and construction.

Figure 4–1 shows that proprietorships appear to be the most profitable form; they received 25 percent of profits on only 6 percent of revenues. Partnerships accounted for 4 percent of revenues but suffered $5.4 billion of *losses*. Corporations received only 75 percent of the profits on 90 percent of the sales. These numbers should be interpreted with caution, however, since proprietorship ''profits'' include net financial return to owners. In a corporation, much of that return would be included in wage and salary expense and deducted from profit.

WHY FORM A PROPRIETORSHIP?

A **proprietorship** is a business
that is owned by one person.

A **proprietorship** is a business that is owned by one person. It is the oldest and most prevalent form of ownership, as well as the least expensive to start. Most small business owners prefer the proprietorship because it is simple to enter, operate, and terminate and provides for relative freedom of action and control—as shown in Figure 4–2. Finally, the proprietorship has a favorable tax status. As will be shown in Chapter 20, it is taxed at the owner's personal income tax rate. In these respects, you may find it an attractive form to use, as millions of proprietors now do.

Notice in the case at the end of the chapter how easy it was for Henry Kloss to begin operating as a proprietor while a student at the Massachusetts Institute of Technology. All he had to do was find a place to produce and sell his cabinets. He probably did not even have to pay taxes. Also, he was independent, with no co-owners to cause him problems.

Figure 4–2 also shows some negative factors that should be considered. First, from a legal point of view, the business and its owner are one and the same and cannot be separated. Consequently, the business legally ends with the proprietor's death, and some legal action must be taken to restart it. Second, if the business does not have enough funds to pay its obligations, the owner must use personal assets to pay them. Figure 4–2 summarizes the major advantages and disadvantages of owning a proprietorship.

WHY FORM A PARTNERSHIP?

A **partnership** is a business
owned by two or more persons
who have unlimited liability for
its debts and obligations.

A **partnership** is a voluntary association of two or more persons to carry on as co-owners of a business for profit. As shown in Figure 4–3, the partnership is similar to the proprietorship but is more difficult to form, operate, and terminate. Partnerships are generally more effective than proprietorships in raising funds and in obtaining better ideas, management, and credit. Also, as with the proprietorship, profits are taxed only once—on each partner's share of the income—not twice, as in the corporation.

Figure 4-2 Weighing the Advantages and Disadvantages of a Proprietorship

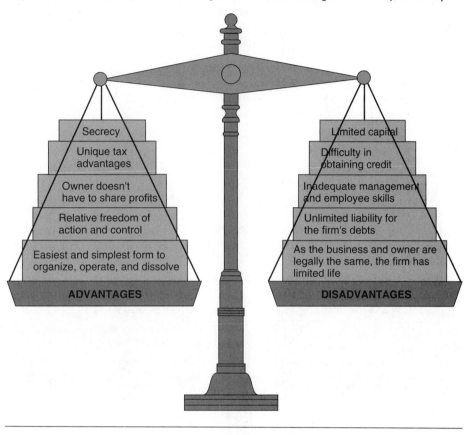

Secrecy

Unique tax advantages

Owner doesn't have to share profits

Relative freedom of action and control

Easiest and simplest form to organize, operate, and dissolve

ADVANTAGES

Limited capital

Difficulty in obtaining credit

Inadequate management and employee skills

Unlimited liability for the firm's debts

As the business and owner are legally the same, the firm has limited life

DISADVANTAGES

Figure 4-3 also shows that the partnership has many drawbacks. For example, the death of any one of the partners legally terminates the business, and legal action is needed to revive it. This disadvantage may be overcome, however, by an agreement among the partners stating that the remaining partner(s) will purchase the interest of the deceased partner. Further, the partnership itself usually carries insurance to cover this contingency.

How a Partnership Operates

Each partner is responsible for the acts of all the other partners. Thus, all partners—except in a limited partnership (see next section)—are liable for all the debts of the firm; even the personal property of each partner can be used to satisfy the debts of the partnership. Nor can a partner obtain bonding protection against the acts of the other partner(s). Therefore, each partner is bound by the actions of the other partners, as the following example illustrates.

Figure 4–3   Weighing the Advantages and Disadvantages of a Partnership

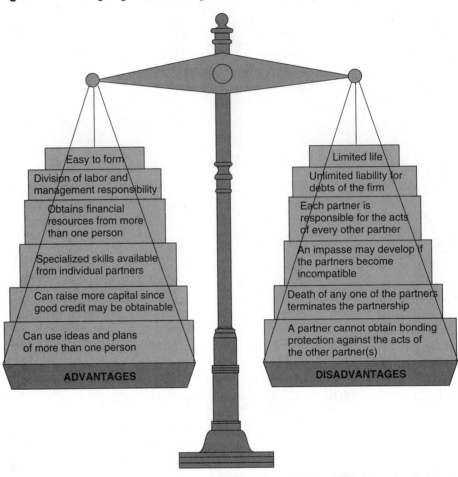

Edward Nickles, a 37-year-old Bostonian, was delighted when his small accounting firm, Pannell Kerr Forster, made him a partner. But his joy was short-lived; after the firm paid $1 million of a $5 million legal settlement, his annual income plummeted from $145,000 to $65,000. Later, the firm dropped its partnership structure and reorganized itself into six separate professional corporations in five states.[1]

An impasse can easily develop if the partners can't agree on basic issues. Consequently, the business may become inoperative (or even dissolve).

This is what happened at Acoustic Research, as described in the case at the end of this chapter. When there was a disagreement over day-to-day operations, Kloss and the others pulled out and sold their interest, but one partner stayed in.

━━━━━━━━━━ USING TECHNOLOGY TO SUCCEED ━━━━━━━━━━

HOW TO FORM A LIMITED PARTNERSHIP

Software is now available with programs to help organize small businesses. One type in particular is available through the Attorneys' Computer Network, Inc. One program is *The Limited Partnerships Library.* By answering relevant multiple-choice, yes/no, and fill-in-the-blank questions, the user can develop the necessary limited partnership agreements, certificates, and various other provisions or options. The options include deferred capital contributions, loans from partners, and reporting requirements.

Other programs offered are *The Shareholders Agreements Library, The Corporate Kits Library,* and many others. Information regarding these programs may be obtained from Attorneys' Computer Network, Inc.; 415 Marlboro Road; Kennet Square, PA 19348. Phone (215) 347-1500.

Source: Jim H. Fernandez, J.D., University of Mobile, Mobile, Alabama.

Types of Partnerships

Partnerships may be general or limited. In a **general partnership**, each partner is known to the public and held liable for the acts of the other partners. In a **limited partnership**, there are one or more general partners and one or more limited partners, whose identity is not generally known. The firm is managed by the general partners, who have unlimited personal liability for the partnership's debt. The personal liability of the limited partners is limited to the amount of capital contributed by them. Limited partners may be employees of the company but may not participate in its management.

> In a **general partnership**, each partner actively participates as an equal in managing the business and being liable for the acts of other partners.

Rights of Partners

If there is no agreement to the contrary, each general partner has an equal voice in running the business. While each of the partners may make decisions pertaining to the operations of the business, the consent of all partners is required to make fundamental changes in the structure itself. The partners' share of the profits is presumed to be their only compensation; in the absence of any agreement otherwise, profits and losses are distributed equally.

> In a **limited partnership**, one or more general partners conduct the business, while one or more limited partners contribute capital but do not participate in management and are not held liable for debts of the general partners.

Ordinarily, the rights, duties, and responsibilities of the partners are detailed in the **articles of copartnership.** These should be agreed on during the preoperating period and should spell out the authority, duties, and responsibilities of each partner. (See Using Technology to Succeed for software that can be used for this purpose.)

> **Articles of copartnership** are drawn up during the preoperating period to show rights, duties, and responsibilities of each partner.

A partnership is required to file Form 1065 with the IRS for information purposes. The IRS can—and sometimes does—challenge the status of a partnership and may attempt to tax it as a separate legal entity.

WHY FORM A CORPORATION?

A **corporation** is a business formed and owned by a group of people, called stockholders, given special rights, privileges, and limited liabilities by law.

In one of the earliest decisions of the U.S. Supreme Court, a corporation was defined as "an artificial being, invisible, intangible, and existing only in contemplation of the law." In other words, a **corporation** is a legal entity whose life exists at the pleasure of the courts. The traditional form of the corporation is called a **C corporation**.

The **C corporation** is a regular corporation that provides the protection of limited liability for shareholders, but its earnings are taxed at both the corporate and shareholder levels.

The formation of a corporation is more formal and complex than that of the other legal forms of business. The minimum number of persons required as stockholders varies with individual state laws, but it usually ranges from three to five. The procedure for formation is usually legally defined and requires the services of an attorney. Incorporation fees are normally based on the corporation's amount of capital.

The corporate form offers several advantages, as shown in Figure 4–4. Since the corporation is separate and distinct from the owners as individuals, the death of one stockholder does not affect its life. Also, each owner's liability for the firm's debts is limited to the amount invested, so personal property can't be taken to pay the debts of the business (with certain limited restrictions, such as loan guarantees, nonpayment of taxes, and malfeasance). Finally, since the owners are not required to help run the firm's operations, large amounts of capital can be raised relatively easily.

Notice in the case at the end of this chapter that Henry Kloss decided to incorporate when he needed more capital but wanted to restrict his liability and reduce the chances of disruption from partners. This made it easier for him to sell his interest to Singer and to raise money from friends when he organized Kloss Video.

The many disadvantages of the corporation, also shown in Figure 4–4, might keep you from choosing it for your business. The main problem is double taxation, as the corporation pays taxes on its profit, and then individual owners pay taxes on their dividends. (As will be shown later, this is one reason for using an S corporation.) Also, the area of operations is limited by the corporation's charter, and the process of incorporation is complex and costly.

How to Form a Corporation

Articles of incorporation are the instrument by which a corporation is formed under the corporation laws of a given state.

To form a corporation, **articles of incorporation** must be prepared and filed with the state in exchange for a **corporate charter**, which states what the business can do and provides other information. Also, the procedures, reports, and statements required for operation of a corporation are cumbersome, and because the owners' powers are limited to those stated in the charter, it may be difficult for the corporation to do business in another state.

A **corporate charter** states what the business can do and provides other organizational and financial information.

Figure 4–4

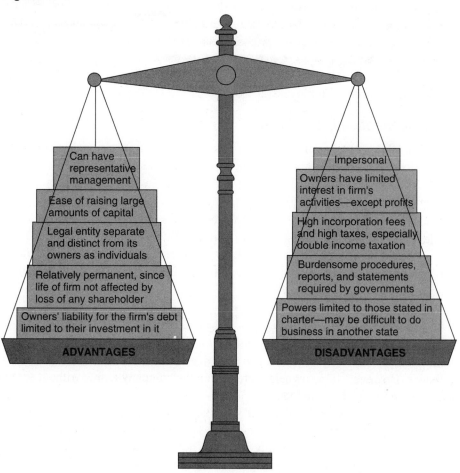

Because the legal requirements for incorporating vary from state to state, it might be advantageous to incorporate in a state favorable to business—such as Delaware. Delaware's incorporation requirements are so lenient that, despite its small size, it charters more corporations than any other state. Texas, however, has fewer filing requirements and simpler forms than any other state.[2]

One danger in any business is that one of the owners will leave and start a competing business. Even if trade secrets are not stolen, the new competitor will have acquired business knowledge at the corporation's expense. It may not be possible to prevent such defections, but incorporators can make provisions during the incorporation process for recovering damages for any loss the firm suffers.

A **buy-sell agreement** explains how stockholders can buy out each other's interest.

One way is to include a **buy-sell agreement** in the articles of incorporation. This arrangement details the terms by which stockholders can buy out each other's interest. Also, if the success of the venture is dependent on key people, insurance should be carried on them. This type of insurance protects the resources of the firm in the event of the loss of these people (see Chapter 22).

Adequate bond and insurance coverage should be maintained against losses that result from the acts of employees and others.

How a Corporation Is Governed

The initial incorporators usually operate the corporation after it is formed. But they are assisted by other stockholders, directors, officers, and executives.

Stockholders

The stockholders are the corporation's owners. In a small company, one or a few people may own most of the stock and therefore be able to control it. In a large corporation, however, holders of as little as 10 percent may be able to control the company. Often, the founders have the controlling interest and can pick the people to be on the board of directors.

Board of Directors

The board of directors represents the stockholders in managing the company. Board members can help set goals and plan marketing, production, and financing strategies. However, some owners prefer to run the company alone, without someone "looking over their shoulder."

There are many sources of effective outside directors, such as experienced businesspeople, investors, bankers, and professionals such as attorneys, CPAs, or business consultants. It is becoming difficult, however, to obtain competent outsiders to serve on boards—especially of small companies—because liability suits may be filed against them by disgruntled stockholders, employees, customers, or other interested parties.[3]

Corporate Officers

While their titles and duties vary, corporate officers usually include the chairman, president, secretary, and treasurer. Within limits set by stockholders and the board, these officers direct the day-to-day operations of the business. (See Using Technology to Succeed (page 67) for software that can help in this respect.) As the business grows, others are often added to constitute an executive committee, which performs this function.

The S Corporation

Corporations with 35 or fewer stockholders and no corporate shareholders or incorporated subsidiaries can, under certain circumstances, reduce the burden of

━━━━━━━━━━━━━━━━━━━ USING TECHNOLOGY TO SUCCEED ━━━━━━━━━━━━━━━━━━━

IT'S LEGAL

Parson's Technology* has developed a software package called *It's Legal,* Version 3.0, which can be used to help perform some of the activities of a corporation. For example, *It's Legal* deals with issues such as election of corporate directors at the annual meeting of the stockholders; preparation of board minutes of official corporate action(s) taken by stockholders or boards of directors; notices/waivers to stockholders and directors as proper notice of upcoming meetings, or waivers regarding voting for certain actions; solicitation of board consent to various actions; and preparation of a corporate worksheet.

These general issues have a ''you-fill-in-the-blanks'' structure, much the same as that of a preprinted will. However, there are some areas that are ''state sensitive,'' which would justify obtaining professional legal guidance.

*One Parson's Drive, P.O. Box 100, Hiawatha, IA 52233-0100.
Source: Bob Leslie, Leslie Enterprises, Fort Walton Beach, Florida.

---

taxes by forming an S corporation (formerly called a *Subchapter S corporation*). The **S corporation** eliminates multiple taxation of income and the attendant paperwork, as well as certain other taxes. For example, regular corporations must deduct Social Security taxes on income paid to owners employed by the firm, as well as pay the employer's share of the taxes. But if an owner receives an outside salary above the maximum from which such taxes are deducted, the S corporation neither deducts nor pays Social Security taxes on the owner's income.

An **S corporation** is a special type of corporation that is exempt from multiple taxation and excessive paperwork.

If the income from corporate operations is distributed to the stockholders of an S corporation, they pay taxes on it at their individual rates. While the payment process is similar to that of a partnership, the corporation must file a special federal income tax return. The maximum individual tax rate of 28 percent is lower than the 34 percent maximum for regular corporations. For this reason, many small businesses have chosen to switch to this ownership form in order to reduce income taxes.

There are, however, significant costs to electing S corporation status. For one thing, these corporations can issue only one class of stock—common. This may limit equity financing in some cases, as other forms of stock—which can't be issued by the S corporation—are preferred by many venture capitalists. Another disadvantage is that all shareholders must be individuals, estates, or some type of personal trust.[4] Therefore, no other corporation or partnership may invest in the company. Finally, tax rules for S corporations are very tough and confusing, as the following example shows.

In 1990, Dallas-based Hartfield & Co., a wholesale distributor of industrial valves, reorganized as an S corporation. While savings in taxes more than justified the switch, George Boles, Hartfield's chief financial officer, had to cope with "one of the murkiest and most volatile aspects of the tax code."[5] According to him, "The Subchapter S rules have got to be some of the toughest in the land."

OTHER FORMS OF BUSINESS

Other legal forms can be used by a small business owner. The most popular of these are the limited-liability company (LLC), the trust, the cooperative, and the joint venture.

The Limited-Liability Company (LLC)

The **limited liability company (LLC)** combines the advantages of a corporation, such as liability protection, with the benefits of a partnership, such as tax advantages.

Since 1977, a few states have authorized the formation of **limited-liability companies (LLCs)** to help entrepreneurs gain the benefit of limited liability provided by the corporation without its double taxation.[6]

The LLC is quite attractive to many small business owners, for without some shield from personal liability, an owner can be held personally liable for the company's debts, which is a major deterrent to prospective proprietors and partners. Like a partnership, an LLC distributes profits and losses directly to owners and investors, who must report them on their personal income tax return. But, like a corporation, it shields their assets from liability claims.

Because of its newness and the limited number of states permitting it, you may run into difficulty if you operate in a state that does not permit the LLC.

Because of worries about environmental problems and the liabilities associated with them, clients of F. B. Kubic, a Wichita, Kansas, accounting firm, used an LLC for an oil and gas venture. They needed the limited-liability protection because of potential lawsuits from environmental problems.[7]

The Trust

A **trust** is established for a specific period of time to hold and distribute assets for the benefit of others.

A trust is designed to overcome some of the disadvantages of the general partnership; it provides continuity of life as well as ease of transferring ownership. It also provides certain tax advantages.

A **trust** differs from a corporation in that it is established for a specific time period or until certain designated events occur. The trust, which receives specific assets from the person(s) establishing it, is administered by a trustee or a board of trustees. The trust covenant defines the purpose of the trust, names the beneficiary or beneficiaries, and establishes a formula for distributing the trust's income and assets.

The Cooperative

A **cooperative** is a business owned by and operated for the benefit of patrons using its services.

A **cooperative** is a business composed of independent producers, wholesalers, retailers, or consumers that acts collectively to buy or sell for its clients. Usually the cooperative's net profit is returned to the patrons at the end of each year, resulting in no profits and no taxes to it. To receive the advantages of a cooperative, a business must meet certain requirements of federal and state governments. The cooperative form of business is usually associated with farm products—purchasing, selling, and financing farm equipment and materials, and/or processing and marketing farm products.

Tasting Delta Pride Catfish
Courtesy of Walter Harrison, Jr., Delta Pride Catfish Inc.

Delta Pride Catfish Inc. of Indianola, Mississippi, the farm-raised catfish capital of the United States, is such a cooperative. Catfish farming—the nation's largest aquaculture industry—is done primarily by small farmers who don't have the expertise or resources to do their own marketing. So they join cooperatives that provide aggressive marketing and financing. Delta Pride, the largest U.S. processor of fresh fish, is a farmer-owned cooperative with nearly 200 members, each of whom receives one share of stock for each acre of land in production. Delta Pride's members own 64,000 acres of catfish ponds.[8]

The Joint Venture

Working relationships between noncompeting companies are quite popular these days and may become even more so in the future. The usual arrangement is a **joint venture**, which is a form of temporary partnership whereby two or more firms join together in a single endeavor to make a profit. For example, two or more investors may combine their finances, buy a piece of land, develop it, and sell it. At that time, the joint venture is dissolved.

Many small businesses are using their research and development capabilities to form joint ventures with larger companies that provide them with marketing and financial clout, as well as other expertise.

A **joint venture** is a form of temporary partnership whereby two or more firms join together in a single endeavor to make a profit.

For example, SolarCare, Inc., a small Bethlehem, Pennsylvania, company, tried—with only limited success—to sell SunSense, a towelette moistened with sunscreen lotion and wrapped in foil. Because of resulting financial difficulties, it tried to attract a venture capitalist, but the 1987 stock market crash dashed hopes for the deal.

SolarCare put together a comprehensive tie-up with the Plough Inc. unit of Schering-Plough Corporation. SolarCare focuses on production and research-and-development work, and Schering uses its greater expertise and resources to market SolarCare's "SunSense by Coppertone." Thus, SolarCare keeps its name on its product and gains a potential distributor for new products while retaining its identity.[9]

In summary, in an endeavor where neither party can achieve its purpose alone, a joint venture becomes a viable option. Usually, income derived from a joint venture is taxed as if the organization were a partnership.

WHAT YOU SHOULD HAVE LEARNED

1. Although your choice of legal form is important, it is not final, for many businesses progress from one form to another. While most small businesses are proprietorships, they generate only a small proportion of business revenues; yet they seem to be quite profitable. Most other U.S. businesses are corporations and partnerships. Corporations account for most of the revenues and profits.

2. A proprietorship is a business owned by one person. It is simple to organize, operate, and dissolve, and gives the proprietor much freedom. The owner gets all the profits (if any), is not required to share information with anyone, and has some unique tax advantages. Since the business is legally inseparable from its owner, it ends when he or she dies. The owner is personally liable for all the debts of the business and may find it hard to raise money or get credit.

3. A partnership is jointly owned by two or more people and is automatically dissolved by the death of any partner. The partners share its profits, its management, and its liabilities. The partnership can combine the resources of several people but can also be difficult to manage if the partners disagree. Moreover, except for limited partners, all partners bear responsibility for the actions of the other partners, and bonding protection against such actions is not available.

4. A corporation is a legal entity separate from its owners. Because owners aren't personally responsible for its liabilities, the corporate form makes it possible to raise large amounts of capital, provides representative management, and assures the continuity of the business regardless of what happens to individual owners. Its main disadvantages are double taxation, the expense and paperwork of incorporation, and the limitations of its charter, which may make it difficult to operate in another state.

   Stockholders have the right to make decisions submitted to them for a vote but may be dominated by a majority of the owners. The board of directors, which is elected by the stockholders, is responsible for running the company, but day-to-day operations are directed by company management.

   For simple businesses, with 35 or fewer shareholders and no corporate shareholders or incorporated subsidiaries, the S corporation offers relief from multiple taxation and some of the burdensome paperwork.

5. Other forms of business include limited-liability companies (LLC), trusts, cooperatives, and joint ventures.

QUESTIONS FOR DISCUSSION

1. What are some of the basic questions to ask when deciding on the legal form to choose for a small business?

2. Define *proprietorship*, *partnership*, *corporation*, *trust*, *cooperative*, and *joint venture*.

3. What are some advantages and disadvantages of a proprietorship?

4. What are some advantages and disadvantages of a partnership?

5. What are some advantages and disadvantages of a corporation?

6. Distinguish between a general partnership and a limited partnership.

7. Distinguish between a C corporation, an S corporation, and a limited-liability company (LLC).

HENRY E. KLOSS: PROPRIETOR, PARTNER, AND CORPORATE OWNER

Henry E. Kloss's first venture into business, as an undergraduate at Massachusetts Institute of Technology, involved designing, making, and selling cabinets for stereos to pay his way through school.

After military service, Kloss returned to Cambridge, where his skills as a cabinetmaker, combined with his interest in electronics and sound, led him to Edgar Villchur, who had an idea for an acoustic suspension system. They formed a partnership, Acoustic Research, in 1954 and pioneered the production of acoustic suspension speakers, which made all other types of loudspeakers obsolete. Half the company stock went to Kloss and

Photo courtesy of Henry E. Kloss.

two other investors, and the other half went to Villchur. Eventually, disagreement over day-to-day management required a separation, so Kloss and the two top managers left.

They sold their interest for about $56,000 and formed KLH Corporation to produce a low-cost, full-range speaker. Later, they expanded their product base by adding items such as the Dolby® noise reduction system. Their sales doubled from $2 to $4 million in the year after they were the first to use transistors in a consumer product — a portable stereo.

In 1964, KLH was sold to Singer for $4.0 million, of which Kloss received $1.2 million. (Unfortunately for him, Singer stock was the second biggest loser on the New York Stock Exchange the next year.) But, over three years, he had sold most of his stock on the open market. Kloss ran KLH for Singer until 1967; but when Singer chose not to enter the TV market,

Kloss left and sold the rest of his stock to Singer for $400,000.

Kloss then founded Advent Corporation to produce projection TV and high-quality, low-priced speakers. Advent lost over $2 million during the first year of production of the TV, so its bankers required new management, and new capital, in 1975.

Kloss spent the next two years perfecting a low-cost method for manufacturing the tubes for his large-screen TV. In 1979, he founded Kloss Video with $400,000 of his own money and $400,000 from private sources. Kloss was president and treasurer. Its two-piece, large-screen projection set, the Novabeam, had sharper and brighter images than those of its competitors. Because of lack of sufficient widespread interest in big TV by the public, Kloss Video reentered the speaker market. Kloss Video's stock declined after reaching its top price in 1983, when Kloss's 60 percent share was worth about $15 million.

By 1987, Kloss Video was interested in emphasizing consumer sales, so the directors asked Kloss to search for a new president from outside the company. Instead, they chose one of their own for the position and appointed Kloss as head of research and development.

Kloss left to start a new company — Cambridge SoundWorks — in nearby Newton, Massachusetts. Its total capital was a $250,000 no-equity loan, from Dr. Henry Morgan, who had been associated with Kloss for several years. Its Ensemble speaker system comprises four separate units: two woofers and two tweeters. The speakers are known for "quality and afford-ability."

In 1992, sales were over $10 million, and net income was over $500,000.

QUESTIONS

1. What caused Henry Kloss's partnership, Acoustic Research, to fall apart? Explain.

2. What inherent problem(s) do you see in having a 50-50 percent ownership (and management) of a company, as was the case in Acoustic Research? Explain.

3. Kloss started and has been involved with four corporations. How might he have avoided the problems he eventually had with his first three corporations? Would you classify Kloss as a success? Why or why not?

4. Assume that you have been hired by Kloss's newest corporation, Cambridge SoundWorks, as a consultant. Your job is to keep Kloss from repeating past mistakes and help him avoid making new ones. What advice and counsel would you give?

5. Putting aside financial considerations, speculate as to which form of business ownership was most rewarding to Kloss.

Source: Correspondence with Henry Kloss and Kloss Video; and various others, such as Kloss Video 10-K filings and proxy statements for the years 1984–1987; and Hans Fantel, "Henry Kloss's Mail-Order Speakers," *The New York Times,* February 19, 1989, p. H32.

II

PLANNING FOR
AND ORGANIZING
A BUSINESS

Part I showed some opportunities in small business, as well as the characteristics of small businesses and their owners. It included some thoughts on studying the economic environment in order to increase the chances of success, but those suggestions presented general ideas rather than precise details. In this part, more specific ideas for planning and organizing a small business are covered. The information presented is considerably more detailed, taking a practical "how to do it" approach to the activities involved in starting such a business.

Owners and managers of small firms must get things done through others, allocate scarce resources, and make decisions so that their objectives are reached. In doing these things, they perform the same five functions as managers in an organization of any size: planning, organizing, staffing, leading, and controlling. Some business textbooks organize individual chapters around these functions, but we will discuss them all in their proper context throughout the text.

We will, however, devote specific chapters to detailed discussion of the activities involved in starting a business. Chapter 5 explains how to become a small business owner; Chapter 6 shows how to do strategic and operational planning; Chapter 7 presents some of the growing opportunities in franchising; Chapter 8 explains how to prepare and present a business plan; and Chapter 9 discusses sources of operating and venture capital.

5

How to Become a Small Business Owner

To start and run a small business, you must know and be many things. —Small Business Administration

There is no such thing as growth industries. There are only companies organized and operated to create and capitalize on growth opportunities. —Theodore Levitt

LEARNING OBJECTIVES

After studying the material in this chapter, you will be able to:

1. Explain how to go into business for yourself.

2. Describe the steps involved in the procedure recommended for going into business.

3. Describe how to search for and identify a product.

4. Describe how to study the market you are entering, including sources of information.

5. Decide whether to start a new business, buy an existing one, or buy a franchise.

JERRY AND MONA SAMUEL: COMBINING OLD-FASHIONED NEWSSTAND AND MODERN GIFT SHOP

Mona and Jerry Samuel started the News 2 U Store in the Muddy Branch Shopping Center in Darnestown, Maryland, in 1988. They went into business with the idea of "running a fun store" that would be different from others. The store is based on the old-fashioned idea of combining good service with a wide selection of goods for customers to choose from.

Photo courtesy of Rick Dugan, in *Bethesda* (Maryland) *Gazette,* August 31, 1989, p. 36.

small gifts. In fact, they even sell "penny candy"—for a dime. According to the Samuels, they added the candy and gifts to make the business more interesting as well as to "provide financial security."

This idea has led to economic success for the couple.

In keeping with the classic newsstand model, the Samuels stock over 1,500 titles of different newspapers and magazines. They carry 40 daily newspapers from around the country; between 70 and 80 computer magazines; and a variety of exercise, health, and running magazines. But it's hard to make a profit with just a magazine store, so the owners added a gift shop with a wide range of candy and

This old-fashioned idea won acceptance even in a fast-paced, high-tech world, leading the Samuels to open two other stores in the fall of 1989. One store is located at the top of L'Enfant Plaza Metro in Washington, D.C., and the other in Rockville, Maryland.

The store is a family business. The parents, aged 42, divide the duties, with Mona selecting the gifts and novelty items and Jerry ordering the books, magazines, and newspapers. Their three children, aged $2\frac{1}{2}$ to 13, assist by accompanying them to shows and testing out the toys and candy.

Source: Jenny Well, "Success of News 2 U Store Prompts Expansion," *Bethesda* (Maryland) *Gazette,* August 31, 1989, pp. 36–37.

Figure 5–1   How a Business Is Formed and Operates

As you can see from the Profile, many opportunities exist for enterprising people to go into business for themselves. As shown in Figure 5–1, the process begins when you have an idea for a new product, such as combining a newsstand and gift shop. Then you decide on the ownership and management of the business and obtain resources—in the form of people, buildings and equipment, materials and supplies, and the money to finance them. You then begin producing and selling the product to obtain revenues to pay expenses and provide you with a profit—so that you can repeat the cycle.

While the concept is simple, the actual process is not as easy as it may appear from the figure or from the Samuels' experience. In fact, the actual process of choosing a business to enter is quite complex, as will be shown in this and the following chapters.

HOW TO GO INTO BUSINESS FOR YOURSELF

Chapter 2 cites many reasons for starting a small business, and Chapter 3 describes some of the available opportunities. Those who do decide to take the important

━━━━━━━━━━ USING TECHNOLOGY TO SUCCEED ━━━━━━━━━━

COMPUTERIZED BUSINESS START-UPS

There is now a host of computer software to help people start a new business. One of the latest is *Venture*, developed by the University of Southern California and Star Software Systems. Used with IBM-compatible systems, it provides a business plan, word processor, file manager, general ledger, spreadsheet, and information on obtaining financing and corresponding with customers. (Note: For further information, call 1-800-242-7827.)

How to Write a Business Plan, developed by the American Institute of Small Business, provides practical information on how to create a business plan. It offers tips on sales forecasting, marketing and competitive analyses, and projected balance sheets, cash flow data, and profit and loss statements. It can be used with Apple's Macintosh as well as IBM-compatibles. (Note: For further information on creating a business plan, call 1-800-328-2906.)

step of starting their own business must do extensive planning in order to increase their chances of success. Now we would like to explain how to actually go into business—if that is what you would like to do.[1]

How to Start a Business

Once the decision is made to go into business, proper planning becomes essential. While there is no one tried-and-true procedure that will work for everyone, you should at least follow some logical, well-thought-out procedure.[2] The next Using Technology to Succeed suggests some shortcuts available if you have a computer.

Steps in Starting a Business

If you *really want to start a new business*, how do you do it? We've tried to compress all the details into the following eight steps:

1. Search for and identify a needed product.*
2. Study the market for the product, using as many sources of information as feasible.
3. Decide whether to start a new business, buy an existing one, or buy a franchise.
4. Make strategic plans, including setting your mission, strategic objectives, and strategies.
5. Make operational plans, including setting policies, budgets, standards, procedures, and methods and planning the many aspects of producing and marketing the product.

*Technically, a product can be either a physical good or a service. To prevent repetition, we will use the term *product* to mean a physical good or a service.

"I had secured sufficient financial backing, I'd set up fine inventory and cash management systems! I was ready for business, then it hit me . . . I had no product or service!"
Source: *Management Accounting,* May 1988, p. 77.

6. Make financial plans, including estimating income and expenses, estimating initial investment, and locating sources of funds.

7. Develop these plans into a detailed business plan.

8. Implement the plan.

The first three of these steps are covered in this chapter. Steps 4, 5, and 6 are discussed in Chapter 6, and steps 7 and 8 are covered in Chapter 8. Implementing the business plan is also covered throughout the text.

IDENTIFYING A NEEDED PRODUCT

Many business owners fail because they see the glamour of some businesses—and the apparent ease with which they are run—and think, "I know I can make a lot of money if I start my own business." While a few do succeed without adequate preparation, the majority fail. While proper planning does not ensure success, it improves the chances of succeeding.

Planning starts with searching for a product to sell. According to William A. Sahlman, who teaches entrepreneurial finance at Harvard, "Being bright-eyed and bushy-tailed isn't necessarily a barometer of success. If people succeed, it's because they really understand an industry and perceive some need or service that no one else has seen."[3] So first find your product!

The list of possible products is almost unlimited, considering the variety of goods and services offered by the nearly 21 million U.S. businesses now in existence. What types of businesses are available? Not all the fields are open, but there is very likely a potential niche for a new business; you just have to find it. Some of the most successful small firms find a "niche within a niche" and never deviate from it.

For example, Tom Turrisi, who plays guitar with his left hand, started a left-handed guitar club. In 1980, the club evolved into a Springfield, Virginia, business—Shane Musical Instruments—which designs and sells guitars for left-handed people.[4]

How to Decide on a Product

How can the right product be found? Most new businesses were at one time uncommon or innovative, such as selling front pouches for parents to carry children in, selling or renting videotapes, and selling computer software. Talking to large companies may help you identify opportunities that can be handled better by a small business. Newspapers are filled with advertisements for "business opportunities"—businesses for sale, new products for sale by their inventors, and other opportunities to become one's own boss. Bear in mind, though, that *these ideas are not always feasible, so proceed with caution.*

Don't forget to look to the past for a "new" product. Consumer tastes run in cycles, so it may be time to reintroduce an old product.

For example, the magazine *Victoria* is devoted to Victorian-style decorating; and old-fashioned clothes for children—at thoroughly modern yuppie prices—are sold in trendy stores and catalogs.

"High Tea"—old-fashioned English tea, scones, French pastries, and fruit trifle—is served daily at the Oak Bay Beach Hotel in Victoria in a picturesque lounge overlooking a bay.

Hobbies, recreation, and work at home require study, training, and practice that can lead to products of new design or characteristics. In addition, the subject of needed products and services often comes up in social conversation. Bankers, consultants, salespeople, and anyone else can be good sources of ideas. But it takes observation, study, vision, and luck to recognize the appropriate product for your business.

The search for and identification of a product require innovative and original thinking, including putting the ideas together in an organized form. For example, if the chosen product is now being provided by competitors, what change is necessary for you to compete successfully—or avoid competition altogether? Can an original approach be used in serving the public? Not always!

For example, things looked good for Steven Freeman, aged 29. He was soon to marry, get his M.B.A. from the Wharton School, and revolutionize Manhattan's real estate market: He would use a computer database to match buyers and sellers. But after working for 18 months and investing $30,000 of his family's money, he quit; not enough people were willing to pay for the service to make it profitable.[5]

Figure 5–2   Questions to Ask to Help Eliminate Possible Businesses

1. How much capital is required to enter and compete successfully in this business?
2. How long will it take to recoup my investment?
3. How long will it take to reach an acceptable level of income?
4. How will I live until that time?
5. What degree of risk is involved? Am I willing to take that risk?
6. Can I make it on my own, or will I need the help of my family or others?
7. How much work is involved in getting the business going? In running it? Am I willing to put out that much effort?
8. Do I want to acquire a franchise from an established company, or do I want to start from scratch and go it on my own?
9. What is the potential of this type of business? What are my chances of achieving that potential?
10. Is sufficient information available to permit reaching a meaningful decision? If so, what are the sources of information?
11. Is it something I would enjoy?

Looking into the future requires extensive reading and contacts with a wide variety of people. Constant questioning of changes that are occurring and critical analysis of products and services being received provide ideas. Innovation is alive and well, and will continue its surge ahead. Each new idea spawns other ideas for new businesses.

Choosing the Business to Enter

In choosing the business to enter, first eliminate the least attractive ideas from consideration and then concentrate on selecting the most desirable one. It is important to eliminate ideas that will not provide the challenges, opportunities, and rewards—financial and personal—that you are seeking. Be rather ruthless in asking, "What's in it for me?" as well as "What can I do to be of service to others?" Questions like those in Figure 5–2 will be helpful. Also, concentrate on the thing(s) you would like to do, not on what someone else wants for you.

After eliminating the unattractive ideas, get down to the serious business of selecting the business to which you plan to devote your energy and resources. One way of doing this is to get a group of friends, a diversified group of small business managers, or a few **SCORE (Service Corps of Retired Executives)** members together and ask them what kinds of products are needed but not available. Try to get them to identify not only existing types of businesses but also new kinds; then consider the market for the kinds of products and businesses they have suggested.

Several self-help groups of entrepreneurs in various parts of the country can be called upon at this stage—as well as later stages. These groups help potential entrepreneurs find their niche and then assist them in surviving start-up, operating, and even personal problems.

SCORE (Service Corps of Retired Executives) is a group of retired—but active—managers from all walks of life that helps people develop their business ideas.

For example, one such group—Master-Mind—operates in Palo Alto, California. It meets twice monthly to help small business owners develop new ideas and cope with "their pressure-cooker world." Master-Mind tries to avoid concerns about direct competition among group members by including a wide variety of businesses. Also, those with new business ideas feel secure in the group because everyone agrees that the discussions are to be confidential.[6]

When obtaining advice from outsiders, though, remember that it is your resources that are at stake when the commitment is made, so the ultimate decision must be yours. *Don't let someone talk you into something you are uncomfortable with.*

After discussing the need for the product with other people, select the business that seems best for you. To be more methodical and objective in your evaluation, you might prepare a checklist similar to the one in Figure 5–3. It is used by a consultant with the MIT Enterprise Forum to help people decide what business to enter. You could use these criteria to help you decide whether suggestions you've received are appropriate for you. If not, make other lists until you find an idea that matches your ability, training, experience, personality, and interests.

Figure 5–3 Business Selection Survey Checklist

Capital required	Degree of risk involved	Amount of work involved	Independent ownership or franchise	Potential of the business	Source of data

Initially you may want to make more than one choice and leave yourself some options. Remember to consider your personal attributes and objectives in order to best utilize your capabilities. Let your mind—not your emotions—govern your decisions.

STUDYING THE MARKET FOR THE PRODUCT

After selecting the product and business, look at the market potential for each one. If a market does not exist—or cannot be developed—don't pursue the project any further. On the other hand, there may be a market in a particular location or a segment of the population that needs your product.

Small businesses usually select one segment of the population for their customers, or choose one product niche, since they do not have sufficient resources to cover the whole market. Also, small businesses cannot include as large a variety of products in their efforts as large businesses can. Hence, a small business must concentrate its efforts on the customers it can serve effectively.

Methods of Obtaining Information about the Market

Marketing research is the systematic gathering, recording, and analyzing of data related to the marketing of goods and services.

There are many ways to identify a market, and all can be generally classified as marketing research. As will be discussed in Chapter 12, **marketing research** consists of gathering, recording, classifying, analyzing, and interpreting data related to the marketing of goods and services. Formal research programs can be very valuable in giving direction, but they can also be expensive. Computers are helping to increase the amount of information gathered while reducing the cost.

Another means of collecting data is a search of existing literature. The first places to look in a library are the "technical section" and the "government documents section." You should examine Census Bureau data on subjects such as population, business, and housing.

The SBA also can be a helpful source of data, as can the research divisions of chambers of commerce, colleges, and trade associations, as well as local business leaders, bankers, and congressional representatives. Talking with others—even potential competitors—can yield useful information.

The U.S. Department of Commerce is another good source of information, as its district offices have well-stocked libraries of census data. The Department of Commerce publishes an especially useful book, *Measuring Markets: A Guide to the use of Federal and State Statistical Data*.[7]

Method Used to Study the Market

There are four things you need to do when estimating your sales and market share. First, determine the size of the industry and market segment you want to enter.

Second, estimate your competition and figure out its market share. Third, determine how you stack up against the competition. Finally, estimate your own sales volume.

Estimating the Size of the Market

Before launching a business, you should find out, by asking the following questions, whether the market for it is large enough to accommodate a newcomer:

- How large is the industry?
- Where is the market for the company, and how large is it?
- Are sales to be made to a selected age group, and, if so, how large is that group?
- What are the size and distribution of income within the population?
- Is the sales volume for this kind of business growing, remaining stable, or declining?
- What are the number and size of competitors?
- What is the success rate for competing businesses?
- What are the technical aspects (state of the art) of the industry?

Estimating the Competition

In studying the market area, the number of similar businesses that have gone out of business or merged with a competitor should be determined. A high number of these activities usually signals market weakness. Analysis of competitors' activities may also indicate how effectively a new company can compete. Is the market large enough for another firm? What features—such as lower price, better product, or more promotion—will attract business? Can these features be developed for the new firm?

Determine the kinds of technology being applied by other firms in the industry. For example, do other machine shops use hand tools, or do they have state-of-the-art equipment, including robots? The level of technology is significant in determining operating costs.

Estimating Your Share of the Market

By now, you should be able to arrive at a ballpark figure for your sales volume and share of the market. First, determine the geographic boundaries of the market area and estimate how much of your product might be purchased. Finally, make an educated guess as to what part of this market you might attract as your share.

Figure 5–4   Which Road to Take?

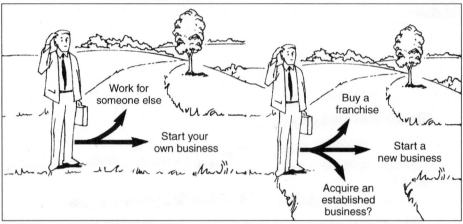

DECIDING WHETHER TO START A NEW BUSINESS, BUY AN EXISTING ONE, OR BUY A FRANCHISE

By now, you have probably decided what type of industry you want to enter and have done an economic feasibility study of that industry and the potential business. The next step is to decide whether to start a new business from scratch, buy an established business, or buy a franchise. As shown in Figure 5–4, many prospective business owners find themselves in a quandary over which direction to take. The material in this section may be helpful in making the choice more effectively.

To Start a New Business?

Most successful small business owners start their own business, because they want others to recognize that the success is all theirs. Often, the idea selected is new, and the businesses for sale at the time do not fit the desired mold. Also, the facilities needed should be new so that the latest ideas, processes, and procedures can be used. Size of company, fresh inventory, new personnel, and new location can be chosen to fit the new venture.

All this is exciting and—when successful—satisfying. But the venture is also challenging because everything about it is new, it demands new ideas, and it must overcome difficulties. Moreover, because everything is newer, a larger investment may be required.

✳ Reasons for Starting a New Business

Some of the reasons for starting a new business lie in the owner's freedom to:

■ Define the nature of the business.

■ Create the preferred type of physical facilities.

- Obtain fresh inventory.
- Have a free hand in selecting and developing personnel.
- Select the competitive environment, to a certain extent.
- Take advantage of the latest technology, equipment, materials, and tools to cover a void in acceptable products available.

For example, Kathy Kolbe raised such a fuss about the lack of stimulating educational materials in her children's schools that she was appointed to head a committee to develop a program for gifted children. Finding no such materials, she wrote and produced her own. She offered these materials to several publishers, but they rejected her offer, considering the market too small to be profitable. So she took $500 from her savings and launched a firm called Resources for the Gifted. She wrote catalogs and sent them to around 3,500 schools and parents. Her first few years were tough, but after six years, she was grossing $3.5 million a year.[8]

Reasons for Not Starting a New Business

Some of the reasons for not starting a new business are:

- Problems in finding the right business.
- Problems associated with assembling the resources—including the location, building, equipment, materials, and a work force.
- The lack of an established product line.
- Production problems associated with starting up a new business.
- The lack of an established market and channels of distribution.
- Problems in establishing basic management systems and controls.

Also, the risk of failure is higher in small business start-ups than in acquiring a franchise or even buying an existing business.

To Buy an Existing Business?

Buying a business can mean different things to different people. It may mean acquiring the total ownership of an entire business, or it may mean acquiring only a firm's assets, its name, or certain parts of it. Keep this point in mind as you study the following material. Also remember that many entrepreneurs find that taking over an existing business isn't always a "piece of cake."

Reasons for Buying an Existing Business

Some reasons for buying an established business are:

- Personnel are already working.
- The facilities are already available.

- A product is already being produced for an existing market.
- The location may be desirable.
- Financial relationships have been established with banks and trade creditors.
- Revenues and profits are being generated, and goodwill exists.

For example, when the owner of the Speedy Bicycle Shop suddenly decided to sell the business, Don Albright, the manager, arranged to buy it. He alerted all the customers who had Christmas layaways to come and collect their purchases before the owner closed the shop.

This gained Don a lot of goodwill when he reopened the shop as his own. Although he had to come up with a lot of capital to purchase new inventory, he had the experience of managing the shop before he owned it.

Reasons for Not Buying an Existing Business

Some reasons for not buying an ongoing business are:

- The physical facilities may be old or obsolete.
- The employees may have a poor production record or attitude.
- The accounts receivable may be past due or uncollectable.
- The location may be bad.
- The financial condition and relations with financial institutions may be poor.
- The inventory may be obsolete or of poor quality.

For example, a group of investors considered buying a coal mine in West Virginia. Because the market for coal was favorable, they thought they had a good deal. However, they found that the local coal was of such poor quality that the market would not accept the firm's product. The group decided not to invest.

To Buy or Not to Buy

Even if there are several businesses to choose from, the evaluation finally comes down to one business that must be thoroughly evaluated before the final decision is made. The steps in this procedure can be compared to these involved in launching a space shuttle, as shown in Figure 5–5. The countdown involves several weeks of intense preparation before the crew climbs into the cabin. Then comes the final countdown. Until the last few seconds, the flight (mission) can be aborted, but from that point on, ''all systems are go.''

The same tends to be true when buying an established business. Up to a given point, the buyer can change the decision to buy. Beyond that point, the decision is final.

Figure 5–5   To Go or Not to Go

Photo courtesy National Aeronautics and Space Administration.

A word of caution is needed here. Past success or failure is not sufficient foundation for a decision of whether or not to buy a given business. Instead, you must make a thorough analysis of its present condition and an appraisal of what the business might do in the future. The following are some important questions to be asked when making the decision to buy an ongoing business.

1. Why is the business available for purchase?   This question should help establish the validity of the owner's stated reason for selling the business. Some reasons provide a challenging opportunity, as this example shows.

Robert Sinclair dropped out of college in his senior year for financial reasons. After working several years for a building supply firm, he went to work as manager of the metal door division for a partnership engaged in diversified construction of commercial buildings. Because the partners were so busy with their other activities, Bob was left to run the division by himself. Finally, he offered to buy the division from the partners, and they accepted. He is now the owner-manager of Sinclair Construction Company.

2. What are the intentions of the present owners?   After selling a business, former owners are free to do what they wish unless restricted by contract. What has been said before the sale and what happens afterward may not be the same. Some questions needing answers are: Will the present owner remain in competition? Does he or she want to retire or leave the area? What is the present owner's physical—and financial—health?

For example, Ron Sikorsky spotted the following in the newspaper one Sunday: "For reasons of health, owner willing to sacrifice successful, profitable sandwich shop, priced for immediate sale." Ron dashed over to the Submariner. The place was full, and business was great. (All the owner's friends just happened to need a sandwich that day.) Following some haggling, Ron and the owner shook hands, and Ron wrote a check for $10,000 of his savings.

A month later, Ron found out the hard way that the business had been ready to fold when he took the bait. The former owner's friends were gone, and business was terrible, but the former owner's (financial) health was miraculously improved!

---

3. Are environmental factors changing?   The demand for a firm's product may rise or fall because of such factors as changes in population characteristics, neighborhood, consumer habits, zoning, traffic patterns, environment, tax law, or technology.

4. Are physical facilities suitable for present and future operations?   To be suitable, facilities must be properly planned and laid out, effectively maintained, and up-to-date.

5. Is the business operating efficiently?   A prospective buyer should know whether a business will need to be "whipped into shape" after purchase. Are the personnel effective? Is waste excessive or under control? Is the quality of the product satisfactory, and is the inventory at the proper level and up-to-date? The following two actual situations are examples of waste and obsolescence.

An example of waste: A potential buyer of a carpet mill noticed that the mill's employees were slicing off one to three inches on each side of the carpets as they were being produced. In the follow-up analysis, he found that if the machines were properly set, the mill could save $10,000 per day.

An example of inventory obsolescence: The owner of a hardware store decided to sell his business. A prospective buyer found 200 horse collars among the antiquated stock.

---

6. What is the financial condition of the firm?   It is important to know whether the firm is a good financial risk. This can be determined by checking variables such as the validity of financial statements, the cash position, the cash flow through the business, various financial ratios, the amount and terms of debt, and the adequacy of cost data.

7. How much investment is needed?   Remember that the investment includes not only the purchase price of the existing firm but also capital needed for renovations, improvements, and start-up activities, such as ordering new stock, advertising and promotion, and legal and license fees.

✳ **8. What is the estimated return on investment?**   This estimate should be realistic and not based on wishful thinking. It should include potential losses as well as potential gains.

Other factors to consider.   One important factor that should always be considered is the price asked for the firm. Sometimes, a successful ongoing business can be bought at a fraction of its value. But while you may be lucky enough to get such a bargain, be wary of pitfalls. For example, a retailer may offer to sell a business for "the current price of assets—less liabilities." But the accounts receivable may be a year or more in arrears, while the inventory consists of unsalable goods. Also, the extent of liability should be verified. Be sure to have a CPA audit the records and verify the inventory and its value.

Another element to consider is your managerial ability. Some people have a special talent for acquiring ongoing businesses that are in economic difficulty and turning them around. If you have—or can develop—this special talent, the ability is valuable to society and profitable to you, the new entrepreneur.

For example, an experienced small businessman sold his business and searched for another business to get involved in. His interests included managerial challenge, economic growth, and profit. After looking at several possibilities, he acquired a small company that manufactured a top-quality airport service vehicle. The company needed additional capital and more effective management. The new owner was able to bring these two ingredients into the company and make it a success.

To Buy a Franchise?

As you will see in Chapter 7, franchising is expanding rapidly and appears to be very successful. Yet franchisors have failed, and some franchisees have suffered severe losses. So the decision to buy a franchise is a serious one.

✳ **Reasons for Buying a Franchise**

Franchise agreements normally spell out what both the franchisor and franchisee are responsible for and must do. Each party usually desires the success of the other. The franchisor brings proven and successful methods of operation and business images to aid the franchisee.

If you decide to become a business owner, you can obtain guidance from experienced people by obtaining a franchise. Franchises are available in a wide range of endeavors, so you may be able to find one that combines your talents and desires, as the following example shows.

David and Tamara Kennedy, of Sausalito, California, once made their living skippering and being a chef aboard yachts around the world. But they were drawn to an ad by a nautical bookstore franchise—Armchair Sailor Bookstore—seeking to expand nationally. "Must have a love of the sea and know how to sail," it said. "While we won't become millionaires," they confessed after buying a franchise, "we love what we're doing and are doing something we know about. It's been a learning experience for both of us."[9]

Another reason for buying a franchise is that it probably has many of the requirements for success. The market niche has been identified, and sales activities are in place. Also, the business may already be located, managed, and running. The questions to ask about franchises are: How much help do I need? Can a franchise help me enough to more than cover the costs of the franchise?

Most potential small business owners do not have the competencies or resources to get started successfully. But the franchisor can provide supplemental help through its experience and concentrated study of the field. These talents come from both successes and failures in the past. A study of the services listed in the contract, in relation to your needs, shows the value to you.

Reasons for Not Buying a Franchise

A franchise is not a guarantee of success. The costs may outweigh the benefits from its purchase. Including expenses such as the initial investments and fees, as well as royalty payments, a franchise can be costly. Also, it may not fit the owner's desires or direction, or it may not give the franchisee enough independence. Also, overpriced, poorly run, uninteresting, and white elephant franchises are potentially disastrous, as the following example illustrates.

A man put up $2,000 as a guaranteed investment for candy machines after the franchisor promised to find good locations for the machines. These failed to materialize, however, because all the desirable locations were already in use. The franchisor disappeared, and the man lost his $2,000.

Even under the best of conditions, franchisors tend to hold an advantage, as shown in Table 5–1. Usually, this relates to operating standards, supply and material purchase agreements, and agreements relating to the repurchase of the

Table 5–1   How Franchising Benefits Both Franchisee and Franchisor

Selected Benefits to the Franchisee	Selected Benefits to the Franchisor
1. Brand recognition	1. Faster expansion and penetration
2. Management training and/or assistance	2. Franchisee motivation
3. Economies of large-scale buying	3. Franchisee attention to detail
4. Financial assistance	4. Lower operating costs
5. Share in local or national promotion	

franchise. Also, there are constraints as to the size of the territory and the specific location. Moreover, you sometimes have no choice about the layout and decor. However, careful study of franchisors' past records and contract offerings can lead to selection of a potentially successful franchise operation.

WHAT YOU SHOULD HAVE LEARNED

1. The first thing to do in becoming a small business owner is to decide whether it is what you *really want to do*. Then, proper planning becomes essential to chart your new venture. The time of starting your new business is also important.

2. Although there is no set procedure for starting a business, there are steps that can be taken to help ensure success. They are *(a)* search for a needed product; *(b)* study the market for the product; *(c)* decide whether to start a new business, buy an existing one, or buy a franchise; *(d)* make strategic plans, including setting a mission, objectives, and strategies; *(e)* make operational plans, including setting up policies, budgets, procedures, and plans for operating the business; *(f)* make financial plans, including estimating income, expenses, and initial investment, and locating sources of funds; *(g)* prepare a business plan; and *(h)* implement the plan. The first three steps were discussed in this chapter.

3. The product to sell can be found by *(a)* reading books, papers, and other information; *(b)* having social and business conversations with friends, support groups, businesspeople, and others; and *(c)* using checklists, questioning people, and doing marketing research.

4. Studying the market for the problem involves estimating *(a)* the size of the market, *(b)* the competition and its share of the market, and *(c)* your own share of the market.

5. Next, you should decide whether to *(a)* start a new business, *(b)* buy an existing one, or *(c)* buy a franchise. There are compelling arguments for and against each of these alternatives. Starting a new business means it is your own, but the process is time-consuming and quite risky.

   When you buy an existing business, you acquire established markets, facilities, and employees. But you must be sure when you buy that all aspects of the business are in good shape and that you are not inheriting someone else's problems.

   Buying a franchise may help bring success in a hurry, since it provides successful management and operating procedures to guide the business. But you must be able to succeed on your own, for a franchise does not ensure success. Also, the cost may be high, or the franchisor may not perform satisfactorily.

QUESTIONS FOR DISCUSSION

1. Is planning really as important in starting a business as the authors say? Defend your answer.

2. What are some important factors to consider in choosing the type of business to enter?

3. How can you identify a business you would like to own? What characteristics do you have that would help make that business successful?

4. How do you go about determining the market for a product? Your share of that market?

5. What kinds of answers to the questions in Figure 5–2 would lead you to eliminate a business from consideration?

6. What are some of the characteristics you should consider in studying the potential market for a proposed business?

7. What are some reasons for and against starting a new business?

8. What are some reasons for and against buying an existing business?

9. What are some reasons for and against buying a franchise?

TIPS FOR BUYING AN EXISTING BUSINESS

Although it may not appeal to true entrepreneurs, buying, rather than starting, a firm does have certain advantages, such as a quicker return on one's investment of time and money. To get those advantages, advises attorney Mitchell Kossoff, whose clients have taken both routes, "Make sure you are buying a business with a good location, an existing plant or facilities, competent employees, some market penetration, a solid base of paying customers, usable inventory and good relations with suppliers and creditors." But Kossoff warns, "This analysis is too complex for an individual to do alone. You'll need the services of lawyers, accountants, business brokers, business appraisers, consultants, and bankers."

"They will examine balance sheets, income tax returns—both federal and local—and other financial statements prepared by a CPA for the seller," says accountant and attorney Stuart Rosenblum. "Have your accountant go over the financial statements and put your attorney to work performing a lien and judgment search on the owners and the hard assets of the business."

Find out why the seller wants to sell. Is the client base diminishing? Are there supply problems or employee problems? Maybe the plant and facilities are obsolete, there are disputes with the landlord, or creditors are after the seller. "Never take the seller's word for why he or she is selling," Rosenblum warns. "Try and dig deep and find the real reason."

Once you have determined the value of the tangibles in the business, you must place a value on the intangibles—often called *goodwill*. This can include its relations with customers, banks, and suppliers.

Next, decide how much the business is worth. "It has to be a better investment than other, more traditional investments," Kossoff says. "Consider the rate of return, analyze the assets, then subtract from them the liabilities."

The financial arrangements you make with the seller are limited only by law and your accountant's creativity.

QUESTIONS

1. Do you agree with Mitchell Kossoff that buying an existing business is so complex that you must have the services of outside experts? Explain.

2. What are some of the reasons a business owner might want to sell the business?

3. How important are "intangibles"?

6

Strategic and Operational Planning

Businesses don't plan to fail, they just fail to plan.—Old business adage

If there's one thing certain about business today, it's change. . . . To meet change head-on, you must predict it, plan for it, and use it.—J. Neal Thomas, head of Arthur Young's Entrepreneurial Services

LEARNING OBJECTIVES

After studying the material in this chapter, you will be able to:
1. Tell why planning is so important—yet so neglected—in small businesses.
2. Distinguish between the two basic types of planning.
3. Explain the role of strategic planning, and give some examples.
4. Explain the role of operational planning, and give some examples of what is involved.
5. Explain the role of financial planning, and give some examples of it.

SPACE SERVICES INC.: USHERING IN THE U.S. COMMERCIAL SPACE INDUSTRY

"Long live free enterprise!" shouted some 300 observers as the 37-foot-long *Conestoga I* rocket lifted off from a makeshift launch pad on the Texas Gulf Coast on September 9, 1982. David Hannah, Jr., chairman of Space Services Inc. (SSI), said to his fellow investors, "I think we're going to make a lot of money with this."

The launch culminated years of effort—and many disappointments. The original *Conestoga,* aptly named for the covered wagons used by early American pioneers, blew up while being tested the week before launch. The firm hired an experienced California contractor and a former astronaut, "Deke" Slayton, as president and flight director. With the help of a $2.5 million investment, these two people, along with six other full-time employees, succeeded in developing the *Conestoga I.*

After spending $6 million to achieve just one successful launch, SSI then raised the $15 million needed to develop, supply, and manage low-cost launch vehicles, launch sites, launch activities, and related services. It plans to offer these commercial systems and services to a broad range of customers in the private sector and government agencies—especially as an alternative to the manned space shuttle. Since the 1986 *Challenger* explosion, there has been renewed interest in unmanned space programs.

By the early 1990s, this privately financed venture was expected to have a fleet of telecommunications and earth-scanning satellites. At least "a dozen" energy companies have expressed interest in doing business with SSI, especially to monitor oil flows at untended offshore wells and to conduct geological surveys from space.

These plans came closer to reality on March 29, 1989, when SSI launched the nation's first private spaceship into a 15-minute suborbital flight that was expected to usher in the age of U.S. commercial space industry. *Consort I*—costing between $1 and $2 million, standing 52 feet tall, and weighing 6,000 pounds at lift-off—was launched from the White Sands Missile Range, New Mexico. It carried six experiments assembled by the University of Alabama—Huntsville's Consortium for Materials Development in Space, which is one of 16 commercial development consortiums sponsored by NASA.

SSI plans several similar launches in the next couple of years and is applying for a license to be the first private contractor to send a satellite into orbit. It believes there is a big future for this type of activity.

Photo courtesy of Space Services Inc.

Sources: Correspondence with Space Services Inc. of Houston, Texas; and others, including "Spaceship's Flight Lasts 15 Minutes," *Mobile* (Alabama) *Register,* March 30, 1989, p. 6-A; and Marcia Dunn, "Astronaut Remembers First Space Flight," *Mobile* (Alabama) *Press Register,* April 28, 1991, p. 11-F.

The Profile illustrates some of the problems and steps involved in planning, organizing, and developing a new business. The first three of those steps were discussed in Chapter 5, and steps 7 and 8 will be covered in Chapter 8. Steps 4, 5, and 6 are explained in detail in this chapter.

THE ROLE OF PLANNING

In order to become an effective business owner-manager, you must look ahead. In selecting the business to enter, as discussed in Chapter 5, you are doing just that—planning for the future.

As shown in Figure 6–1, planning should be the first step in performing a series of managerial functions because it sets the future course of action for the business.

Figure 6–1   How Planning Relates to Other Managerial Functions

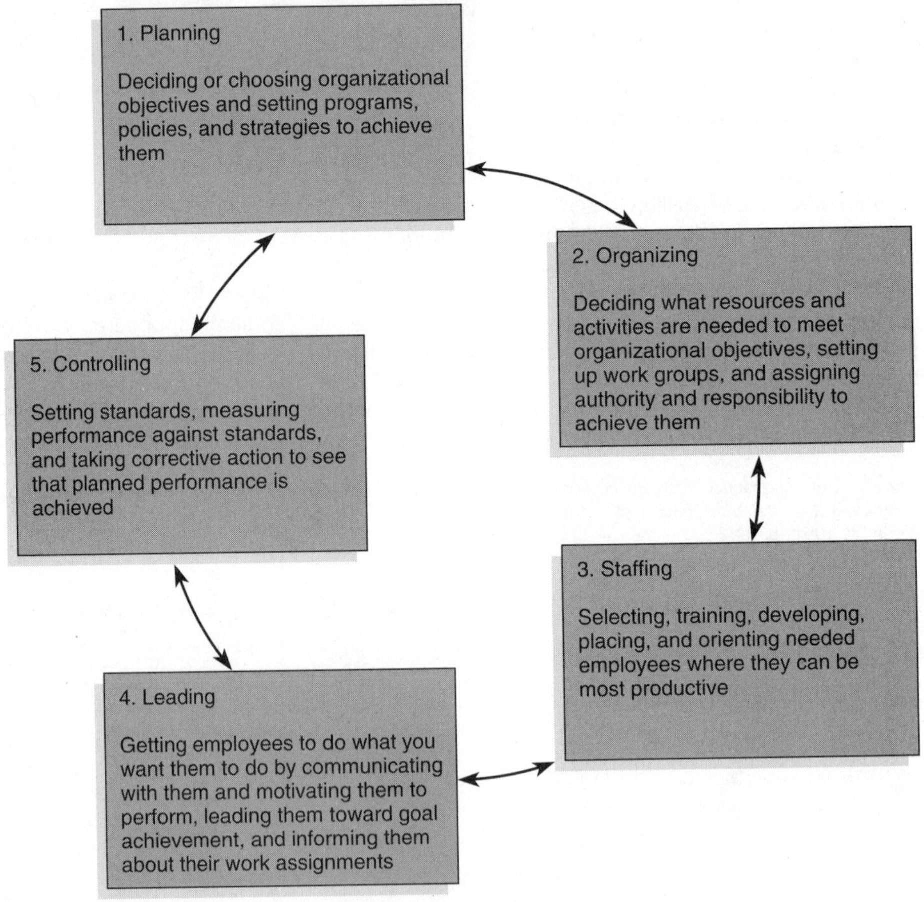

1. Planning

Deciding or choosing organizational objectives and setting programs, policies, and strategies to achieve them

2. Organizing

Deciding what resources and activities are needed to meet organizational objectives, setting up work groups, and assigning authority and responsibility to achieve them

3. Staffing

Selecting, training, developing, placing, and orienting needed employees where they can be most productive

4. Leading

Getting employees to do what you want them to do by communicating with them and motivating them to perform, leading them toward goal achievement, and informing them about their work assignments

5. Controlling

Setting standards, measuring performance against standards, and taking corrective action to see that planned performance is achieved

Planning, which is the process of setting objectives and devising courses of action to achieve those objectives, answers such questions as these: What business am I in? What finances do I need? What is my sales strategy? Where can I find needed personnel? How much profit can I expect?

Planning is the process of setting objectives and determining courses of action to reach them.

Why Small Businesses Need to Plan

Planning is one of the most difficult activities you must do. Yet it is essential that you do it because, before taking action, you must know where you are going and how to get there. Outsiders who invest or lend money need to know your chances of success. Plans provide courses of action, information to others, bases for change, and a means of delegating work. In summary, well-developed plans can (1) interest moneyed people in investing in your business, (2) guide the owner and managers in operating the business, (3) give direction to and motivate employees, and (4) provide an environment to attract customers and prospective employees.

Why Small Businesses Neglect Planning

Although planning is so important, it is one of the most difficult managerial activities to perform. Therefore, small businesspeople, preoccupied with day-to-day operations, often neglect planning. However, they should remember that, while predicting the future is *risky,* doing no planning can be *disastrous.*

Some reasons why so many small business owners neglect planning, despite its importance, are that (1) day-to-day activities leave them little or no time for planning, (2) they fear the problems and weaknesses planning may reveal, (3) they lack knowledge of how to plan, and (4) they feel that future changes cannot be planned for.

In summary, planning requires original thinking, takes time, and is difficult to do, but it does help one prepare to take advantage of promising opportunities and cope with unexpected problems.

Types of Planning

As shown in Table 6–1, planning is usually divided according to the nature of the planning and the distance into the future for which it is done. These criteria set the level in the organization where the planning is usually done and the amount of research required to do it.

The first type, which is long-range, high-level planning, is called **strategic planning.** It consists of (1) setting the company's mission and establishing the objectives that need to be attained in order to accomplish it and (2) determining strategies, which are the methods used to achieve those objectives.

Operational planning is needed to carry out the strategic plans and operate the business. It sets policies, methods, procedures, and budgets.

Strategic planning provides comprehensive long-term direction to help a business accomplish its mission.

Operational planning sets policies, procedures, and standards for achieving objectives.

THE ROLE OF STRATEGIC PLANNING

Strategic planning is perhaps the most important type of planning done by owners and managers of small businesses, for it provides the major, comprehensive, long-term plan that determines the nature of the business. Unfortunately, only about a third of small firms use long-range strategic planning.[1]

Table 6–1 shows that strategic planning consists of two parts: the firm's mission and objectives, and its strategies. The following are some examples of strategic planning:

- Selecting the type of business to enter.
- Formulating the mission of the company.
- Deciding whether to start a new business, buy an existing one, or buy a franchise.
- Choosing the product or service to sell.
- Deciding on the market niche to exploit.
- Selecting the location for the business.

Table 6–1   Some of the Most Important Types of Plans and Planning Functions

Types of Plans and Planning Functions	Examples
Strategic planning:	
Mission: The long-term direction of the business.	To provide financial security at low cost.
Objectives: Shorter-term ends to help achieve the mission.	
For total firm.	Earn a 20 percent return on investment in 1995.
For functional area.	Increase penetration of market by 25 percent by 1996.
Strategies: Means to achieve an end, or courses of action needed to achieve objectives.	
For total firm.	Establish control procedure to control costs by 1995.
For functional area.	Use 1 percent of sales to improve and expand service.
Operational planning:	
Policies: Guides to action that provide consistency in decision making, particularly in repetitive situations.	*Personnel policy:* Promote from within, giving preference to promotions for present employees.
Methods and procedures: Prescribed manner of accomplishing desired output.	*Employee selection:* Complete application form, test, interview, investigate, select.
Budgets and standards: Plans for future activities using measures for control.	*Cash budget:* For planning use of money.

- Choosing the type of organization to use.
- Determining financial needs.

✳ Mission and Objectives

The **mission** is the long-range vision of what the business is trying to become. It is concerned with broad concepts such as the firm's image; with the basic services the firm plans to perform (e.g., "entertainment" instead of just "movies"); and with long-term financial success. Once set, missions are rarely revised.

A business's **mission** is its long-term vision of what it is trying to become.

A clear definition of your mission enables you to design results-oriented objectives and strategies. To deviate from your true mission can have adverse results, as the following example shows.

George Patterson and a partner founded City Gardens Inc. in Boston to sell and maintain plants for offices. Within a few years, however, the partners had opened a retail flower store in Boston; a garden center in Washington, D.C.; and a branch office in Atlanta. "We lost a lot of money, and we were going nowhere," says Patterson.

What business were they in? "Plants" seemed the only way to describe it. What business should they be in? The answer, they decided, was "interior landscaping," since their competitive edge was their expert knowledge of the local market. So they got rid of their non–interior landscaping activities.[2]

Objectives are the goals that give shorter-term direction to the business and serve as benchmarks for measuring performance. Examples of objectives might include: "To increase total sales by 8 percent a year" and "To introduce within the next two years a new product aimed at the middle-class consumer." Objectives are more specific than missions and are revised more frequently. Table 6–2 illustrates how objectives can be set. Choosing the mission and objectives for a small busi-

Objectives are the purposes, goals, and desired results for the business and its parts.

Table 6–2   Example of How Objectives Can Be Set

Firm's Objectives	1994	1995	1996
Total net profit (income) after taxes	$____	$____	$____
Return on investment (ROI) (net income after taxes/total assets)			
Return on equity (ROE) (net income after taxes/equity)	____	____	____
Total sales volume (units)	____	____	____
Total sales volume ($)	____	____	____
Return on sales (ROS) (net income after taxes/sales)	____	____	____
To attain a ____ percent share of market by the end of 1995.			
To have a ____ percent debt-to-equity ratio in the capital structure initially, declining to ____ percent debt-equity at the end of 1995.			
To develop a new product by the end of 1996.			

ness involves two important considerations: the business's external environment and the internal resources that give it a competitive edge.

The External Environment

The external environment includes clients, competitors, the economy, technology, and many other influences. Changes caused by the introduction of videotapes, computer hardware and software, lasers, and population aging, for example, have been a blessing to some companies and a death warrant to others. The expanding communication and transportation systems require that even the smallest companies keep abreast of a constantly widening range of events. The needs and desires of clients, often following fads, may change so rapidly that it's difficult to adjust to them.

For example, Sally Von Werlhof started Salaminder Inc. in 1974 to design, produce, and sell only top-of-the-line American-made western apparel. Growth was steady until the 1980 movie *Urban Cowboy* caused the demand for western wear to skyrocket. Salaminder was swamped with orders and expanded its work force to 60 employees. But sales plummeted in July 1981, when the fad died—just as suddenly as it had begun.[3]

Internal Resources and Competitive Edge

The internal resources found in small businesses include those listed below. Also, to be competitive, the resources must include the characteristics listed.

Human resources are the personnel that make up the business's work force.

1. **Human resources** include both management and nonmanagement people and include key operating employees such as production supervisors, sales personnel, financial analysts, and engineers. To keep the company competitive, these people must be motivated, imaginative, qualified, and dedicated.

Physical resources are the buildings, tools and equipment, and service and distribution facilities that are needed to carry on the business.

2. **Physical resources** include buildings, tools and equipment, and service and distribution facilities. For the company to be competitive, these resources must be strategically located, be productive, be low in operating costs, be effective distributors, and make the proper product.

Financial resources include the cash flow, debt capacity, and equity available to finance operations.

3. **Financial resources** include cash flow, debt capacity, and equity available to run the business. To make the company competitive, company finances must be adequate to maintain current levels of activities and to take advantage of future opportunities.

A **competitive edge** is a particular characteristic that makes a firm more attractive to customers than its competitors.

If a small firm has exceptionally good resources and they are effectively used, it can have a **competitive edge** over its competitors. Therefore, a proper evaluation of available resources may permit you to concentrate on more productive activities and avoid those that appear attractive but are really more costly than profitable.

══════ USING TECHNOLOGY TO SUCCEED ══════

WHAT'S YOUR COMPETITION UP TO?

Miller Business Systems of Dallas plugs information obtained from customers into computer ''profiles'' of its competitors, which it then studies for ways of outmaneuvering these rivals. During a routine scan of those profiles, John W. Sample, Miller's vice-president for sales and marketing, noticed that a competitor had hired nine furniture salesmen in a 10-day period. He believed that was a tip-off to a probable push by the competitor in the office furniture market. Sample had Miller's salesmen make extra calls on their accounts and was able to blunt the competitor's sales drive. His conclusion: ''Your best customers can sometimes be your best sources of information.''

Source: Steven P. Galante, ''More Firms Quiz Customers for Clues about Competition,'' *The Wall Street Journal,* March 3, 1986, p. 21. Reprinted by permission of THE WALL STREET JOURNAL, © 1986 Dow Jones & Company, Inc. All Rights Reserved Worldwide.

For example, in the case of Salaminder Inc., Sally Von Werlhof tried to cope by diversifying beyond the limits of her resources. She found, however, that producing a new line of $5 pot holders took as long as a $50 garment, and a new line of children's clothes cost only $3 less to make than one for adults selling for $40 more. Since the production system was not designed for these changes, Von Werlhof discontinued unprofitable products that did not conform to the company's basic process and concentrated on licensing Salaminder designs to other producers. Sales increased by 50 percent.[4]

As you can see from this example, a small business must align its mission, objectives, and resources with its environment if it is to be effective. The proper evaluation of its competitive edge can make a small firm's planning more realistic and lead to greater profitability.

Strategies

Strategies are the means by which the mission and objectives sought by a small business can be achieved. A basic question in setting strategies is, How should the business be managed in order to achieve its objectives and fulfill its mission? To be most effective, strategies should give a business a competitive advantage in the marketplace (see Using Technology to Succeed). They should combine the activities such as marketing, production or operations, research and development, finance, and personnel in order to use the firm's reources most effectively.

Figure 6–2 shows how a strategy can be set up to fulfill the mission of a small business. Notice that John Smith will provide certain services and policy coverage to clients so that they will have maximum personal financial security at the lowest possible cost.

Strategies are the means by which a business achieves its objectives and fulfills its mission.

Figure 6-2   Mission/Strategy of John Smith
                             General Agent
                             Tulsa, Oklahoma

Mission: To provide the maximum amount of personal financial security at the lowest possible cost while maintaining the highest quality of individualized service.

Objective: To serve the financial needs of businesses, individuals, and their families in the Tulsa area through guaranteed income to meet loss from death or disability, through these services and policy coverages:

■ Estate tax planning.
■ Qualified pension and profit sharing.
■ Group life and health.
■ Ordinary life.
■ Business interruption.

Management by objectives (MBO) is a management technique for defining goals for subordinates through agreement between them and their supervisors.

Management by objectives (MBO) is one method for attaining established goals. Many companies have found MBO programs helpful in aligning the employees' goals with the firm's objectives. MBO emphasizes goal orientation, with employees setting objectives for themselves. Their managers meet with them to discuss, change, and/or reach agreement on those objectives, how they can be accomplished, and how they relate to achieving the firm's overall objectives.

A well-designed MBO program provides each employee with appropriate feedback on results compared with the planned objectives. Employees are expected to overcome obstacles that stand in the way of achieving those objectives. Near the end of a designated period, employees prepare reports for review and discussion with their supervisor.

THE ROLE OF OPERATIONAL PLANNING

Why do so many small businesses fail? Probably the underlying reason in most cases is lack of proper operational planning. Such planning is vital because it helps potential entrepreneurs avoid costly blunders, saves time, and results in a more polished final product. Three types of planning will improve a small business owner's chances of success: (1) operational planning before starting the business; (2) a business plan to attract investors, financiers, and prospective employees; and (3) continuous planning and control after the business starts operating.

As shown in Chapter 5 (Figure 5-1), the business process involves (1) providing the business with the proper financial, physical, and human resources; (2) converting them through some form of operations into goods or services; and (3) distributing them to other processors, assemblers, wholesalers, retailers, or the final consumer. Businesses can be set up to perform any one or more of the parts of this total process.

Setting Up Policies, Methods, Procedures, and Budgets

As you can see from Table 6–1 (page 100), operational planning starts with setting policies, methods and procedures, and budgets, which together form the basis for the other part of operational planning.

Policies guide action. They exist so that managers can delegate work and employees will make decisions based on the thinking and wishes of the business owner. **Methods** and **procedures** provide employees with standing instructions for performing their jobs. They comprise detailed explanations of how to do the work properly, and in what order it should be done. **Budgets** set the requirements needed to follow the strategies and accomplish the objectives. For example, a cash budget shows the amount and times of cash income and outgo. It helps the manager determine when and how much to borrow.

Policies are general statements that serve as guides to managerial decision making and supervisory activities.

Methods and **procedures** provide standing instructions to employees on how to perform their jobs.

Budgets are detailed plans, expressed in monetary terms, of the results expected from officially recognized programs.

Planning to Operate the Business

The second part of operational planning—planning to operate the business—includes:

1. Choosing your location.
2. Planning operations and physical facilities.
3. Developing sources of supply for goods and materials.
4. Planning your personnel requirements.
5. Setting up the legal and organizational structure.
6. Determining your approach to the market.
7. Establishing an efficient records system.
8. Setting up a time schedule.

Choosing a Location

The type of business influences most of your location decisions, as they relate to access to customers, suppliers, employees, utilities, and transportation, as well as compliance with zoning regulations and other laws. The mission of the business is also a basic consideration in seeking the right location. As will be shown in Chapter 16, each type of firm has its own set of factors to consider and gives priority to those that most affect the business.

Planning Operations and Physical Facilities

A firm's ability to sell its product is based on its ability to produce that good or service, as well as on its market potential. Good selection and efficient arrangement of physical facilities, then, are important. Too much capacity increases costs, which can reduce the company's competitive position; too little capacity reduces the availability of goods and causes loss of sales. Therefore, a proper balance between production and sales volume is needed. Planning starts with the estimate of sales and the operations needed to produce the product(s). Using these estimates, the machines and personnel needed for the demand can be determined.

Another important decision is whether to buy facilities outright or lease them. Any such choice between purchase and lease is based on differences in initial investment cost, operating performance and expense, and tax considerations. A photocopier is an example of an item that should probably be leased rather than purchased. Because of rapid improvements—and the need for prompt and proper maintenance—leased copiers will probably give more dependable service than purchased ones. Chapter 16 provides more details on locating and laying out facilities.

Developing Sources of Supply for Goods and Materials

The largest expense for companies selling products usually is purchasing materials, supplies, and/or goods; this cost is often more than 50 percent of the cost of products sold. Therefore, the ability to purchase these at favorable prices can lead to profitability—or vice versa. Lowest-cost materials do not necessarily mean inferior quality, and small firms should take every opportunity to reduce costs. But small businesses usually find it difficult to compete with large ones on the basis of price alone. Instead, they can more successfully compete on the basis of better quality, service, delivery, and so forth. The business must be sure to have sources of supply that meet its standards in all ways, including competitive prices. This topic is covered in greater detail in Chapter 17.

Planning Personnel Requirements

Personnel planning is the process of converting the business's plans and programs into an effective work force.

Personnel planning can be one of the most frustrating tasks facing small businesses, as they are not big enough to hire the specialized people needed. You therefore need to estimate how much time you will spend in the business, for the less time you can devote to the business, the more important it will be to have capable employees. Not only will more employees be needed, but they must be able to work with less supervision than in larger firms. Some important questions to ask yourself are: How many workers are needed? Where will they be obtained? How much must I pay them? These and similar questions are discussed in Chapters 13, 14, and 15.

Setting Up the Legal and Organizational Structure

Your organization structure must be developed, taking into consideration the legal and administrative aspects of the business. Both legal and administrative structures offer several options, so you must select the structure that best serves your needs.

"I believe in keeping things simple and to the point."

Source: Reprinted from *The Wall Street Journal;* permission of Cartoon Features Syndicate

As the accompanying cartoon illustrates, retaining too much authority is one of the best ways to kill your small business.

The legal form of a business, as discussed in Chapter 4, may be a proprietorship, partnership, corporation (C corporation or S Corporation), limited-liability company (LLC), trust, cooperative, or joint venture. The firm's administrative structure should be based on factors such as (1) the strategic plan, including the business mission and objectives; (2) the owner's personal and business objectives; (3) the plans, programs, policies, and practices that will achieve those objectives; and (4) the authority and responsibility relationships that will accomplish the mission or purpose of the firm. These aspects of organization are discussed in greater detail in Chapter 15.

Determining Approach to Market

The volume of sales and income of a small firm depend on its marketing strategies and activities. If a study of the environment determines that there is a sufficiently large market for the firm's product(s), plans must be made to capture enough of that market to be successful. Even if your company's service is the best, you must tell potential customers about it. Many methods of marketing are in use; the ones used must be chosen for the particular business.

For example, some years ago, a man living in New England conceived of a rubber, instead of metal, dustpan. He had a dozen samples of the new product custom-made in a variety of colors and headed to Boston to hawk his wares in Filene's and Jordan Marsh. Neither seemed interested in the dustpan.

Still, because he was sure that housewives would buy his product, he decided to test-market the dustpan by calling on homemakers. Pulling into a residential street, he parked his car and set out to ring doorbells. Just 45 minutes later, he returned to his car with only two pans left.

Convinced that his idea was good, Earl Tupper developed a company—Tupperware—to market the product directly to consumers.

Once a target market is chosen, you must provide for sales promotion and distribution to it. The product to be offered should again be studied carefully to determine answers to the following questions: What qualities make it special to the customer? Are there unique or distinct features to emphasize, such as ease of installation or low maintenance? Should the company use newspaper advertising or mailings to publicize the product? These and other marketing questions are discussed in more detail in Chapters 10, 11, and 12.

Establishing an Efficient Records System

Even in a small business, simple records and information systems must be used. But they must be designed to help you control your business by keeping track of activities and obligations, and also to collect certain types of information demanded by outside organizations such as government agencies. For example, you must maintain records of such data as (1) the date each employee is hired, the number of hours each one works, and the wages and benefits paid; (2) inventories, accounts receivable, and accounts payable; (3) taxes paid and owed; and (4) units of each product sold.

Accounting systems must be designed to keep track of your finances. Incoming revenues and outgoing expenses are processed into accounts that record changing values of assets, liabilities, and equity. The system for planning and controlling the finances can be based on a budget system that sets goals against which actual results can be compared.

The system of records for employees has expanded greatly during recent years as government and legal controls have increased. Efforts to match skills to jobs and promote the proper person require records of factors such as experience, performance, education, and training. Records of accidents help identify unsafe practices.

Many other records are needed to help make the small business operate successfully. Management information systems, covered in Chapter 21, should be selected and designed to aid management in this respect.[5]

Setting Up a Time Schedule

Once you decide to go ahead with the formation of the business, you should establish a time schedule to provide an orderly and coordinated program. The schedule should probably include the prior planning steps. Many of these steps can be and often are performed simultaneously. A SCORE representative can provide valuable assistance.

THE ROLE OF FINANCIAL PLANNING

Financial planning can be quite simple or very complex, as shown in Chapter 9, but it should involve at least the following:

1. Estimating income and expenses.
2. Estimating initial investment required.
3. Locating sources of funds.

Financial planning involves determining what funds are needed, where they can be obtained, and how they can be controlled.

Estimating Income and Expenses

The steps described so far set the stage for determining the profit (or loss) from operating your new business. Income from sales (also called *revenue*) can be estimated by studying the market, and expenses (also called *costs*) can be calculated from past experience and other sources, such as knowledgeable people, a library, or a trade association. After all costs have been estimated, they can be totaled and subtracted from the estimated sales income to obtain the expected **net profit** (or loss), as shown in the worksheet for Dover Enterprises* in Figure 6–3.

When making your estimates, remember two key points. First, these expense and income (or loss) estimates are usually for only the first year of operations. However, if you also make an income analysis for an expected typical year in the future as well as for the first year, the exercise can provide valuable information for planning purposes.

Second, while total expenses do move up and down with sales volume, they do not vary as much. Some expenses, such as materials, which rise in direct proportion to increases in sales volume and drop as sales volume drops, are called **variable expenses.** Other expenses, such as depreciation on buildings, which do not vary in value as sales volume rises or falls, are called **fixed expenses.** Also, there are some expenses, such as supervision, that combine variable and fixed costs.

Changes in sales volume drastically affect the amount of net profit: as sales volume rises (say from 10,000 to 20,000 units), losses are reduced and profits may rise; as sales volume drops (say from 20,000 to 10,000), profits drop and losses may occur. An in-depth discussion of profit planning, including break-even analysis, may be found in Chapters 18 and 19.

Don't forget to also prepare a personal budget! You—and your family—must have enough income to live on during the time you are moving from being an

Net profit is the amount of revenue (sales) over and above the total amount of expenses (costs) of doing business.

Variable expenses change in relation to volume of output: When output is low, the expenses are low, and when output is high, expenses rise.

Fixed expenses do not vary with output, but remain the same.

*An actual company, but the name is disguised at the owner's request.

Figure 6–3

DOVER ENTERPRISES
Worksheet for Estimated Annual Income,
Expenses, and Profit (Loss)*

	Units Sold		
	10,000	**20,000**	**30,000**
Income			
Sales income ($5/unit)	$50,000	$100,000	$150,000
Cost of goods sold:			
Production cost ($1.62/unit)	$16,200	$32,400	$48,600
Shipping boxes and labels ($0.04/unit)	400	800	1,200
Depreciation (mold)	2,500	2,500	2,500
Total production expenses	19,100	35,700	52,300
Gross profit	30,900	64,300	97,700
Other operating expenses			
Salaries	30,000	30,000	30,000
Telephone	3,000	3,500	4,000
Rent	2,100	2,100	2,100
Insurance	400	400	400
Office expense	1,000	1,100	1,200
Sales promotion	7,000	8,000	9,000
Freight	1,000	2,000	3,000
Travel	4,000	4,000	4,000
Taxes and licenses	4,000	4,000	4,000
Miscellaneous	1,000	2,000	3,000
Total operating expenses	53,500	57,100	60,700
Net profit (loss)	($22,600)	$ 7,200	$ 37,000

* Projections for three levels of sales.

employee to being an employer. If your standard of living drops too drastically, it will probably be devastating to your family. So, in addition to determining the expected income and expenses of the business, also estimate your continuing needs—and where you will get the resources to satisfy them.

Estimating Initial Investment

You will need money and/or credit to start your business. You must pay for items such as buildings, equipment, materials, personnel, inventory, machines, business forms, and sales promotion at the outset before income from sales starts providing the means to pay these expenses from internal sources. Credit may be extended to help sell the products, but this only adds to operating expenses.

The worksheet in Figure 6–4 provides a logical method of calculating the initial cash needs of a new business such as Dover Enterprises. The figures in column 1

Figure 6–4

DOVER ENTERPRISES
Estimated Monthly Expenses and Starting Costs
December 1, 19___

Estimated Monthly Expenses

Item	(1) Estimate of Monthly Expenses Based on Sales of $100,000 per Year	(2) Estimate of How Much Cash You Need to Start Your Business (see column 3)	(3) What to Put in (2) (Multipliers are typical for one kind of business. You must decide how many months to allow for in your business.)
Salary of owner-manager	$2,500	$5,000	2 times column 1
All other salaries and wages	—	—	3 times column 1
Rent	175	525	3 times column 1
Travel		1,000	As required
Advertising	700	2,100	3 times column 1
Delivery expense	100	300	3 times column 1
Supplies	100	300	3 times column 1
Recurring inventory and purchases	—	—	Check with suppliers for estimate
Telephone and telegraph	300	900	3 times column 1
Other utilities	—	—	3 times column 1
Insurance		400	Payment required by insurance company
Taxes, including Social Security	325	1,300	4 times column 1
Interest	—	—	3 times column 1
Maintenance	—	—	3 times column 1
Legal and other professional fees	—	—	3 times column 1
Miscellaneous	200	600	3 times column 1

Starting Costs You Have to Pay Only Once

Fixtures and equipment: Telephone, $203; mold, $11,280; computer, $750	$12,233	Enter total from separate list
Decorating and remodeling	—	Talk it over with a contractor
Installation of fixtures and equipment	—	Talk to suppliers from whom you wish to buy these
Starting inventory	5,000	Suppliers will probably help you estimate this
Deposits with public utilities	—	Find out from utilities companies
Legal and other professional fees	—	Lawyer, accountant, and so on
Licenses and permits	(Part of taxes above)	Find out from city offices what you have to have
Advertising and promotion for opening	(Part of advertising above)	Estimate what you'll use
Accounts receivable	1,200	What you need to buy more stock until credit customers pay
Cash	1,000	For unexpected expenses or losses, special purchases, etc.
Other		Make a separate list and enter total
Total estimated cash you need to start with	$31,858	Add up all the numbers in column 2

Source: This basic worksheet is based on *Checklist for Going into Business*, Management Aids No. 2.016 (Washington, DC: Small Business Administration), p. 4.

are estimates that have already been made for the income statement for the first year. The amount of cash needed is some multiple of each of the values in column 1, as shown in column 3. The total of these multiple values is an estimate of the money needed to start the business and is shown in column 2.

Note that the cash needed to start the business—shown in column 2—represents the delay between paying money out for expenses and receiving it back as revenue. The item called *starting inventory* is an illustration of buying goods in one period and selling them in another. But inventories of goods and supplies—in the form of purchases and recurring inventories—continue to exist for the life of the business. Therefore, funds obtained from investments in the business or from loans must continue for its life unless they are paid off.

Because cash does not produce revenue, it should not sit idle but should be used to earn income. The amount of cash a business needs, and has, will vary during the year, since most businesses have busy and slack periods. To keep the investment and borrowing low, **cash flow** projections must be made. The worksheet in Chapter 19 (Figure 19–1) is a form that can be used to make such projections, which can be compared with what actually happens. You might contact your nearest SBA office to get information to help you estimate your start-up costs. Also, various financial firms and certified public accountants have computed some helpful standard figures.

Cash flow is the amount of cash available at a given time to pay expenses.

Locating Sources of Funds

Once the amount of funds needed is known, you must find sources for those funds. The many sources from which to obtain funds to start and operate a business boil down to two: the owner and others. These two sources are discussed in detail in Chapter 9, so only the highlights are discussed here.

Before approaching a funding source, decide how much money you and others will put into the business and how much should come from other sources.

For example, Don Dover started Dover Enterprises with his own money and investments from three relatives. All investors owned the company and made up its board of directors. Don, as president, also managed it on a day-to-day basis.

Using Your Own Funds

Some small business owners prefer to invest only their personal funds and not borrow to start or operate a business. Others believe that they should use little of their own money and instead make as much profit as possible by using their interest in the business as security when obtaining funds from others. Normally, owners control a company; they take the risks of failure but also make the decisions. To maintain control, you must continue to invest more personal funds than all the other investors combined. Moreover, you can maintain control only so long as lenders do not become worried about the safety of their money.

Using Funds from Others

There are several sources of outside funds. These can be generally divided into *equity investors,* who actually become part owners of the business, and *lenders,* who provide money for a limited time at a fixed rate of interest. Both run the risk of losing their money if the business fails, but this gamble is offset for investors by the possibility of large returns if the business is successful. Since the rate of return for lenders is fixed, some security is usually given to offset their risk.

You may be able to find investors interested in a venture opportunity. Such people might be found among relatives, friends, attorneys, bankers, or securities dealers.

You will also find that many people who are not willing to assume the risks of ownership are willing to lend money to a business. They include private individuals, private financial institutions, merchandise and equipment vendors, and government agencies. There are many outright grants available from government agencies to start new businesses, especially for minorities and women.

WHAT YOU SHOULD HAVE LEARNED

1. Planning, one of the key managerial functions, is usually done first, since everything else depends on it. While planning establishes directions and goals for any business, it is especially difficult in small firms, where management is often fully engaged in day-to-day operation and "can't see the forest for the trees." Some barriers to planning in small firms are the fear of learning things you would rather not know, the unpredictability of plans, the uncertainty of plans, and especially the lack of adequate time to plan.

2. Strategic planning—from which other plans are derived—determines the very nature of the business. Next comes operational planning, which sets policies, methods and procedures, budgets and standards, and other operating plans.

3. Strategic planning includes the company's mission, which tells what type of business you are in. Once the mission is determined, a company can establish its objectives, which set the goals it hopes to reach and provide a way of keeping score on its performance. Strategies provide the means to reach objectives.

4. Operational planning, which includes policies, budgets, standards, procedures, and methods, *forms the basis for preparing the business plan.* It involves planning the overall operations of the business, including *(a)* choosing its location, *(b)* planning operations and physical facilities, *(c)*

developing supply sources for goods and materials, *(d)* planning personnel requirements, *(e)* setting up the legal and organizational structure, *(f)* determining the approach to the market, *(g)* establishing an efficient records system, and *(h)* setting up a time schedule.

5. Financial planning involves estimating income and expenses, estimating investment required, and locating sources of funds. Income and expenses should be estimated to ensure that the proposed business will be feasible. Estimates should be based on the firm's first year of operation, as well as a typical ''good'' year, since investors may be willing to assume some risk of loss at the beginning to achieve greater gains later. Also, estimates should be made of personal needs during the transition period. These projections permit the prospective new owner to estimate the initial investment needed. Finally, sources of funds must be determined. The two sources are the business owner(s) and others, either private individuals or lending institutions.

QUESTIONS

1. Explain why planning is so badly needed by small businesses. Why is it so often neglected?
2. Explain the two overall categories of planning. What are the essential differences between the two?
3. Explain the two components of strategic planning.
4. Discuss the factors to be considered in formulating a business's mission.
5. Explain each of the following: policies, methods and procedures, budgets, and standards.
6. In planning to operate the business, what are the factors that must be planned for? Explain each.
7. What is involved in financial planning?
8. What are the two sources of funds for a small business? Explain each.

ARTWATCHES: TURNING A COLLEGE THESIS INTO A $4 MILLION BUSINESS

Geoff Walsh is living proof that not all businesses start with a furrowed brow. Instead, entrepreneurship came easily to him. At age 10, he ran a lemonade stand; at 23, he owned a $4-million-a-year business— ArtWatches.

ArtWatches, selling wristwatches whose faces are reproductions of paintings by Dégas, Picasso, Renoir, and van Gogh, was conceived in 1988, when Walsh was an undergraduate at the University of Pennsylvania's Wharton School of Business. He and his roommate took advantage of the craze for Dan Quayle watches when the vice-presidential nominee was a popular target for the press. After the roommate sold "several hundred" Quayle timepieces, Walsh, seeing that watches with reproductions had a bright future, wrote a business plan for ArtWatches as his undergraduate thesis.

After studying copyright law and searching museums for licensing agreements, he obtained the rights to reproduce eight impressionist works on watches. He started the business in November 1989.

One problem he encountered was in obtaining suppliers and setting up distributors, as there were only about a dozen businesses in the world that controlled the manufacturing side of the industry. Walsh was fortunate to get one of the premier Hong Kong companies to help him out, assembling the watches' Japanese components, with straps made by a Philadelphia company.

His timing was good—and bad. The good news was that demand for watches doubled from 1980 to 1989. The bad news was that the 1990s recession made mincemeat of the $17 million sales estimate in his business plan. Then, in early 1990, Bulova Corporation introduced its Classic Moments line of reproduction paintings, including four that Walsh was also producing.

Walsh countered by changing his market from the upper middle class, who bought the Bulova watch, to mall shoppers—the 18- to 40-year-old suburbanites, who could afford the $45 to $50 price of ArtWatches.

ArtWatches are sold in retail stores, boutiques, museum shops, catalog stores, and department stores and on the QVC Home Shopping Network. Also, through a promotional deal with Toshiba, everyone in Japan who buys one of its big-screen TVs gets a free ArtWatch.

QUESTIONS

1. Which type(s) of planning did Walsh use? Explain.

2. What does this case show about the need for planning?

3. How do you explain Walsh's success?

4. What does the case show about the need for a business plan?

Source: Abstracted from Michelle Osborn, "An Entrepreneur Who's Worth Watching," *USA Today* April 18, 1991, p. 4B. Copyright 1991, USA TODAY. Adapted with permission.

7

Growing Opportunities in Franchising

Buying a franchise is probably the quickest, easiest, and most successful way of becoming an entrepreneur.—Colonel Harlan Sanders, founder of Kentucky Fried Chicken.

Franchising . . . is changing not only our marketing system, but also our way of life.—Peng S. Chan, California State University, Fullerton; and Robert T. Justis, Louisiana State University.

LEARNING OBJECTIVES

After studying the material in this chapter, you will be able to:
1. Discuss the extent of franchising.

2. Define franchising, and describe the two most popular types of franchises.

3. Tell why franchising is growing so rapidly.

4. Explain how to evaluate opportunities in franchising.

5. Discuss the future of franchising, especially in international operations.

PORTERFIELD WILSON: FROM SHINING SHOES TO IMPORTING FOREIGN CARS

In 1978, Porterfield Wilson and his wife, Barbara Jean, obtained franchises to import and sell Hondas and Mazdas—the first black dealers in the United States to sell foreign cars. In 1983, they started Ferndale Honda, near Detroit, which Mrs. Wilson now runs. What makes this achievement so remarkable is Wilson's classic "rags-to-riches" story.

At age 10, though sometimes barefoot himself, Wilson helped support himself by shining shoes in front of the Grand Ole Opry in Nashville, Tennessee. At his death, 46 years later, he was one of the most successful U.S. automobile dealers. His dealership had been recognized by *USA Today* as one of the top 20 black businesses in the nation and was consistently near the top of *Black Enterprise* magazine's

Photo courtesy of Mrs. Porterfield Wilson.

"Top 100 Black-Owned Businesses." Wilson himself was invited to the White House in 1978 to receive a citation for achievement from President Jimmy Carter.

A high school dropout who served as a paratrooper in the Korean War, Wilson moved to Detroit in the 1950s, where he worked on a Dodge assembly line during the day and clerked in a drugstore at night. A customer was so impressed with his outstanding sales ability that he encouraged Wilson to become an automobile salesman, which he did.

Wilson had saved enough money by 1970 to buy a Pontiac dealership and become the first black Pontiac dealer in the Midwest. GM's inventory planners expected him to sell about 300 vehicles that first year; he sold 1,000. "I had never seen a financial statement when I started the company," Wilson recalled, "but I was determined to make the business work."

Wilson ran his own job-training program. He hired uneducated, unskilled people—including minorities—and gave them free courses in such trades as auto mechanics, paying them while they were learning.

His achievements were emphasized when he returned to Nashville after 40 years to receive a key to the city. As he pointed out, "When I was a boy in Nashville, I wasn't allowed to enter the courthouse, and now I have a key to the city. I guess I've come a long way."

Before his death in early 1989, Wilson conceived and launched Porterfield's Marina Village, a $60 million, 63-acre complex featuring 200 luxury apartments and condominiums, a fine riverside restaurant, a public boat launch, and 450 boat slips.

Following Wilson's death, Mrs. Wilson sold the GM, Pontiac, and Mazda operations. But she is still carrying on the work, both at the Honda dealership and with Marina Village.

Source: Correspondence with Mrs. Porterfield Wilson; and others, including *Detroit 90* (a magazine published by the City of Detroit), pp. 45–47.

The Profile illustrates the many exciting opportunities in one of the fastest growing and most important segments of U.S. business: franchising. This attractive alternative to starting a new business has helped tens of thousands of entrepreneurs achieve their dream of owning a business of their own. In Chapter 5, we discussed the reasons to buy—and not to buy—a franchise. In this chapter, however, we present a more detailed look at franchising's role.

EXTENT OF FRANCHISING

The U.S. Department of Commerce estimated that there were 533,000 franchised outlets in the United States in 1990 and that their sales totaled $716 billion. In fact, as you can see from Figure 7–1, franchise sales more than doubled in the last decade, and the number of establishments grew by 21 percent. According to

Figure 7–1   Franchising Takes Off

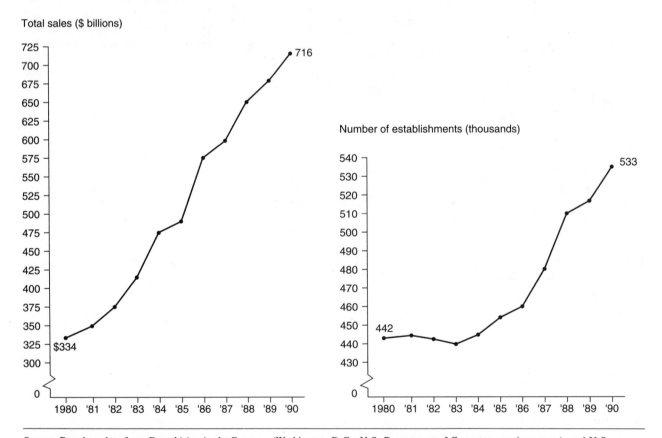

Source: Based on data from *Franchising in the Economy* (Washington, D.C.: U.S. Department of Commerce, various years); and U.S. Bureau of the Census, *Statistical Abstract of the United States, 1991* (Washington, D.C.: U.S. Government Printing Office, 1991), Table 1368, p. 778.

Figure 7–2   Franchising Accounts for 34 Percent of Retail Sales

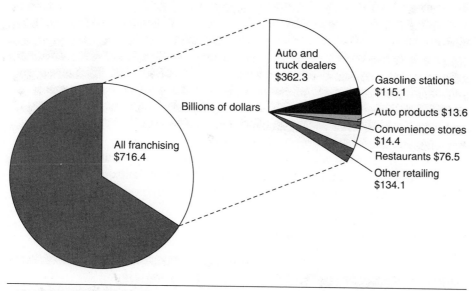

Source: U.S. Department of Commerce, *Franchising in the Economy, 1988–90* (Washington, D.C.: U.S. Department of Commerce, 1990). Exhibit 3, p. 4.

Arthur Karp, chairman of the International Franchising Association (IFA), U.S. franchises create around 300,000 *new jobs* each year, as each new franchise creates 8 to 10 new jobs, and a new franchise opens about every 17 minutes.[1] Franchising also provides direct employment for some 10 million people, including many younger and older workers who otherwise would be unable to find jobs.

Franchising is strong in retailing—especially auto and truck dealers, gasoline stations, and restaurants. As Figure 7–2 shows, franchises accounted for 34 percent of retail sales in 1990, and 87 percent of all franchising receipts come from retailing.[2] Karp estimates that retail sales from franchising will exceed the trillion-dollar mark by 1994 and will account for over 50 percent of total retail sales by the year 2000.[3]

WHAT IS FRANCHISING?

We will define franchising by describing the process and parties involved, and then discuss the two most popular types of franchises.

Definition

Franchising is a marketing system based on a legal arrangement that permits one party—the franchisee—to conduct business as an individual owner while abiding by the terms and conditions set by the second party—the franchisor.

Franchising is a marketing system whereby an individual owner conducts business according to the terms and conditions set by the franchisor.

A **franchise** is an agreement whereby an independent businessperson is given exclusive rights to sell a specified good or service.

The **franchisor** owns the franchise's name and distinctive elements and licenses others to sell its products.

The **franchisee** is an independent businessperson who agrees to sell the product according to the franchisor's requirements.

The **franchise** is the agreement granting the right to do business and specifying the terms and conditions under which the business will be conducted. The **franchisor** is the company that owns the franchise's name and distinctive elements (such as signs, symbols, and patents) and that grants others the right to sell its product. The **franchisee** is usually an independent local businessperson who agrees with the franchise owner to operate the business on a local or regional basis. While the franchisee is given the right to market the franchisor's designated goods or services, that marketing must be done according to the terms of the licensing agreement. The contract specifies what the franchisee can and cannot do and prescribes certain penalties for noncompliance.

While many franchising opportunities exist, they do not automatically spell success. Instead, caution is called for in dealing with franchisors who promise a guaranteed return on your investment, for contracts with these elusive or vanished companies often prove worthless.

Types of Franchising Systems

As shown in Figure 7–3, there are two types of franchising systems: (1) product and trademark franchising and (2) business format franchising.

Product and trademark franchising is an arrangement under which the franchisee is granted the right to sell a widely recognized product or brand. Most such franchisees concentrate on handling one franchisor's product line and identify their business with that firm. Familiar examples include automobile and truck dealerships, gasoline service stations, and soft-drink bottlers. The franchisor exercises very little control over the franchisee's operations; what control there is has to do with maintaining the integrity of the product, not with the franchisee's business operations.

Product and trademark franchising grants the franchisee the right to sell a widely recognized product or brand.

Business format franchising grants a franchisee the right to market the product and trademark and to use a complete operating system.

Business format franchising is a relationship in which the franchisee is granted the right to use an entire marketing system, along with ongoing assistance and guidance from the franchisor. In 1991, there were around 410,000 business format franchises operating in the United States, with sales of $232 billion.[4] The industry groups with the largest volume of sales in this type of franchising are restaurants, retailing (nonfood), hotels and motels, business aids and services, automotive products and services, and convenience stores.

When Ray Kroc set up McDonald's as a franchisor (see the case at the end of this chapter), he controlled the trade name (McDonald's), symbol (golden arches), and operating systems. In turn, he permitted franchisees to use them under controlled conditions—for a fee. Kroc also controlled all aspects of quality that characterized the successful operations of the original drive-in.

WHY FRANCHISING IS GROWING IN IMPORTANCE

If you think of all the franchises you've been involved with during the past week, you can see why they're growing in importance.

Figure 7–3   Types of Franchising Systems

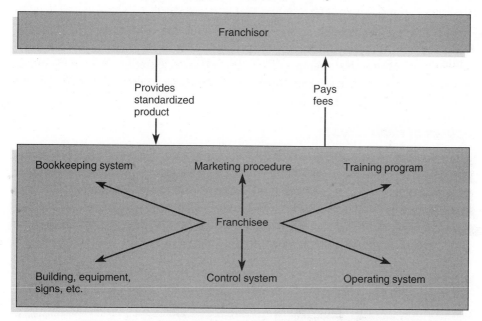

A. Product and trademark franchising

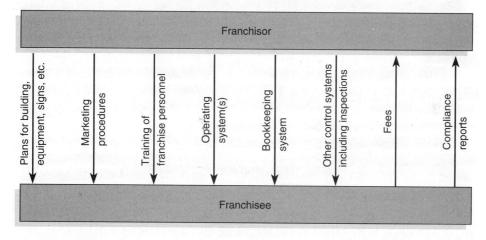

B. Business format franchising

Recent Rapid Growth

Franchising has been one of the fastest-growing areas of U.S. business during the past decade or so. The number of franchise establishments has risen from about 900 in 1972 to about 393,000 in 1990,[5] and this trend is expected to continue through the 1990s. Franchising has become so extensive and diverse that "it's no longer just a way of doing business, it's become a way of life," according to Andrew Kostecka, franchising specialist for the U.S. Department of Commerce's International Trade Association.[6]

Earlier, product and trademark franchising dominated the franchise field, but its role has declined rapidly during the past two decades as business format franchising has skyrocketed. For example, over 100,000 service stations have gone out of business since 1972. But business format franchising has accounted for most of the growth of franchising since then.

Causes of Rapid Growth

There are many reasons why franchising has become so popular. First, a franchisor has already identified a consumer need and created a product to meet that need, as well as a convenient and economical method of marketing it. For example, in single-parent or dual-career homes, few people want to spend precious time preparing meals, so they head for a fast-food outlet such as Wendy's. Reluctance to make dental or doctor's appointments far in advance—with a good chance of spending hours in the waiting room—has led to franchising of walk-in health care services, such as LensCrafters and United Surgical Centers. Increasing leisure time has resulted in franchising of recreational and exercise activities, such as Jazzercise. In other words, franchises have emerged to cater to many consumer and business needs that were not being recognized or satisfied elsewhere.

Second, as Colonel Sanders said in the opening quotation, one of the best ways to succeed in small business is to buy an established franchise, because the failure rate is much lower than for small independent businesses, according to SBA estimates.[7]

A third reason for franchising's popularity is that franchisees have the support of established management systems for bookkeeping, marketing, operations, and control. And these systems give franchisees the benefit of business experience without their having to acquire it for themselves.

A major drawback to franchising, though, is the voluminous paperwork needed to provide disclosure documents to potential franchisees. These statements, required by the Federal Trade Commission (FTC), provide background and financial position information about the franchisor and the franchise offering.

HOW TO TELL WHETHER A FRANCHISE IS RIGHT FOR YOU

While franchising opportunities abound, intensive study and evaluation are needed before you enter into such an arrangement. When you buy a franchise, you're relying not only on your own business expertise and experience but also on the franchisor's business ideas, skills, capital, and ethics.

Two highly publicized failures illustrate this point. Minnie Pearl Chicken failed because the franchisor lacked adequate capital to service the franchisees, and Wild Bill Hamburgers was a "franchising fraud that fleeced millions of dollars from more than 100 investors."[8]

In buying a franchise, is there any way to avoid making a mistake? While nothing is guaranteed to protect you, you can reduce your risks by taking the actions discussed in this section. See Figure 7–4 for some specific questions to ask when checking out a potential franchise.

Look at the Opportunities

In investigating franchises, learn which ones are growing the fastest so as to get in on growth possibilities. You can do this by studying such sources as *Entrepreneur* magazine's annual listing of the best performers and the U.S. Commerce Department's *Franchise Opportunities Handbook,* published annually. Also, your local SBA office or SCORE chapter, schools with small business development centers, chambers of commerce, and libraries can be of great help to you.

See What the Franchise Can Do for You

At this point, you should decide whether you're willing to give up some of your independence by buying a franchise. While you may cherish your freedom to operate as you choose, you might prefer to receive the management training and assistance provided by the franchisor. For entrepreneurs with little business experience, the assistance they can get from the franchisor justifies some sacrifice of their independence.

When you buy a franchise, you'll pay up front to buy a building or rent space, renovate a store or office, lease or buy equipment, buy inventory, and receive other facilities. Then you'll pay the franchisor a one-time franchise fee and regular royalty fees. For these fees and costs—ranging from around 3 to 7 percent—you can expect the kind of help shown in Figure 7–5. Those considering buying a franchise should ask themselves if they are willing to pay these fees, accept the franchisor's regulations, and give up a certain amount of their independence.

Investigate the Franchise

You should investigate the franchisor and the franchise business as thoroughly as possible. First, be sure to look at more than one franchise and investigate similar franchises in the same line of business. Review the brief descriptions of franchises in the Commerce Department's *Franchise Opportunities Handbook,* and consult other guides and literature available from your library or the other sources mentioned above.

Figure 7-4 How to Check Out a Franchise

The franchise
1. Does your lawyer approve of the franchise contract being considered?
2. Does the franchise call upon you to take any steps that your lawyer considers unwise or illegal?
3. Does the franchise agreement provide you an exclusive territory for the length of the franchise, or can the franchisor sell a second or third franchise in the territory?
4. Is the franchisor connected in any way with any other franchise handling similar merchandise or services?
5. If the answer to Question 4 is yes, what is your protection against the second franchisor?
6. Under what circumstances and at what cost can you terminate the franchise contract if you decide to cancel it?
7. If you sell your franchise, will you be compensated for goodwill?

The franchisor
8. How many years has the franchisor been operating?
9. Has it a reputation among local franchisees for honesty and fair dealing?
10. Has the franchisor shown you any certified figures indicating net profit of one or more franchisees that you have personally checked?
11. Will the franchisor assist with:
    a. A management training program?   *d.* Capital?
    b. An employee training program?   *e.* Credit?
    c. A public relations program?   *f.* Merchandising ideas?
12. Will the franchisor help find a good location for the new business?
13. Is the franchisor adequately financed to implement its stated plan of financial assistance and expansion?
14. Does the franchisor have an experienced management team trained in depth?
15. Exactly what can the franchisor do for you that you can't do for yourself?
16. Has the franchisor investigated you carefully enough to be sure of your qualifications?
17. Does your state have a law regulating the sales of franchises, and has the franchisor complied with that law?

The franchisee
18. How much equity capital will you need to purchase the franchise and operate it until it reaches the break-even point? Where are you going to obtain it?
19. Are you prepared to give up some independence in order to secure the advantages offered by the franchise?
20. Do you really believe you have the qualifications to succeed as a franchisee?
21. Are you ready to spend much or all of your remaining business life with this franchise company?

The market
22. Have you determined that an adequate market exists in your territory for the good or service at the prices you will have to charge for it?
23. Is the population in the territory expected to increase, remain the same, or decrease over the next five years?
24. Will the good or service be in greater, about the same, or less demand five years from now than it is today?
25. What is the competition in the territory for the good or service:
    a. From nonfranchised firms?
    b. From franchised firms?

Source: Franchising Opportunities Handbook (Washington, D.C.: U.S. Department of Commerce, January 1988), pp. xxxii–xxxiv.

Figure 7-5   Services Provided by Competent Franchisors

- Start-up assistance, such as market information, site location, building and equipment design and purchase, and financial help.
- A proven and successful system for operating the business.
- A standardized accounting and cost control system for business records. These records are audited periodically by the franchisor's staff. In many instances, standard monthly operating statements are required. The franchisor develops a set of standard performance figures based on composite figures of reporting franchisees and returns a comparative analysis to the franchisee as a managerial aid.
- In some instances, financial assistance to cover land, building, equipment, inventory, and working capital needs.
- Assistance in the purchase of the site and the construction of a standardized structure with a design identified with the franchise.
- A training program to help prepare employees to operate and manage the unit. (The more successful franchisors have their own special training schools, such as McDonald's Hamburger University and the Holiday Inn University.)
- A well-planned and well-implemented national or regional advertising program to establish and maintain a uniform image.
- A set of customer service standards created by the franchisor and its professional staff, who make regular inspection visits to assure compliance by the franchisee.
- Sensitivity and responsiveness to changing market opportunities.
- The advantage of discounts for buying in large quantities.

Study the Franchise Offering Circular

The Federal Trade Commission requires that a franchor give prospective franchisees a formal agreement and a franchise offering circular at least 10 days before the contract is executed or before any money is paid.[9] This **prospectus** or **disclosure statement** should provide background on the franchisor and its financial position; the financial requirements for a franchisee; and the restrictions, protections, and estimated earnings of the franchise.

A **prospectus** or **disclosure statement** provides background and financial information about the franchisor and the franchise offering.

Check with Existing Franchisees

Contact several of the franchise owners listed in the disclosure statement and ask about their franchising experiences. Preferably, seek those who have been in the business for several years. They should be able to give the best advice about what to expect in the first year of operation — typically the period during which the success or failure of a new franchise is determined, as the following example illustrates.

"I'd always wanted to go into business by myself," said Susan McKay, owner of the first Handle With Care packaging store franchise in Florida. She took the plunge after doing a lot of research, planning, "soul searching," and investigating other franchises. Also, as part of her research, she requested disclosure documents and then talked with current franchisees. She warns, "If you have any questions at all, have someone familiar with franchising look at it. Do all your research first!"[10]

Obtain Professional Advice

You should obtain professional assistance in reviewing and evaluating any franchise you consider. The financial statements will reveal to a professional accountant, banker, or financial analyst whether the franchisor's financial condition is sound or whether there is a risk that it will be unable to meet its financial and other obligations. It's also important to check to see whether you'll be required to stock items that you don't need or can't sell, or whether the contract can be terminated for insufficient reason, as the following example shows.

Toni Cironi had a franchise with White Sewing Machine Company to sell its "White" brand machine as well as its "Elna" brand. Last year, Cironi sold $15,000 of the "White" brand and $60,000 of the "Elna" brand. White's national sales manager tried to get him to sell more Whites. Cironi couldn't do so, because a nearby dress shop was buying them for $97 and selling them for $149, while he paid $140 and sold them for $200. White canceled his franchise.[11]

Legal advice is the most important professional assistance you need before investing in a franchise. A lawyer can advise you about your legal rights and obligations in relation to the franchise agreement and may be able to suggest important changes in it that will protect your interest better. A lawyer should also tell you of any laws that may affect the franchise, especially taxation and personal liability aspects.

Know your Legal and Ethical Rights

The International Franchise Association (IFA), the only U.S. international trade association serving franchisors in more than 50 countries, has a code of ethics that covers a franchisor's obligations to its franchisees. Each member company pledges to comply with all applicable laws and to make sure its disclosure statements are complete, accurate, and not misleading. Furthermore, it pledges that all important matters affecting its franchise will be contained in written agreements and that it will accept only those franchisees who appear to possess the qualifications needed to conduct the franchise successfully. The franchisor agrees to base the franchisee's compensation on the sale of the product, not on the recruitment of new franchisees.

In considering the franchisee's rights, what happens if the franchisor attempts to buy back the franchise when it becomes very profitable? Should the franchisee be required to sell, as happened in the following example?

A distributor of Häagen-Dazs ice cream in San Diego said he was forced to sell his franchise to the franchisor at a price he considered unfair. He was allegedly told that the distributor had the right to take over his major customers, whether he sold or not. Häagen-Dazs also terminated a long-term San Francisco area distributor who began distributing two competing local brands of superpremium ice cream.[12]

THE FUTURE OF FRANCHISING

The future of franchising is indeed bright, and the number and variety of U.S. franchises are expected to continue to grow. As indicated earlier, franchises now account for over 34 percent of all retail trade, and the Commerce Department expects this figure to increase to one-half by the year 2000.

Expected Areas of Growth

The industries that especially lend themselves to franchising are restaurants; motels; convenience stores; electronics; and automotive parts, accessories, and servicing. Not all franchises in these categories are of a quality worthy of selection, nor are these categories the only ones worthy of consideration; but they do appear to be good growth areas.

Restaurants

The success of restaurants—especially those offering fast foods—is related to many variables, including demographic factors such as the high percentage of young adults and singles in the population and the increasing number of women working outside the home. Other factors that seem to have had a positive influence on success are product appeal to a growing segment of the market, fast service, a sanitary environment, and buildings and signs that are easily recognizable.

For example, at 26, Vince Millard, a seven-year, multiunit franchisee, expects to be a millionaire before he is 30 years old. He's come a long way since, as a 19-year-old, he was willing to make some sacrifices to invest in his first Sonic Drive-in in Lawrence, Kansas. Having only a few dollars, he sold his interest in his family's hog farm and took in some partners to obtain the $500,000 needed to start the business.

Millard checked into other industries and other fast-food franchises, but he decided on the fast-food industry—for its greater return—and on Sonic, which seemed best for him personally. He liked the '50s-style drive-in, which has been phenomenally successful for him.[13]

Motels

The motel industry has experienced explosive growth since the interstate highway system began in 1956 and the growing affluence and mobility of Americans created a market for quality motels. The industry has grown from mom-and-pop units (with an often questionable image) to one dominated by large corporate empires. These corporations not only sell franchises to independent businesspeople but also operate some of the most profitable units themselves. Best Western is considered to have the largest number of establishments.

USING TECHNOLOGY TO SUCCEED

CAREERS USA, INC.: TAKING THE HIGH-TECH ROAD

"We have to meet our clients' urgent needs if we expect to stay ahead in today's labor market," says Marylin J. Ounjian, president and CEO of Careers USA, Inc., a temporary and permanent placement franchise with 20 locations. "Employers keep work forces lean and add temporary employees when there is a sudden, unexpected surge in business. Our franchisees have to fill positions within hours of the need or risk losing the assignment to another company."

Because the conventional method of manually thumbing through files was too slow to fill its clients' needs, Careers USA invested in "SAM" (for Search, Administrative, and Management), an advanced computer system, to replace the old system. An example of the type of problem SAM can handle would be a request for a bilingual word processor who knows WordPerfect 5.1 and medical terminology. SAM quickly searches for people with those skills and then displays a listing of qualified temps with needed information for the client. For its franchisees, SAM's search capabilities often spell the difference between business lost and business gained.

Source: "Taking the High-Tech Road," *Franchising World,* June 1989, p. 22.

Convenience Stores

While the term *convenience store* is usually associated with food outlets, it may in fact cover other types of specialty shops. Some examples of these franchises are Jitney-Jungle, the Bread Basket, T-Shirts Plus, and Health Mart.

Electronics

With the rapid growth in electronic fields such as music, video, TV, and computers, franchising has naturally followed. Radio Shack has long been a franchise, and its computers are standard equipment for school and business applications. Some other growing franchises are Circuit City, Babbage's, American Software, and Muzak. (See Using Technology to Succeed for an interesting development in the franchising of computer applications.)

Automotive Parts, Accessories, and Servicing

Automotive franchises have been around for a long time as retail outlets for parts and accessories. Some of the units have been affiliated with nationally known tire manufacturers such as General Tire. A comparatively recent entry into the automotive franchise field is the specialty service shop. Some examples are shops specializing in muffler and shock absorber repairs and parts, such as Midas International; shops providing technical assistance and specialized parts for "customizing" vans; and diagnostic centers with sophisticated computerized electronic equipment. Also, the number of automotive service franchises, such as Precision Tune and Jiffy Lube, has been growing as gasoline stations shift from full service to self-service, and many of these franchises use former service station facilities. According to the president of Valvoline Instant Oil Change Co., ''It was the decline of the neighborhood service station that gave rise to our business . . . . Many of the original sites used for our centers were such stations.''[14]

International Franchising

The success achieved by some U.S. franchises has resulted in growing international interest and opportunity. For example, Figure 7–6 shows that nearly 400 U.S.-based franchise companies operate over 35,000 overseas outlets, and that number is rapidly increasing. For example, the IFA found in a 1992 survey that the number of such outlets increased tenfold from 1971 to 1988.[15] Another survey found that an estimated 20 percent of U.S. franchisors operate internationally by means of company units, master licenses, individual franchises, or joint ventures.[16]

Colonel Sanders Goes to Japan
Photo courtesy of KFC International.

For example, KFC has more than 3,600 restaurants outside the United States. They are located on six continents and produce annual sales of over $2 billion. Although it owns more than 1,000 units, KFC's international units are operated primarily through franchise and joint venture arrangements. In these arrangements, KFC holds an equity stake in the operations, from which it earns a percentage of profits.

Through a joint venture with Mitsubishi, more than 800 KFC restaurants operate in Japan, more than in any other country outside the United States. Even in Japan, half a world away from the Colonel's roots, the company's menu, sign, and packaging are nearly identical to those found in U.S. restaurants. As you can see from the photo of KFC's Hiroshima restaurant, the name and image of Colonel Sanders are easily recognizable and transcend language barriers.[17]

U.S. franchisors have been especially successful in Eastern Europe. In fact, many U.S. law firms specializing in franchising are already setting up branches abroad, such as East Europe Law Ltd., in Budapest, Hungary.

Fast-food franchises have been particularly successful abroad. Because the fast-food industry isn't as well developed in other countries, U.S. franchises have a great opportunity to be leaders in many markets. For example, franchises such as McDonald's, Pizza Hut, and Pepsi are flourishing in Eastern European countries. In fact, Pepsi advertises on Russian TV—in Russian.[18]

Figure 7–6   International Franchising

Franchising companies: 374
Number of franchising outlets: 35,046

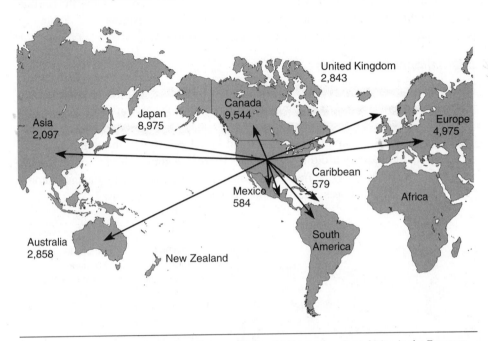

Source: U.S. Department of Commerce, Bureau of Industrial Economics, *Franchising in the Economy, 1988–90* (Washington, D.C.: U.S. Government Printing Office, 1990), p. 99.

Growing franchise industries also include maid and personal services; home improvements; business aids and services (such as accounting, collections, and personnel services); automobile products and services; weight-control centers; hair salons and services; and private postal services.

For example, the California-based Mail Boxes Etc.® franchise, with 1,600 franchisees, was recently granted an exception to the Mexican constitution's ban on private postal services. Each Mail Boxes unit in Mexico pays $1,000 to register as an official post office.[19]

While franchising offers many opportunities overseas, it still isn't as popular in other countries as it is here. For example, franchising accounts for only 10 percent of retail sales in England and 11 percent in France, as opposed to 34 percent in the United States.[20]

Figure 7–7 What's Needed to Become a Franchise Owner

Step-by-step review of what needs to be done and how long it will take to turn the dream of owning your own business into the reality of opening day.

Phase	1 Decide to become a franchisee	2 Make decision and invest $_____	3 Real estate	4 Construction	5 Equipment and inventory
Action items	Investigate and select your franchise	Decide, buy, sign contract; pay $_____	Look for proper store site: *a.* Storefront type *b.* Build to specs, freestanding	Conform to franchise contract: *a.* Leasehold improvements *b.* Construct building per drawings	Order and install all equipment; order opening inventory—goods
Time span	3 months to 2 years	3 months	2 to 12 months	3 to 11 months	1 to 3 months

Phase	6 Hiring	7 Training	8 Pre-opening final check	9 Opening and operations	10 Contract term
Action items	Hire manager or assistant manager; hire crew; fill out state and federal forms	Get your training in franchisor's school; learn procedures and methods	Construction; punch list; permits; bank accounts; marketing plan; inventory	First soft opening; later grand opening Employee daily work schedule Daily sales reports Cash register tapes, money Deposit cash in bank nightly Insure accuracy Pay royalty and advertising fees	Work and manage your own franchise
Time span	2 to 6 weeks	2 weeks to 2 months	1 day to 2 weeks	Select a Friday, Saturday, or Sunday	

Source: Ralph J. Weiger, "Franchise Investigation Time Span," *Franchising World,* March/April 1989, p. 18. Copyright International Franchise Association, Washington, D.C.

Minority Ownership of Franchises

Minority ownership of franchises has made steady progress over the years, especially in automobile and truck dealerships, as the Profile (page 117) illustrates. According to a study of 366 franchise chains in 60 different businesses, 9.5 percent of franchises are operated by minorities.[21]

While the major barriers continue to be lack of financing and expertise, minority ownership is now growing. According to Shingler-Hollis Investment Group, a small business development/franchise consultant, the minority community is insisting on getting more information from franchisors.[22] The result is that franchise executives and government agencies are increasingly alerting potential franchisees to franchise opportunities, including financing, training, and support activities. In fact, some of the larger fast-food chains have programs to target aid to minority buyers, as the following examples illustrate.

Shoney's Inc., which franchises Shoney's, Lee's Famous Recipe Country Chicken, and Captain D's Seafood, defers a big chunk of the initial franchise fee and slashes initial royalties for minority owners. KFC reduces liquidity requirements by over one-half and guarantees loans made by local banks to minority operators of its restaurants.

The **Minority Vendor Profile System** is a computerized database designed to match minority entrepreneurs with available marketing opportunities.

The primary group that implements federal policies benefiting minority entrepreneurship is the Minority Business Development Agency (MBDA). Among its many other activities, it operates the **Minority Vendor Profile System,** a computerized database listing minority firms. The system is designed to match minority entrepreneurs with available marketing opportunities.

TURNING YOUR DREAM INTO A REALITY

We've presented much information to help you decide whether or not you want to go into franchising. You've also been told how to investigate whether a franchise is right for you or not. Now, Figure 7–7 provides a step-by-step review of what is required for you to become a franchisee. It also estimates the time required for each of the steps. While all of these steps may not be required, and the time spans are not universal, the information is a good overview of the activities required by many franchisors and the time it takes to do each of them.

WHAT YOU SHOULD HAVE LEARNED

1. Franchising sales have more than doubled in the last decade, and the number of establishments is also increasing. Franchising is strongest in retailing, accounting for around 34 percent of retail sales and 87 percent of all franchising receipts. It's expected to increase to 50 percent by the year 2000.

2. Franchising is a marketing system that permits the franchisee to conduct business as an individual owner under the terms and conditions set by the franchisor. The two most common franchising systems are *(a)* product and trademark franchising and *(b)* business format franchising. In the first, franchisees acquire the right to sell the franchisor's product and use its trademark, but they are relatively free to use their own operating methods. In the second, the franchisor determines virtually every aspect of the franchisee's operations, including management policies, accounting methods, reporting forms, designs, and furnishings.

3. Business format franchising has increased steadily because it provides a ready market and management system, and the failure rate is lower than for independent businesses.

4. Franchising is a good way for someone to enter business. But you should carefully research the industry and the particular franchise in order to determine whether the assistance provided by the franchisor is worth the sacrifice of independence. You should study the franchise offering circular, check with existing franchisees, and obtain professional advice in order to understand your rights and obligations. Franchisors who belong to the International Franchise Association (IFA) subscribe to a code of ethics that provides protection to their franchisees.

5. The future of franchising looks good, especially for restaurants; motels; convenience stores; electronics; and automotive parts, accessories, and servicing. International franchising is one of the fastest-growing areas of franchising. Minority ownership of franchises is also growing, and special efforts are being made to encourage minority franchising.

QUESTIONS FOR DISCUSSION

1. What distinguishes a franchise from an independent small business?
2. What are the two most important forms of franchising? Describe each.
3. Describe why franchising is growing in importance.
4. How can you decide whether a franchise is right for you? Explain.
5. What are some expected areas of growth for franchising in the future?
6. Why is franchising growing internationally?
7. What is happening to opportunities in franchising for minorities?

RAY KROC: FATHER OF FRANCHISING

Ray Kroc, himself a billionaire, probably made more people millionaires in less time than anyone else in history. And he did it after he was 52 years old and in poor health. Now his "brainchild"–McDonald's–has over 13,000 stores in 65 countries, with over $19 billion in systemwide sales.

Kroc, a high school dropout, sold everything from paper cups in Chicago to real estate in Florida before he wound up selling electric milkshake mixers in the early 1950s. At

McDonald's Founder Ray Kroc
Photo courtesy of McDonald's Corporation.

that time, a hamburger and a shake took about 15 to 30 minutes to prepare at any of the thousands of small, independent drive-ins scattered across the country.

In 1954, Kroc received an order from a drive-in in San Bernardino, California, for eight machines that could make five milkshakes at a time. His curiosity led him to visit Richard and Maurice McDonald to see why they needed to make 40 shakes at a time. He found people lining up at a window, ordering, and leaving in about 30 seconds with bags of hamburgers, fries, and shakes—all for under a dollar. He thought the assembly-line operation, based on clean, instant service with a family atmosphere, was the most amazing merchandising operation he'd ever seen. Kroc persuaded the brothers to let him set up a complete franchising operation, including finding operators and locations, building drive-ins, and ensuring that they maintained the McDonalds' high standards. He left with a contract to franchise McDonald's worldwide and pay the brothers 0.5 percent of restaurant sales.

Kroc opened his first drive-in under this arrangement in Des Plaines, Illinois, in 1955. By 1961, there were 323 of the golden-arches stores, and the McDonalds wanted to retire. Kroc bought their rights for $2.7 million. At the time, sales were $54 million and earnings were around $175,000. Also, the company had some company-owned restaurants. When he died in 1984, at age 81, Kroc was a billionaire. But his franchisees were doing quite well, too. Average store sales were over $1 million and there were before-tax profit margins of 15 to 20 percent.

Kroc did for the fast-food industry what Henry Ford had done for the automobile industry. He was truly the "Father of Franchising."

QUESTIONS

1. Identify and discuss several reasons for the success of the McDonald's franchising operation.

2. What type of franchising system is a McDonald's franchise? Explain.

3. Despite its phenomenal success, speculate as to why one might not want to invest in a McDonald's franchise.

4. You have decided to become a franchise owner. What are some of the factors you must consider before you enter into a franchise arrangement with McDonald's?

5. Based on its past successes, while considering current and future competition, speculate as to the future of the McDonald's chain. Consider opportunities for growth.

Sources: Based on correspondence with McDonald's Corporation, Oak Brook, Illinois; as well as various published sources, such as annual reports.

8

Preparing and Presenting the Business Plan

A completed business plan is a guide that illustrates where you are, where you are going, and how to get there.—Charles J. Bodenstab

A business plan may tell you by the time you're done that this isn't a profitable business. If you go into the business without a path to walk down, without some sort of guidelines, you're in real trouble.—Geoff Walsh

LEARNING OBJECTIVES

After studying the material in this chapter, you will be able to:

1. Tell why a business plan is needed and what purpose it should serve.

2. Explain how to approach the preparation of the business plan.

3. List the components of a business plan.

4. Suggest ways to write and present the plan.

5. Prepare a sample business plan.

JIM BUSBY: PREPARING AND USING A "LIVING BUSINESS PLAN"

James L. Busby has become a legendary figure on the financial scene in Mobile, Alabama. Busby is founder, major stockholder, and CEO of QMS, Inc., a high-tech company that makes and markets computer print systems to meet today's needs for state-of-the-art computer printing. QMS began in 1977 in Busby's son's bedroom. QMS's KISS system is the first intelligent laser printer that is both smart and simple. It produces crisp, near-typewriter-quality output at 400 characters per second and works with Lotus, WordStar, and other software that will print to a Diablo 630, Epson FX-80, or QUME Sprint.

After graduating with an electrical engineering degree from the University of Alabama—where he'd taken computer courses and de-

signed and built his own computer—Busby served in the U.S. Army Signal Corps, working with computers. Afterwards, he worked for four-and-a-half years at International Paper Company and Scott Paper Company, working with computerized systems, while studying for an M.B.A. in the evenings.

He became intrigued by Scott's roll-wrapping system, which was controlled by a computer—except for labeling. On the way home from class one night, he nearly wrecked his car when the solution to the labeling problem struck him. He stayed up all night working out the details. He knew this was his big chance to found his own company, but he needed money.

He prepared a business plan, indicating that he needed $10,000. He went to a stockbroker, who told him to see a banker, who said, "If you can raise $5,000, the bank will match it with a $5,000 loan." Busby called everyone he knew but could not raise the funds. After a week, he called the banker to tell him that he could not get the $5,000. The next day, the banker called and said he was so impressed with Busby's business plan that, if Busby and his wife would co-sign the note, the bank would lend them the $10,000. They agreed and received the loan to start the firm. Busby and his brother-in-law, Mike Dow, started the company while still working full time at other jobs.

QMS was ranked 70th in *Forbes* magazine's 1986 ranking of the 200 Best Small Companies in America, for its 21.7 percent five-year average return on equity. But, like other high-tech growth companies, QMS had to reposition itself after the 1987 crash.

Busby and his staff are now moving QMS into its next growth stage. They regard the company's overall business plan, as well as each department's plan, as the "backbone of the company." It's a "living business plan" that in fiscal year 1991 resulted in over $304 million in sales from its employees worldwide.

Source: Correspondence with QMS; and others, including Bailey Thomson, "Young Company Fights Back," *Mobile* (Alabama) *Press Register,* October 4, 1992, p. 1E.

A **business plan** sets forth the firm's objectives, steps for achieving them, and its financial requirements.

As Jim Busby discovered, a new business results from the prospective owner's having both a good idea for producing and selling a product and the ability to carry out the idea. This truth was confirmed in a survey of the 665 fastest-growing private companies in which 88 percent "succeeded by taking an ordinary idea and pulling it off exceptionally well."[1] Yet other things—such as buildings and machines, personnel, materials and supplies, and finances—are also needed. These needs are developed from the strategic, operational, and financial planning described in Chapter 6. And all that planning needs to be formalized into a **business plan,** which is a tool for attracting the other components of the business formation package—the people and the money. A well-developed and well-presented business plan can provide small business owners with a much greater chance of success—and reduce their chances of failing.

For example, the importance of the business plan was demonstrated in 1989, when Eastern Airlines' unsecured creditors said they would not "give credence to offers to buy the bankrupt firm until the bidder submitted a credible business plan."[2] Even with the plan, however, Eastern still went bankrupt.

PURPOSES OF THE BUSINESS PLAN

The business plan could be the most useful and important document you, as an entrepreneur, ever put together. When you are up to your ears in the details of starting the business, the plan keeps your thinking on target, keeps your creativity on track, and concentrates your power on reaching your goal.

"Dad, have you come to a decision on my comprehensive business plan for my allowance?"
Source: Copyright 1993 by J. Nebesky.

The plan can be a useful money-raising tool to attract venture capital for those entrepreneurs who are willing to dilute control of their company. Although few owners use a plan to attract venture funds, many more use a formal business plan to obtain loans from lending agencies.

For example, when Steven and Barbara Chappell were ready to start up their Our Hero Restaurant franchise, they did not have enough savings to pay the rent and other expenses. So they drew up a 20-page plan—including blueprints, personal data, itemized lists of requirements for materials and supplies, and statistics from the Our Hero franchisor—and presented it to four banks. Since all of them offered to lend the required funds, the Chappells negotiated with the bank that offered the best terms.[3]

But an effective plan does more than just help convince prospective investors that the new business is sound. It provides a detailed blueprint for the activities needed to finance the business, develop the product, market it, and otherwise manage the new business. Business plans are also used for the continuing operations of a firm.

For example, a survey of 1,090 small business owners found that 89 percent of them used the business plan to set employee goals, and 85 percent used it to establish records for management. They also used it to help "run the business," and to serve as a yardstick to measure how the business was running.[4]

Because an effective business plan helps determine the feasibility of an idea, it should include a detailed analysis of factors such as the following:

- The proposed product.
- The expected market for it.
- The strengths and weaknesses of the industry.
- Planned marketing policies, such as price, promotion, and distribution.
- Operations or production methods and facilities.
- Financial aspects, including expected income, expenses, profits (or losses), investment needed, and expected cash flow.

In addition, a properly developed, well-written business plan should answer questions such as the following:

- Is the business formation package complete?
- Would it be attractive to potential investors?
- Does the proposed business have a reasonable chance for success at the start?
- Does it have any long-run competitive advantages to the owner? To investors? To employees?
- Can the product be produced efficiently?

- Can it be marketed effectively?
- Can the production and marketing of the product be economically financed?
- Can the new company's business functions—operations, distribution, finance, and personnel—be properly managed?
- Are the needed employees available?

In summary, a properly developed and written plan provides more than mere facts. Instead, it serves as (1) an effective communication tool to convey ideas, research findings, and proposed plans to others, especially financiers; (2) the basis for managing the new venture; and (3) a measuring device by which to gauge progress and evaluate needed changes. Developing and writing a business plan takes much time, effort, and money, but the results can make the difference between the company's success and failure.

PREPARING THE PLAN

When developing a business plan, you should consider the firm's background, origins, philosophy, mission, and objectives, as well as the means of fulfilling that mission and attaining those objectives.[5] A sound approach is to (1) determine where the business is at present, by recognizing its current status; (2) decide where you would like to be, by clarifying your philosophy about doing business, developing the firm's mission, and setting objectives; and (3) determine how to get to where you want to be, by identifying the best strategies for accomplishing the business's objectives. Figure 8–1 shows one approach to preparing a business plan.

Who Should Prepare the Plan?

If the prospective owner is the only one involved in the business, he or she should prepare the plan, with the advice and counsel of competent advisors. But, if the business is to be organized and run by more than one person, it should be a team effort. In fact, you might encourage each manager to prepare a part of the plan. We

Figure 8–1   How to Prepare a Business Plan

- Survey consumer demands for your product(s) and decide how to satisfy those demands.
- Ask questions that cover everything from the firm's target market to its competitive position.
- Establish a long-range strategic plan for the entire business.
- Develop short-term, detailed plans for all those involved with the business, including the owner(s), managers, and employees.
- Plan for every part of the venture, including operations, marketing, general and administrative functions, and distribution.
- Prepare a plan that uses staff time sparingly.

also recommend having other key employees help in the planning stage, which will improve communication and motivation.

Developing Action Steps

You can collect needed information from the steps discussed in Chapters 5 and 6, as well as from business associates and from legal, management, and financial consultants. Discussions with people both inside and outside the business are useful in gathering and evaluating this information.

The focus of the plan should be on future developments for the business, with steps set up to deal with specific aspects, such as product development, marketing, production or operations, finance, and management. Realistic, measurable objectives should be set, and the plan's steps should be delegated, monitored, and reported regularly.

Questions such as the following are useful in developing action steps: Who will be responsible for each course of action? What is the time frame for achieving each objective? What are the barriers to achieving the objectives? How can those barriers be overcome? Have the necessary controls been considered?

COMPONENTS OF THE PLAN

Because the business plan is such an important document, it should be arranged logically and presented clearly to save the reader time and effort, as well as to ensure understanding. While the information that should be included tends to be standardized, the format to be used is not. (Figure 8–2 presents a typical format.)

Regardless of the specific format chosen, any plan should include at least the following elements:

1. Cover sheet.
2. Executive summary.
3. Table of contents.
4. History of the (proposed) business.
5. Definition of the business.
6. Definition of the market.
7. Description of the product(s).
8. Management structure.
9. Objectives and goals.
10. Financial data.
11. Appendixes.

Cover Sheet

The cover sheet presents identifying information, such as the business name, address, and phone number. Also, readers should know at once who the principals are.

Figure 8–2   Typical Business Plan Format

---

1. Cover sheet
   - Business name, address, and phone number
   - Principals
   - Date
2. Executive summary
   - Abstract–Mission statement
   - Objectives
   - Description of products or services
   - Marketing plan
   - Financial budget
3. Table of contents
4. History
   - Background of principals, or company origins
   - History of products or services
   - Organization structure
   - Company history in brief
5. Definition of the business
6. Definition of the market
   - Target market/area
   - Market analysis
   - Competitor analysis
   - Industry analysis
7. Description of products or services
   - What is to be developed or produced
   - Status of research and development
   - Status of patents, trademarks, copyrights

8. Management structure
   - Who will enact plan
   - Organizational chart
   - Communication flow chart
   - Employee policies
9. Objectives and goals
   - Profit plan
   - Marketing plans
   - Manufacturing plans
   - Quality control plans
   - Financial plans
10. Financial data
    - Pro forma income statements (three years)
    - Pro forma cash flow analyses (first year, by months)
    - Pro forma balance sheets (three years)
    - Cost-volume-profit analyses where appropriate
11. Appendixes
    - Narrative history of firm in detail
    - Résumés of key employees
    - Major environmental assumptions
    - Brochures describing products
    - Letters of recommendation or endorsement
    - Historical financial data (at least three years)
    - Details of:
      - *a.* Products and services
      - *b.* Research and development
      - *c.* Marketing
      - *d.* Manufacturing
      - *e.* Administration
      - *f.* Finance

Executive Summary

The **executive summary** is a brief overview of the most important information in a business plan.

The **executive summary** of your plan must be a real "grabber"; it must motivate the reader to go on to the other sections. Moreover, it must convey a sense of plausibility, credibility, and integrity. Your plan may be one of many evaluated by representatives of lending institutions. They tend to evaluate the worth of the plan on the basis of this summary; if it generates sufficient interest, the remainder of the document may be assigned to other persons for review. The executive summary outlines the entire business plan, its major objectives, how these objectives will be accomplished, and the expected results. Therefore, it is sometimes first sent to

---

Figure 8–3   Sample Outline of an Executive Summary

A. Company
  1. Who and what it is
  2. Status of project/firm
  3. Key goals and objectives
B. Product/service
  1. What it is
  2. How it works
  3. What it is for
  4. Proprietary advantages
C. Market
  1. Prospective customers
  2. How many there are
  3. Market growth rate
  4. Competition (list three to six
     competitors by name and describe)
  5. Industry trends
  6. How the firm will compete
  7. Estimated market share
     a. In one year
     b. In five years

D. Operations
  1. How product/service will be
     manufactured/provided
  2. Facilities/equipment
  3. Special processes
  4. Labor skills needed
E. Channels of distribution: how
   product/service will get to end users
F. Management team
  1. Who will do what
  2. Their qualifications
  3. Availability
G. Sources and application of funds
  1. Present needs
  2. Future needs

One-page profit and loss statement showing annual totals for first three years, including detailed costs of goods sold and overhead (general and administrative) breakdowns.

Source: Entrepreneur Application Profile used by Venture Capital Exchange, Enterprise Development Center, The University of Tulsa, Tulsa, Oklahoma.

potential investors to see if they have any interest in the venture; if so, the entire plan will then be sent to them.

Remember, *the executive summary is just that—a summary—so keep it short!* It may be difficult to get so much information on one or two pages, but try to do so. Also, even though the summary is the initial component of the plan, *it should be written only after the rest of the plan has been developed.*

Figure 8–3 presents a sample outline of the executive summary required of all individuals and firms seeking equity capital from the Venture Capital Exchange of the University of Tulsa. We recommend that your summary also contain sections on the ownership and legal form of the business.

Table of Contents

Because the table of contents provides an overview of what's in the plan, it should be written concisely, in outline form, using alphabetical and numerical headings and subheads.

History of the (Proposed) Business

Background information on the person(s) organizing the business, as well as a description of their contributions, should be discussed at this point. Explanations of how the idea for the product or firm originated and what has been done to develop the idea should also be included. If the owner(s) have been in business before, that should be discussed, and any failures should be explained.

Description of the Business

It is now time for you to describe your business! More information is needed than just a statement of what the firm does—or plans to do—and a listing of its functions, products, or services. This definition should tell what customer needs the business intends to meet. In writing this component, it might be helpful to distinguish between how you perceive the business and what potential customers might think of it. Think about questions such as these:

From the **Owner's** *Perspective:*	From the **Customer's** *Perspective:*
What do you think will sell?	What do you think they need or want to buy?
What is your largest line of inventory?	What is the best-selling item?
Where is your greatest profit made?	On what product or service is most personnel time spent?

Ask yourself whether the answers to these questions are closely aligned and compatible or divergent. If they are divergent, the business may be in trouble. If they are compatible—or can be made compatible—there is a good chance of success, as the following example illustrates.

The sales manager of an FM radio station evaluated the results of efforts to sell advertising and found that advertising customers obtained 45 percent or more of their business volume from the black community. Yet that group made up only a small portion of the station's listening audience, and the station had never attracted the desired volume of advertising. A shift to black disc jockeys and a program format attuned to the black community produced a substantial increase in advertising revenues.

Definition of the Market

While the definition of the market is one of the most important—and most difficult—parts of the plan to develop, it should at least indicate the target of your marketing efforts, as well as the trading area served. It must answer questions such as these: Who buys what and why? What are your customers like? Does the competition have any weaknesses you can exploit?

Description of the Product(s)

This section should describe the firm's existing or planned product(s). The status of all research done and developments under way should be described, along with discussions of any legal aspects, such as patents, copyrights, trademarks, pending lawsuits, and legal claims against the firm. Are any government approvals or clearances needed? Catalog sheets, blueprints, photographs, and other visuals—if available—are helpful and should be included.

Management Structure

This is the place to describe your management structure, especially the expertise of your management team. Explain how its members will help carry out the plan. You could also discuss employee policies and procedures. To repeat: It is important to demonstrate the proven ability and dedication of the owner and staff.

Objectives and Goals

This part outlines what your business plans to accomplish, as well as how and when it will be done and who will do it. Sales forecasts, as well as production, service, quality assurance, and financial plans should be discussed. Other items of interest to potential investors include pricing and anticipated profits, advertising and promotion strategies and budgets, a description of how the product(s) will be distributed and sold, and which categories of customers will be targeted for initial heavy sales effort, and which ones for later sales efforts.

Financial Data

One important purpose of the business plan is to indicate the expected financial results from operations. The plan should show prospective investors or lenders why they should provide funds, when they can expect a return, and what the expected rate of return on their money is. At this point in the new business's development, assumptions—or educated guesses—concerning many issues may have to be made. For example, assumptions must be made about expected revenues, competitors' actions, and future market conditions. Assumptions, while necessary, should be designated as such, and financial projections should be realistically based on how increased personnel, expanded facilities, or equipment needs will affect the projections. The budgetary process to be used is an important part of the business plan. And prices should reflect actual cost figures, as the following example illustrates.

In a college town, a restaurant owner who was in financial difficulty sought aid from the SBA. The first question asked by the SCORE volunteer assigned as a consultant was: "What's the most popular item on your menu?" The owner replied, "Our $5.25 steak dinner." The consultant asked for a scale and a raw steak. He showed the restaurant owner that the raw steak alone cost $4.30. Obviously, the reason for the steak dinner's popularity was the markup of less than 22 percent on the cost of the steak alone. It was also the underlying cause of the business's financial troubles.

Appendixes

Other components needed in the plan are the firm's organizational structure—including organization charts. This part should include résumés of the officers, directors, key personnel, and any outside board members. If any of these have any special expertise that increases the chances of success, this should be mentioned. Historical financial information, with relevant documents, should also be included. Brochures, news items, letters of recommendation or endorsements, photographs, and similar items should be included as well.

PRESENTING THE PLAN

We know a SCORE adviser who tells his clients, "Investors decide during the first five minutes of studying the executive summary whether to reject a proposal or consider it further." Therefore, *presenting the business plan is almost as important as preparing it*. All the work is in vain if potential investors aren't interested in it. Presentation involves both writing the plan and presenting it to the targeted audience.

Writing the Plan

John G. Burch, a writer on entrepreneurship, makes the following suggestions for writing the plan:[6]

1. *Be honest,* not only by avoiding outright lies, but also by revealing what you actually feel about the significant and relevant aspects of the plan.
2. *Use the third person,* not the first person ("I" or "we"). This practice forces you to think clearly and logically from the other person's perspective.
3. *Use transitional words,* such as *but, still,* and *therefore,* and *active, dynamic verbs* as a means of leading the reader from one thought to another.
4. Avoid *redundancies,* such as "*future* plans," since repetition adds nothing to the presentation.
5. *Use short, simple words,* where feasible, so the plan will be easy to understand and follow.
6. *Use visuals,* such as tables, charts, photos, and computer graphics to present your ideas effectively.

The plan should be prepared in an 8½-by-11-inch format, typed and photocopied, with copies for outsiders attractively bound. Most business plans can—and should—be presented effectively in 25 or 30 pages or less. Of course, the plan should be grammatically correct, so have someone proofread it before you present it.

The plan should be reviewed by people outside the firm, such as accounting and business consultants, other businesspeople, and attorneys, before it is sent to potential investors or lenders. Other helpful reviewers might include a professional writer, editor, or English teacher.

When pertinent, the cover and title page should indicate that the information is proprietary and confidential. However, there is always the chance that this practice might offend a potential investor.

The Written/Oral Presentation

In an oral presentation, you should present the plan in person to investors or lenders. Presenting your plan involves creative skills on your part in order to give the impression that you have (or plan to have) a profitable and stable business, and that its chances of continuing that way are good. Your listeners will be looking very carefully at *you,* to see what kind of person *you* are, for *you are the business*—and vice versa. Both written and oral presentations should be very positive and quite upbeat.

The plan should be delivered from the listener's perspective, not yours. Both oral and written presentations should demonstrate that you have a marketable product and that the business has a feasible plan for aggressively marketing it—at a profit. You should provide visual aids for key segments of the plan and be prepared for specific questions concerning the following:

- The adequacy of the research and development behind the product.
- The validity of the market research.
- Your understanding of the business.
- Financial projections and why they will work.
- Relative priority of the objectives.
- Your ability to "make it happen."

The amount of detail in the market data and financial projections will vary according to the plan's purpose. If it is to raise equity or debt financing, more detail is needed; if it's to improve operations and motivate employees, less detail is needed.

Even the best-prepared plan, though, may not be accepted by potential investors. The Using Technology to Succeed illustrates one of business history's classic rebuffs.

IMPLEMENTING THE PLAN

Now you are ready to take the plunge! It is time to get a charter, obtain facilities and supplies, hire and train people, and start operating. Using the capital structure plan and the sources of funds you have developed, obtain the funds and put them in a checking account ready for use. Obtain the services of an attorney to help acquire the charter (if the business is to be incorporated), obtain occupational licenses and permits, and take care of other legal requirements.

━━━━━━━━━━━━━━━ USING TECHNOLOGY TO SUCCEED ━━━━━━━━━━━━━━━

20/20 HINDSIGHT

Forty years ago, J. Presper Eckert, Jr., one of the inventors of the ENIAC®, the first digital computer, fired off a business plan to IBM, hoping it would yield an investment to produce and distribute the UNIVAC®, the first giant electronic computer. IBM president Thomas J. Watson, Sr., after careful review, responded that it was the company's opinion that the world would ultimately need only 12 computers, and Eckert's machine was therefore of no interest to IBM.

Once the funds, charter, and permits are in hand, refer to the timetable and start negotiating contracts; purchasing equipment, materials, and supplies; selecting, hiring, and training employees; establishing a marketing program; setting the legal structure in place; and developing an information system to maintain the records needed to run the business.

You are now a small business owner! You are operating your own business, you have all the risks, and you hope to receive the benefits and rewards of being on your own. Be ready for unforeseen problems, however, that may occur during the start-up period.

SAMPLE BUSINESS PLAN

A sample business plan is presented as an appendix at the end of this chapter. It is a proposal for a new sporting goods business. Notice that it closely follows the form presented in Figure 8–2 (page 142). It was also influenced by several SBA Directory of Business Development Publications.[7]

WHAT YOU SHOULD HAVE LEARNED

1. A business plan is important for obtaining funds and as a blueprint for operating success. The research and analysis required to write an effective plan help you focus on the company's goals, markets, expected performance, and problems that might be encountered. The plan keeps you from jumping into an enterprise without adequate thought and planning, and then serves as a yardstick against which to measure performance.

2. The owner is the best person to prepare the plan, but key personnel should also help with the preparation. They can best define its mission, philosophy, and objectives and determine how it should be organized and operated. Professionals and businesspeople should be consulted for information and advice about specific aspects of the business.

3. The plan should include at least the following: *(a)* cover sheet, *(b)* executive summary, *(c)* table of contents, *(d)* history of the (proposed) business, *(e)* description of the business, *(f)* definition of the market, *(g)* description of the product(s), *(h)* management structure, *(i)* objectives and goals, *(j)* financial data, and *(k)* appendixes. When used to raise funds, detailed financial projections of expected sales, profits, and rates of return should be emphasized.

4. The plan should be honest, logical, interesting, thorough, and easy to understand. It should be reviewed by outsiders qualified to judge its content and/or style before it is presented to potential investors. The plan should be presented from the listener's point of view, using a marketing approach. The important point is to create the impression of a profitable and stable business run by capable and responsible people.

5. From discussions in this and the two previous chapters, you should be able to prepare an effective business plan.

QUESTIONS FOR DISCUSSION

1. What is the purpose of a business plan? Explain.

2. How can a business plan be useful even to a prospective business owner who does not need outside capital?

3. What should the business plan include?

4. Do you think that the preparation of a business plan is as important as the authors claim? Explain.

5. Who should prepare the plan? Why? Why should the writer get help from outside professionals and businesspeople?

6. How should a business plan be written and presented?

USING COMPUTER SOFTWARE TO PREPARE A BUSINESS PLAN

Can a floppy disk substitute for the years at a graduate school of business? Probably not! But a number of software producers have developed programs to help guide unskilled entrepreneurs through business planning, calculating the cash value of a business, preparing business plans, and so forth. These programs help people with no experience, or those from specialized fields, start a new business where knowledge from many areas is needed.

Some of the programs are little more than electronic form letters with spaces for the entrepreneur to complete in order to impress outside capital sources. Others are complete systems that not only ask questions but also give meaningful advice based on the knowledge and beliefs of management experts. For example, Business Resource Software, Inc., a Texas company, has a program called ''Business Insight,'' which costs $495. According to Randy Ziegenhorn, an Illinois wholesale seed dealer, it provided him an insight into better marketing strategies. He said he sold more oats in one month than he had in the previous two years. The program did what his college English literature degree and experience as a farmer could not do—helped him do ''strategic business thinking.''

Value Express's $195 program is designed specifically to calculate the cash value of a business.

The American Institute of Small Business has a program called ''How to Write a Business Plan,'' with accompanying instructions and examples. (See page 79 for more details.)

Entrepreneur magazine has a good plan called ''Developing a Successful Business Plan,''™ which operates on IBM-PCs or compatibles.

In essence, what the programs do is ask questions about the business that the user must answer. This provides a logical approach to business planning.

QUESTIONS

1. To what extent do you think these programs are a substitute for business experience and knowledge? Explain.

2. How would you go about using one of these programs if you were starting a new business?

3. What do you see as the primary use of these programs in the future?

Source: Adapted from William M. Bulkeley, ''With New Planning Software, Entrepreneurs Act Like M.B.A.s,'' *The Wall Street Journal,* June 2, 1992, pp. B1 and B4, and other sources.

A SAMPLE BUSINESS PLAN: BRADLEY'S SPORTING GOODS*

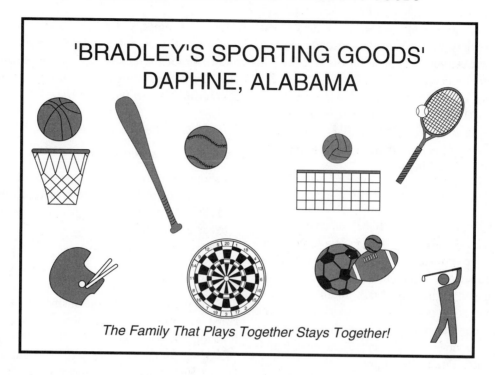

'BRADLEY'S SPORTING GOODS'
DAPHNE, ALABAMA

The Family That Plays Together Stays Together!

EXECUTIVE SUMMARY

The Company

Bradley's Sporting Goods, a retail sporting goods outlet, will offer an array of sporting goods, mainly sporting apparel and equipment—not including hunting, fishing, or marine accessories. The company will offer a full line of athletic equipment at wholesale prices for local schools, parks, and city recreation departments, as well as professional services to buyers. The retail outlet will have 2,500 square feet, with approximately 2,000 square feet used for retail space and 500 square feet of warehousing space for storing bulky items and general merchandise.

Products

Bradley's Sporting Goods will be located off Highway 98 in Daphne, Alabama, four miles south of U.S. Interstate 10. The sporting goods outlet, which will offer a full line of athletic apparel and equipment, will be open from Monday through Saturday. Prices will be moderate in relation to industry markup standards, but slightly higher than discount stores such as Wal-Mart.

Marketing Strategy

The outlet will serve the Baldwin County communities of Daphne, Fairhope, Spanish Fort, Montrose, and Point Clear. The golf courses of Lake Forest and the Grand Hotel, as well as educational institutions ranging from elementary to college level, will be the

*Text and art prepared by Barney Sheppard for Mark and Missy Bradley.

primary targets for sales of athletic goods and supplies. Contracts will be solicited from these establishments prior to, and during, the store's Grand Opening. The economy of the surrounding communities, which have an estimated population of 31,282, will support the retail side of the business.

A billboard at the intersection of Alabama Highway 98 and I-10 will be leased to advertise Bradley's. Prior to the grand opening, ad circulars will be distributed in areas of the immediate store location, such as area shops and parking lots.

Operations

Bradley's Sporting Goods will be managed by the founder/owners, Mark and Missy Bradley. Retail services will be provided by Missy Bradley and two part-time associates, while the wholesale business will be managed entirely by Mark Bradley. He will make contact with potential customers and solicit contracts for equipment needed by such customers as schools, golf courses, hotels, city recreation activities, and parks. The main purpose of the wholesale business will be to provide volume purchasing for those customers.

The Management Team

Each of the Bradleys will own 50 percent of the business, which will operate as a general partnership. Mark will be president and Missy will be both vice president and secretary. The goal of the team is to operate the business at a marginal profit the first two years, but make a substantial profit in the third year. The owners will pay themselves only a moderate salary for the first two years in order to enhance and strengthen the firm's cash flow.

At present, Mark has a full-time job, working a 12-hour, 2/3 rotating shift in a local chemical manufacturing firm. This schedule offers a lot of time off, which will be needed to make the new business succeed. He plans to work at least 40 hours per week in the sporting goods business but anticipates devoting his full time and attention to the business in the long run.

Missy is employed part-time at a local bank. She will keep the company's books while working the retail side of the business with the part-time associates. Sometime during the third year, she plans to devote full time to the business.

Financial Considerations

Sales, Expenses, and Profits

As shown in Exhibit 1, anticipated profits for the first three years of operations are projected to be:

    Year 1: $904.57
    Year 2: $4,388.96
    Year 3: $9,963.27.

Sources of Funds

The sources of funds for the business will be Mr. E. H. Gooden, $50,000.00, and owners' cash, $20,000.00, for a total working capital of $70,000.00. Mr. Gooden, Missy's grandfather, is 78 years old and in very good health. He has been independently wealthy for most of his life, making his fortune in real estate. The owners' cash is from Mark and Missy's savings. The amount financed by the outside source represents 71 percent of the total working capital, which, according to the local SBDC and SBIC, is above the normal 50 percent relationship to owner(s) contributions. Due to the family ties, however, Mr. Gooden will loan Mark and Missy the needed capital to start the business. The loan will be extended for 120 months, which is twice as much as the SBIC extension criteria.

TABLE OF CONTENTS

  I. History and Background
 II. Definition of the Business
III. Definition of the Market
    A. Customers
    B. Competition
    C. Growth Strategy

Exhibit I   Bradley's Sporting Goods Projected Income Statements 1991–1993

BRADLEY'S SPORTING GOODS
Projected Income Statements 1991–1993

	1991	1992	1993
Sales	$192,500.00	$202,125.00	$231,980.00
Cost of goods sold	146,050.00	152,223.75	172,985.00
Gross profit	$ 46,450.00	$ 49,901.25	$ 58,994.60
Controllable expenses			
Salaries	12,000.00	12,000.00	14,400.00
Payroll taxes	1,440.00	1,440.00	1,800.00
Advertising	2,450.00	2,510.00	3,092.75
Dues/subscriptions	50.00	52.50	56.17
Legal & accounting	600.00	630.00	674.04
Office supplies	1,200.00	1,260.00	1,348.20
Telephone	1,500.00	1,575.00	1,653.72
Utilities	3,000.00	3,150.00	3,307.44
Miscellaneous	1,350.00	1,260.00	1,323.00
Fixed expenses			
Insurance	1,944.00	1,944.00	2,040.00
Rent	12,000.00	12,000.00	12,000.00
Tax and license	150.00	150.00	150.00
Interest	4,861.43	4,540.79	4,186.01
Depreciation	3,000.00	3,000.00	3,000.00
Total Expenses	45,545.43	45,512.29	49,031.33
Net Profit (EBIT)	$ 904.57	$ 4,388.96	$ 9,963.27

D. Marketing Strategy: Advertising and Promotion

IV. Description of Products
V. Management Structure
VI. Objectives and Goals
VII. Financial Data
  A. Projected Income Statements
  B. Cash Flow Projections
  C. Pro-Forma Balance Sheet Projections
  D. Comparative Ratios
VIII. Appendixes
  A. Business Advisors
  B. Property

HISTORY AND BACKGROUND

Bradley's Sporting Goods will be a partnership, with Mark and Missy as the partners. Mark is a 29-year-old native Mobilian, with a B.A. degree in physical education from Huntington College in Montgomery, Alabama. While in school, he was very active in all sports but concentrated on baseball for four years and football for two. After graduating in 1984, Mark returned to Mobile to seek employment in his field. Being unable to do so, he joined a local chemical manufacturing firm, M&T, as a chemical operator.

Missy, Mark's wife of three years, is 26 years old and a graduate of Fairhope High School. Over the past five years, she has worked for Delta Airlines and the Grand Hotel. She is currently employed as a bookkeeper at First Alabama Bank in Daphne. After serving a year as a stewardess for Delta, she decided she did not like travel and so resigned to work for the Grand Hotel. She worked in the golf pro shop for three years, having various duties and responsibilities, mainly repairing golf equipment and accessories.

Mark and Missy's backgrounds, and their desire to own an independent business, provide a good basis for running the sporting goods business. With Mark's degree in physical education and Missy's knowledge of golf sales and service, their partnership is suitable to this type of business venture.

DEFINITION OF THE BUSINESS

Bradley's mission is to provide quality athletic goods and services to the Baldwin County area. Its pricing policies, combined with prompt service, should result in an adequate profit.

DEFINITION OF THE MARKET

Retail customers are expected to come from Daphne, Fairhope, Montrose, Spanish Fort, and other Baldwin County communities. The location is accessible to students from several high schools and a community college. The U.S. Census Bureau estimated Baldwin County's 1990 population at 92,300, an increase of 17.5 percent over 1980. Further, the most rapid growth in Baldwin County is occurring along the Eastern Shore area, which is very accessible to Mobile. This area extends 12 miles south from Spanish Fort to Fairhope, with Daphne in the center.

Customers

The larger buyers of athletic equipment and apparel will be the athletic departments of local high schools, city park and recreation units, and Faulkner State Community College. It is expected that 50 percent of the company's volume will come from its wholesale activities. For example, Lake Forest Golf Club has an enrollment of 450 members and hosts 20,000 rounds of golf yearly!

It is anticipated that the "bedroom suburb" characteristics of the local economy will support the business and have a customer base reflected in the demographics shown in Exhibit 2.

The site is well-positioned to serve this market. It has the population base, fronts U.S. 98 (Eastern Shore Parkway)—which is really the area's only major traffic artery—and has abundant parking space. According to the State of Alabama Highway Division, an average of 28,060 cars travel the Parkway daily, with the traffic count on I-10, just four miles north, averaging 38,880. A large market is possible with this traffic volume. The owners believe that about 25 percent of their retail customers will come from I-10 traffic flows, while most others will come from the Baldwin County communities.

Competition

The City of Daphne has no sporting goods outlets, as such, but there is a Wal-Mart within one mile of the business. Although it has an array of sporting goods and equipment, it does not offer such items as uniforms and equipment suitable for team sports.

Two other competitors in the area—Eastern Shore Sporting Goods and Jerry's Sporting Goods—with

Exhibit 2 Daphne Trade Area Population Projections

	3-Mile Radius	5-Mile Radius	10-Mile Radius
1992 population	10,507	20,102	67,940
Percent change (1987–92)	+16.9	+15.0	+2.6
Median age	32.1	32.6	31.5
Median household income (1987)	$32,999	$31,330	$20,212

Source: Urban Decision System, P.O. Box 25953, Los Angeles, CA 90025.

limited sales and inventory, are located within a 10-mile radius of Bradley's. Eastern Shore carries mainly sports clothing, with equipment stocks confined primarily to tennis rackets and caps. Jerry's outlet is located in the Spanish Fort area in a renovated gas station. Because its business is basically seasonal, it concentrates on baseball sales and stocks to conform to local athletic associations' demands, such as Little League baseball. Neither Eastern Shore nor Jerry's advertises widely, nor are they located in prime facilities.

Competitors' Strengths

1. Wal-Mart is a fast-growing, multibillion-dollar retail business, with a very good national and local reputation. Its vast inventories and low prices contribute to its image of "quality goods at low prices." Advertising is heavy, both nationally and locally.

2. Eastern Shore Sporting Goods, located in Fairhope, is patronized by a large number of its elementary and secondary school children. The business is well established and supported by the local economy.

3. Jerry's Sporting Goods is located near I-10, which provides it with excellent visibility. The business has a good reputation for supplying Little League baseball teams with equipment—at reasonable prices.

Competitors' Weaknesses

1. None of the competitors offers the extensive service Bradley's will provide, such as pickup and delivery service for the entire product line.

2. None of the competitors offers a complete line of athletic apparel and equipment, covering all the major sports, including football, baseball, basketball, track, tennis, golf, and swimming.

3. None of the competitors offers a quality product line such as Wilson, Spaulding,

and Russell Athletics, to name a few. Nor do they provide on-site service to customers, give personalized attention to customer needs and desires, or have extensive knowledge in the field of athletics.

Growth Strategy

The projections in Exhibit 2 show that the age and income of potential customers are in line with a growing population representing families, which is the group most likely to "play."

Anticipated sales for the first year are modest, with January sales expected to be $8,000 — or about $266 per day. Year-end sales are expected to be $25,000, or $833 daily. It is anticipated that sales will increase 5 percent in the second year and 12 percent in the third year. These sales figures, based on data obtained from the Eastern Shore Chamber of Commerce and the local SBDC located on the University of South Alabama campus, result from area demographic studies and the history of retail sales.

Marketing Strategy: Advertising and Promotion

The most important consideration in Bradley's marketing strategy will be advertising: by word of mouth, rural route mail circulars, and billboards. The owners believe public relations will be a strong point, since both partners have strong family ties in the area.

Advertising circulars will be important in establishing Bradley's name and in enhancing its sales. On the other hand, the billboard at the intersection of U.S. 98 and I-10 will be an important eye-catcher in pointing out Bradley's location.

Sales promotions will highlight the seasonal changes in athletics. Advertising will be heavy in relation to those seasonal changes, with promotional giveaways used to attract business traffic.

Most sales will be either for cash or major credit cards. Some of the larger wholesale customers will have accounts set up on a 30-day basis. Also, checks from local residents will be accepted, but no out-of-town checks will be accepted.

Exhibit 3   Apparel and Equipment Handled

Football	Basketball
Uniforms	Balls
Protective equipment	Shoes
Shoes	Uniforms
Other as needed	Other as needed
Baseball	Tennis
Shoes	Balls
Uniforms	Rackets
Gloves	Shorts and shirts
Bats and balls	Shoes
Other as needed	Golf
Volleyball	Shoes
Balls	Balls
Nets	Clubs (including repairs)
Uniforms	
Other as needed	

DESCRIPTION OF PRODUCTS

Athletic apparel and sporting goods equipment are shown in Exhibit 3. All sporting apparel will be serviced with on-site ironing of letters and numbers.

MANAGEMENT STRUCTURE

Mark Bradley will serve as president and Missy as vice president and secretary of Bradley's. Both will maintain their present employment, in the short term, while operating the business. However, both hope to be able to devote all of their time to the business after the third year of operations.

OBJECTIVES AND GOALS

The owners' objectives for Bradley's are mainly to improve the financial stability of sales with sustained sales growth that is consistent with the general retail industry of Baldwin County. (This figure is currently 7 percent annually.) They will strive to advertise their product line and maintain service before and after the sale.

The Daphne area, one of the fastest-growing areas in the United States, is expected to grow 40 percent in the next 10 years. Prospects are bright for a retail sporting goods outlet located in the center of this population growth. From this view, the proposed location will serve as a central location for Baldwin County shoppers, which should result in an excellent market for the business.

FINANCIAL DATA

The figures included here are based on assumptions derived from industry norms and area forecasts.

Projected Income Statements

While the owners cannot predict certain success, the profit and loss projections indicate a good probability that the business will grow as follows:

Year 1: $904.57

Year 2: $4,388.96

Year 3: $9,963.27

These figures are presented in more detail in Exhibit 4.

Exhibit 4

BRADLEY'S SPORTING GOODS
Projected Profit and Loss Statement
Year One

	January	February	March	April	May	June	July	August	September	October	November	December	Total
Total sales	$8,000.00	$9,000.00	$12,500.00	$14,000.00	$15,000.00	$16,500.00	$17,000.00	$18,000.00	$18,500.00	$19,000.00	$20,000.00	$25,000.00	$192,500.00
Cost of sales	5,600.00	6,300.00	9,375.00	11,200.00	11,250.00	12,375.00	12,750.00	14,400.00	14,800.00	14,250.00	15,000.00	18,750.00	146,050.00
Gross profit	$2,400.00	$2,700.00	$3,125.00	$2,800.00	$3,750.00	$4,125.00	$4,250.00	$3,600.00	$3,700.00	$4,750.00	$5,000.00	$6,250.00	$46,450.00
Controllable Expenses:													
Salaries	$1,000.00	$1,000.00	$1,000.00	$1,000.00	$1,000.00	$1,000.00	$1,000.00	$1,000.00	$1,000.00	$1,000.00	$1,000.00	$1,000.00	$12,000.00
Payroll taxes	120.00	120.00	120.00	120.00	120.00	120.00	120.00	120.00	120.00	120.00	120.00	120.00	1,440.00
Advertising	1,050.00			350.00				350.00	350.00			350.00	2,450.00
Dues & subscriptions	50.00												50.00
Legal & accounting	50.00	50.00	50.00	50.00	50.00	50.00	50.00	50.00	50.00	50.00	50.00	50.00	600.00
Office supplies	100.00	100.00	100.00	100.00	100.00	100.00	100.00	100.00	100.00	100.00	100.00	100.00	1,200.00
Telephone	125.00	125.00	125.00	125.00	125.00	125.00	125.00	125.00	125.00	125.00	125.00	125.00	1,500.00
Utilities	250.00	250.00	250.00	250.00	250.00	250.00	250.00	250.00	250.00	250.00	250.00	250.00	3,000.00
Miscellaneous	250.00	100.00	100.00	100.00	100.00	100.00	100.00	100.00	100.00	100.00	100.00	100.00	1,350.00
Total controllable expenses	$2,995.00	$1,745.00	$1,745.00	$2,095.00	$1,745.00	$1,745.00	$1,745.00	$2,095.00	$2,095.00	$1,745.00	$1,745.00	$2,095.00	$23,590.00
Fixed Expenses:													
Insurance	$162.00	$162.00	$162.00	$162.00	$162.00	$162.00	$162.00	$162.00	$162.00	$162.00	$162.00	$162.00	$1,944.00
Rent	1,000.00	1,000.00	1,000.00	1,000.00	1,000.00	1,000.00	1,000.00	1,000.00	1,000.00	1,000.00	1,000.00	1,000.00	12,000.00
Tax & license	150.00												150.00
Interest	416.67	414.63	412.06	410.51	408.43	406.33	404.20	402.07	399.91	397.74	395.55	393.33	4,861.43
Depreciation	250.00	250.00	250.00	250.00	250.00	250.00	250.00	250.00	250.00	250.00	250.00	250.00	3,000.00
Total fixed expenses	$1,978.67	$1,826.63	$1,824.06	$1,822.51	$1,820.43	$1,818.33	$1,816.20	$1,814.07	$1,811.91	$1,809.74	$1,807.55	$1,805.33	$21,955.43
Total Expenses	4,973.67	3,571.63	3,569.06	3,917.51	3,565.43	3,563.33	3,561.20	3,909.07	3,906.91	3,554.74	3,552.55	3,900.33	45,545.43
Net Profit	($2,573.67)	($871.63)	($444.06)	($1,117.51)	$184.57	$561.67	688.80	($309.07)	($206.91)	$1,195.26	$1,447.45	$2,349.67	$904.57

Exhibit 4 (continued)

BRADLEY'S SPORTING GOODS
Projected Profit and Loss Statement
Year Two

	January	February	March	April	May	June	July	August	September	October	November	December	Total
Total sales	$8,400.00	$9,450.00	$13,125.00	$14,700.00	$15,750.00	$17,325.00	$17,850.00	$18,900.00	$19,425.00	$19,950.00	$21,000.00	$26,250.00	$202,125.00
Cost of sales	5,880.00	6,615.00	9,843.75	11,760.00	12,600.00	12,993.75	13,387.50	14,175.00	14,568.75	14,962.50	15,750.00	19,687.50	152,223.75
Gross profit	$2,520.00	$2,835.00	$3,281.25	$2,940.00	$3,150.00	$4,331.25	$4,462.50	$4,725.00	$4,856.25	$4,987.50	$5,250.00	$6,562.50	$49,901.25
Controllable Expenses:													
Salaries	$1,000.00	$1,000.00	$1,000.00	$1,000.00	$1,000.00	$1,000.00	$1,000.00	$1,000.00	$1,000.00	$1,000.00	$1,000.00	$1,000.00	$12,000.00
Payroll taxes	120.00	120.00	120.00	120.00	120.00	120.00	120.00	120.00	120.00	120.00	120.00	120.00	1,440.00
Advertising	1,050.00			365.00				365.00	365.00			365.00	2,510.00
Dues & subscriptions	52.50												52.50
Legal & accounting	52.50	52.50	52.50	52.50	52.50	52.50	52.50	52.50	52.50	52.50	52.50	52.50	630.00
Office supplies	105.00	105.00	105.00	105.00	105.00	105.00	105.00	105.00	105.00	105.00	105.00	105.00	1,260.00
Telephone	131.25	131.25	131.25	131.25	131.25	131.25	131.25	131.25	131.25	131.25	131.25	131.25	1,575.00
Utilities	262.50	262.50	262.50	262.50	262.50	262.50	262.50	262.50	262.50	262.50	262.50	262.50	3,150.00
Miscellaneous	105.00	105.00	105.00	105.00	105.00	105.00	105.00	105.00	105.00	105.00	105.00	105.00	1,260.00
Total controllable expenses	$2,878.75	$1,776.25	$1,776.25	$2,141.25	$1,776.25	$1,776.25	$1,776.25	$2,141.25	$2,141.25	$1,776.25	$1,776.25	$2,141.25	$23,877.50
Fixed Expenses:													
Insurance	$ 162.00	$ 162.00	$ 162.00	$ 162.00	$ 162.00	$ 162.00	$ 162.00	$ 162.00	$ 162.00	$ 162.00	$ 162.00	$ 162.00	$ 1,944.00
Rent	1,000.00	1,000.00	1,000.00	1,000.00	1,000.00	1,000.00	1,000.00	1,000.00	1,000.00	1,000.00	1,000.00	1,000.00	12,000.00
Tax & license	150.00												150.00
Interest	391.11	388.86	386.60	384.31	382.00	379.69	377.34	374.98	372.60	370.19	367.78	365.33	4,540.79
Depreciation	250.00	250.00	250.00	250.00	250.00	250.00	250.00	250.00	250.00	250.00	250.00	250.00	3,000.00
Total fixed expenses	$1,953.11	$1,800.86	$1,798.60	$1,796.31	$1,794.00	$1,791.69	$1,789.34	$1,786.98	$1,784.60	$1,782.19	$1,779.78	$1,777.33	$21,634.79
Total Expenses	4,831.86	3,577.11	3,574.85	3,937.56	3,570.25	3,567.94	3,565.59	3,928.23	3,925.85	3,558.44	3,556.03	3,918.58	45,512.29
Net Profit	($2,311.86)	($ 742.11)	($ 293.60)	($ 997.56)	($ 420.25)	$ 763.31	$ 896.91	$ 796.77	$ 930.40	$ 1,429.06	$ 1,693.97	$ 2,643.92	$ 4,388.96

Exhibit 4 (concluded)

BRADLEY'S SPORTING GOODS
Projected Profit and Loss Statement
Year Three

	January	February	March	April	May	June	July	August	September	October	November	December	Total
Total sales	$9,408.00	$10,584.00	$14,700.00	$16,464.00	$17,640.00	$19,404.00	$19,992.00	$21,168.00	$21,756.00	$22,344.00	$23,520.00	$35,000.00	$231,980.00
Cost of sales	6,585.60	7,408.80	11,025.00	12,348.00	13,230.00	14,553.00	14,994.00	15,876.00	16,317.00	16,758.00	17,640.00	26,250.00	172,985.40
Gross profit	$2,822.40	$3,175.20	$3,675.00	$4,116.00	$4,410.00	$4,851.00	$4,998.00	$5,292.00	$5,439.00	$5,586.00	$5,880.00	$8,750.00	$58,994.60
Controllable Expenses:													
Salaries	$1,200.00	$1,200.00	$1,200.00	$1,200.00	$1,200.00	$1,200.00	$1,200.00	$1,200.00	$1,200.00	$1,200.00	$1,200.00	$1,200.00	$14,400.00
Payroll taxes	150.00	150.00	150.00	150.00	150.00	150.00	150.00	150.00	150.00	150.00	150.00	150.00	1,800.00
Advertising	1,140.00			390.55				390.55	390.55			781.10	3,092.75
Dues & subscriptions	56.17												56.17
Legal & accounting	56.17	56.17	56.17	56.17	56.17	56.17	56.17	56.17	56.17	56.17	56.17	56.17	674.04
Office supplies	112.35	112.35	112.35	112.35	112.35	112.35	112.35	112.35	112.35	112.35	112.35	112.35	1,348.20
Telephone	137.81	137.81	137.81	137.81	137.81	137.81	137.81	137.81	137.81	137.81	137.81	137.81	1,653.72
Utilities	275.62	275.62	275.62	275.62	275.62	275.62	275.62	275.62	275.62	275.62	275.62	275.62	3,307.44
Miscellaneous	110.25	110.25	110.25	110.25	110.25	110.25	110.25	110.25	110.25	110.25	110.25	110.25	1,323.00
Total controllable expenses	$3,238.37	$2,042.20	$2,042.20	$2,432.75	$2,042.20	$2,042.20	$2,042.20	$2,432.75	$2,432.75	$2,042.20	$2,042.20	$2,823.30	$27,655.32
Fixed Expenses:													
Insurance	$170.00	$170.00	$170.00	$170.00	$170.00	$170.00	$170.00	$170.00	$170.00	$170.00	$170.00	$170.00	$2,040.00
Rent	1,000.00	1,000.00	1,000.00	1,000.00	1,000.00	1,000.00	1,000.00	1,000.00	1,000.00	1,000.00	1,000.00	1,000.00	12,000.00
Tax & license	150.00												150.00
Interest	362.88	360.39	357.89	355.36	352.82	350.25	347.67	345.05	342.43	339.77	337.10	334.40	4,186.01
Depreciation	250.00	250.00	250.00	250.00	250.00	250.00	250.00	250.00	250.00	250.00	250.00	250.00	3,000.00
Total fixed expenses	$1,932.88	$1,780.39	$1,777.89	$1,775.36	$1,772.82	$1,770.25	$1,767.67	$1,765.05	$1,762.43	$1,759.77	$1,757.10	$1,754.40	$21,376.01
Total Expenses	5,171.25	3,822.59	3,820.09	4,208.11	3,815.02	3,812.45	3,809.87	4,197.80	4,195.18	3,801.97	3,799.30	4,577.70	49,031.33
Net Profit	($2,348.85)	($647.39)	($145.09)	($92.11)	$594.98	$1,038.55	$1,188.13	$1,094.20	$1,243.82	$1,784.03	$2,080.70	$4,172.30	$9,963.27

Cash Flow Projections

Cash flow projections are shown in Exhibit 5. The first year shows eight months with negative cash flows, and there are three months in the second year with negative flows. But there is a strong positive stream of cash for the entire third year.

Pro-Forma Balance Sheet Projections

The balance sheet projections for Bradley's are shown in Exhibit 6. In general, they are:

Year 1: $19,244.25

Year 2: $29,633.21

Year 3: $39,696.48

Comparative Ratios

From the key ratios for the sporting goods industry shown in Exhibit 7, it can be seen that the company's financial ratios are not in line with the industry standards. However, as sales increase with anticipated markups, the ratios improve dramatically over time—reaching those benchmarks more closely by the third year of operations.

APPENDIXES

Business Advisors

- Accountant: Kenneth Strickland
- Lawyer: Benjamin C. Maumenee (Fairhope)
- Insurance: Hank Miner, State Farm Fairhope Agent
- Banker: Craig Jones, VP, First Alabama Bank
- Business consultant: B. E. Sheppard

Property

Bradley's will be housed in 2,500 square feet of the old Ben Franklin Store (recently occupied by the King Arthur Clock Company) located on the Eastern Shore Parkway in Daphne, Alabama, as shown in Exhibit 8 and Exhibit 9. The facilities now available include 15,000 square feet, at a lease purchase price of $5,000.00 monthly.

However, a deal has been tentatively worked out through Cummings & White-Spunner Realty, which handles the lease contracting for the property's owners, under which the sublet owners will subdivide the property to the above dimensions. Because the facilities have been vacant for several years, with the Ben Franklin Company still under contractual obligations to its owners, the firm's officials are eager to deal. Based on this need, a cost-effective contract has been tentatively hammered out by Bradley on a three-year lease for a flat monthly fee of $1,000, with no maintenance fees to the existing property. (For example, Bradley will have to make all repairs to the air conditioning and heating system if needed.) The general construction/renovation will be performed and financed by the sublet owners. In addition, the sublet owners will offer a five-year extension to the original contract of three years, with contract lease increases of 15 percent for the fourth and fifth years and a 20 percent increase for the three years thereafter.

Exhibit 5

BRADLEY'S SPORTING GOODS
Cash Flow Projections
Year One

	Start-up	January	February	March	April	May	June	July	August	September	October	November	December
Beginning cash		$ 3,190.00	$ 772.25	($ 95.50)	($ 538.25)	($ 1,656.00)	($ 1,473.75)	($ 916.50)	($ 234.25)	($ 552.00)	($ 769.55)	$ 412.70	$ 1,844.95
Receipts:													
Cash sales		$ 8,000.00	$ 9,000.00	$ 12,500.00	$ 14,000.00	$ 15,000.00	$ 16,500.00	$ 17,000.00	$ 18,000.00	$ 18,500.00	$ 19,000.00	$ 20,000.00	$ 25,000.00
Loan	50,000.00												
Owner's cash	20,000.00												
Total Receipts	$ 70,000.00	$ 11,190.00	$ 9,772.25	$ 12,404.50	$ 13,461.75	$ 13,344.00	$ 15,026.25	$ 16,083.50	$ 17,765.75	$ 17,948.00	$ 18,230.45	$ 20,412.70	$ 26,844.95
Expenditures:													
Rent		$ 1,000.00	$ 1,000.00	$ 1,000.00	$ 1,000.00	$ 1,000.00	$ 1,000.00	$ 1,000.00	$ 1,000.00	$ 1,000.00	$ 1,000.00	$ 1,000.00	$ 1,000.00
Purchases	$ 50,000.00	5,600.00	6,300.00	9,375.00	11,200.00	11,250.00	12,375.00	12,750.00	14,400.00	14,800.00	14,250.00	15,000.00	18,750.00
Salaries	500.00	1,000.00	1,000.00	1,000.00	1,000.00	1,000.00	1,000.00	1,000.00	1,000.00	1,000.00	1,000.00	1,000.00	1,000.00
Payroll taxes	60.00	120.00	120.00	120.00	120.00	120.00	120.00	120.00	120.00	120.00	120.00	120.00	120.00
Advertising	1,050.00	1,050.00			350.00				350.00	350.00			350.00
Dues & subscriptions	50.00	50.00											
Legal & accounting	500.00	50.00	50.00	50.00	50.00	50.00	50.00	50.00	50.00	50.00	50.00	50.00	50.00
Office supplies	100.00	100.00	100.00	100.00	100.00	100.00	100.00	100.00	100.00	100.00	100.00	100.00	100.00
Utilities	500.00	250.00	250.00	250.00	250.00	250.00	250.00	250.00	250.00	250.00	250.00	250.00	250.00
Telephone	125.00	125.00	125.00	125.00	125.00	125.00	125.00	125.00	125.00	125.00	125.00	125.00	125.00
Insurance	162.00	162.00	162.00	162.00	162.00	162.00	162.00	162.00	162.00	162.00	162.00	162.00	162.00
Tax & license	150.00												
Interest/loan		416.67	414.63	412.58	410.51	408.43	406.33	404.20	402.07	399.91	397.74	395.55	393.33
Principal/loan		244.08	246.12	248.17	250.24	252.32	254.42	256.55	258.68	260.64	263.01	265.20	267.42
Miscellaneous	250.00	250.00	100.00	100.00	100.00	100.00	100.00	100.00	100.00	100.00	100.00	100.00	100.00
Subtotal	51,810.00	10,417.75	9,867.75	12,942.75	15,117.75	14,817.75	15,942.75	16,317.75	18,317.75	18,717.55	17,817.75	18,567.75	22,667.75
Capital purchases	15,000.00												
Total Expenditures	$ 66,810.00	$ 10,417.75	$ 9,867.75	$ 12,942.75	$ 15,117.75	$ 14,817.75	$ 15,942.75	$ 16,317.75	$ 18,317.75	$ 18,717.55	$ 17,817.75	$ 18,567.75	$ 22,667.75
Ending cash	$ 3,190.00	$ 772.25	($ 95.50)	($ 538.25)	($ 1,656.00)	($ 1,473.75)	($ 916.50)	($ 234.25)	($ 552.00)	($ 769.55)	$ 412.70	$ 1,844.95	$ 4,177.20

Exhibit 5 (continued)

BRADLEY'S SPORTING GOODS
Cash Flow Projections
Year Two

	January	February	March	April	May	June	July	August	September	October	November	December
Beginning cash	$ 4,177.20	$ 1,845.70	$ 981.70	$ 663.95	($ 360.05)	($ 809.05)	($ 76.80)	$ 786.70	$ 1,547.70	$ 2,439.95	$ 3,828.45	$ 5,479.45
Receipts:												
Cash sales	$ 8,400.00	$ 9,450.00	$13,125.00	$14,700.00	$15,750.00	$17,325.00	$17,850.00	$18,900.00	$19,425.00	$19,950.00	$21,000.00	$26,250.00
Loan												
Owner's cash												
Total Receipts	$12,577.20	$11,295.70	$14,106.70	$15,363.95	$15,389.95	$16,515.95	$17,773.20	$19,686.70	$20,972.70	$22,389.95	$24,828.45	$31,729.45
Expenditures:												
Rent	$ 1,000.00	$ 1,000.00	$ 1,000.00	$ 1,000.00	$ 1,000.00	$ 1,000.00	$ 1,000.00	$ 1,000.00	$ 1,000.00	$ 1,000.00	$ 1,000.00	$ 1,000.00
Purchases	5,880.00	6,615.00	9,843.75	11,760.00	12,600.00	12,993.75	13,387.50	14,175.00	14,568.75	14,962.50	15,750.00	19,687.50
Salaries	1,000.00	1,000.00	1,000.00	1,000.00	1,000.00	1,000.00	1,000.00	1,000.00	1,000.00	1,000.00	1,000.00	1,000.00
Payroll taxes	120.00	120.00	120.00	120.00	120.00	120.00	120.00	120.00	120.00	120.00	120.00	120.00
Advertising	1,050.00		365.00	365.00				365.00	365.00			365.00
Dues & subscriptions	52.50											52.50
Legal & accounting	52.50	52.50	52.50	52.50	52.50	52.50	52.50	52.50	52.50	52.50	52.50	105.00
Office supplies	105.00	105.00	105.00	105.00	105.00	105.00	105.00	105.00	105.00	105.00	105.00	262.50
Utilities	262.50	262.50	262.50	262.50	262.50	262.50	262.50	262.50	262.50	262.50	262.50	131.25
Telephone	131.25	131.25	131.25	131.25	131.25	131.25	131.25	131.25	131.25	131.25	131.25	162.00
Insurance	162.00	162.00	162.00	162.00	162.00	162.00	162.00	162.00	162.00	162.00	162.00	
Tax & license	150.00											365.33
Interest/loan	391.11	388.86	386.60	384.31	382.00	379.69	377.34	374.98	372.60	370.19	367.78	295.42
Principal/loan	269.64	371.89	274.15	276.44	278.75	281.06	283.41	285.77	288.15	290.56	292.97	105.00
Miscellaneous	105.00	105.00	105.00	105.00	105.00	105.00	105.00	105.00	105.00	105.00	105.00	
Subtotal	10,731.50	10,314.00	13,442.75	15,724.00	16,199.00	16,592.75	16,986.50	18,139.00	18,532.75	18,561.50	19,349.00	23,651.50
Capital purchases												
Total Expenditures	$10,731.50	$10,314.00	$13,442.75	$15,724.00	$16,199.00	$16,592.75	$16,986.50	$18,139.00	$18,532.75	$18,561.50	$19,349.00	$23,651.50
Ending cash	$ 1,845.70	$ 981.70	$ 663.95	($ 360.05)	($ 809.05)	($ 76.80)	$ 786.70	$ 1,547.70	$ 2,439.95	$ 3,828.45	$ 5,479.45	$ 8,077.95

Exhibit 5 (concluded)

BRADLEY'S SPORTING GOODS
Cash Flow Projections
Year Three

	January	February	March	April	May	June	July	August	September	October	November	December
Beginning cash	$ 8,077.95	$ 5,681.23	$ 4,983.48	$ 4,785.53	$ 4,638.03	$ 5,175.08	$ 6,153.13	$ 7,278.18	$ 8,306.68	$ 9,482.18	$11,195.23	$13,202.28
Receipts:												
Cash sales	$ 9,408.00	$10,584.00	$14,700.00	$16,464.00	$17,640.00	$19,404.00	$19,992.00	$21,168.00	$21,756.00	$22,344.00	$23,520.00	$35,000.00
Loan												
Owner's cash												
Total receipts	$17,485.95	$16,265.23	$19,683.48	$21,249.53	$22,278.03	$24,579.08	$26,145.13	$28,446.18	$30,062.68	$31,826.18	$34,715.23	$48,202.28
Expenditures:												
Rent	$ 1,000.00	$ 1,000.00	$ 1,000.00	$ 1,000.00	$ 1,000.00	$ 1,000.00	$ 1,000.00	$ 1,000.00	$ 1,000.00	$ 1,000.00	$ 1,000.00	$ 1,000.00
Purchases	6,585.60	7,408.80	11,025.00	12,348.00	13,230.00	14,553.00	14,994.00	15,876.00	16,317.00	16,758.00	17,640.00	26,250.00
Salaries	1,200.00	1,200.00	1,200.00	1,200.00	1,200.00	1,200.00	1,200.00	1,200.00	1,200.00	1,200.00	1,200.00	1,200.00
Payroll taxes	150.00	150.00	150.00	150.00	150.00	150.00	150.00	150.00	150.00	150.00	150.00	150.00
Advertising	1,140.00											
Dues & subscriptions	56.17			390.55				390.55	390.55			781.10
Legal & accounting	56.17	56.17	56.17	56.17	56.17	56.17	56.17	56.17	56.17	56.17	56.17	56.17
Office supplies	112.35	112.35	112.35	112.35	112.35	112.35	112.35	112.35	112.35	112.35	112.35	112.35
Utilities	275.62	275.62	275.62	275.62	275.62	275.62	275.62	275.62	275.62	275.62	275.62	275.62
Telephone	137.81	137.81	137.81	137.81	137.81	137.81	137.81	137.81	137.81	137.81	137.81	137.81
Insurance	170.00	170.00	170.00	170.00	170.00	170.00	170.00	170.00	170.00	170.00	170.00	170.00
Tax & license	150.00											
Interest/loan	362.88	360.39	357.89	355.36	352.82	350.25	347.67	345.05	342.43	339.77	337.10	334.40
Principal/loan	297.87	300.36	302.86	305.39	307.93	310.50	313.08	315.70	318.32	320.98	323.65	326.35
Miscellaneous	110.25	110.25	110.25	110.25	110.25	110.25	110.25	110.25	110.25	110.25	110.25	110.25
Subtotal	11,804.72	11,281.75	14,897.95	16,611.50	17,102.95	18,425.95	18,866.95	20,139.50	20,580.50	20,630.95	21,512.95	30,904.05
Capital purchases												
Total Expenditures	$11,804.72	$11,281.75	$14,897.95	$16,611.50	$17,102.95	$18,425.95	$18,866.95	$20,139.50	$20,580.50	$20,630.95	$21,512.95	$30,904.05
Ending cash	$ 5,681.23	$ 4,983.48	$ 4,785.53	$ 4,638.03	$ 5,175.08	$ 6,153.13	$ 7,278.18	$ 8,306.68	$ 9,482.18	$11,195.23	$13,202.28	$17,298.23

Exhibit 6

BRADLEY'S SPORTING GOODS
Pro-Forma Balance Sheet

	End of Year 1	End of Year 2	End of Year 3
Assets			
Assets:			
Cash	$ 4,177.20	$ 8,077.05	$17,298.23
Inventory	50,000.00	50,000.00	50,000.00
Equipment	15,000.00	12,000.00	9,000.00
Accumulated depreciation	3,000.00	3,000.00	3,000.00
Total Assets	$66,177.20	$73,077.95	$79,398.23
Liabilities/Owner's Equity			
Liabilities:			
Loan	$46,932.95	$43,444.74	$39,701.75
Total Liabilities	$46,932.95	$43,444.74	$39,701.75
Owner's Equity:			
Paid-in capital	$20,000.00	$20,000.00	$20,000.00
Accumulated earnings	(755.75)	9,633.21	19,696.48
Total owner's equity	$19,244.25	$29,633.21	$39,696.48
Total Liabilities and Owner's Equity	$66,177.20	$73,077.95	$79,398.23

Exhibit 7　Key Business Ratios for the Sporting Goods Industry versus Three-Year Projections

Ratio	STD	Year 1	Year 2	Year 3
Net profit to net sales	5.29	0.5478	1.5265	3.846
Profit to net worth	19.73	1.5936	4.226	11.251
Total debt to net worth	57.40	70.92	59.45	50.06
Current debt to inventory	41.40	92.78	86.89	79.40

Exhibit 8   Map Showing Corporate Limits of the City of Daphne

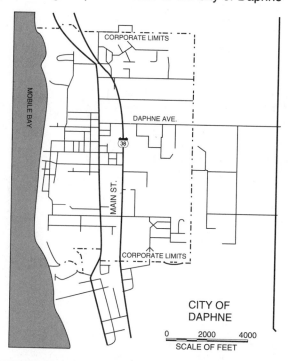

Exhibit 9   Site of Bradley's Sporting Goods

9

Obtaining the Right Financing for Your Business

Money is the seed of money.—Jean-Jacques Rousseau

Many of the financial problems plaguing small businesses are avoidable, provided entrepreneurs analyze their own funding needs objectively and with sufficient lead time to act decisively.—Small Business Administration

LEARNING OBJECTIVES

After studying the material in this chapter, you will be able to:
1. Explain the importance of proper financing for a small business.
2. Tell how to estimate financial needs, and explain some principles to follow in obtaining financing.
3. Explain why equity and debt financing are used, and describe the role each plays in the capital structure of a small firm.
4. Distinguish the types of equity and debt securities.
5. Describe some sources of equity financing.
6. Describe some sources of debt financing.
7. Explain what a lender looks for in a borrower.

ROY MORGAN: PIONEER IN AIR MEDICAL TRANSPORT SERVICES

Roy Morgan, president of Air Methods Corporation of Englewood, Colorado, was a pioneer in providing rapid air medical transport services. After helping to develop the first hospital helipad in Salt Lake City, at Holy Cross Hospital, he brought in the first patient by helicopter, flying him in on the skids of a Bell 47, which was the method used during the Korean War.

Later, after seeing three seriously burned firefighters waiting for primitive medical attention, he saw the critical need to provide rapid medical response for people working in remote areas. After approaching several Colorado hospitals, Roy interested St. Mary's Hospital in Grand Junction in the project. But first he had to have a helicopter.

Roy; his wife, Dorothy; and friends Austin Clark and Ralph Mulford scraped together enough money to form a corporation and make the down payment on a helicopter. Roy and his wife took out a second mortgage on their house; sold a camper, a pickup truck, and stock in Western Airlines; and used their savings account to get the funds. Their friends made similar sacrifices. Air Methods had a Texas company convert the helicopter to provide a medical interior and then started the contract with St. Mary's Hospital AIR

Photos courtesy of Air Methods Corporation.

LIFE in August 1980.

By 1985, Air Methods had started new programs in Greeley, Colorado; Denver, Colorado; Texarkana, Arkansas; Minneapolis/St. Paul, Minnesota, and Bend, Oregon. In order to add another new program with the University of Utah Hospital in Salt Lake City, Utah, Air Methods shareholders expanded to include David and Cheryl Ritchie and Dennis and David Beggrow.

Through this financing, by 1992, Air Methods represented 19 emergency medical programs, serving 43 hospitals in 13 states. It had 25 helicopters and five airplanes (all of which were medically equipped), 250 employees, and revenues of $18.5 million. The average cost of a flight to a hospital is $2,600, which is a small part of the average $160,000 hospital bill.

In November of 1991, Air Methods merged with Cell Technology and became a publicly held corporation. According to Morgan and current chairman and CEO Terry Schreier, "obtaining access to capital is one big benefit to becoming a public company." In fact, the company raised $7.2 million in 1992 by selling shares to help lower debts and increase working capital.

Source: Written by Gayle M. Ross. Other sources include Kevin Maney, "Air Methods Tries to Lift Its Image," *USA Today,* July 15, 1992, p. 3B; and Eugene Carlson, "Airborne Medical-Service Firms See Soaring Growth," *The Wall Street Journal,* July 14, 1992, p. B2.

The Profile shows the importance of a truth that has been shown repeatedly in this text: *Sufficient capital is essential not only for small business start-ups but also for their continued operation.* In fact, one of the main reasons for the high failure rate of small businesses is inadequate or improper financing. All too often, insufficient attention has been paid to planning for financial needs, leaving the new business open to sudden but predictable financial crises. Even firms that are sound financially can be destroyed by financial problems, for one of the difficulties most commonly experienced by rapidly growing firms is that they are unable to finance the investment needed to support sales growth.

ESTIMATING FINANCIAL NEEDS

The degree of uncertainty surrounding a small firm's long-term financial needs primarily depends on whether the business is already operating or is just starting up, as mentioned in the Profile. If a business has an operating history, its future needs can be estimated with relative accuracy, even with substantial growth.

Even for an existing business, however, an in-depth analysis of its *permanent* financial requirements can be valuable. It may show the current method of financing the business to be unsound or unnecessarily risky. As a general rule, small businesses' long-lived assets, such as buildings and other facilities, should be financed with long-term loans, while short-lived assets, such as inventory or accounts receivable, should be financed with short-term loans.

Principles to Follow

Fixed assets are those that are of a relatively permanent nature and are necessary for the functioning of the business.

A new business, or a major expansion of an existing business, should be evaluated with great care, paying particular attention to its capital requirements. For example, the firm's **fixed assets** should be financed with equity funds, or with debt funds having a maturity approximately equal to the productive life of the asset.

Working capital is current assets, less current liabilities, that a firm uses to produce goods and services, and to finance the extension of credit to customers.

No business, however, can be financed entirely with debt funding, nor would such a capitalization be desirable—even if creditors were willing to lend all the funds required. Such a capital structure would be extremely risky, both for the creditors and for the business. This is especially true of **working capital,** which includes the current assets, less current liabilities, that a firm uses to produce goods and services and to finance the extension of credit to customers. These assets include items such as cash, accounts receivable, and inventories. Management of working capital is always a central concern for managers of small firms because they are often undercapitalized and overdependent on uninterrupted cash receipts to pay for recurring expenses. Therefore, small business managers must accurately estimate their working capital needs in advance and obtain sufficient financial resources to cover these needs, plus a buffer for unexpected emergencies.

Using Cash Budgets

An important tool small business managers can use to project working capital needs is a **cash budget.** Such a budget estimates what the out-of-pocket expenses will be during the next year to produce a product(s) for sale and when revenues from these sales are to be collected. In most businesses, sales are not constant over the year, so revenues vary a great deal from one period to another, while the costs of producing them tend to be relatively constant. For example, most retailers have their greatest sales period from Thanksgiving to Christmas. Yet, if they extend their own credit, payments are not received until the following January or February—or even later. Also, small producers may have produced the goods during the previous summer and had to bear the out-of-pocket costs of production for up to six months before actually receiving cash payments.

In general, therefore, when sales are made on credit, *the firm must carry the costs of production itself for an extended period of time.* A cash budget can help the manager predict when these financing needs will be the greatest and plan the firm's funding accordingly. An accurate assessment of seasonal financing needs is especially important if commercial bank loans are used, since bankers usually require a borrower to be completely free of bank debt at least once a year.

Cash budgets project working capital needs by estimating what out-of-pocket expenses will be incurred and when revenues from these sales are to be collected.

REASONS FOR USING EQUITY AND DEBT FINANCING

While **equity** is the owner's share of the firm's assets, the nature of this claim depends on the legal form of ownership. For proprietorships and partnerships, the claim on the assets of the firm is that they are the same as the owner's personal assets. Equity financing in a corporation is evidenced by shares of either common or preferred **stock.**

Common stockholders are the real owners of a corporation, and their financial claim is to the profit left over after all other claims against the business have been met. Because they almost always retain the right to vote for company directors and/or on other important issues, common stockholders exercise effective control over the management of the firm.

Preferred stockholders, on the other hand, have a claim to the firm's profits that must be paid before any dividends can be distributed to the common stockholders; but they often pay for this superior claim by giving up their voting rights.

The other kind of capital, or funding, that a firm uses is called **debt financing,** which comes from lenders, who will be repaid at a specified interest rate within an agreed-upon time span. The lenders' income does not vary with the success of the business, while the stockholders' does.

As discussed in Chapter 4, capital can also be raised by using a limited partnership, which combines the benefits of both debt and equity financing.

Equity is an owner's share of the assets of a company. In a corporation, it is represented by shares of common or preferred stock.

Stock represents ownership in a corporation.

Common stockholders are the owners of a corporation, with claim to a share of its profits and the right to vote on certain corporate decisions.

Preferred stockholders are owners with a superior claim to a share of the firm's profits, but they often have no voting rights.

Debt financing comes from lenders, who will be repaid at a specified interest rate within a specified time span.

Role of Equity Financing

The role of equity financing is to serve as a buffer that protects creditors from loss in case of financial difficulty. In the event of default on a contractual obligation (such as an interest payment), creditors have a legally enforceable claim on the assets of the firm. It takes preference over claims of the common and preferred stockholders. From an investor's point of view, common stock investments should have a higher financial return than debt investments because equity securities are riskier.

Role of Debt Financing

With debt financing, principal and interest payments are legally enforceable claims against the business. Therefore, they entail substantial risk for the firm (or for the entrepreneur if the debt is guaranteed by personal wealth). In spite of the risks involved, however, small firms use debt financing for several reasons. First, the cost of interest paid on debt capital is usually lower than the cost of outside equity, and interest payments are tax-deductible expenses. Second, an entrepreneur may be able to raise more total capital with debt funding than from equity sources alone. Finally, since debt payments are fixed costs, any remaining profits belong solely to the owners. This last strategy, employing a fixed charge to increase the residual return to common stockholders, is referred to as employing **financial leverage.**

> **Financial leverage** is using fixed-charge financing, usually debt, to fund a business's operations.

One type of debt financing that is becoming more popular is leasing facilities and equipment from someone outside the business instead of buying them. A **lease** is a contract that permits you to use someone else's property, such as real estate, equipment, or other facilities, for a specified period of time. While a lease is not usually classified as debt, it is in many respects financially very similar.

> A **lease** is a contract that permits use of someone else's property for a specified period of time.

From the small business owner's point of view, the benefits of a lease are that (1) the payments are tax deductible, and (2) it may be possible for the business to lease equipment when it would be unable to secure debt financing to purchase it, as the following example illustrates.

To bid on construction jobs in 1986, Goudreau Corporation, of Danvers, Massachusetts, had to put up a surety bond (which guaranteed that the company would finish the job satisfactorily). The bonding company would approve only $10 in bonding for every dollar Goudreau had in the bank. Goudreau turned to an equipment leasing company for financing of the trucks, machinery, and other fixed assets needed to continue growing. By 1989, it had sales of $5 million and was using over $200,000 worth of leased equipment.[1]

TYPES OF DEBT AND EQUITY SECURITIES

There are many types of securities used by small companies, some of which are described below. This listing is incomplete but sufficient to illustrate the variety of financial sources that is a hallmark of the American financial system. Potential small business owners should remember that if they have a viable project, financing can be obtained from some source!

Equity Securities

To start operating, all firms must have some equity capital. In corporations, **common stock,** which represents the owners' interest, usually consists of many identical shares, each of which gives the holder one vote in all corporate elections. (See Figure 9–1 for an example of a share of stock in a new small business.) Common stockholders have no enforceable claim to dividends, and the liquidity of the investment will depend largely on whether or not there is a public market for the firm's stock.

A corporation may also issue **preferred stock,** with a fixed par value (the value assigned in the corporation's charter, usually $100 per share). It entitles the holder to a fixed dividend payment, usually expressed as a percentage of par value, such as 8 percent (equal to $8 per year). This dividend is not automatic; it must be

Common stock, representing the owners' interest, usually consists of many identical shares, each of which gives the holder one vote in all corporate elections.

Preferred stock has a fixed par value and a fixed dividend payment, expressed as a percentage of par value.

Figure 9–1   A Share of Stock in a Small Business

Source: Courtesy of Bloomin' Lollipops, Inc.

declared by the firm's board of directors before it can be paid. Nor is it a legally enforceable claim against the business. However, no dividends can be paid to the common stockholders until preferred stock dividends have been paid. Moreover, preferred dividends that have been missed typically cumulate and must be paid in full before payments can be made to common stockholders. Preferred stock usually conveys no voting rights to its holder.

Debt Securities

Debt securities are usually in the form of bonds or loans. In general, publicly issued debt (such as bonds or commercial paper) is more commonly used by larger firms, whereas small companies rely more on private loans from financial institutions such as commercial banks, insurance companies, or finance companies.

Short-term securities mature in one year or less.

Intermediate-term securities mature in one to five years.

Long-term securities mature after five years or longer.

A distinction is usually made among **short-term securities** (those with maturities of one year or less), **intermediate-term securities** (those with maturities of one to five years), and **long-term securities** (those with maturities of more than five years). As we will discuss more thoroughly in the next section, commercial banks prefer to make short- and intermediate-term loans; other financial institutions, such as insurance companies, prefer to make long-term loans.

If a small business manager negotiates a loan from a bank or other single lender, the amount of the loan is simply the amount borrowed. However, if securities are sold to the public or are privately placed with several lenders, most companies will issue the debt in the form of **bonds.** These have a standard denomination, method of interest payment, and method of principal repayment.

A **bond** is a debt security with a standard denomination, method of interest payment, and method of principal repayment.

A **mortgage loan** is long-term debt that is secured by real property.

A **chattel mortgage loan** is debt backed by some physical asset other than land, such as machinery, equipment, or inventory.

Long-term debt secured by real estate property is a **mortgage loan,** whereas a **chattel mortgage loan** is debt backed by some physical asset other than land, such as machinery, transportation equipment, or inventory. Furthermore, many of the "unsecured" loans that banks extend to small businesses require personal guarantees by the manager or directors of the firm. Such loans are implicitly secured by the personal assets of these individuals.

SOURCES OF EQUITY FINANCING

Obtaining sufficient equity funding is a constant challenge for most small businesses, particularly for proprietorships and partnerships. The only way to increase the equity of these two types of firms is either to retain earnings or to accept outsiders as co-owners. For corporations, the choices may be more varied. Some of the more frequently used sources of equity funding are discussed here.

Self

People who start a small business must invest a substantial amount of their own funds in it before seeking outside funding. Outside investors want to see some of the owner's own money committed to the business as some assurance that she or he will not simply give up operating the business and walk away from it. Many owners also prefer using their own funds because they feel uncomfortable risking other people's money or because they do not want to share control of the firm with anyone else.

Small Business Investment Companies (SBICs)

Small business investment companies (SBICs) are private firms licensed and regulated by the SBA to make "venture" or "risk" investments to small firms. SBICs supply equity capital and extend unsecured loans to small enterprises that meet their investment criteria. Because they are privately capitalized themselves (although backed by the SBA), SBICs are intended to be profit-making institutions, so they tend not to make very small investments.

SBICs finance small firms by making straight loans and by making equity-type investments that give the SBIC actual or potential ownership of the small firm's equity securities. SBICs also provide management assistance to the businesses they help finance.

SBICs prefer to make loans to small firms rather than equity investments, so we will discuss them further under the heading Sources of Debt Financing later in this chapter.

> **Small business investment companies (SBICs)** are private firms licensed and regulated by the SBA to make "venture" investments in small firms.

Venture Capitalists

Entrepreneurs often complain that it is "lonely at the top." If so, a venture capitalist can serve as a form of "security blanket" when needed. Traditionally, venture capital firms have been partnerships composed of wealthy individuals who

"I run a small investment firm. . . .
Unfortunately, it used to be a large investment firm!"
Copyright 1989 by Doug Blackwell.

make equity investments in small firms with opportunities for fast growth, such as Federal Express, Apple Computer, and Nike. In general, they have preferred to back fast-growth industries (usually high-tech ones), since the ultimate payoff from backing a successful new business with a new high-tech product can be astronomical.

Venture capitalists *are not a good source of funding for new businesses— especially the mom-and-pop variety.* At least that seems to be suggested by the fact that more than two-thirds of all venture capital goes to expand existing businesses rather than to start new ones.[2]

Foreign stock exchanges are also sources of venture capital. They tend to have easier regulations for listing, require less paperwork, and have lower legal and administrative costs, as the following example shows.

The Vancouver (Canada) Stock Exchange (VSE), is a popular source of venture capital for many small U.S. firms. The VSE specializes in natural resource exploration companies and small new technology firms, such as Neti Technologies Inc., an Ann Arbor, Michigan, software firm, and Sellectek (now operating as Global-Pacific Minerals, Inc.), a Menlo Park, California, software distributor. Sellectek used the VSE to raise $1.5 million.

As of January 29, 1990, with its Vancouver Computerized Trading System (VCT), the VSE became the first North American stock exchange to fully convert from the traditional "outcry market" to a fully automated trade execution system (Figure 9–2). Now, all trading takes place in the offices of member brokerage firms.

The VSE has a "two-tier" system that recognizes the stages of development of companies as they grow and mature. Its rules and regulations are designed to (1) provide a niche for venture companies and (2) maintain the integrity of the marketplace. Also, by using the VSE—rather than making deals with private U.S. venture capitalists—entrepreneurs can keep greater control of their businesses. The VSE has a proven record of performance, as shown by its third-place standing (after the Toronto and New York exchanges) in trading volume among North American stock exchanges.[3]

Many venture capitalists rely more heavily on the executive summary of a business plan (see Chapter 8) than on the plan itself in making investment decisions. So many long and complex plans are presented to them that they need a quick way to evaluate proposals in order to quickly discard those they do not want to consider further. The percentage of business plans accepted by venture capitalists for investment purposes is very low.

You should be aware when approaching either a venture capitalist or an SBIC for possible funding that neither will view your business the same way you do. While you may be content to remain relatively small in order to retain personal control, this is the last thing a professional investor will want. An SBIC or a venture capitalist will invest in a firm with the expectation of ultimately selling the company either to the investing public (through an initial public stock offering) or to a larger company. This potential conflict of goals can be very damaging to the new business owner unless the differences are explicitly addressed before external financing is accepted.

Figure 9–2   Vancouver Computerized Trading System (VCT)

Photo courtesy of Vancouver Stock Exchange.

Angel Capitalists

Entrepreneurs have always tapped financial patrons, such as friends, relatives, and wealthy individuals, for beginning capital. Known as **angel capitalists,** these investors will usually accept lower rates of return on the investments they make than will professional venture capitalists, and they will also make smaller investments. The University of New Hampshire's Center for Venture Research estimated that as many as 90 percent of small businesses are started with the financial help of friends and relatives.[4] It has also been estimated that angel capitalists provide up to four times as much total investment capital for small businesses as do the professional venture capital firms.[5]

Angel capitalists are wealthy local businesspeople and other investors who may be external sources of equity funding.

The New York City Police Pension Fund is an example of an angel capitalist. In 1989, it set aside $50 million to lend to small businesses. These loans were to be guaranteed by the SBA.[6]

Other Sources

In some cases, small business entrepreneurs may be able to acquire financial assistance from business incubators, employee stock ownership plans, their own customers, and others.[7]

Business Incubators

Business incubators are old buildings that have been renovated, subdivided, and rented to new companies by groups desiring to assist young enterprises until they are healthy enough to go out on their own.

A big movement now encouraging the financing and development of small businesses is business incubators. **Business incubators** are usually old buildings, such as factories or warehouses, that have been renovated, subdivided, and rented to new companies by entrepreneurs, corporations, universities, governments, or groups such as chambers of commerce. Their purpose is to shelter young enterprises, offer moral support, and provide support services, including low overhead, until the enterprises are ready to go out on their own. The number of such incubators grew from a handful in 1980 to 470 in 1992.[8]

A classic example of an incubator is Chicago's Fulton-Carroll Center, housed in a 100-year-old former factory. The Center, founded in 1980 by pioneer June Lavelle, provides management assistance, low rent, shared services, and cooperation with other entrepreneurs. Three-fourths of the employees come from within a three-mile radius, and most are minorities. As of 1992, the Fulton-Carroll Center had helped develop 177 new businesses and create 1,500 jobs, 80 percent of them going to local black and Hispanic residents.[9]

Employee Stock Ownership Plans (ESOPs)

Employee stock ownership plans (ESOPs) allow small businesses to reap tax advantages and cash flow advantages by selling stock shares to workers.

For existing small businesses, another source of financing is **employee stock ownership plans (ESOPs)**, to be discussed in Chapter 14. The company reaps tax advantages and cash flow advantages from selling shares to workers. The plan also makes employees think like owners, thereby tending to make them more productive.

Your Customers

Your customers are another source of financing. It happens often, and in many ways. For example, mail-order vendors—especially those who use TV commercials—require the customer to pay when ordering; they then have that money for operations, while the customer waits several weeks for delivery of the goods. Also, it is customary for artisans and contractors to require a substantial down payment before beginning to produce the product.

For example, Diane Allen, a portrait artist, requires a down payment of one-third of the total price before she will begin a portrait. This money not only assures that the contract will be honored but also can be used to buy supplies and cover other expenses.

An innovative new source of start-up financing for high-tech entrepreneurs has become available in recent years. This involves obtaining capital from an established potential client.

An example is Conner Peripherals Inc., of San Jose, California, which entered into a partnership with Compaq Computer of Houston, Texas, whereby Compaq would make two $6 million investments in exchange for 49 percent of Conner's stock. The latter firm, which had only recently been launched by founder Finis Conner, had no revenues, and the partnership agreement with Compaq (which called for the development of advanced-technology disk drives) came only after Conner had approached several venture capitalists without success.[10]

SOURCES OF DEBT FINANCING

Although the more entrepreneurial small businesses may aggressively seek the kinds of equity funding we have been discussing, most small businesses are more likely to use debt financing. This is true at least in part because there are more sources for such financing, several of which are described here.

Trade Credit

Trade credit refers to purchases of inventory, equipment, and/or supplies on an open account in accordance with customary terms for retail and wholesale trade. In general, trade credit is one of the most important sources of debt financing for small business because it arises spontaneously in the normal course of operating the business. Firms seeking new and expanded wholesale and retail markets for goods have the option of using **consignment selling.** Small auto, major appliance, and farm equipment dealers consider consignments a form of trade credit because payments to suppliers are made only when the products are sold rather than when they are received in stock.

Trade credit is extended by vendors on purchases of inventory, equipment, and/or supplies.

With **consignment selling,** payments to suppliers are made only when the products are sold, rather than when they are received in stock.

Commercial and Other Financial Institutions

Traditional financial institutions may provide the small business owner with borrowed funds. The proportion of funds such institutions make available ranges from 25 to 60 percent of the value of the total assets. Usually, the cost of such financing is higher than that of other alternatives, but such funds may be the most accessible.

Commercial Banks

Commercial banks are a good source of credit for business borrowers who have funds of their own and proven successful experience.[11] Rarely will a commercial bank make a conventional commercial loan to a start-up business.

The large demand for funds in recent years has pushed interest rates of bank loans to higher levels and less favorable terms. A well-prepared business plan, as described in Chapter 8, should help lower a firm's interest rate and possibly even extend the term of the loan. Even then, however, you may find it more advantageous to finance the business with a personal loan.

A **line of credit** permits a
business to borrow up to a set
amount without red tape.

If your business is successful, you may want to open up a **line of credit** with
your bank. This is an arrangement whereby the bank permits an ongoing business
to borrow up to a set amount—say $50,000—at any time during the year without
further red tape. The business writes checks against its account, and the bank
honors them up to the maximum amount.

Usually, except for firms with an exceptionally high credit rating, the business
is required to pay up all unsecured debts for a short period—say 10 to 15 days—
each year to prove its credit worthiness. This is usually done when the firm's cash
level is at its highest in order not to inconvenience the borrower too much.

Insurance Companies

Insurance companies may be a good source of funds for a small firm, especially
real estate ventures. The business owner can go directly to the company or contact
its agent or a mortgage banker. While insurance companies have traditionally
engaged in debt financing, they have more recently demanded that they be permitted to buy an equity share in the business as part of the total package.

Small Business Administration (SBA)

One of the primary purposes of the SBA is to help small firms find financing,
including those having trouble securing conventional financing—especially at reasonable rates. Many small firms need "term" loans of up to 25 years, but most
lenders limit their lending to short-term loans.

The SBA helps these small firms in several ways, including offering guaran-
tees on loans made by private lenders and offering direct specialized financing.[12]
As indicated earlier, it also provides some venture capital through SBICs. (See
Using Technology to Succeed for a fast, convenient way to get help from the
SBA.)

Guaranteed Loans

The SBA guarantees 30 to 40 percent of all long-term loans to small businesses
under its 7(a) program. The loans can be used to (1) purchase land, buildings, or
equipment; (2) provide working capital; (3) refinance existing debt; or (4) provide
seasonal lines of credit. To qualify, a business must be unable to obtain private
financing on reasonable terms but must have a good chance of success. Also, the
borrower must meet the size standards shown in Table 9–1.

How does the program operate? The SBA guarantees up to 90 percent of a loan
made by a lender for up to $155,000, and 85 percent of the balance—up to
$750,000. The lender checks with the SBA prior to formal application for "ball-
park" feasibility of the proposed project. The loan terms are usually 5 to 7 years
for working capital and up to 25 years for real estate or equipment. The interest rate
is set at 2.25 to 2.75 percent over the lowest prime rate.

━━━━━━━━━━━━━━━ USING TECHNOLOGY TO SUCCEED ━━━━━━━━━━━━━━━

SBA GOES ON-LINE

The SBA has entered the computer age! Small business owners seeking financial assistance from the SBA can use the SBA On-Line. Entrepreneurs who seek help can log onto the system from their own personal computers, as long as they have modems that allow PCs to connect through phone lines. To use this system, callers from the Washington area dial (202) 205-7265. Owners of 2400-baud modems must dial 1-800-859-INFO, and those with 9600-baud modems need to dial 1-800-697-INFO.

On the first day of operations in October 1992, the system was flooded with 1,000 calls. The response was overwhelming; the 20 toll-free lines were expanded to 41 by the end of the first week.

It is estimated that about 50 percent of small businesses have such capacity. The SBA plans to add on-line counseling and to link the system to other bulletin boards around the country. Sprint paid the $25,000 cost of the toll-free access number for the first year.

Source: Jean Saddler, "Electronic Bulletin Boards Help Businesses Post Success," *The Wall Street Journal,* October 29, 1992, p. B2; and Rhonda Richards, "SBA Goes High-Tech," *USA Today,* October 15, 1992, p. 2B.

Table 9–1   Eligibility for SBA-Guaranteed Business Loans by Industry Type

Type of Industry	Restrictions
Manufacturing	Maximum number of employees may range from 500 to 1,500, depending on the industry in which the applicant is primarily engaged.
Wholesaling	Maximum number of employees not to exceed 100.
Services	Annual receipts not exceeding $3.5 million to $14.5 million, depending on the industry in which the applicant is primarily engaged.
Retailing	Annual sales or receipts not exceeding $3.5 million to $13.5 million, depending on the industry.
Construction	General construction average annual receipts not exceeding $9.5 million to $17 million, depending on the industry.
Agriculture	Annual receipts not exceeding $1.5 million to $3.5 million, depending on the industry.

Source: Lending the SBA Way (Washington, D.C.: U.S. Small Business Administration, 1992), p. 3.

The applicant must provide the lender with (1) the purpose of the loan; (2) history of the business; (3) financial statements for three years (balance sheet and income statements) for existing businesses; (4) amount of applicant's investment in the business; (5) personal résumés; (6) projections of income, expenses, and cash flow; and (7) signed *personal* financial statements.

The lender then forwards the application directly to SBA officers. The SBA looks for (1) management ability and experience in the field; (2) at least a simple, but feasible, business plan; (3) an adequate investment (generally 20–30 percent of equity by the entrepreneur; and (4) ability to repay the loan from projected income.

Specialized Financing

The SBA also makes specialized loans to handicapped persons, disabled and Vietnam-era veterans, small general contractors, and disaster victims. And, as mentioned in Chapter 3, the Women's Business Ownership Act provides SBA-generated miniloans of under $50,000 for women.[13]

Small Business Investment Companies (SBICs)

In addition to indirect equity financing, as previously discussed, SBICs also make qualified SBA loans. The SBA matches each dollar an SBIC puts into a loan. Loans are usually made for a period of 5 to 10 years. An SBIC may stipulate that it be given a certain portion of stock purchase warrants or stock options, or it may make a combination of a loan and a stock purchase. The latter combination has been preferred.

Economic Development Administration (EDA)

The Economic Development Administration (EDA) makes a variety of direct loans to industries located in economically depressed communities or in communities that are declared regional economic growth centers. This financial assistance usually starts where the SBA authority ends, at $750,000.

The direct loans made by the EDA may be used for fixed assets or working capital. In addition, the EDA may extend guarantees on loans to private borrowers from private lending institutions, as well as guarantees of rental payments on fixed assets.

WHAT LENDERS LOOK FOR

What do lenders look for when considering a loan to a small business? In essence the basics apply today as they did in the past. First, if the loan is for a new business, the lender wants to see if you can live within the income of the business. Given your expected revenues and expenses, will you be able to repay the loan? How much collateral can you put up to insure the lender against your inability to repay?

Second, if the money is for an existing business, the lender will look at its track record. If there are problems, you will be expected to explain what's going to

Figure 9–3   How to Improve the Entrepreneur-Investor Relationship

There are at least five steps you should take in order to assure a good working relationship with the investor:
1. Establish the range of funds you will need.
2. Identify the investor's skills and abilities that could help advance your venture.
3. Find an investor with interests and personality traits similar to yours.
4. Find a long-term investor, not one who wants to "make a quick buck" and get out.
5. Find an investor with more to offer you than just money, so that you may avoid having to hire outside consultants.

There are certain things the investor should find out about you:
1. Can you and the investor work together as a team?
2. Do you appear to be flexible and willing to accept new management if the project is highly successful?
3. Are you truly committed to this endeavor, and are you willing to expend the energy and resources to make it a success?
4. Can you accept constructive criticism, feedback, and assistance?
5. Do you have definite, fixed, realistic goals, and where do you plan to be in, say, one year? Five years? Ten years?

happen to make a difference in the future. Do you have a new business plan? Are you going to buy new equipment or technology? Is there a new marketing plan?

To a large extent, your ability to attract money will depend on the lender's perception of your character as well as your ability to return the money. First, *income* is important. Second, the lender will also look at your *stability*, to see how long you've lived in a given residence or neighborhood, as well as how long you've worked at a particular job or run a business.

In summary, your request for financing will almost certainly be checked by some major credit company, using computerized reference services. Therefore, knowing that your credit record will be checked immediately by the computer, you should ask for a credit printout (which can be obtained free or for a few dollars) before you apply for funds. This will give you an opportunity to correct any errors or misunderstandings in your credit record.

Figure 9–3 provides some steps to use in developing a better relationship with investors, along with some questions that the investor should ask you. Remember that, while lenders should have an interest in how financially sound your business is, *they should not have a voice in managing it*. If you permit them to, they in reality become partners and must share responsibility for any failures.

WHAT YOU SHOULD HAVE LEARNED

1. Providing for financial needs is crucial to the success of a small business, which may be undercapitalized and living hand to mouth. Sufficient short-

and long-term financing is needed to provide for fluctuations in sales or an unexpected business slump.

2. For a start-up venture, the assets of a business should be financed with equity, or with debt funds having a maturity about equal to the productive life of the asset. A useful tool for estimating financial needs is the cash budget, which projects the amounts and timing of expenses and revenue for the year.

3. The two major sources of funds are equity and debt financing. Equity financing never has to be repaid and provides an interest in the business, including a share of the profits and a voice in decision making. Debt financing, which must be repaid whether the company is profitable or not, is less expensive than equity financing, since interest payments are tax deductible, and does not require as high a rate of return.

4. The most frequently used types of equity securities are common and preferred stock. Common stock conveys voting rights but has no enforceable claim to dividends. Preferred stock entitles the shareholder to a fixed rate of dividend whenever profits are sufficient, but preferred stockholders usually have no voting rights. Debt securities include short-, intermediate-, and long-term loans and bonds. Loans made by a lender in standard denominations are called *bonds*. Long-term debt secured by real property is a mortgage loan, whereas a chattel mortgage loan is backed by some other physical asset. A lease can also be a form of debt financing.

5. Sources of equity financing include funds from the owner, family and friends, small business investment companies (SBICs), venture capitalists, angel capitalists, business incubators, employees, and customers.

6. Sources of debt financing include trade credit, commercial and other financial institutions, the SBA, SBICs, and the Economic Development Administration (EDA). The SBA finances business ventures through guaranteed loans, direct loans, and participating loans.

7. When deciding whether or not to finance a small business, lenders look for factors such as ability to repay the debt, the owner's and the business's financial and business track record, and the owner's income, stability, and debt management.

QUESTIONS FOR DISCUSSION

1. Discuss the basic rules to follow in financing a business venture.

2. Why should small business managers assess working capital needs in advance?

3. What are some of the reasons small business entrepreneurs use equity financing? Debt financing?

4. What are the factors that determine the classification of debt securities?

5. List and discuss the primary sources of equity financing.

6. List and discuss the primary sources of debt financing.

7. Compare equity financing to debt financing.

8. Evaluate the role of the SBA in providing operating and venture capital.

SHORT OF CASH? TRY BARTERING

Often, the greatest obstacle to success for a small business is inadequate financial resources. In fact, lack of dependable funding results in the closing of thousands of small businesses each year. Some owners of cash-strapped small businesses are taking matters into their own hands by using innovative methods to conserve cash. One such method is bartering.

Bartering, perhaps the oldest form of trade, involves swapping—rather than purchasing—everything from automobiles to health services. It is a creative way to increase sales, move surplus inventory, and utilize excess capacity. Some small firms have even used bartering as a way to collect bad debts, as well as a source of financing.

It works like this: A barter company acts as an intermediary for companies desiring to swap products and services. To become a member of the barter exchange, a company pays a fee averaging about $500 and a 10 percent transaction fee. Once a member, the firm can accumulate "trade dollars" in return for offering products and services on the exchange. A firm can then use the trade dollars to purchase goods or services offered by any other member of the exchange.

For example, Andriana Furs Inc., which sells luxury fur coats, has bartered about $100,000 in furs. According to owner Sohrab Tebyanian, "I can get what I want without paying cash for it." Tebyanian has used his trade dollars to purchase advertising spots on local TV and radio stations, and to acquire new computers and phones for his offices.

The Chicago White Sox baseball team has also used bartering. It bartered thousands of dollars worth of game tickets to pay the company that washed windows in the Comiskey Park skyboxes, as well as to pay for printing and floral arrangements for the opening day.

The use of the barter system as a financial tool for business is definitely on the rise. About 175,000 businesses swap products and services on more than 400 exchanges. In 1990, the estimated value of bartering in the United States amounted to $750 million, nearly double the amount five years earlier, according to the International Reciprocal Trade Association in Alexandria, Virginia.

However, bartering is not a cure-all for cash-poor companies. Depending on the exchange, a business may be limited in its choice of products or services. Also, it may be dangerous if firms don't fully understand the cash cost of a trade dollar. Taxes must still be paid on all sales—just as if cash had been used—and the tax bill can often be a shock!

Bartering is still unfamiliar territory to many firms, but as small businesses face financial difficulties, bartering will continue to gain popularity.

Barter Boom

Estimated value of barter deals through U.S. trade exchanges, in millions of dollars

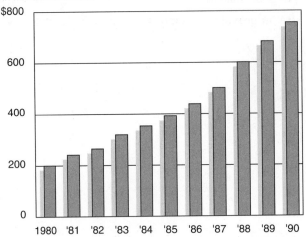

Source: International Reciprocal Trade Association, as reported in *The Wall Street Journal,* November 26, 1990. Adapted with permission of THE WALL STREET JOURNAL, © 1990 Dow Jones & Company, Inc. All Rights Reserved Worldwide.

QUESTIONS

1. Identify and discuss some advantages and disadvantages of the barter system.

2. How might bartering be used as a source of funding for a small business?

3. Would bartering work in all types of businesses? Speculate as to which type of firm might use bartering. Which one might not?

4. You have started the business you always dreamed of having. Describe how you would personally use bartering in your firm.

PART

III

MARKETING GOODS AND SERVICES

To succeed, a small business must effectively perform a number of essential business functions: marketing, organizing and managing, operations, and financing. The last three functions will be covered in Parts IV, V, and VI; this part concentrates on the marketing function.

Marketing involves determining customers' needs, developing goods and services to satisfy those needs, and distributing those products to customers. It is an essential function because, unless the firm has or can develop a market for its product, performing the other business functions is futile.

Chapter 10, "Developing Marketing Strategies," covers the marketing concept; strategy development, including marketing objectives, targets, and mix; types of products and their life cycles; marketing strategies for services; packaging; and pricing strategies.

In Chapter 11, "Marketing the Product," we discuss channels of distribution, using intermediaries or one's own sales force, supporting and controlling sales personnel, and promoting the product.

Chapter 12, "Other Marketing Activities," rounds out the discussion of the marketing function. It discusses marketing research, credit management, physical distribution, and international opportunities.

10

Developing Marketing Strategies

Packaging is the last five seconds of marketing.—John Lester, vice president, Lester Butler Inc.

The buyer needs a hundred eyes, but the seller needs none.—Anonymous

We don't focus enough attention on adequate product differentiation, much less on distribution channels, service organizations, or the reputation of vendors. We tend to forget that those things tremendously influence what someone buys.—William H. Davidow, venture capitalist and author of *Marketing High Technology*

LEARNING OBJECTIVES

After studying the material in this chapter, you will be able to:
  1. Describe the marketing concept, and explain how it can be used by a small business.
  2. Explain how to develop and implement a marketing strategy.
  3. Explain how the product life cycle affects marketing strategies.
  4. Explain how packaging affects marketing.
  5. Describe how prices are set and administered.
  6. Show how marketing services differs from marketing goods.

BYRD SURVEYING: MARKETING A SERVICE

Byrd Surveying is a small land surveying corporation established in 1974 that employs between 20 and 25 people. Its primary business is mortgage loan and boundary surveys, but the firm also does engineering, subdividing, percolations, and construction layout work.

Gerald Byrd, the president and CEO, is licensed in Alabama, Florida, and Mississippi. As in any professional service organization, ethics is a main concern, and many forms of advertising are not considered ethical for this industry. Opportunities for marketing the services are few because professional associations are used to get the word out about the business and its services. Byrd belongs to the Mortgage Bankers Association, the Homebuilders Association, and the Realtors Association.

Photo courtesy of Gerald Byrd.

working member, serving on the various boards and attending all meetings and organizational functions. These associations hold many and various charitable activities, from fishing rodeos to actual construction of buildings and homes. Active members provide services, supplies, and labor for many causes.

In order to maintain an image of friendly professionalism, Byrd also hand-delivers many of his finished jobs. This is a follow-up prospecting function. During this visit to the client, questions can be answered and new projects brainstormed. Pricing, timing, and criteria may also be discussed one-to-one at this time of personal contact. It is also very important that all phone calls and "drop-ins" be treated individually with courtesy and respect. "Let's not forget the quality of the finished product," Byrd says. His business creed is: "A satisfied client is a continuing client."

Such professional memberships can mean many extra hours of service and hard work. Since his membership is a marketing tool, however, Byrd is always an active and

Source: Conversations with Gerald Byrd, his associates, and fellow professionals.

This Profile illustrates an important aspect of the marketing function—marketing a service. It also gives an overview of marketing, including the importance of the marketing concept, product development, and customer service. This chapter is about those and other marketing activities.

THE MARKETING CONCEPT

The **marketing concept** involves giving special consideration to the needs, desires, and wishes of present and prospective customers.

The **marketing concept** helps a business focus its efforts on satisfying customer needs in such a way as to make a satisfactory profit. The concept comprises three basic elements: a customer orientation, a goal orientation, and the systems approach. This concept is based on the truth that the survival of a small business depends on providing service. With such a customer orientation, small firms will try to identify the group of people or firms most likely to buy their product (the target market) and to produce goods or services that will meet the needs of that market. Being consumer oriented often involves exploring consumer needs and then trying to satisfy them, as the following example shows.

In 1982, Pamela Swenson bought Sanitary Dry Cleaners in Laconia, New Hampshire. Not only does she make a living from this business, but she has some very satisfying moments. For example, "a little lady about 75 years old" drives half an hour to trade with her because "she likes spending a little time with us." Another customer said that although he had been trading with a cleaner nearer his home, he changed to Sanitary because "you know my name."[1]

In focusing on consumer orientation, however, the small firm must not lose sight of its own goals. Goals in profit-seeking firms typically center on financial criteria such as profit, return on investment, or market share.

The third component of the marketing concept is the systems approach. In a **system** all parts of the business work together. Thus, consumer needs are identified, and internal procedures are set up to ensure that the right goods and services are produced, distributed, and sold to meet those needs.

In a **system** all parts of the business work in unison.

Determining Customers' Needs

Your understanding of customers' needs starts with the realization that when people buy something, they purchase satisfaction as well as goods or services. Consumers do not simply choose a toothpaste, for example. Instead, some want a decay preventive, some seek pleasant taste, others desire tooth brighteners, and still others will accept any formula at a bargain price. Thus, understanding customers' needs means being aware of the timing of the purchase, what customers like and dislike, or what "turns them on."

Figure 10–1 Factors Affecting Good Service

Employees:
They should be courteous, helpful, and knowledgeable, but not intrusive. There should be an adequate number of salespeople and cashiers. Some retailers, including Wal-Mart Stores Inc., make customer satisfaction part of the employees' job description.

Commissions:
If making customer satisfaction a part of employees' jobs isn't enough, some retailers will offer commission payments to workers who serve their customers well.

Store design:
Store layout should promote shopping efficiency. Merchandise should be in stock and easy to find. Cash registers should be reliable and fast.

Feedback:
Keeping in touch with customers is crucial, especially for mail-order retailers. Toll-free hotlines are effective. Some retailers call or write their customers to solicit their suggestions.

Source: Adapted from Joyce M. Rosenberg, ''Keeping the Customer Satisfied Is Much Easier Said than Done,'' AP report in *Mobile* (Alabama) *Press Register*, August 21, 1988, p. 1-D.

For example, the owner of a ladies' dress shop in a small town has a good business. Many of her customers live as far as 50 miles away. She knows her customers by name, understands their needs, and buys with them as individuals in mind. When she goes to market, she thinks, "This style is perfect for Mrs. Adams," or "Jane would love this." Then she calls Mrs. Adams or Jane when that style comes in.

Meeting Customers' Needs

The marketing concept should guide the attitudes of the firm's salespeople, who should be encouraged to build personal relationships with customers. For example, one retail salesperson, to build a following, writes to 20 customers every day, describing new stock that should appeal to the specific customer.

Small firms should also do little favors for customers. Although people may be uncomfortable with big favors that they cannot repay, small acts of thoughtfulness make them feel that the business cares about them. Customers want a business to be helpful, and outstanding service will often generate good word-of-mouth advertising. One service that harried shoppers especially appreciate is a liberal return policy.

Keeping customers satisfied is more difficult than it seems, because it involves all aspects of the business. As shown in Figure 10–1, customer satisfaction involves not just employees and customers but other factors as well, such as store design and upkeep, method of employee payment, and methods for providing feedback to and from customers.

"It's table 44 on his cellular phone. He wants a waiter."

Source: Reprinted from *The Wall Street Journal*; permission Cartoon Features Syndicate

Implementing the Marketing Concept

In implementing the marketing concept, you should use the systems approach. As mentioned above, all parts of the business must be coordinated and marketing policies must be understood by all personnel in order to avoid problems such as that in the following example.

A store sent its customers a flier urging them to use its credit plan. Yet one customer received the flier in the same mail with a harsh letter threatening repossession of earlier purchases if the customer's account wasn't paid up within 24 hours.

You should try to apply the marketing concept by using one or more of the following ideas.

Be Conscious of Image

You should evaluate the business frequently to see what kind of image it projects — from the customers' point of view. You should ask: Can my customers find what they want, when they want it, and where they want it, at a competitive price?

Practice Consumerism

The major concerns of the consumer movement during the last three decades have been the rights of consumers to buy safe products, to be informed, to be able to choose, and to be heard. **Consumerism** recognizes that consumers are at a disadvantage and works to force businesses to be responsive in giving them a square deal. You can practice consumerism by doing such things as performing product tests, making clear the terms of sales and warranties, and being truthful in advertising.

Consumerism involves prodding businesses to improve the quality of their products and to expand consumer knowledge.

Look for Danger Signals

There are many danger signals that can indicate when the marketing concept is not being followed. Your business is in trouble if, over time, it exhibits one or more of the signs listed in Figure 10–2. An uninterested employee — or manager — turns customers off, as the following example shows.

Thomas Shoemaker was hunting for some Con-Tact paper in a Peoples Drug store in Washington, D.C. He finally gave up the search and was walking out when he saw a man with a Peoples ID badge adjusting some stock on a shelf. When Shoemaker asked him if the store carried Con-Tact paper, the man replied, "I don't know. I don't work here. I'm the manager."[2]

Seeking a Competitive Edge

There is a close relationship between key success factors and the competitive edge that a small business should seek. Some of these factors, based on industry analysis, were discussed in Chapter 6. Your **competitive edge** is something that customers want and only you can supply, which gives you an advantage over your competitors. Some factors that might provide such an advantage are quality, reli-

A **competitive edge** is a particular characteristic that makes one firm more attractive to customers than its competitors.

Figure 10–2 Danger Signals Indicating Marketing Problems

Indicator	*Indication*
Sales	Down from previous period
Customers	Walking out without buying
	No longer visiting store
	Returning more merchandise
	Expressing more complaints
Employees and salespeople	Being slow to greet customers
	Being indifferent to or delaying customer
	Not urging added or upgraded sales
	Having poor personal appearance
	Lacking knowledge of store
	Making more errors
	(Good ones) leaving the company
Store image	Of greed through unreasonable prices
	Inappropriate for market area
	Unclear, sending mixed signals

ability, integrity, and service, as well as lower prices. In some industries, such as electronics or toys, novelty and innovation provide the most important competitive edge; in many small businesses, however it can be as simple a thing as courtesy, friendliness, and helpfulness.

DEVELOPING A MARKETING STRATEGY

As a small business owner, you should develop a marketing strategy early in your business operations. Such a strategy consists of (1) setting objectives, (2) choosing target market(s), and (3) developing an effective marketing mix.

Setting Objectives

Marketing objectives should be tied in with your competitive edge. For example, an image of higher quality than competitors', at comparable prices, may be an objective. To achieve this objective and still make planned profits requires aligning all operations, including the added costs of improved quality, adequate capital, and so forth. Objectives must consider customers' needs as well as the survival of the business. To attain objectives, a target market must be identified and served.

Choosing Target Markets

A **target market** is the part of the total market toward which promotional efforts are concentrated.

The **target market** of a business should be the customers most likely to buy or use its product(s). Only when a clear, precise target market has been identified can an effective marketing mix be developed.

Use Market Segmentation

Market segmentation is identifying and evaluating various layers of a market.

To define a target market requires **market segmentation,** which is the process of identifying and evaluating various layers of a market. Effective market segmentation requires the following steps:

1. Identify the characteristics of two or more segments of the total market. Then, distinguish among the customers in each segment on the basis of such factors as their age, sex, buying patterns, or income level. For example, adults desire a table-service restaurant more than do teenagers and young children, who generally prefer a fast-food format.

2. Determine whether any of those market segments is large enough and has sufficient buying power to generate profit for your business.

3. Align your marketing effort to reach that segment of the market profitably.

For example, Ryka Inc., a 25-employee firm in Weymouth, Massachusetts, was able to take a segment of the $4-billion-a-year athletic shoe market away from giants such as Nike, Reebok, and L.A. Gear by concentrating on athletic shoes for women.[3]

Shifting Target Markets

Choosing and maintaining a target market is becoming more difficult because of changing consumer characteristics. Therefore, small business owners should study the environment for shifts in such factors as population patterns, age groups, and income levels, as well as regional patterns of consumption.

Population, Age, and Income Shifts.   The underlying market factor determining consumer demand is the number and type of people with the purchasing power to buy a given product. In general, the U.S. population is shifting from the East and North to the West and South. Other important population factors are household size and formations, education, and the numbers of married couples, singles, single-parent families, unmarried couples, and children. According to the U.S. Census Bureau, the average size of U.S. households declined from 3.5 in 1940 to 2.7 in 1987 and is expected to be only 2.5 by the year 2000.[4]

Age groups also change. The average age of Americans has been rising and is expected to continue to rise in the foreseeable future. As you can see from Figure 10–3, the percentage of young people and young adults is declining, while the 35-and-over group—especially the 45- to 64-year-old group—is increasing rapidly. As people in each age group differ in their consumption patterns, different marketing strategies are needed.

The most dramatic population shifts now occurring are the aging of the baby boomers and the need to use and conserve the skills and work ethic of older workers. According to one authority, the aging of the ''boomers'' is coinciding with a change in their work ethic. Upon entering their 40s, they're taking stock of their lives and deciding they'll ''pull back from the fast lane.''[5] Members of this group are looking for more personal fulfillment, including more time with family and friends—and more time alone. This trend may cause a change in their spending habits.

For example, by the year 2000, baby boomers are expected to increase spending for food, owned dwellings, and insurance and pensions faster than for home furnishings, health care, sports cars, and education.[6]

The second trend—the need to use and conserve the skills of older workers—is forcing employers to find productive ways to use those who want to keep on working. During the coming decade, employers will have to choose from an aging work force, as shown in Figure 10–3, since there'll be a crunch for younger workers with both basic and technical skills. In fact, the number of 18- to 35-year-olds will decline, which will require redesigning jobs; rehiring retirees as consultants, advisors, or temporaries; using phased-in retirement programs; and aggressively recruiting older workers.

Figure 10–3   Selling to Older Consumers

The growing ranks of older consumers and a decline in the size of the youth market are leading companies to redesign products and sales appeals to capture the increasingly influential senior citizen and aging baby boomer markets.

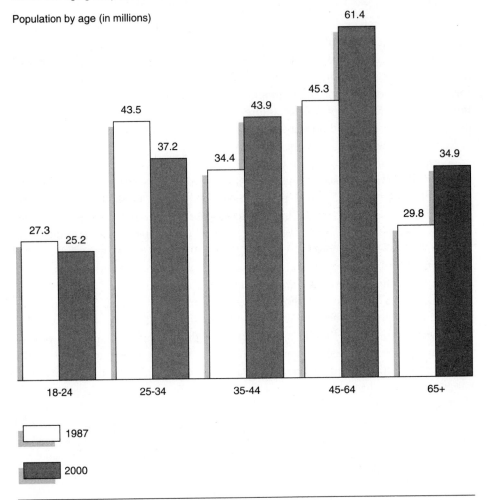

Population by age (in millions)

1987

2000

One of the most important sources of consumer purchasing power is personal income. By the year 2000, the household income of those earning over $35,000 should increase to 43 percent of the total, while that of those earning $15,000 to $35,000 should drop to 33 percent. These estimates are partly explained by the large increases in the number of two-income married couples as a percentage of all married couples. Purchases also vary considerably by region and state, and these variations affect your marketing plans.

Regional Differences in Purchases. Purchasing habits and patterns also vary by region. These variations are significant, for where people live is one of the best clues as to what they buy.

For example, automakers tailor cars to specific regions to exploit regional differences in taste. In the Northeast, which has crowded freeways, drivers are concerned about safety. But in wide-open, less-crowded states such as Wyoming and Nebraska, car owners want to be sure that parts and service will be available. Texas drivers like lots of power and acceleration, while Californians look for dependability and passenger comfort.[7]

Developing an Effective Marketing Mix

A **marketing mix** consists of controllable variables that the firm combines to satisfy the target market. Those variables are the Four Ps: product, place, promotion, and price. The right *product* for the target market must be developed. *Place* refers to the channels of distribution. *Promotion* refers to any method that communicates to the target market. The right *price* should be set to attract customers and make a profit.

> A **marketing mix** is the proper blending of the basic elements of product, price, promotion, and place into an integrated marketing program.

THE PRODUCT LIFE CYCLE

You may find that your most effective strategy is to concentrate on a narrow product line, develop a highly specialized product or service, or provide a product-service "package" containing an unusual amount of service. In setting strategy, competitors' products, prices, and services should be carefully analyzed. This is not easy to do because of the large number of new products introduced each year; for example, there were 17,000 new products introduced in the United States in 1992.[8]

Stages of the Product Life Cycle

Products are much like living organisms: They are brought into the world, they live, and they die. When a new product is successfully introduced into the firm's market mix, it grows; when it loses appeal, it is discontinued. A new product may have a striking effect on the life cycle of other products as well.

Phonograph records are a good illustration of the product life cycle. Although 78 RPM records coexisted with the 45s, they gave way to the long-playing 33s. Now, the compact disc (CD) is threatening all records, even the 45s, which had maintained their hold on jukeboxes. Jukeboxes

Figure 10–4   Life Cycle of a Typical Product

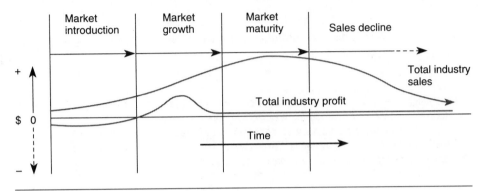

Source: E. Jerome McCarthy and William D. Perreault, Jr., *Basic Marketing,* 11th ed. (Homewood, Ill.: Richard D. Irwin, 1993), p. 288.

that play CDs offer vastly superior quality, along with lower maintenance costs. By 1992, CDs almost entirely supplanted vinyl records.

A **product life cycle** consists of four stages; introduction, growth, maturity, and decline.

As shown in Figure 10–4, a **product life cycle** has four major stages: introduction, growth, maturity, and decline. As a product moves through its cycle, the strategies relating to competition, promotion, distribution, pricing, and market information should be evaluated and possibly changed. You can use the life-cycle concept to time the introduction and improvement of profitable products and the dropping or recycling of unprofitable ones.

Introduction Stage

The introduction stage begins when a product first appears on the market. Prices are usually high, sales are low, and profits are negative because of high development, promotion, and distribution costs. In this stage, it is vital to communicate the product's features, uses, and advantages to potential buyers. Only a few new products—such as home robots (see Using Technology to Succeed)—represent major innovations. More often, a "new" product is an old one in a new form. Many products never get beyond the introduction stage because of insufficient or poor marketing research, design or production problems, or errors in timing the product's introduction.

Growth Stage

During the growth stage, sales rise rapidly and profits peak. As competitors enter the market, they attempt to develop the best product design (the robot in Using Technology to Succeed shows an example of this tendency). During this stage, marketing strategy typically encourages strong brand loyalty. The product's benefits are identified and emphasized in order to develop a competitive niche.

USING TECHNOLOGY TO SUCCEED

YOUR PERSONAL ROBOT

People are getting ready to buy the next household appliance, a personal robot. What is now available may seem crude compared to R2D2 and the other *Star Wars* androids, but with steady advancements in robotics, the ultimate personal robot comes closer to reality than one likes to think.

Several home robots are already on the market. Some popular models include R5BX, sold by RB Robot Corporation of Colorado; Hubot, sold by Hubotics; Stereobot, from Superior Robotics; HERO 2000, from Heath Electronics; Topo and FRED, from Androbot; and GENUS, from Robotics International. Many of them have an IBM-compatible computer, a telescoping arm, a CRT screen in their head, a speech-recognition circuit to respond to voices, built-in sonar for navigation, and a security system to detect intruders, smoke, or fire.

Maturity Stage

Competition becomes more aggressive during the maturity stage, with declining prices and profits. Promotion costs climb; competitors cut prices to attract business; new firms enter, further increasing competition; and weaker competitors are squeezed out. Those that remain make fresh promotional and distribution efforts.

Decline Stage

Sales fall rapidly during the decline stage, especially if a new technology or a social trend is involved. Management considers pruning items from the product line to eliminate unprofitable ones. Promotion efforts may be cut and plans may be made to phase out the product.

For example, the Swanson TV Dinner, developed in 1955, had food to be cooked in an oven on an aluminum tray and eaten while watching TV. It flourished at the height of television's Golden Age but has now been relegated to the Smithsonian Institution for possible display at the National Museum of American History. As VCRs have facilitated "time shifting" of dinner-hour TV programs, the TV Dinner has been replaced by food in a plastic dish, to be popped into a microwave for almost instant cooking.[9]

Need for a Wide Product Mix

The life-cycle concept indicates that many, if not most, products will eventually become unprofitable. Hence, small firms should investigate and evaluate market opportunities to launch new products or extend the life of existing ones. You should have a composite of life-cycle patterns, with various products in the mix at different life-cycle stages; as one product declines, other products are in the introduction, growth, or maturity stages. Some fads may last only a few weeks or months (consider the western clothes example in Chapter 6), while other products (refrigerators, for example) may be essentially unchanged for years.

PACKAGING

Packaging, because it both protects and promotes the product, is important both to you as well as to your customers. Packaging can make a product more convenient to use or store and can reduce spoiling or damage. Good packaging makes products easier to identify, promotes the brand at the store, and influences customers in making buying decisions.

A better box, wrapper, can, or bottle can help create a ''new'' product or market. For example, a small manufacturer introduced a liquid hand soap in a pump container, and it was an instant success. Sometimes, a new package improves a product by making it easier to use, such as motor oil sold in reclosable plastic containers. Packaging can also improve product safety, as when drugs and food are sold in child-proof bottles and tamper-resistant packages.

HOW TO PRICE YOUR PRODUCT

There are three aspects of pricing that you must consider. First, regardless of the desirability of the product, the price must be such that customers are willing—and able—to pay it.

Second, you must set your price to maintain or expand your market share and/or profit. If the new product is successful, competitors will introduce either a better product or a cheaper one.

Third, if you want to make a profit on the new product, the price must be sufficiently greater than cost to cover development, introduction, and operating costs.

Establishing Pricing Policies

As shown in Table 10–1, there's a large variety of pricing policies you can adopt, but the first three deserve particular attention: product life cycle, meet the competition, and cost-oriented pricing.

Effect of Product Life Cycle

A **skimming price** is one set relatively high initially in order to rapidly skim off the ''cream'' of profits.

Notice the role played by the product life cycle, as discussed earlier. When you introduce a new product, you have two alternatives: (1) to set a **skimming price,** which will be high enough to obtain the ''cream'' of the target market before

Table 10–1   Potential Pricing Policies for a Small Business

Policy Area	Description
Product life cycle:	
Skimming price	Aimed at obtaining the "cream" of the target market at a high price before dealing with other market segments.
Penetration price	Intended to try to sell to the entire market at a low price.
Meet the competition	Below the market price. At the competitors' price level. Above the market price.
Cost-oriented pricing	Costs are accumulated for each unit of product, and a markup is added to obtain a base price.
Price flexibility:	
One price	Offering the same price to all customers who purchase goods under the same conditions and in the same quantities.
Flexible price	Offering the same products and quantities to different customers at different prices.
Suggested retail price	Manufacturers often print a suggested price on the product or invoice or in their catalog.
List prices	Published prices that remain the same for a long time.
Prestige pricing	Setting of high prices used, say, by fur retailers.
Leader pricing	Certain products are chosen for their promotional value and are priced low in order to entice customers into retail stores.
Bait pricing	An item is priced extremely low by a dealer, but the salesperson points out the disadvantages of the item and switches customers to items of higher quality and price. (This practice is illegal.)
Odd pricing	Prices end in certain numbers, usually odd, such as $0.95 — e.g., $7.95, $8.95.
Psychological pricing	Certain prices for some products are psychologically appealing; there can be a range of prices that customers perceive as being equal to each other.
Price lining	Policy of setting a few price levels for given lines of merchandise; e.g., ties at three levels: $8, $16, and $25.
Demand-oriented pricing	Potential customer demand is recognized, and prospective revenues are considered in pricing.

competitors enter, or (2) to set a **penetration price,** which will be low enough to obtain an adequate and sustainable market. Small producers sometimes use a combination approach, setting a realistic price but making an initial purchase more attractive by issuing discount coupons.

A **penetration price** is one set relatively low in order to secure market acceptance.

Meeting the Competition

You can also set prices by meeting the competition, that is, following the pricing practices of competitors. But this practice can lead to severe losses if cost and volume of sales aren't taken into account. Small firms with an attractive, possibly unique product should not be afraid to charge what the product is worth, taking into account not only what it costs to provide the product but also what the market will bear.

Cost-Oriented Pricing

Cost-oriented pricing is basic to all pricing policies. Total costs provide a floor below which prices should not be permitted to go, especially for long periods of time. Cost-oriented pricing involves adding a markup to the cost of the item.

Markup is the amount added to the product's cost to determine the selling price.

Markup.   **Markup** is the amount added to the cost of the product to determine the selling price. Usually, the amount of the markup is determined by the type of product sold, the amount of service performed by the retailer, how rapidly the product sells, and the amount of planned profit. Markup may be expressed in terms of dollars and/or cents, or as a percentage.

The way to figure markup percentage on cost is:

$$\frac{\text{Markup as percentage}}{\text{of cost}} = \frac{\text{Dollar amount of markup}}{\text{Cost of the item}}$$

For example, assume that a retailer is pricing a new product that costs \$6. The selling price is set at \$9. Therefore, the total amount of markup is \$3: selling price (\$9) less cost (\$6) equals markup (\$3). The markup percentage, then, is:

$$\text{Markup percentage (cost)} = \frac{\$3}{\$6} = 50 \text{ percent}$$

A **discount** is a reduction from the list price given to customers as an inducement to buy more of a product.

Allowances are given to customers for accepting quality or quantity reductions.

Discounts and Allowances.   Sellers often use discounts and allowances to increase sales. **Discounts,** which are reductions from a product's normal list price, are given to customers as an inducement to buy the item. **Allowances** are given to customers for accepting less of something, or as an adjustment for variations in quality. Some of the more popular discounts and allowances are shown in Table 10–2.

How Prices Are Set by Small Businesses

Prices are set differently by small service firms, retailers, wholesalers, producers, and building contractors. Some of the more popular methods are described here.

By Service Firms

Service firms either charge the ''going rate'' (that is, the usual rate for a given job) or they may set prices according to those prevalent in their industry. They try to set a price based on the cost of labor and materials used to provide the service, as well as direct charges—such as transportation costs—and a profit margin. Many firms charge customers an hourly rate, based on the time required to perform the services, plus any travel expenses. Others incorporate the labor, materials, and transportation costs into an hourly rate, or a rate based on some other variable.

Table 10–2   Discounts and Allowances Provided by Small Businesses

Reduction	*Description*
Cash discounts	Given as a reduction in price to buyers who pay their bill within a specified period of time (e.g., 2/10, net 30 days).
Functional or trade discounts	List price reductions given to channel members for performance of their functions.
Quantity discounts	Reduction in the unit price granted for buying in certain quantities.
Noncumulative	Apply to individual shipments or orders only.
Cumulative	Apply to purchases over a given period (e.g., a year).
Seasonal discounts	Induce buyers to stock earlier than immediate demand would dictate.
Promotional allowances	Provided by manufacturers and wholesalers to retailers for promotion (e.g., point-of-purchase display materials, per case discounts, and cooperative advertisements).
Trade-ins	Allowance provided to customer by retailer in the purchase of, say, a major electric appliance.
Push money or prize money	Allowances provided retailers by manufacturers or wholesalers to be given to salespersons for aggressively selling particular products.

By Retailers

Different types of products are priced differently. Staple convenience goods, such as candy, gum, newspapers, and magazines, usually have customary prices or use the manufacturer's suggested retail price. **Customary prices** are the prices customers expect to pay as a result of custom, tradition, or social habits.

> A **customary price** is what customers expect to pay because of custom, tradition, or social habits.

For example, Hershey Chocolate Company sold candy bars for 5 cents in 1940. As cocoa and sugar became scarce and more expensive because of World War II, the price didn't rise for a while. Instead, the size of the bars was cut in half by the end of 1942.

Some discount and food stores discount prepriced items such as candy, gum, magazines, a set percentage—say 10 or even 20 percent. In fact, Food World discounts all prepriced items 10 percent, and Wal-Mart discounts greeting cards 20 percent and sewing patterns nearly 50 percent.

Fashion goods, by contrast, have high markups but are drastically marked down if they do not sell well. High markups are also used on novelty, specialty, and seasonal goods. When the novelty wears off, or the selling season ends, the price goes down.

For example, early-bird shoppers after holidays expect to find markdowns up to 50 or even 75 percent on Christmas wraps and toys, or on Easter candy and stuffed rabbits. Customers also expect discounts on novelty items marketed as "stocking stuffers," holiday party clothes, and extravagantly priced items intended as gifts.

Unit pricing is listing the product's price in terms of some unit, such as a pound, pint, or yard.

Most grocery stores use **unit pricing** for products such as meats, produce, and deli items, charging so much per ounce or pound for each item. Information about unit prices of other items facilitates comparison shopping by customers.

Although influenced by competitors', vendors', and customary prices, retailers still must determine their own prices for the products they sell. In any case, the retailer's selling price should cover the cost of goods, selling and other operating costs, and a profit margin. In some cases, however, a store might use **loss leaders,** or items sold below cost, to attract customers who may also buy more profitable items.

A loss leader is an item priced at or below cost to attract customers into the store to buy more profitable items.

By Wholesalers

Wholesalers' prices are usually based on a markup set for each product line. Since wholesalers purchase in large quantities and cannot always immediately pass along price increases, price drops can cause heavy losses. Therefore, they may sometimes quote different prices to different buyers for the same products.

By Producers

While meeting competitors' prices is common among small producers, many of them set their prices relative to the cost of production, using a break-even analysis. As shown in Chapter 18, their costs include purchasing, inventory, production, distribution, selling, and administrative costs, as well as a profit margin. Those figures are totaled to arrive at a final price.

By Building Contractors

Cost-plus pricing is basing the price on the basis of all costs, plus a markup for profit.

Most building contractors use **cost-plus pricing.** They start with the cost of the land; add expected construction costs for items such as labor, materials, and supplies; add overhead costs; add financing and closing costs and legal fees; and add the real estate broker's fee. They then total the costs and add on a markup for profit. Figure 10–5 shows how this formula would apply to a $100,000 house being constructed in a big-city suburb.

Other Aspects of Pricing

Product, delivery, service, and fulfillment of psychological needs make up the total package that the customer buys. A price should be consistent with the image the business wants to project. Since customers often equate the quality of unknown products with their prices, raising prices may actually increase sales.

However, the reverse might also be true: Selling at a low price might lead customers to think the product is of low quality. Sometimes, "cheap" can be too cheap, especially when compared to nationally advertised products.

Figure 10–5   Pricing a $100,000 House

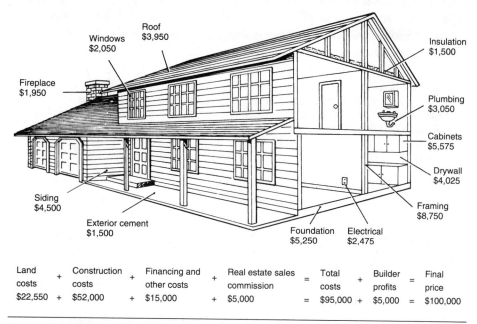

Land costs		Construction costs		Financing and other costs		Real estate sales commission		Total costs		Builder profits		Final price
$22,550	+	$52,000	+	$15,000	+	$5,000	=	$95,000	+	$5,000	=	$100,000

Source: Data from Carol Nanninga, ''Constructing a Price,'' (Bellevue, Washington) *Journal-American,* June 24, 1984, p. G1, as adapted by Louis E. Boone and David L. Kurtz, *Contemporary Marketing,* 5th ed. (New York: Dryden Press, 1986), p. 478. Reproduced with the permission of the *Journal-American.*

In summary, small business owners commonly make two errors in setting prices for their products. First, they charge less than larger businesses and consider themselves price leaders. Because of their relatively small sales, costs per unit tend to be higher for a smaller business than for a larger one. Therefore, *small firms generally should not attempt to be price leaders.*

Second, many firms offering services performed personally by the owner undercharge during the early period of operation. The owner mistakenly believes that prices can be raised later as more customers are secured. However, it is easier to lower prices than to raise them, and raising them usually creates customer dissatisfaction.

STRATEGY FOR MARKETING SERVICES

Because the service sector of our economy is so important and has certain unique features, we will cover strategies for marketing services separately from marketing goods.

Nature of Service Businesses

There are two categories of services: personal and business. **Personal services** include activities such as financial services, transportation, health and beauty,

Personal services are performed by a business for consumers.

Business services are provided to another business or professional.

lodging, advising and counseling, amusement, plumbing, maid services, real estate, and insurance. **Business services** may include some of these, plus others that are strictly business oriented, such as advertising agencies, market research firms, economic counselors, certified public accountants (CPAs), and personal service agents, as the following example illustrates.

ProServ Inc., a Washington-based sports marketing firm, performs various services for professional athletes, such as representing them in salary talks with management, negotiating the contract, handling the player's investment and legal needs, and lining up product endorsements.[10]

Personal services can be performed by individuals or by automated equipment. Two examples of the latter are automatic car washes and computer time-sharing bureaus.

There are many opportunities in service industries because the demand for services is expected to grow faster than for most other types of businesses. Some reasons for increased spending on services include rising discretionary income, services as status symbols, more women working outside the home (and earning more), and a shorter workweek and more leisure time.

On the other hand, service businesses have severe competition, not only from other firms but also from potential customers who perform the services themselves and from manufacturers of do-it-yourself products.

How Services Differ

Since service firms must be chosen on the basis of their perceived reputation, a good image is of utmost importance. There are few objective standards for measuring the quality of services, so they are often judged subjectively. Not only is a service usually complete before a buyer can evaluate its quality, but defective services cannot be returned.

Services cannot be stored in inventory, especially by firms providing amusements, transportation services, and room accommodations. Special features or extra thoughtfulness that create a memorable experience will encourage repeat business in service firms.

The level of customer contact required to provide the service also varies. That is, the longer a customer remains in the service system, the greater the interaction between the server and customer. Generally, economies of scale are more difficult to achieve in high-contact services than in low-contact ones. For example, a beauty salon is a high-contact system, with the receptionist, shampoo person, and stylist all interacting with the customer. On the other hand, an automated car wash may have little contact with a customer.

Developing Service Marketing Strategies

Strategies for marketing services differ according to the level of customer contact. For example, in low-contact services the business doesn't have to be located near the customer. On the other hand, a high-contact service, such as a plumbing firm, must be close enough to quickly meet the customer's needs. Quality control in high-contact services consists basically of doing a good job and maintaining an image and good public relations. Thus, if employees have a poor attitude, the firm may lose customers.

Importance of the Marketing Concept

The marketing concept is more important for service businesses than for other types of businesses, since customers often can perform the service themselves. The business must demonstrate why it is to the customer's advantage to let the service firm do the job.

Pricing Services

The price for a service should reflect the quality, degree of expertise and specialization, and value of its performance to the buyer. As shown earlier, a high price tends to connote quality in the mind of the customer, so lower prices and price reductions may even have a negative effect on sales, particularly in people-based businesses.

The pricing of services in small firms often depends on value provided rather than on cost. Customers will pay whatever they think the service is worth, so pricing depends on what the market will bear. Pricing decisions often consider labor, materials, and transportation costs, as the following example illustrates.

Promoting Services

Word-of-mouth advertising, personal selling, and publicity are usually used by small firms to promote their business. Quite often, the message will have a consistent theme, which is related to the uniqueness of the service, key personnel, or the benefits gained by satisfied customers. Small service firms typically include the Yellow Pages, direct mail, and local newspapers. Specialty advertising, such as calendars with the firm's name, may be considered. Referrals, which ask satisfied customers to recommend the service to friends, can be quite effective. Belonging to professional and civic organizations and sponsoring public events are also important in building a firm's revenues and profitability, as the Profile for this chapter illustrates.

Lynn Brown's Mini-Maid franchise team takes from 30 to 90 minutes to make beds, scour sinks, clean glass doors, sweep and mop or wax floors, vacuum carpets, clean bathrooms, polish furniture, load the dishwasher, wipe cabinets, shine counters, change bed linens, remove garbage, freshen the air, and do general pickup.

Brown furnishes all the cleaning supplies needed, as well as the labor. Depending on the size of the house, her prices range from approximately $25 to $50. Also, in estimating the price—which Brown does on the phone for new customers—she considers the frequency with which customers use her services. The more often they use Mini-Maid, the better their rate.

Brown has a small office in her home with a 24-hour-a-day answering service, but most of her workweek is spent in her minivan. Her biggest expenses are payroll, telephone, transportation, advertising, her answering service, and cleaning supplies. Brown says her success results from doing specific activities, in a specific way, for a specific price—which, as she says, is the Mini-Maid way.[11]

IMPLEMENTING YOUR MARKETING STRATEGY

Now that you have developed your marketing strategy, how do you implement it? Implementation involves two stages: (1) the introductory stage and (2) the growth stage.

The Introductory Stage

When introducing a new product, you should (1) analyze present and future market situations, (2) fit the product to the market, and (3) evaluate your company's resources.

Analyze Market Situations

This step determines the opportunities that lie in present and future market situations, as well as problems and adverse environmental trends that will affect your company. Because market size and growth are vital, potential growth rate should be forecast as accurately as possible.

Fit Product to Market

You should design your products to fit the market and then find other markets that fit those products. A market niche too small to interest large companies may be available.

For example, a small firm manufacturing truck springs found that its product was a standard item produced by larger firms that could benefit from economies of scale. Because price competition was so severe, management decided to specialize in springs for swimming pool diving boards. This change in product strategy proved to be highly profitable.

Evaluate Company Resources

Your company's strengths, as well as its limitations, should be determined at each stage of the marketing process. Financial, cost, competitive, and timing pressures must be viewed realistically, and successes and failures need to be understood and regarded as important learning experiences.

The Growth Stage

Once you begin to grow, you can adopt one of three strategies: (1) expand products to reach new classes of customers, (2) increase penetration in the existing target market, or (3) make no marketing innovations but try instead to hold your present market share by product design and manufacturing innovations.

Expand Products to Reach New Markets

To reach new markets, you may add related products within the present product line, add products unrelated to the present line, find new applications in new markets for the firm's product, or add customized products, perhaps upgrading from low-quality to medium- or high-quality goods. This is **diversification,** or product line expansion, which tends to increase profits; contribute to long-range growth; stabilize production, employment, and payrolls; fill out a product line; and lower administrative overhead cost per unit. The major pitfall of diversification is that the firm may not have the resources to compete effectively.

Diversification involves adding products that are unrelated to the present product line.

Increase Penetration of Present Market

You may want to increase the sales of existing products to existing customers. If so, you might reduce the number and variety of products and models in order to produce substantial operating economies.

Make No Marketing Innovations

The strategy of retaining current marketing practices without trying to innovate may suit your company well if its strength lies in its technical competence. It is often advisable for retail store owners to follow this strategy.

Over the long term, a firm may follow one strategy for several years with the intent to change after certain marketing goals have been reached. But the change should take place if progress is desired.

WHAT YOU SHOULD HAVE LEARNED

1. You use the marketing concept when you focus your efforts on satisfying customers' needs—at a profit. Consumer needs and market opportunities should be identified, and the target market(s) most likely to buy their products should be determined. You should seek a competitive edge that sets your firm apart from, and gives it an advantage over, competitors.

2. A marketing strategy involves setting marketing objectives and selecting target market(s) based on market segmentation. It means knowing consumers' needs, attitudes, and buying behavior, as well as studying population patterns, age groups, income levels, and regional patterns. Finally, the marketing mix, which consists of the controllable variables, product, place, promotion, and price, should weigh heavily in decision making.

   The marketing strategies you can adopt are to expand products to reach new classes of customers, increase penetration in the existing target market, or make no marketing innovation but copy new marketing techniques instead.

3. A product life cycle has four major stages: introduction, growth, maturity, and decline. Strategies related to competition, promotion, distribution, and prices differ depending on the product's stage of the cycle.

4. Packaging both protects and promotes the product. It not only makes products more convenient and reduces spoiling or damage, but also makes products easier to identify, promotes the brand, and makes the purchase decision easier.

5. Pricing objectives should be set in order to achieve your firm's overall objectives. The ''best'' selling price should be cost and market oriented. Some pricing concerns for small businesses are product life cycle, meeting the competition, and cost orientation. Most small businesses use cost-oriented pricing methods, using markups, discounts, and allowances. Different types of small firms use differing pricing practices.

6. The marketing of services differs from the marketing of goods. There are few objective standards for measuring service quality, but quality should be emphasized. Also, price competition in standardized services is quite severe, output of service firms is difficult to standardize, and services cannot be stored.

QUESTIONS FOR DISCUSSION

1. What is the marketing concept, and why is it so important to small firms?

2. How are the key success factors for a firm related to its competitive edge?

3. What is market segmentation, and how can it be made more effective?

4. Discuss some of the characteristics that should be considered in selecting a target market.

5. What controllable variables are combined into a marketing mix to satisfy the target market?

6. What are the major stages of the product life cycle, and how do marketing strategies differ at each stage?

7. In what ways is packaging important to small firms and their customers?

8. What are the three basic aspects that should be considered in pricing products? Explain cost-oriented pricing. What is markup?

9. Explain how service firms, retailers, wholesalers, manufacturers, and building contractors actually set prices.

10. How does the marketing of services differ from the marketing of goods?

FINDING A SPECIAL NICHE

As a future small business owner, you may be asking, "Could I start a business and compete with the big boys without getting stomped?" The answer is often a resounding "Yes!" A small firm can often home in on a market niche and actually take customers away from large businesses. Eastern Connection Inc. (ECI), a small overnight-delivery company, has challenged the overnight-delivery giants, such as Federal Express and UPS, for a "piece of the pie." So far, ECI has experienced phenomenal success, with 1990 profits of over $1 million on revenues of $17.2 million. All this after only seven years in the business.

ECI has developed a simple marketing strategy. Instead of "going head-to-head" with its giant competitors, ECI has developed a regional niche, serving only major East Coast cities. ECI concentrates on high-volume locations and avoids delivering one or two packages to many remote places.

James Berluti, part-owner and manager of ECI, employed a classic marketing strategy. Seeing that there was a need for a low-cost, regional overnight-delivery service, he began to plan how to best meet that need. He chose his target market: regional, high-volume locations. Berluti developed an aggressive marketing mix: lower prices than competitors and guaranteed door-to-door delivery by 9:00 A.M. With $130,000 he had raised, he opened for business.

Berluti realizes that long-term success is not guaranteed. Multibillion-dollar Federal Express and UPS are quite capable of fighting back. ECI cannot even begin to match the millions of dollars spent on advertising by the "big boys." Nor can it hope to match the sophistication of Federal Express's computerized tracking system. Nevertheless, Berluti remains optimistic about the future. Believing that "people want the most purchasing power for their dollar," Berluti is convinced that in the overnight-delivery game he can provide this better than anybody else.

QUESTIONS

1. Explain the marketing strategy employed by ECI.

2. In your opinion, what key factors are responsible for the success of this small business? Discuss.

3. Imagine that you have been hired as the company's new marketing manager. What recommendations would you make to ECI's manager?

4. Speculate as to whether or not ECI should expand out of its market niche and try to "grab a bigger piece of the pie."

5. Speculate as to this company's chances of long-term survival in this competitive market.

Source: Suzanne Alexander, "Small Firm's Single-Coast Strategy Delivers the Goods. Eastern Connection Finds a Regional Niche in Overnight Mail," *The Wall Street Journal,* March 6, 1991, p. B2.

11

Marketing the Product

Don't sell the steak; sell the "sizzle." —Dale Carnegie sales slogan

Sales-management skills are very different from selling skills, and talent in one area does not necessarily indicate talent in the other. —Jack Falvey, management consultant, speaker, and writer

LEARNING OBJECTIVES

After studying the material in this chapter, you will be able to:
1. Describe different channels of distribution used for marketing products and discuss factors to consider in choosing an appropriate channel.

2. Describe the functions of intermediaries used in selling a product.

3. Describe the creative selling process used in personal selling.

4. Describe the use of advertising to promote the sale of a product.

5. Explain the role(s) of merchandising, sales promotion, and publicity in a small business.

6. Discuss some of the opportunities and problems involved in selling to ethnic groups.

MEL FARR: SALES SUPERSTAR

Mel Farr was consensual All-American when he played football for the UCLA Bruins from 1963 to 1967. The number one draft choice of the Detroit Lions in 1967, he was named the NFL's "Rookie of the Year." After being on the All Pro Team in 1967 and 1972, he retired from the NFL in 1974 because of extensive injuries. He was inducted into the prestigious UCLA Sports Hall of Fame in 1988.

Before retiring from the NFL, Farr started preparing for his post-football career. He worked in Ford's Dealer Development Division, played football, and finished his college degree from the University of Detroit in 1971. After retiring from the NFL in 1974, he remained with Ford to help set up its training program for minority dealers. In 1975, Farr and a partner

Photo courtesy of Mel Farr Enterprises.

bought a bankrupt Ford dealership in Oak Park, Michigan. After he bought the partner out in 1978, Farr came up with a brilliant and successful marketing coup for his dealership. For years, he starred in a series of TV ads, dressed in a crimson cape and asking viewers to "See Mel Farr, Superstar, for a Farr better deal." They did! He became the youngest honoree in the "Top 100 Black Businesses in America" when it was first published by *Black Enterprise* magazine in 1978, and he's been listed every year since. He was cited for outstanding achievements in business by President Carter in 1978 and has received numerous other awards and recognitions. In 1992, he headed up the Ford Lincoln-Mercury Minority Dealers Association.

Source: Correspondence with Charlene Mitchell of Mel Farr Enterprises; and others, including Blair S. Walker, "Group: Ford Unfair to Minority Dealers," *USA Today,* November 23, 1992, p. 1B.

The Profile illustrates much of the material covered in this chapter. Mel Farr was creative in his advertising, sales promotion, and personal selling. This chapter deals with those subjects and also covers the channels of distribution to be used, the use of intermediaries for selling your product, other forms of promotion, and the importance of considering ethnic groups in marketing products.

CHOOSING A DISTRIBUTION CHANNEL

A **distribution channel** consists of the marketing organizations responsible for the flow of goods or services from the producer to the consumer.

One of the first things a small business producer of goods or services must do to promote sales of its product is to choose a distribution channel. A **distribution channel** consists of the various marketing organizations involved in moving the flow of goods and services from producer to user. The distribution channel acts as the pipeline through which a product flows. While the choice of distribution channels is quite important, it is not a simple one because of the many variables involved. Also, the channels for distributing consumer and industrial goods differ.

Distribution Channels for Consumer Goods

Figure 11–1 shows the traditional channels for distributing consumer goods. As you can see, a small business has essentially two choices: (1) to sell directly to the consumer or (2) to sell through one or more intermediaries. This decision is usually made (at least initially) when choosing what type of business to enter. The first channel (direct from producer to consumer) is the most frequently used by small firms, probably because it is the simplest.

As shown in Chapter 10, small firms performing services and selling goods at retail usually deal directly with consumers. Most of our discussion in this chapter will concentrate on the remaining channels, which use intermediaries.

Louisiana strawberries are an interesting example of using channel 4. Because strawberries are so perishable, they must be sold quickly. So they are picked, placed in refrigerated railroad cars, and shipped before they are sold. As they travel north, agents or brokers contact wholesalers in cities along the line to Chicago. As the berries are sold, the car(s) carrying them are diverted to the appropriate city, where the wholesaler picks them up and sells them through the remainder of the channel.[1]

Distribution Channels for Industrial Goods

Distribution channels for industrial goods are shown in Figure 11–2. Channel 1 (direct from producer to industrial user) is the most frequently used. In general, items produced in large quantities, but sold in relatively small amounts, move through channel 2. Large, bulky items that have relatively few buyers, or whose demand varies, flow through channel 3.

Figure 11–1   Distribution Channels for Consumer Goods

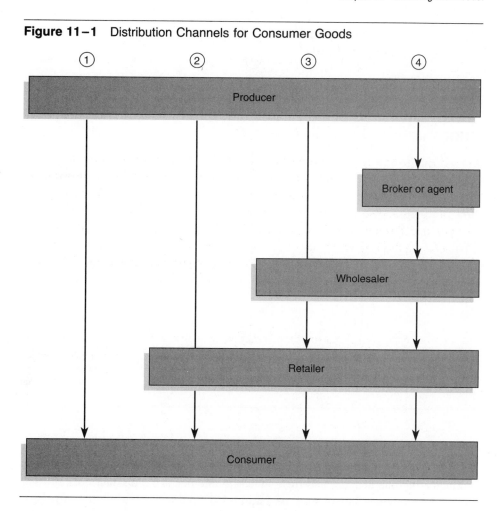

Factors to Consider in Choosing a Distribution Channel

Small business producers should design their own distribution channels, if feasible, in order to attain the optimum income. In doing so, they need to seek a *balance between maintaining control over the flow of the product* and *minimizing the cost involved*. The primary factors to consider include the following:

- Geographical markets and consumer types arranged in order of importance.
- Whether the product will be distributed through many outlets, selected outlets, or exclusive distributors.
- Kind and amount of marketing effort the producer intends to exert.
- Need for receiving feedback about the product.
- Adequate incentives to motivate resellers.

Figure 11–2 Distribution Channels for Industrial Goods

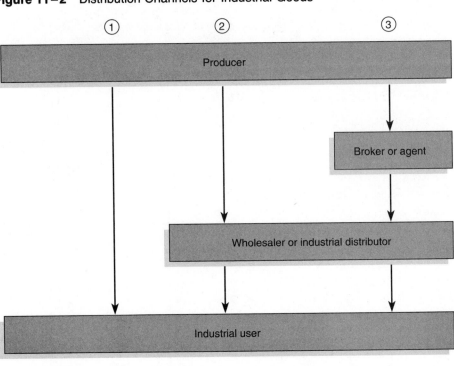

New products commonly require distribution channels different from those used for well-established and widely accepted products. Thus, you may introduce a new product using one channel and then switch to another if the product does not sell well. Also, a new channel may be required if you seek new markets for your products, as the following example illustrates.

When Wendell Ward and Percy Hale bought Bellville Potato Chip Company, a small firm in Bellville, Texas, its annual sales were $275,000, but it was losing $12,000 a year. A year later, Ward and Hale made a profit of over $9,000 on sales of $1 million by selling through distributors instead of directly to retailers. The number of their accounts increased from 12 to more than 700.[2]

Finally, multiple distribution channels can create conflicts, and distribution can be adversely affected unless these conflicts are resolved. This problem should be anticipated and provided for. Choosing the right channel also permits a difference in pricing.

For example, Hill's Science Diet dog and cat foods are so expensive that they could never compete with other pet foods in grocery stores, so they are sold in pet stores and by veterinarians to people who are evidently willing, on the vet's recommendation, to pay the premium price.

SELLING THROUGH INTERMEDIARIES

The usual intermediaries are: (1) brokers, (2) agents, (3) wholesalers, and (4) retailers.

Brokers

A **broker,** for a fee, brings the buyer and seller together to negotiate purchases or sales but does not take title to, or possession of, the goods. The broker has only limited authority to set prices and terms of sale. Firms using brokers usually buy and/or sell highly specialized goods and seasonal products not requiring constant distribution, such as strawberries or crude oil. Also, canned goods, frozen-food items, petroleum products, and household specialty products are often distributed through brokers.

> **Brokers** bring buyers and sellers of goods together to negotiate purchases or sales.

Agents

Because brokers operate on a one-time basis to bring buyers and sellers together, a small business that wants a more permanent distribution channel may use an agent to perform the marketing function. These **agents,** who market a product to others for a fee, are variously called *manufacturers' agents, selling agents,* or *sales representatives (reps),* depending on the industry.

> **Agents** are marketing intermediaries who market a product to others for a fee.

Wholesalers

Wholesalers take actual physical possession of goods and then market them to retailers, other channel members, or industrial users. They maintain a sales force and provide services such as storage, delivery, credit to the buyer, product servicing, and sales promotion.

> **Wholesalers** are intermediaries who take title to the goods handled and then sell them to retailers or other intermediaries.

Retailers

Retailers sell goods and services directly to ultimate consumers. They may sell through store outlets, by mail order, or by means of home sales. Included in this category are services rendered in the home, such as installing draperies and repairing appliances.

> **Retailers** sell goods or services directly to the ultimate consumers.

Some Services Performed by Retailers

Retailers must essentially determine and satisfy consumer needs. They deal with many customers, each making relatively small purchases. Some major decisions of retailers are what goods and services to offer to customers, what quality of goods and services to provide, whom to buy from and sell to, what type of promotion to use and how much, what price to charge, and what credit policy to follow.

Some Current Trends in Retailing

The more traditional retail outlets are department stores, mass-merchandising shopping chains, specialty stores, discount stores, factory outlets, supermarkets, and mail-order selling.

A newer version of the discount house is **off-price retailers,** such as T. J. Maxx and Hit or Miss. They buy designer labels and well-known brands of clothing at less than wholesale prices and pass the savings along to the customers, using mass-merchandising techniques and providing reduced services.

Another new development is self-service fast-food restaurants. Many of these are now following the gasoline companies' move to cheap, self-help "refueling stops."

Off-price retailers are those who buy designer labels and well-known brands of clothing at low prices and sell them at less than typical retail prices.

One such fast-food operation is The Southland Corporation. At many of its stores, customers can select the food they want, heat it in a microwave oven, pay the cashier, and either eat the food there or carry it with them. This practice permits the customer to save time by shopping for gas, groceries, and other staples, while eating.

Using a "refueling stop"
Photo courtesy of The Southland Corporation.

INTERAC CORPORATION: "YOUR ORDER, PLEASE?"

Interac Corporation, of Woodland Hills, California, has devised a new computer system to aid retailers. The system displays, on a laser disk in short segments, information customers can use to decide which product to purchase. For example, the disks display and explain the texture, color, and quality of 2,500 Monsanto Corporation carpets at J. C. Penney stores in the Chicago area. Also, Interac has just installed jukebox-like CD devices in record shops. Customers can hear three 40-second snippets from a selection of 60 to 120 albums, ranging from country to heavy metal. Customers use a touch screen to view and hear selections and then select the one(s) desired.

Source: Kevin Farrell, "Your Order, Please," *Venture,* January 1986, pp. 58 and 60; and Mimi Bluestone, "Thanks to CDs, Listening Booths Are Making a Comeback," *Business Week,* May 9, 1989, p. 107.

Even supermarkets now use this approach. First came self-service, with the customers selecting their own items, taking them to the checkout counter, and paying the checker-cashier. Now customers in some stores can ring up their own groceries.

For example, Ream's Superstore, of American Fork, Utah, installed four U-Scan terminals along a counter in the front of the store. Customers carry their purchases to the counter, pass them over the scanner, and see the items listed on a monitor screen, along with the subtotal of the bill. The customer goes to a cashier, who has a receipt waiting, and pays for the goods. Almost half of Ream's customers use the U-Scan, for which they get 1 percent off their grocery bill. The store expected to save more than $150,000 in labor costs the first year.[3]

Another innovation is similar to automated teller machines (ATMs), namely, computerized video kiosks in shopping malls that replace salespersons. Many retailers are now installing these devices, which utilize existing technologies, such as computer science, video display, laser disks, voice recognition, and sophisticated graphics (see Using Technology to Succeed).

SELLING WITH YOUR OWN SALES FORCE

Selling expertise is needed in all business activities. While advertising may entice customers to desire a product, it alone is not usually sufficient to complete a sale. Customers appreciate good selling and dislike poor service. They believe salespersons should show an interest in them and assist them in their buying. Often, when competing businesses carry the same merchandise, the caliber of the salespeople is the principal reason why one outsells the other. The following letter, which came from a housewife in the Washington, D.C., area, illustrates this point.

I went to the cosmetic counter at Lord & Taylor, intending to get one or—at the most—two items. Instead, the Estée Lauder area sales rep who was there gave me such an overwhelming sales pitch that I ended up buying a horrifying amount of stuff. In addition, they signed me up for the free workshop next week, where they will make me over to show what I should be wearing. After trying *three* Lauder counters in *three* different stores *with no satisfaction,* it was nice to have someone take *a personal interest in me.*

Need for Personal Selling

In self-service operations, the burden of selling merchandise is placed on the producer's packaging and the retailer's display of the merchandise. Some retailers have found that 80 percent of the shoppers who made unplanned purchases bought products because they saw them effectively displayed. Self-service reduces retail costs by having smaller sales salaries and more effective use of store space. However, risks from pilferage and breakage increase.

Some items are packaged differently for self-service. For example, where film is kept behind the counter, the boxes are stacked in bins; but for self-service, the box has a large extra flap with a hole, permitting it to hang on an arm, which increases its visibility and also cuts down on shoplifting. Similarly, the same pens that stand en masse in a bin display in a small office supplies store are packaged in hanging blister packs in drug, grocery, and variety stores.

A quiet revolution is sweeping department store retailing in an effort to counter such factors as apathy, lack of training, and lack of initiative, which have kept salespeople's productivity (and pay) low. Now many retailers are using straight commission, rather than salary or salary plus commission, to pay their salespeople. They hope that the promise of potentially higher pay will motivate existing staff and attract better salespeople (and encourage them to train and develop themselves to be better producers). It seems to be working, as the following example shows.

John L. Palmerio, a veteran salesman in the men's shoe department at the Manhattan Bloomingdale's store, increased his earnings by 25 percent after switching from a straight hourly scale to a 10 percent commission on sales. Similar experiences are being found at other stores, including the Burdines chain in Florida.[4]

The largest promotional expenditure for small businesses is almost always for personal selling. Effective sales personnel are especially important to small businesses, which have difficulty competing with large ones in such areas as variety, price, and promotion. Personal selling is one activity where small firms, particularly retailers, can compete with larger competitors—and win! But effective selling doesn't just happen. Rather, small business managers must work hard to attain a high level of sales effectiveness. They should therefore be aware of what the selling process involves and of the attributes of effective salespeople.

Figure 11-3 Steps in the Sales Process

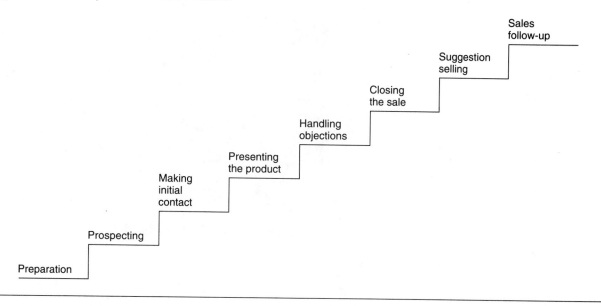

Steps in the Creative Selling Process

The creative selling process, as shown in Figure 11-3, may be divided into eight steps. You should inform your people that these steps are needed for effective selling.

Preparation

Before any customer contact is made, the salesperson should know the company's policies, procedures, and rules; how to operate equipment, such as the cash register; and a great deal about the product, including how and when to use it, its features in comparison with those of other models or brands, and available options (such as color, size, and price).

Prospecting

Prospecting consists of taking the initiative in dealing with new and regular customers by going to them with a new product or service idea. An example of new customer prospecting is when a salesperson contacts a prospective bride or new mother and tells her about goods or services that might be appropriate. Regular customer prospecting is effective because a firm's best prospects are its current customers. A salesperson should periodically call regular customers to tell them about products and services, but not so often that they lose the sense of being *special,* or feel they are being badgered.

Prospecting is taking the initiative in seeking out customers with a new product.

Figure 11-4   Presenting the Product

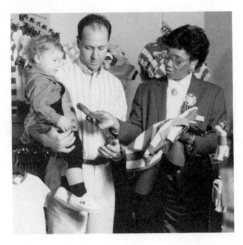

Photo courtesy of William Waldorf.

Making Initial Contact

In the initial contact with a customer, the salesperson should begin on a positive note. The salesclerk might ask, "May I help you?" The customer replies, "No, thank you. I'm just looking." This common, automatic greeting shows no creativity on the part of the clerk. Instead, salespeople should treat each customer as an individual, reacting differently to each one. Initial contact also includes acknowledging customers when they enter the sales area, even if they can't be waited on immediately. For example, you could say, "I'll be with you in a moment." When free, you should be sure to say, "Thank you for waiting." These actions will result in fewer customers leaving without being served and produce a higher sales volume.

Whenever possible, serving customers should be given top priority. Nothing is more annoying to a customer than waiting while a clerk straightens stock, counts money, finishes a discussion with another clerk, or continues a phone conversation.

Presenting the Product

In presenting the product to a customer, you should stress its benefits to the buyer. For example, to a customer interested in the fabric and styling of a suit, you could point out how becoming the color is or that the fabric is especially durable or easy to care for. Get the customer involved in the presentation by demonstrating several features of a garment and then have the customer handle it, as shown in Figure 11-4.

At this stage, you should limit the choices the customer has. For example, you could use the "rule of two" — don't show more than two choices at one time. If more than two items are placed before the customer, the chance of a sale lessens, and the possibility of shoplifting increases. For this reason, many stores limit the number of clothing items that may be taken to a dressing room.

Canned sales presentations are generally ineffective, so you should try to find out how much the customer already knows about the product in order to adapt the presentation to the level of the customer's expertise. A sale can be lost both by boring the customer with known facts and by using bewildering technical jargon.

Handling Objections

Objections are a natural part of the selling process. Thus, if the customer presents objections, you should recognize that as a sign of progress, since a customer who doesn't plan to buy will seldom seek more information in this way. In many cases, an objection opens the way for you to do more selling. For example, if the customer says that a dress looks out of date, you could answer, "Yes, it does look old-fashioned, but that style is back in fashion." This is more diplomatic than a flat contradiction, such as, "That dress was first shown at the market this season. It's the latest thing."

Closing the Sale

Some closing techniques you can use to help the customer make the buying decision are offering a service ("May we deliver it to you this afternoon?"), giving a choice ("Do you want the five-piece or the eight-piece cooking set?"), or offering an incentive ("If you buy now, you get 10 percent off the already low price.").

Suggestion Selling

You should make a definite suggestion for a possible additional sale. Statements such as "Will that be all?" or "Can I get you anything else?" are not positive suggestions. When a customer buys fabric, you should offer matching thread, buttons, and the appropriate interfacing. A supply of bags is a natural suggestion to a vacuum cleaner buyer. And customers' attention should always be drawn to other items in the product line. Many customers like to receive valid suggestions that keep them from having to come back later for needed accessories.

Sales Follow-Up

Follow-up should be a part of every sale. The close, "Thank you for shopping with us," is a form of sales follow-up if said with enthusiasm and sincerity. The customer leaves on a positive note, and the potential for repeat business increases. Follow-up may also consist of checking on anything that was promised the customer after the sale. If delivery is scheduled for a given day or time, you could check to make sure that the promise is met and, if not, notify the customer of the problem.

Attributes of a Creative Salesperson

Many efforts have been made to identify and isolate those personal characteristics that can predict a knack for selling. So far, however, evidence indicates that there is no perfect way to determine who will be successful, for salespeople just do not fit a neat pattern.[5] Still, there are some mental and physical attributes that seem to make some people more effective than others at selling.

Mental Attributes

Judgment—often called common sense, maturity, or intelligence—is essential for effective selling. For example, good salespeople don't argue with customers, nor do they criticize the business in front of customers. Tact is also needed. Good salespeople have a positive attitude toward customers, products, services, and the firm.

Physical Attributes

Personal appearance is important for success. For example, a slim salesperson would be more appropriate than a larger person for a health spa. Poor personal hygiene may lead to lost business. An observant manager should watch out for hygiene problems among the staff and, when necessary, counsel offending employees in private.

ADVERTISING

Advertising informs customers of the availablilty, desirability, and uses of a product.

Advertising informs customers of the availability, desirability, and uses of a product. It also tries to convince customers that the products are superior to those of competitors.

Types of Advertising

Product advertising calls attention to or explains a specific product.

Institutional advertising is selling an idea about the company.

Advertising can be either product or institutional. **Product advertising** is self-explanatory; **institutional advertising** is selling an idea about the company. Most advertising by small firms is a combination of the two. Institutional advertising tries to keep the public conscious of the company and its good reputation while also trying to sell specific products, as the following example illustrates.

Photo courtesy of Wendy's International, Inc.

R. David Thomas, the founder of Wendy's Old Fashioned Hamburgers restaurants, named the business after his daughter, Melinda Lou, nicknamed "Wendy" by her brothers and sisters. In 1989, he began appearing in a series of TV ads built around Wendy. In one ad, he emphasizes quality by saying, "The hamburgers have to be good, or I wouldn't have named the place after my daughter." In another ad, when a voice chides Thomas about his efforts to align a menu board of Wendy's new products, he turns in exasperation and asks, "Wendy, don't you have anything else to do?"

Thomas visits the restaurants and introduces himself with "Hi, I'm Wendy's dad." Market surveys have shown that the consumer identification of Wendy's has jumped about 14 percent, and its nearly 4,000 restaurants increased sales to more than $3 billion in 1992.[6]

Developing the Advertising Program

To be most effective, an advertising program should be used over an extended period of time. The advertising should include preparing customers to accept a new product, suggesting new uses for established products, and calling attention to special sales. Such a program requires four basic decisions: (1) how much money to budget and spend for advertising, (2) what media to use, (3) what to say and how to say it, and (4) what results are expected.

Setting the Budget

Advertising costs should be controlled by an *advertising budget*. The most popular bases for establishing such a budget are (1) a percentage of sales or profits, (2) units of sales, (3) objective (task), and (4) executive decision.

With the *percentage of sales or profits* method, advertising costs have a consistent relationship to the firm's sales volume and/or profit level. Thus, as sales/profits go up/down, advertising expenditures go up/down by the same percentage. One disadvantage of using this method is that advertising may be needed most when sales and profits fall. In the short run, cutting advertising expenses might result in small additions to profit; in the long run, it could lead to a deterioration in net income.

Using the *units of sales method,* the firm sets aside a fixed sum for each unit of product to be sold. It is difficult to use this method when advertising many different kinds of products, for sporadic or irregular markets, and for style merchandise. But, as the following example shows, it is useful for specialty goods and in situations where outside factors limit the amount of product available.

In 1991, with a slump in the ski industry, a weak economy, and much larger rivals hogging market share, Volanti Ski Corporation, of Boulder, Colorado, increased its ad budget to more than $1 million. It set aside nearly $200 per pair to advertise and market 4,800 pairs of stainless steel skis retailing for $425 to $525 each. Calls from interested customers increased to over 4,000 from "a handful" in 1990.[7]

While the *objective (task) method* is most accurate, it is also the most difficult and least used method for estimating an advertising budget. Specific objectives are set, such as "to sell 25 percent more of Product X by attracting the business of teenagers." Then the medium that best reaches this target market is chosen, and estimates are made concerning costs.

With the most popular method of all, the *executive decision method,* the marketing manager decides how much to spend. This method's effectiveness depends on the manager's experience and/or intuition.

Selecting Advertising Media

The most popular advertising media used by small businesses are display ads in newspapers, store signs, direct mail, circulars and handbills, Yellow Pages ads, outdoor signs, radio, and television. Probably the best medium for a small business, though, is word-of-mouth advertising from satisfied customers.

Some Popular Media Used by Small Firms

Display ads in the local newspaper are effective for most retail and service businesses. *Store signs* are useful in announcing sales or special events, and for recruiting personnel. High postage rates are making the use of *direct mail* more expensive. Offset and instant printing have simplified the preparation of small quantities of *circulars* and *handbills;* however, increased printing and distribution

Figure 11–5

"We may not be attractive to boys yet, but we're certainly attractive to advertisers."
Reprinted from *The Wall Street Journal* by permission of Cartoon Features Syndicate

costs and the impact of local ordinances are negative features. *Yellow Pages ads* are effective for special products, services, and repair shops. *Outdoor signs* are useful in announcing the opening or relocation of a business, as shown in the sample business plan in Chapter 8.

Radio advertising is helpful for small businesses in thinly populated areas. *Television* has generally been too costly and wasteful for many small firms to use. Now, however, local cable systems and low-power TV stations, broadcasting only 15 to 25 miles, have rates low enough to permit small firms to use them.[8]

How to Select the Appropriate Medium/Media

The medium (or media) you choose will depend on several factors, including the target market, cost, and availability. The media of choice are those that your *target market* pays most attention to, as Figure 11–5 illustrates.

For example, John Alexander's Los Angeles venture, Dreams Come True, Inc., arranges vacations and other events that thrill jaded globetrotters who've "been everywhere and done everything." As the 1990s recession cut his business by a third, Alexander retargeted his direct mail and promotional activities to people with incomes of over $75,000. His clients dropped from 300 to 100, but the average price of his services increased fivefold, and overall sales and profits increased.[9]

When considering media costs, you must look at both absolute cost and relative cost. *Absolute cost* is the actual expenditure for running an ad. *Relative cost* is the relationship between the actual cost and the number of consumers the message reaches (typically, the cost per 1,000 consumers reached). Finding the lower relative cost should be your objective.

Availability must also be considered, for the local situation will affect the number and kind of media used. Generally, retailers in small communities have fewer options than those in large cities.

Developing the Message

The ideas or information you want to convey should be translated into words and symbols relevant to the target market. To do so, you must decide what is to be said, how it is to be said, what form it will take, and what its style and design will be.

Skilled employees of the chosen medium can help you develop the ads once you have decided on the central idea. Businesses can also get help from an advertising agency or a graphic arts firm.

When and How to Use an Advertising Agency

Most small business managers plan their own ad programs, particularly when they consider the rather high costs of retaining the services of an advertising agency. This practice may be false economy, however, because advertising agencies with experienced specialists can help you by (1) performing preliminary studies and analyses, (2) developing, implementing, and evaluating an advertising plan, and (3) following up on the advertising. Most small agencies tend to specialize in one area. For example, remember from the Profile of Chapter 2 how Try J. Advertising specializes in the automotive field, especially automobile dealerships.

Measuring the Results of Advertising

Immediate-response advertising tries to get customers to buy a product within a short period of time so that response can be easily measured.

Measuring the results of advertising is important. Assume that you want to determine whether your advertising is doing the job it was intended to do. You could do so by using some form of immediate-response advertising. **Immediate-response advertising** attempts to entice potential customers to buy a particular product from the business within a short time, such as a day, weekend, or week. The advertising should then be checked for results shortly after its appearance. Some ways of measuring results of these ads are coupons (especially for food and drug items) brought to the store, letters or phone requests referring to the ads, the amount of sales of a particular item, and checks on store traffic. Comparing sales during an offer period to normal sales, tallying mail and phone orders, and switching offers among different media can help determine which medium was more effective.

MERCHANDISING, SALES PROMOTION, AND PUBLICITY

There are some indications that many businesses are shifting their marketing to other forms of sales promotion.[10] Therefore, merchandising, sales promotion, and publicity are becoming more important in selling a product.

Merchandising

Merchandising is the promotional effort made for a product in retailing firms, especially at the point of purchase. It is the way the product is presented to customers, including items such as window displays, store banners, product label and packaging, and product demonstrations. Window and counter displays are especially effective if they are attractively done and changed frequently. Some manufacturers and wholesalers provide retailers with advice on how to design better store displays and layouts.

Merchandising is promoting the sale of a product at the point of purchase.

Sales Promotion

Sales promotion, or activities that try to make other sales efforts (such as advertising) more effective, includes consumer promotions, trade promotions, and sales force promotions. *Consumer promotions* use coupons, discounts, contests, trading stamps, samples, and so forth. *Trade promotions* include advertising specialties, free goods, buying allowances, merchandise allowances, cooperative advertising, and free items given as premiums. *Sales force promotions* consist of benefits—such as contests, bonuses, extra commissions, and sales rallies—that encourage salespeople to increase their selling effectiveness.

Sales promotion includes marketing activities (other than advertising and personal selling) that stimulate consumer purchasing and dealer effectiveness.

There are many examples of such promotions. Retailers usually promote the opening of their business. A premium (or bonus item) may be given with the purchase of a product. During out-of-season periods, coupons offering a discount may be given to stimulate sales by attracting new customers. Holidays, store remodeling or expansion, store anniversaries, special purchases, fashion shows, or the presence in the store of a celebrity are other events suitable for promotions.

Publicity

Publicity can be considered free advertising. When your product, your business, or you as the owner become newsworthy, publicity may result. Many local newspapers are interested in publicizing the opening of a new store or business in their area. Take the initiative by sending a well-written publicity release to a news editor for possible use. Also, information about a new product or employees who perform various community services may be interesting to the editor.

Publicity is information about a business that is published without charge.

An interesting example of effective public relations is Reed Trencher's rapidly growing New York–based public relations firm, Primetime. He charges clients only if they get favorable coverage. But Trencher reserves the right to turn down clients who do not seem newsworthy.[11]

CONSIDERING ETHNIC DIFFERENCES

There are growing opportunities for small businesses to increase the sales of their product to ethnic groups, for they are growing much faster than traditional markets.

However, ethnic groups may require special attention in promoting your product. Language differences are an obvious example, since more than 10 percent of U.S. families speak a language other than English in their home. Some areas have an even higher percentage. For example, about one out of three households in Miami and San Antonio speaks Spanish. You should be careful, however, not to regard all members of an ethnic group as a single target market. Some minority groups seem to be striving for what they perceive as white middle-income standards in material goods. Others disregard these objectives in favor of their traditional values.

The demographics for ethnic groups may vary, too. The median age of most such groups is much lower than that of whites. And, since more minorities are in the earlier stages of the family life cycle, they constitute a better market for certain goods, especially durable goods. Separate marketing strategies may be needed for these ethnically or racially defined markets.

The second trend is the growing use of advertising on Hispanic TV stations. The two Spanish-language networks, Telemundo Group Inc. and Univision Inc., attract about 5 percent of the total audience during prime-time television viewing. Univision, founded in 1962, reaches about 85 percent of the nation's 6 million Hispanic households. Telemundo, founded in 1986, reaches about 75 percent.[12] Now, companies such as Domino's Pizza have specialized Hispanic media campaigns for selected areas.[13]

WHAT YOU SHOULD HAVE LEARNED

1. Marketing a product begins with deciding how to get it into the users' hands through a distribution channel. A small business essentially has the choice of selling directly to the customer or selling through intermediaries. In making the choice, you should be guided by the nature of the product, traditional practices in the industry, and the size of the business and of its market.

2. The usual intermediaries are brokers, independent agents, wholesalers, and retailers. A broker receives a commission for sales of merchandise without physically handling the goods. Independent agents, such as selling agents and manufacturers' agents (manufacturers' representatives), also represent clients for a commission, but they may do more actual selling than brokers.

Wholesalers take physical possession of the goods they sell and provide storage, delivery, credit to the buyer, product servicing, and sales promotion. Retailers buy goods from manufacturers or wholesalers and sell them to the ultimate consumer. Retailers determine customer needs and satisfy them with choice of location, goods, promotion, prices, and credit policy. The current trends in retailing are toward more self-service and more automation or computerization.

3. Personal selling is required at all levels of the marketing process. All sales personnel should know the steps in the creative selling process, namely, preparation, prospecting, making initial contact, presenting the product, handling objections, closing the sale, suggestion selling, and following up on the sale. A creative salesperson should possess judgment, tact, and a good attitude toward customers, products, services, and the firm.

4. Advertising should be continuous and governed by an advertising budget based on (a) a percentage of sales or profits, (b) a given amount per unit of desired sales, (c) the actual amount required to accomplish the sales objective, or (d) an executive decision. Advertising media include newspapers, store signs, direct mail, circulars and handbills, Yellow Pages ads, outdoor signs, radio, and television. Some factors affecting a company's choice of media are target market, cost, and availability. Using an advertising agency to develop and place advertisements may be desirable. The results of advertising should be measured to determine its effectiveness by some form of immediate-response advertising.

5. Merchandising includes window displays, store banners, product labeling and packaging, samples, and product demonstrations. Sales promotion consists of activities that try to make other sales efforts more effective. Publicity, a form of free advertising, may be achieved when a firm or its owner, products, or employees become newsworthy.

6. Ethnic groups in the United States may require special attention in the promotion of goods and services, but you should not lump all members of an ethnic group together, since many of them are now adopting the values and tastes of middle America and make up a new and distinct ethnic market.

QUESTIONS FOR DISCUSSION

1. What are the traditional channels of distribution for consumer goods? Which one is most frequently used? Why?

2. What are three traditional channels of distribution for industrial goods?

3. What factors should be considered in choosing a channel of distribution?

4. Name two types of independent agents. What are the advantages and disadvantages of using them?

5. Why do small businesses use their own sales force? What are some of the problems involved?

6. Describe the eight steps in the creative selling process.

7. What basic decisions should be made about an advertising program?

8. Distinguish between product and institutional advertising.

9. What are some important functions performed by advertising agencies?

10. What is involved in sales promotion?

11. Describe some opportunities and problems in catering to ethnic differences.

TAKING YOUR STORE TO YOUR CUSTOMERS

There are several channels that producers can use to get their products to the market. Sometimes these distribution channels may be long and complicated, using several intermediaries between the producer and consumer. However, as Sarah Hammet, owner of Feeling Special Fashions, has shown, it does not have to be that complicated.

Hammet sells clothing specially designed for senior citizens. It is called "adaptive" clothing—dresses and separates for seniors whose mobility and dexterity are restricted. Hammet bypasses the usual intermediaries, such as retail stores, and takes her product directly to the customers. She sells clothing at 50 nursing homes and retirement communities in two states and the District of Columbia.

Four days out of the week, every spring and fall, Hammet and an assistant load half a dozen racks of clothes into the back of a van and hit the road. She conducts fashion shows and offers individual consultations at each and every facility they visit. This type of personal selling has been effective for Hammet, who thought up the idea in the early 1980s while visiting her elderly father in a Kentucky nursing home. She was "blown away" by the careless and drab manner in which patients were dressed. Hammet perceived a need and stepped in to fill it.

The clothing she sells is manufactured by Comfort Clothing, Inc., which is located in Canada. The items are stylishly designed and come in various colors and prints. The clothing is different in that armholes are bigger, buttons often hide Velcro® fastenings, and waists are uncinched and come with optional belts. The garments can be stepped into rather than pulled on over the head. They are washable and cost between $40 and $60.

Through a combination of creative merchandising and personal selling, Hammet has established a growing business.

QUESTIONS

1. What type of distribution channels does Feeling Special Fashions use?

2. Should Sarah Hammet consider selling through intermediaries, such as retailers? Discuss the advantages and disadvantages.

3. How would you rate Hammet's selling strategy? Recommend ways she could increase sales.

4. Should Feeling Special Fashions advertise? Discuss the advantages and disadvantages.

5. How do you rate Hammet's chances for success? Why?

12

Other Marketing Activities

Your best customers can sometimes be your best source of information.—John W. Sample, Miller Business Systems

Time and space cannot be discarded, nor can we ignore the fact that we are citizens of the world.—Heywood Broun, author

LEARNING OBJECTIVES

After studying the material in this chapter, you will be able to:
1. Describe the opportunities available to small businesses in international operations.
2. Discuss the need for marketing research in small businesses and describe how to do it.
3. Explain how physical distribution affects marketing strategy.
4. Discuss some of the problems involved in granting credit.

CLARK COPY INTERNATIONAL CORPORATION'S CHINA EXPERIENCE

Otto Clark and representatives of the Chinese government celebrate the signing of the historic contract (April 1982). Left to right: Li Baofeng, Otto Clark, and David Yao.
Photo courtesy of D. C. Heath and Company.

In the early 1980s, China's powerful State Economic Commission launched a major effort to attract small Western enterprises. It was dissatisfied with large firms—especially Japanese ones—that sell expensive consumer items such as VCRs that do little to advance China's backward economy.

This policy helped Clark Copy International Corporation, a small company making plain-paper copiers in a cramped plant in Melrose Park, Illinois, beat out the industry's world leaders to sign a lucrative contract with China. At that time, it had only 14 employees and had earned only $58,000 on $1.5 million of sales for 1982. Clark agreed to sell 1,000 CMC 2000 copiers assembled and ready to use, as well as provide parts and instructions for the Chinese to assemble into another 5,000 machines. Also, Clark would train 1,600 Chinese technicians to manufacture the copiers and other Clark products for domestic and export sales in a new plant in Kweilin in the south of China. Clark—which was to be a full partner with the Chinese—would help lay out and set up the plant.

How did Clark do it? According to Clark's founder and president, Otto A. Clark, a Slovak who emigrated to the United States in 1950, "You can't do business in China on a simple buy-and-sell basis, like most multinationals do. Instead, you have to establish a close human relationship and a commitment to stay." That relationship was established with the help of David Yao, Clark's Far East representative, who was born in Shanghai and speaks fluent Chinese. Yao and Clark went to China eight times to negotiate before closing with China's National Bureau of Instrumentation Industries in April 1982.

In the mid- to late 1980s, the Chinese attitude toward private enterprise and foreign investments changed and Clark wasn't permitted to complete the agreement. By 1991, it was out of business.

Source: Correspondence with Clark Copy International; the Melrose Park, Illinois, Chamber of Commerce; and others, including Michael L. Millenson, ''Ex-Fed Chief's Firm May Buy Clark Copy.'' *Chicago Tribune,* February 9, 1984, p. E13.

The Profile illustrates an area of growing opportunities, and frustrations, for small firms: international operations. That subject, plus marketing research, physical distribution, and credit management round out our presentation of the marketing activities of small businesses.

OPPORTUNITIES FOR SMALL FIRMS IN INTERNATIONAL OPERATIONS

As the opening quote by Heywood Broun indicates, "we are citizens of the world," whether as individuals or as small business owners. Think of the foreign products you use every day. Do you drive an Audi, Honda, Hyundai, Jaguar, Saab, Nissan, or Mazda? If so, you're involved in international operations. Look around you and see how many products originated outside the United States. Your coffee, tea, or cola drink? What type of music system do you use? Where was your television set or VCR produced? Look at the remote control to your electronic system and see if it was "Assembled in Mexico." If you own a personal computer, chances are good that some of its components were designed, manufactured, or assembled in Japan, South Korea, or Taiwan.

Do you get the point? As students, teachers, consumers, and small business people, we're surrounded by the overwhelming evidence of international operations. In fact, we estimate that *over half of you will work in some aspect of international activities during your working life*.

Importing involves purchasing and marketing other nations' products.

Exporting involves marketing our products to other nations.

International marketing has two faces. One is **importing,** which is purchasing and marketing the products of other nations. The other, **exporting,** consists of marketing our products to other nations. We now explore both these facets.

Importing by Small Firms

There are essentially two types of small business importers. First, there are those who engage in actual import activities by importing products and selling them to intermediaries or directly to customers. Second—and much more prevalent—are the millions of small retailers and service businesses that sell international products. Both types are interested in imports for a number of reasons.

Reasons for Importing

First, imported goods may be the product the company sells to customers or the raw material for the goods it produces. The small company must decide whether to purchase U.S. products—if available—or to import foreign products. If the items are imported, does the company purchase them from a U.S. wholesaler or from firms outside the country?

On the other hand, companies from other countries are just as interested in selling to U.S. markets as our producers are in selling to international markets. Thus, imported goods may form the main source of revenue—or competition—for a small business in all stages of buying, producing, and/or selling a product.

Photo courtesy of William Waldorf.

Small business owners capitalize on the fact that some Americans have a preference for foreign goods or services. Goods such as English china, Japanese sports cars, Italian leather goods, Oriental carpets, Russian caviar, and French crystal are eagerly sought by American consumers. Also, small U.S. producers should understand that the increasing flow of new and improved products into the country can improve their output or increase their competitive level.

Some Problems with Importing

The benefits of importing must be weighed against the disadvantages. At present, for example, we see foreign goods flooding U.S. markets at the same time that some of our producers are suffering a lack of customers, or even going out of business. For example, foreign-made automobiles, cameras, stereos, TV sets, VCRs, clothing, shoes, calculators, and home computers are being imported in growing numbers. Although manufactured abroad, these imports provide many opportunities for small firms to sell, distribute, and service them.

While it is probably true that imports generate more jobs than they eliminate, this is small comfort to those small business owners and employees who are adversely affected, as the following example shows.

Kalart Victor Corporation, the last U.S. maker of 16-millimeter movie projectors, called it quits in 1989, a victim of Japanese competition and the popularity of VCRs. Its projectors had been used in school systems and by government bodies around the world. As these groups switched to

VCRs for instructional films, the demand for projectors declined. In 1980, there were five U.S. makers of projectors, with Kalart alone employing 250 people. By 1989, Kalart, the only producer—with fewer than 50 employees—left the market to three Japanese makers.[1]

Exporting by Small Firms

Along with the fascination we have with foreign business, there are many misconceptions concerning it, including the following:

1. *Only large firms can export successfully.* No, small size is no barrier to international marketing. In fact, today's most likely exporters are not the manufacturing giants, but small companies. According to a 1992 survey by Cognetics Inc., 87 percent of the 51,000 exporters it studied employ fewer than 500 workers.[2]

2. *Payment for goods sold to foreign buyers is uncertain.* Not true, as there are fewer credit losses in international sales than there are domestically.

3. *Overseas markets represent only limited sales opportunities.* On the contrary, around 95 percent of the world's population, and two-thirds of its purchasing power, are outside the United States.

4. *Foreign consumers will not buy American products.* Although some goods may not travel or translate well, most American products have a reputation overseas for high quality, style, durability, and many state-of-the-art features. In fact, some products—such as hamburgers, blue jeans, movies, and music albums—are in demand simply because they are American!

5. *Export start-up costs are high.* Not necessarily, since you can begin exporting your products through exporting intermediaries at little real cost to you.

Some Opportunities and Risks

There are many opportunities available for small firms in international operations, but there are also many risks involved, as you can see from Figure 12–1.

In general, the *opportunities* are to expand markets, use excess resources, and increase profits from higher rates of return and possible tax advantages. The *risks* derive from the difficulty of getting earnings out of many countries and the changing political, economic, and cultural conditions. Also, the company can make critical mistakes—such as inadequate research and planning, poor communication, inflexibility, and lack of follow-up—that doom the export efforts.[3] Another major problem is the proliferation of tougher standards in the European Community.[4] If this trend continues, it will freeze many of our exporters out of the European market.

Deciding Whether or Not to Export

If you expect to export, you must be willing to commit the resources necessary to make the effort profitable. Thus, you should make sure that you (1) have a product

---

Figure 12–1   Some Opportunities and Risks in International Operations

---

Opportunities and challenges for small firms:
- Expansion of markets and product diversification
- More effective use of labor force and facilities
- Lower labor costs in most countries
- Availability, and lower cost, of certain desired natural resources
- Potential for higher rates of return on investment
- Tax advantages

Problems and risks:
- Possibility of loss of assets and of earnings due to nationalization, war, terrorism, and other disturbances
- Rapid change in political systems, often by violent overthrow
- Fluctuating foreign exchange rates
- High potential for loss, or difficulty or impossibility of retrieving earnings from investment
- Unfair competition, particularly from state-subsidized firms
- Lower skill levels of workers in underdeveloped countries
- Difficulties in communication and coordination with the home office
- Attitudinal, cultural, and language barriers

Source: Adapted from Leon C. Megginson, Donald C. Mosley, and Paul H. Pietri, Jr., *Management: Concepts and Applications*, 4th ed. (New York: HarperCollins, 1992), Table 19.1, p. 702.

suitable for export, (2) can reliably fill the needs of foreign countries while still satisfying domestic demand, (3) can offer foreign buyers competitive prices and satisfactory credit terms, and (4) are willing to devote the time and skills needed to make export activities a significant part of your business.

Levels of Involvement

There are at least five levels of involvement in exporting, as shown in Figure 12–2. At level 1, you may not even know you're involved in exporting, since the product is sold to an intermediary, who then sells it to foreign buyers. At level 2, you actually make a commitment to seek export business. Level 3 is reached when you make a formal agreement with a foreign country to produce and/or distribute your product there.

For example, Ohio-based Vita-Mix began operating at level 3 in 1991 when it hired an international sales manager. Now, it sells its high-powered blenders to 20 countries, and faxes are pouring in from Norway to Venezuela. Exports accounted for 20 percent of the company's $15 million sales in 1992.[5]

At level 4, you begin to maintain a separate sales office or marketing subsidiary in one or more foreign countries. Finally, you begin to engage in foreign produc-

Figure 12–2   Five Levels of International Operations

Degree of product control	Level		Risk to your company
Great	5	Producing, as well as marketing, your product overseas	Great
	4	Beginning to actually market your product overseas by maintaining an office or subsidiary in a foreign country	
	3	Foreign licensing, involving a formal agreement with a foreign country to produce and/or distribute a product or service	
	2	Becoming actively involved by making a continuing effort to export	
Little	1	Doing some exporting on a casual or accidental basis, usually through an intermediary	Little

Source: Adapted from Leon C. Megginson, Donald C. Mosley, and Paul H. Pietri, Jr., *Management: Concepts and Applications,* 4th ed. (New York: HarperCollins, 1992), p. 707.

tion and marketing at level 5. You can do this by (1) setting up your own production and marketing operations in the foreign country, (2) buying an existing firm to do your business, or (3) forming a joint venture, as discussed in Chapter 4.

Help with Exporting Is Available

In spite of the barriers facing small firms, help with exporting is available from many sources. This help takes two forms: providing information and guidance and providing financial assistance.

Both government and private groups provide practically unlimited information and guidance, including technical expertise. There are 10 different government agencies and some 200 small business development centers, funded by the SBA, that offer export counseling. An SBA pamphlet, *Market Overseas with U.S. Government Help,* provides excellent information on overseas marketing. Other SBA help comes from members of SCORE and ACE, who have many years of practical experience in international trade. Small business institutes also provide export counseling and assistance.

Finally, the U.S. Department of Commerce offers assistance through its International Trade Administration (ITA) and its U.S. and Foreign Commercial Service Agency (USFCSA). The department's computerized market data system has information on 154 nations, and contacts in 67 countries.[6]

For example, a review of the Commerce Department's "best prospects" list turned up some unexpected markets for small firms. It showed that bicycles were needed in sub-Saharan Africa; the United Kingdom needed candles; Cyprus could not get enough hotel furnishings; fast-food franchises were in short supply in Indonesia; and T-shirts illustrating the Heimlich maneuver were in great demand throughout Western Europe.[7]

Small companies needing export-related electronic data processing services can get help from the Commerce Department's Census Bureau.

You can obtain financial assistance for your export program from the Foreign Credit Insurance Association (FCIA) and the Export-Import Bank of the United States (Eximbank). At Eximbank, access to small business programs is determined by size (as defined by the SBA guidelines discussed in Chapter 9). The bank offers small exporters guarantees for short-term working capital loans, backs fixed-rate, medium-term export loans, and offers no-deductible insurance programs. The SBA also offers direct loan programs for small business exporters.[8]

MARKETING RESEARCH

Marketing research is the systematic gathering, recording, and analyzing of data relating to the marketing of goods and services. It is an orderly, objective way of learning about customers or potential customers and their needs and desires. By studying customers' actions and reactions and drawing conclusions from them, you can use marketing research to improve your marketing activities.

> **Marketing research** is the systematic gathering, recording, and analyzing of data relating to the marketing of goods and services.

Marketing research is helpful at several points in the life of your business. Before starting the business, you can use marketing research to find out whether the location and surrounding population are right for your proposed product. After you open the business, marketing research can help you decide (1) whether to develop new or different products, (2) whether to expand at the original location or open additional locations, and (3) when and where to change emphasis on activities such as channels of distribution and advertising and promotion strategy.

How Does Marketing Research Fit into Marketing?

Marketing research is part of a company's overall marketing system. By analyzing marketplace data such as attitudinal, demographic, and lifestyle changes, marketing research can help you plan your strategic efforts. The following are some areas where marketing research is effective:

- Identifying customers for the firm's products.
- Determining their needs.
- Evaluating sales potential for both the firm and its industry.
- Selecting the most appropriate channel of distribution.
- Evaluating advertising and promotional effectiveness.

For example, marketing research techniques are available to correlate data from actual customer purchases, using universal product scanners in supermarkets and drugstores with advertising information. The business owner can see how the amount and type of advertising and sales promotion lead to actual purchases.[9]

How to Do Marketing Research

Marketing research does not have to be fancy or expensive to meet your needs. It deals with people and their constantly changing likes and dislikes, which can be affected by many influences. Marketing research tries to find out how things really are (not how you think they are or should be) and what people really want to buy (not what you want to sell them).

In its simplest form, marketing research involves (1) defining the problem and then (2) gathering and evaluating information. Many small business managers unknowingly do some form of marketing research nearly every day. For example, they check returned items to see if there is some pattern. They ask old customers on the street why they have not been in recently. They look at competitors' ads to find out what the competition is selling, and at what prices.

For example, at a university small business seminar, the owner of a wholesaling firm that sold farm equipment and supplies stated that market research was not relevant in a small business. Later, he told the participants that he visited dealers to learn their needs for shovels and other items before ordering these items for his stock. Without realizing it, he was doing marketing research.

Defining the Problem

Proper identification of the problem, so obvious but often overlooked, is the most important step in the process, since the right answer to the wrong question is useless. Thus, you should look beyond the *symptoms* of a problem to get at the *real cause*. For example, a sales decline is not a *cause* but rather a *symptom* of a marketing problem. In defining the problem, you should look at influences that may have caused it, such as changes in customers' home areas or in their tastes.

Gathering and Evaluating Information

Marketing research can use existing data or generate new information through research. So you must make a subjective judgment and weigh the cost of gathering more information against its usefulness. The cost of making a wrong decision should be balanced against the cost of gathering more data to make a better-informed decision, as shown in Using Technology to Succeed.

━━━━━━━━━━━━━━━━━━━━━━ USING TECHNOLOGY TO SUCCEED ━━━━━━━━━━━━━━━━━

MARKETING RESEARCH VIA TELEVISION

TV won't be just TV much longer! In 1994, the "boob tube" stands ready to be transformed into a multimedia, interactive communications device. TVs, computers, and telephones have been integrated into systems that will revolutionize the way businesses obtain information.

Businesses that decide to invest in this type of technology will have instant access to virtually unlimited amounts and types of data. An incomprehensible amount of market research information will lie at the fingertips of the organizations that purchase this equipment.

Batten down the hatches—it's time for the rocket ride to the next level of the information age.

Source: Kevin Maney, "TVs and PCs to Become Media Centers," *USA Today,* November 19, 1992, p. 1B.

Using Existing Information.   You should "think cheap" and stay as close to home as possible when doing marketing research. Looking at your records and files, such as sales records, complaints, and receipts, can show you where customers live or work or how and what they buy, as the following example illustrates.

The owner of a fabric shop used addresses on checks and cash receipts to pinpoint where her customers lived. She then cross-referenced the addresses with products purchased, which permitted her to check the effectiveness of advertising and sales promotion activities.

Credit records can also yield valuable information about your market, since customers' jobs, income levels, and marital status can be gleaned from them. Employees are a good source of information about customer likes and dislikes, because they hear customers' gripes about the firm's product(s) as well as about its competitors. They are also aware of the items customers request that are not stocked. Outside sources of information include publications such as *Survey of Current Business* and *Statistical Abstract of the United States,* trade association reports, chamber of commerce studies, university research publications, trade journals, newspapers, and marketing journals.

Doing Primary Research.   Primary research can range from simply asking customers or suppliers how they feel about your business to more complex studies such as direct-mail questionnaires, telephone or "on the street" surveys, and test marketing. **Test marketing** simulates the conditions under which a product will eventually be sold. However, even a small market test is costly.

Primary research, which includes studies such as surveys, interviews, and questionnaires, should usually be left to experts. You might use this type of research,

Test marketing simulates the conditions under which a product is to be marketed.

but take care to ask the right questions and obtain unbiased answers. Another type of research involves observing the results of a given action. Sometimes, research methods can be unique, as the following example shows.

During a three-day promotion, a discount merchandiser gave its customers, free of charge, all the roasted peanuts they could eat while shopping in the store. The merchant encouraged customers to "let the hulls fall where they may" and soon had "litter trails" that provided information on the traffic pattern within the store. Trampled peanut hulls littered the most heavily traveled store aisles and were heaped up in front of merchandise displays of special interest to customers. Thus, the merchant learned how customers acted in the store and what they wanted.

Using Specialized Research Techniques.   Other techniques include license plate analysis, telephone number analysis, coded coupons, and "tell them Joe sent you" broadcast ads, not to mention just plain people-watching.

In many states, license plates give information about where a car's owner lives— what city or county, for instance. By recording the origin of cars parked at the firm's location, the trade area can be estimated. Similarly, telephone numbers and ZIP codes can tell where people live. This type of data can be found on sales slips, prospect cards, and contest blanks, as well as on personalized checks used for payment.

Coded coupons and "tell them Joe sent you" broadcast ads can be effective, too. The relative effectiveness of your advertising media can be checked by coding coupons and by including in broadcast ads some phrase customers must use to get a discount on a given sale item. If neighborhood newspapers are involved, you can also get some idea of the area from which customers are drawn. Where they read or heard about the discount offered in the ads may also give information about their tastes.

Using Computerized Databases

A wide variety of information is available at public libraries; many such institutions also offer, for a fee, access to computerized databases, such as Standard & Poor's Daily News and Cumulative News (Corporation Records). By gathering data on selected kinds of companies (such as electronics firms producing home videocassettes) or specific geographic areas (such as firms moving into a particular state or city), you can learn about companies that are expanding operations. Such information may be valuable to small retailers, service businesses, wholesalers, and manufacturers in selecting their target market and marketing strategy.

DISTRIBUTION

Distribution involves the effective physical movement of a product from the production line to the final consumer.

Because of its many cost-saving potentials, distribution should be quite important to you. **Distribution** includes the whole range of activities concerned with the effective movement of a product from the production line into the hands of the final customer. To perform the activity effectively, you must make decisions in such important areas as protective packaging, materials handling, inventory control, transportation (internally and externally), order processing, and various aspects of customer service. Because of space limitations, we'll discuss only storing, order processing, and transportation.

Storing

Until sold or used, goods must be stored by manufacturers, wholesalers, and retailers. While some small manufacturers and wholesalers have their own warehouses, more of them use public warehouses, independently owned facilities that often specialize in handling certain products, such as furniture or refrigerated products. Public warehouses are particularly useful to small firms wanting to place goods close to customers for quick delivery, since the firms then avoid investing in new facilities.

Order Processing

Effective order processing improves customer satisfaction by reducing slow shipment and incorrectly or incompletely filled orders. It begins the moment a customer places an order with a salesperson. The order goes to the office, often on a standardized order form. After the order is filled, the goods are sent to the customer.

Transportation

Transportation involves the physical movement of a product from the seller to the purchaser. Since transportation costs are the largest item in distribution, there are many opportunities for savings and improved efficiency. The two most important aspects are choosing the transportation mode to be used and understanding delivery terms. **Transportation modes** are the methods used to take products from one place to another. A small producer has many choices of ways to move goods to and from its plant and/or warehouse, and each mode has advantages and disadvantages. Which mode you choose to use will depend on speed, frequency, dependability, points served, capability (which includes capacity, flexibility, and adaptability to handle the product), and cost. The use of containers can also affect the transportation system used. The various modes can be evaluated as to their effectiveness on each of these variables.

Transportation modes are the methods used to transfer products from place to place.

Railroads, trucks, oil pipelines, and waterways are the most popular means of transporting bulky and heavy materials. Although the modes of transportation are changing, these still tend to be the primary systems used by small producers.

As you can see from Figure 12–3, railroads are still important movers of goods. Their primary advantage is the capacity to carry large volumes of goods, fairly quickly, at a low cost. The main disadvantage is that they operate only on fixed routes, often on fixed schedules.

Figure 12–3　Share of Freight Carried by Each Transportation Mode

Percentage of tons carried per mile

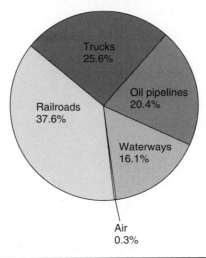

Source: Railroad Facts, as reported in *USA Today*, June 25, 1992, p. 3A.

Trucks are playing an increasing part in shipping because of their flexibility and improved highway systems. However, changing traffic and government rules and regulations also affect their use, as the following example shows.

A Nebraska feed-and-seed store owner spent much time, money, and effort to get the city to rescind a recent ordinance prohibiting tractor-trailers from unloading in front of his store. The extra cost of unloading on the edge of town and transporting sacks of feed and seed to the store would have forced him out of business.

While these modes of transportation are important, the use of air transport is increasing, particularly for items and information that must be delivered in a hurry, as well as for products with a high unit value and low weight and bulk. In such cases, a site near an airport should be considered if the costs are not too high.

Many companies are using a combination of trucks and air to expedite service. For example, Gateway 2000 and many other mail-order computer vendors use Federal Express. UPS is also used by many small businesses.

CREDIT MANAGEMENT

Credit management involves setting and administering credit policies and practices.

Credit management involves (1) deciding how customers will pay for purchases, (2) setting credit policies and practices, and (3) administering credit operations.

The objectives of each of these activities are to increase profits, increase customer stability, and protect the firm's investment in accounts receivable, which is often the largest single asset on the firm's balance sheet.

Methods of Payment

Customers can pay for purchases in a number of ways, and you must decide early in the life of your business which method(s) to accept. Payment methods include cash, checks, and various kinds of credit.

Cash

Given a choice, every business owner would probably prefer to make all sales for cash. Recordkeeping would be easier, and there would be no bad debts. But it is unrealistic to expect buyers to carry cash for every purchase, especially large ones.

Checks

Because accepting checks for payment increases sales, most small business owners think the risks involved are worth it. With proper verification procedures, bad-debt losses can be minimized. Checks can be treated the same as cash in recordkeeping, and they're actually safer to have on hand than cash and easier to deal with in making bank deposits.

Credit

To stimulate sales, various forms of credit may be used, including installment payment plans and credit cards, or a business's own credit plan. Granting your own credit allows you to choose your own customers and avoid fees to credit card issuers. Customer accounts can be paid off every month or can be *revolving charge accounts* such as those used by large department stores. For major purchases, you may give the buyer more time to pay before interest is charged or the account is turned over to a finance company. To extend credit even longer, you may offer an *installment payment plan* that gives the buyer up to a year or more to pay for the purchase. Buyers make a down payment, make regular weekly or monthly payments, and pay interest charges on the unpaid balance.

Whenever you extend credit, though, recordkeeping becomes more complex. Small firms can use manual or computer methods to maintain their charge accounts internally, or they can turn the accounts over to a service firm for handling. Either way, there are costs for billing and collections, as well as bad-debt losses.

Some of these responsibilities and costs can be avoided by accepting bank or corporate *credit cards,* also called *plastic money.* Today's consumers have come to expect most firms of any size to accept the major cards, such as Visa, American Express, Discover, MasterCard, and now GE, GM, and AT&T. This may be especially necessary in resort areas or other places where customers are less likely to have large amounts of cash, local checking accounts, or a store charge account.

Although merchants pay a fee to join and a fee on sales, many find it worth the expense; provided they follow required authorization procedures, sellers are guaranteed payment, largely eliminating bad-debt losses. And authorization, once so cumbersome, is now almost universally automated through the use of readers that scan the card's magnetic strip, dial the number of a database, get authorization for the charge, and record the sale, all in just a few seconds. These readers are often tied into cash registers or other machines that print a receipt that gives not only the date and amount charged but also the cardholder's name and the merchant's name and address.

Setting Credit Policies

While your credit department can contribute to increased sales and profit, several factors should be considered in formulating a credit policy; some are beyond your control. Any credit policy should be flexible enough to accommodate these internal and external factors.

Some credit policies you can use are (1) liberal extension of credit with a liberal collection policy, (2) liberal extension of credit with a strictly enforced collection policy, and (3) strict extension of credit with a collection policy adjusted to individual circumstances. Generally speaking, being liberal in extending credit or in collecting bad debts tends to stimulate sales but increase collection costs and bad-debt losses. Strict policies have the reverse effect. Whatever policy is chosen, you should extend a businesslike attitude toward credit customers.

Carrying Out Credit Policies

The person managing credit for you should have ready access to the accounts receivable records and be free from interruptions and confusion. Several tools this person can use in performing the function include the accounts receivable ledger or computer printout, invoices and other billing documents, credit files, account lists, credit manuals, reference material, and various automated aids.

Classifying Credit Risks

You should begin by classifying present and potential customers according to credit risk: good, fair, or weak. These risks can be determined from information in the customer's file, trade reports, financial reports, and previous credit experience.

Good credit risks may be placed on a preferred list for automatic approval within certain dollar limits. Periodic review of these accounts usually suffices. Fair credit risks will require close checking, particularly on large amounts or in case of slow payment. While weak credit risks may be acceptable, they should be closely watched. You can face many problems when you get involved in unwise extension of credit, as the following example illustrates.

Mr. and Mrs. Neely* invested almost $6,000 of their savings in a venture. They paid $4,000 cash for equipment and set aside the balance to use as working capital.

Sales increased during each of their first 13 months, and all bills were paid. Much capital, however, was tied up in uncollectible accounts receivable. Mr. Neely, who was soft-hearted, said, "I really don't want to offer credit to anyone, but how can I say that to customers without losing their business?"

After they stopped giving credit altogether, their gross profits dropped by almost one-half. They were so discouraged that they sold the business.

Investigating Customers' Creditworthiness

A major cause of bad-debt losses is making credit decisions without adequate investigation. Yet prompt delivery of orders is also important. Thus, your credit-checking method should be geared to need and efficiency to improve the sales and delivery of your product. For new accounts, a complete credit application may be desired. Direct credit inquiry can be effective in obtaining the name of the customer's bank and trade references. Many suppliers and banks cooperate in exchanging credit information, but they should be assured that the information obtained will be treated confidentially. Outside sources of valuable credit information include local credit bureaus, which are linked together nationally through Associated Credit Bureaus, Inc., and others who provide guidelines and mechanisms for obtaining credit information for almost any area in the United States.

Establishing Collection Procedures

The collection of unpaid accounts is an important part of credit management. The collection effort should include systematic and regular follow-up, which is vital to establish credibility with the customer concerning credit terms. The follow-up should be timely, which is now feasible since most businesses have computer capacity to show the age of a bill. For example, a statement sent to a customer may indicate that payment was due on a certain date, but that the bill is, say, 30, 60, or 90 days past due.

When an account is past due, prompt contact with the customer, made tactfully and courteously, generally produces results. If this doesn't work, holding customers' orders can be quite effective. But you should respond rapidly when the customer clears the account so that unnecessary delays in shipping are avoided.

*Name disguised at owner's request.

WHAT YOU SHOULD HAVE LEARNED

1. The opportunities in international marketing are growing rapidly. In fact, all of us—students, teachers, consumers, and large and small businesses—are already involved. Millions of small businesses are importing and selling foreign products. While these imports provide many opportunities for some small firms, they may force some others out of business.

   Benefits of exporting are *(a)* expansion of markets, *(b)* more effective use of resources, particularly personnel, *(c)* potentially higher rates of return on investment, and *(d)* tax advantages. Some problems are *(a)* the difficulty of getting earnings out of the host country, *(b)* unfair competition from state-subsidized firms, *(c)* favorable treatment given to local firms and products, and *(d)* rapidly changing political climates.

   Small firms can become involved in international marketing at one of five levels, namely, *(a)* casual, or accidental, exporting; *(b)* active exporting; *(c)* foreign licensing; *(d)* overseas marketing; and *(e)* foreign production and marketing.

   Considerable help is available to exporters from the SBA, the U.S. Department of Commerce, chambers of commerce and trade associations, the Export-Import Bank, and the Foreign Credit Insurance Association.

2. While relatively few small firms do marketing research, more of them should, because it increases the chance of success and reduces chances of failure. Marketing research does not have to be fancy or expensive. In its simplest form, such research involves defining the problem and gathering and evaluating information. Many small business owners already do market research by checking returned items to see if there is a pattern, correlating consumer addresses with their purchases and payment records, checking to see what types of ads get the best results, and asking customers for suggestions for improving operations. There are many computerized databases for small firms that want to do more formal research.

3. Distribution, which is moving the product from the seller to the buyer, includes the vital functions of storing, order processing, and transporting the product.

4. Credit management includes deciding on customer payment methods, establishing credit policies, and administering credit operations. A credit policy should be flexible and help increase revenues and profits. Customers should be classified according to their creditworthiness—that is, good, fair, or weak. Credit investigations should be conducted, and the collection of outstanding receivables should be systematic and include regular follow-up. The overall results of the credit functions and collection efficiency should be evaluated to see that they are achieving their objectives.

QUESTIONS FOR DISCUSSION

1. Do you believe international marketing is as important as stated? Explain.

2. Do you really believe the statement that over half of you will work in some aspect of international activities in your working life? Explain.

3. What are some reasons for importing? What are some problems?

4. How involved are you, as an individual or a small businessperson, in importing?

5. Name and defend *or* refute the five myths about exporting.

6. List the opportunities available in exporting.

7. Describe some of the risks and problems involved in exporting.

8. Explain the five levels of involvement in exporting.

9. Why should small firms do marketing research?

10. How does a small firm go about doing marketing research?

11. What is the role of distribution in marketing? Describe three components of distribution discussed in this chapter.

12. What is credit management, and why is it so important to small business? Why is the acceptance of credit cards by small businesses increasing?

TO OPEN OR NOT TO OPEN?

The following is an actual example of market research done by a prospective restaurant owner who wanted to determine the feasibility of opening a restaurant in a given location.

First, the prospective owner talked to people who worked near the proposed site to see if they would be interested in eating in his restaurant. Then he surveyed the residents in the area to determine their menu preferences, any dissatisfaction with existing restaurants, and the likelihood of their eating at his prospective restaurant.

After that, he had data gathered about competing restaurants and their menus. Then he made a count of customer traffic flow at the competitors' locations, used a Department of Transportation traffic survey, and studied census data concerning demographics at the proposed site.

On the basis of the results of these efforts, he modified the marketing and financial information on his business plan. Later, this information was used in advertising and media planning after the restaurant opened.

QUESTIONS

1. Evaluate the way the prospective owner did his marketing research.
2. What improvements would you suggest?
3. Is this type of research a valid way of gathering information to use in advertising? Explain.

IV

ORGANIZING AND MANAGING THE BUSINESS

Many management texts begin with a statement such as "Management is getting things done through people." And the annual reports of most companies include statements such as "Our people are our most important asset." Both of these statements are correct: whether the business is large or small, its success or failure depends on having a capable, well-trained, and motivated work force.

In essence, all owners of small businesses are personnel managers. They must decide what work is to be done, determine the type and number of employees needed to do it, recruit those employees, train and develop them, reward them with adequate pay and benefits, and lead and motivate them to perform effectively. How well—or poorly— owners handle this important activity determines the success or failure of their businesses.

Chapter 13 looks at the overall problem of managing human resources in small firms and covers such topics as planning personnel needs, recruiting employees, selecting the right people for the jobs, training and developing them, and complying with equal employment opportunity laws.

In Chapter 14, we discuss leading and rewarding employees and examine the need for good human relations in small businesses. Exercising managerial leadership, communicating with and motivating employees, appraising employees' performance, and compensating them with income and benefits are discussed.

Chapter 15 deals with maintaining relationships with employees. It covers topics such as setting up organizational relationships, protecting employee safety, environmental protection, counseling disturbed employees, handling employee grievances, exercising discipline, and dealing with unions.

13

Managing Human Resources in Small Firms

Small businesses must make wooing and keeping employees as high a priority as attracting and retaining customers. — John L. Ward, Loyola University of Chicago

Good ideas and good products are "a dime a dozen" but good execution and good management — in a word, good people — are rare. — Arthur Rock, venture capitalist

LEARNING OBJECTIVES

After studying the material in this chapter, you will be able to:

1. Explain how small business managers plan personnel needs and develop sources from which to recruit personnel.

2. Name some methods used for recruiting personnel, and describe the steps in the employee selection process.

3. Explain the importance of personnel development, and discuss some development methods.

4. Tell how selection of managers differs from selection of nonmanagerial personnel, and describe some methods of manager development.

5. Discuss the laws that affect personnel recruiting, selection, and development.

COMPU–SCREEN SYSTEMS, INC.: PROVIDING EFFECTIVE PREEMPLOYMENT SCREENING

John B. "Jack" Rucker, left, and George E. "Buddy" Hunter of Compu–Screen Systems, Inc.

With employers losing millions of dollars each year through employee problems such as theft and substance abuse, many are looking for efficient ways to identify potential problem workers. Compu-Screen Systems, Inc., founded by George E. Hunter and John B. Rucker, Jr., two former FBI agents, has developed an effective tool for screening potential employees and finding the ones most likely to rip off the company.

Small employers—as well as large ones—throughout the United States are experiencing unprecedented challenges in employee selection and screening due to various equal employment opportunity laws, especially the Civil Rights Act of 1991 and the Americans With Disabilities Act. If their businesses are to succeed, employers must thoroughly screen applicants and hire the most qualified workers, while complying with laws that often contain undefined and unexplained language that provides little or no guidance.

What can be done to ensure that one's screening methods are accurate, thorough, uniform, easy to administer, not offensive to applicants, not an unnecessary legal risk, and not an honesty or integrity test? Compu-Screen Systems provides "The First Interview," a tape-recorded, timed, preemployment interview that provides the employer with background information that is furnished by the applicant. There is a "Comparison Level" that will alert the employer if the applicant completed the interview in an unrealistic or invalid manner.

The simplicity of administration of "The First Interview" allows those responsible for hiring to interview an applicant within approximately 25 minutes. It has been developed to avoid the legal risks associated with preemployment testing, particularly, preemployment integrity tests. The Civil Rights Act of 1991 makes it easier for individuals to successfully challenge the legality of preemployment integrity tests, resulting in substantial liabilities for employers who use such tests. Preemployment integrity tests have been widely criticized as poor predictors of workplace behavior. As a result, "The First Interview" was developed to provide employers assistance in screening applicants without running the legal risk associated with preemployment tests.

Source: Conversations with officials of Compu-Screen Systems, Inc.; published literature, including Adline Clarke, "Screening Tool for Job Applicants Divised," *Mobile* (Alabama) *Press Register,* March 22, 1987, p. 1-D.

The Profile emphasizes the importance of careful employee selection. You must have a sufficient supply of human resources if you are to succeed. In the late 1800s, a young entrepreneur, Andrew Carnegie, expressed this thought when he said, "Take away all our factories, our trade, our avenues of transportation, and our money, but leave our organization, and in four years, I will have reestablished myself." In other words, while physical and financial resources are *important* to you, human resources are *vital*. This need was emphasized in a recent SBA report, which concluded that if small firms are to succeed, they must "boost wages, increase benefits, hire marginal workers, and invest in labor-saving technology."[1]

Thus, being able to identify and hire good employees can mean the difference between having a successful and an unsuccessful business. This process involves (1) planning for, (2) recruiting, (3) selecting, and (4) training and developing employees, all of which are discussed in this chapter.

PLANNING FOR PERSONNEL NEEDS

You can't wait until you need a new employee to think about your personnel needs. Like larger competitors, small businesses must (1) determine personnel needs and (2) develop sources from which to recruit personnel.

Small businesses find it difficult to carry out these activities, since many are facing absolute labor shortages because of the declining work force. The number of Americans aged 16 to 24 is expected to decrease by more than 7 percent by the year 2000. Because small businesses employ two-thirds of these entry-level workers, they are the first to feel the shortage.

To meet this declining supply of potential employees, many small businesses are changing the way they operate. They are spending more and using new methods to attract more applicants, making their workplaces more attractive, and using employee benefits and other incentives to retain valued employees. Finally, small companies are also stepping up automation and even subcontracting out part of their work to reduce the number of employees needed.[2]

Determining Types of Employees Needed

Job specifications are detailed written statements of work assignments and the qualifications needed to do the job acceptably.

A job description lists the duties and responsibilities of a given job.

When business owners want to construct a building, they obtain a set of blueprints and specifications. When they buy merchandise, materials, and supplies, they develop specifications for those items. In the same way, even the smallest businesses should have **job specifications,** which are statements of the mental, physical, and other qualifications required of a person to do the job. Drawing up job specifications begins with a **job description,** which is a list of the job's duties, responsibilities, and working conditions, as well as relationships between it and other jobs in the organization (see Figure 13–1). When the personal qualities,

Figure 13–1   Sample Job Description

Job Title: Office and credit manager
Supervisor: Store manager
Number of Subordinates: Two

JOB SUMMARY

Responsible for all of the store's office and credit functions, as well as control of the store's assets and expenditures. Helps manager administer store's policies and methods by exercising mature judgment and initiative in carrying out related duties and responsibilities.

Duties	Approximate percentage of work time spent on each duty
1. Prepares bank deposits, listing checks and cash, and takes deposit to bank (daily).	5%
2. Inspects sales tickets for accuracy and completeness of price, stock classification, and delivery information (daily).	5
3. Keeps sales and expenses record sheets, posting sales and expenses and accumulating them for the month.	15
4. Processes credit applications: analyzes financial status and paying record of customers, checks references and credit bureau to determine credit responsibility (daily).	10
5. Sends collection notices to past-due accounts, using mail, telephone calls, and personal visits (if necessary) to collect (daily).	10
6. Checks invoices of outside purchases to verify receipt, quantity, price, etc. Gets store manager's approval (weekly).	5
7. Maintains inventories and their records.	10
8. Does all bookkeeping and prepares periodic financial statements.	20
9. Helps out on sales floor and in other areas when needed.	15
10. Miscellaneous duties.	5

Source: Personnel Management: Administrative Management Course Program, Topic 6 (Washington, D.C.: Small Business Administration, 1965), p. 56, updated.

"Welcome aboard. You're just what we're looking for. Not too bright, no ambition, and content to stay on the bottom of the ladder and not louse things up!"

Source: *Savant*, February/March 1988. Cartoon courtesy of J. Nebesky.

education, training, and experience needed to perform the job are added, the result is a set of job specifications that forms the basis for recruiting and selecting new employees.

Just a word of caution: Job descriptions should be flexible in very small firms to give the owner more freedom in assigning work to available employees, whether the work fits their job description or not.

Don't ask for more than is needed to do the job properly! Ask yourself, "Is a college education really needed, or can a high school graduate do the job?" Or again, "Are three years' experience required, or can an inexperienced person be trained to do the work?" If an inexperienced person can be trained, is there someone to do the training? Increasing education and experience levels raises the starting pay expected, and you may actually be better-off training someone to do things your own way.

Developing Sources of Personnel

As with purchasing supplies for building and running the business, you need sources from which to seek new workers. Some of these sources are shown in Figure 13–2. Not all of them will be appropriate for all small businesses.

Internal Sources

Filling job openings with present employees rather than going outside the business makes good sense. This method raises morale and improves employees' motivation, since they know they can move up in your firm. It also saves time, effort, and money, since outside recruiting is time-consuming and costly.

Figure 13-2 Where to Find Needed Employees

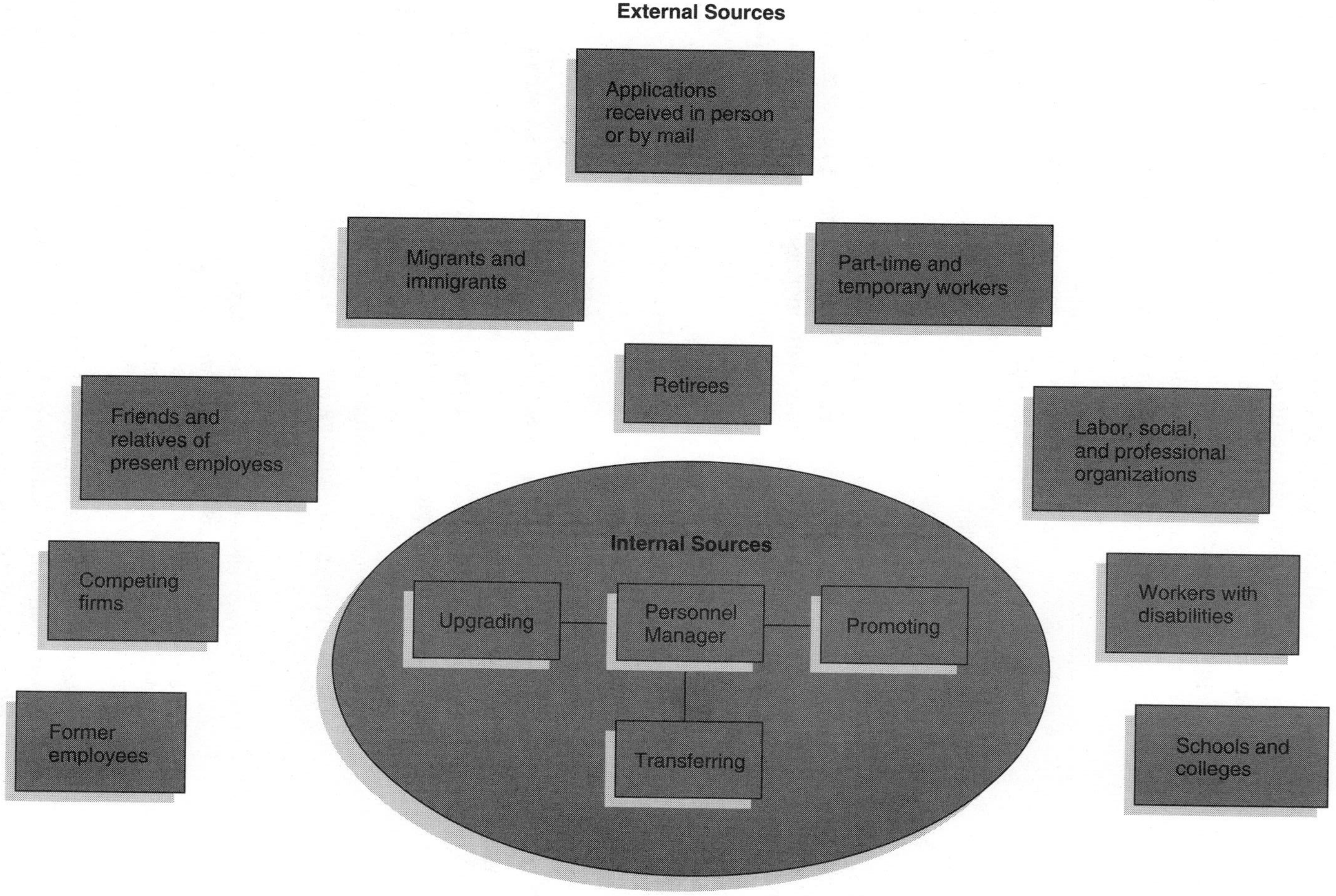

External Sources

Applications received in person or by mail

Part-time and temporary workers

Labor, social, and professional organizations

Workers with disabilities

Schools and colleges

Retirees

Migrants and immigrants

Internal Sources

Promoting

Personnel Manager

Transferring

Upgrading

Friends and relatives of present employees

Competing firms

Former employees

Source: Adapted from Leon C. Megginson, Lyle R. Trueblood, and Gayle M. Ross, *Business* (Lexington, Mass.: D. C. Heath, 1985), p. 239.

Filling jobs from within is also effective because the worker's performance has been observed and evaluated over a period of time. Futher, this method leads to stability. Employees can be upgraded, transferred, or promoted to fill job openings.

Upgrading occurs when an employee who is presently not capable of doing a job that has become more difficult receives training to enable him or her to do the work successfully, as the following example illustrates.

Upgrading involves retraining workers so they can do increasingly complex work.

A small service organization replaced its typewriter with a word processor. The present typist, age 52, had been with the firm for 20 years but didn't know how to use a word processor. Instead of hiring a new operator, management sent the typist to a training program. She mastered word processing in a short time and was soon back at the company using her new skills.

Transferring is moving an employee from one job to another, without necessarily changing title or pay.

Promoting is moving an employee to a higher position, usually with increased responsibilities, title, and pay.

Transferring is moving an employee from one location or department to another, without necessarily changing job title or pay. **Promoting** is moving a person to a higher position, frequently with increased responsibilities, greater status or prestige, a new title, and a higher salary. If the company is family owned, the owners' children can be ''promoted'' as they become capable of assuming more responsibility. The benefits and complications of hiring family members as employees will be covered in detail in Chapter 24.

External Sources

You may need to use external sources as the business grows, especially to fill lower-level jobs. External sources may also be used to provide new ideas and perspectives and to obtain needed skills when necessary, especially for scientific, technical, and professional positions.

Many small firms keep a list of *former employees* as a potential source of trained workers. If a worker left voluntarily and for good reason, is in good standing, and seeks reemployment, rehiring may be a good idea.

Diane Allen worked for Bell Stained Glass and Overlay in Mobile, Alabama. When her husband started teaching at a college 40 miles away, she resigned. While hating to lose a good artist, Bell agreed because its business was slow. Later, when Bell moved to a new location and its business increased, Diane was asked to come back, and she agreed.

As will be shown later, *friends and relatives* of present employees may also be a good source of dependable people. But remember, if a friend or relative is hired but doesn't work out and must be terminated, you've lost a friend as well as an employee.

You should make it a habit to keep *applications that come in either through the mail or in person*. Also, in some areas (especially in shopping centers), workers change jobs frequently, so attracting workers from *other businesses*—even competitors—is another good source.

Managers and technical and professional personnel may be found in various *social and professional organizations*. Also, *schools and colleges* can be a good source for skilled personnel and part-time employees. Contrary to popular belief, the occupations expected to grow most during this decade are not in the sophisticated high-tech fields requiring a college education and years of experience. Instead, they will require skills taught in vocational and technical schools—places that train students for a specific career, such as medical assistants or home health aides, the two fastest-growing areas.[3]

Other sources of employees are *migrants and immigrants, retirees,* and *workers with disabilities*. A company can receive federal tax credits of up to $2,400 for hiring a person with a disability.

Part-time and temporary workers (temps) provide scheduling flexibility, as well as a way of reducing hiring (and benefit) costs. No longer is part-time employment only for students seeking summer jobs or homemakers supplementing the family income. Instead, recent college grads, retirees, corporate dropouts (or those pushed out), and others are taking temporary jobs. One group of such workers are those who wish to work less than 40 hours a week. Thus, they may be hired to work a few hours each day (e.g., as a clerk in a store) or a few days each week (as a bookkeeper or accountant).

For example, Leonard Grey, part owner of a small Birmingham, Michigan, accounting firm, hired Barbara Fitzpatrick as an accountant for $5,000 less than she was offered by a major accounting firm. Ms. Fitzpatrick, who has a young daughter and works in her husband's business on weekends, didn't want to work 70-hour weeks during tax season. She works four days a week—and up to 55 hours during tax time—and thinks it's worth giving up employee benefits and the higher salary.[4]

Leased manpower is another source of part-time employees. These workers may work full time for the leasing firm and only part time for the small employer. This is an especially useful source of employees for clerical, maintenance, janitorial, and food service tasks.

> **Leased manpower** refers to employees obtained from an outside firm that specializes in performing a particular service.

Leasing saves labor costs for a business, because the employees' health insurance and other benefits are paid by the agency that supplies the needed labor. Also, it permits greater flexibility to cut back on staff when business is slack. This group is fast becoming a permanent part of the American work force.[5]

Economic conditions have reshaped our work force in recent years, establishing a smaller "core" of permanent employees surrounded by a flexible border of temporary and part-time workers.

RECRUITING AND SELECTING EMPLOYEES

Once the number, types, and sources of employees needed are known, the small business manager starts looking for them. Don't limit applications to people who drop in and ask for a job; instead, go out and recruit.

Methods of Recruiting Employees

Recruitment is reaching out to attract applicants from which to choose one to fill a job vacancy.

Recruitment, as shown in Figure 13–3, is reaching out to attract a supply of potential employees. It's generally done by advertising, by using employment agencies, by using employee referrals, and by scouting.

Method of Selecting the Right Person for the Job

Selection involves choosing the applicant who has the qualifications to perform the job.

Selection is the process of determining whether an applicant has personal qualities that match the job specifications for a given position. Some of the qualities that working men and women say helped them get ahead are hard work, ability, and high standards.[6]

Figure 13–3   Methods Used to Recruit Employees

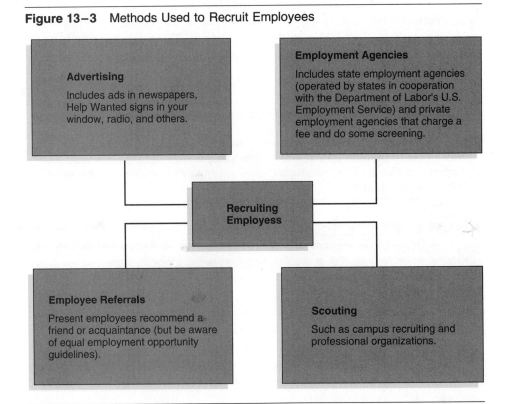

Advertising
Includes ads in newspapers, Help Wanted signs in your window, radio, and others.

Employment Agencies
Includes state employment agencies (operated by states in cooperation with the Department of Labor's U.S. Employment Service) and private employment agencies that charge a fee and do some screening.

Recruiting Employess

Employee Referrals
Present employees recommend a friend or acquaintance (but be aware of equal employment opportunity guidelines).

Scouting
Such as campus recruiting and professional organizations.

No potential employee is perfect! So don't expect to find someone with all of the qualities you ideally want. Instead, find people who have the qualities you need, and be willing to accept qualities you don't need or want, so long as those qualities don't harm the business. The selection procedure involves (1) gathering information about the applicant, (2) making a job offer, and (3) orienting the new employee.

Gathering Information about the Applicant

Many people applying for a job will not be qualified, so try to find out all you can about what they can—and can't—do. In general, what a person has done in the past best indicates future performance. You should therefore use the most appropriate technique(s) to help discover a person's past performance and future possibilities.

The amount of information you need to know about an applicant depends on the type of employee being recruited. Figure 13–4 shows some selection techniques that are frequently used to gather the information, but not all are needed for every job.

You should do some form of *preliminary screening* of applicants early in the selection procedure. This can be done in a formal interview or informally through reviewing a candidate's application form or letter, résumé, or other submitted material. Most firms use some form of interviewing at this point. In general, you should look for such obvious factors as voice, physical appearance, personal grooming, educational qualifications, training, and experience. Many applicants are eliminated at this stage for reasons such as inappropriate dress, attitude, education, or experience.

Biographical information comes from application forms, résumés, school records, military records, credit references, and so forth. You should look for solid evidence of past performance, concrete information upon which to base the decision instead of depending on opinions or assumptions. Having applicants fill out an application form in your presence—in longhand—serves as a simple performance test of their neatness and communications ability, or even simple literacy. No matter how good an applicant's record appears, don't base a decision on her or his unconfirmed statements. Unfortunately, there's a trend toward inflating résumés, so you should make it a point to verify education and employment history and check references.[7]

Several "red flags" may be indications of a phony résumé: gaps in dates or sequences that do not add up, such as the time between getting a degree and a job; degrees from unknown schools; vagueness; and accomplishments that don't make sense, such as years of education and experience that are greater than possible for the applicant's age. In most instances, an employee is not banished for stretching the truth, but it does depend on the degree of exaggeration.

Since 1971, when the U.S. Supreme Court ruled that *employment tests* must be job related, most small firms have minimized their use because of the cost involved

Figure 13–4   Techniques for Gathering Information about Potential Employees

Techniques used to gather data	Characteristics to look for	Applicants who are available as potential employees
		🚶🚶🚶🚶🚶🚶🚶🚶🚶🚶🚶🚶
Preliminary screening*	Not obvious misfit from outward appearance and conduct	🚶🚶🚶🚶🚶🚶🚶🚶🚶🚶🚶
Biographical information from application blank, résumé, etc.	Adequate educational and performance record	🚶🚶🚶🚶🚶🚶🚶🚶🚶🚶
Testing Intelligence test(s)	Meets minimum standards of mental alertness	🚶🚶🚶🚶🚶🚶🚶🚶🚶
Aptitude tests*	Specific capacities for acquiring particular knowledges or skills	🚶🚶🚶🚶🚶🚶🚶🚶
Proficiency or achievement test(s)	Ability to demonstrate capacity to do job	🚶🚶🚶🚶🚶🚶🚶
Interest test(s)	Significant vocational interest in job	🚶🚶🚶🚶🚶🚶
Personality test(s)	Personal characteristics required for job	🚶🚶🚶🚶🚶
In-depth interview	Necessary innate ability, ambition, or other qualities	🚶🚶🚶🚶
Verifying biographical data from references	No unfavorable or negative reports on past performance	🚶🚶🚶
Physical examination*	Physically fit for job	🚶🚶
Personal judgment*	Overall competence and ability to fit into the firm	🚶

*Might be adequate to fill lower-level jobs.

Source: Adapted from Leon C. Megginson, *Personnel Management: A Human Resources Approach,* 5th ed. (Homewood, Ill.: Richard D. Irwin, 1985), p. 203.

A **polygraph** is an instrument for simultaneously recording variations in several different physiological variables.

and the possible legal hassles. A word of caution is needed about the use of a special test, the **polygraph,** or ''lie detector.'' Before 1989, many companies used the polygraph. Because of conflicting results, Congress has since passed a law barring most private employers from using polygraph tests. Now, written and computerized tests for assessing employee honesty are increasingly being produced and sold, as shown in the Profile.

Source: USA Today, August 7, 1985, p. 8A. ©
1985, USA TODAY. Reprinted with permission.

Personnel Decisions Inc. (PDI) in Minneapolis has compiled a list of 10 common mistakes an interviewer makes. The following are suggestions to overcome those mistakes:

- Don't give the candidate too many clues.
- Analyze the job accurately.
- Don't ask the obvious questions.
- Don't ask legally indefensible questions.
- Try not to focus too much attention on the candidate's self-evaluation.
- Don't be afraid of probing the applicant.
- Don't be overly influenced by first impressions.
- Ask the right questions, but be sure to know how to evaluate the answers.
- Don't miss important clues.
- Don't rely too much on past credentials.[8]

References play an important role in gathering information about an applicant. The three most frequently used types of references are: personal, academic, and past employment. For applicants with any work history, the most valued references are from former employers. Using a personal visit, a telephone call, or a personal letter, you can verify work history, educational attainments, and other information the applicant has presented. By law, former employers may, if they choose, limit their responses to information about dates and title of the most recent job and total period of employment. Be sure to get the applicant's permission before contacting the present employer, who may not know the employee is job hunting.

Finally, most employers give some kind of *physical examination* to screen for communicable disease, ability to do the work satisfactorily, and probable high incidence of absenteeism, illness, or accident. As narcotics use and AIDS spread, both large and small employers are increasingly likely to require job seekers to take drug tests. The U.S. Supreme Court has approved drug testing of job applicants by private employers.[9]

Making a Job Offer

When you have decided to hire an applicant, you should make a job offer to him or her. It should include details of working conditions, such as pay, work hours, holidays, vacations, and other employee benefits, as well as the new employee's duties and responsibilities. Given the increasing tendency for workers to sue their employers, you should put job offers in writing and get the applicant to sign, indicating his or her understanding and agreement.

Orienting the New Employee

Selection also should include orienting new employees to the job. A new job is usually a difficult and frustrating experience, even for the best-qualified people. Thus, orientation should include, as a minimum, an introduction to co-workers; an explanation of the business's history, policies, procedures, and benefits; and working closely with the new employee during at least the first pay period. More employees leave a firm during that period than at any other time during their employment, as the following example shows.

After more than 20 years as a full-time wife and mother Elaine Reeves* accepted her first job outside the home. When she reported for work on Monday morning, Elaine was greeted by the business's owner and shown the word processor, other office machines, and the supply cabinet. Then she was left on her own while the owner went to call on several contractors. In these unfamiliar surroundings and with the other employees wrapped up in their own work—which made them seem unfriendly and unhelpful—she felt shaken and discouraged, and was thinking of turning around and going home. The owner walked in just in time to stop her.

TRAINING AND DEVELOPING EMPLOYEES

The continued effectiveness of a business results not only from the ability of the owner but also from (1) the caliber of its employees, including their inherent abilities; (2) their development through training, education, and experience; and

*Name disguised at her request.

(3) their motivation. The first of these depends on effective recruiting and selection. The second results from personnel development. The third, motivation, which will be covered in Chapter 14, results from the manager's leadership abilities.

Need for Training and Development

Not only must new employees be trained, but the present ones must be retrained and upgraded if they are to adjust to rapidly changing job requirements. Some of the results of training and developing workers include (1) increased productivity, (2) reduced turnover, (3) increased earnings for employees, (4) decreased costs of materials and equipment due to errors, (5) less supervision required, and (6) improved employee satisfaction.

Ways of Training Nonmanagerial Employees

You can use many methods to train nonmanagerial employees including (1) on-the-job training (OJT), (2) apprenticeship training, and (3) internship training.[10]

On-the-Job Training

The most universal form of employee development, **on-the-job training (OJT),** occurs when workers perform their regular job under the supervision and guidance of the owner, a manager, or a trained worker or instructor. Thus, while learning to do the job, the worker acts as a regular employee, producing the good or service that the business sells. Whether consciously planned or not, this form of training always occurs. While the methods used vary with the trainer, OJT usually involves:

On-the-job training (OJT) has the worker actually performing the work, under the supervision of a competent trainer.

- Telling workers what needs to be done.
- Telling them how to do the job.
- Showing them how it must be done.
- Letting them do the job under the trainer's guidance.
- Telling—and showing—them what they did right, what they did wrong, and how to correct the wrong activity.
- Repeating the process until the learners have mastered the job.

The main *advantages* of OJT are that it results in low out-of-pocket costs and that production continues during the training. Also, there is no transition from classroom learning to actual production. On the other hand, the *disadvantages* are excessive waste caused by mistakes and the poor learning environment provided by the production area. While most OJT is done by owners and managers, they are not necessarily the best ones to do it, since their primary focus is on running the business. For this reason, another capable employee or even an outside trainer should be assigned this responsibility, if possible.

Apprenticeship Training

Apprenticeship training blends OJT with learning of theory in the classroom.

For workers performing skilled, craft-type jobs, **apprenticeship training** blends the learning of theory with practice in the techniques of the job. If the job can best be learned by combining classroom instruction and actual learning experience on the job, this training method should be used. It usually lasts from two to seven years of both classroom learning and on-the-job training.

Internship Training

Internship training combines OJT with learning at a cooperating school or college.

Internship training combines education at a school or college with on-the-job training at a cooperating business. It is usually used for students who are prospective employees for marketing, clerical, technical, and managerial positions. Co-op programs prepare students for technical positions, provide income to meet the cost of their education, and give them a chance to see if they would like to go to work for the company. This method also gives the small business owner a chance to evaluate the student as a prospective full-time employee.

Outside Help with Training

Many outside programs are available to help you train your employees. For example, the National Apprenticeship Act of 1937, administered by the U.S. Labor Department's Bureau of Apprenticeship and Training, sets policies and standards for apprenticeship programs. Write to this bureau for help in conducting such a program.

Vocational-technical schools, business schools, junior colleges, and small private firms help small companies by conducting regular or special classes. Through such programs, potential employees can become qualified for skilled jobs such as machinist, lathe operator, computer operators (see Using Technology to Succeed), and legal assistants.

SELECTING AND DEVELOPING MANAGERS

Determining the job requirements for someone to be a manager is more difficult than filling other positions because managerial jobs differ so greatly. But one generalization usually applies: *The employee who is a good performer at the nonmanagerial level does not necessarily make a good manager, because the skills needed at the two levels differ drastically.*

Selecting Managers

In small firms, managers are usually promoted from within, but many businesses hire college graduates for management trainee programs. We have found in de-

━━━━━ USING TECHNOLOGY TO SUCCEED ━━━━━

MICRO SUPPORT RESOURCE CORPORATION: TRAINING PEOPLE TO CALL BACK

Deborah Fain and four partners formed Micro Support Resource Corporation (MSR) in Atlanta, Georgia, to train and support employees of client firms using IBM© PCs and/or compatibles.

After one training session of three and a half hours at MSR, the clients' employees can do spreadsheets when they return to their jobs. Afterward, if a problem arises at work, employees are urged to call MSR, whose personnel can answer almost any question about the computer's hardware, software, and peripherals. Once employees are hooked on calling MSR, the company is offered a support contract for future calls.

Fain says her company is ideal for small firms that cannot afford in-house computer troubleshooting.

Source: Jack Hayes, "Telephone Support for PC Users," *Venture,* March 1986, pp. 96–98; and Barbara Krasnoff, "MSR: A New Approach to Software Support," *PC Magazine,* January 13, 1987, pp. 259–65.

veloping, directing, and teaching in management development programs that the characteristics to be developed to produce good managers are creativity, productivity, innovativeness, communication skills (including oral, written, nonverbal, and telephone), self-motivation, and the drive and energy to energize others to achieve consistently large amounts of high-quality work. You can see that these tend to be the same qualities that lead to success as an entrepreneur (see Chapter 2).

Developing Managers

In addition to the usual methods used to develop all employees, some special techniques are used to develop managerial personnel. These include coaching, planned progression, job rotation, and executive development programs, as shown in Figure 13–5.

COMPLYING WITH EQUAL EMPLOYMENT OPPORTUNITY (EEO) LAWS

Federal and state laws and regulations affect almost all aspects of personnel relations. Since state laws vary so widely, only the most significant federal laws affecting recruiting and selecting employees are discussed here.

Since 1963, Congress has passed various acts to create equal employment opportunity and affirmative action. Table 13–1 summarizes this legislation.

Special mention should be made of the **Americans with Disabilities Act (ADA)** of 1992, for it changed the way employers must deal with the 33.8 million U.S. citizens who have physical or mental disabilities. This act mandates the removal of social and physical barriers against the disabled, two-thirds of whom are unemployed. It covers disabilities such as cancer, blindness, arthritis, HIV

The **Americans with Disabilities Act (ADA)** requires the removal of many social and physical barriers to employing the disabled.

Figure 13–5   Methods Used to Develop Managers

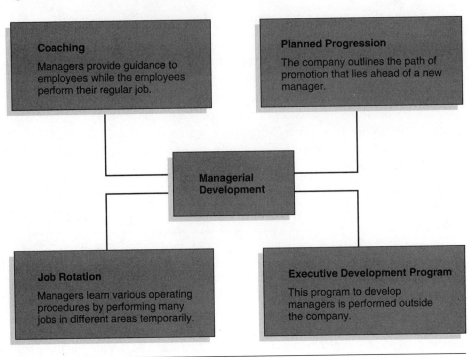

infection, chemical dependency, speech and hearing impairment, learning disabilities, and mental retardation. The act specifically excludes sexual behavior disorders, gambling, kleptomania, and others. This act targets employers with 25 or more workers.

To make sure your company is in compliance, management consultant Towers Perrin suggests that you review the practices shown in Figure 13–6.

Enforcing EEO Laws

You must remember that all employees are entitled to equality in all conditions of employment. Hiring, training, promotions and transfers, wages and benefits, and all other employment factors are covered. Posting available job openings on a bulletin board to give present employees a chance to bid on them has been found to be a good method of complying with EEO laws.

There must be no discrimination in rates of pay, including pensions or other deferred payments. Recreational activities—company sports teams, holiday parties, and the like—should be open to all employees on a nondiscriminatory basis.

Table 13-1 Legal Influences on Equal Employment Opportunity (EEO) and Affirmative Action

Laws	Coverage	Basic Requirements	Agencies Involved
Title VII of Civil Rights Act of 1964, as amended	Employers with 15 or more employees and engaged in interstate commerce; federal service workers; and state and local government workers.	Prohibits employment decisions based on race, color, religion, sex, or national origin.	Equal Employment Opportunity Commission (EEOC)
Executive Order 11246, as amended	Employers with federal contracts and subcontracts.	Requires contractors who underutilize women and minorities to take affirmative action, including setting goals and timetables; and to recruit, select, train, utilize, and promote more minorities and women.	Office of Federal Contract Compliance Programs (OFCCP) in the Labor Department
Age Discrimination in Employment Act of 1967	Employers with 20 or more employees.	Prohibits employment discrimination against employees aged 40 and over, including mandatory retirement before 70, with certain exceptions.	EEOC
Vocational Rehabilitation Act of 1973	Employers with federal contracts or subcontracts.	Prohibits discrimination and requires contractor to develop affirmative action programs to recruit and employ handicapped persons.	OFCCP
Vietnam-Era Veterans Readjustment Act of 1974	Employers with federal contracts or subcontracts.	Requires contractors to develop affirmative action programs to recruit and employ Vietnam-era veterans and to list job openings with state employment services, for priority in referrals.	OFCCP
Americans with Disabilities Act of 1992	Employers generally.	Prohibits discrimination based on physical or mental handicap (affirmative action required).	EEOC

Source: Various government and private publications.

As shown in Table 13-1, the **Equal Employment Opportunity Commission (EEOC)**, is the primary enforcing agency for most EEO laws. Figure 13-7 shows some of the regulations it has issued to prevent discrimination.

The Labor Department's Office of Federal Contract Compliance Programs (OFCCP) requires employers with government contracts or subcontracts to have

The **Equal Employment Opportunity Commission (EEOC)** is the federal agency primarily responsible for enforcing EEO laws.

Figure 13–6   Practices Needing Review to Assure Compliance with the ADA

- *Hiring and job classifications.* Develop job descriptions based on essential job duties and update them. Check recruiting materials and advertising policies.
- *Selection criteria.* Check job application forms. Train interviewers on what or what not to ask. Review tests and other selection criteria to ensure that they are nondiscriminatory.
- *Preemployment exams and questionnaires.* Eliminate all pre-job-offer exams and questionnaires. Ensure that post-offer exams are required for all applicants. Make sure exams are job related. Keep files confidential.
- *Employment moves.* Make sure promotion and termination decisions are based on objective assessments. Document them.
- *Compensation.* Check pay programs to make sure they equal programs for nondisabled. Document reasons for pay disparities.
- *Training.* Ensure that facilities are accessible, without segregating disabled workers. Train supervisors and employees on the importance of ADA.
- *Leaves of absence.* Ensure that medical leave policies are uniformly applied and enforced. Require all employees to present documentation when applying for leave. Grant job reinstatement rights to all workers. Administer policies consistently.
- *General conditions.* Update employee handbooks. Audit work sites periodically and remove barriers blocking access for the disabled. Appoint an ADA liaison. Discuss accommodations with disabled employees and document results. Review workers' comp programs and evaluate substance abuse policies.
- *Contractual arrangements.* Require outside contractors to certify their compliance with ADA and request indemnification clauses in contracts to cover any damages from violations. Review collective bargaining agreements in light of ADA.

Source: Towers Perrin, management consultant, as published in ''Personnel Practices for Firms to Watch,'' *Mobile* (Alabama) *Press Register,* July 26, 1992, p. 1-C. The Mobile Press Register, © 1992. All rights reserved.

Figure 13–7   Principal EEOC Regulations

- Sex discrimination guidelines
- Questions and answers on pregnancy disability and reproductive hazards
- Religious discrimination guidelines
- National origin discrimination guidelines
- Interpretations of the Age Discrimination in Employment Act
- Employee selection guidelines
- Record keeping and reports
- Affirmative action guidelines
- EEO in the federal government
- Equal Pay Act interpretations
- Policy statement on maternal benefits
- Policy statement on relationship of Title VII to 1986
- Immigration Reform and Control Act
- Policy statement on reproductive and fetal hazards
- Policy statement on religious accommodation under Title VII
- Policy guidance on sexual harassment
- Disabilities discrimination guidelines

Source: Adapted from James Ledvinka and Vida Scarpello, *Federal Regulation of Personnel and Human Resource Management,* 2nd ed. (Boston: PWS-Kent, 1991), p. 38.

Affirmative action programs (AAPs) provide guidelines to help firms eliminate discrimination against women and minorities.

affirmative action programs (AAPs) to put the principle of equal employment opportunity into practice. The OFCCP can cancel a guilty firm's contract or prohibit it from getting future contracts if a violation is blatant.

Terminating Employees

While you still have the right to terminate employees for cause, the concept of ''employment at will'' is losing acceptance in courts and legislatures. **Employment at will** essentially means that employers may fire employees with or without

Employment at will means that employers may hire or fire workers with or without cause.

cause at any time they choose. Courts and legislators are now applying instead the ''good faith and fair dealing'' concept, whereby terminations must be ''reasonable'' and not ''arbitrarily'' or ''indiscriminately'' applied. Violating this concept may lead to punitive damages in addition to actual damages that have been sustained by one of the protected employees.[11]

WHAT YOU SHOULD HAVE LEARNED

1. The most important resource for any business is people. Therefore, you must determine the needed number and skills of employees and the sources from which to recruit them. This process begins with a job description and job specifications.

    Employees can be recruited from either internal or external sources. When feasible, it is best to upgrade, transfer, or promote from inside the business, all of which increase employee morale and save time and money; also, employees' past performance is known. External sources include former employees, applications, friends and relatives of present employees, other businesses, social and professional organizations, schools and colleges, retirees, workers with disabilities, and part-time and temporary workers.

2. Employees can be recruited through advertising, employment agencies, employee referrals, and scouting. Newspaper want ads are the most common method of recruiting.

    You can evaluate prospective employees by *(a)* a preliminary screening interview or review of the candidate's application or résumé; *(b)* biographical information from the application or résumé and from school, military, and other records; and *(c)* some form of testing, verifying references, and giving a physical examination.

    Ultimately, the decision of whom to employ involves your personal judgment. Once the decision has been made, a clear—preferably written—job offer should be extended. Orientation can range from a simple introduction to co-workers to a lengthy training process.

3. After employees are hired, they should be retrained and upgraded periodically. Training methods include *(a)* on-the-job training (OJT), *(b)* apprenticeship training, and *(c)* internship training.

4. In selecting managers, you should look for *managerial qualities,* which aren't the same as *nonmanagerial competence.* Techniques used for developing managers include *(a)* coaching, *(b)* planned progression, *(c)* job rotation, and *(d)* executive development programs.

5. You must conform to federal and state laws in your dealings with current and prospective employees. The equal employment opportunity (EEO) provisions of the Civil Rights Act and the requirements of the Americans with

Disabilities Act are especially important. Legislation has been passed to prevent discrimination on the basis of race, color, sex, age, religion, disabilities, or national origin. The Equal Employment Opportunity Commission (EEOC) and the Office of Federal Contract Compliance Programs (OFCCP) enforce these laws.

QUESTIONS FOR DISCUSSION

1. What does personnel planning involve in the small company?
2. What external sources are usually used by small businesses for finding new employees?
3. What are some advantages and disadvantages of filling job openings from within the company?
4. Distinguish among upgrading, promoting, and transferring employees.
5. What does the personnel selection procedure involve?
6. Describe the methods used to gather information about prospective employees.
7. Why should a physical examination be required of an applicant? Why not?
8. What are the primary methods used to train employees? Explain each.
9. What should you look for in a potential manager?
10. What methods can be used to train managers?
11. How do EEO laws affect recruiting and selecting employees?
12. What agencies enforce EEO laws? How do they enforce them?

SUPREME PLUMBING AND HEATING COMPANY: WHERE ARE THE WORKERS?

In the late 1950s, two friendly competitors formed the Supreme Plumbing and Heating Company as a partnership in a rapidly developing industrial area southwest of Houston, Texas. At first, the partners did most of the work themselves, including plumbing, heating, and wiring for both commercial and residential buildings. The business grew rapidly, and several craftsmen and other employees were added. This left the partners devoting almost all of their time to managing the business rather than doing the work themselves.

Supreme competed with six other companies within a 50-mile radius both for business and for the best craftsmen. This became difficult in the 1960s when the Lyndon B. Johnson Space Center was built nearby. Most of the area's skilled workers left their jobs with the companies to work at the center for better pay and benefits, causing a great shortage of craftsmen in the area. At the same time, demand for plumbing, heating, and wiring was increasing. It would have been a good opportunity for Supreme to expand its operations—if the needed workers could have been found.

The partners decided that the only way to have an adequate supply of trained craftsmen was to do their own training, so they started an apprenticeship program. The plan was to hire high school graduates or dropouts to work with some of the older craftsmen as apprentice plumbers and electricians, at the prevailing wage rate, until they learned the trade. When they finished their training, they would train others so there would be a continuous training program.

Although the program gave the young people an opportunity to learn a trade that would be valuable to them in future years, the plan didn't work. The trainees would work for Supreme just long enough to be trained; then they would quit to take another job, go into the armed services, or go back to school. The partners had to reduce the amount of construction work they bid on because of their limited work force. To compensate for this loss of revenue, they started a wholesale plumbing, heating, and electrical supply business.

The worker shortage at Supreme continued until there were only three plumbers, three plumber's helpers, two electricians, and two electrician's helpers left. Because the craftsmen were nearing retirement age and the helpers weren't interested in learning the trade, the owners had to go on with the wholesale business, although they would have preferred to continue in construction.

QUESTIONS

1. Supreme Plumbing and Heating Company limited itself to hiring only high school graduates and even dropouts. What type of preliminary screening should there have been for this type of job, if any? Explain.

2. What types of recruiting methods could have been implemented by the two partners?

3. When the new Space Center was built nearby, what kind of actions should the partners have taken?

4. Although the apprenticeship program seemed to be the route to take, what other options were there?

Source: This case was prepared by Leon C. Megginson.

14

Leading and Motivating Employees

The key to . . . success is superior customer service, continuing internal entrepreneurship, and a deep belief in the dignity, worth, and potential of every person in the organization.—Tom Peters, coauthor of *In Search of Excellence*

The good boss selects people with demonstrated capabilities, tells them what results are expected, largely leaves them alone to decide the means by which they can be obtained, and then monitors the results.—Sanford Jacobs, entrepreneur

LEARNING OBJECTIVES

After studying the material in this chapter, you will be able to:

1. Explain how managerial assumptions affect human relationships with employees.

2. List some barriers to effective communication and show some ways to improve communication.

3. Explain how to improve employee motivation.

4. Tell why personnel appraisals are used.

5. Describe how to compensate employees with money and employee benefits.

MURRY EVANS: DEVELOPING WINNING TEAMS

Murry Evans is both a franchisee and a franchisor. And he has succeeded at both because he developed winning teams. His secret of success: "If you get good people, train them well, work with them, and praise them for good work, you'll have a winning team." He likes to quote one of the late Paul "Bear" Bryant's favorite sayings: "There ain't no fun in anything but winning."

Murry's career as a franchisee began in 1963, when, at age 24, he opened his first Burger King franchise in Mobile, Alabama, with $40,000 he had borrowed from his hardworking father-in-law, an Ohio farmer. His lifetime goal then was "to open five Burger King restaurants." In 1989, with 46 stores, he had far exceeded his goal, owning more franchises than any other individual franchisee in the United States.

Evans attributes much of the success of Midtown Restaurants Corporation to the hard work and dedication he and his wife, Marilyn, put into that first Burger King. After teaching school to support them so he could graduate from The Citadel, Marilyn did everything from cleaning

Photo © 1989 by Thigpen Photography, provided courtesy of SIGNS NOW.

tables and washing dishes to preparing the payroll.

As the chairman of the board and chief executive officer of SIGNS NOW, the original one-day high-tech sign company, Evans is also a successful franchisor. Begun in 1983 to produce computer-generated vinyl signs and lettering in one day, it now has 125 franchises around the world.

Evans believes SIGNS NOW is so successful because it is trying to give people—young and old, male and female—a chance to own a good, solid business that provides a needed service while letting them earn a profit. Franchisees will succeed, he says, if they have a good location, work hard, and are dedicated to the job.

Believing that "if our franchisees are successful, we're successful," he and his team are trying to help them succeed. Having been a franchisee himself for 30 years, Evans is sympathetic to their problems and can help them solve those problems.

Evans is living proof that having big ideas, a good team, motivation, and willingness to work hard leads to success.

Source: Correspondence and discussions with John E. Carpenter, Director of Franchise Sales for SIGNS NOW, and others.

The opening quotations and Profile illustrate the importance of leading and motivating people in small firms. These activities include:

- Practicing "good" human relations.
- Using enlightened leadership in dealing with them.
- Communicating openly and truthfully with them.
- Using positive motivation.
- Compensating them fairly.
- Evaluating their performance.

GOOD HUMAN RELATIONS IS NEEDED IN SMALL FIRMS

Defining the term *human relations* is difficult, for it means different things to different people. Dr. Alfred Haake, lecturer for General Motors, would begin his lectures on human relations by saying, "Some people say that good human relations is treating people as if it were your last day on earth." "Ah, no!" he would continue. "Good human relations is treating people as if it were *their* last day on earth."

Human relations is involves the interaction of people in an organization, especially in the areas of leadership, communications, and motivation. Regardless of the definition used, your success as a small business owner is based upon your practicing good human relations.[1]

> **Human relations** involves the interaction among people in an organization.

For example, Keith Dunn started his own restaurant because of the poor treatment he'd received from his employers. After he tried and failed at using motivational techniques, such as contests and benefits, he started including his employees in decisions affecting the business. Now that they are a vital part of the business, the annual turnover rate has dropped from 250 percent—normal for the industry—to 60 percent.[2]

EXERCISING EFFECTIVE LEADERSHIP

While management and leadership are similar, there are some significant differences. Leading is an important part of managing—but not the whole of it. **Leadership** is the ability of one person to influence others to strive to attain goals or objectives. Management, while requiring the use of leadership, also includes the other functions of planning, organizing, staffing, and controlling. Leadership is especially important for small business owners: without it, they can't get workers to strive to achieve their goals or the business's objectives.

> **Leadership** is the ability of the supervisor to influence individuals to attain objectives.

It is tempting to say that one leadership style is better than another for small business owners. Yet experience has shown that no one style is ideal at all times. Instead, the best approach depends on the situation and the people involved.

COMMUNICATING WITH EMPLOYEES AND OTHERS

Communication, the process of transferring meaning—that is, ideas and information—from one person to another, is your number one job. Studies show that verbal communications take up about 80 percent of a manager's time.[3]

Communication is important because people need and want to know what is going on so they can do their jobs properly. Owners, employees, customers, vendors, and others need to coordinate their work, so communication must be clear and complete. In addition, speaking pleasantly and persuasively makes people want to do good work. A Japanese proverb says, ''One kind word can warm three winter months.''

Communication is the transfer of meaning from one person to another.

What Happens When You Communicate?

While explaining a process as complex as communication is difficult, Figure 14–1 shows that the process involves: (1) someone (the source) having an idea, thought,

Figure 14–1 The Communication Process

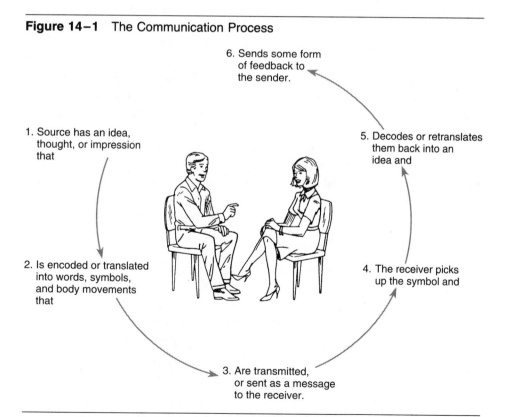

6. Sends some form of feedback to the sender.

1. Source has an idea, thought, or impression that

5. Decodes or retranslates them back into an idea and

2. Is encoded or translated into words, symbols, and body movements that

4. The receiver picks up the symbol and

3. Are transmitted, or sent as a message to the receiver.

Source: Adapted from Leon C. Megginson, *Personnel Management: A Human Relations Approach,* 5th ed. (Homewood, Ill.: Richard D. Irwin, 1985), p. 335.

or impression that (2) is encoded or translated into words or symbols that (3) are transmitted, or sent as a message, to another person (the receiver), who (4) picks up the symbols and (5) decodes, or retranslates, them back into an idea and (6) sends some form of feedback to the sender. Feedback completes the process, because communication cannot be assumed to have taken place until the receiver demonstrates understanding of the message. Since communication is an exchange of meaning rather than words or symbols, many forms of nonverbal communication convey meaning through signals, signs, sounds (other than words), and facial expressions.

Barriers to Effective Communication

Despite the importance of communication and the amount of time we spend communicating, it's not always effective. One study showed that up to 70 percent of all business communication fails to achieve the desired results.[4] There are many causes of this ineffectiveness, especially some barriers erected by the business itself or by the people involved.

First, because of the owner's position of authority, employees tend to believe what the owner says, regardless of whether it is true or not. In addition, the status of the communicator either lends credibility to what is being said or detracts from it, for messages of higher-status people tend to carry greater credibility than those of lower-status people.

The imprecise use of language also serves as a barrier. Have you noticed how frequently people use the expression *you know* in daily communications or adopt buzzwords (especially those from high-tech fields) without really knowing what they mean? For example, such terms as *outplacement* and *replacement* are used often to soften the impact on the employee being dismissed.

Perhaps the greatest barriers to effective communication are simply inattention and poor listening. Small business owners, as well as managers of bigger companies, are often so preoccupied with running their business that they may not pay attention to employee feedback.

How to Improve Communication

You can become a more effective communicator by clarifying ideas, considering the environment in which the communication occurs, considering emotional overtones as well as the message, following up on communication, and being a good listener. As we have emphasized, communication is a two-way street. Even more important than getting your meaning across are listening to and understanding what the other person says.

MOTIVATING EMPLOYEES

Before reading the following material, complete the exercise in Figure 14–2. This exercise helps explain why motivation is so complex and why it is so difficult to

Figure 14–2   What Do You Want from a Job?

Rank the employment factors shown below in their order of importance to you at three
points in your career. In the first column, assume that you are about to graduate and are
looking for your first full-time job. In the second column, assume that you have been
gainfully employed for 5 to 10 years and that you are presently employed by a reputable
firm at the prevailing salary for the type of job and industry you are in. In the third
column, try to assume that 25 to 30 years from now you have "found your niche in life"
and have been working for a reputable employer for several years. (Rank your first choice
as "1," second as "2," and so forth through "9.")

Ranking of Selected Employment Factors

Employment Factor	As You Seek Your First Full-Time Job	Your Ranking 5–10 Years Later	Your Ranking 25–30 Years Later
Fair adjustment of grievances			
Good job instruction and training			
Effective job supervision by your supervisor			
Promotion possibilities			
Recognition (praise, rewards, and so on)			
Job safety			
Job security (no threat of being dismissed or laid off)			
Good salary			
Good working conditions (nice office surroundings, good hours, and so on)			

Source: Adapted from Leon C. Megginson, Donald C. Mosley, and Paul H. Pietri, Jr., *Management:
Concepts and Applications*, 4th ed. (New York: HarperCollins, 1992), p. 447.

motivate some employees. You must use different incentives to motivate different
people at different times in their working lives. Yet it is difficult for us to always
know what a given employee wants at a given time. Understanding those needs,
and understanding how to use the appropriate motivation, are the secrets of successful small business ownership and management.

What Is Motivation?

You can use **motivation** to bring out the best in your employees by giving them
reasons to perform better, but it's not easy. First of all, you are *always* motivating

Motivation is the inner state
that activates a person,
including drives, desires, and/or
motives.

employees—either positively (to perform) or negatively (to withhold performance)—even when you're not conscious of doing so. When you give employees a reason to perform better, you create positive motivation; on the other hand, if you say or do something that annoys, frustrates, or antagonizes employees, they'll react negatively and either withhold production or actually sabotage operations.

For example, a customer went into an ice cream shop in a college town and ordered a banana split. When it came, something was obviously wrong. There were five scoops of ice cream, double portions of fruit and nuts, and a huge serving of whipped cream, with several cherries on top. The customer asked the young employee, "What's wrong?" The young man didn't even pretend not to understand. "I'm mad at the boss," he promptly replied. A few months later, the shop went out of business.

The best way for you to succeed in business is to increase employee productivity and efficiency. While there is a limit to improvements in employee productivity, effective motivation can have a positive effect. However, *because there are many factors that affect productivity, motivation alone is not enough.*

In general, employee performance is a product of the employee's ability to do the job and the application of positive motivation; that is,

$$\text{Performance} = \text{Ability} \times \text{Motivation}$$

Most employees go to work for a company expecting to do a good job, receive a satisfactory income, and gain satisfaction from doing a good job. However, performance and satisfaction are dependent on the *ability* to do the job. If your employees are not performing as you would like them to, they may be unsuited for the job, inadequately trained, or unmotivated. If they are unsuited, move them to a more suitable job, and if untrained, train them. If they are both suited and trained, try harder to motivate them.

Why Motivate Employees?

One reason managerial motivation is so difficult to use is that there are different purposes for motivating people, each of which requires different incentives. Usually managers use motivation to (1) attract potential employees, (2) improve performance, and (3) retain good employees.

Attracting Potential Employees

If you want to encourage potential employees to work for you, you must find and use incentives that appeal to a person needing a job. These incentives usually include a good income, pleasant working conditions, promotional possibilities, and sometimes a signing bonus.

Figure 14–3   The Motivational Process

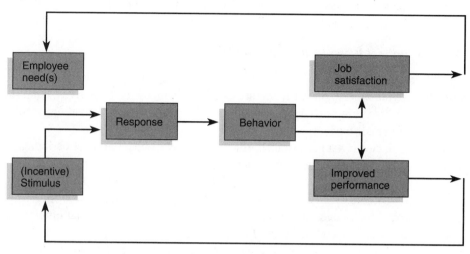

The exercise in Figure 14–2 has been used with junior- and senior-level business students since 1957. With very few exceptions, "good salary" has been the primary consideration in looking for a first job in over 200 surveys reviewed, while "promotion possibilities" and "good working conditions" are a close second and third. How did you rate these factors?

Improving Performance

You can also use motivation to improve performance and efficiency on the part of present employees. You can do this by praising good work, giving employees more responsibility, publicly recognizing a job well done, and awarding merit salary increases.

Notice in the Profile that Murry Evans treated his people well in order to bring out the best in them. He gave them personal attention and helped them with their problems.

Retaining Good Employees

Motivation can also be used to retain your present employees. This is accomplished primarily through the use of employee benefits, most of which are designed to reward employees who stay with the company.

How to Motivate Employees

The theory of motivation is relatively simple (as shown in Figure 14–3). An employee has a need or needs, and you apply some kind of incentive (or stimulus) that promises to satisfy that need. Your main problem in motivating employees is to know them well enough to know what they need and what incentives will stimulate them to perform.

Some Practical Ways to Improve Motivation

Some tried-and-true ways of improving motivation are (1) quality circles (2) zero defects programs, (3) job enrichment, (4) management by objectives, and (5) variable work schedules. These techniques offer promise for motivating people, especially in small businesses.

Quality circles (QCs) are small, organized work groups that meet periodically to find ways to improve quality and output. They motivate by getting employees involved and taking advantage of their creativity and innovativeness.

The **zero-defects** approach is based on getting workers to do their work "right the first time," thus generating pride in workmanship. It assumes that employees want to do a good job, if permitted to.

Job enrichment emphasizes giving employees greater responsibility and authority over their job as the best way to motivate them. Employees are encouraged to learn new and related skills or even to trade jobs with each other as ways of making the job more interesting and therefore more productive.

As discussed in Chapter 6, the purpose of *management by objectives (MBO)* is for managers and employees to work together to set goals for the company and themselves, and then to use those goals as a guide to performance and as a means of evaluating it.

Variable work schedules permit employees to work at times other than the standard workweek of five eight-hour days.[5] Such schedules are being extensively used by small firms to motivate employees. **Flextime** allows employees to schedule their own hours as long as they are present during certain required hours, called *core time*. This gives employees greater control over their time and activities. **Job splitting** is dividing a single full-time job into distinct parts and letting two (or more) employees do the different parts. In **job sharing,** a single full-time job is shared by two (or more) employees, with one doing all aspects of the job at one time and the other at another time, as the following example shows.

Cheryl Houser, burned out after selling ads for the *Seattle Weekly* for four years, wanted time to travel, do volunteer work, and eventually have a baby. Carol Cummins, a co-worker expecting a baby, also wanted to work part time. Being good salespeople, they talked their boss, Jane Levine, vice-president of advertising and marketing, into letting them share one full-time job. Houser works on Mondays and Thursdays, Cummins works on Wednesdays and Fridays, and both come in on Tuesdays. In exchange for lighter work duties, since the two women each work only three days a week, the paper gets two seasoned workers for the price of one.[6]

Quality circles (QCs) are small employee groups that meet periodically to improve quality and output.

A **zero-defects** approach uses pride in workmanship to get workers to do their work "right the first time."

Job enrichment is granting workers greater responsibility and authority in their jobs.

Flextime is an arrangement under which employees may schedule their own hours, around a core time.

Job splitting occurs when employees divide a single job into two or more different parts.

Job sharing occurs when a single full-time job is shared by two or more employees.

Small business owners are faced with a dilemma when considering such motivational programs. They may believe that using one or more of the new methods will improve employee performance and hence increase profits. But they may not have the knowledge, time, money, or personnel to implement the method or methods.

Does Money Motivate?

Some management scholars say that money doesn't motivate and that psychological rewards may be more significant than monetary rewards.[7] But, as shown, our research indicates that most students say ''good salary'' is the first thing they'll be looking for in their first job. Also, several studies indicate that money does motivate. For example, one study revealed that 60 percent of women say money motivates them to achieve a better life.[8] In summary, we believe that money motivates, but so do many other factors, as indicated in the Profile.

Motivation Is More than Mere Technique

Successful motivation of employees is based more on a managerial philosophy than on using a given technique. Thus, you should try to create an environment in your firm in which employees can apply themselves willingly and wholeheartedly to the task of increasing productivity and quality. This thought was expressed by Clarence Francis, chairman of General Foods, when he said, ''You can buy a man's time; you can buy a man's physical presence at a given place; you can even buy a measured number of skilled muscular motions per hour or day; but you cannot buy enthusiasm; you cannot buy initiative; you cannot buy loyalty; you cannot buy devotion of hearts, minds, and souls. You have to earn these things.''[9]

APPRAISING EMPLOYEES' PERFORMANCE

You need an effective **performance appraisal** system (also called *employee evaluation* or *merit rating*) to help you answer the question ''How well are my people performing?'' Under such a system, each employee's performance and progress are evaluated, and rewards are given for above-average performance. Often, this method is used in determining merit salary increases.

Performance appraisal is evaluating workers to see how well they're performing.

Employee appraisals are usually based on such factors as quantity and quality of work performed, cooperativeness, initiative, dependability (including attendance), job knowledge, safety, and personal habits.

Employee evaluations should be related to promotions and salary increases in addition to identifying marginal workers and designing training activities for them. They can also be used to motivate employees, if the evaluations are adequately translated into rewards.

COMPENSATING EMPLOYEES

Another aspect of leading and rewarding employees is providing what employees consider fair pay for their activities. Their earnings should be high enough to motivate them to be good producers, yet low enough for you to maintain satisfactory profits.

Legal Influences

There are many federal and state laws that affect how much small business owners pay their employees (see Table 14–1 for the primary federal laws involved). According to the Wage and Hour Law, 14 is the minimum working age for most nonfarm jobs. Thus, you can hire workers aged 14 and 15 for nonhazardous jobs for up to three hours on a school day and eight hours on any other day, but no more

Table 14–1 Legal Influence on Compensation and Hours of Work

Law	Coverage	Basic Requirements	Agencies Involved
Public Construction Act (Davis-Bacon Act)	Employers with federal construction contracts or subcontracts of $2,000 or more.	Employers must pay at least the prevailing wages in the area, as determined by the Secretary of Labor; overtime is to be paid at 1½ times the basic wage for all work over 8 hours per day or 40 hours per week.	Wage and Hour Division of the Labor Department.
Public Contracts Act (Walsh-Healy Act)	Employers with federal contracts of $1,000 or more.	Same as above.	Same as above.
Fair Labor Standards Act (wage and hour law)	Private employers engaged in interstate commerce; retailers having annual sales of $325,000. (Many groups are exempted from overtime requirements.)	Employers must pay a minimum of $4.25 per hour and 1½ times the basic rate for work over 40 hours per week and are limited (by jobs and school status) in employing persons under 18.	Same as above.
Equal Pay Act	All employers.	Men and women must receive equal pay for jobs requiring substantially the same skill, working conditions, effort, and responsibility.	Equal Employment Opportunity Commission.
Service Contracts Act	Employers with contracts to provide services worth $2,500 or more per year to the federal government.	Same as Davis-Bacon.	Same as Davis-Bacon.

Source: Various government and private publications.

than 18 hours per week from 7:00 A.M. to 7:00 P.M. during the school term. Those aged 16 and 17 can work an unlimited time on nonhazardous jobs.

Certain retail and service companies don't have to comply if their annual sales are less than $500,000. Laundry, fabric care, dry cleaning, and some construction firms also qualify for exemptions, while those who hope to receive tips face a minimum wage of only $2.34.[10]

Since state laws vary so much from each other and from the federal law, we won't try to discuss them. You should check the laws for the state in which you operate.

Setting Rates of Pay

In addition to legal factors, many variables influence what employees consider a fair wage. First, they feel that they should be paid in proportion to their physical and mental efforts on the job. The standard of living and cost of living in the area also matter. And unions help set wages in a geographic area through collective bargaining, whether the company itself is unionized or not. The economic factors of supply and demand for workers help set wages. Finally, the employer's ability to pay must be considered.

In actual practice, most small businesses pay either the minimum wage or the same wages that similar businesses in the area pay. If you pay less than the prevailing wage, you will have difficulty finding employees. Conversely, you cannot afford to pay much more unless your employees are more productive. In the final analysis, you pay whatever you have to in order to attract the people you really need—and can afford.

Using Money to Motivate

Many small businesses use some form of financial incentive to motivate their employees to use their initiative and to perform better. Some of the more popular financial incentives are (1) merit increases, (2) incentive payments, and (3) profit sharing. Figure 14–4 shows the results of a survey of 1,598 small and large manufacturing and service companies by the American Productivity and Quality Center. Notice how popular profit sharing, lump-sum bonuses, and individual incentive payments are.

Merit Increases

Merit increases, which base a person's wage or salary on ability and merit rather than on seniority or some other factor, tend to be effective motivators. Merit programs identify, appraise, and reward employees for outstanding contribution toward your company's profit. Thus, an employee's wage or salary relates directly to that person's efforts to achieve your objectives.

Merit increases are based on the employee's ability and performance.

Figure 14–4   Incentive Pay Programs Grow Popular

Pay raises are not the only way companies reward employees any more. Here's the percentage of U. S. companies using non-traditional forms of compensation:

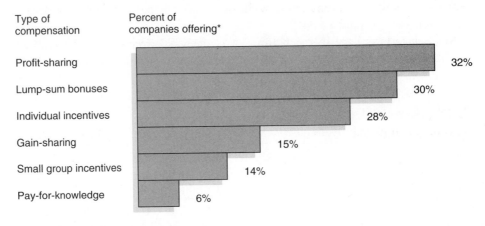

Type of compensation / Percent of companies offering*

- Profit-sharing — 32%
- Lump-sum bonuses — 30%
- Individual incentives — 28%
- Gain-sharing — 15%
- Small group incentives — 14%
- Pay-for-knowledge — 6%

*Some companies offer more than one plan.

Source: ''Plans Become Labor's Latest Battleground,'' *USA Today,* November 7, 1989, p. 1B. Copyright 1989, USA TODAY. Adapted with permission.

Incentive Payments

Incentive payments can be paid in the form of incentive wages, push money, and so forth.

An **incentive wage,** which is the extra compensation paid for all production over a specified amount, is effective in situations where a worker can control the volume of sales or production. Piece rates, commissions, and bonuses are forms of incentive payments. Under a *piece-rate system,* an employee's earnings are based on a rate per unit times the number of units produced. But you should give some form of guaranteed base rate to ensure that the employee earns at least a minimum amount. Piece-rate systems, which are usually used in production- or operations-type activities, can be quite effective, as the following example illustrates.

An **incentive wage** is the extra compensation paid for all production over a specified amount.

A study of the use of piece rates in the corrugated shipping container industry found that 16 of 18 operations showed significantly increased productivity after use of such incentives. On the average, productivity per employee increased around 75 percent.[11]

A **commission** is incentive compensation directly related to the sales or profits achieved by a salesperson.

Commissions, which consist of a given amount per sale or a percentage of sales, are used extensively to reward salespeople, especially in retailing. They are particularly useful in rewarding door-to-door selling of items such as encyclopedias and magazine subscriptions, but they are also used by most department stores and similar retail outlets and are the only form of compensation for real estate agents.

Bonuses are amounts given to employees either for exceeding their production quotas or as a reward on special occasions. Many production or sales personnel have work quotas and receive bonuses if they exceed that amount.

> A **bonus** is a reward to employees for special efforts and accomplishments.

Another form of incentive payment is called *push money (PM),* which is a reward given to employees for selling an item the business is making a special effort to sell—in other words, pushing.

Profit Sharing

In **profit sharing,** employees receive a prearranged share of the company's profits. Profit sharing can be quite effective in motivating employees by tying rewards to company performance. Not only does it reward good performance, but a good plan can also reduce turnover, increase productivity, and reduce the amount of supervision needed.

> **Profit sharing** is an arrangement whereby employees receive a prescribed share of the company's profits.

If you can afford to do so, you might want to use an **employee stock ownership plan (ESOP),** which is a modification of profit sharing. In general, an ESOP borrows money, purchases a block of the company's stock, and allocates it to the employees on the basis of salaries and/or longevity. These plans are particularly attractive to small companies because they provide a source of needed capital, boost the company's cash flow, raise employee morale and productivity, and provide a very beneficial new employee benefit.

> An **employee stock ownership plan (ESOP),** a form of profit sharing, borrows money, purchases some of the company's stock, and allocates it to the employees on the basis of salaries and/or longevity.

Compensating Managerial and Professional Personnel

In general, managers of small businesses are paid on a merit basis, with their income based on the firm's earnings. Many small companies also use profit sharing, bonuses, or some other method of stimulating the interest of managerial and professional personnel.

For example, managers of Radio Shack stores receive a share of profits if their store's profit margin is 10 percent or more. If a given store has, say, an 11 percent profit margin, the manager gets 11 percent of those profits as a bonus; with a 15 percent profit margin, the manager takes home an extra 15 percent of profits.[12]

Employee Benefits

Employee benefits (sometimes called *fringe benefits*) are the rewards and services provided to employees in addition to their regular earnings. Figure 14–5 shows some of the most popular employee benefits. In general, these benefits increase in importance as employees' lifestyles expand and it takes more than just wages to

> **Employee benefits** are the rewards and services provided to workers in addition to their regular earnings.

Figure 14–5   Some of the Most Popular Employee Benefits

1. Legally required
   Social Security/Medicare
   Unemployment insurance
   Workers' compensation
   Family and medical leave
2. Voluntary, private
   a. Health and accident insurance
      Eye care and eyeglasses
      Chiropractic care
      Dental and orthodontic care
      Health maintenance—diagnostic
         visits/physical exams
      Major medical/hospitalization
      Psychiatric and mental care
      Accident and sickness insurance
   b. Life and disability insurance
      Accidental death and dismemberment
      Group term life insurance
      Long-term disability
   c. Sick leave, including maternity leave
   d. Income maintenance
      Severance pay
      Supplemental unemployment
         benefits (SUBs)
      Pensions
   e. Pay for time off
      Holidays
      Personal time
      Sabbatical leaves
      Union activities
      Vacations

   f. Employee services and others
      Alcohol and drug rehabilitation
      Auto insurance
      Child care and day-care centers for
         other family members
      Christmas bonuses
      Clothing and uniforms
      Company car
      Credit unions
      Discount privileges on organization's
         products or services
      Loans and financial assistance
      Food services and cafeteria
      Group tours and charter flights
      Gymnasium and physical training
         center
      Legal assistance
      Liability coverage
      Matching gifts to charitable
         organizations or schools
      Matching payroll deductions and
         savings plans
      Moving and transfer allowances
      Personal counseling and financial advice
      Recreation center
      Service awards
      Stock purchase and profit-sharing plans
      Transportation and parking
      Tuition for employee and/or family
         members

Source: Various government and private publications.

satisfy them. But benefits are costly! And once given, they are difficult—if not impossible—to take back. Moreover, their cost is rising much faster than wages. Yet employees want and expect them, almost as much as they do their salary!

Legally Required Benefits

Small employers are legally required by the Social Security Act to provide retirement, disability, survivors, and medical benefits; unemployment insurance; and workers' compensation. Also, employers with 20 or more employees must continue health insurance for up to 18 months for employees when they leave—either voluntarily or otherwise—and up to 36 months for widows, divorced or separated spouses, and employee dependents.

Under the **Social Security** system, you act as both taxpayer and tax collector, as you must pay a tax on employees' earnings and deduct an equal amount from their paychecks. In 1993, the tax rate was 7.65 percent (6.2 percent for Social Security and 1.45 percent for Medicare), and the taxable wage base was $57,600 for Social Security and $57,600 to $135,000 for Medicare; so employers and employees each had to pay a maximum of $4,200. Self-employed people must pay the entire cost themselves, which is twice the listed amount.

Social Security is a federal program that provides support for the retired, widowed, disabled, and their dependents.

State governments receive most of the **unemployment insurance** tax, which can be as high as 4.7 percent of the first $8,000 of each employee's pay, while the rest goes to the U.S. government for administrative costs. If the business can lower its unemployment rate, the tax is reduced under a merit rating system. Using funds from the tax, the state pays unemployed workers a predetermined amount each week. This amount varies from state to state.

Unemployment insurance provides some financial support to employees laid off for reasons beyond their control.

Employee losses from accidents and occupational diseases are paid for under state **workers' compensation** laws. Each employer is required to pay insurance premiums to either a state fund or a private insurance company. The accumulated funds are used to compensate victims of industrial accidents or work-related illnesses. A firm's premiums depend on the hazards involved and the effectiveness of its safety programs. The amount paid to an employee or to his or her estate is fixed according to the type and extent of injury. According to the National Council on Compensation Insurance, the costs of these programs more than doubled between 1986 and 1992, from just over $30 billion to over $60 billion.[13] *This trend threatens small firms, which may not be able to bear the increasing costs.*

Workers' compensation involves payments made to employees for losses from accidents and occupational diseases.

Employers with 50 or more workers within 75 miles must guarantee workers up to 12 weeks of unpaid leave a year for births, adoptions, or the care of sick children, spouses, or parents. The Family and Medical Leave Act, passed February 5, 1993, covers employees on the job at least one year, but the employer can exclude the top-paid 10 percent of employees. Employees are required to give 30 days' notice when practical, such as births and adoptions, and may be required to use vacation or other leave time first. Couples employed at the same place may be restricted to 12 weeks total leave each year. Employers must continue to provide health insurance during leave and guarantee workers the same or an equivalent job upon return.[14]

Other Employee Benefits

As shown in Figure 14–5, there are many voluntary benefits in addition to the legally required ones. Health, accident, life, and disability insurance are especially popular with small businesses and their employees. In trade and service businesses, discounts on the firm's goods or services are also well received.

Pension programs were common in small firms until the passage of the *Employee Retirement Income Security Act (ERISA)* in 1974. Because the law proved too complex and difficult for small businesses to conform to, many of them gave up their voluntary pension programs, especially after it was amended in 1989.[15]

For example, Ronald Turner, a third-generation lumber company owner in Clarksburg, West Virginia, dropped his employee pension plan, saying that the changes made the benefit program too costly and complex to maintain. He gave his employees the cash due them from the fund. He said he had tried to obey the law, but quit after the required paperwork grew from 35 to 77 pages and the IRS disqualified the plan "on a technicality."[16]

Individual retirement accounts (IRAs) are accounts open to employees to replace pension programs; they may provide tax benefits.

Many small firms have decided to let their employees establish private pension programs using **individual retirement accounts (IRAs).** Any employee who is not covered by a qualified employer retirement plan, and has a taxable income of less than $40,000 for a married couple filing jointly or $25,000 for a single taxpayer, may make a deductible contribution of $2,000 annually to a qualified IRA account (plus $250 to the spouse's account).[17]

A **Keogh retirement plan** permits self-employed persons and partnerships to set aside a certain amount of their earnings and deduct it from income taxes.

Another benefit permits self-employed persons and partnerships to set up tax-deferred retirement programs. Up to $30,000 a year—but no more than 25 percent of the person's eligible total earnings—can be put into a **Keogh retirement plan** and deducted from income taxes.[18] Or they may choose a *simplified employee pension (SEP) plan,* whereby employees open their own IRAs—at a place of their choice. Then the employer pays 15 percent of each employee's salary, or $3,000, whichever is less, into that employee's IRA account each year. In this way, workers can take their pensions with them if they leave their employers. There are, however, some restrictions.[19]

401(k) plans permit workers to place up to a certain amount of their wages each year in tax-deferred retirement savings plans.

Finally, some employers have **401(k) plans,** which permit workers to place up to $7,000 of their wages annually in tax-deferred retirement savings plans. Employers can match the employees' contributions (and often do) on a one-for-one basis. According to the U.S. Chamber of Commerce, more than half of all U.S. employers use this type of plan.[20]

A survey of 500 small and midsize companies found that health insurance was provided by 96 percent of them; life insurance by 82 percent; tuition refunds for job-related courses, 70 percent; dental insurance, 68 percent; profit sharing, 66 percent; 401(k) plans, 52 percent; and pension/retirement plans, 34 percent.[21]

Flexible Approach to Benefits

A *cafeteria-style benefit plan* can help you reduce your annual increase in benefit costs. Under this system, you tell your employees the dollar value of benefits they are entitled to receive. Each employee then tells you how to allocate the money among a variety of available programs. This system increases employee awareness

━━━━━━━━━━━━ USING TECHNOLOGY TO SUCCEED ━━━━━━━━━━━━

COMPUTER SPECIALISTS, INC.: FLEXIBLE SPENDING ACCOUNTS

Computer software has made it technically and economically feasible for small companies to use cafeteria-style benefit programs. The employees at Computer Specialists, Inc., a contract programming business in Monroeville, Pennsylvania, have such a flexible spending account. They can choose from a menu of benefits that includes both the typical ones, such as medical and dental insurance and vacation days, and not-so-typical ones, such as car payments, adoption assistance, and a clothing allowance. One employee was ''frightened to death'' of driving, so the company picked up her $105 monthly cab bill, in addition to paying for her new eyeglasses, a pair of shoes, and a dress. Incidentally, she had to pay income tax on the last three items.

Source: Ellen Kolton, ''Fringe Benefits: True Flexibility,'' *Inc.*, July 1985, p. 104.

of the value of the benefits and offers freedom of choice and a personalized approach (see Using Technology to Succeed).

NEED FOR AN INTEGRATED APPROACH

We would like to end this discussion of leading and motivating employees by returning to the ideas expressed in the Profile. As a small business owner, you need to use more than just financial rewards to get your employees to perform. Instead, you need to hire good people, train them well, communicate with them, let them make suggestions, provide them with an equitable income, and offer innovative employee benefits.

WHAT YOU SHOULD HAVE LEARNED

1. To be successful, you must provide the kind of leadership and motivation that will inspire workers to perform productively. Part of the secret lies in good human relations. Leadership is the ability to inspire others to reach objectives that aren't necessarily their personal goals.

2. Managers spend around 80 percent of their time communicating, that is, in exchanges of meaning. Barriers to effective communication include the status of the communicator (lack of credibility), imprecise use of language, and poor listening. You can become a better communicator by identifying the audience and environment of the communication, and by being a good listener.

3. You can increase employee productivity and improve employee satisfaction through effective motivation. Your problem is to know your employees well

enough to know what incentives will stimulate them to perform. Different incentives must be used according to the purpose of the motivation.

Some currently popular motivational techniques include quality circles, zero-defects programs, job enrichment, management by objectives (MBO), and variable work schedules. Motivation is more than mere technique, and the best motivators are based on a managerial philosophy that recognizes the worth of employees and expects the best from them.

4. Appraising employees' performance is an important part of your job. Merit raises and promotions should be based on such performance appraisals, and they can also point up possible training and development needs in specific areas.

5. Money is an important motivator, so you must pay your employees not just the minimum wage, but enough to attract and keep them. You can use merit increases, incentive payments, and profit sharing to motivate your employees.

Employee benefits, which are increasingly important to both employees and employers, are quite costly. While Social Security, Medicare, unemployment insurance, and workers' compensation are legally required, pension plans and various kinds of insurance are popular voluntary benefits.

QUESTIONS FOR DISCUSSION

1. How would you define (or explain) *good human relations?*
2. Why is communication so important in a small business? What are some barriers to effective communication? How can these barriers be overcome?
3. What is motivation? Why is it so important to a small business manager?
4. What are some practical ways to improve employee motivation?
5. How would you explain the role of money in employee motivation?
6. What is the purpose of personnel appraisals? Why are they so important?
7. What are some legal restraints that affect how much a company pays its employees?
8. What are some of the other factors that affect the amount and form of compensation paid to employees?
9. How can wages be used to motivate employees to perform better?
10. Explain the four legally required employee benefits. What are some of the other benefits frequently used by small businesses?

PERSONNEL POLICIES HELP INTERMATIC GROW

Jim Miller, CEO of Intermatic, Inc., claims his company's personnel policies and programs have been the key to its growth, profitability, and survival. In fact, he thinks this philosophy saved the Spring Grove, Illinois, producer of timing devices and low-voltage lighting from disaster.

Several years ago, when Intermatic was on the verge of bankruptcy, Miller, a former employee, was asked to return as president. To save the company, he reduced the work force by 50 percent, closed down one division, restructured the staff, consolidated positions, and instituted the employee relations policies and programs that have since assured the firm's success.

An incentive system for production workers earns them about 135 percent of their base pay, and some of the unusual employee benefits are (1) programs that pay workers to shed pounds, (2) free eye examinations and glasses, (3) aerobics classes, (4) golf lessons, (5) an outside exercise course, (6) an indoor track, (7) tennis courts, (8) membership in arts-and-culture clubs, (9) shopping at company-subsidized stores for items such as jeans, T-shirts, and baseball caps, and

Jim Miller
Photo courtesy of Intermatic, Inc.

(10) reimbursement of tuition for college courses.

In addition, Miller is quite open in his communications with employees, telling them what has to be done and why it must be done. He also is available to help people with their personal problems, knows them by name, and knows their family situations. The payoff? Turnover is only 3 percent, compared to over 5 percent for similar firms, and it has become such a popular place to work that there's a waiting list of people seeking employment with Intermatic.

QUESTIONS

1. How do you explain the increased performance at Intermatic?

2. Would Jim Miller's methods work at all companies? Explain.

3. Do you think all the employee benefits are needed?

4. How would you like to work at Intermatic?

Source: Correspondence with Intermatic, Inc.

15

Maintaining Good Relationships with Employees

The highest and best form of efficiency is the spontaneous cooperation of a free people.—Woodrow Wilson

You can't manage people—you can only work with them. For your business to succeed, you must work closely with them and take exceedingly good care of them.—Paul Hawken, *Growing a Business*

LEARNING OBJECTIVES

After studying the material in this chapter, you will be able to:
1. Discuss some basic organizational concepts and show how small firms can use them.

2. List some factors influencing employee health and safety, and tell how to safeguard employees in small firms.

3. Define counseling and discuss some of the areas in which it may be needed in small firms.

4. Outline procedures for handling employee complaints and imposing discipline.

5. Discuss some of the complexities of dealing with unions.

MARY H. PARTRIDGE AND MICHAEL LEVY: "HIS AND HERS" BUSINESSES

Michael Levy and Mary H. Partridge, a married couple in The Woodlands, Texas, have separate businesses but share the same office and telephone. He owns and operates Michael Levy & Associates, consultants in training and organization development; she owns and is president of The Woodlands Consulting Group, consultants in personnel administration and human resource development.

Having separate businesses not only allows them to have their own sense of ownership and direction but also permits them to develop their own clients and expertise. When they choose, or need, to use each other's specialized abilities, they collaborate. But when they do this, they try to keep clear who the practical decision maker is, while using the other as a creative resource. They find it "a nice mix."

Photo courtesy of Michael Levy and Mary H. Partridge.

As the environment has changed, the owners have adjusted their activities. The "fat trimming" of the oil industry, their primary clients, has led to an emphasis on developing the team after layoffs, transfers, and terminations. They also help the remaining employees adjust to the need to do more and varied work with fewer employees. They refocus the managers' and employees' emphasis on the mission, objectives, and values of the business.

Much of their time is spent on executive coaching, which involves individual consultations with managers to improve their management approach, communication abilities, and leadership style.

Practicing what they preach, the two consultants avoid hiring staff and incurring lots of overhead. Instead, they use a network of familiar independent contractors, as needed.

Their traditional activities include training trainers for both small and large companies. They do this through formal group seminars or by working one-on-one to coach a company's supervisors or other persons responsible for training personnel. They also conduct seminars on training and development for middle managers.

Levy and Partridge have developed workable relationships with their own personnel—each other and hired free-lancers—and they are able to translate their knowledge and experience to benefit the companies they serve.

Source: Correspondence and discussions with Mary H. Partridge and Michael Levy.

In previous chapters you have seen how to recruit, select, train, and motivate employees. You will now find out how to organize them, protect their health and safety, counsel them, discipline them, and deal with labor unions.

✳ SETTING UP THE ORGANIZATIONAL STRUCTURE

The organizational structure of a business governs relationships between the owner, managers, and employees. **Organizing** involves determining the activities needed to achieve the firm's objectives, dividing them into small groups, and assigning each group to a manager with the necessary authority and expertise to see that they are done. A major problem for many small business owners is that they don't organize their activities properly. The following material should help you understand how best to organize a business.

*margin: **Organizing** is determining those activities that are necessary to achieve a firm's objectives, and assigning them to responsible persons.*

Some Basic Organizational Concepts

There are at least three basic organizational concepts that apply even to small businesses: (1) delegation, (2) span of management, and (3) specialization. While these concepts should be applied to businesses as they grow larger, they must often be adjusted when applied to mom-and-pop businesses.

Delegation

Delegation means assigning responsibility to subordinates for doing certain activities, giving them the authority to carry out the duties, and letting them take care of the details of how the job is done. Many owners and managers of small firms find it difficult to delegate authority. Yet you need to learn to delegate if you answer yes to most of the questions in Figure 15–1.

When you delegate work to subordinates, try to delegate sufficient authority to them to carry out their responsibilities. Otherwise, they lack the means of performing their duties.

*margin: **Delegation** is assigning responsibility to subordinates for certain activities, and giving them the authority to perform those activities.*

Figure 15–1   How Well Do You Delegate?

1. Do you do work an employee could do just as well?
2. Do you think that you are the only one who actually knows how the job should be done?
3. Do you leave work each day loaded down with details to take care of at home?
4. Do you frequently stay after hours catching up?
5. Are you a perfectionist?
6. Do you tell your employees how to solve problems?
7. Do you seem never to be able to complete the work assigned to you?

Source: Claude S. George, *Supervision in Action: The Art of Managing Others,* 4th ed., © 1985, p. 283. Reprinted by permission of Prentice Hall, Inc., Englewood Cliffs, New Jersey.

Except in very small mom-and-pop shops, you should give employees a *job description,* which is a written statement of duties, responsibilities, authority, and relationships (see Chapter 13 for details). When you delegate authority to employees to do certain duties, you must be willing to let them do it; yet you can't relinquish your responsibility for seeing that those duties are performed.

Another important aspect of delegation is that decisions are best made by the person closest to the point of action, since he or she usually knows more about what is going on.

Span of Management

A manager's **span of management,** which is the number of employees reporting directly to him or her, should be limited. Being responsible for too many people, or for too many different types of work, will reduce the manager's ability to handle the work. In general, those with fewer activities to control can successfully manage more people, and vice versa. For example, supervisors may have 10 or more employees reporting to them because of the similarity and repetitive nature of their work. On the other hand, middle managers may have fewer subordinates, doing very dissimilar jobs. Don't try to supervise too many people personally, or the operation of the business could be severely hampered.

Span of management is the number of employees that report directly to a manager.

Specialization

You should try to use **specialization,** whereby employees do the work they are best suited for. But, while it may lead to increased expertise, specialization can also lead to problems such as boredom, fatigue, alienation, and lack of initiative. This concept is hard to apply in very small businesses, where rigid specialization can result in some employees being idle while others are overworked. You must exercise judgment in assigning job responsibilities according to employees' talents and desires, without neglecting an equitable distribution of work.

Specialization is using employees to do the work that they are best suited for.

Some Organizational Problems in Small Firms

A common problem in small firms is the owner's reluctance to delegate. This practice prevents the owner from devoting time to more pressing needs while also preventing others from developing into well-rounded workers.

For example, the owner of a small wholesale company was chairman of the board, president, and treasurer. He handled all financial affairs; supervised accounting operations, wages, salaries, and sales commissions; and made recommendations to the board on the payments of dividends. Yet the company also had a vice-president, sales manager, and operations manager.

This example describes an owner who does not delegate authority. But another problem is an owner who is afraid to make decisions, so the business becomes paralyzed. Then there's the owner who reverses decisions made by others. Perhaps he hasn't developed policies to cover the major repetitive situations and business functions.

The following are some other indications of organizational trouble:

- Sales or production can't keep up with its work load.
- The owner holds too many meetings attended by too many people, resulting in wasted hours and excessive costs.
- Administrative expenses grow more rapidly than sales.
- The owner spends too much time following proper procedures or resolving conflicts rather than "getting production out."
- The attention of key people is not directed toward key activities of the firm and their performance.

Failure to delegate places an immense burden on you, making it impossible for you ever to be absent from the business and virtually guaranteeing its failure should you become incapacitated for a long time, since no one else has been trained to perform management tasks.

Some Ways of Organizing a Small Business

You can organize your business in many ways, but the most frequent ways are by (1) types of authority granted and (2) activities to be performed.

Organizing by Types of Authority

The organizational forms based on types of authority are (1) the line organization and (2) the line-and-staff organization. Within these types of organization is found another type—the informal organization.

As was shown in Figure 3–6 (page 52), a business may start with the owner doing all the work and then hiring a few people who do a variety of duties in producing, financing, and selling the firm's product. The owner is directly responsible for seeing that the employees do these things. This is called a **line organization,** as shown in Figure 15–2.

As the firm grows and becomes more complex, specialized workers—called *staff*—are hired to advise and perform services for those doing the operations, financing, and selling. Some examples are accountants (or controllers), personnel officers, and legal staff. This type of organization is called a **line-and-staff organization** (see Figure 15–3).

An **informal organization** always exists within the formal structure of a business. It involves the many interpersonal relationships that arise on and off the job. Two examples are the *informal leader* and *grapevine communication* systems. You can't fight it, so if you're wise, you'll determine who the informal leaders are and get their support for your activities.

In a **line organization**, the owner has a direct line of command over employees.

A **line-and-staff organization** is one that has specialists to advise and perform services for other employees.

The **informal organization** is the set of interpersonal relationships that come about as a result of friendships that develop on and off the job.

Figure 15–2   A Simplified Line Organization

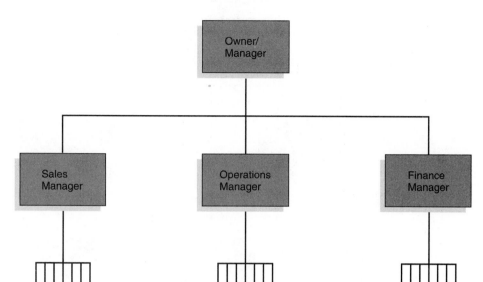

For example, what informal organizations do you belong to? A morning coffee group? A study group? A social get-together once a week?

Organizing by Activities to Be Performed

When you set up your formal organization structure, you can group the activities into small, workable groups according to:

1. *Function performed,* such as production, sales, or finance, as shown in Figure 15–2.
2. *Product sold,* such as menswear, ladies' wear, and so forth.
3. *Process used,* such as X-rays, operating room, and food service in a hospital.
4. *Area served,* such as urban, suburban, or rural.
5. *Types of customers served,* such as industrial, commercial, institutional, or governmental.
6. *Project being managed,* such as constructing a store and an apartment complex.

Preparing an Organization Chart

There is no one structure that is best for all businesses, either large or small. However, the following discussion may help you organize your business to achieve its objectives.

Figure 15–3   A Simplified Line-and-Staff Organization

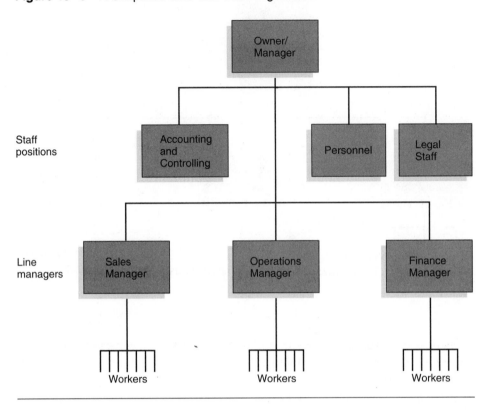

Begin by setting up a series of authority and responsibility relationships expressed in a formal **organization chart,** as shown in Figure 15–2 and Figure 15–3. Even in a small business, a chart can be useful in establishing present relationships, planning future developments, and projecting personnel requirements. Therefore, a list of job titles and job specifications should accompany the chart (see Chapter 13 for details).

An **organization chart** shows the authority and responsibility relationships that exist in a business.

If the business is small and unincorporated, a tight, formal organizational structure could stifle creativity and reduce initiative. Instead, you might have a structure similar to that shown in Figure 15–4.

PROTECTING EMPLOYEES' HEALTH AND SAFETY

Totally safe working conditions are impossible to provide, so employee safety is a condition involving *relative* freedom from danger or injury. This section looks at how small business owners can maintain working conditions in which employees not only *are* safe but also *feel* safe. In other words, employees need to know that you care about their safety.

Figure 15–4 Organization of a Small, Unincorporated Mom-and-Pop Business

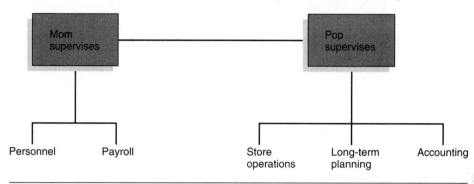

Factors Influencing Workers' Health and Safety

Many factors affect healthy, safe working conditions, but we cover only the most significant ones: (1) organization size, (2) type of industry and occupation, and (3) human variables.

Organization Size

The smallest and largest businesses tend to be the safest places to work; those with either under 20 or over 1,000 employees are safer than those in between. The most dangerous places to work are those with 50 to 1,000 workers.[1]

Type of Industry and Occupation

Although their safety records change periodically, the *least safe industries* usually include longshoring, meat and meat products, roofing and sheet metal, lumber and wood products, and miscellaneous transport.[2]

The type of occupation also affects safety. Workplace dangers and injuries that were once considered likely only in construction and factories have now invaded offices and stores. For example, back injuries are quite prevalent among hotel and motel workers, as well as health care workers who must frequently lift patients or mattresses. According to the Bureau of Labor Statistics, while the illness and injury rate in the private sector averages 8.6 per 100 workers, it is 10.4 for hotel and motel workers, 7.3 for health services, and 44.9 in shipbuilding.[3]

A growing health problem for small firms is called *repetitive-stress injuries (RSIs)*. These muscular or skeletal injuries to the hand, wrist, and other areas that bear the brunt of repeated motions have nearly doubled since 1985.[4] They are now responsible for 56 percent of all workplace illnesses. Aetna Life & Casualty estimates that workers' compensation claims from employees such as reporters, telephone operators, data processors, and checkout clerks using scanners may soon cost as much as $20 billion a year. And the Americans with Disabilities Act may make it easier for victims of RSIs to sue their employers.

Human Variables

The most important human variables influencing safety are job satisfaction, personal characteristics, and management attitudes. Studies indicate a close relationship between safety and employees' satisfaction with their work. Other studies indicate that where top management actively supports safety programs, the accident frequency and severity rates are lower. Finally, most industrial injuries occur in persons 20 to 24 years old, especially males; fewer occur among the married.[5]

✳The Occupational Safety and Health Act

The **Occupational Safety and Health Administration (OSHA)** establishes specific safety standards to assure, to the extent feasible, the safety and health of workers.

The Occupational Safety and Health Act created the **Occupational Safety and Health Administration (OSHA)** to assure — to the extent feasible — safe and healthful working conditions for U.S. employees. The law covers businesses that are engaged in interstate commerce and *have one or more employees,* except those covered by the Atomic Energy Act or the Federal Mine Safety Act.

Employee Rights

First, if workers believe their employer's violation of job safety or health standards threatens physical harm, they may request an OSHA inspection without being discharged or discriminated against for doing so. Second, they can participate in any resulting hearings and can protest if they think the penalty is too light. Third, they can request that the Department of Health and Human Services check to see if there is any potentially toxic substance in the workplace and have safe exposure levels set for that substance.

Employer Obligations and Rights

OSHA encourages increased examination and questioning of management's staffing decisions and equipment selection. To illustrate, employees may claim that a crew size is unsafe or that a machine is potentially dangerous. Also, even though many accidents result from the employees' own lack of safety consciousness, employees usually don't receive citations. Instead, OSHA holds employers responsible for making employees wear safety equipment (see Case 15 for an example).

Employers are subject to fines for unsafe practices regardless of whether any accidents actually occur. Therefore, you should provide safety training for your employees, encourage and follow up on employee compliance with safety regulations and precautions, and discipline employees for noncompliance. Assistance may be obtained from OSHA and National Safety Council chapters. Also, your workers' compensation carrier may be helpful in suggesting ways to improve safety and employees' health. You may obtain useful information from equipment manufacturers, other employers who have had an inspection, trade associations, and the local fire department.

Some Generalizations about OSHA Enforcement

Firms with fewer than eight employees don't have to maintain injury and illness records, except where a fatality occurs or an accident hospitalizes five or more persons. Also, OSHA doesn't inspect firms with 10 or fewer employees in "relatively safe" industries, which exempts nearly 80 percent of firms from inspections. Finally, inspectors concentrate on workplaces with unsatisfactory records.

Since 1988, small businesses have found that the paperwork burden makes it especially difficult for them to comply with OSHA's Hazard Communications Standard. It requires every employer in the country to identify hazardous substances in the workplace, list them, and train employees to use them safely. At first, the law applied only to manufacturers, but now the rule applies to all—"from accountants to zookeepers."[6]

Because the inspection program and its technical nature constantly change, you're advised to use the resources suggested previously, as well as local chambers of commerce, area planning and development commissions, and local offices of the SBA and OSHA. As indicated in Chapter 9, SBA loans may be available to help meet safety and health standards.

Environmental Protection

The *Environmental Protection Agency (EPA)* was created to help protect and improve the quality of the nation's environment. Its mandate includes solid-waste disposal, clean air, water resources, noise, pesticides, and atomic radiation. Environmental protection, though beneficial to society, can be hard on small firms. Many marginal plants have closed because of EPA requirements that pollution control equipment be installed. You owe it to your employees, for humanitarian reasons as well as financial ones, to protect their environment. As shown in Using Technology to Succeed, environmental protection efforts can also give your company a competitive edge.

✳ COUNSELING TROUBLED EMPLOYEES

Counseling is designed to help employees do a better job by helping them understand their relationships with supervisors, fellow workers, and customers. While most small firms don't have formal counseling programs, they counsel employees on a day-to-day basis. The information in Figure 15–5 should help you do informal counseling. If you don't feel qualified to perform this activity, specialized employees may be used.[7]

Counseling helps to provide people with an understanding of their relationships with their supervisors, fellow workers, and customers.

━━━━━━━━━━━━━━━━━━━━ USING TECHNOLOGY TO SUCCEED ━━━━━━━━━━━━━━━━━━━━

COMBINING IDEALISM WITH OPPORTUNISM

In the past, the computer industry has enjoyed a reputation for being environmentally clean—especially when compared to industries such as metals, paper, and petrochemicals. But groups such as the Silicon Valley Toxics Coalition have shown that computer waste products also pollute the air, soil, and ground water. The primary problem is CFCs (chlorofluorocarbons), used as a solvent to wash the residue from printed circuit boards.

Inmos, a chip manufacturer located in the United Kingdom, has been using IPA (isopropyl alcohol) to replace CFCs. Unfortunately, it is highly flammable and is potentially dangerous—especially if used in the same quantities as CFCs.

While computers and peripherals are themselves rarely tossed into landfills—causing an environmental problem—such is not true of consumables, such as batteries, disk media, paper, printer ribbons, and toner cartridges. While waste from computers makes up a small amount of municipal garbage, its proportion has grown every year since the advent of the personal computer. In order to prevent such waste from becoming a public relations problem, several companies have announced programs to recycle laser-printer toner cartridges. For example, Apple began its program to recycle toner cartridges in 1991. Cartridges bought in the United States include a prepaid shipping label that lets you return them when you're through with them. For every cartridge you return in the United States, Apple will donate $1 to one of two environmental organizations.

Source: Andy Reinhardt et al., "The Greening of Computers," *Byte,* September 1992, pp. 147–58.

Figure 15–5   How to Approach a Troubled Employee

---

1. Establish the standards of job performance you expect.
2. Be specific about behavioral criteria, such as absenteeism and poor job performance.
3. Restrict criticism to job performance.
4. Be firm and consistent.
5. Be prepared to deal with resistance, defensiveness, or even hostility.
6. Point out the availability of internal or external counseling services.
7. Explain that only the employee can decide whether or not to seek assistance.
8. Discuss drinking only if it occurs on the job or the employee is obviously intoxicated.
9. Emphasize the confidentiality of the program.
10. Get a commitment from the employee to meet specific work criteria and monitor this with a plan for improvement based on work performance.

Areas Needing Counseling

While counseling involves all areas of employee relations, most counseling needs fall into the categories of (1) job-related activities, (2) personal problems, and (3) employee complaints.

Reprinted from *The Wall Street Journal*; permission
Cartoon Features Syndicate

Job-Related Activities

The activities that need counseling most are (1) performance, (2) safety, (3) retirement or termination, and (4) discipline, which will be treated separately.

Performance Appraisal. As discussed in Chapter 14, you should evaluate your employees' performance periodically, and discuss the results with them to help each see his or her strengths and weaknesses more clearly. The procedure—especially the follow-up discussion—should try to motivate workers to build on their strengths and minimize their weaknesses.

Health and Safety. As shown earlier, the whole area of health and safety requires considerable counseling and guidance. Because safety is largely a matter of attitude, your role is to counsel employees on the need for safe operations and to actively support all safety efforts.

Retirement or Termination. Employees need considerable preparation for retirement, especially with regard to the benefits coming to them. But counseling is even more urgently needed when an employee must be terminated—with or without cause. Now that U.S. businesses are more concerned with cost saving, primarily because of foreign competition, terminations are more frequent. When employees just can't produce, or when the business can't afford to keep them, termination is often the only option. But, as shown in Chapter 13, you might want to help the worker find other employment. Even with such help, though, termination is still traumatic for the worker, and counseling is needed.

Personal Problems

It's estimated that around a fifth of employees suffer personal problems, which reduce productivity by as much as 25 percent and result in ''astronomical'' dollar

Figure 15–6   Drug Problems in the Workplace

Percentage of problems caused by drugs at 102 companies:

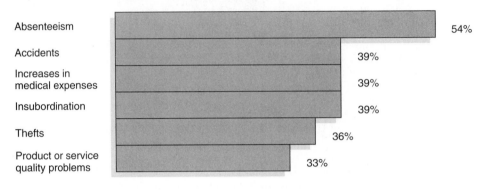

Absenteeism	54%
Accidents	39%
Increases in medical expenses	39%
Insubordination	39%
Thefts	36%
Product or service quality problems	33%

Source: Hoffmann-La Roche Inc., October 1989, as reported in *USA Today,* December 7, 1989, p. 1A. © 1989, USA TODAY. Adapted with permission.

losses.[8] Two-thirds of those problems are drug and alcohol related, while the others tend to be emotional problems. Figure 15–6 shows some problems that can result from drug abuse. One way employers are coping with these problems is through counseling, referral to trained professionals, and employee-assistance programs.

Since 1989, small businesses with federal contracts and grants have been required to have a substance abuse policy that conforms to the Department of Defense's *Drug-Free Workforce Rules,* which impose sweeping new obligations on contractors and grantees.[9] While the cost of such a drug-free environment is unknown, many small firms may be unable to bear the cost.

Dealing with Employee Complaints

Because complaints will inevitably occur, you should encourage employees to inform you when they think something is wrong and needs to be corrected. An effective procedure to do this should provide (1) assurance to employees that expressing their complaints will not jeopardize their employment, (2) a simple procedure for presenting their complaints, and (3) a minimum of red tape and time in processing complaints and determining solutions.

Unresolved complaints can lead to more problems, so you should listen patiently and deal with them promptly even if they seem to be without foundation. You should analyze the complaint carefully, gather pertinent facts, make a decision, inform the employee of it, and follow up to determine whether the cause of the problem has been corrected. Detailed, written records of all complaints (and disciplinary actions), as well as how they were resolved, should be maintained in employees' files as a defense against legal charges that may be brought against you.

IMPOSING DISCIPLINE

Employees like to work in an environment where there is **discipline**—in the sense of having a system of rules and procedures and having them enforced fairly. You can achieve such an orderly, disciplined environment by either (1) motivating employees to exercise self-discipline or (2) imposing discipline on them.

Discipline involves fairly enforcing a system of rules and regulations to obtain order.

Encouraging Self-Discipline

To be effective, your employees should have confidence in their ability to perform their job, see good performance as compatible with their own interests, and know that you will provide support if they run into difficulties. Therefore, you should encourage self-discipline among employees rather than rely on direct control. In this respect, the personal example of the owner will be important in influencing employee discipline, as the following example illustrates.

The owner of a small firm selling and installing metal buildings had a problem with employees taking long lunch breaks. When he asked his supervisors to correct this practice, one of them had the courage to say, "That would be easier to do if you didn't take two-hour lunches yourself."

We've heard managers of small firms say that traditional discipline doesn't work for them. Instead, some are using *positive discipline* to improve morale and lower turnover. Under this approach, employees who commit some breach of conduct receive an oral "reminder," not a reprimand. Then there is a written reminder, followed by a paid day off to decide whether they really want to keep their job. If the answer is "yes," the employee agrees in writing to be on his or her best behavior for a given period of time. The employee who doesn't perform satisfactorily after that is fired. Since the cases are fully documented, employees usually have little recourse.

How to Discipline Employees

Most employees rarely cause problems. Yet if you don't deal effectively with the few who violate rules and regulations, employees' respect for you will decline. An effective disciplinary system that meets union and legal guidelines involves:

- Setting definite rules and seeing that employees know them.
- Acting promptly on violations.

- Gathering pertinent facts about violations.
- Allowing employees an opportunity to explain their behavior.
- Setting up tentative courses of action and evaluating them.
- Deciding what action to take.
- Taking disciplinary action, while observing labor contract and EEO procedures.
- Setting up and maintaining a record of actions taken, and following up on the outcome.

The procedure should distinguish between major and minor offenses and consider extenuating circumstances, such as the employee's length of service, prior performance record, and the amount of time since the last offense.

DEALING WITH UNIONS

The percentage of the U.S. work force belonging to unions has dropped drastically in the last four decades—from over 33 percent in 1955 to 16.1 percent in 1991.[10] And only 11.9 percent of the private sector work force is unionized.[11] Yet unions are quite powerful economically and politically, so they affect you one way or another.

While union organizers have tended to concentrate their organizing efforts on larger firms, because they are easier to unionize, they're now also trying to organize smaller firms, because that's where potential new members are. Also, small business owners are more active in lobbying Congress and state legislatures, through groups such as the National Federation of Independent Business (NFIB), for laws and regulations unions oppose.[12] Therefore, you need to know something about unions and how to deal with them.

Laws Governing Union-Management Relations

The *National Labor Relations Act (NLRA)* (also called the *Wagner Act),* as amended, requires management to bargain with the union if a majority of its employees desire unionization. (See Table 15–1 for the provisions of this and related laws.) Managers are forbidden to discriminate against employees in any way because of union activity. The *National Labor Relations Board (NLRB)* serves as the labor court. Its general counsel investigates charges of unfair labor practices, issues complaints, and prosecutes cases. The union or management can appeal a ruling of the board through a U.S. circuit court all the way up to the U.S. Supreme Court.

Right-to-work laws permit states to prohibit unions from requiring workers to join a union.

In some states a *union shop clause* provides that employees must join the recognized union within 30 days after being hired. But under **right-to-work laws** in effect in 21 states, the union shop is not legally permitted.[13]

Table 15–1 Some Laws Governing Union-Management Relations

Laws	Coverage	Basic Requirements	Agencies Involved
National Labor Relations Act of 1935, as amended (also called the Wagner Act)	Nonmanagerial employees in nonagricultural private firms not covered by the Railway Labor Act, and postal employees.	Employees have the right to form or join labor organizations (or to refuse to), to bargain collectively through their representatives, and to engage in other concerted activities such as strikes, picketing, and boycotts; there are unfair labor practices in which the employer and the union cannot engage.	National Labor Relations Board (NLRB).
Labor-Management Relations Act of 1947, as amended (also called the Taft-Hartley Act)	Same as above.	Amended NLRA; permits states to pass laws prohibiting compulsory union membership; sets up methods to deal with strikes affecting national health and safety.	NLRB; Federal Mediation and Conciliation Service.
Labor-Management Reporting and Discourse Act of 1959, as amended (also called the Landrum-Griffin Act)	Same as above.	Amended NLRA and LMRA; guarantees individual rights of union members in dealing with their union; requires financial disclosures by unions.	U.S. Department of Labor.

Source: Various government and private publications.

What Happens When the Union Enters

Unions exist to bargain with the employer on behalf of their members for higher wages, fringe benefits, better working conditions, security, and other terms and conditions of employment. In order to do this, the union must first organize the company's employees.

The first thing you should do if your employees want to form a union is to recognize that it's because they believe they need the protection the union offers. You should therefore ask yourself such questions as: Why do my employees feel that it is necessary to have a union to represent them? Is it a lack of communication, or have I failed to respond to their needs? Am I treating them arbitrarily or unfairly? Studies of successful nonunionized companies find that management and employees participate in the business process as a team rather than as adversaries.

The second thing you should do is call in a competent consultant or labor lawyer. Small firms are increasingly turning to advisors to deal with unions, as the following example indicates.

When employees tried to organize Persona Inc., a Watertown, South Dakota, manufacturing firm, its president called in Henry N. Teipel of St. Paul, Minnesota, as a consultant. He helped the personnel manager prepare for meetings with union representatives. The advice, which cost $4,000, "saved a tremendous amount of money . . . by keeping the battle short and the union out," according to the president.[14]

If your company is unionized, you should be prepared for certain changes. Your actions and statements may be reported to union officials, and the union may file unfair labor practice charges with the NLRB. Your best defense is to know your rights under the prevailing laws—and to maintain favorable relationships with employees.

Negotiating the Agreement

Negotiating an agreement with the union requires much preparation, as well as the actual bargaining, and these require patience and understanding, so again it's advisable to consult your labor lawyer.

Preparing for the Bargaining

Preparation may well be the most important step in negotiating the agreement. Obtaining facts about the issues before sitting down at the bargaining table should improve your position. You should collect information on other contracts in the industry and in the local area. Disciplinary actions, complaints, and other key matters that arose before the union's entry should be studied. Current business literature concerning business in general and the status of union-management relations in the industry can be useful. A carefully researched proposal should be developed well in advance of the first bargaining session.

Bargaining with the Union

If you've prepared properly, you should be in a positive negotiating position instead of a defensive stance against the union's proposals. The "I don't want to give away any more than I have to" attitude generally leads to poor bargaining. All too frequently, however, fear seems to overcome the owner's willingness to develop in advance a proposal with attractive features that will appeal to employees, while protecting the company's position.

You should recognize the negotiation step as critical: it must be handled properly, preferably with outside assistance. Also remember that anything given away will be difficult to take back.

Be prepared to bargain over at least the following:

- Union recognition.
- Wages.
- Vacations and holidays.
- Working conditions.
- Layoffs and rehiring.

- Hours of work.
- Management prerogatives.
- Seniority.
- Arbitration.
- Renewal of the agreement.

Specific agreements must be reached in each of these areas, and rules established that should be obeyed by the company and the union. The *management prerogatives clause* is very important because it defines the areas in which you have the right to act freely as an employer, without interference from the union.

Living with the Agreement

Because the agreement becomes a legal document when it's signed, you must learn to live with its provisions until time for renegotiation. Your managers should be thoroughly briefed on its contents and implications. Meanings and interpretations of each clause should be reviewed and the wording clearly understood. Supervisors' questions should be answered to better prepare them to deal firsthand with labor matters.

Information and advice can be obtained from government sources, such as federal and state mediators, NLRB regional offices, state industrial relations departments, and members of SCORE. Private sources include employer groups, trade associations, labor relations attorneys, and labor relations consultants.

WHAT YOU SHOULD HAVE LEARNED

1. Some important organizational concepts that apply to small firms as they grow are delegation, span of management, and specialization. Following these principles helps you delegate, tends to eliminate tensions, and eases employee frustrations.

   You can organize your business by *(a)* type of authority used or *(b)* activities performed. The simplest structure is the line organization, where orders are handed down from the top to the bottom. With growth, specialized people are needed to do activities not strictly related to operations, selling, or finance, resulting in a line-and-staff structure. Informal organizations, found in all businesses, shouldn't be ignored, because their informal leaders and grapevine communications can affect your activities.

2. Employee health and safety varies with the size of the organization, the industry and occupation involved, and personal characteristics of the owner and employees. OSHA, the government agency responsible for promoting safe and healthful working conditions, concentrates on the businesses most likely to be unsafe or unhealthy.

While environmental protection is undoubtedly beneficial, the costs of required equipment and/or procedures can be a hardship for small businesses.

3. Counseling may involve listening to an employee gripe about some petty grievance, or it may be needed to correct a serious work problem. Counseling is needed in the job-related areas of performance appraisal, health and safety, and retirement or termination, as well as the personal areas of illness, mental and emotional problems, and substance abuse.

4. While some complaints from employees are inevitable, they can often be handled informally, but an established procedure is needed to discipline unsatisfactory employees. In the ideal work situation, employees discipline themselves, but for those who don't, a procedure should be set up to take into account the severity of the offense and the number of times it has been committed, as well as other factors and extenuating circumstances. Positive discipline, which challenges employees to discipline themselves, is being used in many small firms.

5. Dealing with a union is a challenge most owners and managers of small businesses don't want to face, and most will try to keep the union out. However, when a union does enter, many things change. Many laws govern labor-management relations, so hire a good consultant to help you. Negotiating an agreement with the union requires much preparation. After agreement is reached, supervisors should be briefed on the terms of the contract, and instructed on how to deal with labor matters. Managers can get help in dealing with a union from many government and private sources.

QUESTIONS FOR DISCUSSION

1. Explain some of the basic organizational concepts used in organizing a small business.

2. Describe some of the organizational problems small firms have.

3. Distinguish between organizing the business by type of authority and by grouping of activities.

4. Discuss the most significant factors that influence safe working conditions. What can a small business owner do about them, if anything?

5. Briefly discuss the Occupational Safety and Health Act and its application by OSHA.

6. Discuss the areas requiring counseling. What, if anything, can a small business manager do to improve counseling in those areas?

7. Explain the differences between self-discipline and externally imposed discipline.

8. Explain how national labor laws affect small businesses. Should you, as a small business owner, favor or oppose your employees' unionizing? Defend your answer.

THE CASE OF SAM SAWYER

Sam Sawyer was a top-rated operator in a building where a material with caustic soda was processed. The five stages were located on five separate floors. Operators moved the material in open buggies from the first stage to a chute in the floor and dumped it onto equipment on the floor below, where the next stage took place.

Because of the corrosive nature of the material, close-fitting goggles were provided. Until a year earlier, safety rules had required that goggles be worn only when removing material from equipment, because that was where the greatest possibility of injury existed. Their use at other times was up to the discretion of each operator.

At two stages in the process, though, the material was light and fluffy, and occasional backdrafts through the chutes caused it to fly. After this had resulted in three cases of eye irritations, the rules were changed, and operators were required to wear goggles whenever they were near exposed material.

Dave Watts, supervisor of operations for two years, had worked on all stages of the operation his first year out of engineering school. He had gotten along well with the men, was grateful to them for teaching him the "tricks of the trade," and might have been tempted to be lenient with them. Watts's boss, however, was very safety minded and insisted that safety rules be followed to the letter.

Sam Sawyer, who had worked on the operation for 20 years, was an outstanding operator and was looked up to by his fellow workers. His safety record was one of the best in the plant, as he had had only one minor injury in all his years of service.

Source: Prepared by Bruce Gunn, Florida State University.

When the new safety rule went into effect, Dave was bothered because everyone went along with it except Sam, who contended that it was unnecessary to wear goggles except when unloading equipment. This caused problems for Dave, because the others followed Sam's example. After much discussion, however, Sam agreed to go along with the rule.

Dave had a strong feeling that Sam was complying with the rule only while he was around. On half a dozen occasions he thought that Sam had put on the goggles just as he came on the floor. Before the rule change, Sam had worn the goggles around his neck when they weren't needed, but he had recently started wearing them pushed up on his forehead.

Dave's doubts were confirmed today when he came upon Sam unexpectedly and saw him bob his head to shift the goggles from his forehead to his eyes.

QUESTIONS

1. What does the case show about the need for emphasis on safety by management?

2. How can you explain the workers' lack of interest in their own safety?

3. What would you do if you were the supervisor?

4. How would you explain it to an OSHA inspector?

5. What does this case illustrate about the role of informal leaders?

V

OPERATING THE BUSINESS

Up to this point, we have been concerned with the challenge of owning a small business: planning for, organizing, and managing the business; marketing the product; and organizing and managing the work force. Now it is time to look at the process of actually operating the business.

Many different activities are required to carry on operations. Your business must determine what products to sell; decide whether to purchase them from someone else or produce them; plan, acquire, lay out, and maintain the physical facilities needed for operations; procure and produce the right quality of the right products, at the right time and at the right cost; control the quality and quantity of inventory; control the quality of your output; maintain a work force; and do *all of this as efficiently and economically as possible!*

All these activities make operating a business interesting, challenging, and rewarding—but also quite frustrating. To help meet this challenge, this part will cover designing operating systems for production and service. Locating and laying out facilities are discussed in Chapter 16. Chapter 17 covers purchasing, operations, and quality control.

16

Locating and Laying Out Operating Facilities

Production is not the application of tools to materials, but logic to work.—Peter F. Drucker

You know your company is ready for robots when you recognize that automating is cheaper than relocating in South Korea or Taiwan.—Bruce H. Kleiner, management professor

LEARNING OBJECTIVES

After studying the material in this chapter, you will be able to:

1. Explain what an operating system is and how it functions.

2. Discuss how to determine the right location for a small business.

3. Describe the important factors involved in choosing a retail site.

4. Describe the most important factors involved in choosing a manufacturing site.

5. Identify the steps in planning the layout of physical facilities and show how to implement them.

6. Explain how to set and use performance standards.

TEAGUE BROTHERS: CLEANING PERSIAN CARPETS

"We are in business to provide a needed service," said Joe Teague, who with his wife, Margaret, owns and operates Teague Brothers Carpet Cleaning and Sales, Inc. "First we sell carpets, and then we clean them."

Joe Teague operated a moving company before opening the carpet business in 1959. His wife joined him in 1962, when their children were in school. The rug-cleaning business declined sharply in the mid-1960s and early 1970s, when wall-to-wall carpeting became popular, but has since recovered. The Teagues' daughter, Dottie, now runs the family moving business (see Chapter 24), while the parents concentrate on the carpet business.

The Teagues operate in a building containing a showroom, an office, two production rooms, and a warehouse. The sales and cleaning activities require two different operating systems. New rugs and carpeting are on display in the showroom, along with chairs and desks for customers and sales personnel. After purchase, the rugs are delivered, or the carpeting and runners are installed.

While cleaning Oriental rugs may seem simple and easy, it's really quite complicated and difficult, according to Mrs. Teague.

Photo by Jay Ferchaud. © 1986, The Mobile Press Register. All rights reserved.

The process starts on a long cylinder called a beater vacuum. The rug, inserted upside down, literally has the dirt beaten out of it by a series of leather "fingers." The vacuum then sucks the dirt away.

Next, the carpet is laid flat on the sloping floor, spot-sprayed with cleaning fluid, and thoroughly doused with a mixture of cleaner and water from a wooden container 15 feet above the floor. An electric cleaning machine is repeatedly passed over it; then the carpet is rinsed clean, and the cleaner and water are drained into a gutter around the edge of the floor.

Then, two men pick up the carpet and feed it into slots on the rolling machine (see photo). Rollers feed the rug through while it is rinsed to get out any remaining dirt or cleaning mixture; the rollers squeeze it to extract excess water. The carpet then is hung up to dry at a temperature of 140 degrees. While only one carpet can be cleaned at a time, up to 60 can be dried simultaneously.

This process may seem a peculiar way to clean a valuable carpet, but that's the way they are cleaned after being woven in Iran, Turkey, Pakistan, and Afghanistan.

Teague Brothers is the only carpet cleaner in the area that is a member of the National Institute of Rug Cleaners.

Sources: Visits to Teague Brothers; Marion Valentino, ''Taking an Old Favorite to the Cleaners,'' *Mobile* (Alabama) *Press Register,* August 24, 1986, p. 14-F; and Carol Cain Lynn, ''Business All in the Family,'' *Mobile* (Alabama) *Press Register,* August 6, 1989, p. 3-E.

As the Profile illustrates, all businesses produce some product, either selling a good or providing a service. A retailer forecasts demand and then purchases merchandise and displays, sells, and delivers it to customers. A producer forecasts demand and then purchases material, processes it into products, and sells and delivers the products to customers. A service business tries to satisfy the needs of customers by providing a needed service. This chapter examines what you must do to produce your product, how to choose the right location to produce it, how to plan and lay out physical facilities, and how to constantly improve operations.

DEVELOPING OPERATING SYSTEMS

The steps required to start a business, as discussed in Chapter 5, are (1) searching for a product, (2) studying the market for the product, (3) deciding how to get into business, (4) making strategic plans, and (5) making operational plans, including planning the many aspects of operating the business once it's started. This last step involves setting up your operating systems, and providing building(s), materials, equipment, and people to produce the product.

Operating systems in different businesses are really quite similar, although the sequence of events and activities may vary as each business adjusts the system to fit its own needs. Also, support systems, such as accounting, personnel, and cash flow systems, must be integrated into the overall producing system.

Operating systems have the following productive elements: (1) a system for changing form, place, or time; (2) a sequence of steps to change the inputs into outputs; (3) special skills, tools, and/or machines to make the change; (4) instructions and goods identification; and (5) a time frame within which the work is to be done.

What Are Operating Systems?

Operating systems consist of the inputs, processes, and outputs of a business.

Inputs are materials, people, money, information, machines, and other productive factors.

Processes convert these inputs into products customers want.

Outputs are the products produced and the satisfactions to employees and the public.

An **operating system** consists of inputs, processes, and outputs. The **inputs** include materials, people, money, information, machines, and other factors. The **process** involves converting these inputs into the goods or services the customers want, using the employees, machines, materials, and other factors. The **outputs** consist of the goods and services required by the customers; desired outputs also include satisfying the needs of employees and the public.

Figure 16–1 shows some examples of how inputs are processed into outputs. Note that each process represents a major operation: cloth, thread, and buttons are sewn into shirts; dirty carpets (as shown in the Profile) are cleaned; or a request for data is converted into a computer program.

Figure 16–1 Examples of Operating Systems

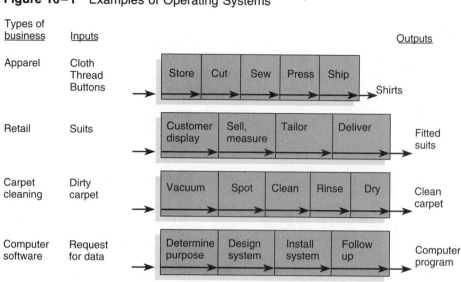

How Operating Systems Work

Operations, or **production,** includes all the activities from obtaining raw materials through delivering the product to the customers. Thus, the word *operations* refers to those activities necessary to produce and deliver a service or good.*

All businesses usually have systems other than the production system, and as the following example shows, these systems must be coordinated for the best production.

Operations, or **production,** is converting inputs into outputs for customers.

For example, the objective of fast-food operations is to supply food quickly and with little customer effort. At Burger King, for example, there are three systems:

1. *A marketing system.* The order for a Whopper is taken from the customer and money received to pay for it.
2. *A production system.* The order is given to someone to prepare the hamburger and package it, while someone else prepares drinks.
3. *A delivery system.* The completed order is handed to the customer.

These three systems are coordinated to provide quick service and to keep the line moving. Figure 16–2 shows how the production system operates. Notice how the inputs—such as rolls, meat patties, mayonnaise, lettuce, onions, and pickles—are processed by cooking, assembling, and wrapping into the output—a Whopper—which is then delivered to the customer.

---

*There are three activities that must be performed by all businesses, regardless of their nature. They are (1) *marketing,* (2) *finance,* and (3) *operations.* In manufacturing and similar plants, operations is called *production,* but in retail and service-type firms the activity is called *operations.*

Figure 16–2   Operations Involved in Producing a Hamburger

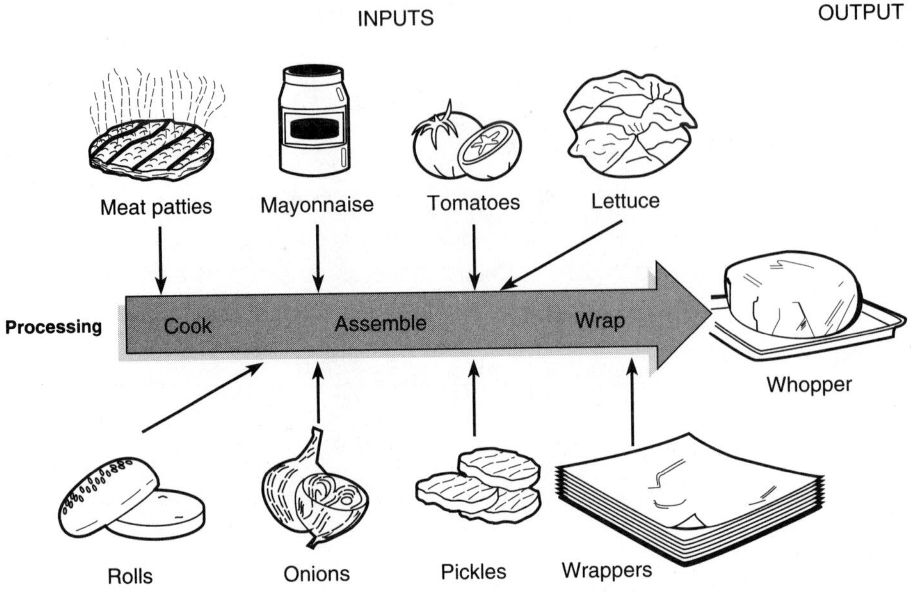

Source: Adapted from Leon C. Megginson, Lyle R. Trueblood, and Gayle M. Ross, *Business* (Lexington, Mass.: D. C. Heath, 1985), p. 202.

How to Begin Operations

You are now ready to begin operations, which involves (1) choosing the right location, (2) planning physical facilities, (3) deciding on a layout, and (4) implementing your plans.

CHOOSING THE RIGHT LOCATION

As shown in Chapters 6 and 8, you must define the character of your business and decide upon your business strategies before you begin to investigate available locations for your business. You must then ask yourself such questions as: Do I plan to have just one store or to grow regionally or nationwide? Do I intend to concentrate on one product area or expand into several? The answers to these questions will focus your search.

Why Choosing the Right Location Is So Important

Location is one of the factors that can make the difference between success and failure for a small business. Sales come from customers who find it advantageous to buy from you rather than someone else. All of these advantages, including convenience, cost, reliability, and good service, are influenced by location. Therefore, you should evaluate your specific location requirements very carefully.

When you choose a location, you usually expect to stay there for some time. It is very expensive to move to another location, customers follow established patterns of activity and do not like changes, and employees are affected in the same way.

Some Important Factors Affecting Location Choice

Information on which to base a location decision can come from a wide variety of sources, as discussed in Chapters 5 and 12. You should consider two sets of factors when choosing a location for your business. There are some general factors that affect all types of businesses, but there are also some factors that pertain to specific types of businesses.

General Factors Affecting All Businesses

The more important general factors are:

1. Access to a capable, well-trained work force.
2. Availability of electricity, gas, water, sewerage, and other utilities.
3. Availability of adequate and affordable supplies and services.
4. Availability, type, use, and cost of transportation.
5. Taxes and government regulations.

Specific Factors to Consider for Various Businesses

The type of business—retailing, producing, or service—influences most location decisions because it determines the relative importance of the general factors mentioned above. For example, location of customers may be more important to a large department store, while location of employees will be more important to a manufacturing plant. Table 16–1 shows some of the specific factors to be considered in making location decisions. Although the factors have been separated into retail and producer, many of them apply equally to retailing, producing, and service organizations.

Retailers are concerned with people who come to—or are drawn into—the store for the purpose of making a purchase. Therefore, location is concerned with people's movement, attention, attitudes, convenience, needs, and ability to buy. In other words, which location will provide sales at a reasonable profit?

Producers are not usually concerned with the flow of people coming in to buy goods because sales are made by salespeople or through some other method of promotion for delivery at some future date. The plant and customer can be some distance apart, so other factors become more important. Still, nearness to customers and suppliers helps to keep costs down and permit satisfactory service. Primary emphasis in locating, though, is placed on cost and service.

Table 16-1   Some Important Location Factors

	Factors Affecting Selection of	
City	**Area in City**	**Specific Site**
Retail:		
Size of trade area	Attraction power	Traffic passing site
Population trends	Competitive nature	Ability to intercept traffic
Purchasing power	Access routes	Compatibility of adjacent stores
Trade potential	Zoning regulations	Adequacy of parking
Competition	Area expansion	Unfriendly competition
Shopping centers	General appearance	Cost of site
Producer:		
Market location	Zoning	Zoning
Vendor location	Industrial park	Sewer, effluent control
Labor availability	Transportation	Transportation
Transportation		Terrain
Utilities		Utilities
Government, taxes		Labor availability
Schools, recreation		

Source: U.S. Small Business Administration, *Choosing a Retailing Location,* Management Aid No. 2.021 (Washington, D.C.: U.S. Government Printing Office), p. 2.

Service companies have some of the characteristics of both retailing and producing. These companies perform specialized services to individuals and organizations. The location of services requiring customers to come to the business location, such as a hairdresser, depends upon convenient travel. Services going to the home of a customer have more latitude, but they should try to locate near where customers are clustered. In fact, service businesses that cannot attract enough customers to a central location may acquire more by taking their show on the road.

For example, after grooming dogs for 27 years from a fixed location, Ronnie and Martell White, owners of On the Spot Dog Grooming, now use a "grooming van." With a small office in their home, they cover an area of about 100 square miles. The van is fully loaded with an extensive unit for all aspects of dog grooming, including a built-in bathtub. On an average day, the Whites service eight dogs or more at a cost of $15 or $20 each.[1]

Many small service businesses start and continue to operate out of the owner's home. This is a logical arrangement since the owner may be tentative about going into business and may not want to have the fixed expense of an office. Also, the owner tends to go to the clients to perform the service. Finally, as will be shown in Chapter 20, there are tax benefits.[2]

Figure 16–3 Rating Sheet for Sites

Grade each factor: 1 (lowest) to 10 (highest)
Weigh each factor: 1 (least important) to 5 (most important)

Factors	Grade	Weight
1. Centrally located to reach my market.	_____	_____
2. Raw materials readily available.	_____	_____
3. Quantity of available labor.	_____	_____
4. Transportation availability and rates.	_____	_____
5. Labor rates of pay/estimated productivity.	_____	_____
6. Adequacy of utilities (sewer, water, power, gas).	_____	_____
7. Local business climate.	_____	_____
8. Provision for future expansion.	_____	_____
9. Tax burden.	_____	_____
10. Topography of the site (slope and foundation).	_____	_____
11. Quality of police and fire protection.	_____	_____
12. Housing availability for workers and managers.	_____	_____
13. Environmental factors (schools, cultural, community atmosphere).	_____	_____
14. Estimate of quality of this site in five years.	_____	_____
15. Estimate of this site in relation to my major competitor.	_____	_____

Note: Copies of this *Aid* and other publications are available from the SBA for a small processing fee. Order forms 115A and 115B can be obtained free from SBA, P.O. Box 15434, Fort Worth, TX 76119. *Aids* may be condensed or reproduced. They may not be altered to imply approval by SBA of any private organization, product or service. Material courtesy of Small Business Administration.

Source: U.S. Small Business Administration, *Locating or Relocating Your Business,* Management Aid No. 2.002, p. 6.

At some point, the data collected must be analyzed to provide the information necessary for a decision. A score sheet like that in Figure 16–3 can be valuable in comparing possible locations. Evaluations can sometimes be quantitative, such as number of households times median income times percentage of income spent on store items times some special factor for this store. Others are ratings, grading factors from 1 for the lowest to 10 for the highest.

Some factors are very important and should be given more weight than others. In fact, one factor in a given site might be so intolerable that the site must be eliminated from consideration.

LOCATING RETAIL STORES

In choosing a site for a retail store, two interrelated factors are important: the type of store (i.e., the type of goods sold) and the type of location.

Types of Stores

Customers view products in different ways when selecting the store from which to buy. Therefore, stores can be grouped into (1) convenience, (2) shopping, and (3) specialty stores, according to the type of goods they sell.

Convenience Goods Stores

Convenience goods are
products that customers buy
often, routinely, quickly, and in
any store that carries them.

Convenience goods are usually low-priced items that are purchased often, are sold in many stores, are bought by habit, and lend themselves to self-service. Examples are candy bars, milk, bread, cigarettes, and detergents. Although the term *convenience goods* may make you think of *convenience stores* (small markets with gas pumps out front), convenience goods stores are better typified by the grocery and variety stores where we regularly shop for consumable items. Convenience goods stores are interested in having a high flow of customer traffic, so they try to get people to remember their needs and come in to purchase the items currently on display. The quantity of customer flow seems more important than its quality. These stores are built where the traffic flow is already heavy.

Nearly 70 percent of women have been found to patronize stores within five blocks of their residence.[3] Store hours are also very important.

Shopping Goods Stores

Shopping goods are goods that
customers buy infrequently,
after shopping at only a few
stores.

Shopping goods are usually higher-priced items, which are bought infrequently, and for which the customer compares prices. People spend much time looking for these items and talking to sales personnel. Therefore, capable salespeople with selling ability are required (see Chapter 11 for more detail). Examples of these goods are suits, automobiles, and furniture.

Specialty Goods Stores

Specialty goods are bought
infrequently, often at exclusive
outlets, after special effort by
the customer to drive to the
store.

Specialty goods are high-priced shopping goods with trade names that are recognized for the exclusive nature of the clientele for the goods. By their very nature, specialty goods stores often generate their own traffic, but customer flow can be helped by similar stores in the vicinity. Some examples of specialty goods are quality dresses, precious jewelry, and expensive video and sound equipment. In essence, people do not comparison shop for specialty goods, but just buy the name on the item.

Types of Locations

In general, the types of locations for retail businesses are (1) downtown business districts, (2) freestanding stores, and (3) community shopping centers or malls.

Downtown Business District

Changes in retail locations have occurred as discounters have located their stores outside the downtown area. Now, governments, financial businesses, and the head offices of large firms provide most of the downtown business for downtown retail stores.

A downtown location has many advantages, such as lower rents, better public transportation, and proximity to where people work. But the disadvantages include limited shopping hours, higher crime rates, poor or inadequate traffic and parking, and deterioration of downtown areas.

Freestanding Stores

A freestanding location may be the best for customers who have brand or company loyalty, or for those who identify with a given shop, where a business has a competitive edge over its competitors, where the character of customers and growth objectives blend well. Low costs, good parking, independent hours and operations, and restricted competition in these locations tend to fit the more entrepreneurial types of businesspeople. However, in order to attract customers, especially new ones, you may have to do considerable advertising. Moreover, acquiring a suitable building and land may be difficult.

Shopping Centers

Shopping centers are planned and built only after lengthy and involved studies. These centers vary in size from small neighborhood and strip centers, to community centers, to the large regional malls.

Why Shopping Centers Are So Popular.   Shopping centers are designed to draw traffic according to the planned nature of the stores to be included in them. The design of the centers ranges from small, neighborhood convenience goods stores to giant regional centers with a wide range of goods and services, which may or may not be specialized. Shopping centers offer many services, such as specialized activities to bring in traffic, merchant association activities, parking, utilities, and combined advertising. A current trend is for large "power centers" to compete with one another to be the largest.

Enclosed malls have eliminated weather problems for customers. Also, older and handicapped people are encouraged to use the mall to exercise in a controlled climate.

The typical shopping center has two **anchor stores.** These stores, often large department stores, are strategically located in the center or at the primary corners of the mall in order to generate heavy traffic for themselves and for the small stores between them. The photo on the next page illustrates an anchor store.

Anchor stores are those that generate heavy traffic in a shopping center.

Some malls may have a "theme" that stores are expected to conform to. The purpose of the theme is to pull the stores together and have them handle products of similar quality. For example, the center may have regulations on shopping hours, how to use the space in front of the store (what to display and how), and so on.

Photo courtesy of William Waldorf.

Drawbacks of Shopping Centers.   Although the above advantages are considerable, there are also disadvantages to locating in a center. Some of the most significant of these are cost, restrictions imposed by the center's theme, operating regulations, and possible changes in the center's owners and managers, which could bring policy changes.

There is now a "total rent" concept for cost that must be considered in evaluating the costs of renting space in a shopping center. These costs may include dues to the merchants' association, maintenance fees for the common areas, and the cost of special events or combined advertising. The most common rental is a basic rent, usually based on square footage, plus a percentage of gross sales (usually 5 to 7 percent). These costs tend to be high and often discourage tenants, as the following example shows.

For several years, Kitty* operated her medium-priced ladies' wear shop in a small shopping area across from one of the community's larger shopping malls. A representative of the mall tried to persuade Kitty to move to the mall. After hearing the rental terms, however, Kitty was appalled. The basic rent was $21.75 per square foot with an additional charge of 5 percent of the gross sales. Later Kitty told a friend, "Do you know that just the basic rent would have cost me $2,400 a month, to which I would have had to add on 5 percent? Can you imagine what I would have had to charge for my clothes in order to make a profit after paying that kind of rent? I think I'd better stay put."

LOCATING MANUFACTURING PLANTS

Manufacturing involves making or processing materials into finished goods.

Manufacturing usually involves making, or processing, raw materials into a finished product. The materials may be those extracted from the ground, or they may be outputs of other companies (such as metal plates, silicon chips, or ground meat for hamburgers), which are changed in form or shape, or assembled into a

*Name disguised.

USING TECHNOLOGY TO SUCCEED

AUTODESK, INC.: DESIGNERS GET INTO THEIR DESIGNS

A few years ago, designers found that with computers they could tinker with, test, and perfect their work on screens before going into costly prototypes. Some of the fancier systems even showed animated designs in three dimensions. Now, a Sausalito, California, company, Autodesk, Inc., believes engineers will want to go even further—getting inside their designing.

The company, which sells software to mechanical designers (including the popular AutoCAD program), is working on a product that creates a design "Never-Never Land" called *Hyperspace*. When the software is coupled with a high-powered computer and special electronic eyeglasses and gloves are used, the designer has the impression that he or she is walking inside the project being designed. With this system, engineers can design not only a building but also its environment, and explore it while the designing is still being done.

Source: G. Pascal Zachary, "New Software Invites Designers into Designs," *The Wall Street Journal,* August 4, 1989, p. B1. Reprinted by permission of THE WALL STREET JOURNAL, © 1989 Dow Jones & Company, Inc. All Rights Reserved Worldwide.

---

different type of product. The location of a manufacturing plant is usually selected with the aim of serving customers properly at the lowest practical cost. Of the factors to consider in locating a manufacturing plant (See Table 16–1), the most important ones are nearness to customers and vendors, and availability and cost of transportation.

Of considerable importance to manufacturers is the time and cost of transporting finished goods to the customers and acquiring raw materials from vendors. The success of a given location can hinge on the availability and cost of the proper mode(s) of transportation, as discussed in Chapter 12.

PLANNING PHYSICAL FACILITIES

Once you've selected your location, you must begin planning, acquiring, and installing facilities. These **facilities**, which include the building, machines and other equipment, and furniture and fixtures, must be designed or selected to produce the desired product at the lowest practical cost. As the above Using Technology to Succeed shows, computers are now being used in this type of design operation.

> **Facilities** are the buildings, machines and other equipment, and furniture and fixtures needed to produce and distribute a product.

These activities include four steps: (1) determine the product to be sold and the volume in which it is to be produced, (2) identify the operations and activities required to get the product to the customer, (3) determine space requirements, and (4) determine the most effective layout of the facilities.

Determine Product to Be Produced

Facilities should be planned for the future so as to avoid early major changes. Projections for five years are normal, and industry standards for the space required for planned sales or production volume can be a good start in planning.

Identify Operations and Activities to Be Performed

You will remember that operations include all the activities from buying the materials through delivering the finished product to the customer. These activities include (1) purchasing materials and parts for production or goods to sell, (2) performing operations needed to produce the product, and (3) carrying out support activities.

Sequences of operations may be fixed (e.g., producing the hamburger in Figure 16–2) or may change from order to order, as happens in retail stores or service businesses.

Determine Space Requirements

Space is required for materials, equipment, and machines, as well as the movement of customers and employees. Space is also needed for carts and trucks, inventory, displays, waiting areas, personal facilities, maintenance and cleaning, and many other services. The number and size of all these areas are dependent on the volume of output planned.

Decide on the Best Layout

The objective in layout planning is to obtain the best placement of furniture and fixtures; tools, machines, and equipment; storage and materials handling; service activities such as cleaning and maintenance; and places for employees and customers to sit, stand, or move about.

Figure 16–4 shows a tentative layout of a company making metal signs. Notice the placement of facilities, such as ovens, presses, benches, and paint booths. Also, notice the lines with arrows showing the flow of traffic.

Types of Layout

The two general types of layout are product and process, although actual layouts often combine the two types.

A **product layout** has the facilities laid out according to the sequence of operations to be performed.

Product Layout.   In a **product layout,** facilities are arranged so that materials, workers, and/or customers move from one operation to another with little backtracking, such as the school cafeteria shown in Figure 16–5A. The advantages of the product layout plan include specialization of workers and machines, less inventory, fewer instructions and controls, faster movement, and less space needed

Figure 16–4   Tentative Layout for a Metal Sign Company

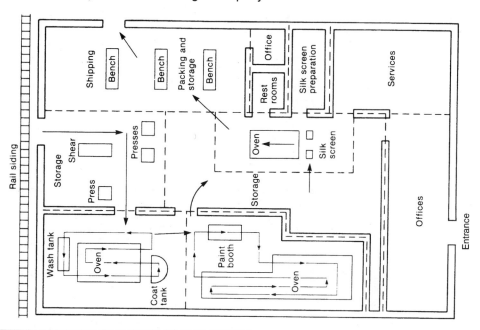

for aisles and storage. This arrangement tends to improve efficiency and maximize sales, especially in the automobile and fast-food industries.

For example, notice in Figure 16–2 (p. 324) that if you order a Whopper, its production moves forward from cooking the meat to assembling, wrapping, and delivering the Whopper to you.

 Process Layout.   The **process layout** groups together machines performing the same type of work and workers with similar skills such as the cafeteria shown in Figure 16–5B.

The process layout requires more movement of material or people, as is shown by the figure, and requires a larger inventory. But it also provides flexibility to take care of change and variety, often can use the same general-purpose machines and equipment for several steps in the operation, and permits more efficient scheduling of equipment and workers.

Few layout plans are totally product or process layouts. Instead, most layout plans combine the two to obtain the advantages of both, as shown in Figure 16–4.

A **process layout** groups together the facilities doing the same type of work.

Determining the General Layout

The next step in the design process is determining the general layout by grouping together machines, products, or departments. This helps to establish the general

Figure 16–5   Product and Process Layout Comparison of Cafeterias

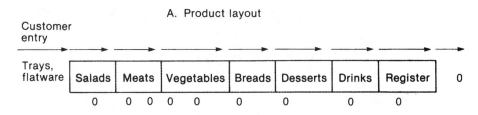

A. Product layout

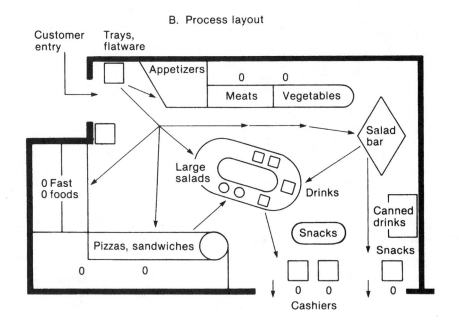

B. Process layout

arrangement of the plant, store, or office before spending much time on details. Using similar layouts as an example, you can estimate the space needed.

Notice in Figure 16–4 that the broken lines outline the spaces set aside for particular operations and activities. Space should also be provided, where appropriate, for maintenance, planning, and food and other needed services. Each service should be placed conveniently near the units that use it.

Entrance locations are important in the layout of retail and service establishments. Customers usually enter downtown stores from the street, parking lot, or corridors, and goods usually enter from the back. External factors to consider include entrances for employees, parking for customers, connections to utilities, governmental restrictions, and weather factors.

Figure 16–6   Questions to Ask about a Production Layout

1. *Space for movement.* Are aisles wide enough for cart and truck movement? Is there enough room for lines that form at machines and checkout stations? Can material be obtained easily and shelves restocked conveniently?

2. *Utilities.* Has adequate wiring and plumbing, and provision for changes, been planned? Has provision been made for proper temperature? Does the area meet Environmental Protection Agency (EPA) standards?

3. *Safety.* Is proper fire protection provided, and are Occupational Safety and Health Administration (OSHA) standards being met? Are proper guards on machines, in aisles, and around dangerous areas planned?

4. *Working conditions.* Do workers have enough working space and light? Is there provision for low noise levels, proper temperature, and elimination of objectionable odors? Are workers safe? Can they socialize and take care of personal needs?

5. *Cleanliness and maintenance.* Is the layout designed for effective housekeeping and waste disposal at low cost? Can machinery, equipment, and the building be maintained easily?

6. *Product quality.* Has provision been made to assure proper quality and to protect the product as it moves through the plant or stays in storage?

7. *Aesthetics.* Is the layout attractive to customers and employees?

In manufacturing and large retail and wholesale warehouses, materials-handling devices such as conveyors, carts, hand trucks, and cranes are used to move materials. The objective is to move the items as quickly as possible, with a minimum of handling, and without increasing other costs.

Determining the Final Layout

If your performance is to be efficient, the final layout must be planned in detail, so examine each operation to assure easy performance of the work. If workers spend too much time in walking, turning, twisting, or other wasted motion, the work will take longer and be more tiring. Tools and other items to be used should be located close at hand for quick service. Some specific factors to consider when doing your final layout are shown in Figure 16–6.

Since the first of these, space for movement, is particularly important, you should ask questions such as: Is there enough room if a line forms? Can shelves be restocked conveniently? Are aisles wide enough for one- or two-way traffic?

For example, grocery store aisles are designed to allow passage of two carts, but they often become blocked by special displays of new or sale items. Similarly, it may be difficult to squeeze between the display racks in department stores, and office planners often fail to allow enough space for storage of accumulated files.

The last consideration, aesthetics, is also important, so ask yourself: Are the layout and surroundings attractive to workers and customers?

The Gloucester, Virginia, ServiStar Hardware Store, which once was patronized primarily by men, was dank, dark, and ugly. With more women becoming do-it-yourselfers and buyers of more hardware store items, ServiStar decided to change its image. It installed bright lights, chrome gridwork, and even murals. "Some of the old guys come in and kid us about being a disco," says Robert Fitchett, whose family owns the store, "but our sales are up 33 percent from last year."

Implement Your Plans

Finally, you should test your layout plans to see if they are sound. One way to do this is to have employees, customers, or other knowledgeable people review the plans and make suggestions.

Finally, construction of a new building requires consideration of the type and method of construction, arrangements for vehicular movement and parking, provision for public transportation, if available, and landscaping.

HOW TO IMPROVE OPERATIONS

Products and methods of operation are constantly changing, and competition pushes out obsolete or inefficient businesses. However, some tools are available in the disciplines of work simplification and industrial engineering to help you keep up-to-date and constantly improve your operations.

The steps used in designing and improving work are (1) state the problem, (2) collect and record information, (3) develop and analyze alternatives, and (4) select, install, and follow up on the new work method. Computers are now used to help improve operations, particularly through the use of software that simulates operations.

State the Problem

As usual, it is best to begin by clearly stating *the problem—not a symptom* of it. Ask questions such as: Is the cost of the work too high? Is the quality of the service low? Is the service to customers delayed?

Collect and Record Information

This step consists of collecting information for the *what, how, where, who, why,* and *when* of the work being done. Observing the work being performed, talking with knowledgeable people, and studying available data are methods of obtaining information.[4]

Develop and Analyze Alternatives

Listing the available alternatives is basic to any type of analysis and a critical step in decision making. All work and services can be performed in many ways, and products can be made from many different materials.

Some questions that might be used in improving work performance include:

- Who performs the activity, what is it, and where is it being done?
- Why is the activity being performed?
- Can the activity be performed in a better way?
- Can it be combined with another activity (or activities)?
- Can the work sequence be changed to reduce the volume of work?
- Can it be simplified?

Select, Install, and Follow Up on New Methods

Using your objectives, such as lower costs or better service, as a guide, pick the method that best suits your goals. Installing this new method includes setting up the physical equipment, gaining acceptance, and training workers. Test the method to see that it works and follow up to see that workers are familiar with it and are following procedures.

SETTING AND USING PERFORMANCE STANDARDS

One of the most difficult problems you'll face in your business is measuring the performance of employees, since there are few precise tools for establishing standards against which to measure it. Instead, you must rely heavily on the judgment of people. Physical work can be measured more precisely than mental work, but doing so still requires judgment.

Performance standards can be set up by (1) estimates by people experienced in the work; (2) time studies, using a watch or other timing device; and (3) synthesis of the elemental times obtained from published tables. Most small business owners use the first method, using estimates of experienced people. These estimates should be recorded and given to workers for their guidance. The standards should allow for the time needed to do the work at normal speed, plus time for unavoidable delays and personal requirements. A good set of standards can be determined this way at a minimal cost.

WHAT YOU SHOULD HAVE LEARNED

1. All businesses have operating systems, which transform inputs of people, money, machines, methods, and materials into outputs of goods, services, and satisfactions.

2. Some general factors to be considered in locating any business are access to *(a)* the work force, *(b)* utilities, *(c)* vendors, and *(d)* transportation, as well as *(e)* taxes and government regulations.

3. The most important factors to consider in choosing a retail site are the type of business and the type of location. The type of business largely determines

the location. Convenience goods stores are usually located where the traffic flow is high, shopping goods stores where comparison shopping can be done. Specialty goods stores often generate their own traffic but are helped by having similar stores in the vicinity.

The types of retail locations are downtown, in freestanding stores, and in shopping centers.

4. Among the most important factors in choosing a manufacturing site are nearness to customers and vendors, and the availability and cost of transportation.

5. In planning physical facilities you *(a)* determine the desired product and volume to produce, *(b)* identify the operations and activities required to process it, *(c)* estimate the space needed, and *(d)* determine the best physical arrangement and layout of those facilities. The types of layout are product and process, or a combination of both.

Physical facilities must be laid out to provide for a smooth flow of work and activities, space for movement, adequate utilities, safe operations, favorable working conditions, cleanliness and ease of maintenance, product quality, and a favorable impression.

6. The method of setting and/or improving performance standards includes *(a)* stating the problem; *(b)* collecting and recording information; *(c)* developing and analyzing alternatives; and *(d)* selecting, installing, and following up on the new methods.

QUESTIONS FOR DISCUSSION

1. What are some characteristics of an operating system? What are some of the inputs into an operating system? What are some of the outputs resulting from the operating processes?

2. Explain some of the more important general factors affecting location choice.

3. Explain the two most important factors in choosing a retail site.

4. Explain the two most important factors in locating a manufacturing plant.

5. Explain the steps involved in planning facilities.

6. Explain the three different types of layout.

7. What are some of the characteristics of an effective layout?

8. Explain the four steps involved in improving operations.

9. Which of the two cafeteria layouts in Figure 16–5 do you think would be more effective? Why?

10. Do you remember your movements during course registration the last time? What improvements could you make in the process?

MANUFACTURING SMART PHONES

Competition in the pay telephone industry has resulted in the manufacture and use of "intelligent pay phones." The main difference between smart pay phones and standard ones is computerization. Because the standard phone is a transceiver linked to others by the phone company, busy signals, no answer, and so forth are relayed to each phone from a central location. Tiny computer chips inside smart phones perform this function within the telephone itself.

One of the oldest manufacturers of smart phones is Telecommunications Technology Inc., of Mobile, Alabama (TTI). According to Phil Hardy, founder

Photo by Adline Clarke. © 1986, The Mobile Press Register, Inc. All rights reserved.

and marketing director, it originally had no intention of manufacturing phones. Instead, the founders thought they would have a vending phone business. But being unable to find a coin-operated phone of the quality it wanted to vend, and faced with having to pay an excessively high tariff to use Bell telephone lines, TTI began developing and making its own pay phone—the TTI Model 400K.

Designed by TTI, Model 400K is assembled by a company in Tallahassee, Florida, which also makes other telecommunications products. The phones are then shipped to Mobile, where TTI engineers and technicians program them to do what buyers want them to do. For example, they can either limit the calls to three minutes or have no time limits. The phones can also be programmed to block out undesirable numbers such as Dial-a-Porn or to allow callers to place toll-free calls. The phone also has a voice that says, "Please deposit 25 cents."

TTI sells its phones through a distributor network selling TTI equipment exclusively. Entrepreneurs buy the smart phones from TTI, place them in businesses, and then share the profits with the owners of the businesses.

TTI sells its phones primarily in Illinois, New York, Texas, and Washington.

QUESTIONS

1. Do you think TTI did the right thing in producing its own phones? Why or why not?

2. Could you suggest ways for improving its production of the phones? How?

3. What other activities would you recommend for TTI?

Source: Adline Clarke, "TTI of Mobile Manufacturing Smart Phones," *Mobile* (Alabama) *Press Register,* Octoer 12, 1986, p. 1-C.

17

Purchasing, Inventory, and Quality Control

With the automation we have today, an agent can do five times the work he could do only six years ago.—William Quartermaine, business leader, in 1885

Resources must be employed productively and their productivity has to grow if the business is to survive.—Peter F. Drucker

LEARNING OBJECTIVES

After studying the material in this chapter, you will be able to:

1. Discuss the importance of purchasing.

2. Explain the need to choose suppliers carefully.

3. Describe how to establish an effective purchasing procedure.

4. Discuss how to establish and maintain effective inventory control.

5. Explain what is involved in operations planning and control.

6. Describe how to maintain quality control.

ANDERS BOOK STORES: DEALING WITH HUNDREDS OF SUPPLIERS

Bob and Kathy Summer find owning and managing Anders Book Stores (ABS) "frustrating—but fun!" They purchased the store from Jim Anders in 1982 after spending several years working for him and learning some of the ins and outs of running the business.

The Summers have divided the responsibilities so that Bob specializes in college-level books and Kathy handles everything associated with textbooks and supplies for 12 private schools. After ordering and receiving the books, she groups them by grade, sells them, and returns unsold copies to publishers. In handling these activities, as well as being responsible for materials and supplies, she deals with "over 1,000 suppliers each year."

Bob handles sales to the University of South Alabama,

which has its own bookstore a few blocks away, to other colleges in the area, and at the Anders branch on the University of Mobile campus, about 15 miles away. Bob receives the book orders from faculty members; buys, receives, and sells the books; reorders if necessary; and returns unsold books to the publishers.

A major problem Anders faces is estimating how many copies of each text to order. Each book order has the estimated number of students in the class; so taking into consideration that some students will share a book and some won't buy a text, Bob estimates how many copies of each text to order.

Bob buys used books from students and used-book wholesalers; new textbooks come from their publishers. The problem is that ABS has 1,200 publishers listed in its computer, although it regularly buys from "only" about 300 to 400 in any one year. When you consider that Kathy also buys from "over 1,000" suppliers, you can understand

why they say that "buying and bookkeeping problems are horrendous."

About six to eight weeks before classes start, orders are sent to publishers via computer modem. Publishers then ship the books, either UPS or freight, sometimes as much as six weeks before they're needed.

Another problem is not having enough textbooks to meet student needs. When this happens, Bob reorders and books are shipped UPS. The supplier usually ships the books one to seven days after the order is received. If needed immediately, a book can be shipped second-day express—at a charge of up to $10 more. One year, enrollment increased so rapidly that Bob had to place over 50 reorders, for about 25 percent of the books sold.

Even worse is the problem of unsold books. Even when publishers allow returns for a refund, there is usually a restocking fee. And in the present economic climate of rapid mergers, sometimes the publisher that sold the books has been acquired by another house, so where should the books be returned? Given the already low gross profit margin of only 15 to 20 percent, returns put a severe financial strain on the business.

Poor-quality books pose another problem. In one order, some books had the first 78 pages glued together. In another, some sections came unglued and fell apart. Although the publisher replaces books, replacement is inconvenient and time-consuming.

Most of the large publishers send out an annual evaluation form for their dealers to complete. Since doing this, Bob and Kathy have noticed an improvement in service from the publishers.

Source: Discussions with Kathy and Bob Summer.

The Profile shows that the profitability of a small business depends largely on effective purchasing, inventory, operations, and quality control. Most small firms have many potential sources of supply for goods and services, each of which requires close study to secure the proper quality, quantity, timing, price, and service needed. This chapter emphasizes the strategies and procedures needed for effective purchasing, as well as inventory, operations, and quality control.

THE IMPORTANCE OF PURCHASING

Your business will need products that are provided by someone else, and the wide variety of items available requires careful study to ensure that proper selection is made. Some items, such as electricity, come from only one supplier but even they require a careful analysis in order to obtain them at the lowest cost. Others, such as insurance, machines, and equipment, also require special attention because they are often expensive and are purchased infrequently. Still other items, such as paper clips and welding rods, are relatively cheap, and they're purchased routinely. Finally, materials that are part of the company's main product and have a high cost relative to revenue will take up a large amount of your time. This chapter is primarily concerned with this last group, those that are an important part of your main product.

What Purchasing Involves

Purchasing determines the company's needs and finds, orders, and assures delivery of those items.

Obtaining all items, including goods and services, in the proper form, quantity, and quality, and at the proper place, time, and cost, is the main objective of **purchasing.** Purchasing identifies the needs of the company and finds, negotiates for, orders, and assures delivery of those items. Thus, you should coordinate your needs with the operations of suppliers, establish standardized procedures, and set up and maintain controls to ensure proper performance. Notice that Bob and Kathy Summer do all of these things in buying for Anders Book Stores.

In retail stores, buying requires coordinating the level of stock of many items with consumer demands, which change as factors such as styles, colors, technology, and personal identification change. (And many customers may expect to buy year-round certain "standard" items that don't reflect fashion changes.) Each type of item may be handled differently, so the person(s) doing the buying must work closely with those doing the selling to satisfy these differing needs.

Purchasing for a manufacturing plant involves getting the proper materials and processing them into finished goods, while maintaining inventory and quality control. Thus, those doing the purchasing must work closely with those doing the production and selling.

Why Purchasing Is So Important

The cost of materials and other goods and services needed to produce a product is about half the revenue received for it. This means that all other costs, plus profit, just about equal the cost of purchases. In many cases (Mead Pharmaceutical is one example), the cost of purchases is as much as two-thirds of sales revenues.[1]

While the price of purchases is important, other aspects can be just as critical. For example, obtaining **just-in-time delivery**—where the materials are delivered to the user just at the time they are needed for production—can save on inventory costs. Close coordination between you and your supplier can greatly improve efficiency.

Just-in-time delivery is having materials delivered to the user at the time needed for production.

Although neither is small, Wal-Mart Stores has an agreement with Procter & Gamble (P&G) that is expected to revolutionize the way manufacturers deal with even small retailers. P&G already shares a computer-to-computer inventory system with Wal-Mart, but it is making changes to move the flow of goods from raw materials through manufacturing to the product supply division more efficiently in order to expedite deliveries and drive down costs to the retailer.[2]

In summary, not having the appropriate stock—the right style, at the right price, at the right time, and of the proper quality—properly displayed for customers can result in costs and lower profits.

For example, Chrysler had to recall the first 4,000 of its popular new midsize LH cars to fix a 5-cent part. A defective washer in the steering system could disintegrate, making it harder to control the car.[3]

☀ MAKING SOMEONE RESPONSIBLE FOR PURCHASING

While capable subordinates, such as specialty buyers, may be delegated the authority to order in their areas of expertise, in general, one person should be given the overall purchasing responsibility. But that person should ask for—and get—the help of people knowledgeable in the area where the items are needed.

Those doing the purchasing should be aware of trends and special situations that can affect operations and should call situations such as the following to your attention:

1. *Expected changes in price.* Buying later for expected decreases in price or buying increased quantities for expected inflation in price can result in savings. However, **stockouts,** which are sales lost because an item is not in stock when customers want it, and inventory costs that are too heavy should be guarded against.

Stockouts are sales lost because an item is not in stock.

2. *Expected changes in demand.* Seasonal products and high-fashion items fall into this category.

3. *Orders for specialty goods.* The quantity ordered should match expected demand, so that no material is left over. Because demand for these items is unknown, forecasts should include estimates of losses that may occur from stockouts or old and stale inventory.

4. *Short supply of materials,* as the following example illustrates.

In the Salaminder, Inc., example in Chapter 6, you learned that the demand for high-quality (and high-priced) western clothing skyrocketed because of the popularity of the movie *Urban Cowboy.* The small producer had to overcome the short supply by rapidly expanding operations—only to have to cut back severely the next summer, as demand plummeted.

SELECTING THE RIGHT SUPPLIER(S)

You will be more successful in purchasing if you can find several acceptable sources of goods and services. Because reliability in delivery and quality affects nearly all operations, suppliers can be valuable sources of information for various aspects of operations, and suppliers can provide valuable service.

You can find many good sources by consulting the Yellow Pages, the *Thomas Register of American Manufacturers,* the *McRae Bluebook,* newspapers, trade journals, and publications of research organizations. In addition, visits to trade shows and merchandise marts give you an opportunity to view exhibits and talk with salespeople. Electronic networks can be set up and used to obtain information on possible sources. Many small firms are now hiring expert consultants when purchasing becomes complex.[4]

Types of Suppliers

As discussed in Chapter 11, you can purchase from brokers, jobbers, wholesalers, producers, or others. Each provides a particular type of service. Notice that Anders Book Stores buys new books from the producers (the publishers) but buys used ones from wholesalers (used-book companies) and students. Also, supplies and other items are ordered from a variety of sources.

Use Few or Many Suppliers?

Should you buy from one, a few, or many suppliers? A single source of supply can result in a closer and more personalized relationship so that when shortages occur, you should receive better service than when many sources are used. Also, discounts may be obtained with larger-volume buying. If one seller can supply a wide assortment of the items needed, the cost of ordering is reduced. On the other hand, multiple sources provide a greater variety of goods and often better terms. Most small firms use several sources. Notice also that Anders Book Stores buys from some 2,000 different suppliers.

Sometimes it's desirable—or even necessary—to use a single source for specialized items, as the following example illustrates.

Several years ago, Wynton M. and Carolyn Blount donated the land and money to build the Wynton M. Blount Cultural Park in Montgomery, Alabama, where the Alabama Shakespeare Festival is located. Because they were great admirers of Queen Elizabeth II's beautiful black swans, they inquired as to where she had found them. The answer came back from England that they'd been bought at a farm just a few miles from Montgomery—the only known source of supply of the beautiful birds shown here.

Photo by Alabama Shakespeare Festival photographer Phil Scarsbrook. Used with permission.

Investigating Potential Suppliers

Potential sources can be checked for factors such as quality of output, price, desire to serve, reliability, transportation, terms of payment, and guarantee and warranties; because all of these factors affect your company's performance, a minimum standard must be set for each.

Suppliers should not be chosen on the basis of price alone, for quality and/or service may suffer if the supplier has to lower prices to obtain your order. Instead, they should be chosen to meet carefully set quality and service standards. These standards can be used to ensure acceptable quality without paying for quality higher than needed.

Evaluating Supplier Performance

Just as you investigate potential suppliers, you should also evaluate their performance. While it requires some time and effort, you could develop some type of rating system to use in selecting, evaluating, and retaining suppliers. Some such rating systems pick out important factors such as quality, service, and reliability, as well as price, and then use those to evaluate each supplier.

For example, Sharp Corporation uses this kind of rating system in its Memphis Plant to evaluate its 70 suppliers, most of which are small firms. A copy of its creed, "Practice Sincerity and Creativity," is given to each potential supplier with a statement that Sharp expects "100% quality parts," delivered precisely on schedule. Suppliers who agree to this stipulation become Sharp's suppliers and receive a periodic report card showing how they rate on satisfying quality, price, prompt delivery, and other standards.[5]

ESTABLISHING AN EFFECTIVE PURCHASING PROCEDURE

In addition to deciding on the supplier(s) to use, you must establish a purchasing procedure to ensure effective purchasing. While there is no "one best way," Figure 17–1 presents a computer flow chart of a well-designed purchase order system. The diagram shows the basic process but doesn't include the many variations needed for special conditions. For example, some companies order standardized units, while others order specially designed ones.

Requisitioning Goods or Services

The request to purchase goods or services (item 1 in Figure 17–1) can originate from many sources. If a service is needed, the request usually comes from the user of that service, as when the accounting manager requests an outside audit, the personnel manager needs to install or change an insurance program, or the marketing manager needs to place an ad with an agency. But when goods are needed, the request can originate in any of several ways, such as when (1) someone observes that inventory is low; (2) it's the prescribed time to order the item; or (3) an operating manager requests it, a customer requests a given item, or the purchasing manager observes some special condition(s) that indicate the need to purchase an item.

Purchasing by retailers poses different problems from purchasing by a producer. Figure 17–2 shows a suggested schedule for a retailer to buy and sell style goods. The procedure operates as follows.

Figure 17–1   Purchase Order Process Flow Chart

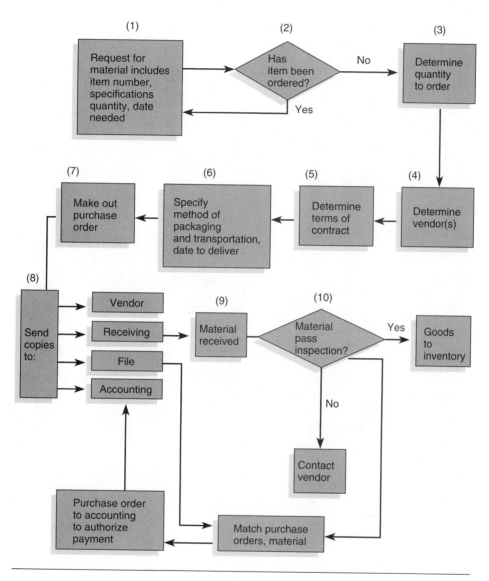

In August 1993, the retailer visits a trade show—or consults suppliers—and places orders based on evaluation of styles and plans. Between August and February, plans for the spring and summer are completed. Goods are received in time for the selling seasons; inventory and sales are checked to consider placing orders to replenish stock. End-of-season sales are run in late winter 1994 to remove stock from inventory. Planning is started during this time in preparation for the fall and winter (1994–95) seasons.

Figure 17–2   Suggested Schedule for Purchasing and Retailing Style Goods

Activity	1993 Fall	1993–94 Winter	1994 Spring	1994 Summer
Retailer	F&W 1993-94			
Plans	Planning S&S 1994 sales			
	Selects styles and orders	Plans sales and promotion (Reorders, F&W, 1993-94)		
and			Planning F&W 1994-95 sales	
			Plans styles and sales	Selects styles and orders	Plans sales and promotion (Reorders, S&S 1994)
Orders				(S&S 1995) Plans styles and sales
Retailer	S&S 1993			
Sells	Receives goods	Selling F&W 1993-94 goods		
		Regular sales Markdown sales		
Goods			Receives goods	Selling S&S 1994 goods
				Regular sales Markdown sales
Producer	F&W 1993-94			
Produces	Producing S&S 1994 goods			
Goods				Producing F&W 1994-95 goods

Legend: S&S = Spring and summer; F&W = Fall and winter.

A **purchase order** tells the supplier to ship you a given amount of an item at a given quality and price.

Standing orders set predetermined times to ship given quantities of needed items, at a set price.

Making and Placing the Purchase Order

There are many ways of placing orders for needed goods (item 7 in Figure 17–1), depending on your needs and the supplier's demands. Issuing **purchase orders** is very common, since they become legal records for the buyer and seller. Establishing **standing orders** with the supplier simplifies the purchasing procedure and allows for long-range planning. It involves setting schedules for delivery of goods in predetermined quantities and times, and at agreed-to terms.

Receiving the Items

Receiving goods and placing them in inventory (item 9 in Figure 17–1), is the last step in the purchasing procedure. A copy of the purchase order, including the desired specifications, is sent to those receiving the goods. Upon arrival, the condition of the goods is checked, and they are checked against the order to make sure that they are the desired items, in the correct color or material, size, quantity, and so on. Proper receiving procedure can detect deviations from these standards. The prices are also checked. The person who ordered the items, as well as the accountant, is informed that the items have been received and are ready for processing.

Using Computers to Aid Purchasing and Inventory Control

Small companies are increasingly using computers to keep track of inventory items, spot replenishment needs, identify sources of supply, and provide information needed for ordering. In most cases, computers provide information needed by the purchaser to use in the ordering process.

The prompt availability of updated computer information reduces errors and processing time compared to manual systems. The computer also expands the types and amount of information for potentially better and faster processing of orders. For example, many computer installations are designed to perform automatically, for selected items, the purchasing steps numbered 1 through 7 in Figure 17–1.

CONTROLLING INVENTORY

Inventory is carried in order to disconnect one segment of the operating process from another so that each part can operate at its optimum level. A crude example is in your home. If you didn't have a supply of food, you would have to go out, find some, buy it, bring it home, and prepare it every time you were hungry. Having surplus food in your pantry or refrigerator, however, you can buy more food at your convenience, keep it as inventory, and then process it when you get hungry.

The same holds true in a manufacturing plant. Figure 17–3 shows what happens from the receipt of raw materials, through each of three operations, to final sale to customers. Notice that inventories are shown at different levels at different stages of the operation and that the inventory level at a given stage depends on what activities have occurred in the operations process.

Figure 17–3   Diagram of Material Flow and Inventory

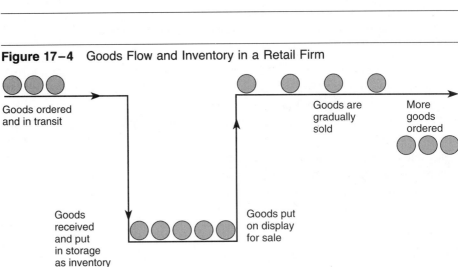

| Materials received and stored | Materials sent to Operation 1 for processing into parts, which are placed in inventory | Parts sent to Operation 2 for further processing and the results put in inventory | Semi-finished product sent to Operation 3 to be converted into finished product, which goes into inventory | Finished product sold to customers |

Inventory   Inventory   Inventory   Inventory

Figure 17–4   Goods Flow and Inventory in a Retail Firm

Goods ordered and in transit

Goods received and put in storage as inventory

Goods put on display for sale

Goods are gradually sold

More goods ordered

A similar situation occurs in retail stores. Retailers receive goods, store them, put them on display for sale, sell them to customers, and then order more of the goods. The level of inventory at any given time depends on the amount of goods bought—and stored in inventory—relative to the quantity sold. Thus, a retailer must have enough goods in inventory after an order is received to last until the next order is placed and received. Figure 17–4 illustrates this process. Notice that when the goods on the left are received, they're stored with similar goods, as inventory. Then, after being put on display and gradually sold, they're replaced with other goods.

Types of Inventory

Inventories exist in small firms at all times in one or more of the following forms: (1) finished items on display for sale to customers; (2) batches of goods, such as materials, parts, and subassemblies, awaiting processing or delivery; (3) repair parts awaiting use; (4) supplies for use in offices, stores, or shops, or for use in processing other goods; and (5) miscellaneous items, such as tools placed in a toolroom.

These inventories, especially the first two kinds, represent a major investment by all businesses—large ones as well as small. Many companies have failed because their inventory tied up too much money or the items in inventory became obsolete, damaged, or lost, as the following example illustrates.

In 1985, Chris Hoelzle's Los Angeles computer repair store and computer salvage operation had 35 employees and $35 million annual revenues. Then, with the computer "bust," profits turned to losses, and Hoelzle was bankrupt—without declaring bankruptcy. He slashed staff and sold inventory—which had become "200 tons of electronic junk"—at bargain prices. Three years later, however, he had 15 employees, $3 million in annual revenues, and three times his pre-1986 profits.[6]

Costs of Carrying Inventory

Having inventory on hand costs a small business more than most people realize. These costs consist of (1) the cost of providing and maintaining storage space, (2) insurance and taxes, (3) profits lost because money is tied up in inventory (called *opportunity cost*), (4) theft and destruction, and (5) obsolescence and deterioration of the items.

Determining When to Place an Order

Figure 17–3 showed the changing inventory levels as materials were ordered, processed, stored, and sold. Figure 17–4 showed how levels change as a retailer orders goods, stores them, and then sells them. The real problem in both these instances is knowing when is the most appropriate time to order needed items.

The optimum inventory level at which to order goods can be estimated or actually calculated. It is the point where the sum of the costs of carrying inventory and the costs of stocking out is the lowest. This calculation isn't easy, and you'll make mistakes, but with rational analysis, practice, and a certain amount of intuition, you'll make it.[7]

Determining How Much to Order

The order quantity is determined by the level of inventory and the order interval. When orders are placed at *certain, regular intervals,* the order quantity should be set to bring the inventory level up to a predetermined amount. When *inventory level* determines the time to order, the order quantity is a fixed amount called the *economic order quantity (EOQ)*. The EOQ is determined by balancing (1) the cost of placing an order with (2) the costs of carrying the inventory.[8]

OPERATIONS PLANNING AND CONTROL

As shown in Chapter 6, operations planning and control begins when you determine what business you're going into, what product(s) you'll sell, and what resources are needed to produce the quantity you expect. If you're to have products available when demanded, you must carefully forecast and plan for sales. Predicting the sales of a small company with any degree of accuracy is difficult, but even crude estimates are better than none, since considerable cost is involved in trying to serve customers if the items they seek aren't in stock.

Handling Variations in Demand

Demand for products varies from one period to another for such reasons as changing lifestyles, economic conditions, and seasons. In fact, most sales of goods have seasonal variations. Some examples of complementary seasonal goods are summer and winter clothing, furnaces and air conditioners, sweaters and swimsuits, and many types of construction items. If a small business chooses a narrow marketing niche for one of these products—as is often recommended—sales will probably vary considerably during the year. Therefore, you may be constantly hiring, training, and laying off employees; not using facilities efficiently; and facing cash flow problems and product shortages.

There are several operating plans that may be used to cope at least partially with seasonal variations. The most popular such plans are these:

1. Allow operations to rise and fall according to changing sales demands.
2. Use self-service to reduce the number of employees and hire temporary or part-time workers during peak periods.
3. Use inventory buildups—or drawdown—to smooth out operations.
4. Carry complementary products.
5. Subcontract out production during maximum demand periods.
6. Lose sales by not expanding operations to meet increased demand.
7. Use special inducements to stimulate sales during periods of low demand.

Scheduling Operations

Scheduling is setting the times and sequences required to do work.

Scheduling involves setting the times and sequences needed to perform specialized activities, including when and how long it takes to do it. You are often faced with this problem of scheduling. For example, you try to schedule your classes to minimize inconvenience and for your greatest benefit. Then you have to schedule appointments with the doctor or dentist around them. Figure 17–2 showed a schedule of the steps involved in selling style items.

A major entertainment event poses massive scheduling challenges, including scheduling the design and creation of clothing and costumes.

The 1989 Miss USA Pageant was such an event. As you saw in the Profile for Chapter 3, the contestants' evening gowns were designed by Sherri Hill of Norman, Oklahoma.

Some of the other costumes were designed and produced by Los Angeles costume designer Pete Menefee. In addition, he took 12 to 14 of Mrs. Hill's dress designs and made them in different fabrics. Since each contestant required a different pattern, 120 different dresses were made for the girls to choose from.

The dresses, made in Los Angeles, were shipped to the contest site in Mobile, Alabama, where Menefee altered them with the help of local seamstresses. The results are shown in the photo (left). In addition, he saw that each girl had the proper hosiery, shoes dyed to match, and costume jewelry to go with the gowns.[9]

Computers are now being used effectively by small businesses to perform scheduling operations. Using Technology to Succeed shows what happens when a small travel agency uses a computerized system to book a traveler.

Controlling Operations

Even if you make the best of plans, communicate them effectively, and use the best workers and materials to perform the work effectively, controls are still needed. Without the exercise of adequate control over the operations, the process will fail.

In simple systems, the comparison of planned performance with actual performance can be made informally by personal observation. Usually, though, a system of formal checks is needed. Standards are set, data on actual performance are collected, standards and actual data are compared, and exceptions are reported.

━━━━━━━━━━━━━━━ USING TECHNOLOGY TO SUCCEED ━━━━━━━━━━━━━━━

INSTANT TRAVEL SCHEDULING

Kari Givens and her co-workers at Springdale Travel, Vacation World, and Cruise Quarters can schedule your business or pleasure travel with a wink and a keyboard. Thanks to a system called Worldspan, which is completely supported by Delta Airlines (software, hardware, and user support), your travel can be scheduled, reservations made, and confirmations received almost instantaneously.

Similar systems are provided by three other airlines: Sabre by American, Covia by United, and System One by Continental. In addition, there are services provided by international airlines and many third-party software systems. The third-party systems are subscription services designed for small travel agencies.

Worldspan taps into about 650 airlines, 150,000 routes, 15,000 hotels, and 19 car rental agencies. Because of the speed and quality of the system, Springdale Travel, Vacation World, and Cruise Quarters can issue your tickets on the spot. You can either pick them up or have them mailed or delivered to you by special courier. Itineraries can be faxed immediately so that you—the traveler—can see the whole picture and complete schedule of your proposed excursion.

Source: Murray Cape, Owner, Springdale Travel Inc.

QUALITY AND ITS CONTROL

In recent years, American consumers have shown increasing concern about the quality of U.S. goods and services, since so often foreign companies produce and sell us products of superior quality. Now, though, many U.S. companies are taking steps to improve the caliber of their products. This is particularly true of small companies, as shown in Chapter 12.

While small businesses must compete in the market with large companies, many are finding that emphasizing quality and reliability and designing output to match customer needs are better tactics than lowering prices.

What Is Quality?

Quality can have at least two meanings. First, it refers to characteristics of products being judged. Second, it means the probability that products will meet established standards. In the discussion that follows, we will use the meanings interchangeably.

Assessment of the quality of a product is relative; it depends on the expectations of the evaluator—the customer. Customers who are used to high-quality goods and services tend to be much more critical of purchases than those accustomed to lower standards. Because small companies usually cannot cater to all quality levels, they must set their sights on the level demanded by their customers.

Quality involves many characteristics of a product: strength, color, taste, smell, content, weight, tone, look, capacity, accomplishment, creativity, and reliability, among others. Part of the quality of service are such factors as salespersons' smiles, attentiveness, friendly greetings, and willing assistance. Standards to meet the desires of customers must be established for each characteristic.

Customers tend to want high quality, but often they want to pay only a limited price for the product. Still, some qualities, such as a friendly greeting, cost little; others, such as precision jewelry settings, cost much. Quality-level analysis is thus based on the value of quality to the customer and the cost of producing that level of quality. To make the decision, you must ask the following questions: Who are my customers? What quality do they want? What quality of product can I provide, and at what cost?

How do you determine where to set the quality level? Market research, questionnaires, talking to customers, comparison with competitors' products, and trial and error are a few of the methods.

Improving and Controlling Quality

There are many ways a small business can improve quality, but we will discuss only three: (1) setting up quality circles, (2) designing quality into the operations processes, and (3) installing a good quality control process.

Establishing Quality Circles

Many progressive companies report good results from using quality circle programs. In **quality circles,** a small group of workers meets regularly to identify and develop ways to solve company problems, especially quality. The members, who are usually not supervisors, receive training in areas such as problem identification, communications, and problem solving. Also, as they meet, they may have access to resource people who can provide further expertise. Quality circles seem to be more successful when top management gives them unrestricted support.

Quality circles are small work groups meeting periodically to find ways to improve quality and performance.

Designing Quality into the Process

Since quality is achieved during the production of a product, the processes must be designed to produce the desired quality. Machines must be capable of turning out the product within set tolerances, workers must be trained to produce that level of quality, and materials and goods must be purchased that meet the stated standards. In service companies, employees must be trained to understand a customer's needs and to perform the work to the customer's satisfaction. If the process or employees cannot produce the proper quality of output, no type of control can correct the situation.

Installing a Quality Control Process

Quality control, or quality assurance, is the process by which a producer ensures that the finished goods or services meet the expectations of customers. Therefore, quality control involves at least the following steps:

Figure 17–5   Example of Feedback Quality Control in a Restaurant

Management Encourages Your Comments

Date 5/19/92

Waiter or waitress *Phyllis*

Please circle meal   Breakfast (Lunch) Dinner

	Yes	No
1. Were you greeted by host or hostess promptly and courteously?	✓	
2. Was your server prompt, courteous, and attractive in appearance?	✓	
3. Was the quality of food to your expectations?		✓
4. Was the table setting and condition of overall restaurant appearance pleasing and in good taste?	✓	
5. Will you return to our restaurant?		✓
6. Will you recommend our restaurant to your friends and associates?		✓

Comments

Food was overcooked. Potatoes were left-overs. Meat was tough. This was my second visit and I brought a friend with me. We were both very disappointed.

Name and address
(if you desire)

Please drop this in our quality improvement box provided as you exit room.

Thank you and have a good day.

- Setting standards for the desired quality range.
- Measuring actual performance.
- Comparing that performance with established standards.
- Making corrections when needed.

Some standards may be measured by instruments, such as rulers or gauges for length; but color, taste, and other standards must be evaluated by skilled individuals. Measurement may be made by selected people at selected spots in the process—usually upon receipt of material and always before the product goes to the customer. Quality can also be controlled by feedback from customers, as shown in Figure 17–5.

WHAT YOU SHOULD HAVE LEARNED

1. Purchases are a small company's largest single type of cost. Goods and services must be obtained at the proper price, quality, and time, and in the proper quantity.

2. Sources of supply must be found and investigated, and one or more suppliers selected. Reliability in delivery and quality affect nearly all operations. You must decide whether to use one or multiple suppliers.

3. An effective purchasing procedure consists of *(a)* determining the items needed, in what quantity, from whom to purchase, and the terms of the contract; *(b)* sending the purchase order; *(c)* receiving the goods; *(d)* inspecting them, and *(e)* paying for them.

4. Inventory is carried in order to disconnect one part of the operating process from another so that each part can operate effectively. Inventory takes many forms, from raw materials to finished products. The cost of carrying inventory consists of providing and maintaining storage space, insurance and taxes, profits lost from money tied up in it, obsolescence and deterioration, and theft and destruction. The cost of inadequate inventory is dissatisfied customers from stockouts.

5. Operations planning and control start with a forecast of sales from which operating plans are developed. Alternative plans for seasonal sales include *(a)* producing to demand, *(b)* using self-service and part-time workers to help meet peak demand, *(c)* producing at a constant rate and inventorying for future demand, *(d)* carrying complementary products, *(e)* subcontracting high demand, *(f)* not meeting high demand, and *(g)* using off-season sales inducements.

   Scheduling is setting the times and sequences required to do work. Control of operations is obtained by reacting to exceptions to plans.

6. In small firms, the emphasis should be on quality of goods and services rather than on low price. The term *quality* refers both to acceptable characteristics and to reliability of the product. Quality circles have been used by small companies to improve performance.

   Quality control steps include setting standards, measuring performance, comparing actual performance with standards, and making corrections.

Sampling inspections and customer feedback are used to check performance or quality.

QUESTIONS FOR DISCUSSION

1. Discuss the advantages and disadvantages of buying locally versus buying from a distant seller.

2. What are the advantages and disadvantages of shopping at a single store rather than at several?

3. In what ways can inventories serve to reduce costs? To increase costs? To change income?

4. How would you make an economic study to determine the quantity of a food item to buy for your family on each trip to the store? How often should purchases be made?

5. In some parts of the country, building construction varies seasonally. *(a)* Is this a problem for company management? *(b)* What decisions must management make concerning these variations?

6. Many times, sales personnel do not practice good selling relations. How would you control the quality of this type of service?

7. What is quality? How can it be measured? How can it be controlled?

8. Outline instructions for installing a new quality circle.

TO MAKE, BUY, OR LEASE?

When small producers become dissatisfied with the quality, cost, or timing of purchased materials, they may be tempted to make their own. This usually requires a substantial investment in facilities to produce them. Still, when producers make their own goods, they have more control over the process and quality, there's less idle machine and personnel time, and more growth is possible in the form of new products.

For example, Kimball International, formerly the nation's premier piano maker, now churns out regular orchestra instruments and produces office furniture as well. The latter is the largest contributor to sales and profits. Kimball's staying power is based on "making its own." It owns some hardwood forests, has its own sawmills, and produces its own lumber and plywood. It also makes plastic accessories for its products and operates a fleet of delivery trucks.

Yet it's impossible for producers to make all goods and provide all services, so some must be bought. When this happens, both capital investment (in machines) and personnel costs are lower; management can specialize, devoting company time to producing its main product; and planning, directing, and controlling are less complex.

But problems may be encountered in matching inventory and production whether one decides to "make" or "buy," so inventory control is needed to ensure a continuous, timely supply of parts and materials.

For example, when Gillette did a superb job of promoting its new Sensor razor in early 1990, there weren't enough razors to satisfy retailers' needs. Part of the problem was that the assembly line at its South Boston plant was unable to provide enough cartridges, which contained nine parts and required microlaser welding and complex assembly.

A rapidly growing trend for obtaining facilities, supplies, and services is to lease or rent them. A growing number of organizations find leasing to be an effective way to save on wear and tear—and taxes. Almost anything that can be bought can be leased, including offices; plants; stores; vehicles, such as trucks, locomotives, and cars; office machines and equipment; and even people.

For example, Norman Hart, owner of a small Tampa print shop, hated the hassle of paperwork and bookkeeping but enjoyed building up his business. So he "fired" himself, his manager-daughter, and six other employees. The next day, Print 'n Go owners and workers were back on the job, but Miami-based Action Leasing was handling the administrative details.

QUESTIONS

Which of these methods do you think is best for each of the following, and why do you think so?

1. A small producer of high-tech equipment for sale on a long-term contract to a successful large drug company.

2. A small producer using standard parts that can be bought from many suppliers at a reasonable cost.

3. A small service firm trying to break into a new industry by selling to foreign importers.

Sources: Keith Hammonds, "It's One Sharp Ad Campaign, but Where's the Blade?" *Business Week,* March 5, 1990, p. 30; Kenneth R. Sheets, "Firms Now Lease Everything but Time," *U.S. News & World Report,* August 14, 1989, pp. 45–46; and Julianne Slovak, "Companies to Watch: Kimball International," *Fortune,* March 12, 1990, p. 90.

VI

FINANCIAL PLANNING AND CONTROL

As we have shown throughout this text, the requirements for success in small business include an understanding of the importance of financial management; knowledge of how financial relationships affect profit or loss; and the devotion of time, energy and initiative to planning and controlling financial activities. We discuss in this part how such planning and control ensure that the business will not only survive but also grow and develop.

Chapter 18 explains the need for, and methods of, planning for a profit, guiding you through the steps of planning the profit for a hypothetical company. It also covers the basic financial structure of a business.

Chapter 19 explores the basic structure of control and shows how to collect information and compare actual performance with standard performance. The design and use of budgets and budgetary control are also covered, along with the use of ratio analysis.

Chapter 20 focuses on the taxes that a small business must pay. It also deals with how to collect, handle, and report those taxes.

Chapter 21 discusses the management information system needed for decision making. It covers the importance of gathering and maintaining information, and how to record it. It also emphasizes the need for, and how to use, computers in small firms.

18

Planning for Profits

Never mind the business outlook; be on the outlook for business.—Anonymous

Earning a profit—staying in business—is still the No. 1 thing. Unless you can make money, you cannot do any of the other things.—Irving Shapiro, on his retirement as chairman of Du Pont

LEARNING OBJECTIVES

After studying the material in this chapter, you will be able to:
1. Explain the need for profit planning for a small business.
2. Discuss what causes changes in the financial position of a company.
3. Understand the financial structure of a business.
4. Learn how to plan to make a profit.
5. Plan for a profit for an actual small business.

CHECKERS DRIVE-IN RESTAURANTS

Jim Mattei, cofounder, president, and CEO of Checker's Drive-In Restaurants, Inc., of Clearwater, Florida, and former director and co-founder Mark Reed decided to build a fast-food restaurant because they were dissatisfied with other fast-food restaurants. Mattei was a builder by profession and was director, CEO, and president of Mattei Companies. Reed, who is no longer active in the organization, was Mattei's attorney prior to the founding of Checkers. The idea for Checkers originated in 1984–85, and the first restaurant opened on April 14, 1986, in Mobile, Alabama. The second store followed on May 14, 1986, and the third store approximately four months later.

Photo courtesy of Checkers Drive-In Restaurants, Inc.

The main thrust of Checkers was to avoid the different types of menus that other fast-food restaurants offer, especially breakfast menu items. Instead, the founders wanted a place where someone could get a high-quality "hamburger with the works" in a hurry!

In the beginning, Checkers' business plan called for seven stores in two years. Only five stores materialized during that time. By 1993, however, the business had grown to 224 units in 18 states including 101 company-owned units, 123 franchised units, and a strong modular construction component that designs and builds the restaurant buildings.

The funds originally used to found the business were from Mattei's personal savings. Mattei was told by the banks that they did not like to lend money to people just starting out in the fast-food business because of its high risks. As you might suspect, Checkers almost did go broke, and short-term personal bank loans were used to keep it afloat. When asked what he would do differently if they could start all over again, Mattei said he "would not change a thing. Without funding, we learned to be patient and refine our operations."

Under Checkers' unit franchise agreement, each franchise is generally required to pay a unit franchise fee of $25,000 for each restaurant opened by the franchisee. Each franchisee is also usually required to pay the franchisor a semimonthly royalty of 4 percent of each restaurant's gross sales and to expend 2 percent of gross sales monthly for local advertising and promotion.

Numerous problems occurred in the start-up process. The first three years were very rocky; in fact, there was no profit for several years, until 1989. In 1986, 1987, and 1988, the company lost money, and in 1989 it made its first profit ($71,000). The result was that the partners were drained financially during those years.

One of the major tools Checkers uses to maintain and enhance profitability is a point-of-sale computer system. This unique system monitors sales, labor, food costs, customer counts, and various other data on a daily basis. The speed of this process provides the company the appropriate control in the various areas. In addition, the company is very selective and strict with franchisees. They, too, are monitored and controlled. Mattei says that the key to successful profits is in selective site evaluations, an outstanding management team, and financial stability. In other words, grow conservatively! Checkers, which went public in 1991, continues to prosper as one of the nation's fastest-growing fast-food chains.

Source: Conversations and correspondence with Jim Mattei and other Checkers executives.

Profit cannot be left to chance in small firms. Yet all too frequently it is, because small business owners tend to know little about finance.[1] Even when efforts *are* made to plan for profit, they are often inadequate, for owners tend to assume that history repeats itself—that past profits will be repeated in the future. Instead, small business managers must learn to identify all income and costs if they are to make a profit. Therefore, each item must be realistically priced, as shown in Chapter 10, and each cost should be accurately computed.

NEED FOR PROFIT PLANNING

To make a profit, your prices must cover all costs and include a markup for planned profit. This chapter will help you (1) determine how much profit you want and how to achieve it; (2) learn how to set up an accounting system for your firm and how to read, evaluate, and interpret its accounting and financial figures;[2] and (3) evaluate, or estimate, your firm's financial position.

A lack of accurate cost information, a recurring problem among small business owners, usually results in profits of unknown quantity—or even a loss. Also, it can foster the illusion of making a greater profit than is really earned, if any.

The owner of Children's Party Caterer* illustrated this point. During the first interview with a SCORE counselor, she said she had "around $800 worth of party materials" in her pantry at home. But when asked the cost of materials used, and the time involved in preparing for each party, she couldn't answer. The counselor gave her a "homework assignment" to determine the time she spent preparing for and giving each party, as well as the cost of materials.

She was surprised to find that she spent around 18 to 20 hours per party, and the cost of materials ranged from $40 to $50. Also, she hadn't included the cost of transportation or the $10 to $12 baby-sitting cost for her two children. Yet she charged only about $40 to $50 for each party. To the suggestion that she raise her prices to cover these costs, plus a markup for profit, she responded, "People won't pay it." When the advisor replied, "You aren't in the charity business," her exuberant reply was, "Oh, but I enjoy doing it!"

HOW A BUSINESS'S FINANCIAL POSITION CHANGES

The operations of a small business result from decisions made by its owner and managers and the many activities they perform. As decisions are made and operations occur, the firm's financial position constantly changes. For example, cash received for sales increases the bank balance; credit sales increase accounts receivable; and purchases of material, while increasing inventory, also increase accounts payable or decrease the bank balance. At the same time, machines decrease in value, materials are processed into inventory, and utilities are used.

*Name disguised.

USING TECHNOLOGY TO SUCCEED

GAINING POWER OVER YOUR MONEY

Many entrepreneurs are finding that the financial software package *Quicken* meets their accounting needs. The program, produced by Intuit Inc., is user-friendly and affordable. It can be used to budget, write checks, and keep track of expenses and investments. There is room for as many as 255 accounts. It can also generate any needed reports. The company provides a toll-free telephone help line.

Source: Dan Gutman, "Gain Power over Money: A Secret Weapon That Is Also Cheap," *Success,* April 1992, p. 14.

Consequently, because the financial position of the business is constantly changing, those changes should be recorded and analyzed.

Tracing Changes in a Company's Financial Position

Throughout its operations, the important question to small business owners is whether their business is improving its chances of reaching its primary objective—to make a profit. However, some small firms make a profit and still fail, since profits are not necessarily in the form of cash. Accounts receivable may reflect profits, but many of those accounts may not be collectible. Too much money may be tied up in other assets and not available to pay bills as they come due. In other words, focusing only on net income may be foolhardy, unless other variables are also considered.[3] The "bottom line" is not an end in itself, but it is the beginning of the more difficult process of tracking cash flow. (See Chapter 19 for more details.)

You may have—or have had—similar problems with your personal finances. Your allowance, earnings, and/or other income may be adequate to pay for food, clothing, and other operating expenses, but you may have an unexpected expense, such as replacing a worn-out car, for which you must make a cash down payment. If your funds are invested in a fixed asset, such as a mortgage on your car, they are not available for paying bills. The same is true of a small business. In fact, as the Using Technology to Succeed example indicates, you can use the same computer programs to handle both your business and your personal finances.

Importance of Accounting

Accounting is quite important in achieving success in any business, especially a small one. Therefore, your accounting records must accurately reflect the changes occurring in your firm's assets, liabilities, income, expenses, and equity. The continued operation of your business also depends—as Irving Shapiro pointed out

"*See no evil, hear no evil, speak no evil. . . . I like that in an accountant, Mr. Farouche.*"
Reprinted from *Management Accounting,* January 1988, p. 13.

in the opening quotation—on maintaining the proper balance among its investments, revenues, expenses, and profit. Because profit margins are so critical to the success of a business, any decline in them should trigger an immediate search for the cause.

Many small business owners don't realize their business is in trouble until it's too late, and many fail without knowing what their problem is—or even that they have a problem. All they know is that they end up with no money and can't pay their bills. Timothy O'Donnell, a CPA, calls these owners "seat-of-the-pants operators" because they fail to monitor all aspects of their businesses. They often consider financial statements "a necessary evil" and think everything is fine as long as sales are increasing and there is money in the bank. "They don't realize that what they do in their businesses is reflected in the financial statements. They tend not to pay much attention to the information accountants give them."[4] One young entrepreneur found this out the hard way.

For Richard Huttner, the hardest problem in running New York's Parenting Unlimited Inc. was doing the accounting necessary in running its new acquisition, *Baby Talk* magazine. Although *Baby Talk* had revenues of several million dollars a year, it had no financial management, accounting system, general ledger, or bank account when it was acquired. Consequently, while trying to master an ongoing business, Huttner had to spend nearly a third of his time the first three months paying bills and doing accounting. He lamented, "Stanford didn't teach me how long it takes out-of-state checks to clear. At first, that caused us constant cash flow problems.[5]

In discussing financial management in this chapter, we have used a real small business, which we have disguised as The Model Company, Inc., to illustrate the concepts. Assume throughout the following discussion that, while the company is owned by Mr. Model, you manage it for him. Therefore, you must make the management decisions called for.

WHAT IS THE FINANCIAL STRUCTURE OF A BUSINESS?

The assets, liabilities, and equity of a business are reflected in its financial structure. These accounts, which are interrelated and interact with each other, represent the **financial structure** of a firm, which changes constantly as business activities take place. Always keep in mind that *the total of liabilities plus owners' equity always equals the total assets of the firm.*

At regular intervals, a **balance sheet** is prepared to show the assets, liabilities, and owners' equity of the business. See Figure 18–1 for the arrangement and amounts of the accounts for our hypothetical business, The Model Company.

Assets

Assets, which are the things your business owns, are divided into current and fixed assets.

Current Assets

Current assets are expected to turn over — that is, to change from one form to another — within a year. **Cash** includes the bills and coins in the cash register(s), deposits in a checking account, and other deposits that can be converted into cash immediately. A certain level of cash is necessary to operate a business; however, holding too much cash reduces your income, because it doesn't produce revenue.[6] The question is, What is the correct level? The following example suggests a partial answer.

Alan Goldstein, a partner in Touche Ross & Company's Enterprise Group in Boston, which helps small firms decide how much cash is needed, answers the question "When do everyday nuisances turn into disaster?" by saying, "When you're about to run out of cash."[7]

Accounts receivable result from giving credit to customers, as shown in Chapter 12. While selling on credit helps maintain a higher level of sales, care must be taken to select customers who will pay within a reasonable length of time.

Inventory provides a buffer between purchase, production, and sales (as discussed in Chapter 17). You must maintain a certain amount in order to serve customers. But carrying an excessive amount of inventory places a financial burden on the small firm because inventory isn't an income-producing asset. Thus, the amount of inventory to carry depends on a judicious balancing of income and costs.

Other current asset accounts often are called *short-term investments,* and *prepaid expenses.* Usually, these make up only a small part of the current assets of a small business and need little attention (for example, refer to Figure 18–1).

Financial structure describes the relative proportions of a firm's assets, liabilities, and owners' equity.

A **balance sheet** is a statement of a firm's assets, liabilities, and owners' equity at a given point in time.

Assets are the things a business owns.

Current assets are those that are expected to change from one form to another within a year.

Cash includes bills, coins, deposits in a checking account, and other deposits that can be converted into cash immediately.

Accounts receivable is an asset resulting from selling a product on credit.

Inventory consists of tangible goods a firm expects to sell or use up in a short period of time.

Figure 18–1

THE MODEL COMPANY
Balance Sheet
December 31, 19—

Assets

Current assets:

Cash	$ 7,054	
Accounts receivable	60,484	
Inventory	80,042	
Prepaid expenses	1,046	
Total current assets		$148,626

Fixed assets:

Equipment	$100,500		
Building	40,950		
Gross fixed assets		141,450	
Less: accumulated depreciation		16,900	
Net fixed assets			124,550
Total assets			$273,176

Liabilities and Owners' Equity

Current liabilities:

Accounts payable	51,348	
Accrued payables	3,060	
Total current liabilities		$ 54,408

Long-term liabilities:

Mortgage payable	20,708	
Total liabilities		$ 75,116

Owners' equity:

Capital stock	160,000	
Retained earnings	38,060	
Total equity		198,060
Total liabilities and owners' equity		$273,176

Fixed Assets

Fixed assets are relatively permanent items the business needs for its continued operations.

Items a business expects to own for a long time—such as buildings, machinery, store fixtures, trucks, and land—are included among its **fixed assets.** Part of their cost is written off each period as depreciation expense. Different types of fixed assets have different lengths of useful life.

As was shown in Chapter 9, some small firms find it desirable to lease fixed assets instead of owning them. For example, a retailer may rent a store to reduce the need to make a large investment in it, as will be shown in the Profile for Chapter 23.

Liabilities

As discussed in Chapter 9, a business can obtain funds by owner investment and by borrowing, which is creating an obligation to pay. The first, which is necessary, increases *owners' equity,* or the *owners' interest* in the business. The second results in a **liability** of the business to pay back the funds—plus interest. Borrowing from creditors is divided into current and long-term liabilities.

Liabilities are the financial obligations of a business.

Current Liabilities

Obligations to be paid within a year are **current liabilities.** They include accounts payable, notes payable, and accrued items (such as payroll), which are for services performed for you but not yet paid for.

Current liabilities are obligations that must be paid within a year.

Accounts payable are obligations to pay for goods and services purchased, and are usually due within 30 or 60 days, depending on the credit terms. Since any business should maintain current assets sufficient to pay these accounts, maintaining a high level of accounts payable requires a high level of current assets.[8] Thus, you should determine whether or not early payment is beneficial; some sellers offer a discount for early payment, such as 1 or 2 percent if bills are paid within 10 days. This is a good return on your money!

Accounts payable are obligations to pay, resulting from purchasing goods or services.

Notes payable, which are written obligations to pay, usually give the business a longer time than accounts payable before payment is due. An example is a 90-day note.

Notes payable are written obligations to pay, usually after 90 days to a year.

Long-Term Liabilities

Bonds and mortgages are the usual types of **long-term liabilities,** which have terms of more than a year. A business usually incurs these liabilities when purchasing fixed assets. Long-term loans may be used to supply a reasonable amount of **working capital,** which is current assets less current liabilities. This type of borrowing requires regular payment of interest. The need to make these payments during slack times increases the risk of being unable to meet other obligations, so both short- and long-term strategies should be used. In general, small firms use long-term borrowing as a source of funds much less frequently than large ones do.[9]

Long-term liabilities are obligations to pay someone after one year or more.

Working capital is a firm's current assets minus current liabilities.

Owners' Equity

Owners' equity is the owners' share of (or **net worth** in) the business, after liabilities are subtracted from assets. The owners receive income from profits in the form of dividends or an increase in their share of the company through an increase in retained earnings. Owners also absorb losses, which decrease their equity. (See Chapters 9 and 20 for further details.)

Owners' equity is the owners' share of (or **net worth** in) the business, after liabilities are subtracted from assets.

As shown in Chapter 9, when owners invest in a corporation, they receive shares of stock, and the *owners' equity account*—common stock—is increased on the firm's balance sheet.

Retained earnings are the profits kept in the business rather than being distributed to the owners. Most firms retain some of the profits to use in times of need or to provide for growth. Many small firms have failed because the owners paid

Retained earnings are profits kept in the business rather than distributed to owners.

themselves too much of the profits, thereby reducing their assets. Definite policies should be set as to what part of your earnings should be retained and what part distributed to you as income.

PROFIT-MAKING ACTIVITIES OF A BUSINESS

The profit-making activities of a business influence its financial structure. These activities are reflected in the revenue and expense accounts, as shown by the following formula:

$$\text{Net income (profit)} = \text{Revenue (income)} - \text{Expenses (costs)}$$

During a given period, the business performs services for which it receives revenues. It also incurs expenses for goods and services provided to it by others. These revenues and expenses are shown in the **income statement,** also known as the **profit and loss statement** (see Figure 18–2).

An **income statement (profit and loss statement)** periodically shows revenues, expenses, and profits from a firm's operations.

Revenue and Expenses

Revenue (sales income) is the return to the firm from selling a good or performing a service.

Revenue (also called **sales income**) is the return from services performed or goods sold. The business receives revenue in the form of cash or accounts receivable.

Figure 18–2

THE MODEL COMPANY
Income Statement
January 1 through December 31, 19—

Net sales	$463,148	
Less: Cost of goods sold	291,262	
Gross income		$171,886
Operating expenses:		
Salaries	$ 83,138	
Utilities	6,950	
Depreciation	10,050	
Rent	2,000	
Building services	4,920	
Insurance	4,000	
Interest	2,646	
Office and supplies	6,550	
Sales promotion	11,000	
Taxes and licenses	6,480	
Maintenance	1,610	
Delivery	5,848	
Miscellaneous	1,750	
Total expenses		146,942
Net income before taxes		24,944
Less: Income taxes		5,484
Net income after taxes		$19,460

Expenses, the costs of paying people to work for you (or for goods or services provided to you), include such items as materials, wages, insurance, utilities, transportation, depreciation, taxes, supplies, and advertising. As these costs are incurred, they are deducted from revenue.

Expenses are the costs of labor, goods, and services.

There are two types of expenses (costs): (1) fixed and (2) variable. **Fixed expenses (costs)** are those that are incurred periodically, regardless of whether operations are carried on or not. These include such items as depreciation, rent, and insurance. **Variable expenses (costs)** vary according to the level of operations. Thus, if there are no operations, there are no variable expenses. These expenses include such items as labor and material to produce and sell the product, plus sales promotion and delivery costs.

Fixed expenses (costs) do not vary with changes in output.

Variable expenses (costs) vary directly with changes in output.

Profit

Profit, also called **income,** is the difference between revenues earned and expenses incurred. Depending on the type of expenses deducted, profit may be called *gross income, operating profit, net income before taxes,* or *net income.*

Profit is the difference between revenue earned and expenses incurred.

Your profit margins indicate the relationship between revenues and expenses; therefore, a decline in them should trigger a search for the cause. The problem could be a rise in expenses, a per unit sales revenue decline caused by discounting or pricing errors, or changing the basic operations of the business.

HOW TO PLAN FOR PROFIT

According to a Dun & Bradstreet report, a well-managed small business has at least the following characteristics:

- It is more liquid than a badly managed company.
- The balance sheet is as important to the owner(s) as the income statement.
- Stability is emphasized, instead of rapid growth.
- Long-range planning is important.

Need for Profit Planning

As you study the income statement in Figure 18–2, you may interpret it as saying, "The Model Company received $463,148 in net sales, expended $291,262 for costs of goods sold, paid out $146,942 in total operating expenses, and had $24,944 left over as net income (or profits) before income taxes." Under this interpretation, *profit* is a "leftover," not a planned amount. While neither you nor Mr. Model can do anything about the past, you can do something about future operations. Since one of your goals is to make a profit, you should plan the operations now in order to achieve your desired profit goal later. So let's see how you can do it!

Steps in Profit Planning

To achieve your goal during the coming year, you need to take the following steps:

1. Establish a profit goal.
2. Determine the volume of sales revenue needed to make that profit.
3. Estimate the expenses you will incur in reaching that volume of sales.
4. Determine estimated profit, based on plans resulting from Steps 2 and 3.
5. Compare the estimated profit with the profit goal.

If you are satisfied with the plans, you can stop at this point. However, you may want to check further to determine whether improvements can be made, particularly if you aren't happy with the results of Step 5. Doing Steps 6 through 10 may help you to understand better how changing some of your operations can affect profit.

6. List some possible alternatives that can be used to improve profits.
7. Determine how expenses vary with changes in sales volume.
8. Determine how profits vary with changes in sales volume.
9. Analyze your alternatives from a profit standpoint.
10. Select an alternative and implement the plan.

Need for Realism in Profit Planning

Be realistic when going through these steps, or you may be unable to reach the desired profit goal. You may feel the future is too uncertain to make such plans, but *the greater the uncertainty, the greater the need for planning*.

For example, the president of a small firm said that his forecasts were too inaccurate to be of any help in planning operations, so he had stopped forecasting. His business became so unsuccessful that he had to sell out.

The owner of another small business recently stated that she can't forecast the next year's revenue within 20 percent of actual sales. However, she continues to forecast and plan, for she says she needs plans from which to deviate as conditions change.

✳PROFIT PLANNING APPLIED IN A TYPICAL SMALL BUSINESS

This section uses the above steps to plan profits for The Model Company. As manager, you must start planning for the coming year several months in advance so you can put your plans into effect at the proper time. In order to present a systematic analysis, assume that you are planning for the company for the first time.*

*Actually, you should be planning for each month at least six months or a year ahead. This can be done by dropping the past month, adjusting the rest of the months in your prior plans, and adding the plans for another month. Such planning gives you time to anticipate needed changes and do something about them.

"You didn't consider our paper profits real—why do you consider our paper losses real?"

Reprinted from *The Wall Street Journal;* permission Cartoon Features Syndicate

Step 1: Establish the Profit Goal

Your desired profit must be a specific target value. To begin with, as you manage the business, pay yourself a reasonable salary. Also, Mr. Model should receive a return on his investment—not only his initial investment but also any earnings left in the business—for taking the risks of ownership. To do this, compare what you would receive as salary for working for someone else and the income Mr. Model would receive if the same amount of money were placed in a relatively safe investment, such as U.S. government bonds or high-grade stocks. Each of these investments provides a return with a certain degree of risk—and pleasure. If Mr. Model could invest the same amount of money at an 8 percent return, with little risk, what do you think the return on his investment in The Model Company should be?

Mr. Model originally invested $160,000 in the company and has since left about $40,000 of his profits in the business. He made about 10 percent on his investment this past year, which he thinks is too low for the risk he is taking; he feels that about a 20 percent return is reasonable. So, as Step 1 in Figure 18–3, you enter his investment, desired profit, and estimate of income taxes (from the past and after consultation with his accountant). You determine that he must make $52,000 before taxes, or a 26 percent return on his investment, if he is to reach his desired profit. After you and Mr. Model have set this goal, you should turn to the task of determining what the profit before taxes will be from your forecast of next year's plans.

Step 2: Determine the Planned Sales Volume

A **sales forecast** is an estimate of the amount a firm expects to sell during a given period. In preparing operating and sales budgets, these forecasts are used to estimate revenues for the next quarter, for the year, or perhaps even for three to five

> A **sales forecast** is an estimate of the amount of revenue expected from sales for a given period in the future.

Figure 18–3

THE MODEL COMPANY, INC.
Planning for Profit for the Year 19___

Step Description	*Analysis*	*Comments*
1. *Establish your profit goals.*		
Equity invested in company	$160,000	
Retained earnings	40,000	
Owners' equity	200,000	
Return desired, after income taxes	40,000	20% × $200,000
Estimated tax on profit	12,000	
Profit needed before income taxes	$ 52,000	
2. *Determine your planned volume of sales.*		
Estimate of sales income	$530,000	530 units × $1,000/unit
3. *Estimate your expenses for planned*		
volume of sales.	Estimated, 19___	Actual, last year
Cost of goods	$333,900	$291,262
Salaries	88,300	88,138
Utilities	7,100	6,950
Depreciation	10,000	10,050
Rent	2,500	2,000
Building services	5,100	4,920
Insurance	5,000	4,000
Interest	3,000	2,646
Office expenses	6,000	5,550
Sales promotion	11,800	11,000
Taxes and licenses	6,900	6,480
Maintenance	1,900	1,610
Delivery	6,500	5,848
Miscellaneous	2,000	1,740
Total	$490,000	$437,204
4. *Determine your estimated profit, based on*		
Steps 2 and 3.		
Estimated sales income	$530,000	
Estimated expenses	490,000	
Estimated net profit before taxes	$ 40,000	
5. *Compare estimated profit with profit goal.*		
Estimated profit before taxes	$ 40,000	
Desired profit before taxes	52,000	
Difference	−$ 12,000	

6. *List possible alternatives to improve profits.*
   A. Change the planned sales income:
      (1) Increase planned volume of units sold.
      (2) Increase or decrease planned price
          of units.
      (3) Combine (1) and (2).
   B. Decrease planned expenses.
   C. Add other products or services.
   D. Subcontract work.

Figure 18–3   (*concluded*)

7. *Determine how expenses vary with changes in sales volume.*

Expense Item	Sales Volume of 364			Sales Volume of 530		Sales Volume of 700	
	Fixed Expenses	*Variable Expenses*	*Total Expenses*	*Variable Expenses*	*Total Expenses*	*Variable Expenses*	*Total Expenses*
Goods sold		$229,200	$229,200	$333,900	$333,900	$440,789	$440,789
Salaries	$50,000	26,304	76,304	38,300	88,300	50,585	100,585
Utilities	6,000	755	6,755	1,100	7,100	1,453	7,453
Depreciation	10,000		10,000		10,000		10,000
Rent	2,500		2,500		2,500		2,500
Building services	4,000	7,555	4,755	1,100	5,100	1,453	5,453
Insurance	5,000		5,000		5,000		5,000
Interest		2,060	2,060	3,000	3,000	3,962	3,962
Office expenses	2,800	2,198	4,998	3,200	6,000	4,226	7,026
Sales promotion		8,104	8,104	11,800	11,800	15,585	15,585
Taxes and licenses	5,000	1,305	6,305	1,900	6,900	2,509	7,509
Maintenance	800	755	1,555	1,100	1,900	1,453	2,253
Delivery		4,464	4,464	6,500	6,500	8,585	8,585
Miscellaneous	2,000		2,000		2,000		2,000
Total	$88,100	$275,900	$364,000	$401,900	$490,000	$530,600	$618,700

8. *Determine how profits vary with changes in sales volume.*

	Sales Volume of 364	Sales Volume of 530	Sales Volume of 700
Revenue @ $1,000 per unit	$364,000	$530,000	$700,000
Expenses			
Fixed	$ 88,100	$ 88,100	$ 88,100
Variable	275,900	401,900	530,600
Total	364,000	490,000	618,700
Estimated profit before income tax	$000,000 (Break-even)	$ 40,000	$ 81,300

9. *Analyze alternatives from a profit standpoint.*
   Increase income by increasing price? Decreasing price?
   Increase income by increasing advertising?
   Decrease variable costs?
10. *Select and implement the plan.*

---

years. Learning how to forecast accurately can spell the difference between growth and stagnation for your business.[10]

Different parts of the business use these forecasts for planning and controlling their parts of the operations. Thus, the forecasts influence decisions about purchasing materials, scheduling production, securing financial resources, purchasing plant or equipment, hiring and paying personnel, scheduling vacations, and planning inventory levels.

In our example, you would probably forecast sales for the coming year on estimates of several factors, such as market conditions, level of sales promotion, estimate of competitors' activities, and inflation. Or you could use forecasts appearing in specialized business and government publications. Also, your trade association(s), banker, customers, vendors, and others can provide valuable information. Using all this information—and assuming 6 percent inflation for the coming year—you estimate that sales will increase about 8 percent, to $530,000 ($1,000 per unit × 530 units), which you enter as Step 2 in Figure 18–3.

Step 3: Estimate Expenses for Planned Sales Volume

To estimate expenses for the coming year, you record last year's figures as part of Step 3. You should then adjust them for changes in economic conditions (including inflation), changes in expenses needed to attain the planned sales, improved methods of production, and a reasonable salary for the services of the owner.

You then compute that about 63 percent of your revenue is to pay for materials and labor used directly to produce the goods you will sell. Using this figure—adjusted 6 percent for inflation—you enter the result, $333,900, as "cost of goods." You then estimate the amount of each of the other expenses, recognizing that some expenses vary directly with volume changes, while others change little, if at all. Enter each expense figure in the appropriate place. The total of all expected expenses is $490,000.

Step 4: Determine the Estimated Profit

In this step, you first deduct the figure for estimated expenses from the estimated sales income; then, add the total of any other income, such as interest. You calculate this amount and find that profit before taxes is estimated to be $40,000 ($530,000 − $490,000), which is higher than the $24,944 made last year.

Step 5: Compare Estimated Profit with Profit Goal

Next, you compare the estimated profit ($40,000) with your profit goal ($52,000). Because estimated profit is $12,000 less than you would wish, you decide to continue with Steps 6 through 10.

Step 6: List Possible Alternatives to Improve Profits

As shown in Step 6 of Figure 18–3, you have many alternatives for improving profits. Some of these are as follows:

A. Change the planned sales income by:
   1. Increasing planned volume of units sold by increasing sales promotion, improving the quality of the product, making it more available, or finding new uses for it.
   2. Increasing or decreasing the planned price of the units. The best price may not be the one you're using.

3. Combining (1) and (2). On occasion, some small business owners become too concerned with selling on the basis of price alone. Instead, price for profit and sell quality, better service, reliability, and integrity.

B. Decrease planned expenses by:

1. Establishing a better control system. Spotting areas where losses occur and establishing controls may reduce expenses.

2. Increasing productivity of people and machines through improving methods, developing proper motivators, and improving the types and use of machinery.

3. Redesigning the product by developing new materials, machines, and/or methods for improving products and reducing costs.

C. Reduce costs per unit or add other products or services by:

1. Adding a summer product to a winter line of products.

2. Selling as well as using parts made on machines with idle capacity.

3. Making some customarily purchased parts.

D. Subcontract work.

Having listed possible alternatives, you must evaluate each of them and concentrate on the best one(s).

Step 7: Determine How Expenses Vary with Changes in Sales Volume

Although you have estimated your planned sales volume at 530 units (at $1,000 per unit), you will probably want to see what happens to expenses if you sell fewer or more units. This can be done by reviewing your expected expenses in Step 3 and varying them up and down, remembering that some are fixed and some vary with level of sales. We've done this in Step 7 at three levels: 364, 530, and 700 units. Notice that total expenses increase from $364,000 at 364 units, to $490,000 at 530 units, and to $618,700 at 700 units.

While an analysis of past costs is helpful in projecting future expenses, be aware that

1. The relationships exist only within limited changes in sales volume. Very high sales volumes may be obtained by extraordinary and costly efforts, low volumes result in extra costs from idle capacity, lost volume discounts, and so forth.

2. Past relationships may not continue in the future. Inflation or deflation, changing location of customers, new products, and other factors can cause changes in the unit costs.

Step 8: Determine How Profits Vary with Changes in Sales Volume

As you notice in Step 8 of Figure 18–3, profit (or loss) can be estimated for different levels of sales. We've done that for the three levels— 364, 530, and 700

Figure 18–4   Break-Even Chart for The Model Company

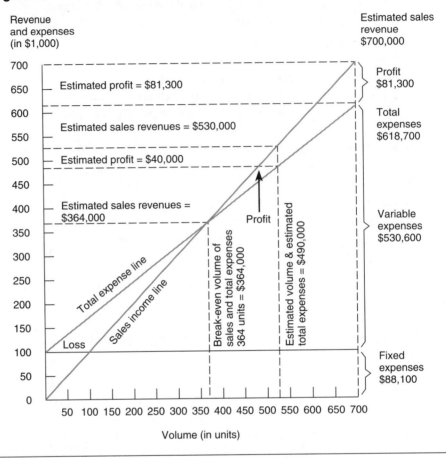

units—using fixed expenses, variable expenses, and the resulting profit before income taxes.

These figures were then incorporated into a chart (Figure 18–4) to show what sales volume would result in The Model Company's neither making nor losing money on its operations. This figure, called the **break-even point,** was 364 units, where sales revenues and total expenses were $364,000.

Step 9: Analyze Alternatives from a Profit Standpoint

The **break-even point** is that volume of sales where total revenue and expenses are equal so that there is neither profit nor loss.

Using the information you've generated so far, especially from Steps 6, 7, and 8, you can analyze some alternatives, such as the following, to increase profits:

1. How much can you reduce your sales price to bring in more sales volume?

2. Is it profitable to increase advertising?

Figure 18–5

THE MODEL COMPANY, INC.		
Income Statement for the Year 19___		
Sales income		$530,000
Less:		
Cost of goods sold	$327,200	
Other expenses	156,100	
Total expenses		483,300
Net profit before taxes		$46,700
Pretax return on equity		23.4%
Pretax profit margin		8.8%

3. What would a reduction in variable costs do to profit?

4. Which product is most profitable?

Other alternatives can be evaluated in much the same manner. Then, having made these economic analyses, you will be ready to make your final plan for action.

Step 10: Select and Implement the Plan

The selection of the plan for action depends on your judgment as to what will most benefit the business.[11] The results of the analyses made in the prior steps provide the economic inputs. These must be evaluated along with other goals. Cost reduction may result in laying off employees or in reducing service to customers.

Mr. Model has just read this text and has been studying some other management literature. After hearing you present the above analyses to him, he believes that the company can reduce the cost of goods sold by about 2 percent. Figure 18–5 shows a simplified statement of the planned income and outgo for the next year, based on the work you and he have done. How does it look to you?

WHAT YOU SHOULD HAVE LEARNED

1. Not only do small business owners often fail to plan for a profit, but they sometimes don't even know whether or not they are making a profit. Because healthy sales income doesn't guarantee a profit, it's important to determine the true cost of a product in order to set a fair price and budget and plan accordingly.

2. A business's financial position is not static. Every time a product is sold, money comes in, inventory is bought, or credit is given, assets and liabilities fluctuate. Rapid growth and ''paper profits'' can be the downfall of small

business owners who don't keep accurate records and don't listen to the conclusions accountants draw from the figures.

3. A company's financial structure consists of its assets, liabilities, and owners' equity. Assets are the things that a company owns. Current assets, which turn over within a year, include cash, accounts receivable, and inventory, as well as short-term investments and prepaid expenses. Fixed assets—such as buildings, machinery, store fixtures, trucks, and land—are things the company expects to own for a longer time. Part of their cost is written off each year as depreciation expense.

   Liabilities are obligations created by borrowing or buying something on credit. Current liabilities, payable within one year, include accounts payable, notes payable, and accrued expenses. Long-term liabilities, with terms of a year or longer, should be used to pay for fixed assets and to acquire working capital.

   Owners' equity is the owners' share of a business after liabilities are subtracted from assets. Profits may be distributed to owners as cash or dividends, or accumulated in the business in the form of retained earnings.

4. A company's profit (net income) is what is retained after expenses—the costs of doing business—are subtracted from revenues—the proceeds from sales. When sales increase, not only does sales income rise, but variable costs change as well, and it may sometimes be necessary to increase fixed costs.

   To plan for a profit, you must go through at least the first 5 of the following 10 steps: (1) establish the profit goal, (2) determine the planned volume of sales, (3) estimate the expenses for the planned sales volume, (4) determine estimated profit for the planned sales volume, and (5) compare the estimated profit with the profit goal. If the results of (5) are unsatisfactory, (6) list possible alternatives that can be used to improve the profit position, (7) determine how costs vary with changes in sales volume, (8) determine how profits vary with changes in sales volume, (9) analyze alternatives from a profit standpoint, and (10) select an alternative and implement the plan.

5. The chapter concluded by illustrating these steps for a hypothetical company.

QUESTIONS FOR DISCUSSION

1. Why is planning for profit so important to a small business?

2. In analyzing the changing financial position of a small business, what are some of the things you should look for?

3. "If a small firm is making a profit, there's no danger of its failing." Do you agree? Why or why not?

4. What is a firm's financial structure? What are the components of this structure?

5. Explain each of the following: *(a)* assets, *(b)* current assets, *(c)* fixed assets, *(d)* liabilities, *(e)* current liabilities, *(f)* long-term liabilities, *(g)* owners' equity, *(h)* retained earnings, *(i)* income (profit and loss) statement, *(j)* balance sheet, and *(k)* profit.

6. What steps are needed in profit planning?

7. How do you establish a profit goal?

8. How do you determine planned volume of sales?

9. How do you determine planned expenses?

10. What are some alternatives that could improve planned profits? Explain each.

WHAT IS PROFIT?

The Powell Company* was started in a small metal building in Louisiana two years ago to sell and service small boats. The company needed to hire some experienced personnel from an established competitor. Phil Powell, the owner, approached several of these people and offered them the same wages they were earning from their current employers. Because there were no immediate benefits from changing jobs, they were told of the advantages of getting in on the ground floor of the newer, though smaller, business. They were told that as the firm grew and sales and profits increased, it would be management's policy to pay a higher basic wage and also larger employee benefits. Several of these employees joined Powell.

During the first year, sales didn't come up to expectations. Powell decided that in order to increase sales he should move to a more desirable location, where modern equipment and facilities could improve production. The search for a new location was begun, and the employees were excited at the prospect of being located in a newer building with expanded facilities and the latest tools and equipment.

While the new facilities were being readied, morale was high and employee performance was superior. When the facilities were occupied, morale improved even further. During the first few months, more orders were obtained by the sales force than the firm was able to fill, but production quotas were met and surpassed. It appeared to all concerned that the company was well on its way to becoming a leader in its field.

With the new and expanded facilities, though, came new and unexpected problems. For example, overhead greatly expanded and there was a larger tax burden. Also, costs incurred for insurance, utilities, and personnel increased, which significantly increased expenses. So, while revenues were obviously increasing, expenses were increasing faster, and the business wasn't even breaking even, much less making a profit.

Powell felt he couldn't keep his promise to increase wages and add more employee benefits. He told the employees that they would just have to wait until the financial position improved before receiving what he had promised them. He said that the increases wouldn't be given until the company's sales were sufficiently higher than expenses to provide a profit.

Bob Benjamin, the production manager, agreed with Powell that wages couldn't be raised at that time, but he believed that unless the employees were shown a detailed report of expenses, they would continue to believe that the firm was making a substantial profit and had gone back on its word.

Powell, although he realized that this was true, said he also felt the employees had no justification for looking into the company's financial situation. In view of this, he said, he knew of but one alternative—the one he had previously outlined.

QUESTIONS

1. What does this case show about the relationships among income, expenses, and profits (losses)?

2. What did the move to new facilities do to the firm's break-even point?

3. Should the owner show the books to the employees? Why or why not?

4. What would you do now if you were the owner?

*Name disguised at the request of the owner.
Source: Prepared by Gayle M. Ross, Ross Publishing Company.

19

Budgeting and Controlling Operations

In dealing with accountants, never ask whether something can be done. The correct question is, "How can we do this?"—Robert Dince, former Pepperdine University professor

Let us watch well our beginnings, and the results will take care of themselves.—Alexander Clark

LEARNING OBJECTIVES

After studying the material in this chapter, you will be able to:

1. Explain how managers exercise control in a small business.

2. Describe the characteristics of control systems.

3. Tell what a budget is, explain the different types, and tell how they are prepared and used.

4. Describe how budgetary control operates.

5. Discuss how information on actual performance can be obtained and used.

6. Explain how ratios can be used to evaluate a firm's financial condition.

M & I FORD: "WE DON'T HAVE A BUDGET"

In the spring of 1980, James M. Wooten purchased M & I Ford, which was then primarily a distributor of Ford industrial engines. With Mr. Wooten serving as president, M & I Ford, Inc., grew very rapidly and in 1986 moved from its inner-city location to a rural setting in Baldwin County, Alabama. After moving into this new 21,000 square-foot building, M & I added Ford tractors and farm equipment to its product line.

Expanding into new businesses, while sticking with the basic blue of the Ford Power Products and Farm Equipment has been a way of life for James Wooten. He has been associated with Ford for over 40 years, beginning as a manager of a Power Products distributorship.

This rapidly growing company now has a total inventory of about $1.3 million, with over $600,000 in parts, over $200,000 in engines, and over $400,000 in tractor inventory. The size of this inventory and the service necessary to support this line of equipment has proved to be a financial challenge to the relatively new and small business. However, it has developed a reputation for supplying reliable products and quick, dependable service in the southern Alabama and northwest Florida areas.

Providing the engines for various types of logging equipment and forklifts is still a large part of M & I's busi-

James Wooten, right, demonstrates a tractor to a potential client.

ness, even after moving to the more rural, farming environment. The reliability of the products and the stability of the company helped M & I enter the business of supplying engines to a local producer of aircraft de-icers. M & I has shown a 500 percent increase in sales and service over its short history. One thing that Mr. Wooten has learned during his long association with Ford and the tractor and equipment business is that inventory control is very important.

When asked about the budgetary controls of M & I Ford, the first answer from Wooten was, "We don't have a budget." Under further examination it was discovered that, while not having a formal full-year budget, M & I does use a rolling budget. A projection is made each month based on the performance of that same month the previous year. Subjective adjustments are made to this projection based on the judgment of Mr. Wooten and his partners, B. J. Long and Bill Estes, relating to the local conditions facing area farmers and current economic conditions.

Mr. Wooten is proud of the fact that, even though he is involved in a very seasonal business, the firm has never had to lay off an employee. This is due to sound financial planning based on what to expect in the near future.

Source: Prepared by Dr. Walter Hollingsworth, University of Mobile.

The Profile illustrates what this text has stressed throughout—especially in the previous chapter—namely, the importance of controlling your firm's operations. In this chapter, we emphasize the nature, objectives, and methods of control, along with the design and use of budgets and the importance of budgetary control.

WHAT IS INVOLVED IN CONTROL?

Profit planning alone is not enough! Instead, after developing plans for making a profit, you must design an operating system to implement those plans. As you will see, that system, in turn, must be controlled to see that plans are carried out and objectives reached.

The Role of Control

Control is the process of assuring that organizational goals are achieved.

We continually exercise **control** over our activities and are, in turn, subject to controls. We control the speed of the car we drive; signal lights control the traffic flow. We control our homes' thermostats, which keep the temperature within an acceptable range. Ropes in an airport terminal guide passengers to the next available clerk. As you can see, controls that have been established to help accomplish certain objectives are found everywhere.

As shown in Chapter 5, planning provides the guides and standards used in performing the activities necessary to achieve company goals. Then, a system of controls is installed to ensure that performance conforms to the organization's plans. Any deviation from these plans should point to a need for change—usually in performance, but sometimes in the plans themselves, as the following example shows.

A machine-shop owner, with a special machine to produce wooden display stands for art objects, arranged to display the machine at a trade show for art dealers in a nearby city. The reception of this new equipment was good, and he received orders for 10 machines. Returning home, he took a year to raise capital, set up production, and produce the machines. By that time, his orders had evaporated. Since no advance payment had been received, he found himself with 10 unsold machines and an additional materials inventory of $27,500 to $31,750. A system of controls to align delivery with customer needs and to obtain advance payments would have prevented the problem.

Steps in Control

The control process consists of five steps:

1. Setting up standards of performance.
2. Measuring actual performance.
3. Comparing actual performance with planned performance standards.

4. Deciding whether any deviations are excessive.

5. Determining the appropriate corrective action needed to equalize planned and actual performance.

These steps are performed in all control systems, even though the systems may be quite different. Later in this chapter, these five steps are covered in detail, but the first step should be strongly emphasized at this point.

Setting Performance Standards

Performance standards tell employees what level of performance is expected of them. They also measure how well employees meet expectations. Performance standards are usually stated in terms of (1) units consumed or produced or (2) price paid or charged. Some examples are *standard hours per unit* to produce a good or service, *miles per gallon* of gasoline used, *price per unit* for purchased goods, and so on. There are many ways of developing these standards, such as intuition, past performance, careful measurement of activities, and comparison with other standards or averages.

Once standards of performance are set, they should be communicated by means of written policies, rules, procedures, and/or statements of standards to the people responsible for performance. Standards are valuable in locating sources of inefficient as well as efficient performance.

> **Performance standards** set acceptable levels to which employee performance should conform.

✳CHARACTERISTICS OF EFFECTIVE CONTROL SYSTEMS

Effective control systems should be (1) timely, (2) cost-effective (3) accurate, (4) quantifiable and measurable, and they should (5) indicate cause-and-effect relationships, (6) be the responsibility of one individual, and (7) be generally acceptable to those involved with them.[1]

Timely

To keep control systems timely, checks should be made frequently and as quickly as feasible. You can't wait until the end of the year to find out whether sales meet expectations.

Cost-Effective

Any control system requires the time of a person or of some equipment, both costly. But the cost of a control system should be balanced against its value. Some systems are simple; others are more complex and costly. While you should try to reduce the time and paperwork needed to collect information, the system must do what it's supposed to do—control. A simple inspection of shelf stock may give enough information for inventory control without having a clerk provide a tabulated summary, but there are times when the extra cost of the tabulated summary may be justified.

Accurate

If controls are to be useful, they must be reliable; to be reliable, they must be accurate. Thus, a basic tenet of any control system or procedure is to obtain accurate data and then use them correctly.

Quantifiable and Measurable

Although quality must sometimes be judged subjectively, it's much easier to measure and control things that can be expressed in quantitative terms, so the choice of measuring the unit of control is vital. Sales can be measured in dollars, pounds, tons, barrels, gallons, grams, kilograms, meters, or other units.

Indicative of Cause-and-Effect Relationships—When Possible

A report of increasing costs of a product may indicate the actual situation but not tell *why* costs increased. On the other hand, a report showing that the cost per unit of raw materials is higher than planned because a supplier raised prices not only pinpoints the problem but also identifies its cause.

The Responsibility of One Individual

Because you won't have time to control all activities yourself, you'll need to delegate the authority for some aspects of control to subordinates. As shown in Chapter 15, you should give those people authority, provide the necessary resources, and then hold them responsible for achieving the desired control.

Acceptable to Those Involved with Them

People tend to resent controls, especially those they consider unnecessary, unreasonable, unfair, or excessive. They show their resentment by rebelling, that is, by finding a way to "beat the system." Therefore, if controls are to be accepted, it is important for those involved to clearly understand the purpose of the controls and feel that they have an important stake in them.

USING BUDGETS TO COMMUNICATE STANDARDS

A **budget** is a detailed statement of financial results expected for a given future period.

Performance standards serve as building blocks for the preparation of the **budget,** which is a detailed statement of financial results expected for a given future period. The time period may be a month, a quarter, or a year. The budget is expressed in monetary terms but may also include other measurements, such as number of units expected to be sold, units of inventory used, and labor hours worked. The budget should be based on realistic goals that can be achieved during the planning period.

Types of Budgets

The three most important types of budgets are (1) capital budgets, (2) operating budgets, and (3) cash flow budgets.

The **capital budget** reflects a business's plans for obtaining, expanding, and replacing physical facilities. It requires that management preplan the use of its limited financial resources for needed buildings, tools, equipment, and other facilities.

The **operating budget** is based on profit plans for the budget period. It contains a forecast of the amounts and sources of sales income and the materials, labor, and other expenses that will be needed to achieve the sales forecast.

The **cash flow budget** is a forecast of expected cash receipts and necessary cash payments. It shows whether sufficient cash will be available for timely payment of budgeted expenses, capital equipment purchases, and other cash requirements. It also tells whether arrangements need to be made for external sources of cash, such as borrowings or owner investments. The lack of ready cash resources is the primary reason that firms are forced into liquidation. Thus, effective forecasting is essential.[2]

Neil Churchill, professor of entrepreneurship at Babson College, thinks the biggest crisis for small business is lack of cash. Therefore, dealing quickly with cash flow problems can mean the difference between success and failure. His tips on how small firms can cope with this problem are given in the case at the end of this chapter. Also, the SBA has a form called "Monthly Cash Flow Projection," with instructions for its use, which should be of help to you.

MASTER BUDGETS

A **capital budget** plans expenditures for obtaining, expanding, and replacing physical facilities.

An **operating budget** forecasts sales and allocates expenses for achieving them.

A **cash flow budget** forecasts the amount of cash receipts and cash needed to pay expenses and make other purchases.

Preparing the Operating Budget

The objective of the operating budget is to plan and control revenue and expenses to obtain desired profits. Therefore, the *sales budget* is planned first, giving consideration to the production and personnel functions. The *production budget* is then set to meet the sales budget plans. This budget includes production, purchasing, and personnel schedules and inventory levels. It includes units such as amount of materials and personnel time, as well as their costs. Next, a *personnel budget* is developed for the number of people needed to produce the product, any costs of training them, their pay and benefits, and other factors needed. The amount of detail in each of these budgets depends on its value to the company.

The sales budget is the most basic consideration. As you saw in Figure 18–3, Step 2, the sales budget must be prepared first before you can plan your production and personnel budgets. Because it was discussed in detail there, we'll not discuss it further in this chapter.

Preparing the Cash Flow Budget

It surprises some small business owners that their businesses may be making profits and yet fail because they don't have the cash to pay current expenses. Therefore, provision must be made for adequate cash to pay bills when they are due and payable. This cash planning takes two forms: (1) the daily and weekly cash requirements for the normal operation of the business and (2) the maintenance of the proper balance for longer-term requirements.

Planning Daily and Weekly Cash Needs

The first type of planning tends to be routine and is done on a daily or weekly basis.[3] For example, you may have a fairly constant income and outgo, which you can predict. Thus, you can establish policies for the amount of cash to maintain and set up procedures to control that level of cash. These routine demands represent a small part of the needed cash on hand, and they tend to remain fairly constant.

Planning Monthly and Yearly Cash Needs

The second type of planning requires a budget for, say, each month of the year. Payments for rent, payroll, purchases, and services require a regular outflow of cash. Insurance and taxes may require large payments a number of times each year. A special purchase, such as a truck, will place a heavy demand on cash. So, it takes planning to have the *right* amount of cash available when needed.

Procedure for Planning Cash Needs

Figure 19–1 shows the form used by The Model Company to budget its cash for three months ahead. Each month is completed before the next month is shown. Items 1 through 4 give estimates of cash to be received. For example, The Model Company expects to receive 20 percent of its monthly sales in cash (item 1). A check of its accounts receivable budget can provide an estimate of the cash to be received in January (item 2). Other income (item 3) might come from interest on investments or the sale of surplus equipment. Item 4 shows the expected total cash to be received.

Expected cash payments, items 5 through 18, show the items The Model Company might list in its planned budget (see Step 3 in Figure 18–3). Cash is often paid in the month during or after which the goods are received or the service is performed. Examples include payments for electricity and for material purchases. Some cash payments can be made at any one of several times. For example, payments on a new insurance policy can be set up to come due when other cash demands are low.

Figure 19–1

THE MODEL COMPANY Cash Budget For Three Months Ending March 31, 19___						
	January		February		March	
Items that Change Cash Level	Budget	Actual	Budget	Actual	Budget	Actual
Expected Cash Receipts 1. Cash sales						
2. Collections—accounts receivable						
3. Other income						
4. Total cash receipts						
Expected Cash Payments 5. Goods purchases						
6. Salaries						
7. Utilities						
8. Depreciation						
9. Rent						
10. Building services						
11. Insurance						
12. Interest						
13. Office expenses						
14. Sales promotion						
15. Taxes and licenses						
16. Maintenance						
17. Delivery						
18. Miscellaneous						
19. Total cash payments						
Cash Balance 20. Cash balance—beginning of month						
21. Change—item 4 minus item 19						
22. Cash balance—end of month						
23. Desired cash balance						
24. Short-term loans needed						
25. Cash available—end of month						
Cash for Capital Investments 26. Cash available—line 25						
27. Desired capital cash						
28. Long-term loans needed						

USING TECHNOLOGY TO SUCCEED

THE CHECK IS IN THE COMPUTER

"The whole name of the game is being able to use your money more effectively," said Jayne Palmer, who manages the money in about 20 accounts for Response Communications, an Atlanta telemarketing company.

To use money more effectively, several new businesses have grown up to manage other people's money. For example, Martin Tudor uses a personal computer in his office to (1) manage the business affairs of several New York actors, (2) check their bank balances, (3) see if a check or deposit has cleared, and (4) move funds between interest-earning and bill-paying accounts. His computer is hooked into his bank's computer system. In effect, he has a branch of the bank in his office.

Neither Palmer nor Tudor uses home banking services to pay bills. Palmer uses a separate computer for that, and Tudor uses checks in order to have proof of payment.

Source: Michael Totty, "Small Businesses Find Electronic Banking Can Be a Useful Tool in Managing Money," *The Wall Street Journal,* July 22, 1986, p. 33. Reprinted by permission of THE WALL STREET JOURNAL, © 1986 Dow Jones & Company, Inc. All Rights Reserved Worldwide.

As shown in Figure 19–1, the cash budget shows when payments are to be made. For example, the cash balance on the first of January (item 20), plus the month's receipts (item 4), less the month's cash payments (item 19), provide an expected cash balance at the end of January as follows:

$$\frac{\text{Balance at}}{\text{beginning of month}} + \frac{\text{Total cash}}{\text{receipts}} - \frac{\text{Total cash}}{\text{payments}} = \frac{\text{Balance at}}{\text{end of month}}$$

A negative balance will require an increase in cash receipts, a decrease in payments, or the floating of a short-term loan. A company should have a certain amount of cash to take care of contingencies. Item 23 shows the desired amount of cash needed as a minimum balance.

A three-month projection is probably the optimum time estimate for a cash budget. If sales are seasonal or you expect heavy demands on the cash balance, longer periods may be necessary.

Rationale for Cash Flow Budgeting

The cash flow budget controls the flow of cash into your business so you can make needed payments and not maintain too high a cash balance. Many small business people, though, don't realize the importance of moving money through their systems as quickly and effectively as possible. Everything else being equal, the faster you can move your money and turn it over in sales and income, the greater the profits and the less the interest payments should be.

The Using Technology to Succeed above illustrates the use of electronic banking in small business, which has many advantages, as well as drawbacks.[4] Because the name of the game is using money most effectively to make more money, many small and medium-sized companies don't use electronic transfer of funds to pay their bills. Instead, they prefer to take maximum advantage of *float time,* which is the time it takes for a check to go to the receiver, be deposited, and clear the banks. Robert Anton of Sages Electric Supply Company in Hingham, Massachusetts, explains it this way: "We write checks one or two days before they are due. Then we have two days until the check clears the bank. With electronic transfer, we'd lose those two days of float."[5]

USING BUDGETARY CONTROL

By itself, a budget is only a collection of figures or estimates that indicate plans. When it's used for control purposes, though, it becomes **budgetary control,** which involves careful planning and control of all the company's financial activities. This includes frequent and close controls in the areas where poor performance most affects a company. Other areas may be controlled less often. For example, the cost of goods sold by The Model Company is planned for 63 percent of the sales dollar, and utilities are 1.34 percent of sales (see Steps 2 and 3 in Figure 18–3). Cost of goods sold may be divided into material and labor and checked weekly, while utilities might be checked monthly.

Budgetary control is the careful planning and control of all financial activities of a firm.

Controlling Credit, Collections, and Accounts Receivable

As shown in Chapter 12, extending credit increases the potential for sales—and losses from bad debts. You may have found that the amount of accounts receivable for The Model Company was large relative to its credit sales (see Figures 18–1 and 18–2). Waiting until the end of the year to find this out is potentially dangerous, since the average retailer loses more from slow accounts than from bad debts. Checks should be made often enough to identify customers who are slow in paying and to determine the reason(s) for it. In general, the longer an account goes unpaid, the less the chance of collection. A rule of thumb is that you can expect to collect only a quarter of accounts over two years old, and none after five years.

The best control of bad debt losses starts with investigating the customer's ability and willingness to pay, and by providing clear statements of terms. Then, proctor past-due accounts each month so that each slow account is followed up promptly.

You may decide to write off some accounts as a bad debt expense, while providing some incentive for earlier payment by slow-paying customers. Uncollectible accounts receivable create a misstatement of income and therefore an unjustified increase in business income tax liability. Unless there exists a reasonable expectation of collecting the account, a good rule of thumb is to *write off all accounts receivable over six months old at tax time.*

Other Types of Budgetary Control

Many other types of budgetary control can be used to restrain a company's activities and investments. Any expense can increase gradually without the change being recognized. Have you noticed how fast the cash in your pockets disappears? You know you must control this, but it's very hard to do. Some call it being "nickeled and dimed to death." A small business has similar problems. Contributing to this creeping increase in the firm's costs may be such diverse situations as a clerk added to process increased paperwork, a solicitor asking for donations, a big customer requesting special delivery, an employee who uses company stamps for personal letters, rising energy costs, and inflation-increased costs. These costs must be controlled if the firm is to survive.

Using Audits to Control the Budget

An **audit** is a formalized examination and/or review of a company's financial records.

An **audit** of a company consists of a formalized, methodical study, examination, and/or review of its financial records, with the intent of verifying, analyzing, informing, and/or discovering opportunities for improvement.[6] There are three main types of audits: (1) financial, (2) internal, and (3) operations audits.

In *financial auditing,* an outside certified public accountant (CPA) examines the records and provides financial statements of a company once a year. This audit furnishes the owner(s) with information on the company's financial status and operations and provides authenticity for anyone using the financial statements.

A new wrinkle in auditing is using compact discs for storing information to send to auditors. The discs are the same as those used for music. The primary advantages are reduced storage space and ease of finding citations when doing research. The main disadvantages are that indexing of audit materials is time-consuming and that, to keep current, new discs must be sent to auditors as frequently as every three months.[7]

Internal auditing is an independent appraisal of accounting, financial, and/or operations activities with the intention of measuring and evaluating the effectiveness of controls. Such audits function primarily as a service to management for the improvement of its financial controls.

An *operations audit* studies the basic operations of a company to identify problem areas. It may include studies of functional areas (marketing, finance, production, organization structure, personnel, and planning). Closely related to internal auditing, operations auditing emphasizes operations more than financial activities.

In summary, a company should be audited annually to ensure continued proper financial reporting. Bankers often require financial statements audited by a CPA before they will loan money. If any questions arise as to proper controls, inefficient operations, or lost opportunities, some form of internal or operations audit should also be considered.

OBTAINING AND USING PERFORMANCE INFORMATION

Information on actual performance comes through some form of **feedback:** observation, oral reports, written memos or reports, and/or other methods.

Feedback is the response a receiver gives through further communication with the sender of the message or some other person.

Obtaining the Information

Observation will probably be most satisfying because you are at the scene of action and have direct control over the situation. However, this method is time-consuming, and you can't be in all places at one time. But you can justify using this method if your knowledge is needed, your presence may improve the work, or you are present for other purposes.

Oral reports, the most prevalent type of control used in small firms, are also time-consuming, but they provide two-way communication.

Written memos or reports are prepared when a record is needed or when many facts must be assembled. This type of feedback is costly unless the reports are the original records. A good record system, as will be discussed in Chapter 21, is a valuable aid, and it should be designed to be a ready source of reports.

Comparing Actual Performance with Standards

The ability to keep costs low is one of the primary advantages of small businesses. To do this, an effective cost accounting system and cost-sensitive controls are vital. Information about actual performance, obtained through feedback, can be compared with predetermined standards to see if any changes are needed.

Simple, informal controls can usually be used by small firms. Performance measures are carried in the owner's head; comparisons are made as feedback is

"Never mind the dramatics, Snodgrass—just read the treasurer's report!"
Reprinted from *The Savant* (a SCORE publication), March 1989.

received, and decisions are made accordingly. This type of control follows the same steps as the more formal types of control needed when delegating authority. Examples of the use of standards were discussed in Chapter 17 and follow the same pattern as control through the use of budgets.

Determining Causes of Poor Performance

Poor performance can result from many factors, both internal and external, including the following:

- Having the wrong objectives.
- Customers not buying the company's product.
- Poor scheduling of production or purchases.
- Theft and/or spoilage of products.
- Too many employees for the work being performed.
- Opportunities lost.
- Too many free services or donations.

Once management isolates the true cause(s) of the firm's poor performance, remedies can probably be found, as the following example shows.

A small company oriented toward research and development (R&D) was providing customers with special R&D service without reimbursement for the thousands of dollars spent in this manner. After the policy was changed, the company's profits improved.

EVALUATING THE FIRM'S FINANCIAL CONDITION

Ratios are relationships between two or more variables.

The **current ratio** is the amount of current assets divided by the amount of current liabilities.

Having considered the financial structure and operations of a company, we now consider the methods of evaluating its financial condition. Look at Figures 18–1 and 18–2 (pp. 368 and 370), which show the financial statements of The Model Company. Is the company in a good financial position? How can you tell? You can do so by establishing and analyzing **ratios,** which are relationships between two or more variables. For example, the amount of current assets needed depends on other conditions of a company, such as the size of its current liabilities. So the **current ratio**—current assets divided by current liabilities—shows how easily a company can pay its current obligations.

Unfortunately, no standard figures have been determined for successes or failures, but reasonable evaluations are possible. Two sets of values can be used for evaluation purposes: (1) a comparison of the current value of your firm's operations with those of the past and (2) a comparison of your operations with those of similar businesses.

Comparing Your Company's Current and Past Performance

A change in the value of selected ratios for a business indicates a change in its financial position. For example, suppose the *current ratio* for The Model Company has moved gradually from a value of 1:1 to its present value of 2.73:1 (which is $148,626 ÷ $54,408 in Figure 18–1). In the past, a ratio of 2:1 has been used as a rule of thumb for the current ratio. However, no one value of a ratio is favorable for all companies. For example, The Model Company has decided to have more current assets than current liabilities, so it looks good. However, this improvement may be due to keeping old, uncollectible accounts on the books. In that case, appearances are deceiving. Analysis is needed to determine the causes and to help the company decide what to do.

Comparing Your Company with Similar Companies

Average values and ranges of values for the ratios are published for a variety of small to large companies. These provide a guide to what your competitors are doing. Suppose the *current ratio* for companies with assets of $300,000 or less is found to be 1.3:1, while The Model Company has a ratio of 2.73:1. Again, the company's ratio looks good, but it may be losing income by maintaining too many nonproductive assets in a period of high interest rates.

SOME IMPORTANT RATIOS AND THEIR MEANINGS

Some of the more important ratios, and the ways to compute them, are shown in Table 19–1. Spaces are provided for computing the ratios for The Model Company, using the data provided in Figures 18–1 and 18–2. Comparable figures for the industry are provided for comparative purposes.

These ratios will help you answer such questions as the following: (1) Are profits satisfactory? (2) Are assets productive? (3) Can the business pay its debts? (4) How good are the business's assets? and (5) Is your equity in the business satisfactory?

Are Profits Satisfactory?

Is the owner of The Model Company getting an adequate or reasonable return on his investment? The ratio of *net profit (income) to owners' equity* (Ratio 1 in Table 19–1)—often called **return on equity (ROE)**—is used to evaluate this, but several other ratios should be considered in profit planning and decision making.

How much return does your company make on its sales dollar? The ratio of *net profit (income) to net sales* (Ratio 2) provides this information. Suppose The Model Company now makes 4.3 cents profit (after taxes) per dollar of sales. Is the trend up or down? How does it compare with the experience of similar companies? If it is dropping, why? Costs may be increasing without an increase in price; competitors may be keeping their prices lower than The Model Company; it may be trying

Return on equity (ROE) is the percentage of net profit your equity earns, before taxes.

Table 19–1   Financial Ratios

Ratio	Formula	The Model Company	Industry Average*
1. Net profit to owners' equity	$\dfrac{\text{Net profit before taxes}}{\text{Owners' equity}}$	= _____	18.4%
2. Net profit to net sales	$\dfrac{\text{Net profit before taxes}}{\text{Net sales}}$	= _____	3.1
3. Net sales to fixed assets	$\dfrac{\text{Net sales}}{\text{Fixed assets}}$	= _____	5.8
4. Net sales to owners' equity	$\dfrac{\text{Net sales}}{\text{Owners' equity}}$	= _____	7.5
5. Current ratio	$\dfrac{\text{Current assets}}{\text{Current liabilities}}$	= _____	1.3
6. Acid test (quick ratio)	$\dfrac{\text{Current assets} - \text{Inventory}}{\text{Current liabilities}}$	= _____	1.0
7. Receivables to working capital†	$\dfrac{\text{Accounts receivable}}{\text{Working capital}}$	= _____	1.2
8. Inventory to working capital	$\dfrac{\text{Inventory}}{\text{Working capital}}$	= _____	0.4
9. Collection period	$\dfrac{\text{Accounts receivable}}{\text{Average daily credit sales‡}}$	= _____	43.0 days
10. Net sales to inventory	$\dfrac{\text{Net sales}}{\text{Inventory}}$	= _____	22.0
11. Net sales to working capital	$\dfrac{\text{Net sales}}{\text{Working capital}}$	= _____	10.0
12. Long-term liabilities to working capital	$\dfrac{\text{Long-term liabilities}}{\text{Working capital}}$	= _____	0.7
13. Debt to owners' equity	$\dfrac{\text{Total liabilities}}{\text{Owners' equity}}$	= _____	1.6
14. Current liabilities to owners' equity	$\dfrac{\text{Current liabilities}}{\text{Owners' equity}}$	= _____	1.1
15. Fixed assets to owners' equity	$\dfrac{\text{Fixed assets}}{\text{Owners' equity}}$	= _____	1.2

*Times unless otherwise specified
†Working capital = Current assets minus current liabilities.
‡If 80 percent of sales are on credit, average daily credit sales are: Annual sales ÷ 365 × 0.80 = _____.

to obtain a large sales volume at the expense of profit. An increase in sales volume with the same investment and net profit per dollar of sales will increase ROE; a decrease will reduce ROE.

Are Assets Productive?

Does your company obtain enough sales from its producing assets? The answer is reflected in the ratio of *net sales to fixed assets* (Ratio 3)—fixed assets representing the producing units of the company. So many variables exist (such as leasing instead of owning fixed assets) that this ratio can change with changes in policy.

Does your company have enough sales for the amount of investment? The ratio of *net sales to owners' equity* (Ratio 4) provides an answer. This ratio can be combined with the *net profit to net sales* ratio (Ratio 2) to obtain the *return on equity (ROE)* ratio (Ratio 1).

Can the Business Pay Its Debts?

Can your business pay its current obligations? A number of ratios can help answer this question. As mentioned earlier, the best known is the *current ratio* (Ratio 5), which is the ratio of current assets to current liabilities. You may be making a good profit but not be able to pay your debts, for cash doesn't necessarily increase when you make a profit. The **acid test (quick) ratio** (Ratio 6), which is the ratio of current assets minus inventory to current liabilities, is an even more rigorous test of the ability to pay debts quickly.

Another check is obtained by using **working capital,** or current assets less current liabilities, as a basis.[8] Working capital is the margin of safety a company has in paying its current liabilities. The ratios of *accounts receivable to working capital* (Ratio 7) and *inventory to working capital* (8) provide an insight into the riskiness of the company's ability to make current payments.

The **acid test (quick) ratio** is the ratio of current assets, less inventory, to current liabilities.

Working capital is the amount of current assets less current liabilities.

How Good Are the Business's Assets?

How good are your assets? Cash in hand is the best asset, but it doesn't produce any revenue. *Accounts receivable* represent what you will receive in cash from customers sometime in the future. However, as indicated earlier, the older an account, the greater the chance of loss. So the *collection period* ratio (Ratio 9), accounts receivable to average daily credit sales, provides a guide to their quality.

Inventories can be evaluated in about the same way as accounts receivable. Because goods in inventory become obsolete if not sold within a reasonable time, they should be turned over at least once during the year. The turnover rate is expressed by the ratio of *net sales to inventory* (Ratio 10). If your company turns its inventory over too slowly, you may be keeping obsolete or deteriorating goods. Too high a ratio may result from an inventory so low that it hurts production or from not providing satisfactory service to customers.

For example, Bayview Fabrics had a "going-out-of-business" sale recently; some of the inventory had been in the store 10 years or longer.

To get an idea of the support that you receive from your current assets, compute the ratio of *net sales to working capital* (Ratio 11). Accounts receivable and inventory should increase with an increase in sales, but not out of proportion.

Increases in payroll and other expenses require a higher level of cash outflow. On the other hand, too low a ratio indicates available surplus working capital to service sales.

Is Your Equity in the Business Satisfactory?

How much equity should you have in your company? Assets are financed either by equity investments or by the creation of debt—a liability. Thus, any retained earnings, which are part of your equity, can be used to increase your assets or decrease your liabilities. You can maintain a high level of equity, with a relatively low level of risk, or a relatively high level of liabilities with a higher expected return on equity, but greater risk.

Most small companies don't like to maintain a large amount of long-term debt, since the risk is too great. The ratios commonly used to check the company's source-of-funds relationships are *long-term liabilities to working capital* (Ratio 12), *debt to owners' equity* (Ratio 13), *current liabilities to owners' equity* (Ratio 14), and *fixed assets to owners' equity* (Ratio 15). An extremely high value for any of these puts your company in a risky situation. While a bad year will probably decrease your income, the obligation to pay continues. On the other hand, a very good year results in large returns to you.

Ratios Are Interrelated

While each ratio indicates only part of the firm's position, the ratios overlap because a company is a complex system, and a change in the size of one of the accounts, such as cash, affects other values.

The financial ratios for the items on the profit and loss statement can be expressed in percentages of sales. This information is usually hard to obtain from competing small firms. High cost of goods sold as a percentage of sales income may indicate a poor choice of vendors, inefficient use of material or labor, or too low a price. A high percentage of salaries may indicate overstaffing of the company.

WHAT YOU SHOULD HAVE LEARNED

1. Small firms must have specific goals and standards for performance, know how their performance compares with those goals and standards, and take steps to ensure conformity with standards. The job of controls is to do these things.

2. Controls should be timely, cost-effective, accurate, quantifiable and measurable, show cause-and-effect relationships, be administered by one individual, and be acceptable to those involved in their use. Before controls

can be used, standards of performance must be set and communicated to those responsible for meeting them.

3. A budget is a summary of planned expenditures and income for a given period of time. Small businesses need at least a capital budget, an operating budget, and a cash flow budget. Sales estimates provide the basis of production and personnel budgets. A cash flow budget is needed to help a company have enough cash on hand to meet current demands and to avoid maintaining a cash balance that is higher than needed.

4. Budgetary control is needed to control accounts receivable, since uncollectible debts reported as assets will be taxed along with the best-paying accounts. Budgetary control can also be used to control the activities and investments of the company, as well as expenses and inventory.

     An audit, which is a formalized, methodical examination of the company's financial records, can be used to control financial condition. Outside CPA firms usually perform financial audits, but internal audits can also be used to measure and evaluate the effectiveness of controls. A financial audit is needed at least once a year.

5. Information on actual performance can be obtained by observation or from oral or written reports. Actual performance can be compared to standards to determine the causes of poor performance.

6. Various ratios can be used to compare the company's current and past performance, as well as its performance relative to competitors. They can help determine whether profits are satisfactory, whether assets are productive, how able the company is to pay its debts, how good its assets are, and how much equity the owner(s) have.

QUESTIONS FOR DISCUSSION

1. What is control? List the steps in an effective control process.
2. What are some characteristics of effective control systems?
3. What are performance standards? Why are they used?
4. What are some benefits of using a well-planned budget? Discuss the different types of budgets.
5. What is budgetary control? How can it be used by a small business?
6. How can auditing be used to control the budget of a small firm?
7. How can information about actual performance be obtained in a small firm?
8. Compute the ratios listed in Table 19-1 for The Model Company, using the data in Figures 18-1 and 18-2.

9. Evaluate the financial condition of The Model Company.

10. Evaluate your personal financial situation and operations, using material developed in this chapter.

11. Develop a budget for yourself for the coming year.

HOW TO DEAL WITH CASH FLOW PROBLEMS

According to Neil Churchill, a finance expert, the best way to deal with cash flow problems is to:

1. Make finances your number one priority. Monitor cash flow daily if possible.

2. Consider replacing the person who handles your company's finances. Look for a "tough son-of-a-gun" who knows how to keep tighter control over costs.

3. Speed up cash flow into the company. One way: Offer discounts to customers who pay their bills within 10 to 15 days versus 30 to 60 days.

4. Turn as much inventory as possible into cash, even if it means selling inventory to your competitors.

5. Put as many unpaid bills as possible on hold. But be sure to negotiate with your suppliers and your bank to stretch out payments. Don't leave lenders hanging.

6. Cut employment. About 80 percent of potential costs savings will come from reducing your work force. As you cut back, though, try to keep your most productive workers.

7. Cut your rental costs. Move to cheaper office space or cut back on the amount of space you use.

8. Get rid of unproductive assets that cost money, such as outdated machinery that requires costly maintenance.

QUESTIONS

1. How feasible are these suggestions?

2. Which one do you think would be *most effective* in dealing with the cash flow problem? Why?

3. Which one(s) would *not* work? Why?

4. What other suggestions do you have? Explain.

Source: Neil Churchill, as reported in David E. Gumpert, "Watch the Purse Strings," *USA Today,* May 8, 1989, p. 10E. Copyright 1989, USA TODAY. Excerpted with permission.

20

Taxes and Their Treatment

Noah must have taken two taxes into the ark—and they have been multiplying ever since!—Will Rogers

Our Constitution is in actual operation; everything appears to promise that it will last; but in this world nothing can be said to be certain but death and taxes.—Benjamin Franklin

LEARNING OBJECTIVES

After studying the material in this chapter, you will be able to:

1. Explain how the U.S. tax system operates.

2. Name and describe the taxes imposed on the small business itself.

3. Name and describe employment-related taxes.

4. Explain how the ownership of the business results in direct taxation of the owner.

5. Show how taxes may be reduced by careful estate planning.

6. Understand the importance of record keeping and tax reporting.

JACK BARES: ESTATE PLANNING TO MINIMIZE TAXES

Jack Bares is an unusual entrepreneur. Not only did he establish his own company—Milbar Corporation, a Chagrin Falls, Ohio, hand-tool manufacturing company—but he also started planning his estate at the birth of his first child, shortly after starting Milbar. He worked out a practical three-stage approach to correspond with the life cycle of his growing family and business.

In 1960, in the first stage, he wrote a will leaving the new business and his other assets to his wife—and "bought plenty of life insurance." Then he set up a family partnership with his wife and children, combining a standard family partnership agreement with a sale-leaseback strategy. After placing Milbar's few assets in the partnership, the corporation leased the assets back from the partnership. The result was that the corporation basically owned only its working capital, while the family partnership owned everything else.

The parents made annual tax-free contributions of $10,000 (the IRS limit) to the partnership in each child's name. The parents were the general partners, operating and controlling the partnership's business. Because of the

Milbar Corporation CEO Jack Bares
Photo courtesy of Jack Bares.

leasing strategy, the income earned by the partnership, which was primarily leasing fees, was taxed at a personal rate—which was then lower than the corporate rate.

When their first child went to college, Bares entered the second stage of his estate plan by concentrating on the best tax-saving device available at that time, namely, the estate freeze (no longer legal). Under a stock recapitalization plan, he transferred nonvoting common stock to the children, while he retained the voting stock. Thus, he continued to run, build, and profit from the business while passing along the ownership of the company to the children, at large tax savings.

He recently entered the third stage. He and his wife reduced their share of the business to only 0.5 percent each, and the remaining shares were split equally among the children. He promoted a vice-president to the president's spot and named three outside businesspeople as board members. The role of these four people is either to ensure a smooth transition to new family management or, if none of the family want to stay involved, to sell the company.

Source: Jill Andresky Fraser, "Planning Ahead: Estate Planning Isn't Just for Your Heirs, It Can Save Your Company," *Inc.*, August 1989, pp. 125–27. Adapted with permission of *Inc.* magazine. Copyright © 1989 by Goldhirsh Group, Inc., 38 Commercial Wharf, Boston, MA 02110.

Taxes are charges levied by a
government on persons and
groups subject to its jurisdiction.

The Profile dramatizes small business owners' need to lower their **taxes,** which are charges levied by a government on persons and groups subject to its jurisdiction. Therefore, we'll try to explain how the U.S. tax system affects you and your small business.

THE U.S. TAX SYSTEM

The U.S. tax system includes all the federal, state, and local tax systems, each of which has at least two parts. The first part is the system for determining what the taxes will be and who will pay them. The second part is the system for collecting the taxes.

Who Pays the Taxes?

Indirect taxes are not paid by a
person or firm, but by someone
else.

Direct taxes are those paid
directly to a taxing authority by
the person or business against
which they are levied.

Taxes can be either indirect or direct. **Indirect taxes** are paid not by the person or firm against which they're levied but by someone else. Since indirect taxes are part of the cost of doing business, they must either be added to the price of the firm's product(s) or shifted backward to the persons who produced the product(s).

　　Direct taxes are paid directly to the taxing authority by the person or business against which they're levied.

For example, the owner of a building containing a retail shop pays the property tax (direct) to the tax collector, but the amount of the tax is included in the rent paid by the retailer to the owner (indirect). In turn, the retailer includes this tax in the price that a customer pays for the goods or services that are being sold (indirect).

　　Also, as will be shown later, you pay tax on your income (direct) even though your employer may withhold it and send it to the tax collector for you.

　　Table 20–1 gives an overview of some selected taxes on small businesses. It shows the kind of tax, the taxpayer, the point of collection, and the governmental unit collecting the tax.

How Taxes Affect Small Businesses

Taxes affect almost every aspect of operating a small business. First, there is the direct taxation of business income, whether in the form of sales taxes levied as a tax on business receipts or as an income tax on corporate profits.

　　Second, employers must withhold—and often match—a variety of employment-related taxes levied on their employees, such as federal and state taxes on personal wage and salary incomes, and federal taxes levied to fund the Social Security/Medicare system.

Table 20–1   Some Selected Direct Taxes Paid by Small Firms

Kind of Tax	Taxpayer	Point of Collection	Collecting Agency
Corporate income tax	Corporations	Tax collectors	Internal Revenue Service State revenue departments City tax collectors
Corporate franchise tax (on capital stock)	Corporations	Tax collectors	States
Undistributed profits tax	Corporations	District IRS office	Internal Revenue Service
Customs duties	Corporations	Customs agents	U.S. Customs Service
Excise taxes	Businesses Customers	Utility companies Wholesale distributors Tax collectors	Internal Revenue Service State revenue departments
Motor fuel taxes	Businesses	Wholesale distributors	Internal Revenue Service State revenue departments
Highway use tax	Motor transport businesses	Interstate Commerce Commission	Interstate Commerce Commission
Unemployment compensation	Employers	Internal Revenue Service	Internal Revenue Service
Licenses, permits	Businesses	Tax collectors	City tax collectors State revenue departments CAB, ICC, FCC, etc.
Old Age, Survivors, Disability, and Hospital Insurance (OASDHI)	Employers Employees	Businesses	Internal Revenue Service
Sales and use taxes	Customers	Businesses	City and state revenue departments
Property tax	Businesses	Local tax collectors	City and county tax collectors
Inventory or floor tax	Businesses	Local and state tax collectors	City and county tax collectors
Public utility taxes	Utility companies	City, county, and state tax collectors	City, county, and state tax collectors

Note: This table applies to direct taxes only; the shifting of taxes from the point of collection backward or forward is not considered.

Third, owners must pay personal taxes on their salaries and other ownership-related income they withdraw from the business. And, if part of their wealth is invested outside the business, they face taxes on the investment income they receive.

Fourth, taxes are levied on the transfer of ownership of the business, so the owner must do careful estate planning in order to minimize the tax bite on an inheritance, as shown in the Profile, and as will be discussed later.

Fifth, taxes also affect business decisions on other levels as well. For example, as shown in Chapter 4, the choice of the best form of business largely depends on the profitability of the business and the tax status of the owner(s).

Finally, the administrative cost of being a tax collector for the government is becoming burdensome. As shown in Table 20–1, it's the responsibility of the business owner to collect several taxes for the government by withholding sums from employees' paychecks or by adding the tax (such as sales or use taxes) to the price of products sold to customers. These administrative costs become very expensive in terms of personnel, time, and money.

Get Professional Help!

The purposes of this chapter are to make you aware of the current tax environment in which you will operate and to raise some basic tax issues important to every business owner. *It is very important for someone in every small firm to understand the tax system in order to take advantage of the opportunities available for deductions, credits, and tax savings.* Therefore, it is wise to hire a competent advisor on tax matters. However, the final responsibility for determining and paying your taxes rests with you.

While the U.S. Internal Revenue Service, as well as state and local agencies, will willingly help you determine whether you owe additional taxes, *they accept no responsibility for the accuracy of their advice.* The responsibility is yours, so get professional help! Also, you should familiarize yourself with the *Tax Guide for Small Business,*[1] which covers income, excise, and employment taxes for individuals, partnerships, and corporations.

Types of Taxes

Since it is impossible to discuss all the taxes you will have to pay, we've grouped them into four categories: (1) taxes imposed on the business itself, (2) employment-related taxes, (3) personal taxes that owners pay, and (4) estate taxes.

TAXES IMPOSED ON THE BUSINESS ITSELF

Numerous taxes are imposed on the small firm as a condition of its doing business. We've grouped these together as (1) taxes and fees paid for the "right" to operate the business; (2) excise and intangible property taxes; (3) state and local taxes on business receipts; and (4) federal, state, and local income taxes.

Taxes and Fees Paid to Operate the Business

Some license fees, incorporation taxes, and the cost of permits must be paid before the business actually begins operating. Figure 20–1 lists some of the most important of these. These fees and permits are often intertwined with taxes, insurance, capital requirements, and the nature and scope of the business itself.

Figure 20–1   Selected Licenses, Permits, and Registrations Required of Small Firms

- *Business license (city, county, state).* Generally, you must apply for one or more business licenses. Often a tax identification number will be printed on your business license, and you'll use the number when filing various tax returns. Your state department of revenue can assist you in defining your reporting requirements.
- *Employer's federal ID number (SS–4)(federal).* A federal ID number is needed to identify an employer on all federal tax filings. Some local jurisdictions also require the federal ID number on various filings. The SS–4 form is available from the IRS.
- *Incorporation or partnership registration (state).* You should plan on using an attorney to assist with registering your company as a corporation or partnership. If it is a corporation, you'll also need articles of incorporation, bylaws, stock certificates, a corporate seal, and other items.
- *Trade name registration (state).* You'll need to register any trade names used in your business (e.g., if your legal incorporated name is Superior Semiconductors of California, Ltd., but you generally go by the name "Superior," you'll need to register your alternative name).
- *Zoning permits (city or county).* If your business constitutes an "alternative use" or other special case, you'll need appropriate zoning permits.
- *Building permits (city or county).* If you are doing any remodeling, construction, or related work, be sure you have the appropriate permits.
- *Mailing permits (federal).* Check with your post office about any bulk, presorted first class, business reply mail, or other mailing permits.
- *Professional registrations (state).* Generally, these are employee specific, such as registered engineer, notary public, and so forth. You may, however, wish to reimburse employees for any job-related expenses.

Source: Building the High Technology Business: Positioning for Growth, Profitability, and Success (New York: Peat Marwick Main & Co., 1988), p. 59.

Excise and Intangible Property Taxes

The federal government places an **excise tax** on many items such as tires for automobiles and other moving vehicles, cigars and cigarettes, and alcoholic beverages. Many states also apply such taxes. Taxes on intangibles such as copyrights, patents, and trademarks are another source of income for many states. Some states even have a tax on inventories in stock.

> An **excise tax** is an additional tax on certain items imposed by the federal government.

State and Local Sales and Use Taxes

Many states and localities have sales and use taxes, which generate large sums. **Use taxes** are usually imposed on the use, consumption, or storage of goods within the taxing jurisdiction. This type of tax is often applied to automobiles and other moving vehicles that are purchased outside the jurisdiction and brought in for future use.

> A **use tax** is a tax on the use, consumption, or storage of goods within a taxing jurisdiction.

Sales taxes are usually based on the gross amount of the sale for goods sold within the taxing jurisdiction. A new trend is to tax sales in other locations as well, so you will need to check for your liability for sales taxes in those locations. Exemptions from sales taxes are often provided for goods to be resold and for machinery or equipment used exclusively in processing or assembling other goods. Service businesses are often totally exempt, as are drugs, unprepared foods, and agricultural products in certain states. For example, in Maryland, not only are

> A **sales tax** is a tax added to the gross amount of the sale for goods sold within the taxing jurisdiction.

drugs and food items in grocery stores exempt but also prepared foods under $1 (such as concession sales and restaurant orders such as a cup of coffee).

One word of caution: Even if you do not collect these taxes from your customers or clients, you will probably be held liable for the full amount of the uncollected taxes.

Federal, State, and Local Income Taxes

Almost everyone, businesses and individuals alike, is concerned about income taxes—those presently in effect and those that may result from proposed changes. Because of the variation and complexities of the state and local laws, we'll discuss only the federal law.

From the very beginning of your business, you should have a qualified accountant to provide you with information and help you make important decisions, compile facts for accurate tax returns, and protect you from costly errors. There are three major decisions involving these taxes that you must make at the start, namely: (1) the method of handling your income and expenses, (2) the time period for paying taxes, and (3) the form of business to use.

Accounting Method and Tax Period

Choosing the appropriate accounting method and the period of your business "year" can save your company unnecessary future tax liabilities.

The **accrual method** of accounting permits income and expenses to be charged during the period in which they occur.

As discussed in Chapters 18 and 21, using the **accrual method** of accounting, income and expenses are charged to the period in which they occur, regardless of whether the money has been received or paid out. Thus, if you sell goods on credit and they have not been paid for, you still record them as income during the period when they were sold.

The accrual method *is required* for inventories that are significant in amount, and for corporations and partnerships with annual gross receipts of more than $5 million.

Tax returns for your business may be prepared on a calendar- or fiscal-year basis. If the tax liability is calculated on a calendar-year basis, the tax return must be filed with the IRS no later than April 15 each year. However, in order to pick a more favorable filing month, many firms use a fiscal-year basis.

How the Form of a Business Affects Its Taxes

As discussed in Chapter 4, the amount and methods of handling income taxes affect the choice of business form.[2] Thus, you may choose a partnership or proprietorship rather than pay higher taxes on corporate income and then pay additional individual taxes on dividends.

U.S. tax laws permit some corporations to seek S corporation status. S corporation shareholders (individuals, estates, and certain trusts) are taxed at individual

Table 20–2   Federal Tax Rates for Corporations

Taxable Income	Tax Rate
$0–$50,000	15%
$50,000–$75,000	25%
$75,000–$100,000	34%
$100,000–$335,000	34% + 5% (39%)*

*Additional tax, which "phases out" the lower marginal rates.

Source: U.S. Department of the Treasury, Internal Revenue Service, *Tax Information on Corporations* (Washington, D.C.: U.S. Government Printing Office, December 1991), p. 1.

rates, which are lower than corporate rates; yet they still enjoy the legal protection that comes with corporate status.[3] But remember: S corporations do have disadvantages, such as restrictions on benefit plans and a limit of 35 shareholders.

Finally, as shown in Chapter 9, the use of employee stock ownership plans (ESOPs) can lead to tax advantages as well as cash flow advantages.

Treatment of Federal Corporate Income Taxes

There are three questions small corporations need to answer when handling their federal income taxes:

1. What tax rate applies to the business?
2. What is taxable income?
3. What are deductible expenses?

What Tax Rate Applies?

As shown in Table 20–2, there are three tax rates on small corporations: 15, 25, and 34 percent. There's also an additional tax of 5 percent (total, 39 percent) on net income of $100,000 to $335,000.

What Is Taxable Income?

For income tax purposes, **taxable income** is defined as total revenues minus deductible expenses. While this definition sounds simple, problems arise in measuring both income and expenses. While the government has set the rules for calculating income for tax purposes, the firm may have discretion in reporting income to its stockholders.[4]

Taxable income is total revenues minus deductible expenses.

What Expenses Are Deductible?

Normally, deductions from income are classified as *cost of goods sold, selling expenses,* and *administrative expenses.* The following are the expenses most frequently deducted from revenue to determine net income: (1) administrative expenses; (2) depreciation; (3) inventory valuation; (4) interest payments; (5) business lunches, entertainment, and travel; and (6) automobile, home, and computer expenses.

Administrative Expenses.   Administrative expenses are those needed to run a business office, such as rent, accounting and legal expenses, telephone and other utilities, dues and subscriptions to business publications, and professional services.

Depreciation.   The determination of the amount of depreciation to be deducted from income tax each year is an example of the effect that different accounting procedures can have on income. For example, you can use cash-value depreciation or tax-related depreciation.[5]

Cash value depreciation is based on the difference between the cost of a piece of equipment and its fair market value at the end of a given period of time. *Tax-related depreciation*, on the other hand, can be used to maximize the allowable deduction permitted by tax laws in figuring your net taxable income.

Inventory Valuation.   Another accounting decision you must make is how to value inventory that is used during the year. The problem is particularly acute when prices are changing and/or when a firm holds inventory for long periods of time. As shown in Chapter 21, the three methods of computing inventory used in production are (1) the *first-in, first-out (FIFO) method,* (2) the *last-in, first-out (LIFO) method,* and (3) the *average-cost method*. In general, when prices are rising, small firms tend to use the LIFO method to save taxes. For example, by switching to LIFO, the Chicago Heights Steel Company lowered its income taxes by 5 to 10 percent.[6]

Interest Payments.   The U.S. Revenue Code favors the use of debt by small firms, since interest on debt is deductible while dividends paid to stockholders are not. The total amount of interest paid is deducted from revenue to find taxable income.

Business Lunches, Entertainment, and Travel.   Meals are 100 percent deductible if business is discussed before, during, or after the meal. Otherwise, only 80 percent of the cost of business meals and entertainment expenses is deductible. To deduct any meals and entertainment expenses, you must keep records of (1) whom you entertained, (2) the purpose of the meeting, (3) the amount spent, and (4) when and where it took place.

Travel, food, and lodging expenses for out-of-town business travel are deductible if you stay overnight. Such costs as air, bus, or auto transportation; hotel cost; meals; taxes; and tips are deductible. The cost of seminars, conferences, and conventions is also deductible.

Automobile, Home, and Computer Expenses.   Many small business owners operate out of their home, and certain expenses—such as automobile, utilities, repairs and maintenance, computer operations and maintenance, and home insurance and taxes—can be deducted from income taxes if they are business related. The deductions are quite beneficial to the owner, but there are restrictions, which are enforced. For an automobile, you can either deduct the actual cost of running your car or truck, or take a standard mileage rate. You must use actual costs if you use more than one vehicle in your business. In 1992, the standard mileage rate was 28 cents per mile up to 15,000 miles, and 11.5 cents for each mile after that, in addition to parking fees and tolls.

When you work out of your home, you can claim *actual business-related expenses,* such as telephone charges, business equipment and supplies, postage, photocopying, computer paper and magnetic media, and clerical and professional costs.[7] A deduction is also allowable for any portion of your home used "exclusively" and "regularly" as your principal place of business. For example, you can deduct expenses for taxes, insurance, and depreciation on that portion of your home that is used exclusively as your office. The IRS rule is this: The home must be the principal place of business for your trade or business, or a place of business used by clients, patients, or customers.[8]

The *Deficit Reduction Act of 1984* limits the conditions under which computers used in the home can be deducted as business expenses. The simple test is this: If you use a home computer for business purposes over 50 percent of the time, it qualifies for the appropriate credits or deductions.

EMPLOYMENT-RELATED TAXES

As shown in Chapter 14, employers are legally required to provide their employees with *Social Security/Medicare, unemployment compensation insurance,* and *industrial insurance* (commonly called *workers' compensation*). In addition, the employer must withhold taxes from employees for city, county, state, and federal income taxes. Also, since 1986, the *Employee Retirement Income Security Act (ERISA)* has required employers with 20 or more employees to continue health insurance programs for limited periods for employees who are terminated and for widows, divorced spouses, and dependents of employees.

Income Tax Withholding

The IRS and certain states, counties, and localities require you to withhold the appropriate amount of income tax from each employee's earnings during each pay period. The amount of this pay-as-you-go tax depends on each employee's total wages, number of exemptions claimed on his or her withholding exemption certificate, marital status, and length of pay period. Each employee must complete and sign a W–4 form for your files.[9] See Figure 20–2 for the more important employee-related forms needed by small firms.

The amount withheld from all employees must be submitted to the IRS, along with Form 941, on a quarterly basis. However, if $3,000 or more has been with-

Figure 20–2   Selected Employee-Related Tax Forms Needed by Small Firms

A. Federal Tax Forms
  For companies with paid employees:
  - Form SS–4, Application for Employer Identification Number
  - Form W–2, Wage and Tax Statement
  - Form W–2P, Statement for Recipients of Periodic Annuities, Pensions, Retired Pay, or IRA Payments
  - Form W–3, Transmittal of Income and Tax Statements
  - Form W–4, Employee's Withholding Allowance Certificate, for each employee
  - Form 940, Employer's Annual Federal Unemployment (FUTA) Tax Return
  - Form 941, Employer's Quarterly Federal Tax Return
  - Form 1099–MISC, Statement for Recipients of Nonemployee Compensation

  Income tax forms and schedules, which vary depending on your organizational status, type of income/losses, selection of various elections, etc.
  ERISA Form 5500 series, depending on your status under the Employee Retirement Income Security Act

B. State and Local Forms
  Income and/or business and occupation taxes
  Industrial insurance ("workers' compensation")
  Unemployment compensation insurance

held from employees during the month, that deposit must be made within three banking days following the end of the month.

Form W–2, Wage and Tax Statement, must be completed and mailed to each employee by January 31 immediately following the taxable year. As shown in the Using Technology to Succeed, employers submitting 250 or more W–2 or W–2P forms must transmit those forms to the IRS by magnetic media.

Social Security/Medicare Taxes

As shown in Chapter 14, the Social Security program requires employers to act as both tax collectors and taxpayers. Therefore, not only do you have to withhold a certain percentage of each employee's income, but you must also match it with a payment of your own. These taxes are technically for the *Federal Insurance Contributions Act (FICA)* but are usually referred to as the Social Security and Medicare taxes. In 1993, the employer had to collect 6.2 percent of an employee's total earnings—up to $57,600—and then match that amount out of business revenues. Another 1.45 percent of earnings up to $135,000, must be collected for Medicare.[10] These taxes are sent to the IRS each quarter, along with Federal Form 941, Employer's Quarterly Federal Tax Return. Self-employed people must pay the combined employee's and employer's amount of taxes, which amounted to 15.3 percent in 1993.

Unemployment Compensation Insurance

The **federal unemployment tax** is a tax paid to the federal government to administer the unemployment insurance program.

Unemployment compensation insurance has two parts. First, a small basic amount is paid to the U.S. government as a **federal unemployment tax** to administer the

━━━━━━━━━━━━━━ USING TECHNOLOGY TO SUCCEED ━━━━━━━━━━━━━━

MAGNETIC MEDIA REPORTING

Beginning in 1988, for the tax year 1987, employers reporting 250 or more Forms W–2 or W–2P must transmit those forms by magnetic media. You can file your W–2 data on magnetic film or diskette, but Form W–2P data must be filed on magnetic tape. The IRS has certain waiver requirements if an employer can show undue hardship.

Many service bureaus have agreed to prepare these magnetic reports and submit them directly to the Social Security Administration, saving their customers the time and trouble of filing their own reports on copy A of the W–2.

For more information, write to Magnetic Media Reporting, Social Security Administration, P.O. Box 2312, Baltimore, MD 21203.

Source: A Message from Social Security to All Employers, SSA Pub. No. 05-10155, January 1988, pp. 10–11.

program. A second part, which is determined by the states, builds up a fund from which employees are paid in case they are laid off. Federal Form 940, Employer's Annual Federal Unemployment (FUTA) Tax Return, must be filed annually. However, you may be liable for periodic tax deposits during the year.

Workers' Compensation

Employers are required to provide industrial insurance for employees who are harmed or killed on the job. These payments are usually funded through an insurance program, with higher rates for higher-risk employees.

PERSONAL TAXES PAID BY OWNERS THEMSELVES

There are several ways of withdrawing cash from the business for your own use. Some of these are taxable to you, and some are taxable to the firm.

Taxes on Amounts Withdrawn from the Business

First, salaries and bonuses received from the business are an expense to the business. But individual income taxes are also paid on those sums, at the rate shown in Table 20–3. You can also withdraw cash from a proprietorship or partnership, and these sums are also taxable to you as an individual.

When owners receive a dividend from a corporation, it is taxed twice. The corporation pays taxes on it but gets no tax deduction, and owners must pay taxes at their individual rates.

Although not in the form of cash, employees can also receive tax-free benefits from the business, which are deductible by the firm. These include such things as

Table 20–3   Federal Income Tax Rates for Nonbusiness Individuals

Single Individual				Married, Filing Jointly, or Qualifying Widow(er)			
If taxable income is over	*But not over*	*The tax is*	*Of the amount over*	*If taxable income is over*	*But not over*	*The tax is*	*Of the amount over*
$0	$20,350	. . . 15%	$ 0	$ 0	$34,000	. . . 15%	$ 0
20,350	49,300	$3,052.50 + 28%	20,350	34,000	82,150	$5,100.00 + 28%	34,000
49,300	. . .	11,158.50 + 31%	49,300	82,150	. . .	18,582.00 + 31%	82,150

Source: U.S. Department of the Treasury, Internal Revenue Service, *1991 Forms and Instructions, 1040* (Washington: U.S. Government Printing Office, 1991), p. 47.

medical and legal reimbursements, tuition assistance, and other fringe benefits, as well as travel and entertainment expense reimbursements.

Finally, there are many pension and profit-sharing plans, the payment of which is deductible by the business. Payments from the plans are not taxable to the recipients until they are received.

Taxes on Amounts Received from Sale of the Business

Usually, when entrepreneurs sell their companies, the contracts contain the following important provisions: (1) a noncompeting clause from the seller; (2) warranties and representations by the seller about the debt and liabilities of the company being sold; and (3) the purchase price—whether it is paid in cash, with a promissory note, in stock in the acquiring company, or with some combination.

Under the Tax Reform Act of 1986, most sales of assets are subject to double taxation, both corporate and personal, as shown earlier, so many transactions now involve the exchange of stock. Therefore, the form in which the proceeds are to be received can be as critical as the price and should be included in negotiations between buyer and seller, as the following example illustrates.

Jan and Al Williams started Bio Clinic Co. in their garage in southern California in the early 1960s. By 1985, it was so successful that Sunrise Medical Inc., a Torrance, California, company, offered $7.2 million for it. The Williamses, who were in the process of divorcing at the time, wanted different things when they negotiated the terms of sale. Jan wanted stock, since she expected the stock of Sunrise to grow in value. Al, on the other hand, wanted as much cash as possible. The parties worked out a compromise—$2 million in stock, and $5.2 million in cash.[11]

In summary, the tax consequences from the sale of a business are that either (1) you pay an immediate capital gains tax on cash payments from the sale (at rates that, for 1992 income, were the same as the individual tax rate), or (2) if you receive part of the payment in stock, you may be able to defer some taxes to a later period.

ESTATE PLANNING TO MINIMIZE TAXES

No one wants to pay more taxes than necessary; especially when you're trying to pass the benefits of the estate you've built up over the years to your family, you want to reduce taxes to the minimum so that they will get the maximum. Notice that Jack Bares (in the Profile) did that for his children. He planned his estate for 29 years so they would gain control of the business but pay only a minimum in taxes.

To give you an idea of the problem, in 1993, the tax on gifts and bequests between $2.5 million and $3 million was $1.026 million, plus 53 percent of the amount over $2.5 million. For gifts and estates from $3 million to $10 million, the rate was even higher: $1.291 million, plus 55 percent of amounts over $3 million. So you can see that it becomes almost impossible to pass the estate on to your children and leave them a viable business.

Estate Planning Issues

For entrepreneurs, there are several issues involved in estate planning. The most important of these are (1) trying to minimize taxes, (2) retaining control of the business, and (3) maintaining flexibility of operations.

Estate Planning Techniques

While it is impossible to avoid all estate taxes, the following can be used to minimize them: (1) family gifts, (2) family partnerships, (3) stock sales to family members, and (4) living trusts.

Make Gifts to Family

One way to reduce taxes on your estate is to start giving parts of it to your family as soon as feasible. The rules are:

1. The gifts must be of "present interest," such as a direct cash gift, rather than a "future interest," such as gifts of cash that go into a trust fund for later distribution.
2. The first $10,000 in gifts made by each spouse to each person during the year is tax free.
3. Lifetime gifts of up to $300,000 by a single person, or $600,000 from a couple, are essentially tax free, so you can exhaust this privilege in 30 years.
4. The gifts, which are based on the fair market value of the property, can be cash, bonds, real estate, the family business, interest in a partnership, and so forth.[12]

Establish Family Partnerships

You can form a family partnership to take money out of your company at lower tax rates. It must be a passive partnership that owns some type of property but does not operate the business. Because this type of tax shelter is very complex, don't try to do it by yourself; get professional help.[13]

Sell Stock to Children

You can also sell all or a part of your business to your children, but, like establishing a family partnership, this is complicated. First, your children will need a source of income to make nondeductible payments to you for the stock. And second, you must pay capital gains tax on the stock you sell. You may want to combine this method with gifts to the family. If the value of your business is greater than the amount you can give as gifts during your lifetime, you may want to give up to the maximum and sell stock for the rest of the business.

Establish a Living Trust

A **living trust** is a legal document that provides for distributing and managing of personal assets upon the maker's death or disability.

A **living trust** resembles a will but, in addition to providing for distributing personal assets upon the maker's death, also contains instructions for managing those assets should the person become disabled.

Living trusts are more difficult to contest than wills. Also, the firm's assets can be immediately and privately distributed to the beneficiaries. Finally, a living trust can save on estate taxes.[14] For example, if you have a will for an estate valued at more than $600,000, federal estate taxes must be paid at your death, at a rate beginning at 37 percent. A living trust, on the other hand, lets you and your spouse pass on up to $1.2 million to your beneficiaries tax free. When one of you dies, the trust is divided into two separate trusts, each with a $600,000 estate tax exemption.

But there are some *disadvantages* of a living trust. First, when you establish such a trust, you must also change the title on all real estate, securities, and other assets to the name of your trust. From a legal point of view, you no longer own these properties, so there is nothing to probate when it becomes time to distribute your assets. You (and your spouse) may find it advantageous to become joint trustees in order to bypass the probate process. Finally, if you need to refinance your home or other assets, some lenders may refuse to refinance it if it is in a trust.

In order to avoid the many pitfalls of this device, hire an experienced trust attorney and select a capable and trustworthy trustee. Also, carefully weigh the benefits against the time and effort required.[15]

RECORD KEEPING AND TAX REPORTING

The importance of record keeping has been emphasized throughout this text. There are essentially two reasons for keeping business records. First, tax and other records are required by law; second, they help you manage your business better. While the IRS allows some flexibility in records systems, it does require that records be kept, be complete, and be separate for each individual business.

Table 20–4   List of Selected Tax-Reporting Periods

Tax	Reporting Period
Estimated income tax deposits	Quarterly
Income tax withholding deposits	Quarterly
FICA tax deposits	Quarterly
FUTA tax deposits	Quarterly
Income tax	Annually
Income tax withholding	Annually
Self-employment tax	Annually
FICA (Social Security) tax	Annually
FUTA (unemployment) tax	Annually

Note: Even though tax deposits are made quarterly, a return (which reports income and the bases for calculating the tax due) is filed only annually. Reporting periods and payment dates differ. Please consult Circular E, *Employers' Tax Guide*, for instructions.

Maintaining Tax Records

When you start your business, as shown in Chapter 5, you should set up the kind of records system most suitable for your particular operations. Also, keep in mind that the records should be readily available to compute, record, and pay taxes as they become due and payable.

The IRS requires that tax records be retained for up to three years after a tax return is filed. If there's reason to suspect fraud, it may look at your tax records for longer periods. Fraud may be suspected when deductions seem excessive or appear to have been claimed with the intent to defraud the government out of tax revenues, or when income seems unnaturally low. While the IRS has up to three years to look at your records, you also have up to three years from the date of filing to straighten out tax matters as the circumstances demand. If changes are needed, you may file a one-page amended return on Form 1040X.

Reporting Your Taxes

All federal, state, and local governments having jurisdiction over your business require that you submit a written monthly, quarterly, or annual report on income. Since the requirements vary so much for state and local agencies, we will list only the federal reporting requirements, which are shown in Table 20–4.

WHAT YOU SHOULD HAVE LEARNED

1. The U.S. tax system is very complex. Federal, state, and local governments impose taxes directly on individuals and businesses and require them to collect taxes from others. The four types of business taxes are *(a)* those

imposed on the business itself, *(b)* employment-related taxes, *(c)* personal taxes paid by the owners, and *(d)* estate taxes.

2. Taxes imposed on the business itself include *(a)* taxes paid for the right to operate the business, *(b)* excise and property taxes, *(c)* taxes on business receipts, and *(d)* income taxes.

   Taxes paid to operate the business include fees paid for a business permit or license, state incorporation or partnership registration, zoning variances, building permits, mailing permits, occupational or professional registration, and other such licenses.

   Excise and intangible property taxes are paid on such items as tires; cigars, cigarettes, and alcoholic beverages; and intangibles such as copyrights, patents, and trademarks. Sales and use taxes are imposed on the purchase, use, consumption, or storage of goods. Exceptions are often made for service businesses, drugs, and industrial goods. The three important questions regarding the federal corporate income tax are *(a)* What tax rates apply to your business? *(b)* What is income? and *(c)* What are deductible expenses?

3. You are required to provide Social Security, Medicare, unemployment insurance, and workers' compensation for your employees, and to withhold taxes from them. Each employee must complete a W–4 form. The withheld amounts must be submitted to the IRS periodically. A Form W–2 must be mailed to each employee by January 31 of the following year. Unemployment insurance payments build up a fund from which a state can pay employees if they are laid off.

4. The owners themselves must also pay taxes on funds withdrawn from the business by *(a)* receiving salaries or bonuses, *(b)* withdrawing sums from a proprietorship or partnership, *(c)* receiving dividends from a corporation, *(d)* receiving tax-free benefits from the business, and *(e)* receiving pension and profit-sharing benefits. When you sell the business, you must pay taxes on the capital gain received.

5. Estate planning can be used to minimize taxes by *(a)* giving gifts from the business to the family, *(b)* forming family partnerships, *(c)* selling stock to family members, and *(d)* setting up a living trust. All have advantages and disadvantages, so get professional help in using them.

6. From the time you begin your business, you should maintain complete and accurate tax records. For tax purposes, records must be retained up to three years after the date of filing the return. If for any reason the IRS suspects fraud, there is no time limitation.

QUESTIONS FOR DISCUSSION

1. What is included in the U.S. tax system?

2. Name the three main types of taxes a small firm must pay.

3. Name and explain at least five taxes a firm must pay for the right to do business.

4. How does the form of a business affect its taxes?

5. Name and explain the three types of employment-related taxes.

6. How can funds be withdrawn from a small business, and how are they treated for tax purposes?

7. What are the three main issues in estate planning? What are the ways a small business owner can reduce estate taxes?

8. Why are records so important for tax purposes?

HOW TO REDUCE YOUR BUSINESS TAX BURDENS

There are several strategic moves a business can make at year-end to reduce its tax burden. The first consideration is choosing the right form for the business. Many small firms use the S corporation form because it can be taxed similarly to a proprietorship or partnership. For an S corporation, the business income or loss is reported directly by the shareholders, not by the business. Also, the business is not subject to the personal holding company or accumulated earnings penalty taxes that apply to regular corporations. An existing corporation can elect S corporation status; however, it may have to pay tax on income reported in the 10-year period following the conversion if the income is attributable to a "built-in gain."

Next, there are several year-end tax-saving moves that involve income shifting. Perhaps the most time-honored year-end planning strategy involves shifting income and expenses between years. If it appears that your income will be high this year, shift some of your income to future years or prepay some expenses for future years.

Another way to reduce the business tax burden is to "keep it in the family." Having your business employ and make salary payments to your children shifts income from you to them, where it is subject to little or no income tax. Of course, services must actually be performed by the children, and their salaries must be reasonable and well documented.

QUESTIONS

1. What do you think of these methods?

2. Which one would you favor?

3. Can you think of others?

21

Using Computers and Management Information Systems*

Smart companies get rich using technology; small ones go bankrupt selling it.
—Thomas Doerflinger, Paine Webber executive

Farms, factories, even tiny one-person businesses are reaping the benefits—and surviving the frustrations—of computerization.—Jared Taylor, business consultant

LEARNING OBJECTIVES

After studying the material in this chapter, you will be able to:
1. Explain the importance of information to a small business.

2. Discuss the need for a management information system (MIS).

3. Describe the growing role of computers in small business.

4. Discuss how accounting is part of a small business's management information system.

*The authors thank Charles E. Scott, Loyola College in Maryland, for his original contributions to this chapter, and Walter H. Hollingsworth of the University of Mobile for his revision of it.

THE MAINE LINE COMPANY: OBTAINING AND USING ACCURATE INFORMATION

The Maine Line Company, based in Rockport, Maine, publishes greeting cards, note cards, and memo pads. Established in 1980 by Joyce Boaz and Perri Ardman and employing 18 people, the company operated for five years without computers. To obtain and use information more efficiently, and thereby increase employee creativity, the company decided to look into a computer system suitable for its needs and budget.

After a seven-month search, the Maine Line Company had an Altos system installed in May 1985. The system is used primarily for inventory control, billing, accounts receivable, and general ledger. The Altos allows the company to know exactly how much stock is on hand

Joyce Boaz and Perri Ardman, co-owners of Maine Line.

Photo courtesy of *Bangor Daily News.*

and precisely when to restock. Because word processing slowed the primary functions of the system, Maine Line purchased two Sperry PCs to be used independently of the Altos system.

Aside from word processing, the personal computers distribute spreadsheet functions, and employees can analyze information on sales and account activity. With the Altos system and the two PCs, Maine Line can trace sales activity in each store selling its products for a quick review of marketing efforts.

Maine Line was acquired by a large New Jersey corporation a few years ago. Since then, the Rockport, Maine, store has scaled back operations.

Source: ''The Maine Line Company,'' *Venture,* November 1986, p. 80.

The Profile illustrates how two people have taken advantage of a computer system to modernize their information systems. This chapter is designed to study how the computer and management information systems are used in small businesses.

IMPORTANCE OF INFORMATION

Have you ever considered how many records you keep or generate? You probably have in your possession at least a driver's license, credit card(s), student ID, Social Security card, and checkbook. Without these items, you would find it difficult to transact much of your daily business. Also, whenever you use one of these items, records (or entries in the records) are generated. For example, when you use a credit card, it generates a sales or credit slip, a monthly statement, and a record of payment. You use the statement to write a check and to deduct the amount from your bank balance. All the while, you keep some information (such as your Social Security number) in your head to save time in filling out forms.

As you can see, information is a most important resource for a small business, as well as for a person. It should help provide answers to such questions as: Is the product selling properly? Will the cash flow be adequate? Are the employees paid the correct amounts, and are the employment taxes handled properly?

Obviously, these questions cannot be answered without the appropriate data. Just as your personal records provide data for your personal decisions, your company must also collect data for its operations.

An efficient information system is needed by small firms—as well as large ones—to convert data to information so management can use it to operate the company. And, as you will see, many of these information systems are now computerized, even in the small business.

ELEMENTS OF A MANAGEMENT INFORMATION SYSTEM (MIS)

A **management information system (MIS)** collects, records, processes, reports, and/or converts data into a usable form.

As shown in Chapter 16, all types of systems involve the same basic elements: inputs, processes, and outputs. A **management information system (MIS)** is designed to collect, record, process, report, and/or convert data into a form suitable for management's use. For example, as will be shown later, an accounting system records data, processes data, and produces reports. A system may be entirely manual or, at the other extreme, almost entirely machine or computer operated.

All these systems start with inputs, process the inputs, and furnish outputs. Whether or not computers are used, an organized MIS is necessary for the efficient operation of any business. Figure 21–1 diagrams a system that can be manually or computer operated—or can use some combination of both. Defining the needs of each part of a business for information and its processing and use is the first step in designing an information system.

Figure 21–1   Accounting for Sales

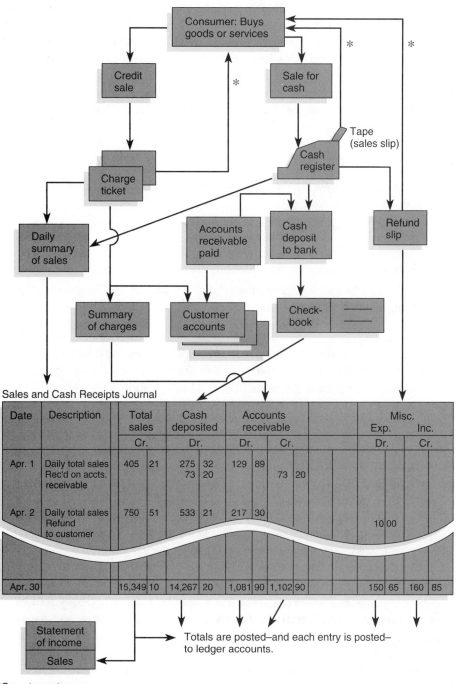

Sales and Cash Receipts Journal

Date	Description	Total sales		Cash deposited		Accounts receivable				Misc.			
										Exp.		Inc.	
		Cr.		Dr.		Dr.		Cr.		Dr.		Cr.	
Apr. 1	Daily total sales Rec'd on accts. receivable	405	21	275	32	129	89						
				73	20			73	20				
Apr. 2	Daily total sales Refund to customer	750	51	533	21	217	30			10	00		
Apr. 30		15,349	10	14,267	20	1,081	90	1,102	90	150	65	160	85

Totals are posted–and each entry is posted–
to ledger accounts.

*Copy to customer.

What Information Is Needed?

Everyone in the small firm should consider the questions "What do I need to know in order to do my job better?" and "What information do I have that will help others do their jobs better?" The accumulation of these pieces of information, with analysis of what data are reasonably available, is the initial step in forming an information system. Emphasis should be on developing a system adapted to present needs yet flexible enough to accommodate future changes. An obvious but often overlooked bit of advice: Even the best information system is of no value if it is not used—and used properly.

Purposes for Which Information Is Used

In determining what information is needed, you should ask yourself why you want it. The usual answers are:

1. *To plan a course of action,* such as deciding the number of items to purchase.
2. *To meet obligations,* such as repaying borrowed money.
3. *To control activities,* such as assuring that ordered materials have arrived.
4. *To satisfy government regulations,* such as conforming to safety, employment, and ethical standards.
5. *To evaluate performance.*

In addition to determining the information needed, you must know how to use it. This involves classifying it into a usable form and establishing systems and procedures to assure the availability of critical information.

Examples of Needed Information

The kinds of information you might need are too numerous to discuss, but the most important are (1) records of service provided to customers and (2) records of services performed for the business.

Services to customers provide revenue in the form of cash, checks, or promises to pay. Figure 21–1 shows a diagram of a system for recording sales of goods or services. Both real-time and delayed transactions occur in this system. For example, when products are sold, sales slips are made out to give to customers. Later, the slips are used as daily summaries of sales, sales taxes, and so forth, which are then recorded in journals. Unlike direct sales, rental of items requires additional transactions.

Services performed for the business must also be recorded. Goods sold to, or services performed for, a firm are its expenses of doing business, and payments must be made for them. In addition, payments are made to increase assets and reduce obligations.

Even very small businesses need formal systems for keeping records. In the past, very simple record-keeping systems such as manila folders, shoe boxes, and entries in a checkbook have been used for this purpose. These methods are simple and easy to understand but in many cases do not meet the demands of today's competitive marketplace.

Timing of Information Flow(s)

Data from activities may be needed (1) at the time of transaction (real-time processing) or (2) after transactions accumulate (batch processing). For example, as shown in Figure 21–1, a customer is given a sales slip on completion of the sale, which is *real-time processing*. An MIS can be designed to take care of such immediate feedback. For example, portable computers, modems, mobile phones, electronic wands or scanners, and radios can be used to collect and provide information quickly, as in the following example.

Ernest Gore, an architect, visited Jean Soor, who was interested in building a house. During the discussion, Ernest opened his laptop computer and laid out the house plan as Jean described her ideas. Several times, they discussed "what ifs," and he made the changes to show their effects. He left with the plans well developed. Ernest attributes a great deal of his success in making the sale and satisfying the customer to this type of rapid feedback.

Batch processing is done after more than one transaction has occurred, such as at the end of an hour or at the end of the day, as shown in Figure 21–1, when the daily sales are summarized.

Slower turnaround may meet the requirements of the system and be less expensive, so you should balance the speed and convenience of real-time processing with the economy of batch processing. Many restaurants, such as Checkers (Chapter 18) now use computers to store orders. This method is also objective and effective.

Choosing an MIS

Figure 21–2 presents a checklist you can use to define your company and the types and volume of information it needs. Completion of this checklist should help you form a better idea of the system to install, including assessing needs, determining reliable suppliers, setting up a budget, and implementing the system.

THE ROLE OF COMPUTERS IN SMALL BUSINESS

As their capabilities mushroom and costs decline, computers are rapidly taking over the roles of recordkeepers, clerks, and analysts. Through the use of computers, data can be quickly received, collected, processed, and reported. Even some of the smallest firms now use computers. As a business grows, computers become more essential because of the increased volume of relevant information.

Figure 21–2   Defining What a Company Needs in an MIS

Type of Business
    Retail _____ Wholesale _____ Mfg. _____ Professional services _____
    Real estate _____ Agriculture _____ Nonprofit _____ Other _____

Business Size
    Gross income _____ Net profit as percent of gross income _____

Types of Information Needed
    Numerical _____ Textual _____ Graphics _____ Communications _____

Location(s)
    Single _____ Dispersed _____ Franchise _____ Subsidiary _____

Transaction Volume
    Invoices/month _____ Average accounts receivable _____ Average inventory _____
    Inventory turnover _____ Number of inventory items _____
    Number of customers _____ Number of employees _____

Current Information System (Describe.)
_____
_____

Trouble Areas (Rank each according to importance and number of people involved. Use more paper if needed. Be as complete as possible.)
_____
_____
_____

Potential Future Needs (Include all possible needs, as they may be economically feasible in any system designed.)
_____
_____

Applications
   Business Areas to Be Addressed (Number in order of priority.)
     Accounting _____ Financial reporting _____ Inventory management _____
     Cash flow planning _____ Market and sales analysis _____ Decision support _____
     Billing _____ Scheduling _____ Quality control _____ Payroll _____
     Employee benefits _____ Commissions _____ Customer tracking _____
     Portfolio management _____ Legal defense _____ Long-term planning _____
     Tax reporting _____ Word processing _____ Other (be specific) _____

Computer Skills Available in Company
_____

Proposed Budget for MIS
    $ _____ Maximum _____

Time Frame
    Desired start _____ Latest allowed start _____

The Development of Computers for Small Businesses

A modern computer information system consists of hardware, software, and people. The **hardware** consists of a central processing unit (CPU), a monitor, a keyboard, and other parts that you can see, feel, and touch. (The CPU is the part

Hardware consists of the CPU, monitor, keyboard, and other parts that you can see and touch.

of the computer hardware that controls all other parts of the system. See the Appendix at the end of the chapter for other computer-related terms.)

Software is the programs, manuals, and procedures that cause the hardware to operate in a manner desired by the problem solver. Of course, neither of these components is of any use without the people to use and operate them.

> **Software** is the programs, manuals, and procedures that cause the hardware to operate in a desired manner.

Early Use of Computers by Business

The first business application of a computer was the Univac, a giant mainframe installed by Sperry-Rand Univac at GE's Louisville, Kentucky, plant in 1954. But such computers were too big, powerful, and expensive for small business use. Digital Equipment Corporation (DEC), formed in 1957, developed the minicomputer and marketed its first model, the PDP-1, in 1960.

It was the microcomputer, however, that finally made computer use feasible for small firms. Because of the abundance of inexpensive microcomputer hardware and software available to small businesses, we will limit our discussion of computers to this type.

The Microcomputer—The Small Business Computer

The terms *microcomputer, personal computer,* and *desktop computer* are used interchangeably to refer to computers based on the *microprocessor,* which is a miniaturized computer processor stored on a silicon chip.

The introduction of the microcomputer made the computer available to small businesses and to individuals. The machines that had been very large and expensive became relatively inexpensive and fit on a desktop, although they were not immediately adapted for personal and small business use. The first microcomputers were sold as kits and were of very little practical use. They were primarily marketed to hobbyists who viewed the computer as an end in itself. The first mass-produced fully assembled microcomputer was the Radio Shack TRS-80, introduced by Tandy Corporation in the early 1970s; it was followed by the Commodore Pet 2000 and the Apple.

The development of small and inexpensive CPU chips made possible the development of the microcomputer. All of the so-called personal computers have used these "computers on a chip" as the heart of their system, and continuing improvement of the microprocessor chip has made possible more and more powerful computers in smaller and smaller boxes. The first TRS-80 had an internal memory of about 4,000 characters and sold for $599. In computer terms, it had *4K RAM,* meaning the ability to store 4,000 characters in random access memory.* The first Apple had internal storage of 16K, while the first Commodore Pet had a very small keyboard and 4K memory.[1]

---

*Actually four (binary) thousand (4 × 1,024) characters.

Apple and Commodore based their computers on a different chip from that used in the TRS-80. This required different software, since the computers were not compatible, and programs that would run on the Apple would not run on the TRS-80 and vice versa.

Tandy and Apple soon emerged as the two major competitors, and they fought vigorously for market share. User groups sprang up for both computers, and brand loyalty was sometimes very intense.

Because of the ease of entry into the computer market, the number of companies mushroomed. Machines made by the emerging new companies were "hardware compatible" with the TRS-80 or Apple but not "software compatible" with either machine.[2]

IBM's strategy, as in the mainframe industry, was not to be a technology leader but to follow the market with improved design and the best marketing and service in the industry. So, with the exception of its Model 5100, a large and expensive machine, IBM largely ignored the microcomputers during the mid- to late 1970s.

In 1981, IBM introduced its Personal Computer (IBM® PC), which soon became the standard of the industry. While there was nothing technologically new in the IBM PC,[3] IBM did have an exceptional advantage in the business market because of its large market share in the mainframe business (about 80 percent from the mid-1950s to the mid-1980s). The IBM PC used the Intel 8088 chip, which was similar to the older chips already in use, so the computer was compatible with existing technology.

The introduction of the IBM PC was something of a paradox. It gave instantaneous credibility to the personal computer market, but it also slowed innovation as other manufacturers rapidly followed IBM's lead.[4] While Apple, Atari, and some others continued to use the Motorola chip, Tandy and most of the rest of the industry followed the IBM lead and produced computers based on the Intel chip. This did permit some standardization of hardware and software, allowing prices to fall.

Microcomputers have undergone many changes over the past decade. IBM computers and their clones largely use the same series of Intel chips and operating systems created by Microsoft® under the designation *MS-DOS*®. In rapid succession, 8088 computers were followed by those based on the 80286, 80386, and 80486 chips. The 80586—marketed under the tradename Pentium®—was introduced in early 1993.

Most advances in computer technology have been designed to make the machines faster and more powerful, with more RAM, larger disk storage, and a variety of ingenious peripherals, including printers, modems, fax machines, and so on. One recent development being marketed with some success for business use is the "multimedia" computer, which includes, at a minimum, a sound board and a CD-ROM drive. ROM (read-only memory) disks, which resemble audio CDs, can store whole encyclopedias of print information, plus pictures and sound—even moving pictures and animation. Other devices allow users to capture images from videotapes or live television broadcasts for use in documents or other applications.

A kindergarten student learns to use a laptop computer.

If any innovation is really taking the business world by storm, though, it is the notebook computer. Although still comparatively expensive for their power, these literally notebook-sized devices, most with an LCD screen, combine a keyboard, "pointing device," hard disk, and floppy disk drive in a battery-operated package that can be taken anywhere. For salesmen on the road or engineers in the field, they are ideal, since records or computations can be made on the spot and stored for later transfer to a desktop computer either by modem or directly. They are also ideal for introducing students to the computer world.

Strengths and Weaknesses of Computers for Small Firms

The key to the usefulness of a computer to a small firm is the use to be made of it. Given the currently available technology, the computer itself is not likely to limit its usefulness. The primary limitation is the availability of software that can economically accomplish the desired tasks. Figure 21–3 gives a list of the activities for which software is currently available.

Notice that the areas in which a computer can be an asset are repetitive, high-volume, quantitative tasks. By contrast, the areas where computers are less useful are the unstructured, open-ended types of activities where human creativity or judgment is required. While the latter are more innovation- or people-oriented activities, the former are the boring, detail-oriented jobs once assigned to lower-paid employees. Now, smart business owners will delegate this category of activ-

---

Figure 21-3   What Computers Do Best—and Worst

The computer is most helpful in the following applications, for which software is readily available:

■ Repetitive, data-oriented operations, such as accounting, record keeping, or mailing lists.

■ Organizing data into information, such as financial reporting.

■ Codifying and monitoring procedures, such as technical manuals and production control.

■ Calculations, such as financial ratios and tax analyses.

■ Forecasting, such as trend projection and materials requirements planning.

The computer is less valuable, and may even be a liability, in operations of the following types:

■ Solving unstructured problems or those that are not clearly defined, as in invention or innovation.

■ Defining and/or establishing true authority in a company, such as leadership roles.

■ Identifying new markets or products. The computer can be a major asset here, but only as a tool to assist human workers.

■ Interpersonal relations, such as contract negotiations or establishing corporate culture.

■ Defining the corporate mission.

---

ities to the computer, with competent staff supervising its activities, freeing themselves to handle the more interesting, long-term problems,[5] as the following example illustrates.

In 1983, four advertising veterans founded Rossin Greenberg Seronick & Hill (RGS&H), an advertising agency in Boston. Neal Hill, as CEO, was responsible for creating an organization to support the others so they could be creative. He soon found that most of the people's time involved moving information around, leaving little time to create ads.

Hill computerized the noncreative work, but the employees resisted the change. Then Hill got top managers to use word processors. According to one partner, who used one only reluctantly, "My capacity to do the paperwork quadrupled." After that, the partners were able to motivate all the employees to use computers.

In a year and a half, billings doubled, while personnel increased only 25 percent![6]

The computer can do nothing that humans can't do; it simply assists the user in the accomplishment of routine duties. Ideally, the computer and human skills can be combined for more effective performance.

Manual versus Computer MIS

The discussion of computers so far has been quite general. It has been phrased in terms of computer versus manual systems instead of discussing the more realistic

Table 21–1 Manual versus Computer Processing of Employees' Hours

Manual Using Time Cards	Partially Computerized Using Time Cards	Fully Computerized
Workers clock out.	Workers clock out.	Workers key out.
Clerk collects time cards and records time; calculates regular and overtime; obtains wage rate; calculates pay, taxes, and other deductions, and net pay; records in accounting records.	Clerk collects time cards and records time, selects software, and runs software.	Hours are automatically entered in computer system.
	Computer calculates.	Computer calculates pay and makes entries in accounting records.
	Clerk makes entries in accounting records.	
Clerk makes out checks.	Clerk makes out checks.	Computer prints checks.
Resources needed for each process:		
Time clock, cards, pen, paper, clerk's time, checks, accounts.	Time clock, cards, software, computer, clerk's time, checks, database, accounts, pen.	Time clock attached to computer, computer, software, database, printer, accounts.

systems that are partly manual and partly computer operated. All management information systems have some elements of manual operations and some of mechanization. But computers are increasingly involved in the mechanized portion of the MIS. Table 21–1 compares three levels of mechanization of a company's payroll. The one to choose depends on the comparative output and cost, as well as the company situation.

Some Potential Problems

There are many advantages and disadvantages to implementing a computer system. Therefore, careful planning is needed to assure accuracy, acceptability, and adaptability. Errors or inadequacies that develop in the system are much easier to detect and correct if the system is carefully designed and if employees are supportive and motivated to make it work. But even when errors and malfunctions are detected, they may not be easy to correct. Have you ever tried to get a computer-generated error on a credit rating report corrected?

According to Betty Shaffer, doing freelance bookkeeping in her Richardson, Texas, home was "driving me insane," so she bought an IBM PC and an accounting program. Even after she learned to run the program—by reading the instruction manual—the system would not copy data from one magnetic disk to another. Naturally, it had all worked fine at the outlet where she had bought it.

After several painful months nursing the sick computer, Shaffer persuaded the store manager to make a house call. He found that the machine worked well when the display monitor was moved from the top of the drive unit and put on a table. He suspected the screen must have been mistakenly given a magnetic coating.

With her computer "cured," Shaffer's business "took off." Because the computer does the calculations and prints the reports, she can do three times as much work—for three times more income.[7]

Another need caused by the introduction of computerized operations is the need to upgrade your employees' skills. This need can be partially met by other small firms that provide training courses and computer support.

Computers Require Added Security

Computers are used for generating and storing important, often confidential, records, which makes controlling access an important issue. Some steps that can be taken to provide security include physical control of facilities, such as guards and emergency power; access control, such as identification of users and specifying authority; and backups, such as appropriate saving of data.

Just as important as the security of the information you are storing is the integrity of that information. "Hackers" (computer programmers who experiment to see what they can do) have created computer "viruses" that can destroy your data and programs without your being able to stop them. These are programs which "hide" in other programs and are transmitted from one computer to another through disks used on one computer and then used on another. *In order to protect your system, you need to get antiviral programs along with the system and minimize the use of programs and/or disks of unfamiliar origin.*

Choosing Software, Hardware, and Employee Training

The primary software applications likely to be needed by a small business include word processing, spreadsheet analysis, account processing, file management, and electronic mail/messaging.[8] It is easy to assume that your business is unique and requires a specially designed system to match your needs. Be wary of this approach, however, because there are many "off-the-shelf" programs (already designed and available) that, while they may not satisfy all your needs, will likely provide a cost-effective solution to most of them.

Having defined your computer needs and the software desired, you must then choose the hardware. A wide range is available, from simple, inexpensive micros to complicated, expensive mainframes. Most small companies need a system somewhere in the middle—one that is not too costly but does the work satisfactorily (see Using Technology to Succeed). We suggest that you focus primarily on personal computers because their recently increased speed and capacity make them capable of handling most of the needs of a small business. Figure 21–4 lists some selected sources of information to help you choose hardware, software, and employee training.

THE ACCOUNTING SYSTEM AS AN MIS

There are many parts to the MIS of a small business. For example, forecasting; reporting to tax authorities, management, and workers; inventory control; and personnel records. These require collecting, storing, and analyzing data. One

===== USING TECHNOLOGY TO SUCCEED =====

THE HAWTHORNE HOTEL: 19TH-CENTURY HOTEL, 20TH-CENTURY TECHNOLOGY

The Hawthorne Hotel, a stylish 89-room inn located in Salem, Massachusetts—where the 17th-century witch hunts took place—has spent over $2 million restoring its appearance to what it must have been in the 19th century. The hotel's manager, Kenneth Boyles, states that the beauty of his hotel is its history, charm, and grace.

To reap the benefits of 20th-century technology, Boyles bought an Apple® computer. Initially purchased for bookkeeping, its workload has steadily increased. Boyles added financial projections using income statements and balance sheets;

later, he began controlling the food and beverage inventory. Recently, Boyles added an IBM® PC to the inn's system to be used as part of a new reservation system and for night audits. He also integrated the dining room into the system.

Boyles credits his success to two things: a step-by-step implementation of the computer and help from Tod Riedel, president of First Micro Group Inc. of Boston. Riedel believes that starting small is the best approach for small companies: "It gets technology in the door."

The Hawthorne, Salem's new hotel, circa 1920
Photo courtesy of Hawthorne Hotel.

major MIS is the accounting system, which, because of its highly quantitative nature, has historically been the first system to be computerized even in very small companies.

The rest of this chapter traces the flow of data for selected transactions in the accounting system. The discussion is based on the flow shown in Figure 21–1. Note the level of detail needed to design systems and how the logical flow of data

---

Figure 21–4   Sources of Information about Computer Hardware, Software, and Training

---

The following sources can be used to obtain information to help in choosing hardware, software, and training.

- *Computer stores and consultants.* These can provide need-specific advice, packaged systems, and ongoing support, but they may be more oriented toward their sale than to your needs. The quality of advice may vary. Future availability of recommended systems is critical.

- *Friends or peers, user groups, bulletin boards, and seminars or workshops.* These can give more specialized advice, though it may not match your needs. Since hands-on experience is often possible, you may gain a better understanding of your needs, if not a specific answer. These are good sources of answers to technical questions, but beware of sales pitches.

- *Magazines, books, and libraries.* Although these are good sources of background information and comparative evaluations of hardware and software, the volume and technical nature of the information may create information overload problems, and the information is usually not tailored to your needs.

- *Computer company promotional material and mail order.* This is more oriented to specific hardware and software than to your needs, but it permits comparison of detailed technical specifications. Some mail-order firms offer ongoing support, but be sure to check, because this is important.

- *Industry associations.* These may have systems already fully designed to handle your specific problems and data that could be useful to you, but they may include a membership cost or licensing fee.

- *Government publications and SCORE/SBA.* These are inexpensive sources of information, data services, consultant referrals, and possibly even funding, but the quality may vary and may not include the most recent technology.

---

tends to lead to computerization. An expert may be needed to help on the more complex transactions.

Sales

Profits result from the sale of goods or the performance of a service, for which a record must be kept. Figure 21–1 showed how a record of sales and cash receipts can be made and accounted for.

The sale of a product generates a sales slip, on which the number and type of items, unit price, and total price are entered. When cash registers are used, cash sales can be recorded on a tape to be used as the sales slip. Cash registers and computers can record and total sales variables including types of product, salesperson, and department.

Information on the sales forms is used to accumulate the sales income, to reduce inventory, to make analyses for future plans, and—in the case of a credit sale—to enter in the accounts receivable a record for the customer. A computer is particularly needed to help keep records and warn of late-paying customers.

Daily summaries of sales, sales on account, cash received (including charges to bank credit cards), sales by department, and other vital data can be recorded on multicolumnar or computer paper. Then, periodically, the total is entered in the ledger account. An analysis of this sheet can provide valuable information on the sales trends.

Cash Income and Outgo

Recorded sales totals must equal the total of recorded cash, credits, and other values if your accounts are to balance. Since cash is highly negotiable, the system for recording it should be designed and established with care so as to minimize mishandling and consequent losses. For cash sales, goods sold and cash received should be recorded independently of each other—if possible—for control purposes.

For example, a waitress makes out the bill for a customer at a restaurant, and a cashier receives the money. The cash register, placed in view of customers paying their bill, allows them to check the cash recording.

Also, to maintain control, only certain people should be allowed to handle the cash and then only on an individual basis: each person starts with a standard amount for change, and the cash balance is reconciled each day—or more often, if feasible. The reconciliation assures that cash on hand equals the beginning cash on hand, plus cash sales, less cash returns.

At the end of each day, businesses usually deposit in the bank the cash received that day, less the change needed for the next day's operations. The deposited amount is added to the checkbook stub. The business then makes payments by check. Each check is entered in the cash journal to identify the account to which it is charged.

Accounts Receivable

When customers buy goods using open accounts or a store's credit card, each sale is entered on a customer account record, as shown in Figure 21–1. At the end of each period—usually a month—customers' accounts are totaled and bills sent requesting payment. As payments are received, the amount is posted to each customer's account and totaled for entry in the sales and cash receipts journal. Sales to customers using outside credit cards are treated as cash sales and processed as cash through the bank.

Accounts Payable

A business incurs many obligations for materials purchased, utilities, wages, and taxes. The bills and invoices for these are entered in the purchases or expense

Figure 21–5   Examples of Recording and Adjusting Transactions

1. (a) Receive shipment of material X, $100, entered in books when received.
   (b) Used $80 of material X, entered at end of period.

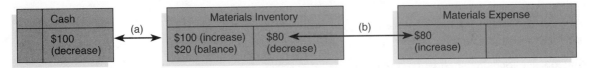

2. (a) Paid insurance policy premium of $600, entered when paid.
   (b) Monthly expense of insurance, $50 (1/12 of annual $600), entered at end of period.

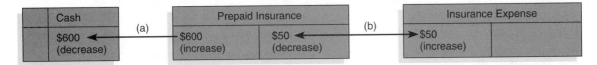

3. Have machine which cost $1,300. From machine records, machine expense, $20 = (Machine cost [$1,300] – Estimated scrap value [$100]) ÷ Estimated life (5 years [60 months]).

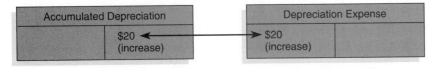

journal or computer and may be filed by date to be paid. The journals can be multicolumnar to show how the money is spent. Columns are for categories with many similar items, such as material purchases, and the miscellaneous column is for categories, such as insurance, that require few entries. Individual files keep track of whom to pay, when to pay, and how much to pay. After payment, the bills are filed for future reference. The paid bill amount is entered on the check stub and in the purchases and cash disbursements journal.

Inventory

Among the most troublesome records to keep are those dealing with inventory. While the physical planning and control of inventory were discussed in Chapter 17, we will discuss here the accounting aspects of inventory.

When materials are received, their costs are recorded as materials inventory and paid for with cash, as shown in 1(a) in Figure 21–5. Inventory increases by $100, and cash decreases by $100. As the materials are used, it's recorded as an expense of $80, leaving an inventory balance of $20 at the end of the month. In another method, often used by high-volume purchasers, purchases are charged to expense as they are received, and then, at the end of the month, the unused portion is moved to inventory.

A business selling a high volume of many items—a grocery store, for example—depends on periodic visual inspection of the items on the shelves. Holograph scanners, connected to a computer, are often used to read the product number, comparing the amount in inventory with expected needs and entering the amount that needs to be ordered. The introduction of computers and point-of-sale scanners has made the use of *perpetual inventory records,* for timely control, more feasible.

Expenses

A business purchases services and goods from other businesses, and these become expenses. Material is transformed and sold, electricity is used, machines decrease in value, and insurance protection lapses. The payment interval for these costs of doing business varies from one day to several years. To determine true profit—say for the month of March—income and expenses must be determined for that month. This can be done on a *cash* or *accrual* basis.

Many small businesses compute their profit on the cash rather than accrual basis because the cash basis is simpler. The **cash basis** assumes that payments and use occur in the same time period. But payment is not always received (or made) in the same period in which services are performed—as in the case of credit sales, for example. The **accrual basis** makes adjustments to reflect the actual expense of a service and the income received for it in a given time period, not past expenses or anticipated income. In deciding which method to use, *balance the value of accuracy against the cost of each method.*

> The **cash basis** assumes that payments and use occur in the same time period.
>
> The **accrual basis** makes adjustments to income and expenses to reflect actual expenses incurred and income earned during the period.

To calculate expenses by the accrual method, (1) obtain the values of all assets, payments, and obligations; (2) determine how much of each has been used during the period; and (3) transfer the used portion to expense and reduce the asset or increase the obligation. Items 2 and 3 in Figure 21–5 are examples of the accrual method.

Insurance may be paid monthly, quarterly, or annually. Usually, annual payments reduce the cost and are prorated as shown in Figure 21–5, example 2. In the illustration, $600 is charged to prepaid insurance (an asset) when it is paid by the small firm, with 1/12, or $50, charged to expenses each month.

Machinery, equipment, and buildings are used over a number of years, so their value is only gradually used up. In order to assign a part of their expense to each period, an accounting method must reflect their **depreciation,** which is the amount of value a facility loses over a period of time. The most common method, *straight-line depreciation,* depreciates a machine at a constant rate over its useful life. The amount to be charged for each month may be determined by the following formula:

> **Depreciation** is the gradual loss of value of a facility.

$$\frac{\text{Cost of machine} - \text{Disposal value (sell or scrap) at end of expected life}}{\text{Expected life (in months)}}$$

The amount that has already been charged to *depreciation expenses* is called *accumulated depreciation*. Figure 21–5, example 3, shows the adjustment of the two depreciation accounts by the amount thus arrived at. Many other items of expense and income need the same types of adjustment just discussed.

Financial Statements

As shown in Chapter 18, financial statements, prepared from accounting records discussed in this chapter, aid you in making these analyses. They are usually the balance sheet and income statement. Income statements should be prepared monthly, while the balance sheets can be prepared less often. Tax reports are completed for the various government divisions many times during the year. These include reports for income, sales, Social Security, and excise tax.

WHAT YOU SHOULD HAVE LEARNED

1. Information is an important resource for small businesses as well as for people. Companies collect and process data, make decisions, act on those decisions, and start the cycle anew.

2. A management information system (MIS) collects, processes, records, reports, and/or converts data into a usable form for management. Data can be processed in *real time,* with instantaneous feedback, or *batch processed* later at a lower cost.

3. Microcomputers, which now have the processing power of the mainframes and minicomputers of a few years ago, are increasingly important in small firms because they can process data so quickly. A computer (hardware) is physical equipment used for storing, processing, and presenting large quantities of data. Programs (software) direct the computer to process the data.

   In a small business, computers are used to process data related to such areas as accounting, employees, forecasting, and operations. Most systems involve both manual and computer operations, and the choice of the appropriate system depends on output, cost, and the situation in the business. In choosing a computer system, analyze the present situation in terms of available software, hardware, and employee training.

4. Accounting systems are part of a firm's MIS. The sale of goods starts a series of accounting entries using sales slips; cash register receipts; credit card receipts; multicolumnar paper (or computer files); and ledgers to record

changes in cash, sales, and accounts receivable. Computers can facilitate this process and enhance its value.

When a sale is made on credit, the amount of the sale is entered into accounts receivable, and the customer is billed later.

Bills for purchases and other items used are recorded in suppliers' accounts for proper payment. Monthly, the amount used during the month is moved to an expense account. Keeping track of inventory can be one of the greatest challenges for any business. Expenses can be recorded on either the cash or the accrual basis. The simpler cash basis charges items as they are actually paid. The accrual basis assigns the amount of revenue and expenses to the period in which they occur.

QUESTIONS FOR DISCUSSION

1. What are some of the management decisions owners of small businesses must make?

2. What types of information do they need to make those decisions?

3. What are some of the sources of the needed information?

4. Present a *short* history of the development of the microcomputer.

5. Discuss manual versus computer processing in a company you are acquainted with.

6. How might a computer be used by a realtor, a drugstore, or a fast-food restaurant?

7. Distinguish between the cash and accrual methods of handling expenses.

HERMAN VALENTINE: CUSTOMIZING COMPUTERS FOR MILITARY USE

Herman Valentine, chairman and president of Systems Management American (SMA) Corporation, remembers the time years ago when he shined shoes on the corner of Monticello and Market streets in downtown Norfolk, Virginia. His best customers were executives working in the four-story department store and the 16-story Maritime Towers office building across the street. He now owns the entire block, including the store—which serves as headquarters for his company—and the office building.

SMA is a computer systems integrator serving the government and private industry. Its capabilities include manufacturing, installation, integrated logistics support, software/hardware development, configuration management, command and control, image processing, and data conversion services.

SMA has grown from a one-man operation in 1970 into a national corporation with a staff of 430. Not realizing how difficult it was going to be, Valentine "put in long hours, borrowed often from banks, and spent a lot of time on proposals for contracts he did not get." SMA is now one of the largest black-owned businesses in the United States.

An outstanding high school basketball player, Valentine wanted to play in college and the NBA, but he wanted a car more! So he took part-time jobs to buy one, finished high school, went into the army, mar-

Herman Valentine, chairman and president of Systems Management American Corporation.

Photo courtesy of Systems Management American Corporation.

ried, and at age 23 returned to Norfolk. After earning a bachelor's degree from Norfolk State University in three years (paid for by more part-time jobs), he became an executive officer for the U.S. Department of Agriculture and later business manager for Norfolk State.

In 1970, he opened Systems Management Associates, a consulting firm for black businesses, with $5,000 he had saved. With an answering service, a post office box, and a part-time secretary, Valentine sold administrative and financial advice to black entrepreneurs and performed data processing and programming for them. Two years later, with 12 employees (mostly part-timers), he began bidding on—and winning—small government data processing jobs.

But his business really took off in 1981, when he snagged a contract to design, install, and maintain sophisticated record-keeping computers aboard navy ships. The navy thought the job was too big for him, but he persuaded them to send an evaluation team, which found no reason why he couldn't do the job. Revenues skyrocketed for a while, and they have been as high as $60 million. Valentine has pared down his operations somewhat, but SMA continues to bid on—and be awarded—government contracts.

Valentine is concentrating on more contract diversification—which includes the government—as well as the private sector, as military budget cuts begin to affect the computer industry. After closing three small offices around the country and cutting $4 million out of overhead, he and his staff are "lean and competitive."

He trains his employees—many of whom are unskilled workers—to be computer technicians and high-tech specialists. He also encourages other minorities to become entrepreneurs.

QUESTIONS

1. How do you explain Valentine's success?

2. To what extent do you think his diversification plan will work? Explain.

3. What suggestions would you make to him for adjusting to the changing economic environment?

Source: Correspondence with Systems Management American Corporation; *Inside Information/Employee Publication of SMA,* December 1988, p. 8; and various others, including Lewis Giles, Jr., "Success: Minority Entrepreneurs Help Their Communities," *Minority Business Today,* May 1989, pp. 19–20.

SOME FREQUENTLY USED COMPUTER TERMS

bit Binary digit, smallest unit of computer information.

bulletin board Computer network with data and programs available to others.

byte Unit of information for PCs (equals 8 bits).

CAD/CAM Computer-Assisted Design/Computer-Aided Manufacture—hardware and software.

chip Processing unit for computer.

CPU Central processing unit—"brains" of the computer.

CRT Cathode ray tube—video display of a PC.

desktop publishing package Software that combines graphics and text into camera-ready printout.

disk drive Large-capacity storage device; can be floppy disk or hard disk/card.

DOS Disk operating system—software to start and run other programs.

floppy disk See disk drive.

hard disk/card See disk drive.

laptop Small portable computer.

LCD Lliquid crystal display—a display activated by applying a low voltage to a liquid crystal material commonly used in battery operated computers such as lap tops and notebooks.

mainframe Large multiuser computer.

MB Megabyte—binary million bytes—common unit of storage.

megahertz Unit of computer processing speed.

microcomputer or **personal computer (PC)** Small, desktop computer.

minicomputer Small multiuser computer.

modem Modulator/demodulator; device to connect a computer with another over a telephone line; needs communications package to use.

mouse External mechanical device to move cursor on a computer screen to select options.

MS-DOS Microsoft's DOS—an industry standard.

OS/2 New Microsoft DOS designed for new technology.

RAM Random access memory—usable internal computer memory.

ROM Read-only memory—unchangeable computer memory used for specialized applications.

spreadsheet Program for tabular manipulation of numeric data.

terminal Input/output device; includes keyboard and video display.

word processors "Intelligent typewriter" software.

workstation Single-user, special-purpose micro-computer.

VII

PROVIDING PRESENT AND FUTURE SECURITY FOR THE BUSINESS

We have covered most of the general information about managing a small business in the preceding parts. Now, we need to present some special considerations to you before we are through.

First, Chapter 22 discusses your need to minimize the risks incurred in owning and operating a small business. Most losses can be minimized by establishing insurance and reserves. With properly planned operations and crime prevention, including security measures, the chances—or magnitude—of other losses can be reduced.

Chapter 23 covers some of the most important laws affecting small firms. It also discusses the need for social responsibility and the practice of business ethics.

Chapter 24 deals with the need to provide for management succession. It also discusses family and manager problems in small firms. Many business owners do not like to talk about the question of succession. However, to assure the continuance of your business or to provide a going concern for family members to operate, you must look at this question objectively and realistically.

22

Risk Management, Insurance, and Crime Prevention

Everything is sweetened by risk.—Alexander Smith

Carrying liability insurance these days is almost a liability in itself. . . . Premiums are rising at a fantastic rate . . . [and] in some cases insurance coverage has become impossible to obtain—at any cost.—Charles W. Patchen, CPA and writer

LEARNING OBJECTIVES

After studying the material in this chapter, you will be able to:
1. Define risk and explain how to manage it.
2. Explain what insurance is and show how it can be used to minimize risk.
3. Show how crime prevention can reduce risk and protect assets.
4. Describe how to safeguard employees with preventive measures.

BUSINESS RISKS INTERNATIONAL INC.: CORPORATE PROTECTION

Recent years have witnessed a dramatic increase in white-collar crime, substance abuse by employees, terrorist threats against corporate executives, and other criminal risks facing business. A new breed of entrepreneur has come forth to help companies navigate through this minefield of shady risks—the private security specialist. Many of these people, and their newly formed companies, have successfully carved a niche in the U.S. security industry, which is growing at an 8 to 12 percent annual rate.

Don Walker, a lawyer and former FBI agent, founded Nashville-based Business Risks International Inc. (BRI) in 1985. Previously he had been director of security for several firms and assistant general counsel at Genesco.

Don Walker
Photo courtesy of Business Risks International Inc.

BRI now has offices in the United States, London, Bangkok, Hong Kong, the Philippines, Singapore, and Taiwan. The company has benefited from trends that cause other companies major headaches, such as the growth of crime and terrorism. BRI helps firms reduce their exposure to risks. Companies, increasingly aware of the costs associated with these risks, often use outside resources to identify and eliminate or reduce the problem—just as they use other resources, such as attorneys, accountants, and management consultants. Small firms use BRI's services instead of starting their own security department; larger companies use them to supplement their current staff. In either case, BRI reduces the business's hiring costs and overhead expenses.

Among the services that BRI provides is investigating prospective employees and potential business associates. The pervasiveness of alcohol and drug abuse among employees has caused a dramatic increase in the demand for effective screening and investigation of workers, especially since federal law severely restricts (and usually prohibits) polygraph tests in preemployment screening. Also, the Drug-Free Omnibus Act of 1988 requires firms with a contract of $25,000 or more with the U.S. government to have a "drug-free workplace" program. This affects *many* small companies.

Walker tells of a case where BRI agents, working under cover, purchased cocaine from employees manufacturing equipment for the U.S. military. In another case, BRI investigated a prospective foreign business partner for one of his clients. A South American businessman was on the verge of being awarded a franchise for a major fast-food chain when BRI discovered that the man was a key figure in one of the Colombian cocaine cartels.

The future definitely looks bright for security firms such as BRI. As the nation girds itself for a major new war on drugs, demand for their services should continue to skyrocket. In fact, BRI was so successful that it merged with Kroll Associates, Inc., a high-profile investigation firm, in September 1991, and its stock was bought by Pinkerton® on November 1, 1991.

Source: Jack Cavanaugh, "Running Scared," *Venture,* January 1989, pp. 31–33; correspondence with Business Risks International Inc.; and Laurence Hooper, "Kroll Associates, Rival Firm BRI Agree to Merge," *The Wall Street Journal,* July 19, 1991, p. B38.

We will discuss in this chapter some of the most prevalent risks—such as those mentioned in the Profile—facing you as a small business owner, and we will show how you can cope with them. The first part deals with risk and its management; the second part, with using insurance to minimize loss due to risk; the third part, with crime prevention; and the last part explains how security systems can protect your assets.

RISK AND ITS MANAGEMENT

Small business losses of money and property occur as a result of such things as fire, severe weather, theft, lawsuits, bankruptcy, and politics, as well as the death, disability, or defection of key personnel. For example, a physical peril like a hurricane, fire, or tornado may destroy your property outright. Or remodeling, street repairs, or flooding may temporarily close your business and reduce income. Goods may be stolen, damaged, destroyed, or spoiled in transit, for which the common carrier isn't liable. Banks may either call in, or refuse to renew, loans. Customers may be unable to pay accounts receivable. The government may cut back on military spending. A competitor may hire one of your key employees. Given this rogues' gallery of lurking perils, what's a small business to do?

Risk management is the process of conserving earning power and assets by minimizing the shock from losses.

The answer is to use **risk management,** which is the process of conserving a firm's earning power and assets by minimizing the financial shocks of accidental losses. It lets a firm regain its financial balance and operating effectiveness after suffering an unexpected loss.

Types of Risk

There are two primary types of risk you will face as a small business owner. A **pure risk** is uncertainty as to whether some unpredictable event that can result in loss will occur. Pure risk always exists when the possibility of a loss is present but the possible extent of the loss is unknown. For example, the consequences of a fire, the death of a key employee, or a liability judgment against you cannot be predicted with any degree of certainty. Many of these risks, however, can be analyzed statistically and are therefore insurable.

Pure risk is the uncertainty that some unpredictable event will result in a loss.

Speculative risk is the uncertainty that a voluntarily undertaken risk will result in a loss.

On the other hand, a **speculative risk** is uncertainty as to whether a voluntarily undertaken activity will result in a gain or a loss. Production risks, such as building a plant that turns out to have the wrong capacity or keeping an inventory level that turns out to be too high or too low, are speculative risks. Speculative risk is the name of the game in business.

For example, Levi Strauss risked selling its jeans through mass merchandisers such as Sears and Penney's, only to have department stores turn to Lee jeans.

Some business risks are insurable and others uninsurable. And, as you know, the greatest risk facing any small business—the ever present possibility that it will be unprofitable—is uninsurable. Other uninsurable risks are associated with the development of new products, changes in customers' preferences, price fluctuations, and changes in laws. In this chapter we deal only with *insurable risks*.

Ways of Coping with Risk

The main ways you can cope with risk are (1) risk avoidance; (2) risk prevention, or loss control; (3) risk transfer; and (4) risk assumption.

Risk avoidance is refusing to undertake—or abandoning—an activity in which the risk seems too costly. For instance, a New York bank experimented with having depositors of less than $5,000 either pay a fee to see a teller or use an automatic teller machine. When customers rebelled, the project was dropped as too risky.[1]

Risk prevention, or **loss control,** consists of using various methods to reduce the probability that a given event will occur. The primary control technique is prevention, including safety and protective procedures. For example, if your business is large enough, you might try to control losses by providing first-aid offices, driver training, and work safety rules, not to mention security guards to prevent pilferage, shoplifting, and other forms of theft.

Risk transfer means shifting the consequences of a risk to persons or organizations outside your business. The best-known form of risk transfer is **insurance,** which is the process by which an insurance company agrees, for a fee (a premium) to pay an individual or organization an agreed-upon sum of money for a given loss. But, because of escalating health-care costs, many companies are shifting part of the risk to their employees, who must pay higher deductibles and a larger percentage of nonreimbursed expenses.[2]

Risk assumption usually takes the form of **self-insurance,** whereby a business sets aside a certain amount of its own funds to meet losses that are uncertain in size and frequency.[3] This method is usually impractical for very small firms, because they do not have the large cash reserves needed to make it feasible.

Generally, more than one method of handling risks is used at the same time. For example, a firm may use self-insurance for automobile damage, which costs relatively little, while using commercial insurance against liability claims, which may be prohibitively great.

> **Risk avoidance** is refusing to undertake an activity where the risk seems too costly.
>
> **Risk prevention (loss control)** is using various methods to reduce the possibility of a loss occurring.
>
> **Risk transfer** is shifting a risk to someone outside your company.
>
> **Insurance** is provided by another company that agrees, for a fee, to reimburse your company for part of a loss.
>
> **Risk assumption or self-insurance** is the process of setting aside funds to meet losses that are uncertain in size and frequency.

USING INSURANCE TO MINIMIZE LOSS DUE TO RISK

The principal value of insurance lies in its reduction of your risks from doing business. In buying insurance, you trade a potentially large but uncertain loss for a small but certain one (the cost of the premium). In other words, you trade uncertainty for certainty. But, if the insurance premium is a substantial proportion of the value of the property, don't buy the insurance.

Figure 22–1   How to Determine Whether You Need Insurance

To determine how to handle business risks, ask yourself, What will happen if:

1. I die or suddenly become incapacitated?
2. A fire destroys my firm's building(s), machines, tools and equipment, and/or inventories?
3. There is theft by an outsider, a customer, or an employee, or an employee embezzles company funds?
4. My business is robbed?
5. A customer is awarded a sizable settlement after bringing a product or accident liability suit against me?
6. Someone, inside or outside the business, obtains unauthorized information from my computer?

A well-designed insurance program not only compensates for losses but also provides other values, including reduction of worry, freeing funds for investment, suggestions for loss prevention techniques, and easing of credit.

In deciding what to do about business risks, you should ask yourself questions such as those shown in Figure 22–1. Often, when such disasters occur in small companies with inadequate insurance protection or none at all, either the owners are forced out of business or operations are severely restricted.

Types of Insurance Coverage

Because there are so many types of insurance, we will discuss those you will need most as a small business owner.

The basic *fire insurance policy* insures only for losses from fire and lightning and those due to temporary removal of goods from the premises because of fire. In most instances, this policy should be supplemented by an *extended-coverage endorsement* that insures against loss from windstorm, hail, explosion, riot, aircraft, vehicle, and smoke damage.

To ensure reimbursement for the full amount of covered losses, most property insurance contracts have a **coinsurance** provision. It requires policyholders to buy insurance in an amount equal to a specified percentage of the property value—say, 80 percent.

Business interruption coverage should also be provided through endorsement, because such indirect losses are frequently more severe in their eventual cost than are direct losses. For example, while rebuilding after a fire, the business must continue to pay fixed expenses such as salaries of key employees and such expenses as utilities, interest, and taxes. You also need this type of insurance for other types of business interruption.

Coinsurance is having the business buy insurance equal to a specific percentage of property value.

For example, Ali Kamber, executive vice president for Ferromin International, a metals and minerals trading company with four employees, said his company lost $100,000 during the week following the bombing of the World Trade Center in early 1993. The company "lacked insurance for business interruptions," he said.[4]

Casualty insurance consists of automobile insurance (both collision and public liability) plus burglary, theft, robbery, plate glass, and health and accident insurance. Automobile liability and physical-damage insurance are necessary because firms may be legally liable for vehicles used on their behalf, even those they do not own. For example, when employees use their own cars on company business, the employer is liable in case of an accident.

Product/service liability insurance protects a business against losses resulting from the use of its product. It is particularly important for small firms because in conducting business companies are subject to common and statutory laws governing negligence to customers, employees, and anyone else with whom they do business. One liability judgment, without adequate insurance, can easily result in the liquidation of a business. It is estimated that such liability adds 50 percent to the cost of a stepladder and increases the cost of some vaccines for children's diseases 20-fold.[5] As a result, premiums for liability coverage are becoming almost prohibitive. In fact, the crisis has reached such proportions that some companies are dropping products rather than face the danger of bankruptcy.

Product/service liability insurance protects a business from losses resulting from the use of its product.

For example, after spending more than $100 million defending itself against charges that Bendectin, an antinausea drug used by millions of pregnant women for decades, caused birth defects, its only producer quit making it in 1983.[6]

Another growing problem for small firms is what to do about liability when sponsoring athletic teams or some potentially dangerous activities. Employers are facing the problem in two ways. Some are trying to get reasonably priced insurance coverage. When this isn't feasible, many small firms are abandoning the practice.

Workers' compensation policies typically provide for medical care, lump sums for death and dismemberment, and income payments for disabled workers or their dependents.

The workers' comp problem is rapidly getting "out of control" because of "unrestrained medical costs, excessive legal disputes in what is supposed to be a no-fault system, broadening definitions of what are job-related injuries, and rampant fraud and abuse."[7] As shown in Table 22–1, the average medical cost for each injury to an employee increased 14 percent per year from 1980 to 1990, while the medical component of the consumer price index increased only 8 percent. The result: premiums for such coverage increased from $22.3 billion to $56 billion (see Table 22–2). This is now *the biggest insurance expense* for American businesses.[8]

Table 22–1   The High Cost of Workplace Injury

The medical cost per injury paid by workers' compensation insurers has increased an average of 14 percent a year, compared with 8 percent for the medical component of the consumer price index.

Year	Average Medical Cost per Claim
1980	$1,748
1981	$2,243
1982	$2,472
1983	$2,982
1984	$3,564
1985	$3,673
1986	$3,848
1987	$4,516
1988	$5,207
1989	$5,863
1990	$6,611

Source: National Council on Compensation Insurance. Reprinted by permission, *Nation's Business*, July 1992. Copyright 1992, U.S. Chamber of Commerce.

Table 22–2   Employers' Premiums for Workers' Comp ($ billions)

Year	Total Premiums
1960	$ 2.1
1970	4.9
1980	22.3
1982	22.8
1984	25.1
1986	34.3
1988	43.3
1989	48.0
1990*	56.0
1991*	62.0

*Estimate

Source: John Burton's *Workers' Compensation Monitor*, May/June 1992, Reprinted by permission, *Nation's Business*, July 1992. Copyright 1992, U.S. Chamber of Commerce.

Figure 22–2   Percentage of Companies Providing Employees with Health Insurance

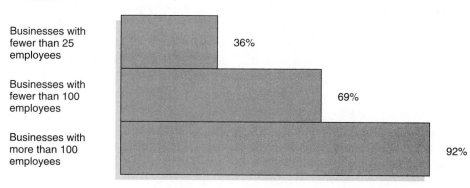

Businesses with fewer than 25 employees — 36%

Businesses with fewer than 100 employees — 69%

Businesses with more than 100 employees — 92%

Source: Bureau of Labor Statistics, ''Employee Benefits in Medium and Large Firms, 1989,'' and ''Employee Benefits in Small, Private Establishments, 1990.''

Group health and life insurance for employees are also important in small firms. *Life insurance* provides protection for an employee's estate when he or she dies while still in the income-producing years, or lives beyond that time but has little or no income. *Health insurance* provides protection against the risk of medical expenses, including doctor and hospital bills and prescription expenses.

Health insurance is one of the most important benefits offered by small firms, but it's also one of the costliest. As shown in Figure 22–2, while 92 percent of large firms provide this coverage, only 69 percent of those with fewer than 100 employees and 36 percent of those with fewer than 25 employees provide such coverage.

A major cause of the low coverage by small firms is the cost. Health insurance costs have increased at more than twice the inflation rate for over a decade, and some small firms have experienced 25 to 50 percent annual increases. Widely recognized as an acute problem for the entire country, this is critical for small businesses.[9]

Finally, insurance companies treat large and small businesses differently. If a big company has a bad year, with a high total health bill, the insurer regards it as a natural occurrence and assumes that costs will decline the following year. But it's common for rates at a very small business—one with 10 to 20 people covered—to skyrocket if just one employee racks up huge health claims during the year.

For example, Mike Lower has had trouble finding an insurer for his two Corydon, Indiana, businesses. The spouse of one of his three employees has a serious illness, which seems to be under control. Still, insurers willing to cover him would charge an expensive $300 a month or more per employee.[10]

Business owner's insurance is another important protection you need. It consists of (1) protection of owner or dependents against loss from premature death, disability, or medical expenses and (2) provision for the continuation of a business following the death of an owner. Also, *business continuation life insurance* is used in closely held corporations to provide cash on the death of an owner. The cash can be used to retire the interest of a partner or, in case of death, to repurchase the stock of a closely held corporation.

Insurers issue fidelity and surety bonds to guarantee that employees and others with whom the company transacts business are honest and will fulfill their contractual obligations. *Fidelity bonds* are purchased for employees occupying positions that involve the handling of company funds. *Surety bonds* provide protection against the failure of a contractor to fulfill contractual obligations. Problems with bonding restrict the growth of many small contractors.

For example, in a poll of 150 contractors in New York and New Jersey, more than three-fourths of them said that difficulty in getting bonded limited their access to jobs, especially the bigger and more profitable ones.[11]

Guides to Selecting an Insurer

In choosing an insurer, consider the financial characteristics of the insurer, the insurer's flexibility in meeting your requirements, and the services rendered by the agent. While insurance companies have agents representing them, independent agents represent more than one company. These independent agents use the following logo:

Financial Characteristics and Flexibility of Insurer

The major types of insurers are stock companies, mutual companies, reciprocals, and Lloyd's groups. While mutuals and reciprocals are cooperatively organized and sell insurance ''at cost,'' in practice their premiums may be no lower than those of profit-making companies. In comparing different types of insurers, you should use the following criteria:

- Financial stability and safety.
- Specialization in your type of business.
- Ability to tailor policy to meet your needs.
- Cost of protection.

Valid comparisons of insurance coverage and its costs are difficult to make, but your insurance brokers, independent insurance advisors, or agents can assist you. In addition, the following are a few things you can do to ease the pain when your insurance comes up for renewal:

- Consult your agent for methods of minimizing your premium.
- Consider boosting your policy deductibles to keep premium costs within manageable limits.
- Before renewal time arrives, shop around among several agents for coverage.
- Find out if your professional organization offers lower-cost coverage for its members.
- Check out the special-risk pools.
- Consider alternatives to insurance coverage, such as self-insurance or coinsurance.

Services Rendered by the Agent

Decide which qualifications of agents are most important, and then inquire about agents among business friends and others who have had experience with them. In comparing agents, look for contacts among insurers, professionalism, degree of individual attention, quality of service, and help in time of loss. Choose an agent who is willing and able to (1) devote enough time to your individual problems to justify the commission, (2) survey exposure to loss, (3) recommend adequate insurance and loss prevention programs, and (4) offer alternative methods of insurance.

Noninsurance Methods for Dealing with Risk

Methods you can use for handling risk other than insurance include noninsurance and loss prevention. One or both of these methods, combined with insurance, may reduce costs related to risks.

Noninsurance is used to some extent by all firms, for they must inevitably assume some risks. To cover all potential losses is simply impossible. Noninsurance makes sense when the severity of the potential loss is low and when the risks are predictable, preventable, or reducible.

Loss prevention programs, by design, reduce the probability of loss. Examples include programs for preventing fire and burglary. Such programs usually result in reductions in insurance premiums, but they add to other expenses.

Figure 22–3   The Five Most Common Security Problem Areas for Small Firms

1. Easily defeated door locks.
2. Lack of (computerized) information backup system.
3. Little or no control over distribution of keys or access codes.
4. False sense of security provided by insurance.
5. Improperly secured equipment.

Source: Paul Gassaway, ''Identifying Security Risks,'' *Business Age,* April 1989, p. 29.

CRIME PREVENTION TO PROTECT ASSETS

Small business owners need to practice crime prevention as a way of reducing risks and protecting their assets. Not only do you need to prevent major crimes, such as armed robbery, theft, and white-collar crimes, but you also need protection from trespassing, vandalism, and harassment.

An awareness of the potential dangers helps to minimize the risks involved and reduces losses from crime. It's impossible to have a security program that will prevent all criminal acts, so you can only hope to minimize their occurrence and severity. Figure 22–3 lists the five most common security problem areas for small businesses. The source article of the figure also describes steps that can be taken to address these problem areas.

Law enforcement agencies and the business community are learning to identify areas particularly susceptible to crime. Crimes appear to fall into patterns. Armed robbery may occur frequently in one type of neighborhood, theft in another, and both in a third. A prospective business owner needs to evaluate a potential site with this problem in mind. Examples of sites that appear to be particularly vulnerable to criminal acts are public housing projects, low-rent neighborhoods, areas of high unemployment, and areas with a high incidence of illiteracy.

Criminal acts have forced not only small but even large businesses into insolvency. Armed robbery, theft, and white-collar crimes are the major crimes affecting small firms.

Armed Robbery

In recent years, the number of armed robberies has increased significantly. An armed person enters the premises with the intent of obtaining cash or valuable merchandise and leaves as quickly as possible in order to minimize the risk of identification or apprehension. Since time is critical in such circumstances, locations that afford easy access and relatively secure escape routes seem most vulnerable. This type of criminal usually wants to be in and out of the location in three minutes or less, and the pressure of the situation tends to make the robber more dangerous.

Several measures can be taken to reduce the chances of being robbed. They include modifying the store's layout, securing entrances, using security dogs, controlling the handling of cash, and redesigning the surrounding area.

Modifying Store Layout

Location of the cash register and high visibility inside and from outside the store are important in preventing armed robbery. If robbers cannot dash in, scoop up the cash, and dash out again within a short time, they aren't as likely to attempt the robbery, as the following example shows.

One convenience food chain removed from the windows all material that would obstruct the view into the store. In addition, it encouraged crowds at all hours with various gimmicks and attracted policemen by giving them free coffee. The average annual robbery rate dropped markedly.

Securing Entrances

The security of entrances and exits is extremely important in preventing robbery. Windows and rear doors should be kept locked and barred. In high-crime neighborhoods, many businesses use tough, shock-resistant transparent materials in their windows instead of glass.

Using Security Dogs

Security dogs are trained to be vicious on command. Businesspeople have found these animals to be effective deterrents against armed robbers. For example, when 589 convicted criminals were asked how best to foil burglars, the largest number— 15.8 percent—said, "Have a dog."[12] However, health and sanitation regulations in some jurisdictions may prevent the use of dogs.

Controlling the Handling of Cash

Making daily cash deposits, and varying the deposit time from day to day are highly recommended. Perhaps you have been in a supermarket checkout line when the cash register signals "too much cash" and will not operate until another employee has removed the excess to a safe and reset the register with a key. Banks and other businesses rigidly enforce minimum-cash-on-hand rules for cash drawers in order to reduce losses in the event of an armed robbery. Many businesses hide safes in unobtrusive hiding places and limit knowledge of their combinations to only one or two people. It is not uncommon for a sign to be posted on the safe, or near it, advising that the person on duty does not have access to the combination or saying, "Notice: Cash in drawer does not exceed $50." Other stores, such as gas stations, use locked cash boxes and accept only correct change, credit cards, and/or payment through secured windows during certain hours.

"The salesman said it was the most effective home security system on the market."

Reprinted from *The Wall Street Journal*; permission Cartoon Features Syndicate

Redesigning the Surroundings

Well-lighted parking lots help deter robbers. If possible, try to keep vehicles from parking too near the entrance to your business. Armed robbery can be reduced by making access less convenient. For example, many convenience food store parking lots have precast concrete bumper blocks so distributed as to deter fast entry into and exit from the lot. Also, some businesses use silent alarms, video cameras to photograph crime in action, or video cameras tied to TV monitors in a security office.

Theft

Theft has become a serious problem for businesses for numerous reasons: drug use, inflation, and unemployment, for example, as well as the challenge theft offers. Because of the extent of the problem, many national merchandising businesses add 2 to 3 percent to their prices to cover the cost of theft, but even this may not be enough to compensate for the total loss.

Types of Theft

The two major types of theft are (1) that done by outsiders, usually known as shoplifting, and (2) that done by employees, employee theft, as shown in Figure 22–4. Retailers sometimes refer to losses from both kinds of theft as *shrinkage*.

Shoplifting. *Shoplifting* is a major problem for retailing establishments. While some losses are due to amateurs and kleptomaniacs, professional shoplifters cause the greatest prevention problems for businesses. The amateur may be a thrill seeker who takes an item or two to see whether or not he or she can get away with it. (This

Figure 22–4 Look Who's Stealing

Sources of inventory loss in the retail industry

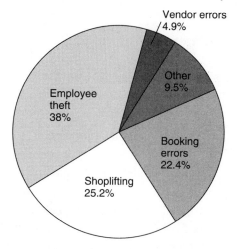

Source: Survey of 456 retailers sponsored by the National Retail Foundation and others, as reported in *The Wall Street Journal,* October 5, 1992, p. B2. Adapted with permission of THE WALL STREET JOURNAL, © 1989 Dow Jones & Company, Inc. All Rights Reserved Worldwide.

is often the case with children and teenagers.) The *kleptomaniac* has an uncontrollable urge to take things, whether they are needed or not. Kleptomaniacs are more easily detected than the *professional shoplifter,* who may wear specially prepared or large garments, carry a large handbag, or ask for an empty box to conceal stolen merchandise. Business owners and managers often find the various techniques that people use to remove merchandise from their premises shocking, as the following example illustrates.

A well-known matron was at the checkout counter. Upon inspection, her large purse was found to contain several prepackaged steaks and packages of luncheon meat. The store owner observed, "I thought she was one of our best customers. She has been coming here for years. I wonder how much she has taken."

Retailers are now striking back at shoplifters by means of a new tactic called *civil recovery,* or *civil restitution,* whereby they send letters to shoplifters or their parents demanding payment for the items taken. Some states permit not only recovery of the amount stolen but also damage awards for additional costs of crime prevention, damage to displays, or injuries resulting from the act. Civil Demand Associates, of Sherman Oaks, California, which specializes in this type of recovery, has clients nationwide.[13]

Figure 22–5   Stealing at Work

A study of 453 employees caught stealing from their company showed that:

- 90 percent are under 30 years old.
- 78 percent steal without an accomplice.
- 63 percent are male.
- 60 percent are full-time workers.
- 60 percent steal merchandise.

Source: Security Management magazine, as reported in *The Wall Street Journal,* November 11, 1986, p. 39. Reprinted by permission of THE WALL STREET JOURNAL, © 1986 Dow Jones & Company, Inc. All Rights Reserved Worldwide.

Employee Theft.   As shown in Figure 22–4, employee theft is the major source of inventory loss in the retail industry. It may range from the simple act of an individual who takes only small items (such as pens or paper clips) to raids by groups that remove truckloads of merchandise. Surveys have found as many as 50 percent of employees admit stealing from their employer.[14]

Also, employees sometimes conspire with outsiders to steal from their employer. They may do this in various ways—for example, by charging the outsiders a lower price or by placing additional merchandise in their packages.

How serious is employee theft? It has been estimated that it costs all businesses between $70 and $100 billion annually.[15]

Who Steals?

Research has shown that employees who think their income is too low, or stagnating, steal more often and in greater amounts than other employees. For example, as you can see from Figure 22–5, one study showed that those who steal tend to be young, full-time employees operating alone, and they steal merchandise more often than cash.

Techniques for Preventing Theft

Retail establishments have found the use of some of the following measures effective in reducing theft:

1. Wide-angle and one-way mirrors to observe employee or customer behavior.
2. TV cameras, tied to monitors, to observe a large area of the store.
3. Electronic noise activators—some visible, some not—to warn of unprocessed merchandise leaving the store.
4. Using paper-and-pencil tests of a potential employee's honesty, such as the Compu-Scan Pre-Employment Risk Analysis (see Profile for Chapter 13).

5. Security guards, if economically feasible.

6. Security audits, such as the following:

   a. Unannounced spot checks of critical activity areas, such as cash registers, employees' packages, car trunks, lunch pails, and waste disposal holding areas.

   b. Visible security surveillance of work activities.

   c. Weekly, monthly, or quarterly physical inventory checks.

In addition to using dogs and security guards (discussed earlier), construction contractors have found the following measures effective:

1. Scheduling operations and purchasing materials for just-in-time delivery.

2. Scheduling lower inventory levels on weekends.

3. Fencing and lighting storage yards and clearing the area adjacent to the fence.

4. Using locking systems that are difficult to jimmy.

5. Unannounced rotation of the person responsible for receiving materials.

6. Assigning a trusted employee the responsibility for checking materials into the job site, to prevent problems such as that in the following example.

A contractor purchased a mobile concrete mixer and sent it to the site of one of his jobs. Those responsible for the mixer left it outside the fenced-in area that night, and it was stolen. Later, the contractor found that a subordinate had failed to record it for insurance coverage.

White-Collar Crime

Another category of serious abuse against business is white-collar crimes, which have been rising rapidly.

Types of White-Collar Crimes

White-collar crimes are committed by managerial, professional, and technical employees. They include the falsification of accounts; fraudulent accessing and manipulating of the computer; bribery of purchasing agents and other officials; collusion that results in unrecorded transactions; sale of proprietary information; and sabotage of new technology, new or old products, or customer relations. According to the FBI special agent-in-charge in Cleveland, Ohio, white-collar crime adds 15 percent to the price of everything we buy. It costs us at least $200 billion each year, which is far more than robbers take.[16]

Computer security is becoming a real problem for small firms. The two main problems are fraudulent use and unintentional destruction of data. Not only has the number of such crimes increased; so has their magnitude. For example, Steve

White-collar crimes are those committed by managerial, professional, and technical employees.

Albrecht, of Brigham Young University, has estimated that thieves working with computers average $500,000 each time they strike, as opposed to an average of $23,500 for other white-collar crimes, and only $250 for armed robbery.[17]

A new kind of white-collar criminal you should be aware of is called the *credit doctor.* These computer con artists gain access to credit bureau computer files and steal the personal data of people who have good credit histories, which they sell to people with bad credit records. Lenders then grant credit to these poor risks and end up footing the bill when a credit applicant stops making payments or vanishes.[18]

Ways to Minimize White-Collar Crime

Special measures must be taken to minimize crimes by white-collar personnel. Some deterrents you can use include audits, being aware of employee work habits, identification, and bonding. Also, as mentioned above, small firms that use computers may need the services of a firm with computer security expertise.

Audits of data such as past sales transactions, inventory levels, purchase prices, and accounts receivable may uncover undesirable activities.

You should be aware of your white-collar employees' *work habits*. They may all be open and aboveboard, but they should be checked. You should ask such questions as: Do they work nights regularly? Do they never take a day off? Do they forgo their usual vacation? Standards of living, dress, car, housing, entertainment, and travel that seem to cost more than an employee should be able to afford often signal economic misconduct.

Proper identification, along with a device that takes pictures of a check and the person cashing it, tends to discourage bad-check artists. Although this practice may be too expensive for your small firm, your bank may assist in developing effective identification procedures. Many states have passed "*bad-check laws,*" which permit a business that receives a bad check to collect not only its face value but also double to triple damages in small claims court.

Since credit cards are frequently stolen, additional identification should be required. Be sure that the signature corresponds to the one on the card. Also, you should be sure to ascertain the validity of trade documents, such as invoices and securities. Each year, millions of dollars are lost by businesspeople through carelessness that allows others to palm off bogus documents.

Fidelity bonding helps insure against employee fraud or theft. The employer pays a premium to an insurance company, which then assumes the risk and reimburses the company for any loss.

Document Security

Our personal experience in working with small businesses, as well as press releases in recent years, has made us aware of the importance of document security. As

━━━━━━━━━━━━━━━ USING TECHNOLOGY TO SUCCEED ━━━━━━━━━━━━━━━

KROY SIGN SYSTEMS: WATCH THAT SIGN—IT MAY BE WATCHING YOU

Kroy Sign Systems of Scottsdale, Arizona, has proposed the security system of the future. According to John Glitsos, Kroy's vice-president and general manager, the computer and burglar alarm system that "sees" all would implant motion-detecting sensors in hallway signs and link them to a central computer. A tiny microchip transmitter would be installed in employees' and visitors' name badges. Anyone walking in the area without a valid name tag would activate the sensors, which would set off an alarm.

Source: "Computer 'Watches' Where You Go," *USA Today,* November 24, 1986, p. 4B. © 1986, USA TODAY. Reprinted with permission.

shown in Chapter 21, *information is a vital factor in managing and controlling business activities,* and its management and maintenance help to assure the continuation of the business. The life of your business depends on the appropriate recording of information, its transmission to the appropriate person, and its security. Records with confidential information should be stored in bank lockboxes, safes, or restricted areas, and only authorized persons should have access to them. And all records should be protected by backups.

The proprietary nature of confidential business records and various documents makes it essential that you protect them from unauthorized eyes and hands. The trade secrets and competitive advantage of your business may be lost if this information passes into the wrong hands. Therefore, a list of authorized personnel should be prepared and provided to those responsible for document security.

An unbending rule should be that under no circumstance is it permissible to remove confidential material from the restricted area or from the business premises. Some business owners think they can save on personnel costs by permitting material to be carried to an employee's residence where the employee works on the firm's records after hours. The chance of loss, the opportunity for access by unauthorized persons, and the risk of a claim for adequate compensation make this practice inadvisable.

A *computerized security system* has been proposed for helping prevent theft and other types of unauthorized activity by employees and outsiders (see Using Technology to Succeed).

SAFEGUARDING EMPLOYEES WITH PREVENTIVE MEASURES

Within a business, various types of accidents and health problems occur, causing potential losses. The use of insurance to eliminate or minimize disastrous financial losses in a company was discussed earlier in this chapter. In addition, safeguards can be instituted to reduce human suffering as well as costs to a company and employees. Employees are a valuable resource that you should protect through proper safety procedures as shown in Chapter 15. These procedures should be preventive in nature. Not only should you provide a safe place for workers but, in addition, they must work safely, since most accidents occur because of human error, such as driving an automobile carelessly or handling equipment improperly.

Guards over moving tools, devices to keep hands away or stop machines, employee protective gear, warnings of unsafe conditions, and medical treatment are some safeguards used to protect employees from accidents and health problems and to prevent lawsuits.

WHAT YOU SHOULD HAVE LEARNED

1. One of the greatest challenges for small businesses is dealing with risk. Risk management minimizes financial shocks. Pure risk is uncertain but is often measurable and insurable. Speculative risk occurs with voluntary decisions. Risk may be avoided, prevented, assumed, or transferred.

2. Insurance can be used to minimize losses due to risks. Small businesses usually need insurance for (*a*) fire, (*b*) casualty, (*c*) product/service liability, (*d*) workers' compensation, (*e*) employee life and health, and (*f*) business continuation, as well as (*g*) fidelity and surety bonds.

   In choosing an insurer, consider its financial characteristics, flexibility in meeting your requirements, and the services it renders. An insurance company can be judged on financial stability, specialization in types of coverage, flexibility in the offering of coverage, and cost of protection.

   Alternatives to insurance include noninsurance and loss prevention.

3. Although businesses should be insured against losses, they should also take steps to prevent crimes, such as armed robbery, theft, and white-collar crime, especially computer crimes. Measures that can reduce the chances of being robbed include modifying the store's layout, securing entrances, using security dogs, controlling the handling of cash, and redesigning the surrounding area.

   Theft includes shoplifting by outsiders and employee theft. Security measures to reduce theft include mirrors, TV cameras, electronic noise activators on merchandise, screening of prospective employees, security guards, and security audits.

   White-collar crime includes removal of cash; falsification of accounts; fraudulent computer access and manipulation; bribery; collusion resulting in unrecorded transactions; sale of proprietary information; and sabotage of new technology, products, or customer relations. Ways to deal with white-collar crime include auditing of records, observing employees' work habits, requiring proper identification with checks and credit cards, and fidelity bonding. Confidential documents should be stored in bank lockboxes, safes, or restricted areas.

4. A small firm has a special responsibility to protect employees, to provide a safe workplace, and to encourage employees to maintain safe work habits.

QUESTIONS FOR DISCUSSION

1. What is meant by risk management?

2. Distinguish between pure risk and speculative risk as they apply to small businesses.

3. Discuss four ways small firms can cope with risk.

4. What are some considerations in determining a small business's need for insurance?

5. What types of insurance are commonly carried by small businesses? Describe each type of coverage.

6. What criteria should you use in choosing an insurer?

7. Discuss some methods a small business can use to reduce the chances of being robbed.

8. What is meant by white-collar crime? What are some ways to minimize it?

9. What are some methods used to safeguard employees?

BEWARE OF "SOFTLIFTING"

These days, even the smallest of businesses are making use of computers. As mentioned in Chapter 21, the microcomputer has replaced the file cabinet, resulting in a great need for computer security. When we think about computer security we generally think in terms of protecting the equipment or the data on the hard disk. However, there is another aspect of computer security that business owners must be aware of and guard against, namely, "softlifting." A business owner who has more than one computer may be tempted to buy one copy of the needed software and install it on all the computers in order to save money. *DON'T DO IT!*

This is softlifting and it's a very common problem. According to the Software Publishers Association (SPA), one in five personal computer programs in use today is an illegal copy. Software bootlegging costs U.S. software publishers $1.2 billion each year, on sales of only $6 to $7 billion. This is why "Software Police" are cracking down hard and the penalties are harsh. Softlifting recently became a felony with penalties of up to $250,000 and up to five years in jail.

The University of Oregon Continuation Center in Eugene, Oregon, thought it would "save a few bucks" by softlifting. But it got caught and had to pay a $130,000 fine and hold a national conference on copyright laws and software use.

Parametrix Inc., of Seattle, also learned the hard way. It was raided by the "Software Police," who had a search warrant and were accompanied by a U.S. marshall. The raid turned up dozens of bootlegged copies of software programs. Parametrix agreed to pay fines totaling $350,000.

How does the SPA find out about these abuses? The tipoff usually comes from a call to the SPA's toll-free Piracy Hotline. Quite often the caller is an ex-employee or a disgruntled employee who is seeking revenge. Regardless, more and more companies are getting caught. Obviously, thousands and thousands don't get caught, but since 1984 the SPA has conducted 75 raids and filed more than 300 lawsuits.

The best advice is: STAY LEGAL! Don't risk losing the business you've worked so hard to build just to "save a few bucks," because according to the SPA, if you're softlifting you are definitely living on borrowed time.

QUESTIONS

1. How severe do you perceive this problem to be? Why or why not?

2. Are you aware of any organizations who have participated in "softlifting"? If so, do they deserve to be caught and punished, in your opinion?

3. How can a small business owner prevent employees from making bootlegged copies of software programs for themselves?

4. You have a small business with a total of five computers. Your old software is obsolete and must be replaced, but your business is struggling financially. Would you risk buying one copy of the software and installing it on all five machines? Explain why or why not.

Source: "Companies, Beware of 'Software Police'," Associated Press release, in *The Mobile Press Register,* November 16, 1992, p. 5B.

23

Business-Government Relations and Business Ethics

No man shall be judged except by the legal judgment of his peers or the law of the land.—Magna Carta (1215)

Business has a soul, and management has social responsibilities as a major partner in the community, alongside capital and labour.—Oliver Sheldon, *The Philosophy of Management* (1923)

I want as few government mandates on small business as possible.—Susan Engeleiter, former SBA administrator

LEARNING OBJECTIVES

After studying the material in this chapter, you will be able to:
1. Understand the legal system in which small businesses operate, and explain some basic business laws affecting them.
2. Discuss the role played by government assistance.
3. Describe some of the burdensome aspects of government regulation and paperwork.
4. Explain how to choose a lawyer.
5. Describe what is ethical and socially responsible behavior.

GEORGIO CHERUBINI: SCORE SCORES A HIT!

Georgio Cherubini, an Italian immigrant living in Minneapolis, Minnesota, had long dreamed of owning his own restaurant. But since he needed the security of a steady income, the restaurant had to wait while he earned a living. However, his security was shattered when economic conditions forced cutbacks at his company and he was laid off. Fortunately, with the help of Marcel Sutton, a SCORE counselor, he was able to turn misfortune into opportunity and use his vision

Georgio Cherubini and SCORE counselor Marcel Sutton.
Photo courtesy of the late Marcel Sutton.

and motivation to enter the restaurant business.

Cherubini's success was not based on luck, although that did come into play, as you will see. But he was also well prepared, since he had received his training as a cook and in restaurant operation in his native Florence. After immigrating to the United States, he worked as an engineer until 1985, when he lost his job. He took a job as a waiter at the Rosewood Room, one of Minneapolis's finer dining spots.

On December 5, 1985, Cherubini contacted SCORE for counseling. His case was turned over to Marcel Sutton, who counseled Cherubini at the SCORE office a week later. After that, Sutton worked with Cherubini several times, including telephone discussions.

Cherubini's proposed 60-table restaurant, specializing in regional Tuscan cooking, would require about $300,000 for leasehold improvements, equipment, decor, and other start-up needs. Because Cherubini had only $10,000 available for investment, Sutton tried to get him an SBA-guaranteed bank loan, but it couldn't be negotiated because of the lack of required capital investment and collateral needed for a $300,000 loan.

However, there was one possible way Cherubini could open such a restaurant with his limited capital. First, he had to find a suitable location where a previous restaurant had gone into bankruptcy; then, he had to lease the location with all the existing equipment as part of the lease. Thus, the $10,000 would be enough for his initial operating capital. After a year and a half, he found such a restaurant in a good downtown location.

Hosteria Fiorentina opened in May 1987 and succeeded immediately. It showed a profit by the end of its second week of operation. By September, it had received the *Minneapolis Star-Tribune*'s coveted three-star rating, and Cherubini had to turn customers away on weekends.

Source: Correspondence and discussions with the late Marcel Sutton; and others, including ''Success in SCORE: Engineer-Turned Restaurateur Cooks Up 3-Star Recipe,'' *The Savant,* March 1989, p. 8.

Your small business will operate in a legal and governmental environment that sets rules and regulations for activities from starting the business to going out of business. Throughout the book, we've talked about the operation of a small business within the framework of government assistance and regulation. Now we would like to go into greater detail about this environment. We will look at some of the most important government laws and regulations affecting small firms, as well as show how governments provide assistance and control. Then we will discuss how to choose a lawyer and how to maintain ethical and socially responsible behavior.

UNDERSTANDING THE LEGAL ENVIRONMENT

Because it is so important to know and obey government laws and regulations, we will give you an overview of the subject. For further coverage, you should obtain competent legal assistance from someone familiar with local business conditions.

You're already familiar with some of the most basic legal principles, such as *Everyone is equal under the law, Everyone is entitled to his or her day in court,* and *A person is presumed innocent until proven guilty.* Table 23–1 provides a closer look at some basic legal principles and terminology.

All laws affecting small businesses are based on the federal or a state constitution. However, the making, administering, and interpreting of laws are separated into three distinct branches of government: *legislative, executive,* and *judicial.* Moreover, laws are made at all levels of our government, including federal, state, county, and municipal levels. These levels are generally referred to as *multiple levels of government,* and each level administers its own laws. Occasionally some of these laws are contradictory, so be prepared to retain competent legal representation.

SOME BASIC BUSINESS LAWS

The most important laws, as far as small firms are concerned, are those dealing with (1) contracts; (2) sales; (3) property; (4) patents, copyrights, and trademarks; (5) agency; (6) negotiable instruments; (7) torts; and (8) bankruptcy. Influencing all of these—and, in turn, influenced by them—is the Uniform Commercial Code (UCC).

The Uniform Commercial Code (UCC)

Since laws affecting business vary greatly from state to state, an effort was made to draft a set of uniform model statutes to govern business and commercial transactions in all 50 states.[1] The result was the **Uniform Commercial Code (UCC),** consisting of the following 10 parts: (1) general provisions, (2) sales, (3) commercial paper, (4) bank deposits and collections, (5) letters of credit, (6) bulk transfers, (7) documents of title, (8) investment securities, (9) secured transactions, and (10) effective date and repealer.

The **Uniform Commercial Code (UCC)** is a set of uniform model statutes to govern business and commercial transactions in all states.

Table 23–1 Selected Basic Legal Terminology

Common law	Unwritten law derived from judicial decisions based on customs and usages accepted by the people.
Statutory law	Body of laws passed by federal, state, and local governments.
Interstate commerce clause	Gives Congress the right to "regulate commerce with foreign nations, and among the several states."
Police power	States' right to regulate business, including the right to use the force of the state to promote the general welfare of citizens. All laws must be based on the federal or a state constitution.
Due process	Implies that everyone is entitled to a day in court, and all processes must be equal and fair.
Legislative branch of government	The U.S. Congress, state legislature, county/city council, or any other body that passes laws.
Executive branch of government	President, governor, mayor, or any other who enforces the laws through regulatory agencies and decrees.
Judicial branch of government	The court system, or those who interpret the laws and supervise enforcement.
Public law	Deals with the rights and powers of the government.
Criminal law	Deals with punishing those who commit illegal acts.
Private law	Is administered between two or more citizens.
Civil law	Deals with violations against another person who has been harmed in some way.

The code has been adopted by all 50 states, the U.S. Virgin Islands, and the District of Columbia, with minor exceptions. For example, Louisiana, which still has many laws based on the Code Napoléon, the French Civil Code that has been in effect there since the Louisiana Purchase, has adopted only Articles 1, 3, 4, and 5 of the UCC.

Instead of trying to describe the entire UCC, we will look at the most important of the business laws.

✳ Contracts

The law of contracts deals with legal business relationships resulting from agreements between two or more individuals or businesses. A **contract** is an agreement between two individuals or groups that is enforced by law. A contract may be valid and enforceable whether it is oral or written. Without contracts there would be no business as we know it, for contract law affects almost all business operations.

A **contract** is an agreement between two individuals or groups that is enforced by law.

For a contract to be legal in the United States, the following conditions must be met:

✳1. Both parties must be legally competent to act. This means not only being of sound mind but also being the authorized representative of a group or corporation.

2. The agreement must not involve illegal actions or promises.

Figure 23–1 A Simple Contract

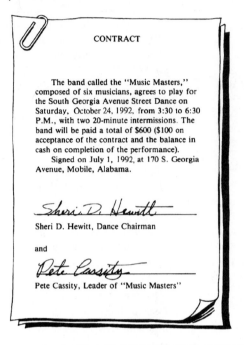

CONTRACT

The band called the "Music Masters," composed of six musicians, agrees to play for the South Georgia Avenue Street Dance on Saturday, October 24, 1992, from 3:30 to 6:30 P.M., with two 20-minute intermissions. The band will be paid a total of $600 ($100 on acceptance of the contract and the balance in cash on completion of the performance).

Signed on July 1, 1992, at 170 S. Georgia Avenue, Mobile, Alabama.

Sheri D. Hewitt

Sheri D. Hewitt, Dance Chairman

and

Pete Cassity

Pete Cassity, Leader of "Music Masters"

3. A valid offer to enter into an agreement must be made by one party, in a serious manner, not in jest. The offer may be explicit—an automobile salesperson may offer to sell you the Super Deluxe Whizbang for "only $15,000 plus your old car." Or it may be implicit—a retailer marks a VCR on display "$299.99."

4. The second party must voluntarily accept this offer, equally seriously, without duress (physical force or other compulsion) or "undue influence."

5. Each party must promise the other something of value, such as money, services, goods, or the surrender of some legal right.

6. The contract must be in a legal form, even if oral, but may be quite simple (as Figure 23–1 illustrates). It must contain at least four elements to be a valid contract—the identity of the two parties, an offer, consideration, and acceptance—but little else is needed.

Notice in the sample contract that (1) both Pete Cassity, the leader of the band, and Sheri Hewitt, elected by the residents of Georgia Avenue, were authorized representatives; (2) the dance was legal; (3) there was a valid offer—to provide music for the dance—which (4) was accepted; and (5) there was something of value offered by each party—a payment of $600 in return for three hours of music.

Sales

Laws affecting the sale of products are really part of contract law, except that when we pay the stated price for a product without negotiation, we don't usually realize that we are actually entering into an **implied contract,** which can be inferred from the actions of the parties involved. If two parties negotiate and reach an agreement, an **express contract** is formed, even if nothing is written down.[2]

An **implied contract** is an unwritten contract that results from the actions of the parties involved.

An **express contract** results when two parties negotiate and reach an agreement.

For example, if you go to a physician, state your symptoms, and receive treatment, a valid *implied contract* can be inferred. If a prospective buyer makes an offer on a house and it is accepted by the seller, an *express contract* exists.

Warranties

A **warranty,** which is a representation made by the seller to the buyer regarding the quality and performance of a product, may be express or implied. *Express warranties,* which are specific representations made by the seller regarding the product, often come in the form of warranty cards to be completed and returned by the buyer. *Implied warranties* are those legally imposed on the seller. For example, the FDA defines what is meant by ''ice cream'' as opposed to ''ice milk,'' and ''cheese'' as opposed to ''pasteurized process cheese food''; a seller who labels a product with one of those names implies that the buyer has a right to expect that it will be as defined. Unless implied warranties are disclaimed before the sale, in writing, by the seller, they are automatically applied. The law of warranties for sales transactions is set forth in the UCC.

A **warranty** is a representation made by the seller to the buyer regarding the quality and performance of a product.

Product Liability

As shown in Chapter 22, a serious problem you face these days is product liability. An ever present question facing a small business is: How safe *should* the product be? Much attention is now being focused on the design of products and quality control to ensure product safety. But if all possible safety precautions were built into all products and their production, they'd be prohibitively expensive—and sometimes impossible to use. Thus, the degree of safety required depends on the product itself. While a defective compact disc may present only a minor inconvenience, the proper functioning of a heart pacemaker is a matter of life and death, so each pacemaker must be perfect.

For example, Cordis Corporation, a medical equipment manufacturer, pleaded guilty in 1989 to charges of selling thousands of defective pacemakers and batteries prone to corrode. In all, Cordis agreed to pay $564,000 in claims and penalties.[3]

Table 23–2   Some Selected Components of Property Law

Real property	Land or anything permanently attached to it.
Personal property	Anything of value that can be individually owned, other than land.
Deed	Transfer of ownership of real property.
Lease	Allows limited use of a property granted by the owner in writing.
Tangible property	Material good or product that can be touched, seen, and felt.
Intangible property	Represents ownership; examples are a stock certificate and a bank deposit book.
Title	Proof of ownership that may be conveyed.

Property

Property law involves the rights and duties resulting from the ownership or use of personal or real property. Contract, sales, and other types of law also apply to the transfer of such property. Table 23–2 presents some selected aspects of property law.

Patents, Copyrights, and Trademarks

The legal protection of personal property also includes protecting patents, copyrights, and trademarks.

A **patent** is a grant from the U.S. Patent and Trademark Office giving the inventor of a product the exclusive right to make, use, or sell the invention in the United States for 17 years from the date it is issued. After that time, the patent expires and cannot be renewed. In order to be patented, a device must be new, useful, and not obvious to a person in the related field of ordinary skill or knowledge. Inventors can enhance their chances of getting a patent by following the basic steps suggested by the Patent and Trademark Office.[4]

A **copyright** is the exclusive right that protects creators of "original works of authorship" such as artistic, literary, dramatic, and musical works. It protects only the form in which the idea is expressed, not the idea itself. While you can copyright something merely by claiming the right to do so, *Form TX must be filed with the Copyright Office of the Library of Congress to register the copyright.* A valid copyright lasts for the life of the creator plus 50 years. When a copyright expires, the work becomes public property and can be used by anyone, free of charge. The internationally recognized symbol © is used to designate a copyrighted work.

A **trademark** is any distinctive name, term, word, design, symbol, or device used to identify the origin of a product, or to distinguish it from other products on the market. Registration of a trademark prevents others from employing a similar mark to identify their products. In the United States, a trademark cannot be

A **patent** is a grant giving the inventor of a product the exclusive right to make, use, or sell it in the United States.

A **copyright** is the exclusive right that protects creators of "original" artistic, literary, dramatic, and musical works.

A **trademark** is a distinctive name, term, word, design, symbol, or device used to identify a product or to distinguish it from other products.

reserved in advance of its use. Instead, the owner must establish the right to a trademark by actually using it.

A registered trademark cannot keep anyone else from producing the same item, or from selling it under a different trademark. It merely prevents others from using the same or a confusingly similar trademark for the same or a similar product.

To register a trademark, the applicant must prove that it is distinctive. As long as a producer continues to use a trademark, no one can legally infringe upon it. But an owner may lose the exclusive right to a trademark if it loses its unique character and becomes a generic name. *Aspirin, cellophane, thermos,* and *shredded wheat* were once enforceable trademarks but, because of common usage, can no longer be licensed as a company's trademark. On the other hand, Velcro®, Kelly Girl®, Xerox®, and Kleenex® are still valid trademarks fiercely protected by their owners.

Agency

The term *agency* describes the legal relationship between a principal and an agent. The **principal** is the person who wants to do something but is unable or unwilling to do it personally. The **agent** is the person or company engaged to act on behalf of the principal. All types of business transactions, and many personal ones, involve agency.

> The **principal** is one who wants to do something but is unable or unwilling to do it personally.
>
> The **agent** is the person or company engaged to act on behalf of the principal.

Negotiable Instruments

Special laws are needed to deal with buying, owning, and selling negotiable instruments. A **negotiable instrument** is some form of financial document, such as a check, bank draft, or certificate of deposit, that is transferable from one party to another. The law requires that negotiable instruments be written, not oral; signed by the maker; good for the promise of a specified sum of money; and payable when endorsed by the payee.

> A **negotiable instrument** is a financial document that is transferable from one party to another.

Torts

A **tort** is a wrongful act by one party, not covered by criminal law, that results in injury to a second party's person, property, or reputation, for which the first party is liable. Laws dealing with torts provide for the performance of duties and compensation for the physical, mental, or economic injuries resulting from faulty products or actions of employees. This usually involves some form of economic restitution (monetary payment) for damages or losses incurred.

> A **tort** is a wrongful act by one party, not covered by criminal law, that results in injury to a second party's person, property, or reputation, for which the first party is liable.

For example, a man who tried to commit suicide by throwing himself in front of an incoming New York Metropolitan Transit Authority subway train won a $650,000 settlement because the train's operator "demonstrated negligence."[5]

Bankruptcy

Under **bankruptcy law**, people or businesses can petition the courts to be relieved of the obligation to pay debts they can't repay.

Under **bankruptcy law,** people or businesses can petition the courts to be relieved of the obligation to pay debts they can't repay. There are two types of bankruptcy, voluntary and involuntary. *Voluntary bankruptcy* occurs when a debtor files an application with a court claiming that debts exceed assets and asks to be declared bankrupt. When one or more creditors file the bankruptcy petition against the debtor, it's called *involuntary bankruptcy.* The Bankruptcy Reform Act of 1978 provides for quick and efficient handling of both types.

Chapter 11 provides for reorganizing a bankrupt business, whether the bankruptcy petition is filed voluntarily or involuntarily.

Chapter 11 of this act contains a provision for reorganizing the bankrupt business, whether the bankruptcy petition is filed voluntarily or involuntarily. Thus, the firm can continue to operate while its debts are being repaid. If the business is so far gone that it can't keep operating, it must be liquidated.

You should consult a lawyer as soon as possible, if your business is ever faced with a bankruptcy situation.

GOVERNMENT HELP FOR SMALL BUSINESSES

Many examples of assistance to small businesses have been given throughout this text. Because most such help is provided by the SBA and the U.S. Department of Commerce, their assistance will be summarized.

Small Business Administration (SBA)

As was shown in Chapter 9, the SBA provides many types of direct and guaranteed loans for small firms. Its publications, such as its series of Management Aids; local workshops; small business development centers; and small business institutes provide help for small firms. Also, information on overseas marketing is provided.

In addition, the SBA sponsors the *Service Corps of Retired Executives* (*SCORE*). SCORE's 750 chapters and satellites nationwide comprise 13,000 volunteer members who specialize in helping people develop their business ideas. As shown in the Profile, SCORE can match one or more of these counselors to a specific business. It can also call on its extensive roster of public relations experts, bankers, lawyers, and the like to answer the important and detailed questions you might have about setting up a business. They'll even work with you as long as you need after you start your business. Some clients consult with SCORE counselors for several years.

Another way the SBA helps is by encouraging small business owners to try to perform more effectively. It does this by making state and national awards for the "Small Business Persons of the Year." Figure 23–2 shows (former) president George Bush announcing the 1991 awards at the White House.

Figure 23–2   Former President George Bush Presenting Awards at White House Ceremonies for 1992 Small Business Week

Photo courtesy of Susan Biddle, The White House, May 12, 1992.

U.S. Department of Commerce

As indicated in earlier chapters, the U.S. Department of Commerce offers assistance through its International Trade Administration (ITA), its U.S. and Foreign Commercial Service Agency (USFCSA), and its Minority Business Development Agency (MBDA). Finally, the department's Census Bureau furnishes much demographic information. For small firms in a hurry, data may be obtained electronically, as shown in the Using Technology to Succeed.

Other Government Agencies

Among the other agencies helping small business are the U.S. Department of Agriculture—which provides assistance through the Cooperative Extension Service, the Federal Land Bank Association, the Production Credit Association, and the Farmers Home Administration—and the IRS. In addition, a wide range of state and local agencies provide help when contacted.

HANDLING GOVERMNENT REGULATIONS AND PAPERWORK

As we mentioned in Chapter 1, if you want to see a small business person become incensed, mention government regulations and paperwork, which are a growing

━━━━━   USING TECHNOLOGY TO SUCCEED   **━━━━━**

THE COMMERCE DEPARTMENT REPORTS BY COMPUTER

Many small business owners need information and economic reports from the government much more quickly than they can receive them by mail. Now, the U.S. Department of Commerce makes electronic data available to small businesses that have computers and modems. Data can be obtained on subjects such as consumer prices, trade figures, retail sales, housing starts, gross national product, and other timely topics of interest.

The department charges small firms a $35 registration fee, which includes $12 worth of access time. The charge for time is approximately 20 cents per minute in the daytime and 5 cents per minute at night. For more details about this service, call the Commerce Department at (202) 482-1986 and request the Economic Bulletin Board (EBB).

problem. At one time, smaller firms were exempt from many federal regulations and even some state and local ones. Today, though, these firms tend to be regulated the same as their larger competitors. These regulations are numerous, complex, costly, and often confusing or contradictory, as the following example illustrates.

According to Ron Smith, Colorado director of the National Federation of Independent Business, his state recently repealed laws requiring retail stores to get special licenses to sell ice or foil packages of aspirin. Still on the books, though, is a regulation saying hospitals will be fined if they don't present their annual budgets to the Colorado Hospital—which "was abolished four years ago."[6]

It is difficult to understand and comply with governmental requirements. While most businesspeople are willing to obey the law, compliance is often very complex, arduous, time-consuming, and expensive. Rochester Institute of Technology economist Thomas Hopkins, a former Office of Management and Budget deputy administrator, puts the 1991 pricetag of U.S. regulations for all U.S. businesses at "a half-trillion dollars—nearly 10 percent of the nation's gross domestic product."[7] Murray Weidenbaum, a Washington university professor, found that 150,000 small firms will have to spend more than $10,000 each *just* for pollution permits under the 1990 Clean Air Act.[8]

As an example of these costs, Mereco Technologies Inc., a Rhode Island maker of adhesives for the aerospace and electronics industries, "had to hire three chemists to work 40 hours a week for six months to write" information on more than 800 chemical products in order "to satisfy an array of overlapping state and federal rules."[9]

Dealing with Regulatory Agencies

In theory, a *regulatory agency* is more flexible and sensitive to the needs of society than Congress can be, since less time is needed for an agency to develop and issue new regulations than for Congress to enact new legislation. Experience, however, doesn't seem to support this theory. Many small business managers believe, for example, that on occasion an agency's findings may be arbitrary or may protect its own security or that of the industry it's supposed to regulate.

Some Benefits of Regulation

Do the benefits of government regulation outweigh the costs? Since there's no profit mechanism to measure this, as there is in private business, and since both costs and benefits are hard to determine, estimates must be made. Even with these measurement limitations, though, it's been shown that some regulations are truly cost-effective.

For example, air pollution requirements have provided economic benefits that far outweigh the costs of complying with them, according to the White House Council on Environmental Quality.[10]

Finally, when regulations are imposed on one industry or business they often generate opportunities for other small entrepreneurs.

For example, when the EPA announced standards for replacements for automobile catalytic converters six years ago, it created a market for replacement models that could be made more cheaply, because they didn't have to last as long. Perfection Automotive Products Corp., of Livonia, Michigan, broadened its product line to make them. It added nearly 100 employees, doubling its previous work force, to serve the market.[11]

Some Problems with Regulation

There are at least three areas of concern that small firms have with government regulations. The first problem *is the difficulty of understanding some of the regulations,* as well as the confusing and often restrictive nature of some laws and regulations, as the case at the end of this chapter illustrates. A second problem is *the enormous amount of paperwork involved in preparing and handling the reports needed to comply with government regulations and in maintaining the records needed to satisfy the regulators.* A third problem is *the difficulty and cost of complying with the regulations.* The costs are greater than just the administrative expenses; bringing actual operations into compliance with the regulations is also expensive, as the following example illustrates.

Some states require more than $1 million of liability insurance for the entrepreneur who selects bungee jumping for a product. All states now have very strict regulations and stiff inspection fees. These new requirements are rapidly weeding out a lot of small businesses involved in bungee jumping. In 1991, bungee jumping businesses were soaring beyond anyone's wildest dreams; now they are simply bobbing along very cautiously.[12]

How Small Firms Can Cope with Regulations

What can small business managers do about burdensome government regulations and paperwork? There are several approaches to consider.

1. Learn as much as you can about the law, particularly if it is possible that a law can help you.

2. Challenge detrimental or harmful laws, perhaps by joining organizations such as the National Federation of Independent Business, the National Small Business Association, or National Small Business United.

3. Become involved in the legal-political system to elect officials of your choosing who will help change the laws. Close to 40 members of the National Federation of Independent Business ran for Congress in 1992, with the encouragement of the Small Business Legislative Council.[13]

4. Find a better legal environment, if possible, even if it means moving to a different city, county, or state.

5. Learn to live with the laws and regulations.

CHOOSING AND USING A LAWYER

You can see from the previous discussion that, from a legal point of view, it isn't easy to start and operate a small business. Therefore, one of the first things you should do when forming a business is to retain a competent lawyer. Actually, your attorney should be retained at the time you are developing your business plan, as well as when you are obtaining financing—not when you get in trouble.

Choosing the Lawyer

You should choose a lawyer as you would a consultant, an accountant, or anyone else who provides services. Comparison shop! Check the credentials of different attorneys! Discuss fees with them candidly! And, whatever you do, don't forget to talk with them about the wisdom of retaining legal counsel. For example, does it make sense to spend $500 in legal fees and court costs to recover a $300 bad debt?

Where to Look

How do you look for a lawyer? The first and most obvious step is to define the nature of your legal problem. Once you have defined the problem, there are a number of ways to find a lawyer to help you with it. The American Bar Association recommends four sources:[14]

1. *Personal referral* from someone whose opinion you value, such as your banker, your minister, a relative, or another lawyer.

2. The *Martindale-Hubbell Law Directory,* which is the most nearly complete roster—as up-to-date as possible—of the members of the bar in the United States and Canada.

3. *Lawyer Referral and Information Services* (*LRS*), which are provided by most bar associations in larger cities.

4. *Advertising,* since lawyers can now advertise certain information in newspapers and the Yellow Pages and on radio and television.

What to Look For

First, look for appropriate experience with your type of small business. While you may not necessarily rely on the lawyer for business advice, the one chosen should at least have sufficient background and information about the particulars of your business and its problems to represent you effectively.[15]

Second, since there should be compatibility between lawyer and client, observe the lawyer's demeanor, the style and atmosphere of his or her office, and any clients—if possible (Does the lawyer represent a competitor?)—before making your choice.

Third, does the lawyer have time for you and your business? If you have difficulty getting an appointment or are repeatedly kept waiting on the phone, you should probably look elsewhere.

Finally, since cost is an important consideration, do not hesitate to discuss fees with the prospective attorney, for performance must be balanced against the cost of the service provided. Lawyers' time is expensive!

Maintaining Relationships with Your Attorney

Lawyers usually have three basic ways of charging for their services. First, a flat fee may be charged for a specific assignment. Thus, the cost of the service is known, and funds can be allocated for it. Second, the lawyer may charge an hourly fee based on the type of activities to be performed and the amount of staff assistance required. Third, a contingency fee may be set. If the stakes are really high, and if time and risks are involved, the attorney may charge a percentage (say 30 percent) of the negotiated settlement, or even more if the amount is obtained through a trial (as high as 50 percent), as shown in the sample contract in Figure 23–3.

Also, the lawyer will expect to be reimbursed for expenses. In long, involved cases, the lawyer should provide periodic reports, including a statement of expenses.

Figure 23–3　A Sample Contract for a Lawyer's Services

I, Jane Doe, hereby agree to employ the law firm of Richard Roe to represent me and act on my behalf and in my best interest in presenting a claim for any and all damages, including my personal injury, resulting from an accident which occurred on or about June 29, 1993, near Bethesda, Maryland.

I agree to pay to said firm an amount equal to 30 percent of any and all sums collected by way of settlement or from legal action. In the event of trial (as determined as of the time a jury is impaneled), I agree to pay said firm an amount equal to 50 percent of any amounts received.

Be it further understood that no settlement will be made without consent of client.

It is understood that if nothing is obtained on client's behalf, then client owes nothing to said law firm, except for the expenses associated with handling this case.

Said law firm agrees to act on client's behalf with all due diligence and in client's best interest at all times in prosecuting said claims.

DATED this _____ day of _____, 19___

Richard Roe
By:_____

SOCIALLY AND ETHICALLY RESPONSIBLE BEHAVIOR

While most small business people have long accepted—and practiced—social responsibility and ethical behavior, considerable external emphasis is now being placed on these topics.

Social Responsibility

Social responsibility is a business's obligation to follow desirable courses of action in terms of society's values and objectives.

Social responsibility is a business's obligation to set policies, make decisions, and follow courses of action that are desirable in terms of the values and objectives of society. Whether that term is used or not, it means that the business acts with the best interests of society in mind, as well as those of the business.

Social responsibility as practiced by small firms usually takes the form of (1) consumerism, (2) employee relations, and (3) environmental protection.

Consumerism

Consumerism is the organized efforts of independent, government, and business groups to protect consumers from undesirable effects of poorly designed and produced products.

Consumerism is the organized efforts of independent, government, and business groups to protect consumers from undesirable effects of poorly designed and poorly produced products. As shown in Part III, the consumerism movement became popular during the 1960s and 1970s. The Child Protection and Toy Safety Act set up the Consumer Product Safety Commission (CPSC) to set safety standards, require warning labels on potentially unsafe products, and require recall of products found to be harmful.

Employee Relations

Enlightened **employee relations** involves a concern for employee rights, especially as to meaningful employment; training, development, and promotions; pay; and health and safety. As shown in Part IV, there is now a greater effort to hire qualified persons without regard to race, sex, religion, color, creed, age, or disabilities. While much is still to be done, small firms have made tremendous strides in this area.

Enlightened **employee relations** is showing interest in and concern for employees' rights.

Environmental Protection

Environmental protection is trying to maintain a healthy balance between people and their environment. It takes two forms, namely, conserving natural resources and preventing pollution. The problem is very complex; it involves balancing our current use of natural resources and also conserving them for future use. The real problem—from a small business perspective—is balancing environmental needs with economic ones. This is becoming increasingly difficult; for example, recent court rulings have held banks liable when their customers pollute, so banks are demanding an environmental audit and proof that you've never polluted.[16]

Environmental protection tries to maintain a healthy balance between people and their environment.

In 1980, the Bank of Montana—Butte lent $275,000 to a local firm that coated telephone poles with PCP and other chemicals to protect against bugs and rot. The firm left behind a heavily contaminated site when it failed in 1984. Projected cost of the cleanup was $10–$15 million, which regulators tried to obtain from former owners—including the bank, whose total capital was $2.4 million.[17]

Business Ethics

Business ethics are the standards used to judge the rightness or wrongness of a business's relations to others. Small business people are expected to deal ethically with employees, customers, competitors, and others. For example, ethical behavior is expected in decisions concerning bribery, industrial theft and espionage, collusion, tax evasion, false and/or misleading advertising, and conflicts of interest, as well as in personal conduct, such as loyalty, confidentiality, respecting others' privacy, and truthfulness.[18]

Business ethics are the standards used to judge the rightness or wrongness of a business's relations to others.

Many large and small companies are embracing business ethics in order to be socially responsible, while others do it to enhance profits. How do social responsibility and ethical behavior affect profits? While the final answer isn't in yet, it can be answered in the negative: "Doing the wrong thing can be costly."[19]

In general, if you launch a business-ethics program solely to enhance profits—*or* only to be socially responsible—the program will fail at the first sign of trouble.[20] Instead, socially responsible behavior and profits are both needed.

Figure 23–4   Low-Grade Government

Percentage of people who feel these groups have good moral and ethical standards:

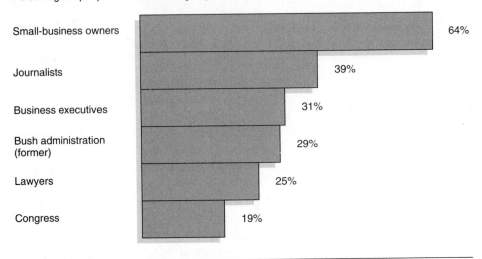

Small-business owners   64%

Journalists   39%

Business executives   31%

Bush administration
(former)   29%

Lawyers   25%

Congress   19%

Source: Harris Poll of 1,256 adults, as reported in *USA Today,* September 3, 1992, p. 1A. © 1992, USA TODAY. Adapted with permission.

What course are you to follow, then? As a minimum, the public expects small business owners and managers to obey both the letter and the spirit of laws affecting their operations. Finally, they should go beyond laws and social responsibility to behavior based on ethical considerations. Sometimes, though, it is difficult for the small business to act ethically and still satisfy the customer. Apparently, as shown in Figure 23–4, small businesses are succeeding better than big business executives, lawyers, Congress, and others.

Perhaps your best test of ethical behavior is Rotary International's Four-Way Test. In making a decision, ask yourself:

1. Is it the truth?
2. Is it fair to all concerned?
3. Will it build goodwill and better relationships?
4. Will it be beneficial to all?

WHAT YOU SHOULD HAVE LEARNED

1. The U.S. legal system is based on many principles, including (*a*) everyone is equal under the law, (*b*) everyone is entitled to a day in court, (*c*) a person is presumed to be innocent until proven guilty, and (*d*) there are multiple levels of government—and laws. The most important areas of business laws for

small firms are (*a*) contracts; (*b*) sales; (*c*) property; (*d*) patents, copyrights, and trademarks; (*e*) agency; (*f*) negotiable instruments; (*g*) torts; and (*h*) bankruptcy. Many of these laws, which differ in the various states, have been codified into the Uniform Commercial Code.

2. Both the federal and local governments provide considerable assistance for small businesses. The SBA, U.S. Department of Commerce, U.S. Department of Agriculture, Internal Revenue Service, and other agencies provide assistance.

3. There is considerable regulation and paperwork from government agencies, which causes problems for small firms, including (*a*) difficulty of understanding some of the regulations, which may be confusing and even contradictory; (*b*) enormous amounts of paperwork needed to comply with them; and (*c*) the difficulty and cost of complying with the regulations.

    Small firms can cope with regulation by (*a*) learning about the laws and using them for their benefit; (*b*) challenging detrimental or harmful laws and trying to get them modified or repealed; (*c*) becoming involved in the legal-political system; (*d*) finding a better legal environment, if possible; and (*e*) learning to live with the laws.

4. In choosing a lawyer, look for one who's familiar with small business activities, as well as with the problems you are facing. You can use the local lawyer referral service, talk to friends, or use word of mouth in searching for a competent lawyer. Some criteria for choosing a lawyer are to be sure that (*a*) the lawyer is knowledgeable about your type of business, (*b*) you and the lawyer are compatible, (*c*) the lawyer has time to deal with you and your business, and (*d*) the costs are not prohibitive.

5. Small businesses are expected to act in an ethical and socially responsible manner in dealing with employees, customers, and the public, and to consider not only the owners but also others in making decisions that affect them. Most small businesses have always acted ethically and responsibly—and continue to do so. As a minimum, small business owners are expected to obey both the letter and the spirit of laws affecting them.

QUESTIONS FOR DISCUSSION

1. What is the Uniform Commercial Code?
2. What is a contract? What are the elements necessary to make a contract legal?
3. What is a warranty? Distinguish between *express* and *implied* warranties.
4. What are a patent, a copyright, and a trademark? How are these protected under U.S. law?

5. Distinguish between voluntary, involuntary bankruptcy, and Chapter 11 bankruptcy.

6. Describe some of the assistance available to small firms from government agencies.

7. Explain the five ways in which small firms can cope with regulations.

8. Describe the characteristics you should look for in a lawyer. How would you find such a lawyer? How are lawyers compensated for their services?

9. What is social responsibility? Why is it important to small firms?

10. What are business ethics, and why are they so important?

THE GROUNDED CHARTER BOAT SERVICE

For 18 years, Wilfred Allick, Jr., like his father before him, ran a charter boat service to the Buck Island Reef National Monument near St. Croix in the U.S. Virgin Islands. But in the mid-1970s, believing there were too many charter boat operators carrying tourists to Buck Island, the National Park Service (NPS) began licensing operators and regulating charter rates to stop "predatory price cutting." According to Leonard Hall, in charge of concessions for the Park Service in the southeastern United States, including the Virgin Islands, Allick is one of the best operators around and has done nothing to harm the national monument.

In 1982, however, when Allick took longer than the Park Service allowed to replace the mast on his sailboat, the agency terminated his permit. Allick worked for other charter boat operators for a while and then reapplied for a Buck Island permit in 1988, but it was denied.

Buck Island Reef National Monument, Virgin Islands
Photo courtesy of the National Park Service.

Explaining, "I just want to make an honest living," Allick felt very frustrated. In 1989, he was trying to start his own charter service to other sites in the area. Also, he considered filing suit against the Park Service.

The Park Service's policy of stopping price cutting has apparently worked, for where there were once 23 operators, there were only 7 in 1989. In fact, according to Hall, the Park Service was then more worried about "price gouging" than price cutting.

QUESTIONS

1. What does this case show about the nature of government regulation?

2. What would you do now if you were Mr. Allick?

3. If the Park Service were truly interested in preventing "price gouging," what could it do about it?

Source: John R. Emshwiller, "Agencies Block Competition by Small Firms," *The Wall Street Journal,* July 26, 1989, pp. B1, B2. Reprinted by permission of THE WALL STREET JOURNAL, © 1989 Dow Jones & Company, Inc. All Rights Reserved Worldwide.

24

Planning for the Future

Time present and time past
Are perhaps both contained in time future,
And time future contained in time past.
—T. S. Eliot

And 'tis a shameful sight,
When children of one family
Fall out, and chide, and fight.
—Isaac Watts

LEARNING OBJECTIVES

After studying the material in this chapter, you will be able to:

1. Discuss some of the problems involved in organizing and operating small family-owned businesses.

2. Explain how family relationships can affect the business.

3. Discuss the importance and method of preparing for management succession.

4. Describe the activities needed to prepare the next generation to enter the firm.

5. Discuss the need for tax and estate planning in small companies.

KEEPING THE BUSINESS IN THE FAMILY

Joe Teague and his wife, Margaret, owned and operated Teague Brothers Carpet Sales & Service and Teague Brothers Transfer & Storage Co., Inc. (See Profile of Chapter 16 for details.) Because of the pressure of running both businesses, the Teagues decided to sell the moving company in 1988. Their daughter, Dottie Teague Wesley, who had handled the business aspects of the moving company for four years, bought it from them. Her reason: "My father started it in 1955, and because it carried my family's name, and was part of my life, I decided to accept the challenge." Now, she's the boss and runs all aspects of Teague Brothers Transfer & Storage Co., Inc.

Dottie Teague Wesley bought Teague Brothers Moving & Storage Co. to keep the business in the family.

Photo by J. P. Schaffner, The Mobile Press Register, Inc. © 1993. All Rights Reserved.

When Dottie started working in the trucking business in 1984, she and her father had several "knock-down, dragouts," since he didn't think she knew how to run a "man's business." But when he saw that she could do the job, he began to respect her abilities and helped her learn to communicate and work with the men and women in the moving industry. In fact, in 1989, she was a winner of the Career Club "Outstanding Career Woman" award. And now, she tries to be assertive in an appropriate manner while retaining the feminine aspect—the kind and gentle part.

She laughingly says her previous experience was selling Amway products and Girl Scout cookies, and taking several basic business courses. And, as a kid, she worked at the company doing packing and running errands. Now, she runs the entire business! In two years, her employees increased from 5 to 12, along with some part-timers.

Her children have been very supportive, as have her parents. During the time she was learning to run the business, the American Business Women's Association helped her, through its seminars, to expand her business potential, in addition to providing her with many business contacts.

After working in the office doing accounting and scheduling work for two years, she hired a secretary to handle the phone calls, which allowed her to go out and make sales calls. Keeping in touch with former customers, regardless of what you may have done for them in the past, is necessary if you want to continue getting their business, she says.

Source: Conversation with Joe and Margaret Teague, Dottie Teague Wesley, and other sources, including Marion Valentino, "Taking an Old Favorite to the Cleaners," *Mobile* (Alabama), *Press Register,* August 24, 1986, p. 14–F; Carol Cain Lynn, "Business All in the Family," *Mobile* (Alabama) *Press Register,* August 6, 1989, p. 3–E; and Kathy Jumper, "She's a Real Mover and a Shaker," *Mobile* (Alabama) *Press Register,* November 11, 1990, p. 1–E.

Many small business owners aren't as fortunate as the Teagues. Instead of providing for their business to continue, they put off selecting a successor until it is too late. Many family-business executives, facing possible retirement, feel that finding a successor can be done quickly. But the odds are against them. It has been estimated that fewer than one-third of U.S. family businesses pass successfully from the first to the second generation, and only 15 percent make it to the third generation.[1]

Over 80 percent of all U.S. businesses—large, medium, and small—are family owned, and they account for 50 percent of our gross national product, as well as half of our work force.[2] Yet, as indicated, only about one out of seven of them makes it to the third generation, often because of unwillingness or inability to deal with the challenges that are unique to family-run enterprises.[3] But most small business owners don't like to talk about the question of succession. Perhaps this reflects a denial of their own mortality, the same instinct that makes people reluctant to make a will. However, to be realistic in assuring the continuation of your business, or in providing an ongoing concern for family members to operate, you must look at this question analytically. We do that in this chapter.

ROLE OF FAMILY-OWNED BUSINESSES

While family-owned businesses provide a living and personal satisfaction for many people, they must be managed just like any other small firm if they are to succeed. Family businesses are the backbone of America, but they can also be a source of unresolved family tensions and conflicts, which can create obstacles to achieving even the most basic business goals.[4] When close relatives work together, emotions often interfere with business decisions. Also, unique problems, such as the departure of the founder-owner, develop in family-owned firms. When more than one family member is involved, emotions and differing value systems can cause conflicts between members.[5]

The Family and the Business

We usually think of family businesses as being started, owned, and operated by the parents, with children helping out and later taking over. This has been the normal pattern, as many examples in the text have shown. Now, though, two contrary trends are developing. First, many young people are going into business for themselves—and tapping their parents for funds to finance their ventures. In return, the children often give one or both parents an executive position in the company, including a seat on the company's board. Also, many retirees want to work part-time for the children's businesses, without assuming a lot of responsibility.

For example, the two brothers who run the Levy Organization in Chicago employ their mother as a hostess at one of their restaurants. They even named a deli after her and use her recipes. According to Mark Levy, the company's vice chairman, "My mom is a very integral part of our business."[6]

Another trend is the large number of spouses doing business together. We used to think of married couples running a small neighborhood store, toiling long hours for a modest living. Now, though, a new breed of husband-and-wife entrepreneurs has emerged. They typically run a service enterprise out of their home and use computers, modems, and phone lines as the tools of their trade. As shown in Chapter 2, while there was a 42 percent increase in all proprietorships during a recent period, the SBA found that joint proprietorships of husbands and wives jumped 63 percent.

Although ownership of a small firm is usually controlled by one or a few family members, many others in the larger family are often involved. The spouse and children are vitally interested because the business is the source of their livelihood. In addition, some relatives may be employed by the firm, some may have investments in it, and some may perform various services for it.

The founder-owner may set any one or more of a variety of goals, such as adequate income and perpetuation of the business, high sales, service to the community, support of family, and production of an unusual product, just to name a few. This variety of goals exists in all companies, but in family firms strong family ties can improve the chances of consensus and support, while dissensions can lead to disagreement and/or disruption of activities.

Family Interactions

Usually the founder—or a close descendant—is the head of a small business. Relatives may be placed in high positions in the company, while other positions are filled by nonfamily members. In some cases, it is expected that the next head of the firm will be a family member and other members will move up through the ranks, according to their position in the family. Family ties can cause friction when ownership and management are not dealt with separately. When family members are treated preferentially, nonfamily employees may become disgruntled or quit.[7]

Family members' sense of ''ownership'' can be a strong, positive motivator in building the business and leading to greater cooperation, as happened with Bloomin' Lollipops, in the Profile in Chapter 4. The opposite can also be true, however. Conflicts can occur because each relative looks at the business from a different perspective. Relatives who are silent partners, stockholders, or directors may see only dollar signs when judging capital expenditures, growth, and other important matters. On the other hand, relatives involved in daily operations may

Cartoon © 1989 by Doug Blackwell. Reprinted with permission.

judge those matters from the viewpoint of marketing, operations, and personnel necessary to make the firm successful.

How to Deal with Incompetent Family Members

A related problem can be the inability of family members to make objective decisions about one another's skills and abilities. Unfortunately, their quarrels and ill feelings may spread to include nonfamily employees. One possible solution is to convince family members, as well as nonfamily employees, that their interests are best served by a profitable firm with strong leadership, as the following example illustrates.

The Chapman House grew into a profitable chain of restaurants, motels, and textile industries. In time, the second generation took over many activities from the matriarch, and the third generation began its entry into the business. This resulted in an overexpansion of activities, an increase in internal conflicts, and a decrease in profitability. The death of the matriarch was followed by 90 days of internal strife.

Then a third-generation family member with an M.B.A. and previous employment experience in a major industrial corporation developed some centralized objectives and an organizational structure appropriate to reaching the objectives. After that, most family members recognized that they should keep the business intact and expand only in those areas offering the best return on investment.

Some members want to become chief executive officer of the business but do not have the talents or training needed. Some others may have the talents, but because of their youth or inexperience, these talents may not be recognized.

Family members with little ability to contribute to the firm can be placed in jobs where they do not disturb other employees. Sometimes, though, relatives can demoralize the business by their dealings with other employees or customers or by loafing on the job, avoiding unpleasant tasks, or taking special privileges. They may be responsible for the high turnover rate of top-notch nonfamily managers and employees. Such relatives should be assigned to jobs allowing minimal contact with other employees. In some cases, attitudes may be changed by formal or informal education.

How to Compensate Family Members

Compensating family members and dividing profits among them can also be difficult because some of them may feel they contribute more to the success of the firm than others. Compensation should therefore be based on job performance, not family position. Fringe benefits can be useful as financial rewards, but they must conform to those given to nonfamily employees. Stock can be established as part of the compensation plan. Deferred profit-sharing plans, pension plans, insurance programs, and stock purchase programs can all be effective in placating disgruntled family members.

Family Limitations

Entrepreneurs tend to be specialists in an activity such as marketing, production, or finance, so they aren't usually good general managers. While managerial skills can be developed over a period of time through training and/or experience, the skill of sometimes saying no to family members wanting to enter the business may still be missing.

Another problem is that family managers may feel it is necessary to clear routine matters with the top family member. Also, bottlenecks that work against efficient operations can be caused by personality clashes and emotional reactions. Therefore, lines of authority and responsibility in the company must be clear and separated from those in the family. This is an important distinction because a person's age often determines the lines of authority in a family, while ability must be the primary guide in a business.

The number of competent family members from whom to choose the managers of the company is usually limited. Some members do not want to join—or are not capable of joining—the company in any position; some are only capable of filling lower-level jobs; and some are not willing to take the time or expend the effort to prepare themselves for a management position. So it's amazing that so many family businesses have such good leadership—family and nonfamily. But, as the leader grows older, he or she must keep up with the times and guard against letting past successes lead to conforming to the things of the past by trying to maintain the status quo.

For example, the five stockholders of Donald & Asby, engineers, established a policy of encouraging growth. One of the younger stockholders suggested using media advertising to obtain new business. But Mr. Donald, who had helped found the firm 30 years earlier, said that this would produce an undesirable type of growth. He suggested that they continue to depend on the company's reputation to expand requests for job proposals. How do you think the stockholders decided? Why?

Some families form their businesses into corporations and hire professional managers to run them when no members are in positions to manage or no agreement can be reached on who should run the company. This solution has the advantages of using professional management, freeing family time for other purposes, reducing friction, and having employees treated more fairly. However, the disadvantages are loss of a personal touch, reduced family employment, lower income, concentration of power in small cliques, and difficulties in finding and keeping a good management team.

Family Resources

The amount of capital available within the family may limit expansion. While family resources and contacts may be adequate for a small business, as the company grows, the borrowing power is limited by the amount of family assets. Then, family members may disagree about such issues as the following: Should money be obtained by borrowing, issuing stock, selling assets, or other financial techniques? Should planning be for the short or long run? Because of the diversity of opinion, even the choice of a consultant can be controversial.

Preparing the Next Generation

It might be assumed that children (or grandchildren) automatically want to enter the family business. But this isn't always true. A growing problem facing many small family businesses today is apathy on the part of offspring. Often, children who are reared in a small business become bored or uninterested, or simply lack the drive and desire to succeed that their parents displayed. They may feel that since the business has supported them in the past, it will continue to do so in the future.

What does lead children to follow in their parent's footsteps? A survey by Nancy Bowman-Upton of Baylor University found that the two primary reasons were money and liking the business. Figure 24–1 shows the importance of these and other reasons for joining the family business.

Start at Part-Time or Full-Time Job(s)?

One way to prepare children to take over the family business is to let them work on simple jobs, or on a part-time basis, which provides insights that may influence

Figure 24–1   Reasons Why Children Join Family Businesses*

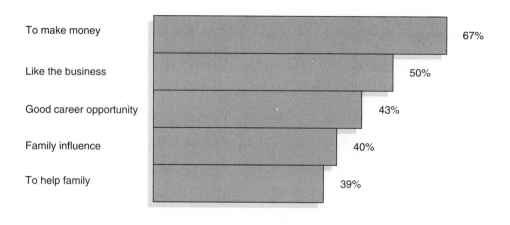

To make money	67%
Like the business	50%
Good career opportunity	43%
Family influence	40%
To help family	39%

*Respondents could give more than one answer.
Source: Survey by Nancy Bowman-Upton, Baylor University, as reported in *The Wall Street Journal,* May 19, 1989, p. B1. Adapted with permission of THE WALL STREET JOURNAL, © 1989 Dow Jones & Company, Inc. All Rights Reserved Worldwide.

them into— or away from— the business. The experience often encourages them to finish their education, in order to be better prepared when it's their turn to run the business.

Another form of preparation is working for another company in order to broaden their training and background. Such experience helps justify moving a family member into the family business at a higher level. For example, a study by the Los Angeles accounting firm of Laventhal & Horwath found that the vast majority of owners of family firms thought children should have outside experience, either as their own boss or working for someone else, before joining the family business. As you can see from Figure 24–2, 65 percent of respondents felt this way.

Start at Entry-Level or Higher-Level Position(s)?

Should a family member start in an entry-level job in order to learn the business from the ground up? There is some disagreement on this point, but none about the need for knowing the business, regardless of how it's done. The following are some techniques that have worked for others:

- Never allow a child to work in senior management until he or she has worked for someone else for at least two years.
- Rotate the person in varying positions.
- Give promotions only as they are earned.

Figure 24–2   When Should Children Join Family Businesses?

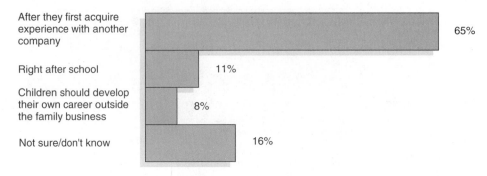

When asked when their children should join the company, surveyed owners of family businesses said:

After they first acquire experience with another company — 65%

Right after school — 11%

Children should develop their own career outside the family business — 8%

Not sure/don't know — 16%

Source: Laventhal & Horwath, as reported in *The Wall Street Journal,* December 19, 1989, p. 25. Adapted with permission of THE WALL STREET JOURNAL, © 1988 Dow Jones & Company, Inc. All Rights Reserved Worldwide.

- Devote at least half an hour each day to face-to-face teaching and training.
- Don't take business matters home.[8]

If the newcomer is really to learn the business, true responsibility must be given. Otherwise, the person cannot learn to manage the business, as the following example shows.

A son who took over his father's business said, "My father had difficulty trusting me. It's not what you might think. He just didn't want to see me fail. When he saw that something I was doing might not pan out, he would step in and take over. I never had a chance to fail."

Thus, when he took over the business, making it work was very difficult, but he finally succeeded.[9]

PREPARING FOR MANAGEMENT SUCCESSION

Any business must be ready for changes in its top management. It's not enough to select a person to step into the top job when it becomes vacant. That key job requires much training and experience, because the decisions the person makes can vitally affect the company and its future. Thus, every transfer of ownership and power is an invitation to disaster. In order to prevent that from happening, the owner should do two things: *Plan early and carefully, and groom a successor!*

Why Succession Is a Problem

When preparing someone for management succession, many small business owners have some grave concerns about passing the business on to their children. In the

Figure 24–3   Who Will Take Charge?

Family-business owners with two or more children working for the company were surveyed. Here's a breakdown of how they said they intend to resolve the issue of who will take over when the owners step aside:

35% plan to groom one child from an early age to take over.

25% plan to let the children compete and to choose one or more successors with help from the board of directors.

15% plan to let the children compete and choose one or more successors without input from a third party.

15% plan to form an "executive committee" of two or more children.

10% plan to let the children choose their own leader or leaders.

Source: John Ward, professor at Loyola University of Chicago's Graduate School of Business, as reported in Buck Brown, "Succession Strategies for Family Firms," *The Wall Street Journal,* August 4, 1988, p. 23. Reprinted by permission of THE WALL STREET JOURNAL, © 1988 Dow Jones & Company, Inc. All Rights Reserved Worldwide.

previously mentioned survey by Nancy Bowman-Upton, it was found that the main concern was treating all children fairly. Of the entrepreneurs surveyed, 31 percent gave this as their main concern. Another 22 percent were concerned about the reaction of nonfamily employees. And 20 percent gave family communication, conflict, and estate taxes as concerns.[10]

Another trend is having two or more children succeed the parent in running the business. As Figure 24–3 shows, a study by John Ward, a professor at Loyola University's Graduate School of Business, found that 55 percent of family-owned firms say they want to include two or more children in future ownership or management of the family business.

For example, when Somer Obernauer retired, his daughter Lorie and her brother, Somer, Jr., split ownership and management of the firm. She became executive vice-president, in charge of sales, while he became president, in charge of accounting. They were already essentially running the Keystone Ribbon & Floral Supply Company, according to Lorie: "I was in charge out front, and he was in charge in back. We each had our own territory."[11]

If family members are going to be used to run the business, rather than bring in outsiders, ongoing training should begin early. Early on, one or more replacements should be started on the path toward taking over the reins of the firm. This process sometimes works, but sometimes it does not, as the case at the end of the chapter illustrates.

When the choice of replacements is limited, the owner may consider reorganizing the present assignments and using present managers more effectively. The job specifications for a new manager may be written more broadly to widen the range of choices. All present managers—family and nonfamily—should partici- pate in this planning so that they feel they have contributed to the decision.

An Overlooked Problem

In most firms, the development of managerial personnel and the provision for management succession are greatly neglected, often until it is too late to do anything about it. According to one expert, "The lack of planning for the company's future is the most common, and most fatal, flaw in family businesses."[12]

Yet research studies indicate that most entrepreneurs simply don't want to face the inevitable. For example, in interviews with 400 owners of small companies across the United States, Peter Collins, head of Buckingham Associates, a New York consulting firm, found that 85 percent *had no formal plan* to leave their business. Moreover, 31 percent had "no idea at all how they would exit their business."[13]

In another survey of fast-growing small companies, Coopers & Lybrand found that only 51 percent of the CEOs of small businesses had a management-succession plan in place, and only 38 percent had put it in writing.[14]

PLAN AHEAD!

Management succession occurs when the family leader (1) dies, (2) becomes incapacitated, (3) leaves the company—voluntarily or otherwise—or (4) retires. Therefore, in order to avoid family succession problems, entrepreneurs should start planning for their replacements as much as 10 to 15 years ahead of the actual passing of power, according to John Schoen of Baylor University's Institute for Family Business in Waco, Texas.[15] Such a comprehensive succession plan in- volves more than just laying out the role of the younger generation in the business and ownership of the business. Instead, operating authority must pass from one generation to the next. These plans should be flexible enough to include (1) a sudden departure or (2) a planned one.

Sudden Departure

A successful business must continue to operate even when the owner/manager leaves, for whatever reason. Plans can easily be made for vacations because they are of short duration, they require a limited number of decisions, and the vaca- tioner is available if needed. In fact, when the owner takes a vacation, a form of on-the-job training is provided for those left in charge. Those persons can take over temporarily under those circumstances.

But the sudden death or incapacity of the owner can be very disruptive if not adequately provided for. If the owner has left no will or instructions on what to do, family members will probably have conflicting opinions about what should be done. For this reason, an owner should make a will and keep it current, including instructions about what should be done in—or with—the business.

As shown in Chapter 22, the firm can take out life insurance on the owner(s), the proceeds from which will go to the company in case of death. This money can be used to help the business operate until it recovers from the loss of its owner-manager.

Planned Departure

When owners plan to leave or retire, they have a number of options, as shown in Figure 24–4. If the company is a corporation, there will probably be less controversy, because the replacement top officer should be known by the time the owner departs, and the transition should go smoothly. The board of directors can select a family or nonfamily employee, or an outsider, for the top job. The handling of the stock can be delayed, but stock retention may give the new key executive the feeling that the departed one is still looking over his or her shoulder.

The entire family tends to become involved in the replacement decision in proprietorships and partnerships. Therefore, in planning for departure, the owner should look for someone in the family able and willing to take over. This person(s) may already be recognized as the "heir apparent."

Notice in the Keystone Ribbon & Floral Supply Company example that both the daughter (Lorie) and the son (Somer, Jr.) were designated "heirs apparent."

Selling to Family Member(s)

If the transition is to be complete, the business should be sold to the offspring so that full responsibility is handed over to them. The advantages of this type of change for the original owner are as follows:

- The business stays in the family.
- It provides a source of employment for family members.
- The family's stature is maintained.
- The former owner is free to relax or travel.
- There is pleasure when the successor is successful.
- It can strengthen family bonds rather than produce additional family friction.

Selling to Outsiders

If no relative will assume responsibility for the running of the business, the owner can sell out to a partner or an outsider, or can even close the business.

Figure 24–4   Options for Replacing Family Management

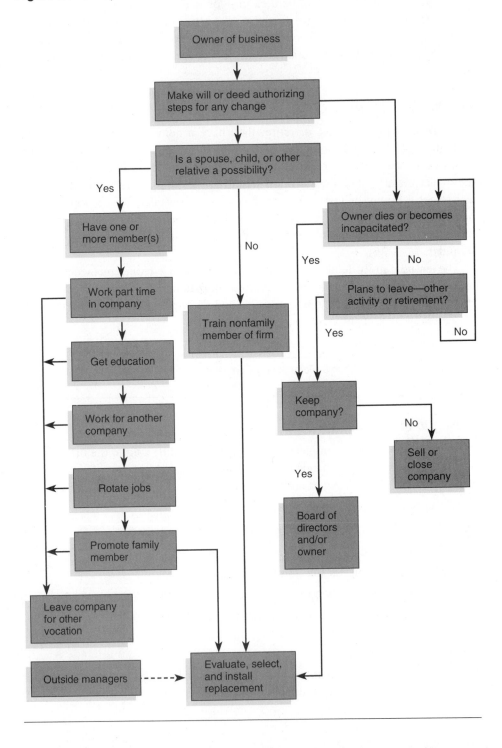

Reasons for Selling to Outsiders

There are many advantages to turning the reins over to an outsider.[16] Among these are the following:

- Assured income.
- Lack of worry about what subsequently happens.
- Possible opportunity to consult.
- Release of family tension.
- Relief from further responsibility.

Selling to someone outside the family can mean loss of family identification and resulting sadness, since it marks the end of years of effort and the loss of something the founder built. Still, selling to outsiders can have a beneficial effect on family relationships, as the following example illustrates.

When a troubled family business was sold, the reaction of one child was: "A number of financially enmeshed families were liberated to pursue individual courses. A company had shed its burdensome past and could look forward to a renewal under new leadership. Ray, Joyce, and I are no longer wrangling siblings polarized in an ugly triad. We are free to be friends."[17]

Helpful Hints on Selling Your Business

When you've decided to sell the business, you've done the easy part. The difficult part is going through with it. It can take a year or longer to negotiate a trouble-free transfer of ownership—so start planning early![18]

Ric Zigmond, head of the small business practice at Laventhal & Horwath, a Los Angeles tax accounting firm, lists the following as the most important basic considerations:[19]

1. Decide on your goal. If you plan to retire immediately, this may reduce the firm's attractiveness, because some buyers want to keep the founder around during the transition.
2. Set a price, with specialized help in evaluating assets.[20] (See Using Technology to Succeed.)
3. Shift some assets to your heirs, to lower or spread out taxes.
4. Build up profits, to make the company more attractive to buyers.
5. Update financial records to truly reflect your firm's worth.
6. Consider what you'll lose by selling—such as pension, health insurance, company car, and club dues—and set the selling price accordingly.
7. Check tax considerations such as the state sales tax on assets, or transfer taxes, as well as state and federal income taxes.

■■■■ USING TECHNOLOGY TO SUCCEED ■■■■

LET YOUR COMPUTER VALUE YOUR BUSINESS

One of the most difficult problems in deciding to sell your business is determining a price that is acceptable to you and the buyer. While there are many methods of doing this, Valuesource, a San Diego software company, has developed a highly specialized spreadsheet designed specifically to calculate the cash value of a business. Its simplified version, called *ValueExpress,* sells for $195 and is very popular with buyers, estate planners, and even divorce lawyers, among others.

Valuesource has developed a more sophisticated version of the package for the IRS that's linked to databases that contain information on businesses with comparable values.

Source: William M. Bulkeley, "With New Planning Software, Entrepreneurs Act Like M.B.A.s," *The Wall Street Journal,* June 2, 1992, p. B1.

Making the Transition Easier

What preparations should you make when you plan to turn the business over to someone else? Too often, a small firm suffers under these circumstances, and sales may decrease or production lag.

For the Owner

To make transitions easier for themselves, owners need to broaden their focus. The narrower the owners' experience and skills, the more difficult it will be to make a smooth transition to other activities after leaving their business. Owners should also begin to devote more time to hobbies and outside group activities, which should help develop a sense of worth apart from the business.

Finally, the transition can be made in phases, by gradually turning part of the business over to the successors.

For the New Manager

To minimize the problems for the new owner or manager, be prepared to have him or her pick up where you leave off. The key is to make available to the successor the specialized knowledge you have accumulated over the years. To accomplish this, an inventory of the various kinds of information can be developed, including your goals and objectives, facts about the general management of the company, data concerning the firm's finances, and information about operational and technical aspects. This type of inventory should also help in estimating the value of the firm at any time and in making projections of cash flow and profit or loss.

The Moment of Truth

Ultimately, the moment arrives when you must turn over to someone else the business you have created by your own ambition, initiative, and character. Built well, it will survive as a testament to that creativity. But a successful changeover requires advance preparation and transition.

TAX AND ESTATE PLANNING

As shown in Chapter 20, in projecting the future of your business, planning is needed to minimize estate taxes. A business and its assets may appreciate in value much more than the owners are aware, and inheritance taxes can be devastating. Therefore, estate plans should be reviewed frequently, along with possible estate tax liability and the provisions for paying such taxes.

Tax Planning

In planning your firm's future activities, consider the influence taxes will have on profits and the business's capital structure. Since tax laws and regulations change frequently, stay current in the knowledge of these matters. You should probably have an annual planning conference with a CPA well versed in business tax matters.

Estate Planning

Estate planning prepares for the transfer of the equity of an owner when death occurs. The major concern here is the perpetuation of a small or family business. Tax rates on estates are now such that the assets bequeathed to beneficiaries may be needed to pay taxes, resulting in removal of equity from a business. By planning for the transition, this problem can be minimized.

From the small firm's standpoint, estate planning can (1) reduce the need for beneficiaries to withdraw funds, (2) help maintain beneficiaries' interest in keeping funds in the firm, and (3) provide for a smooth transition. As discussed in Chapter 20, estate planning for the above objectives can be in the form of (1) gifts to children, (2) family partnerships, (3) stock sales to family members, and (4) living trusts.

In carrying out those planning steps, appropriate steps should be taken to assure compliance with IRS regulations, especially the valuation of the business. Three methods for determining the true value of a business are (1) determining the value of a comparable business that is publicly traded, (2) ascertaining the business's value by capitalizing its earnings, and (3) estimating the business's value by determining its book value.

Certain actions are possible to assure that the IRS is bound by a predetermined agreement. One way of accomplishing this is to use a predetermined shareholder

A **buy/sell agreement** provides for the corporation to buy back a shareholder's stock when he or she leaves the company.

buy/sell agreement, whereby the corporation agrees to buy back the stock or sell it for the shareholder. Such an agreement becomes binding on the IRS. In addition, a properly prepared buy/sell agreement assures a market for the stock. It also provides protection for the minority stockholder. If such a stockholder is terminated without such an agreement, he or she may be placed at a serious disadvantage, as the following example illustrates.

A young woman held 28 percent of the stock in her employer's corporation; a majority of her personal assets were tied up in the stock. Without warning, she lost her job, and her unsympathetic ex-employer was unwilling to redeem the stock.

A number of references may be used to aid in estate and tax planning, but we recommend using the services of a lawyer, accountant, and/or professional tax planner as well.

WHAT YOU SHOULD HAVE LEARNED

1. This chapter shows that members of family-owned firms have different viewpoints depending on their relationships in the family and the business. Founders expect that some family member(s), especially their children, will follow them into the firm.

2. To the extent feasible, ownership and management should be separated from family affairs in order to be fair to nonfamily employees and to reduce friction. Accepted upward movement of family and other employees in the business can generate positive motivation, but evaluation of family members' skills is difficult. Disruptive members should be isolated, delegation should be practiced, and compensation should be based on job performance, if possible.

3. Family businesses are usually limited in the number and caliber of people from whom to choose managers, and in the money available for expansion. Age may hamper the progress of younger family members and may lead to disagreements on money matters. Forming a corporation tends to lessen family stress within the company. Ongoing training—including early employment in the business and personal contact with the owner—is recommended for developing younger members.

4. Start planning for succession early in the game in order to help smooth any sudden transition. If the new CEO is known early, planning has been good; if not, selection must be made under adverse conditions. Transfer of the firm to other family members has many advantages, including continuity and family support.

5. Planning for the future should also include estate planning to minimize the tax burden of the business owner's heirs. Strategies to reduce beneficiaries' need to withdraw funds, maintain their interest in leaving funds in the firm, and provide for a smooth transition include gifts to children, setting up a family partnership, selling stock to family members, and setting up a living trust. In all such planning, owners are advised to consult professionals such as lawyers, accountants, or professional tax planners, and to assure that IRS regulations are met.

QUESTIONS FOR DISCUSSION

1. Why is management succession so important an issue for any small firm? For a family firm?

2. Why is it often difficult to make reasonable decisions in a family business? What problems are caused by a family organization structure?

3. What problems face a company when a key officer leaves suddenly?

4. If you start a business when you are in your 20s or 30s, should you do anything about your replacement? Explain.

5. Suppose you have a successful business now but decide you want to leave it. What might be some reasons for leaving it? What alternatives do you have for the business?

6. How important is estate planning? How can you do it?

THE SON-IN-LAW

Fred Clayton, a college graduate with a degree in sociology, was inducted as a commissioned officer in the U.S. Navy. While in the service, he married the daughter (and only child) of Art Carroll, a prosperous manufacturers' agent in the electronics industry.

When Fred completed his military service, he accepted a sales position in his father-in-law's organization, the Carroll Sales Company. Carroll had high hopes that Fred would take an interest in the business and eventually relieve him of some of the managerial responsibilities. Fred was trained for a short while in the home office and was assigned a territory in which to make sales calls and to promote the products offered by his company. A new car and a liberal expense account were provided. He presented a pleasing personal appearance to the customers. However, it was soon evident to Carroll that Fred did not possess the necessary characteristics to become a good salesman.

For a number of years, Fred continued to receive a share of the available business in his area with little sales effort. This condition was primarily due to the tremendous demand for electronic equipment, which far exceeded the supply at that time.

Carroll was concerned about the fact that Fred was not spending sufficient time in his territory. He would frequently leave town on Tuesday and return on Thursday of the same week after attempting to cover an area which, to be properly serviced, would normally take from Monday through Friday. Fred's expenses were extremely high for the time he spent in the field. On occasion, Carroll would discuss Fred's progress with him. Carroll requested that his son-in-law, as a future officer in the company, set an example for the other sales personnel by putting in more time in his territory and by cutting down on his weekly expenses. After these talks, Fred would improve, but within a short time he would return to his original routine.

The company continued to prosper and expand due to good sales effort from most of the sales force and because of the continued demand for their products. Five years ago, the company covered a sales area comprising nine states. At that time, the son-in-law was appointed district sales manager of a two-state territory and was responsible for the supervision of a warehouse and five salespeople. Fred did not work closely with any of his sales personnel, but he took time to scrutinize all expense accounts and often returned them with items marked "not approved." The salespeople felt he was very petty about this and were frequently infuriated by his actions. He also controlled all their correspondence and information flowing to and from the territory. The other sales districts within the company had more liberal expense accounts, and salespeople could make decisions on their own. The district under the supervision of Fred Clayton never led the company in sales, although it had the greatest potential of all the districts.

Carroll was quite disappointed in the lack of sales progress in Fred's division. He was also very concerned over the results of a survey indicating that Fred's district had an unusually high turnover of sales personnel.

About a year ago, Carroll took his son-in-law out of sales. He still hoped that there might be some position in the firm where the younger man would be a real asset. With this thought in mind, he placed Fred in charge of operations to supervise and regulate the operation of the warehouses. Fred was to control inventories. He continued to have problems with personnel, causing so much unrest among employees that a number of key employees talked of leaving.

A year later, Carroll realized that the situation was critical. He asked himself, "Why, after 16 years with the company, is Fred unhappy? Is he completely unmotivated to succeed because he thinks he doesn't have to? Doesn't he feel at least a moral obligation to try to get along with his associates? How have I failed to give his best abilities an opportunity? How far must I go in trying to fit him into the situation?

QUESTIONS

1. Comment on Fred's capabilities for managing a small business.
2. What could Carroll do to help Fred become a better manager?

Prepared by Gayle M. Ross of Ross Printing Company.

3. Who was responsible for developing Fred into a capable executive? Has Fred or Carroll succeeded or failed? Explain the success or failure of each.
4. How would you answer each of Carroll's questions?
5. What does the case show about the problem of management succession in a small family-owned business?

I. INTRODUCTION

A. WHAT IS A BUSINESS PLAN?

The business plan is probably the most useful and important document you, as a present or prospective small business owner, will ever put together. It is a written statement setting forth the business's mission and objectives, its operational and financial details, its ownership and management structure, and how it hopes to achieve its objectives.

B. WHAT IS THE PURPOSE OF A BUSINESS PLAN?

A well-developed and well-presented business plan can provide you with a "road map to riches"—or at least a pathway to a satisfactory profit. There are at least five reasons for preparing a business plan, which include the following:

1. It provides a blueprint, or plan, to follow in developing and operating the business. It helps keep your creativity on target and helps you concentrate on taking the actions that are needed to achieve your goals and objectives.
2. It can serve as a powerful money-raising tool.
3. It can be an effective communication tool for attracting and dealing with personnel, suppliers, customers, providers of capital, and others. It helps them understand your goals and operations.
4. It can help you develop as a manager, because it provides practice in studying competitive conditions, promotional opportunities, and situations that can be advantageous to your business. Thus, it can help you operate your business more effectively.
5. It provides an effective basis for controlling operations so you can see if your actions are following your plans.

In summary, the plan performs three important functions: (1) being an effective communication tool to convey ideas, research findings, and proposed plans to others, especially financiers; (2) serving as a blueprint for organizing and managing the new venture; and (3) providing a measuring device, or yardstick, by which to gauge progress and evaluate needed changes.

C. WHAT IS INCLUDED IN A BUSINESS PLAN?

Regardless of the specific format used, an effective plan *should include at least* the following:
1. Cover sheet.
2. Executive summary.
3. Table of contents.
4. History of the (proposed) business.
5. Description of the business.
6. Description of the market.
7. Description of the product(s).

8. Ownership and management structure.
9. Objectives and goals.
10. Financial analysis.
11. Appendixes.

II. HOW TO PREPARE A BUSINESS PLAN

You should start by considering your business's background, origins, philosophy, mission, and objectives. Then, you should determine the means for fulfilling the mission and obtaining the objectives. A sound approach is to (1) determine where the business is at present (if an ongoing business) or what is needed to get the business going, (2) decide where you would like the business to be at some point in the future, and (3) determine how to get there; in other words, determine the best strategies for accomplishing the objectives in order to achieve your mission.

The following is one feasible approach you can use in preparing a business plan:

1. Survey consumer demands for your product(s) and decide how to satisfy those demands.
2. Ask questions that cover everything from your firm's target market to its long-run competitive prospects.
3. Establish a long-range strategic plan for the entire business and its various parts.
4. Develop short-term detailed plans for every aspect of the business, involving the owner(s), managers, and key employees, if feasible.
5. Plan for every facet of the business's structure, including finances, operations, sales, distribution, personnel, and general and administrative activities.
6. Prepare a business plan that will use your time and that of your personnel most effectively.

III. HOW TO USE THIS BUSINESS PLAN WORKBOOK

This workbook is a detailed, practical, how-to approach to researching and preparing an actual business plan. It is designed so that you can answer the questions that are asked or find the information that is called for, record it in the spaces provided, and prepare the final plan.

A. SOURCES OF INFORMATION

There are several possible sources of information you can use in preparing this workbook. First, we have included a case study of an actual business (the name has been disguised at the request of the owner) that contains most of the information—except the location—that you will need to complete the workbook. A second source is a business with which you trade, the business of a friend or relative, or some other business that will be willing to provide the information.

Finally, you may want to come up with a possible business to start on your own. In that case, you would start from scratch, gathering the information you need to complete the workbook.

B. COMPLETING THE WORKBOOK

The workbook should be completed essentially in two stages. The first stage is to gather the information beginning with Item 4, History of the Business, and going through Item 11, Appendixes.

After this information is gathered and recorded, come back and complete Item 1, Cover Sheet; Item 2, Executive Summary; and Item 3, Table of Contents.

Finally, type (or word process) the information from the worksheet into a final form (such as the example at the end of Chapter 8).

Item 1, Cover Sheet

On the cover sheet you should include identifying information so that readers will immediately know the business name, address, and phone number; the names and titles of the principals; and the date the plan was prepared.

1. Cover Sheet
   Business name, address, and phone number:

   _____

   _____

   _____

   Principals:

   _____

   _____

   _____

   Date: _____

Item 2, Executive Summary

The executive summary should be a succinct statement of the purpose of the plan. Thus, it should be designed to motivate the reader to go on to the other sections of the plan. It should convey a sense of excitement, challenge, plausibility, credibility, and integrity. Even though the summary is the second item in the plan, *it should be written last, after the rest of the plan has been developed*. Remember, *the executive summary is just that—a summary—so keep it short!*

2. Executive Summary

   Brief summary of plan

Major objectives

Description of product(s)

Marketing strategy

Financial projections

Item 3, Table of Contents

Because the table of contents provides the reader an overview of what is contained in the plan itself, it should be written and presented concisely, in outline form, using numerical and alphabetical designations for headings and subheadings.

3. Table of Contents (each section listed, with subheads)

Item 4, History of the (Proposed) Business

The history of the (proposed) business should include a discussion of how the idea for the business, or product, originated and what has been done to develop the idea up to this point. If the owners or managers have been in business before, and their experience is pertinent to the success of the business, include that information. Other relevant background information on the persons, products, capitalization, source(s), funds, and anything else of potential interest to the readers should also be included.

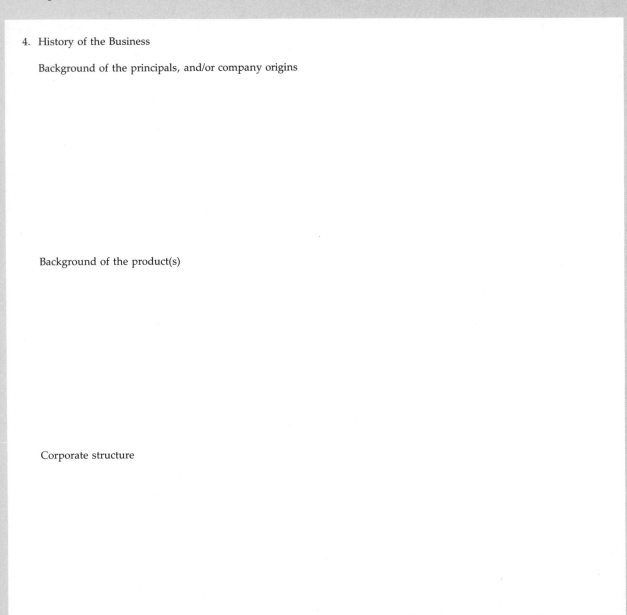

4. History of the Business

Background of the principals, and/or company origins

Background of the product(s)

Corporate structure

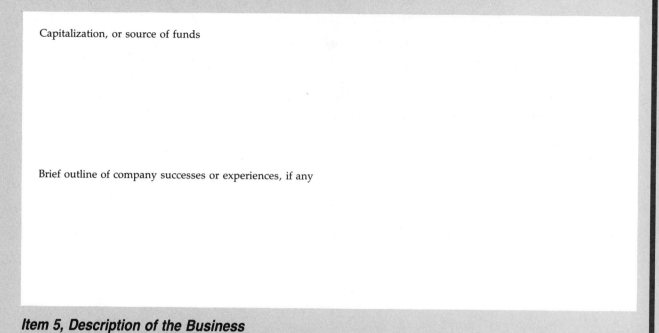

Capitalization, or source of funds

Brief outline of company successes or experiences, if any

Item 5, Description of the Business

Item 5 is the place to define your business, as you see it. Therefore, you should essentially answer such questions as: What business am I in? What services do I provide? This item should include more than just a statement of plans and a listing of activities. It should tell readers what customer needs the business intends to meet. In writing this component, try to put yourself in the position of the reader and include information that potential investors, customers, employees, and community members in general might need to assess your plan.

5. Description of the Business

Item 6, Description of the Market

The description of the market is one of the most important—but most difficult—items of the plan for you to develop. In it, you should try to answer such questions as: Who will buy my product? Where is my market? What is my sales strategy? What marketing strategy(ies) will I use? Who buys what, when, where, and why? What are my customers like? Who constitutes my target market (or what special niche am I aiming for)? You should also look at your competition and appraise it carefully, showing any weaknesses it has that you are able to, and plan to, exploit.

6. Description of the Market

   Target market: Who? How many?

   Market penetration projections and strategies

   Analysis of competition: How many? Strengths and weaknesses?

Item 7, Description of the Product(s)

Item 7 should describe all of your existing or planned products, including services to be performed as well as goods to be produced. You should also look at any research-and-development activities and new plans to improve or redevelop the product, along with any patents, trademarks, and copyrights you hold — or that are pending.

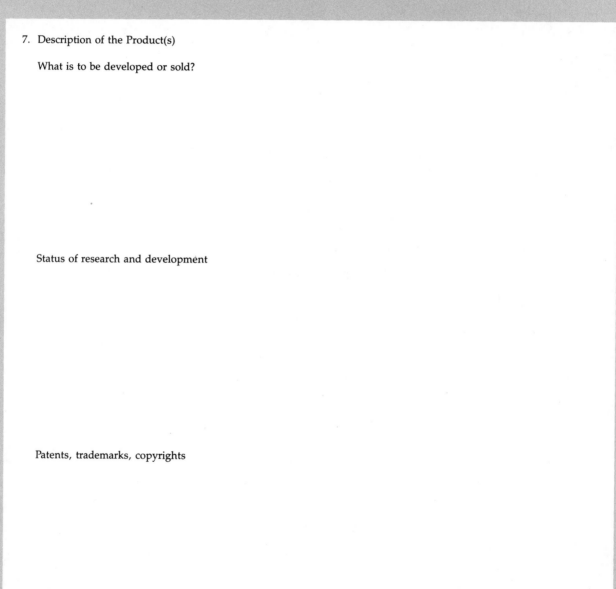

7. Description of the Product(s)

What is to be developed or sold?

Status of research and development

Patents, trademarks, copyrights

Item 8, Ownership and Management Structure

Item 8 is the place to describe the owner(s), including those you identified by name and title in Item 1. Here you would want to give more detail about their experience and expertise. Also, you should describe your management team, along with their abilities, training and development, and experience. Then, designate who will carry out the plan once it is enacted. Finally, something should be included about organizational structure, including employee policies and procedures.

8. Ownership and Management Structure

    Owners and their expertise

    Managers and their abilities, training and development, and experience

    Organizational structure

Item 9, Objectives and Goals

In essence, your objectives and goals outline what you plan to accomplish in your business, as well as showing how it will be done. Include such items as sales and revenue forecasts; marketing plans, including how sales are to be made and what advertising, sales promotion, and publicity will be used; manufacturing plans, including provisions for quality assurance and control; and financial plans (but not the specific financial data, ratios, or analyses, which are in the next item).

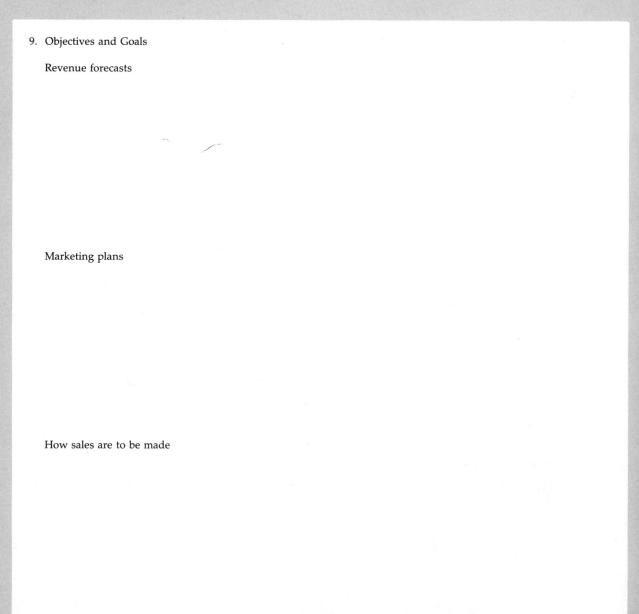

9. Objectives and Goals

   Revenue forecasts

   Marketing plans

   How sales are to be made

Advertising and sales promotion

Manufacturing plans

Quality assurance plans

Financial plans

Item 10, Financial Analyses

Since one purpose of the plan is to attract prospective investors or lenders, Item 10 is the place in the plan where you can indicate the expected financial results of your operations. It should show prospective investors or lenders *why* they should provide funds, *when* they can realistically expect a return, and *what* the expected return on their money *should* be. While you must make assumptions—or educated guesses—at this point, you should at least try to include projected income statements and balance sheets for up to three years, as well as projected cash flow analyses for the first year by months. There should be an analysis of costs/volume/profits, where appropriate. Finally, you should provide projected statements of changes in financial position that you anticipate. If practical, you might want to provide some financial ratios.

10. Financial Data

    Projected income statements (three years)

    Projected balance sheets (three years)

    Projected cash flow analyses (first year, by months)

Cost/volume/profit analyses, where appropriate

Projected statements of changes in financial position

Financial ratios, if practical

Item 11, Appendixes

In the appendixes you can include pertinent information about yourself and your business that is not included elsewhere in the plan. Some possible details to include are (1) narrative history of firm; (2) organizational structure (if not done in Item 8), including management structure, organization chart(s), and résumés of key people; (3) major assumptions you have made in preparing the plan; (4) brochures or other published information describing the product(s) and services you provide; (5) letters of recommendation or endorsement; (6) historical financial information, for the past three years (if not done in Item 10); (7) details of objectives and goals; and (8) catalog sheets, photographs, or technical information.

---

11. Appendixes

　　Use separate sheet(s) of paper to write this information.

IV. SAMPLE CASE: CLEANDRUM, INC.

For nine years, Sue Ley served as a forklift truck operator for a local oil company. Then she drove a tractor-trailer for the company for four more years. Tiring of this type of work and thinking she'd like to get into selling, she applied to participate in the company's education program, which pays tuition for employees taking college courses, and was accepted.

Sue enrolled in the marketing program at the local university. While continuing to drive the truck, she completed her marketing course work in three years and graduated with a bachelor's degree in business administration. But when she applied for a transfer to the marketing department, she was told that it would be "four or five years" before there'd be an opening for her.

Sue's uncle, who had taken over her grandfather's steel oil drum cleaning business, suggested that she start a similar business. Assuring her that she could make around $100,000 per year ($300,000 by the third year) if she founded a business of this sort, he offered to help her get the business started. She could not see any future with the oil company in marketing and did not want to drive trucks the rest of her life. Having saved $25,000 that she could put into the business, she decided to take a chance and start her own company.

History of the Business

Sue approached the local Small Business Development Center (SBDC) to find out if there was a large enough market for such a company in her area. The center's survey of 200 firms confirmed that a sufficient market existed for a "quality operation." While other firms were performing the service, their quality was not high enough.

In 1990, using information furnished by her uncle, Sue had an accounting firm prepare projected balance sheets, income statements, and changes in cash for five years. Sales projections were for 31,000 units in 1990 and up to 50,000 in 1994. Sales were estimated to be $367,000 in 1990, up to $588,000 in 1994, and net income was estimated to increase from $9,000 to $62,000.

Armed with these projections, and at the request of her banker, she approached potential customers and obtained letters indicating their willingness to do business with her "if high quality, good service, and competitive prices were offered."

She then prepared a business plan. On the basis of the SBDC report, financial projections, the letters, a personal history, and interviews with the loan officer, the bank approved a $60,000 loan. Adding her $25,000, Sue had a lawyer draw up incorporation papers for CleanDrum, Inc. Sue was now ready to go into the business of buying, straightening, cleaning, painting, and selling used 55-gallon steel drums and buying, cleaning, and selling used plastic drums for transporting and storing oil, chemicals, and similar products.

She started by renting a building. Then her uncle arranged for purchase of the necessary machinery (at a "special" price of $59,000). (She later learned that he had bankrupted her grandfather's business and that the quality of the equipment he had purchased was suspect.) When the machinery arrived, he failed to come to supervise its installation. It took Sue three months to hire mechanics, plumbers, and electricians to set up and connect the equipment. She also hired and trained six laborers to operate the machinery. She studied her uncle's plant for two weeks to learn enough to enable her to run her own company. All this delayed her start-up and drained much of her cash.

Sue had sales of only 500 drums during the first month of operation, which provided insufficient income to cover her direct labor costs. In the first four months, she drove a truck during the daytime hours four days a week and ran the drum-cleaning operations until 11:00 each night. The rest of the time, she was on the road selling CDI's drum-cleaning service.

She concentrated her sales activities on the firms that had responded positively to the SBDC survey. She had expected her uncle to help her sell, but he didn't. CDI's losses continued. Her banker insisted that she quit her truck driving and devote her full energies to her business or close it.

At the end of 1990, CDI had cleaned and sold about 18,000 drums, but it was still $30,000 in the hole. The bank loaned her another $12,000, and she mortgaged her home for more funds.

Management, Ownership, and Personnel

Early the next year, when the financial situation was the lowest, Edie Jones became interested in investing in the company. Edie had no business experience herself, but she was married to the owner of a successful business. She invested $32,000 in CDI in return for 50 percent ownership.

In early 1993, CleanDrum employed six workers in the plant. In addition, Sue's daughter and two sons worked in the office, drove the semi, and did some selling.

Not only is Sue a co-owner, but she also manages CDI. Among her many duties, she supervises production, trains workers, buys drums, and spends two to three days a week on the road selling the drums. The plant workers move, lift, turn, paint, and inspect drums and control the operations of the machines. The plant operates 40 hours per week.

Shortly after Edie joined CDI, the partners became concerned about its losses. Edie felt that labor costs should be reduced and a supervisor hired. Sue argued, however, that despite already low wages the employees were producing quality output efficiently. During the first year they had worked for the minimum wage. However, she said, "In the past, when I came to work, I often found a breakdown, a lack of materials, or that an employee hadn't shown up. It was as if my hands were tied and I couldn't get out and sell."

By the second year, the workers' pay had improved because of the training and stability of the work force and an increase in the minimum wage. "None of them had families dependent on them. Now, the group leader, who has been with me since I started, is paid $7 per hour, another long-timer earns $6; while a third one, a skilled worker, makes $5.50. The other three, who have been with me less than two years, earn minimum wage. One competitor in another city is paying only minimum wage, but another, a mechanized plant in another area, is paying over $10 an hour."

Social Security, workers' compensation, and unemployment insurance are the only employee benefits provided, but two of the workers are making health insurance payments on their own.

Sue says that the company has not had enough money to hire a supervisor. She has, however, discussed the possibility of giving the workers a bonus to recognize and encourage good work. The problem is, she says, "How could we pay for it?"

Product Line and Production Process

CDI performs two types of services. First, it buys steel and plastic drums with the intention of processing and selling them. This requires finding, pricing, purchasing, transporting, and selling drums. It owns the drums until they are sold. Second, it has an ongoing drum exchange, whereby it delivers processed drums and picks up drums to be processed. CDI does not own these drums at any time. Sales are about evenly split between the two types of services, and steel drums make up about 85 percent of those handled.

Drums not meeting customers' standards are converted into waste or parts receptacles by drilling or removing their tops. These are processed and sold to other customers.

The company rents a 4,000-square-foot building, where operations are conducted. (See Exhibit 1.) Sue estimates that the machinery can process about 5,000 drums a month and that current production averages about 3,000 drums per month. The machines are not fastened to the floor, but have electrical and pipe connections.

The drums are brought to the plant in trailers, pulled by CDI's only tractor; 267 drums make up a trailer load. The company has three trailers so that two can stay at the plant to be unloaded and loaded while the other is delivering clean drums to customers. CDI tries to move drums in full trailer loads—sometimes requiring several stops. However, CDI has learned that orders for fewer than 50 drums are not profitable and does not accept them unless the customer pays the transportation costs.

The operations and their sequence for processing *steel drums* are shown in Exhibit 2. The production process involves the following steps.

1. Drums are received and unloaded over a period of several days. The bungs (stoppers screwed in the top of the drums) are removed and the drums checked for quality. The drums are stacked, moved to a waiting area, or moved to first flush. About 300 drums are in each of the receiving and shipping areas.
2. Each drum is upended on a pipe and flushed with steam and a chemical.
3. Each drum is righted, a light is lowered into it, and the drum is inspected for rust. Rusty drums are rolled to a separate room, where the rust is removed, and then returned for further processing.
4. Drums needing straightening are run through the chimer.
5. Drums are placed on a conveyor and rolled into a vat for cleaning. Six drums can be cleaned at the same time.

Exhibit 1   Layout of CleanDrum Plant

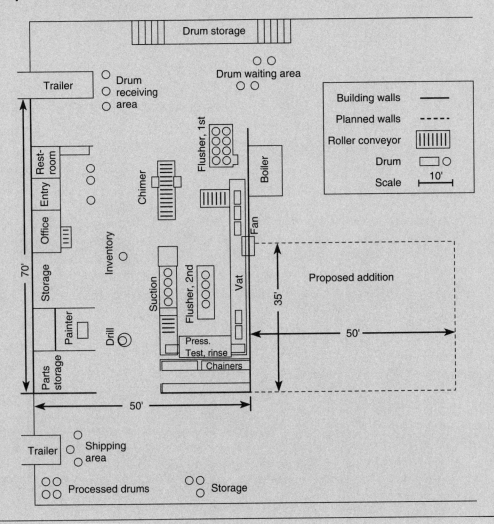

6. Drums are mechanically lifted, turned, and rolled into the outside rinser.
7. Drums are pressure tested. Those not meeting the pressure test are removed from the process.
8. Drums roll down the conveyor, where a worker lifts and upends each onto a steam pipe for final flushing.
9. Each drum is righted and placed on the floor, where a suction pipe is inserted to dry the inside (see Exhibit 3).
10. Final inspection for rust is made.

Exhibit 2   Sequence of Operations at CleanDrum

Operations

Steel Drums	Plastic Drums	Machines	Time in Drum
1. Receive	1. Receive	Trailer	
2. First flush	2. First flush	Flusher	3 minutes
3. Inspect for rust; if so, clean with chain		Visual	3 minutes
		Chainer*	15 minutes
4. Straighten		Chimer	1 minute
5. Clean		Vat	10 minutes
6. Outside rinse		Rinser	3 minutes
7. Pressure test; if not passed, cut out top		Forced air	20 seconds
		Hand cutter	10 minutes
	3. Pressure test	Hand tester	2 minutes
8. Last flush	4. Flush	Flusher	4 minutes
	5. Wash outside	Hand washer	3 minutes
9. Dry		Suction	2 minutes
10. Inspect for rust; if not passed, cut 9″ hole		Visual	2 minutes
		Drill press	10 minutes
11. Paint (90%)		Paint booth	4 minutes
12. Ship		Truck	

*About 5 percent

Exhibit 3   The CleanDrum Flushing and Drying Operation

11. Drums are rolled to the paint booth for individual spray painting while being turned. A label is affixed to signify that the drum has gone through the entire cleaning process and conforms to established standards.
12. Drums are put into a waiting trailer for delivery or are moved to storage.

Plastic drums follow a separate path, which causes "some confusion." After the first flush, they are manually pressure tested, flushed again, and washed on a mobile cradle.

At times, space around the machines is crowded with drums (some stacked) awaiting the next operation. During the summer, the plant is extremely hot even with the draft through the open ends of the building, augmented by a six-foot-diameter fan placed in the wall by the vat. In rainy weather, workers in receiving and shipping wear raincoats or other protective wear.

Sue and the owner of the building have decided to enlarge it by 50 percent to provide more "breathing room" for the workers, and expand production. The additional space will raise the rent 50 percent, from $600 to $900 per month. The owner of the building has made available some lengths of roller conveyor totaling about 100 feet for moving the drums.

Marketing and Sales Promotion

Since the start of the company, Sue has spent part of her time on the road selling CDI's service. In 1992, she spent two to three days each week on the road making contact with customers. Although she also makes many phone calls to her clients, she says that these can't replace face-to-face contacts. Sue plans her itinerary, within a 200-mile radius, to minimize travel time and mileage.

The 200-mile radius is considered the extent of CDI's market. This area is served by five companies, and market size is estimated to be 13,000 drums a month. Currently, CDI's sales volume places it in the middle of the group. Sue estimates that she has over 100 customers, about 50 percent of the companies that originally indicated a need. About 75 percent of the sales have come from competitors' customers.

Oil and chemical companies are the major customers. Some call in to alert CDI to their need for its service. For example, one of the major customers may call to say, "We have 100 drums ready to be cleaned, and will have 200 by the end of next week." Several companies order twice a month, and some once every six months.

Sue has been selling service on 2,500 to 3,000 drums a month and has her eye on sales of 5,000 per month. She explains that it's possible for several reasons. First, the number of customers has increased steadily since CDI opened. Second, a competing company recently went bankrupt, and Sue picked up most of its customers. Finally, as will soon be discussed, several customers and sales reps from other, noncompeting companies have "boosted" CDI.

Presently, Sue feels that quality and service should be the main selling emphasis. Even though CDI has chosen to compete on these points, however, it must also compete with price cutting by some competitors. Pricing practices vary. Sue has heard reports that one competitor quotes a high price for the purchase of good drums and then finds enough wrong with them to drive the purchase price down so it can sell the processed drums for lower prices.

Sue says she has seen delivered drums, processed by others, that have been carelessly processed, while others have not been pressure tested. Early on, CDI "almost lost a good customer because a part-time worker left some refuse in some drums." (Sue has consistently emphasized to the authors how important the workers' performance is to the company.) Sue also cited a customer that was lost because somebody tampered with some of CDI's delivered drums. She hopes to convince potential customers who are currently buying substandard processing that it's in their best interest to obtain quality service.

Some companies, having received poorly processed used drums, now use only new drums. Sue has approached some of these companies asking for a chance to demonstrate the quality of CDI's delivered drums.

Although she hasn't had much success, she says she plans to continue trying. Also, her satisfied customers and others are referring other companies to CDI. CDI, which does only limited advertising and sales promotion, distributes magnetic calling cards and is the only company listed under "Barrels & Drums—Equipment & Supplies" in the Yellow Pages of the local telephone directory. Sue does not know of any other publication in which it would be worthwhile to advertise.

Financial Affairs

Ben, a member of SCORE, was contacted for counseling about the company's finances. Company information indicated to Ben that CDI was losing about $1,000 a month and that overhead (as a percentage of sales) was high, labor and material costs were low, and apparently greater sales volume was needed. He suggested that CDI do some advertising and/or hire a sales representative to help increase sales. Sue said that the company couldn't afford either of those plans. Ben pointed out, "There's no way you can solve your problem by 'economizing.' Your overhead—not your direct costs—is your problem, and it's practically irreducible." He suggested that a 5 percent reduction in price would produce a 15 to 20 percent increase in sales, allowing CDI to make a profit.

They then discussed CDI's pricing policies. While CDI's price structure varies, it is about as follows. Used drums are purchased from various sources for about $4 apiece, depending on their condition. Those needing straightening and/or rust removal can be purchased at lower prices. After processing, a cleaned and painted drum is sold for about $12 to $13.

Customers' drums are processed and returned to them for about $7 a drum—again depending on the condition before processing. Drums sold for waste and parts storage are sold for about $5 each. Sue feels that CDI's pricing is in line with that of its competitors. (One competitor sells drums at a lower price, but he doesn't pressure test and appears to obtain dirty drums at lower prices than CDI.)

During the early years of the company, Sue used her checkbook to do the accounting. When cash was received, she entered it in the checkbook; when she paid a bill, she paid it by check. She used sales and shipping slips to keep track of sales and invoices received. At the end of the year, she took all the slips, invoices, and checks to the firm's accountant and received in return a financial package, plus completed tax forms.

Archie, another SCORE member, revised the system so that Sue now fills in a multicolumnar sheet as income is received and expenses are paid. At the end of the month, she totals the columns and prepares a profit and loss sheet. Of the new system, Sue says, "Until Ben and Archie came in, I didn't know how many units CDI needed to sell each month to break even. We have figured that that level is 2,000 to 3,000 drums. Any units sold beyond this level will be making a profit."

Sue decided at the end of this past year to have the accounting firm do the tax preparation as usual, but not the annual reports—in order to save $1,000.

During 1992, losses continued to mount—even with sales of about 30,000 clean drums. More money had to be borrowed, and Sue had to sell her house to keep herself and the business going. Acting under necessity, she stabilized her work force and called upon Ben for further counseling. This time, Ben and Archie joined forces in analyzing costs and seeking solutions to CDI's problems. As one practical way of helping, Archie helped design and install a simple accounting system. (See Exhibits 4 and 5 for CDI's financial statements for its first three years in business.)

Recently, Sue obtained a state loan to replace numerous loans that, because CDI's rating was low, were at rates of interest above the prime. (The state loan program has been made available to start or operate small

Exhibit 4

CLEANDRUM, INC.
Balance Sheet
December 31, 1992
($000s)*

	1990	1991	1992
Assets			
Current assets:			
Cash in bank	$ —	$ —	$ 6.7
Accounts in bank	26.7	22.7	12.8
Inventory	10.5	14.7	7.7
Total current assets	37.2	37.4	27.2
Property and equipment:			
Equipment	87.2	78.5	78.5
Leasehold improvements	—	5.5	5.5
Less: accumulated depreciation	−52.8	−36.1	−19.8
Net property and equipment	34.4	47.9	64.2
Total assets	$ 71.6	$ 85.3	$ 91.4
Liabilities and Stockholders' Equity			
Current liabilities:			
Accounts payable	$ 28.2	$ 36.1	$ 38.9
Current long-term debt	25.0	25.0	16.4
Notes payable	85.0	85.1	59.0
Accruals	5.4	9.4	11.8
Total current liabilities	143.6	155.6	126.1
Long-term debt	91.0	80.0	96.5
Total liabilities	234.6	235.6	222.6
Stockholders' equity			
Common stock	1.0	1.0	1.0
Added paid-in capital	16.7	9.0	9.0
Accumulated deficit	(180.7)	(160.3)	(141.2)
Total stockholders' equity	(163.0)	(150.3)	(131.2)
Total liabilities and stockholders' equity	$ 71.6	$ 85.3	$ 91.4

*Values have been converted to thousands for ease of study.

businesses that need help.) CDI has a loan for two years at 8.5 percent interest. During the year, when CDI didn't have $3,000 to pay a bill, Sue paid it from her own bank account but didn't record it on CDI's books.

In 1992, sales per month ranged from around 2,500 to 3,000 units. While CDI's sales and financial operations had improved, it had lost money from the beginning. Sue was discouraged! But the first-quarter results for 1993 (Exhibit 6) indicate a turnaround. This was the best financial quarter that CDI has ever had. "We have been selling well over 3,000 drums each month—3,400 last month and 2,000 in the first half of this month. If we can maintain these sales levels, we should soon be in good shape," Sue said. While sales volume is not yet up to the 44,000 drums set for 1992 in the initial proposal for the firm, the past quarter does indicate a trend toward the 50,000 drums set for 1993.

Exhibit 5

CLEANDRUM, INC.
Profit and Loss Statements
($000s)*

Item	1990	1991	1992
Sales	$ 161.2	$ 303.3	$ 320.4
Cost of sales:			
Materials	98.9	104.2	99.1
Labor	64.6	86.2	64.6
Freight	—	19.3	42.0
Total cost of sales	147.0	209.7	205.7
Gross profit	$ 14.2	$ 93.6	$ 114.7
Operating, administrative, and selling costs:			
Depreciation	15.9	16.4	16.7
Payroll taxes	6.4	10.4	10.0
Repair and maintenance	11.3	3.9	14.5
Rent	13.3	7.2	7.2
Utilities	13.2	19.6	18.0
Salaries	13.0	15.7	20.9
Insurance	11.0	11.2	14.5
Office expense	1.5	1.5	3.6
General tax, legal, accounting	4.3	2.9	0.5
Selling, travel, automobile	3.2	3.4	10.4
Telephone	3.8	4.6	7.6
Sales taxes	—	—	—
Miscellaneous	2.9	1.8	0.5
Total operating, administrative, and selling costs	99.8	98.6	124.4
Operating profit	(85.6)	(5.0)	(9.7)
Income-legal	—	—	10.1
Interest expense	17.6	14.0	19.9
Net income	$ (97.4)	$ (19.0)	$ (19.6)

*Values have been converted to thousands for ease of study.

In early 1993, Sue started preparing monthly financial statements according to the new bookkeeping system designed and implemented by Archie. Sue hadn't had monthly statements before. She said she found it quite easy to total the columns at the end of the month and draw off the profit and loss statements.

The Future

CDI is still having trouble with its cash flow, as indicated by the delay in paying for some drums. However, it had raised its cash balance from zero to $6,700 at the beginning of 1993. Also, during the quarter, it was able to make large payments due on a loan and on past sales tax.

The increased volume of sales required increased production, which, in turn, increased the number of drums in process. At times, drums stored between operations hamper movement in the plant, While the plant is to be expanded, construction hasn't yet begun. This change will increase the rent, and moving and installing machines is also expected to be expensive. Sue plans to use the plant workers for most of the machine movement and installation.

Exhibit 6	**CLEANDRUM, INC.** **Profit and Loss Sheets** **1993** **($000s)***

	Months		
Item	*January*	*February*	*March*
Sales	$ 30.0	$ 34.7	$ 31.0
Cost of sales:			
Beginning inventory	$ 10.4	$ 8.9	$ 8.7
Drums purchased	4.0	10.4**	4.6
Paint	—	1.5	—
Miscellaneous supplies	0.1	2.1	0.6
Direct labor	3.8	4.7	5.7†
Freight	2.0	3.0	2.8
Less ending inventory	−8.9	−8.7	−6.8
Total cost of sales	$ 11.4	$ 21.9	$ 15.6
Gross profit	$ 18.6	$ 12.8	$ 15.4
Operating, administrative, and selling costs:			
Payroll taxes	$ 2.0	$ 1.8	$ 2.1
Repair and maintenance	—	1.6	0.8
Rent	0.6	0.6	0.6
Utilities	1.1	1.7	1.4
Salaries	1.3	1.3	2.0
Insurance	0.6	0.6	1.9
Office expenses	0.3	0.6	0.1
General tax, legal, and accounting expenses	—	0.2	0.1
Selling (travel and auto) expenses	0.5	0.8	0.5
Telephone	0.4	1.1	0.4
Interest	—	1.0	1.0
Sales taxes‡	5.9	0.4	0.4
Miscellaneous (loan principal)	6.3	1.3	1.3
Total operating, administrative, and selling expenses	$ 19.0	$ 13.0	$ 12.6
Net income	$ (0.4)	$ (0.2)	$ 2.8

*Values have been converted to thousands for ease of study.
**Paid Coger Bros. $5,600 for drums purchased in 1992.
†Three payrolls in this month.
‡In January, accumulated unpaid sales taxes were paid.

Sue is elated by the increase in sales, yet her financial situation still appears to be unsettled.

Source: Prepared by William M. Spain, SCORE, and Charles R. Scott, University of Alabama.

Note: The following SBA documents were helpful to us in preparing this plan: MP4, *Business Plan for Small Manufacturing;* MP5, *Business Plan for Small Construction Firms,* and MP 11, *Business Plan for Small Service Firms.* See also MP 15, *The Business Plan for Homebased Business.* MP4, 5, and 15 can be obtained from the U.S. Small Business Administration, P.O. Box 15434, Fort Worth, TX 76119, for $1 each; MP11 costs only $0.50.

ENDNOTES

Chapter 1

1. *USA Today,* October 25, 1985, p. 1A.

2. "Millions of New Jobs to Be Created in '86, Survey Shows," *Mobile* (Alabama) *Register,* March 31, 1986, p. 3-A.

3. "When You Start Your Own Business . . . ," *Parade Magazine,* August 21, 1988, p. 12.

4. As reported in *USA Today,* May 8, 1989, p. 1E.

5. *Your Business and the SBA* (Washington, D.C.: U.S. Small Business Administration, September 1990), p. 2.

6. See "College Prof Says Entrepreneurship Coachable," *Mobile* (Alabama) *Register,* November 28, 1988, p. 3-B; and Mindy Fetterman, "Hot Line: Callers Eager to Be Own Boss," *USA Today,* May 9, 1989, p. 1A.

7. "Millions of New Jobs," p. 3-A.

8. R. Wendell Moore, "The Smaller They Are the Better They Grow," *USA Today,* March 20, 1992, p. A13; and Constance J. Pritchard, "Forget the Fortune 500," *The Wall Street Journal,* "Managing Your Career," Fall 1992, p. 12.

9. "For New Jobs, Help Small Business," *The Wall Street Journal,* August 10, 1992, p. A10; and "Small Companies Are Still Afraid to Add Workers," *Business Week,* August 3, 1992, p. 16.

10. Robert L. Bartley, "On Clinton's Recipe for Growth," *The Wall Street Journal,* July 16, 1992, p. A10.

11. "Odds and Ends," *The Wall Street Journal,* July 17, 1992, p. B1.

12. *USA Today,* February 12, 1985, p. 18.

13. "The American Dream: Your Own Business," *Nation's Business,* November 1988, pp. 10–11.

14. "Building a Better Entrepreneur," *The New York Times Magazine,* March 22, 1992, p. 6A.

15. Roger Ricklefs, "Schools Increase Courses to Help Entrepreneurs," *The Wall Street Journal,* February 6, 1989, p. B1.

16. Suzanne Alexander, "Student Entrepreneurs Find Road to Riches on Campus," *The Wall Street Journal,* June 23, 1989, p. B1.

17. Steven P. Galante, "Corporate Executives Quitting to Buy Rust Belt Businesses," *The Wall Street Journal,* April 28, 1986, p. 27.

18. Bethany Kanel, "South-Bronx Teen-Ager Relishes Being Known as 'Mr. Hot Dog,'" *USA Today,* May 9, 1988, p. 9E; and "ABC Evening News," November 14, 1989.

19. Katie Gardner, "Student Entrepreneurs: Minding Their Own Businesses," *Washington Post Education Review,* April 9, 1989, pp. 5–7.

20. Reported in Shelley Liles, "New Business Owners Smart, Experienced," *USA Today,* May 8, 1989, p. 3E.

21. From *Meeting the Special Problems of Small Businesses* (New York: Committee for Economic Development, 1974), p. 14.

22. W. B. Barnes, *First Semi-Annual Report of the Small Business Administration* (Washington, D.C.: Small Business Administration, January 31, 1954), p. 7.

23. Correspondence with MicroFridge, Inc.

24. *Fortune,* February 18, 1985, p. 91; and communication with Digital Network Inc.

25. U.S. Bureau of the Census, *Statistical Abstract of the United States, 1991,* 111th ed. (Washington, D.C.: U.S. Government Printing Office, 1991), Table 861, p. 525.

26. As reported by Paul Craig Roberts, "Trickle-Down Triumph: In the '80s, the Poor Got . . . Riches," *Business Week,* July 13, 1992, p. 18; and Frederic Smoler, "The Man Who Would Bring Back the 1980s," *Andarity,* Winter 1993, pp. 14–26.

27. Reported in Shelley Liles, "More Small Businesses Succeeding," *USA Today,* May 8, 1989, p. 1E.

28. Cited in *USA Today,* March 13, 1987, p. 13.

29. Stephen M. Pollan and Mark Levine, "Playing to Win: The Small Business Guide to Survival and Growth," Special Advertising Section, *U.S. News & World Report,* December 12, 1988, p. A20.

30. David S. Evans, "The Effects of Access to Capital on Entry into Self-Employment," *Small Business Research Summary,* No. 116, November 1991.

Chapter 2

1. Reported in *USA Today,* October 16, 1985, p. 1D.

2. "Labor Letter: They're Different!" *The Wall Street Journal,* May 2, 1989, p. 1.

3. Tait Trussell, "The Untypical Typical Millionaire," *Nation's Business,* November 1988, pp. 62ff.

4. Nelson A. Aldrich, Jr., "Private Lives: Staubach Co.," *Inc.,* December 1985, pp. 66–68.

5. *The State of Small Businesses: A Report to the President* (Washington, D.C.: U.S. Government Printing Office, March 1983), p. 54.

6. Hal B. Pickle and Brian S. Rungeling, "Empirical Investigation of Entrepreneurial Goals and Customer Satisfaction," *Journal of Business,* April 1973, pp. 268–73.

7. Joanne Davidson, "Broken in Body, Not Spirit," *U.S. News & World Report,* July 4, 1983, pp. 38–39.

8. Nancy Madlin, "The Venture Survey: Probing the Entrepreneurial Psyche," *Venture,* May 1985, p. 24.

9. T. R. Fletcher, "It's No Secret—Mystery Bookshop Offers 12,000 Volumes," *Bethesda* (Maryland) *Gazette,* March 16, 1989, p. A-45.

10. John H. Johnson with Lerone Bennett, Jr., *Succeeding against the Odds* (New York: Warner Books, 1989).

11. Lynn Langway, "Like Fathers, Like Daughters," *Newsweek,* January 16, 1984, pp. 78–80.

12. Robert Lewis, "More Spouses Doing Business Together," *Mobile* (Alabama) *Register,* August 6, 1989, p. 2-D.

13. "Handmade Brooms Sweep Up Sales," *USA Today,* February 10, 1989, p. 12B, Copyright 1989, *USA Today.* Adapted with permission.

14. "Personality Traits Distinguish Employees from Entrepreneurs," *Mobile* (Alabama) *Press Register,* September 27, 1992, p. E-4.

15. Janice Castro, "Big vs. Small," *Time,* September 5, 1988, pp. 48–50.

16. Eric Morganthaler, "Snuggling Business Booms as Babes in Pouches Proliferate," *The Wall Street Journal,* April 23, 1982, pp. 1, 29.

17. Mark Robichaux, "Fledgling Honeybee Learns to Fly with the Big Guys," *The Wall Street Journal,* May 12, 1989, p. D2; and Tom Waters, "The Robot's Reach," *Discover,* October 1990, pp. 68–74.

18. As reported in Carrie Dolan, "Entrepreneurs Often Fail as Managers," *The Wall Street Journal,* May 15, 1989, p. B1.

Chapter 3

1. Richard Greene, "Do You Really Want to Be Your Own Boss?" *Forbes,* October 21, 1985, p. 91.

2. Marcia Staimer, "Hottest Business Areas," *USA Today,* May 10, 1989, p. 1B.

3. David Gumpert, ''Entrepreneurial Edge: 10 Hot Businesses to Start in the '90s,'' *Working Woman,* June 1991, pp. 55–56 and 96.

4. Small Business Administration estimate, reported in Julia Lawlor, ''Women Start Firms Faster Than You Can Say 'Glass Ceiling,' '' *USA Today,* May 6, 1991, p. 3E.

5. Susan Rook, ''Beyond the Glass Ceiling,'' Special CNN Report, November 15, 1992.

6. ''A Woman's Work,'' *Fortune,* August 24, 1992, p. 59.

7. Lawlor, ''Women Start Firms Faster.''

8. Neuharth, ''Risk-Taking Women Create Own Ceiling.'' .

9. ''Women Entrepreneurs: Who Are They?'' *USA Today,* June 21, 1989, p. 12D.

10. Mark Robichaux, ''Business First, Family Second,'' *The Wall Street Journal,* May 12, 1989, p. B1.

11. ''She's the Boss,'' *USA Today,* June 21, 1989, p. 1A.

12. ''The Immigrants,'' *Business Week,* July 13, 1992, pp. 114–21.

13. According to the latest SBA survey of minority-owned firms, conducted in 1987.

14. Kent Gibbons, ''Black-Owned Firms Feel Pinch of Law, Economy,'' *USA Today,* May 6, 1991, p. 3E.

15. John Emshwiller, ''Former TV Actor Stars as Entrepreneur,'' *The Wall Street Journal,* July 10, 1992, p. B1.

16. ''The Top 100,'' *Black Enterprise,* June 1989, pp. 57ff.

17. Kevin Johnson, ''McDonald's Recruits Duo to Make Its McCroutons,'' *USA Today,* January 27, 1989, p. 7. Copyright 1989, *USA Today.* Adapted with permission.

18. As reported in Andrea Stone, ''Asian Growth: 105% in 10 Years,'' *USA Today,* February 27, 1991, p. 11A.

19. Alfredo Corchado, ''Hispanic Supermarkets Are Blossoming,'' *The Wall Street Journal,* January 23, 1989, p. B1.

20. As reported in Margaret L. Usdansky, ''Asian Businesses Big Winners in '80s,'' *USA Today,* August 2, 1991, p. 1A; and John D. Kasarda, ''Why Asians Can Prosper Where Blacks Fail,'' *The Wall Street Journal,* May 5, 1992, p. A20.

21. Stone, ''Asian Growth: 105% in 10 Years.''

22. Robert Lewis, ''Asian Immigrants Find Large Profits in Small Stores,'' *Mobile* (Alabama) *Press Register,* March 5, 1989, p. G-1.

23. ''Asian Entrepreneurs: Success Isn't Cultural,'' *The Wall Street Journal,* April 3, 1989, p. B1.

Chapter 4

1. Lee Berton and Joann S. Lublin, ''Seeking Shelter: Partnership Structure Is Called in Question as Liability Rises,'' *The Wall Street Journal,* June 10, 1992, pp. A1, and A9.

2. ''New Businesses in Some States Have Less Red Tape to Fight,'' *The Wall Street Journal,* June 7, 1983, p. 33.

3. Laurie Baum and John A. Byrne, ''The Job Nobody Wants,'' *Business Week,* September 8, 1986, pp. 55–61.

4. For more details, see Steven P. Galante, ''Tax Package Would Enhance Attractions of S Corporations,'' *The Wall Street Journal,* September 15, 1986, p. 37.

5. ''Corporate Structure: Protecting Subchapter S Status,'' *Inc.,* January 1992, pp. 107–8.

6. For more details, see Thomas L. Barton and Michael A. Dillon, ''A New Menu for VCs: The Limited Liability Company,'' *Venture Capital Journal,* January 1992, pp. 52–55; and Barbara L. Bryniarski, ''Structuring for Limited Liability,'' *Nation's Business,* April 1992, pp. 46 and 48.

7. Bryniarski, ''Structuring for Limited Liability,'' p. 46.

8. Correspondence with Carolyn Ann Sledge, Assistant Director of Marketing for Delta Pride.

9. Cecile Sorra, ''SolarCare Resorts to a 'Big Brother' to Lighten Its Task,'' *The Wall Street Journal,* July 14, 1989, p. B2.

Chapter 5

1. This section is based on F. J. Roussel and Rose Epplin, *Thinking about Going into Business?,* U.S. Small Business Administration Management Aid No. 2.025. This and other publications are available for a small processing fee.

2. An excellent guide to use is the SBA's *Checklist for Going into Business,* Management Aid No. 2.016. To obtain this aid, contact your nearest SBA office.

3. Keith H. Hammonds, ''What B-School Doesn't Teach You about Start-ups,'' *Business Week,* July 24, 1989, p. 40.

4. Jeanne Saddler, ''Specialized Firms Stick to the Straight and Very Narrow,'' *The Wall Street Journal,* May 19, 1989, p. B2.

5. Hammonds, ''What B-School Doesn't Teach You about Start-ups,'' p. 41.

6. Jeanne Saddler, ''Entrepreneurs' Support Group Eases Stress,'' *The Wall Street Journal,* April 27, 1989, p. B2.

7. You can order this and other U.S. Census publications from the Bureau of the Census, U.S. Department of Commerce, Washington, DC 20233. Other documents can be bought from the U.S. Government Printing Office, Washington, DC 20402.

8. Otto Friedrich, ''Seven Who Succeeded,'' *Time,* January 7, 1985, pp. 40–44.

9. ''Franchising: The Take-Out Recipe for Success,'' *Small Business Success* 11 (1989): 28.

Chapter 6

1. *The Wall Street Journal,* October 31, 1986, p. 37.

2. ''Where to Start: The Best Way to Begin the Planning Process Is to Challenge Basic Assumptions,'' *Inc.,* November 1985, p. 132.

3. Donn Fenn, ''Growing by Design,'' *Inc.,* August 1985, p. 86.

4. Ibid.

5. See *Keeping Records in Small Business,* Management Aid No. 1.017, which can be obtained free from the Small Business Administration, Box 15434, Fort Worth, TX 76119.

Chapter 7

1. Arthur G. Sharp, ''Enfranchising Europe,'' *TWA Ambassador,* January 1991, p. 52.

2. U.S. Department of Commerce, *Franchising in the Economy, 1988–1990* (Washington, D.C.: Government Printing Office), p. 4.

3. Sharp, ''Enfranchising Europe.''

4. Robert S. Bond and Christopher E. Bond, *Franchising Opportunities, 1991–1992 Edition* (Homewood, Ill.: Irwin, 1992), p. 3.

5. International Franchise Association, *Franchising in the Economy,* 1989–1992, p. 115.

6. Constance Mitchell, ''Franchising Fever Spreads,'' *USA Today,* September 13, 1985, p. 4B.

7. Barbara Marsh, ''Franchisees Frolic but Focus on Deals at Annual Meeting,'' *The Wall Street Journal,* February 9, 1989, p. B2. For other estimates, see Jeffrey A. Tannenbaum, ''Dispute Grows over True Rate of Franchisee Failures,'' *The Wall Street Journal,* July 3, 1992, p. B2.

8. Constance Mitchell, ''Franchisees Shielded from Fraud,'' *USA Today,* September 13, 1985, p. 5B.

9. *Franchising Opportunities* (Babylon, N.Y.: Pilot Industries, Inc. 1992), p. 76.

10. "So You Want to Make It on Your Own," *Franchising World,* April 1989, pp. 10–15.

11. See Leon C. Megginson, Charles R. Scott, and William L. Megginson, *Successful Small Business Management,* 6th ed. (Homewood, Ill.: Irwin, 1991), pp. 113–15, for further details.

12. Sanford L. Jacobs, "Häagen-Dazs Distributors Find Big Profits, but Little Security," *The Wall Street Journal,* November 18, 1985, p. 33.

13. "So You Want to Make it on Your Own," pp. 10–11.

14. "Lube Shops on Corner Stations," *Mobile* (Alabama) *Register,* October 4, 1992, p. 8-E.

15. Sharp, "Enfranchising Europe," p. 48.

16. Carol Steinberg, "Franchising: A Global Concept," *USA Today,* April 9, 1992, p. 5B.

17. Correspondence with Richard Detwiler, director, public affairs, KFC International.

18. Richard W. Stevenson, "Pepsi to Show Ad in Russian," *New York Times,* January 20, 1989, p. C5.

19. "Moving South of the Border," *USA Today,* April 9, 1992, p. 7B.

20. Sharp, "Enfranchising Europe," p. 52.

21. *Franchising in the Economy, 1989–1992,* p. 19.

22. As reported in Carol Steinberg, "Minority Recruitment Efforts Underway," *USA Today,* June 25, 1992, p. 4B.

Chapter 8

1. "Behind Success: Ordinary Ideas," *USA Today,* May 30, 1989, p. 7B.

2. Christi Harlan, "Judge Clears Sale of Eastern Air Shuttle, Slates Monday Hearing on Rival Bids," *The Wall Street Journal,* May 17, 1989, p. A4.

3. See "Our Hero Restaurant (B)" in Leon C. Megginson, Charles R. Scott, and William L. Megginson, *Successful Small Business Management,* 6th ed. (Homewood, Ill.: Richard D. Irwin, 1991), pp. 251–54, for further details.

4. Cynthia C. Ryans, *Managing the Small Business* (Englewood Cliffs, N.J.: Prentice Hall, 1989), p. 73.

5. The SBA has several free publications to help you in preparing a plan. For example, SBA Management Aids No. 2.007 is a *Business Plan for Small Manufacturers*.

6. John G. Burch, *Entrepreneurship* (New York: John Wiley & Sons, 1986), pp. 377–82.

7. MP4 *Business Plan for Small Manufacturers,* MP5 *Business Plan for Small Construction Firms,* and MP15 *The Business Plan for Homebased Business* can be obtained from the U.S. Small Business Administration, P.O. Box 15434, Fort Worth, TX 76119, for $1.00 each. MP11 *Business Plan for Small Service Firms* can be obtained for $0.50 from the same source.

Chapter 9

1. Don Nichols, "For Sale or Rent, No Money Down," *Venture,* April 1989, p. 54.

2. Kathleen Devlin, "Disbursements Hit 10-Year Low," *Venture Capital Journal,* June 1992, p. 29.

3. Correspondence with the Vancouver Stock Exchange.

4. Ellie Winninghoff, "The Trouble with Angels," *Working Woman,* March 1992, p. 57.

5. Ellen J. James, "Desperate for Dollars," *Venture,* May 1988, p. 64.

6. "Pension-Fund Money Goes to Small Business," *The Wall Street Journal,* August 25, 1989, p. B1.

7. See Gibson Heath, *Funding Options for Small Business* (Denver: dba/USA Press, Inc., 1990); and Joan C. Szabo, "Alternative Ways to Find Capital," *Nation's Business,* April 1992, pp. 33–35, for some of these sources.

8. Udayan Gupta, ''Venture-Capital Funding Falls, but 'Incubators' Thrive,'' *The Wall Street Journal,* February 11, 1992, p. B2.

9. Correspondence with June Lavelle; and Bradford McKee, ''A Boost for Start-Ups,'' *Nation's Business,* August 1992, pp. 40–42.

10. Joel Katkin, ''Natural Partners,'' *Inc.,* June 1989, pp. 67–80; and David Webb, ''A Buyer-Supplier Alliance That Really Works,'' *Electronic Business,* March 30, 1992, p. 137.

11. See Gibson Heath, *Doing Business with Banks* (Lakewood, Col.: dba/USA Press, Inc., 1991), for some excellent suggestions for small business borrowers.

12. This discussion is based on the SBA publications *Lending the SBA Way* (no date) and *Your Business & the SBA* (September 1990), unless otherwise noted. Since Congress periodically passes new legislation that determines the kind of assistance the SBA provides, contact the nearest SBA district office to determine what types of assistance are currently available to you.

13. Mindy Fetterman, ''Callers Ignite the Hot Line,'' *USA Today,* May 10, 1989, p. 2B.

Chapter 10

1. ''You Know My Name,'' *Forbes,* October 21, 1985, p. 94.

2. Bob Levy, ''The Prime Offender: Business Itself, *Washington Post,* May 12, 1988, p. D20.

3. Suzanne Alexander, ''Tiny Ryka Seeks a Foothold with Sneakers for Women,'' *The Wall Street Journal,* July 31, 1989, p. B2.

4. Reported in *USA Today,* November 28, 1989, p. 1A.

5. Anita Manning, ''Boomers Are Ready to Loll into Decade,'' *USA Today,* December 13, 1989, pp. 1D, 2D.

6. Thomas R. King, ''Catering to the Maturing Baby-Boom Generation,'' *The Wall Street Journal,* Centennial Edition, 1989, p. A7.

7. *The Wall Street Journal*, October 14, 1982, p. 1; and ''Targeting You by ZIP,'' *USA Today,* March 16, 1989, p. B1.

8. ''17,000 Ideas Can't Be All Bad,'' *USA Today,* December 21, 1992, p. 3B.

9. Tom Shales, ''It Came, It Thawed, It Conquered,'' *Washington Post,* April 16, 1987, pp. C1, C6.

10. ''ProServ Inc.,'' *New York Times,* February 21, 1989, p. C8.

11. Discussion and correspondence with Ms. Brown; and Susan French Cone, ''Business Circle: Their Housework Not Just Routine; They Find No Two Days the Same,'' *Baldwin* (County, Alabama) *Press Register,* July 10, 1989, p. 5.

Chapter 11

1. Sometimes they are not sold by the time they reach Chicago, the train's destination, and must be sold at distressed prices or allowed to rot. Then the farmers not only lose the value of their crop but must pay transportation costs as well.

2. Lloyd Gite and Harriet C. Johnson, ''Pair Cooks Up Success in Potato Chip Business,'' *USA Today,* June 20, 1986, p. 4B.

3. Martin Sloane, ''Shoppers Ring Up Groceries,'' *Mobile* (Alabama) *Press Register,* May 25, 1986, p. 18-F.

4. Correspondence with Professor Russell Eustice, Husson College, Bangor, Maine.

5. Walter Kiechell, ''How to Manage Sales People,'' *Fortune,* March 14, 1988, pp. 179–80.

6. Correspondence with Sue Willis of Wendy's International, Inc.; and Guy Boulton, ''Wendy's Keeps Eye on Basics,'' *Mobile* (Alabama) *Register,* December 6, 1992, p. 16-E.

7. Marj Charlier, ''Upstart Ski Maker Plows Money into Ads amid Slump,'' *The Wall Street Journal,* November 25, 1991, p. B2.

8. William Smith, ''Local Cable Comes of Age,'' *Marketing & Media Decisions,* October 1988, p. 28; and Peter Pae, ''Low-Power TV Expands, Fed by New Programming,'' *The Wall Street Journal,* May 30, 1989, p. B1.

9. David D. Jefferson, ''Travel Concern Keeps Dreams Alive Despite Recession,'' *The Wall Street Journal,* April 3, 1992, p. B2.

10. William F. Allman, ''Science 1, Advertisers 0,'' *U.S. News & World Report,* May 1, 1989, p. 60.

11. ''The Ultimate in Pay for Performance,'' *Fortune,* May 25, 1987, p. 14; and Deborah Quilter, ''P.R.'s Odd Man Out,'' *Columbia Journalism Review* 27 (January–February 1989), p. 12.

12. Joanne Lipman, ''Nielsen to Track Hispanic TV Ratings,'' *The Wall Street Journal,* July 24, 1989, p. B4.

13. Alfredo Corchado, ''Demand for Hispanic Ads Outstrips Specialists in Field,'' *The Wall Street Journal,* June 29, 1989, p. B1.

Chapter 12

1. ''VCRs Cause Failure of Firm,'' *Mobile* (Alabama) *Register,* July 31, 1989, p. 2-A.

2. Reported in William J. Holstein and Kevin Kelley, ''Little Companies, Big Exports,'' *Business Week,* April 13, 1992, p. 70.

3. Kamvan Kashani, ''Beware the Pitfalls of Global Marketing,'' *Harvard Business Review* 67 (September/October 1989): 91–98.

4. Patrick Oster, Vince Gagetta, and Rob Hoff, ''10,000 New EC Rules,'' *Business Week,* September 7, 1992, pp. 48 and 50.

5. Holstein and Kelley, ''Little Companies, Big Exports.''

6. Its hotline can be reached at 800-872-8723.

7. ''Markets You May Have Missed,'' *Inc.,* November 1985, p. 162.

8. See Bill Holstein, ''An Export Service of Great Import,'' *Business Week,* September 28, 1992, p. 38, for some other practical sources.

9. Magrid Abraham, ''Getting the Most out of Advertising and Promotion,'' *Harvard Business Review* 68 (May/June 1990): 50–52.

Chapter 13

1. Barbara Marsh, ''Small Firms' Disadvantage in Hiring Likely to Grow,'' *The Wall Street Journal,* November 27, 1989, p. B1.

2. Udayan Gupta and Jeffrey A. Tannenbaum, ''Labor Shortages Force Changes at Small Firms,'' *The Wall Street Journal,* May 22, 1989, p. 1B.

3. U.S. Department of Commerce, Bureau of the Census, *Statistical Abstract of the United States, 1990* (Washington, D.C.: Government Printing Office, 1990), p. 398.

4. Marsh, ''Small Firms' Disadvantage,'' p. B2.

5. Timothy D. Schellhart, ''Temporary-Help Rebound May Prove Permanent,'' *The Wall Street Journal,* July 28, 1992, p. B4.

6. *Working Woman,* October 1985, as reported in *USA Today,* November 7, 1985, p. 1B.

7. Ward Howell International Inc., as reported in *The Wall Street Journal,* June 17, 1985, p. 1.

8. ''When You Are Face to Face,'' *Personnel* 67 (October 1990): 6.

9. Ted Gest, ''Testing, Testing,'' *U.S. News & World Report,* March 13, 1989, p. 52; and ''Green Light on Drug Tests for New Hires,'' *USA Today,* June 20, 1989, p. 1A.

10. For an excellent approach to training, see Iris Randall, ''10 Ways to Train Your Staff on a Tight Budget,'' *Black Enterprise,* February 1991, pp. 165–68.

11. Amy Dockser, ''Wrongful-Firing Case in Montana May Prompt Laws in Other States,'' *The Wall Street Journal,* July 3, 1989, p. 11.

Chapter 14

1. Douglas McGregor, *The Human Side of Enterprise* (New York: McGraw-Hill, 1960).

2. Joshua Hyatt, ''The Odyssey of an Excellent Man,'' *Inc.* February 1989, pp. 63–69.

3. For more information on this topic, see Rosemary Stewart, *Managers and Their Jobs* (New York: Macmillan, 1967); and Henry Mintzberg, *The Nature of Managerial Work* (New York: Harper & Row, 1973), p. 38.

4. Ralph W. Weber and Gloria E. Perry, *Behavioral Insights for Supervisors* (Englewood Cliffs, N.J.: Prentice Hall, 1975), p. 138.

5. *The Wall Street Journal,* February 18, 1992, p. B1.

6. Amy Saltzman, ''One Job, Two Contented Workers,'' *U.S. News & World Report,* November 1988, pp. 74 and 76.

7. Stanley Sloan and David E. Schrieber, ''Incentives: Are They Relevant? Obsolete? Misunderstood?'' *Personnel Administrator,* January–February 1970, pp. 25–27.

8. *U.S. News & World Report,* October 28, 1991, p. 16.

9. Clarence Francis, ''Management Methods,'' speech given in 1952; reprinted in *Management Methods Magazine,* 1952.

10. *The Wall Street Journal,* August 7, 1992, p. A14.

11. Donald L. McManis and William G. Dick, ''Monetary Incentives in Today's Industrial Setting,'' *Personnel Journal* 52 (May 1973): 387–89.

12. Margaret Magnus, ''Personnel Policies in Partnership with Profit,'' *Personnel Journal* 66 (September 1987): 102–9.

13. As reported in *Business Week,* February 3, 1992, p. 72.

14. See Julia Lawler, ''Landmark Act Leaves Some Businesses Fuming,'' *USA Today,* February 8, 1993, p. 4B, for an excellent analysis of the law.

15. Bryna Brennan, ''Small Firms Dropping Pension Plans; Laws Too Complex,'' *Birmingham* (Alabama) *News,* December 17, 1989, p. 2D.

16. Ibid.

17. Since the requirements are complex and change frequently, check with your accountant before setting up an IRA or any other type of retirement plan.

18. See ''Retirement,'' *U.S. News & World Report,* November 18, 1985, p. 55, for a fuller explanation of IRAs and Keogh plans.

19. Carol Lee Morgan, ''You *Can* Take It with You,'' *Parade Magazine,* May 7, 1989. pp. 22–23.

20. *Nation's Business,* February 1992, p. 43.

21. ''Beyond the Pay Envelope,'' *Inc.,* December 1991, p. 158.

Chapter 15

1. New York (state), Department of Labor, Division of Research and Statistics, *Injury Rates in Factories* (New York, 1966).

2. *Accident Facts* (Chicago: National Safety Council).

3. U.S. Bureau of the Census, *Statistical Abstract of the US, 1991,* pp. 422–23.

4. Michele Galen et al., "Repetitive Stress: The Pain Has Just Begun," *Business Week,* July 13, 1992, p. 142. OSHA is preparing *ergonomics standards,* but they won't be ready for years. These standards will force employers to provide appropriate furniture and equipment (for example, chairs and keyboards) to help relieve maladies such as RSI.

5. Leon C. Megginson, *Personnel Management: A Human Resources Approach,* 5th ed. (Homewood, Ill.: Richard D. Irwin, 1985), pp. 407–9.

6. Sanford L. Jacobs, "Small Business Slowly Wakes to OSHA Hazard Rule," *The Wall Street Journal,* November 22, 1988, p. B1.

7. See "Norton Delegates Personnel Affairs to the Workers," *International Management* 30 (June 1975): 48–50, for an example.

8. Stuart Elliott, "Workers' Woes Give Firms Financial Fits," *USA Today,* June 13, 1989, p. 1B.

9. Contact your nearest SBA office for more information on these laws.

10. Megginson, *Personnel Management,* p. 558; and *Mobile* (Alabama) *Register,* June 10, 1992, p. 6-A.

11. Ron Suskind, "Tough Vote: Threat of Cheap Labor Abroad Complicates Decisions to Unionize," *The Wall Street Journal,* July 28, 1992, p. A1.

12. Albert R. Karr, "Small Business Scores Big in Congressional Lobbying," *The Wall Street Journal,* October 3, 1988, pp. B1, B2.

13. Those states are Alabama, Arizona, Arkansas, Florida, Georgia, Idaho, Kansas, Louisiana, Mississippi, Nebraska, Nevada, North Carolina, North Dakota, South Carolina, South Dakota, Tennessee, Texas, Utah, Virginia, and Wyoming.

14. Jeffrey A. Tannenbaum, "Consultants, Small Business Come to Need One Another," *The Wall Street Journal,* September 28, 1989, p. B1.

Chapter 16

1. Jeffrey Theodore, "They Groom Dogs 'On the Spot,' " *Baldwin* (County, Alabama) *Press Register,* June 12, 1989, p. 4.

2. See Karen Levine, "Making Money from Home," *Parent's Magazine,* November 1991, pp. 89–92, for more details.

3. Leon C. Megginson, Lyle R. Trueblood, and Gayle M. Ross, *Business* (Lexington, Mass.: D. C. Heath, 1985), pp. 344–46.

4. Consult any basic industrial engineering text for a detailed discussion of this process, along with sample forms.

Chapter 17

1. Leon C. Megginson, Donald C. Mosley, and Paul H. Pietri, Jr., *Management: Concepts and Applications,* 4th ed. (New York: HarperCollins, 1992), p. 662.

2. "Wal-Mart Plans 'Just-in-Time' Delivery System," *Birmingham* (Alabama) *Post-Herald,* February 14, 1989, p. B1.

3. Micheline Maynard, "5-Cent Part Defect Forces LH Recall," *USA Today,* September 4, 1992, p. 1B.

4. "Consultants: For a Complex Purchase, an Outside Expert May Be Just What You Need," *Inc.,* October 1991, pp. OG 65-OG 66.

5. Leon C. Megginson, Lyle R. Trueblood, and Gayle M. Ross, *Business* (Lexington, Mass.: D. C. Heath, 1985), p. 213.

6. David E. Gumpert, "Lighten Load, Trim Sails to Ride Out the Storm," *USA Today,* May 8, 1989, p. 10E.

7. For an example of the use of intuition, see "Bush as the Nation's Manager," *USA Today,* February 8, 1991, pp. 1B and 2B.

8. See any current marketing or production management text for formulas to use.

9. Kathy Jumper, ''Menefee Wants His Clients to Be Happy, Look Good,'' *Mobile* (Alabama) *Register,* February 20, 1989, p. 1-B.

Chapter 18

1. Mary Rowland, ''Why Small Businesses Are Failing,'' *The New York Times,* August 11, 1991, Sec. 3, p. 16.

2. Gus Gordon, *Understanding Financial Statements* (Cincinnati, Ohio: South-Western, 1992).

3. Jeffrey M. Lademman, ''Earnings, Schmernings—Look at the Cash,'' *Business Week,* July 24, 1989, pp. 56–57.

4. Sanford L. Jacobs, ''Watch the Numbers to Learn If the Business Is Doing Well,'' *The Wall Street Journal,* August 26, 1985, p. 19.

5. Roger Ricklefs and Udayan Gupta, ''Traumas of a New Entrepreneur,'' *The Wall Street Journal,* May 10, 1989, p. B1.

6. Roberta Maynard, ''Smart Ways to Manage Cash,'' *Nation's Business,* August 1992, pp. 43–44.

7. David M. Gumpert, ''Don't Let Optimism Block Out Trouble Signposts,'' *USA Today,* May 8, 1989, p. 10E.

8. ''Strategies that Pay Off,'' *Inc.,* March 1991, p. 74.

9. M. K. Kolay, ''Managing Working Capital Crises: A System Dynamics Approach,'' *Management Decisions* 29 (September 1991): 46–52.

10. Jill A. Fraser, ''On Target,'' *Inc.,* April 1991, pp. 113–14.

11. See Michelle L. Singletary, ''Trimming the Fat,'' *Black Enterprise,* June 1991, pp. 246–49, for some helpful suggestions as to how to do this.

Chapter 19

1. See ''The Five Cardinal Rules of Financial Control,'' *Inc.,* May 1992, p. 156, for a different set of characteristics.

2. See Alan Wilson, ''Effective Cash and Profit Forecasting,'' *The Accountant's Magazine,* August 1990, pp. 45–47, for some techniques you can use.

3. Teri Lammers, ''The Weekly Cash-Flow Planner,'' *Inc.,* June 1992, pp. 99–102.

4. See Ripley Hotch, ''Not Just the Numbers,'' *Nation's Business,* January 1992, pp. 42–44; and William F. Zachmann, ''Beware the Shrink-Wrap Fallacy,'' *PC Magazine,* September 15, 1992, p. 105, for some of these.

5. ''Financial Tactics: The Check Is in the Mail,'' *Inc.,* June 1985, p. 123.

6. For some suggestions on how you can best use auditors, see John E. McEldowney, Thomas L. Barton, and Edward J. Todd, ''The Audit of a Small Business: War Stories and Dreams,'' *The CPA Journal,* November 1990, pp. 32–36.

7. G. Paschal Zachary, ''CDs to Store Data Are Music to Auditors' Ears,'' *The Wall Street Journal,* August 4, 1989, p. B1.

8. Dean Planeaux, ''Factoring Guarantees Cash Flow for Diaper Startup,'' *Corporate Cashflow Magazine,* August 1991, p. 42.

Chapter 20

1. U.S. Department of the Treasury, Internal Revenue Service, *Tax Guide for Small Business,* Publication 334 (Washington, D.C.: U.S. Government Printing Office, 1992).

2. Kurt R. Majette and Thomas P. Rohman, ''Choice of Business Entity after the Tax Reform of 1986: The Brave New World,'' *Review of Taxation for Individuals,* Winter 1988, pp. 38–65.

3. See U.S. Department of the Treasury, Internal Revenue Service, *Tax Information on S Corporations,* Publication 589 (Washington, D.C.: U.S. Government Printing Office, 1991), for more details.

4. Gordon Alexander and William F. Sharpe, *Fundamentals of Investments* (Englewood Cliffs, N.J.: Prentice Hall, 1987), pp. 72–73.

5. Eugene Willis et al., *West's Federal Taxation: Comprehensive Volume, 1993 Edition* (St. Paul, Minn.: West, 1992), p. A10.

6. "Inflation Jitters Prompt Companies to Shift Accounting Methods," *The Wall Street Journal,* April 27, 1989, p. A1.

7. See U.S. Department of the Treasury, Internal Revenue Service, *1992 Forms and Instructions, 1040* (Washington, D.C.: U.S. Government Printing Office, 1992).

8. Willis, *West's Federal Taxation: Comprehensive Volume, 1993 Edition,* pp. 9–26.

9. For more information, see U.S. Department of the Treasury, Internal Revenue Service, *1991 Federal Employment Tax Forms,* Publication 393 (Rancho Cordova, Calif.: IRS, 1991).

10. John D. McClain, "Social Security Recipients to Receive Bigger Checks," *Mobile* (Alabama) *Register,* October 16, 1992, p. 5-A.

11. Sandra Salmans, "Cutting the Deal," *Venture,* January 19, 1988, pp. 32, 34.

12. See Irving L. Blackman, "Family Gifts," *Inc.,* January 1989, p. 125, for details.

13. See Irving L. Blackman, "Family Partnerships as Tax Shelter," *Inc.,* April 1988, p. 131, for further details and illustrations.

14. Louis Austin, Vickie Schumaker, and Jim Schumacher, "Living Trusts Replace Wills as Estate Planning Tools," *Small Business Reports,* March 1989, p. 93.

15. Diane Weber, "A Living Trust Can Be Great If You Dodge These Pitfalls," *Medical Economics,* August 20, 1992, pp. 90–95.

Chapter 21

1. Michael Edelhart and Douglas Garr, *The Complete Computer Compendium* (Menlo Park, Calif.: Addison-Wesley, 1984), p. 57.

2. JDR Microdevices advertisement, *Byte,* November 1984, p. 568.

3. Lawrence J. Curran and Richard S. Shuford, "IBM's Estridge," *Byte,* November 1983, p. 89.

4. "Inside the IBM PC," *Byte,* November 1983, p. 76.

5. See Mark Stevens, "Six Small-Business Problems Computers Can Solve," *Working Woman,* September 1987, pp. 33–36, for more uses of computers in small firms.

6. Tom Richman, "Break It to Me Gently," *Inc.,* July 1989, pp. 108–10.

7. Jared Taylor, "Keeping Up with the Computer," *The Wall Street Journal,* Special Report, May 20, 1985, p. 84C.

8. "Office Technology: Software Use," *Inc.,* May 1989, p. 123.

Chapter 22

1. "Citibank's Test of Paying to See Tellers Doesn't Pay," *The Wall Street Journal,* May 26, 1983, p. 6.

2. "Making Insurance Cost Shifting Less Painful," *Inc.,* March 1992, p. 104.

3. David Scott, "How Much Risk Can Your Company Stand?" *Risk Management,* June 1991, pp. 85–88.

4. Rob Wells, "Trade Center Firms Struggle to Resume Business Activity," AP bulletin to *Mobile* (Alabama) *Register,* March 2, 1993, p. 6-A.

5. Linda Chavez, "Suits Are Big Problem," *USA Today,* September 10, 1992, p. 14A.

6. Ibid.

7. Roger Thompson, "Workers' Comp Costs: Out of Control," *Nation's Business,* July 1992, pp. 22–30.

8. Terri Thompson, "Premium-Priced Controversies," p. 47.

9. Various sources, but especially Roger Thompson, "How to Buy Health Insurance," *Nation's Business,* October 1992, pp. 16–22.

10. Ben Z. Hershberg, "The Ills of Small Firms," *USA Today,* September 25, 1989, p. 3B.

11. Udayan Gupta, "Enterprise," *The Wall Street Journal,* April 21, 1992, p. B2.

12. "To Stop a Thief," *U.S. News & World Report,* May 1, 1989, p. 76.

13. Arlene Levinson, "Retailers Strike Back at Shoplifters via Letter Campaign," *Mobile* (Alabama) *Press Register,* May 13, 1989, p. 5-A.

14. John R. Emshwiller, "Employers Lose Billions of Dollars to Employee Theft," *The Wall Street Journal,* October 5, 1992, p. B2.

15. Peter Pae, "Small Firms Are Easy Prey for Embezzlers," *The Wall Street Journal,* August 3, 1989, pp. B1, B2.

16. "White-Collar Crime Deserves Jail Time," *USA Today,* October 27, 1989, p. 14A.

17. "High-Tech Success," *The Wall Street Journal,* November 22, 1988, p. 1A.

18. Bob Kirby, "New Kind of Doctor. . . ," *Mobile* (Alabama) *Register,* May 18, 1989, p. 1-B.

Chapter 23

1. For some selected sections from the UCC, see Douglas Whitman et al., *Law and Business* (New York: Random House, 1987) pp. 781–855.

2. Ibid., p. 83.

3. "Selling Faulty Pacemakers Costs Firm Plenty," *Mobile* (Alabama) *Register,* March 29, 1989, p. 2-A.

4. For more details on how to get a patent, call the U.S. Patent Office at (703) 557-3158. To register a trademark, write the U.S. Trademark Association at 6 East 45th Street, New York, NY 10017.

5. *Fortune,* January 23, 1984, p. 31.

6. Brent Bowers, "The Doozies: Seven Scary Tales of Wild Bureaucracy," *The Wall Street Journal,* June 19, 1992, p. B2.

7. Louis Richman, "Bringing Reason to Regulation," *Fortune,* October 19, 1992, p. 94.

8. Jeanne Saddler, "Small Businesses Complain That Jungle of Regulations Jeopardizes Their Futures," *The Wall Street Journal,* June 11, 1992, p. B1.

9. Ibid.

10. U.S. Department of Commerce, *Survey of Current Business* (Washington, D.C.: U.S. Government Printing Office, August 1983), p. 24.

11. Jeffrey A. Tannenbaum, "Government Red Tape Puts Entrepreneurs in the Black," *The Wall Street Journal,* June 12, 1992, p. B2.

12. Paul J. Lim, "Bungee Jumping's Unencumbered Cord Gets Tangled," *The Wall Street Journal,* August 11, 1992, p. B2.

13. Jeanne Saddler, "Small Business Owners Increase Their Political Activity," *The Wall Street Journal,* April 2, 1992, p. B2.

14. *How to Choose and Use a Lawyer* (Chicago: American Bar Association, 1990). For information contact the ABA at 750 N. Lake Shore Drive, Chicago, IL 60611.

15. Jeffrey A. Tannenbaum, ''Small-Business Owners Must Pick a Lawyer Judiciously,'' *The Wall Street Journal,* February 15, 1989, p. B2.

16. Gary Hector, ''A New Reason You Can't Get a Loan,'' *Fortune,* September 21, 1992, pp. 107–12.

17. Ibid.

18. The Annenberg/CPB Project has a new audio and video series entitled ''Ethics in Business.'' A preview can be arranged by writing The Annenberg/CPB Project, % Intellimation, P.O. Box 4069, Santa Barbara, CA 93140, or calling 1-800-LEARNER.

19. Kenneth Labich, ''The New Crisis in Business Ethics,'' *Fortune,* April 20, 1992, p. 172.

20. W. Michael Hoffman and Edward S. Petry, Jr., ''Abusing Business Ethics,'' *Phi Kappa Journal,* Winter 1992, pp. 10–13.

Chapter 24

1. Hank Gilman, ''The Last Generation,'' *The Wall Street Journal,* May 20, 1985, p. 29C; and Terence Pare, ''Passing on the Family Business,'' *Fortune,* May 7, 1990, pp. 81–82.

2. Wendy C. Handler, ''Key Interpersonal Relationships of Next-Generation Family Members in Family Firms,'' *Journal of Small Business Management* 29 (July 1991): 21.

3. ''When Business Is All in the Family,'' *Mobile* (Alabama) *Press Register,* February 23, 1986, p. 1-C.

4. Jean K. Mason, ''Selling Father's Painful Legacy,'' *Nation's Business,* September 1988, p. 30.

5. Margaret Crane, ''How to Keep Families from Feuding,'' *Inc. Magazine's Guide to Small Business Success,* 1987, pp. 32–34.

6. ''The New Business: Smith & Parents,'' *The Wall Street Journal,* December 8, 1988, p. B1.

7. Daniel M. Morris, ''Why Family Businesses Fail,'' *Business Credit,* February 1989, p. 47.

8. David L. Epstein, ''Prepare Your Heir,'' *Restaurant Business,* January 20, 1988, p. 70.

9. ''So You're Going to Take Over the Family Business,'' *Agency Sales Magazine,* July 1988, p. 34.

10. John R. Emshwiller, ''Handing Down the Business,'' *The Wall Street Journal,* May 19, 1989, p. B1.

11. Sharon Donovan, ''Boss's Daughter, Son Get Down to Business,'' *USA Today,* May 8, 1989, p. 10E.

12. Priscilla Donegan, ''A Fight for Survival,'' *Progressive Grocer,* September 1988, p. 22.

13. ''Entrepreneurs Neglect One Type of Planning,'' *The Wall Street Journal,* April 8, 1992, p. B1.

14. Ibid.

15. ''Planning Ahead Can Ease Succession,'' *The Wall Street Journal,* May 19, 1989, p. B1.

16. K. Von Kreisler-Bomben, ''The Outsiders,'' *Entrepreneur,* December 1991, pp. 172–75.

17. Mason, ''Selling Father's Painful Legacy,'' p. 35.

18. Robert L. Kuhn and David H. Troob, ''When It's Time to Sell the Firm,'' *Nation's Business,* July 1992, pp. 47–49.

19. Harriet C. Johnson, ''Ready to Sell? Helpful Tips from Experts,'' *USA Today,* May 9, 1988, p. 11E. Also, see Paul Sperry and Beatrice Mitchell, *The Complete Guide to Selling Your Business* (Dover, N.H.: Upstart, 1992), for a comprehensive step-by-step guide through the process of selling your firm, from deciding to sell through negotiating the final terms.

20. Richard K. Berkowitz and Joseph A. Blanco, ''Putting a Price Tag on Your Company,'' *Nation's Business,* January 1992, pp. 29–31.

Accounting; *see also* Inventory; Liabilities
  accounting system as MIS, 436–42
  accounts payable, 396
  accounts receivable, 367, 399, 439
  accrual method, 410, 441
  assets, 367
    current assets, 367
    fixed assets, 368
  balance sheet, 367
  cash basis method, **441**
  depreciation, 414
    straight-line depreciation, 414–15
  financial structure, 367
  importance of, 365–67
  owner's equity, 369
  retained earnings, 369
Accounts payable, 396
Accounts receivable, 367, 399
  computers and, 439
Accrual method (accounting), **410, 441**
ACE (Association of Collegiate
    Entrepreneurs), 7–8, 242
Acid test (quick) ratio, 398, **399**
Acoustic Research, 62, 72
Action Leasing, 359
ADA; *see* Americans with Disabilities Act
Advent Corporation, 72
Advertising, **226,** 226–30
  advertising agencies, 230
  budget for, 227–28
  immediate-response advertising, 230
  institutional advertising, 226
  media for, 228–30
  product advertising, 226
Aetna Life and Casualty, 305–6
Affirmative action programs (AAPs), 274
Agents, 219, 477
  agency law, 477
Air pollution requirements, 401
Albrecht, Steve, 463–64
Albright, Don, 88
Alexander, John, 229
Alexander, Suzanne, 212
Allen, Diane, 176, 262
Allick, Wilfred, Jr., 489
Allowances, 202
American Association of Community and
    Junior Colleges, 6
American Business Information, 45
American Business Women's Association,
    491
American Institute of Small Business, 79,
    150
American Motors, as small business, 9

American Productivity and Quality Center,
    289
American Software, 128
Americans with Disabilities Act (ADA) of
    1992, 257, **271,** 271–72, 274, 306
American Women's Economic Development
    Corporation, 47
Anchor stores, 329
Anders Book Stores, 341
Anderson, Kevin, 8
Andriana Furs Inc., 184
Androbot, 199
Angel capitalists, 175
Aplin, Lisa, 31
Apple Computer, 174, 308
Apprenticeship training, 270
Ardman, Perri, 425
Armchair Sailor Bookstore, 91
Armed robbery, as business risk, 458–60
Arnst, Catherine, 3
Arthur Young's Entrepreneurial Services, 96
Articles of copartnership, 63
Articles of incorporation, 64
ArtWatches, 115
Asian-Americans, business opportunities,
    49–51
ASK Computer Systems, 8
Assets, 367
  current assets, 367
  fixed assets to owner's equity ratio, 398,
    400
  net sales to fixed assets ratio, 398–99
Association of Collegiate Entrepreneurs
    (ACE), 7–8, 242
Attorneys' Computer Network, Inc., 63
Audit, 394
  for budget control, 394–95
  for crime prevention, 464
  internal auditing, 394
  operations audit, 394
Authority, organization by, 302
Autodesk, Inc., 331
Average cost inventory method, 412

Babbage's, 128
Baby Talk (magazine), 366
Bacon, Francis, 40
Balance sheet, 367
Baldwin Press Register, 208
Bank of Montana, 485
Bares, Jack, 405
Bartering, 184
Bartimo, Jim, 3

Bartley, Robert L., 5
Basic Marketing (McCarthy and Perreault),
    198
Beggrow, David, 167
Beggrow, Dennis, 167
Bellevue Journal-American, 205
Bell Stained Glass and Overlay, 262
Bellville Potato Chip Company, 218
Bennett, Robert, 10
Berluti, James, 212
Best Western, 127
Bethesda Gazette, 77
Biddle, Susan, 479
Bio Clinic Co., 416
Black Enterprise, 5, 48, 117, 215
Blacks
  in business, 22, 117, 137–38, 215,
    444–45
  business incubators and, 176
  opportunities for, 47–48
Blackwell, Doug, 173, 494
Bloomingdale's, 222
Bloomin' Lollipops, Inc., 57, 171, 493
Blount, Carolyn, 345
Blount, Wynton M., 345
Bluestone, Mimi, 221
Boaz, Joyce, 425
Bodenstab, Charles J., 136
Boles, George, 67
Bond, 172
Bonus (as incentive pay), **291**
Boone, Louis E., 205
Boone, Sherron, 31
Bowman-Upton, Nancy, 496–97, 499
Boyles, Kenneth, 437
Bradley, Mark, 151
Bradley, Missy, 151
Bradley Sporting Goods, business plan,
    151–65
Bread Basket, 128
Break-even point, 378
Brokers, 219
Broun, Heywood, 236
Brown, Buck, 499
Brown, Lynn, 207
Bryant, Paul (Bear), 279
Buckingham Associates, 500
Budgets, 105, 388
  advertising and, 227–28
  audit (for budget control), **394,** 394–95
  budgetary control, 393, 393–95
    internal auditing, 394
    operations audit, 394
  capital budget, 388

Budgets—*Cont.*
cash flow budget, 388
to communicate standards, 388–95
operating budget, 388, 389
personal budget, necessity of, 109–10
types of, 389
Building the High Technology Business, 409
Bulkeley, William M., 150, 504
Bulova Corporation, 115
Burch, John G., 146
Burdines, 222
Bureau of Apprenticeship and Training (US DOL), 270
Bureau of Labor Statistics, 305
Burger King, 279, 323
Burke, Edmund, 56
Burton, John, 454
Busby, James L., 137–39
Bush, George, 478–79
Business (Megginson, Trueblood, Ross), 324
Business Age, 458
Business continuation life insurance, 456
Business ethics, 485, 485–86
Business format franchising, 120
Business incubators, 176
Business Insight (software), 150
Business interruption insurance coverage, 452
Business laws, basic, 472–78
agency law, 477
agent, 477
principal, 477
bankruptcy law, 478
Chapter 11, 478
contract, 473, 473–74
legal terminology, 473
negotiable instrument, 477
product liability, 475
property law, 476–77
copyright, 476
patent, 476
trademark, 476, 476–77
sales laws
express contract, 475
implied contract, 475
tort, 477
Uniform Commercial Code (UCC), 472, 472–73
warranty, 475
Business owner's insurance, 456
Business plan, 136–65, 138
components of, 141–46
presentation of, 146–47
sample plan, 151–65
software for preparation, 79, 150
Business Resource Software, Inc., 150
Business Risks International, Inc., 449
Business services, 206

Business Week, 3, 221, 359
Newsletter for Family-Owned Businesses, 5
Buy-sell agreement (corporate), **66, 506**
Byrd, Gerald, 199
Byrd Surveying, 199
Byte, 308

Cadwell, Carlton, 56
Cafeteria-style benefit plan, 294–95
Cambridge Soundworks, 64, 72–73
Cape, Murray, 354
Capital; *see also* Financing
capital budget, 389
locating funds, 112–13
long-term liabilities to working capital ratio, 398, 400
for new businesses, 15, 32–33
working capital, 399
Capital debt financing, 170–71
Captain D's Seafood, 132
Careers USA, Inc., 128
Carlson, Eugene, 167
Carnegie, Andrew, 258
Carnegie, Dale, 214
Carpenter, John E., 279
Carter, Jimmy, 117, 215
Caruth's Institute of Owner-Managed Business, 31
Cash basis (accounting), **441**
Cash budget, 169
Cash flow, 112
cash flow budget, 389, 390–93
problems with, 403
Casualty insurance, 453
Cavanaugh, Jack, 449
C corporation, 64
Cell Technology, 167
CERA Economics Consultants, Inc., 15
CFCs (chlorofluorocarbons), 308
Chan, Peng S., 116
Chapman House, 494
Chappell, Barbara, 139
Chappell, Steven, 139
Chattel mortgage, 172
Checker's Drive-In Restaurants, Inc., 363
Checklist for Going into Business (SBA), 111
Cherubini, Georgio, 471
Chicago Tribune, 237
Chicago White Sox, as barterer, 184
Child Protection and Toy Safety Act, 484
Choosing a Retailing Location (SBA), 326
Chrysler, 343
Churchill, Neil, 389, 403
Circuit City, 128
Cironi, Toni, 126
Civil Demand Associates, 461

Civil recovery (civil restitution), 461
Civil Rights Act of 1991, 257
Clark, Alexander, 384
Clark, Austin, 167
Clark, Otto, 237
Clark Copy International Corporation, 237
Clarke, Adline, 257, 339
Clean Air Act of 1990, 480
Cloud 9, 51
Cognetics, Inc., 43, 240
Coinsurance, 452
Collection period ratio, 398, 399
Collins, Peter, 500
Comfort Clothing, Inc., 235
Commission (as incentive pay), **290**
Committee for Economic Development, 9
Common stock, 171
Common stockholders, 169
Communication, 281
with employees, 281–82
grapevine communication systems, 302
Compaq Computers, 177
Competitive edge, 102, 193
Comprehensive Accounting Corporation, 5
Compu-Screen Systems, Inc., 257
Computer Specialists, Inc., 295
Computers for small business; *see also* Management information system (MIS); Software for
computer terms, 446
hardware, 430
history of development, 431–33
inventory control and, 440–41
security of, 436, 463–64
softlifting, 468
software, 431
sources of information about, 438
strengths and weaknesses, 433–34
Conner, Finis, 177
Conner Peripherals Inc., 177
Consignment selling, 177
Consumerism, 192–93, **193, 484**
Consumer Products Safety Commission, 484
Contemporary Marketing (Boone and Kurtz), 205
Contract, 473, 473–74
express contract, 475
implied contract, 475
Control, 386; *see also* Budgets
control systems, characteristics of, 387–88
performance standards, 387
role of, 386
steps in, 386–87
Convenience goods, 328
Cooperative, 68, 68–69
Coopers & Lybrand, 500
Copyright, 476
Cordis Corporation, 475

Corporate charter, 64
Corporate income taxes, 411–13
The Corporate Kits Library (software), 63
Corporation, 64, 64–67
   articles of incorporation, 64
   buy-sell agreement, 66, 506
   C corporation, 64
   corporate charter, 64
   S corporation, 66–67, 67
Cost-oriented pricing, 202
Cost-plus pricing, 204
Counseling (of employees), **307,** 307–11
Credit cards, 249–50
   crime prevention and, 464
   taxis and, 44
Credit doctor, as white-collar crime, 464
Credit management, 248, 248–51
Crime prevention, 458–64
   armed robbery, 458–60
   theft, 460–63
   white collar crimes, 463, 463–64
Cuisine Express, 46
Cummins, Carol, 286
Cumulative News (S&P), 246
Current assets, 367
Current liabilities, 369
Customary price, 203

D. C. Heath and Company, 237
Daily News (S&P), 246
Davidow, William H., 188
Debt financing, 169, 170–71
   debt securities
      bond, 172
      chattel mortgage, 172
      intermediate-term securities, 172
      long-term securities, 172
      mortgage loan, 172
      short-term securities, 172
   sources of, 177–78
Debt to owner's equity ratio, 398, 400
Deficit Reduction Act of 1984, 413
Delaware, incorporation laws, 65
Delegation, 300, 300–301
Dell, Michael, 3–4
Dell Computer Corporation, 3–4
Delta Pride Catfish, Inc., 69
Depreciation, 414, 414–15
Detroit 90, 117
Deutschman, Alan, 3
Digital Network, Inc., 11
Dince, Robert, 384
Direct mail advertising, 228
Disabled veterans, SBA loans for, 180
Disaster victims, SBA loans for, 180
Discipline (of employees), **311,** 311–12
Disclosure statement (prospectus) (for
   franchising), **125**
Discontinuance (of business), **52**

Distribution, 246, 246–48
   distribution channel, 216, 216–19, 240
Diversification, 209
Document security, 464–65
Doerflinger, Thomas, 424
Domino's Pizza, 232
Donald & Asby, 496
Dow, Mike, 137
Dreams Come True, Inc., 229
Drucker, Peter F., 320, 340
Drug-Free Workforce Rules (DOD), 310
Dugan, Rick, 28, 77
Dunn, Keith, 280
Dunn, Marcia, 97

Eastern Airlines, 138
Eastern Connection, Inc., 212
East Europe Law Ltd., 129
Ebony, 28
Eckert, J. Presper, Jr., 13, 148
Economic Bulletin Board (US DOC), 480
Economic Development Administration
   (EDA), 180
Economic order quantity, 352
Electronic scanners, 34
Eliot, T. S., 490
Employee (fringe) **benefits, 291,** 291–95
   cafeteria-style benefit plan, 294–95
   401(k) plans, 294
   **individual retirement accounts (IRAs),
      294**
   Keogh retirement plan, 294
   simplified employee pension (SEP) plan,
      294
   Social Security, 293
   unemployment insurance, 293
   workers' compensation, 293
Employee Retirement Income Security Act
   of 1974 (ERISA), 294, 413
Employees; *see also* Employee (fringe)
   benefits; Equal Employment
   Opportunity (EEO) laws
   compensation of, 288–91
   laws and, 288–89
   complaints of, 310–11
   counseling (of employees), **307,** 307–11
   discipline, 311, 311–12
   employee relations, 298–317, 485
      organizational concepts and, 300–304
      organization by activities, 304
      organization by authority, 302
      organization chart, 303, 303–4
   leadership (of), **280**
      communication, 281, 281–82
   managers
      compensation of, 291
      selecting and developing, 270–71
   motivation, 283, 283–87

Employees—*Cont.*
   older workers, 195
   part-time and temporary, 263
   performance appraisal, 287
   performance standards, 337, 387
   personnel needs, planning for, 258–67
   recruiting and selecting, 264–68
   safeguarding at workplace, 304–7,
      465–66
   termination of, 274–75
   theft by employees, 463
   training and developing, 268–70
   unions and, 312–15
**Employee stock ownership plan (ESOP),
   176, 291**
   taxes and, 411
Employment at will, 274–75
Emshwiller, John R., 489
Engeleiter, Susan, 470
Enterprise Development Center, 143
Enterprise Group, 367
Entrepreneur (magazine), 5, 123, 150
Entrepreneur Application Profile, 143
Entrepreneurial Woman, 5
Entrepreneurship, 6–7
   entrepreneur, 10
   entrepreneurial venture, 10
      versus small business, 9–11
   entrepreneur-investor relationship, 181
   Kiam on success, 38–39
   test for potential of, 31
Environmental protection, 307–8, 485
Environmental Protection Agency, 307
Equal Employment Opportunity (EEO) laws,
   271–75
   **affirmative action programs (AAPs),
      274**
   Americans with Disabilities Act (ADA)
      of 1992, 257, **271,** 271–72, 274,
      306
   employment at will, 274–75
   **Equal Employment Opportunity
      Commission (EEOC), 273**
Equity, 169
   equity investors, 113
   equity securities, 171–72
   sources of, 172–77
**ESOPs (employee stock ownership plans),
   176**
Estate planning, 505–6
   living trust, 418
   taxes and, 417–18
Estée Lauder, 222
Estes, Bill, 385
Ethics of business, 485–86, 485–96
Evans, Marilyn, 279
Evans, Murry, 279, 285
Excise tax, 409
Executive decision method, for advertising,
   228

Executive summary (of business plan), **142**, 142–43
Eximbank (Export-Import Bank of United States), 243
Expenses, 371
  fixed expenses (costs), 371
  variable expenses (costs), 371
Export-Import Bank of United States (Eximbank), 243
Exporting, 238, 240–43
Express contract, 475
Extended-coverage (insurance) endorsement, 452

Facilities, 331
  physical facilities, planning of, 331–36
Failure (of business), 15–16, **52**, 96
Fain, Deborah, 271
Falvey, Jack, 214
Family Business, 5
Family and Medical Leave Act of 1993, 293
Family-owned business, 492–505
  management succession of, 498–501
Fantel, Hans, 73
Farr, Mel, 215
Farrell, Kevin, 221
FCIA (Foreign Credit Insurance Association), 243
Federal Express, 174, 212, 248
Federal Insurance Contributions Act (FICA), 414
Federal Trade Commission (FTC), paperwork for franchisors, 122
Federal unemployment tax, 414, 414–15
Feedback, 395
Feeling Special Fashions, 235
Ferchaud, Jay, 41
Fernandez, Jim H., 63
Ferndale Honda, 117
Ferromin International, 453
Fidelity bonds, 455
  for crime prevention, 464
Filene's, 108
Financial condition of business; *see* Financial ratios
Financial leverage, 170
Financial planning, 109
  profit planning, 364–80
  role of, 109–13
Financial ratios
  acid test (quick) ratio, 398, **399**
  collection period ratio, 398, 399
  current liabilities to owner's equity ratio, 398, 400
  current ratio, 396, 396–97, 398, 399
  debt to owner's equity ratio, 398, 400
  fixed assets to owner's equity ratio, 398, 400
  long-term liabilities to working capital ratio, 398, 400

Financial ratios—*Cont.*
  net profit (income) to owner's equity ratio, 397, 398
  net sales to fixed assets ratio, 398–99
  net sales to inventory ratio, 398, 399
  net sales to working capital ratio, 398, 399–400
  ratios, 396
  receivables to working capital ratio, 398
  return on equity (ROE) ratio, 397, 397–87
  working capital, 399
Financial structure, 367
Financing, 166–85; *see also* Capital debt financing
  debt securities, 172
    sources of, 177–80
  equity financing, 170
    equity, 169
    equity investors, 113
    equity securities, 171–72
    sources of, 172–77
Fire insurance, 452
  extended-coverage endorsement, 452
First-in, first-out (FIFO) inventory method, 412
"The First Interview" (tape recording), 257
First Micro Group, Inc., 437
Fitchett, Robert, 336
Fitzpatrick, Barbara, 263
Fixed assets, 168, **368**
Fixed expenses, 109
Flextime, 286
Food World, 203
Forbes, 137
Ford, Henry, 134
Ford Aerospace, 34
Ford Lincoln-Mercury Minority Dealers Association, 215
Foreign Credit Insurance Association (FCIA), 243
Formal failure (of business), **52**
Fortune, 3, 8, 359
  "Fortune Fast 100," 3
401(k) plans, 294
Four-Way Test, of Rotary International, 486
Franchise Opportunities Handbook (US DOC), 123, 124
Franchising, 116–34, **119**
  business format franchising, 120
  evaluating a franchise, 91–93, 122–26
  extent of, 118–19
  franchise, 120
  franchisee, 120
  franchisor, 120
  future of, 127–29
  international franchising, 129–30
  minorities and, 117, 132
  product and trademark franchising, 120

Franchising—*Cont.*
  prospectus (disclosure statement), 125
  types of, 120
  women and, 132
Franchising in the Economy (US DOC), 118, 119, 130
Franchising World, 128, 131
Francis, Clarence, 287
Franklin, Benjamin, 404
Frank, Mark, 6
Fraser, Jill Andresky, 405
Freeman, Steven, 81
FTC; *see* Federal Trade Commission
Fulton-Carroll Center, 176

Gaites, Dorothy J., 49
Galante, Steven P., 103
Gassaway, Paul, 458
Gates, William (Bill), 3, 8
Gateway 2000, 248
General partnership, 63
General Tires, 128
George, Claude S., 300
Giles, Lewis, Jr., 445
Gillette, 359
Givens, Kari, 354
Glitos, John, 465
Global-Pacific Minerals, Inc., 174
Going for It! How to Succeed as an Entrepreneur (Kiam), 38–39
Goldstein, Alan, 367
Goodwill, value of, 95
Goudreau Corporation, 170
Government
  help for small business, 478–79
    other agencies, 479
    Small Business Administration (SBA), 478–79
    U.S. Department of Commerce, 479
  regulation of small business, 16, 33–34, 479–80
    employee compensation and, 288–89
    regulatory agencies, 481–82
    union-management relations and, 312–15
Grapevine communication systems, 302
Grey, Leonard, 263
Group health and life insurance, 455
Grove, Andrew, 47
Growing a Business (Hawken), 298
Gu, Bob, 54–55
Gu, Mai, 54–55
Gumpert, David E., 46, 403
Gunn, Bruce, 317
Gutman, Dan, 365

Häagen-Dazs, 126
Haake, Alfred, 280

Hale, Percy, 218
Hall, Leonard, 489
Hammett, Sarah, 235
Hammonds, Keith, 359
Handicapped persons, SBA loans for, 180
Handle With Care, 125
Hannaford Brothers company, 34
Hannah, David, Jr., 97
Hardy, Phil, 339
Harrison, Walter, Jr., 69
Harris Poll, 486
Hart, Norman, 359
Hartfield & Co., 67
Hawken, Paul, 298
Hawthorne Hotel, 437
Hayes, Jack, 271
Health insurance, group, 455
Health Mart, 128
Health and safety of employees, 304–7, 465–66
   Occupational Safety and Health Administration (OSHA), 303, 303–7
Heath Electronics, 199
Hershey Chocolate Company, 203
Higher Education Research Institute, 6–7
Hill, Sherri, 41, 353
Hill's Science Diet, 219
Hispanic Business, 5
Hispanics
   business incubators and, 176
   business opportunites, 48–49
   television targeting, 232
Hit or Miss, 220
Hoelzle, Chris, 351
Hofer, Charles W., 20
Hoffman-La Roche Inc., 310
Hollingsworth, Walter, 385, 424
Honeybee Robotics, 34–35
Hooper, Laurence, 449
Hopkins, Thomas, 480
Hosteria Florentina, 471
Houser, Cheryl, 286
*How to **Really** Create a Successful **Business Plan*** (Gumpert), 46
How to Write a Business Plan (software), 79, 150
Hubotics, 199
Huffy Corporation, 32
Human relations, 280
Human resources, 102; *see also* Employees
Hunter, George E. (Buddy), 257
Huttner, Richard, 366

IBM, 13–14
IFA (International Franchising Association), 119, 126
Immediate-response advertising, 230
Implied contract, 475

Importing, 238, 238–40
Inc., 3, 4, 295, 405
Incentive payments, 290–91
   bonus, 291
   commission, 290
   employee stock ownership plan (ESOP), 291
   incentive wage, 290
   profit sharing, 291
Income statement (profit and loss statement), 370
Income taxes, 410–11
   corporate income taxes, 411–13
   income tax withholding, 413–14
Individual retirement accounts (IRAs), 294
Informal organization, 302
Informal (personal) failure (of business), **52**
Inmos, 308
Inputs, 322
In Search of Excellence (Peters and Waters), 40, 278
Institute for Family Business (Baylor), 500
Institutional advertising, 226
Insurance, 451, 451–57; *see also named types*
   coinsurance, 452
   insurance agents, 457
   selecting insurers, 456–57
   types of insurance, 452–56
Intel, 47
Interac Corporation, 221
Intermatic, Inc., 297
Intermediate-term securities, 172
Internal audit, 394
Internal Revenue Service (IRS)
   small business definition, 11
   Tax Guide for Small Business, 408
International franchising, 129–30
International Franchising Association (IFA), 119, 126
International operations
   exporting, 238, 240–43
   levels of involvement, 241–42
   franchising, 129–30
   importing, 238, 238–40
International Reciprocal Trade Association, 184
International Trade Administration (ITA, of DOC), 242
International Trade Association (US DOC), 122
Internship training, 270
Intuit, Inc., 365
Inventory, 349–52, **367**
   average cost method, 412
   federal income taxes and, 412
   first-in, first-out (FIFO) method, 412
   inventory control and computers, 440–41
   last-in, first-out (LIFO) method, 412

Inventory—*Cont.*
   net sales to inventory ratio, 398, 399
   taxes and, 412
IPA (isopropyl alcohol), 308
Irwin, Scott W., 21
ITA (International Trade Administration of DOC), 242
It's Legal (software), 67

J. C. Penney, 221
J. D. Power, 3
Jacobs, Sanford, 278
Jet, 28
Jiffy Lube, 129
Jitney-Jungle, 128
Job description, 258, 258–60, 301
Job enrichment, 286
Job sharing, 286
Job specifications, 258
Job splitting, 286
Jobs, Steven, 2, 51
Johnson, George, 48
Johnson, John H., 28
Johnson Publishing Company, 28
Joint venture, 69
Jones, Craig, 160
Jones, Dell, 44
Jones, Judith Anne, 21
Jones, Louis V., 21
Jordan Marsh, 108
Journal of Small Business Management, 5
Jumper, Kathy, 41, 491
Just-in-time delivery, 343
Justis, Robert T., 116

Kalart Victor Corporation, 239–40
Kamber, Ali, 453
Karp, Arthur, 119
Kemper Financial Services, 5
Kennedy, David, 91
Kennedy, Tamara, 91
Kentucky Fried Chicken, 129, 132
Keogh retirement plan, 294
Keystone Ribbon & Floral Supply Company, 499, 501
Kiam, Victor K., II, 27, 38–39
Kimball International, 359
Kleiner, Bruce H., 320
KLH Corporation, 62, 72
Kloss, Henry, 60, 62, 64, 72–73
Kloss Video, 64, 72
Kolbe, Kathy, 87
Kolton, Ellen, 295
Kossoff, Mitchell, 95
Kostecka, Andrew, 122
Krasnoff, Barbara, 271
Kroc, Ray, 120, 134
Kroll Associates, Inc., 449

Kroy Sign Systems, 465
Kubic, F. B., 68
Kurtz, David L., 205
Kurtzig, Sandra, 8

Last-in, first-out (LIFO) inventory method, 412
Lavelle, June, 176
Laventhal & Horwath, 497–98, 503
Lawyer(s), 482–84
    franchising and, 126
    referral sources, 483
    union negotiations and, 314
Leadership (of employees), **280**
Lease, 170
Leased manpower, 263
Ledvinka, James, 274
Lee Jeans, 450
Lee's Famous Recipe Country Chicken, 132
Legal terminology, 473
LensCrafters, 122
Leslie, Bob, 67
Leslie Enterprises, 67
Lester, John, 188
Levine, Jane, 286
Levi Strauss, 450
Levitt, Theodore, 76
Levy, Mark, 493
Levy, Michael, 299
Levy Organization, 493
Lewis, Robert, 50
Ley, Sue, 18
Liabilities, 368–69, **369**
    current liabilities, 369
    liability insurance, 453, 482
    long-term liabilities, 369
    notes payable, 369
Li Baofeng, 237
Life insurance
    business continuation, 456
    group, 455
Limited-liability company, 68
Limited partnership, 63
The Limited Partnership Library (software), 63
Lindsey, Barbara, 48
Lindstrom, Addie, 26
Line-and-staff organization, 302
Line of credit, 178
Line organization, 302
Live to Win (Kiam), 38–39
Living trust, 418
Locating or Relocating Your Business (SBA), 327
Location of business
    for manufacturing, 330–31
    selection of, 324–31
Long, B. J., 385

Long-term liabilities, 369
    long-term liabilities to working capital ratio, 398, 400
Long-term securities, 172
Lord & Taylor, 222
Los Angeles Black Enterprise Expo, 48
Loss control (risk prevention), 451
Loss leader, 204
Lower, Mike, 455
Lynn, Carol Cain, 321, 491

M & I Ford, Inc., 385
McAuley, Roy C., 257
McCarthy, E. Jerome, 198
McDonald, Maurice, 134
McDonald, Richard, 134
McDonald's, 120, 129, 134
    blacks and, 48
McKay, Susan, 125
McMillen, Jean, 28
McMillen, Ronald, 28
McRae Bluebook, 344
Magna Carta, 470
Mail Boxes franchises, 130
Maine Line Company, 425
Management: Concepts and Applications (Megginson, Mosley, Pietri), 241, 242, 283
Management by objectives, 104, 286
Management information system (MIS), 426, 426–29; *see also* Computers for small business
    accounting system as, 436–42
    elements of, 426–29
Management prerogatives clause, of union contract, 315
Managers
    compensation of, 291
    selecting and developing, 270–71
Maney, Kevin, 167, 245
Management Accounting, 80, 366
Manufacturing, 330, 330–31
    plants, locating of, 330–31
Marina Village, 117
Market, studying for a product, 84–85
Marketing; *see also* Advertising; International operations
    credit management, 248, 248–51
    distribution, 246, 246–48
    distribution channel, 216, 216–19
        intermediaries and, 216, 219–21
    ethnicity and, 232
    marketing concept, 190, 190–94
    marketing mix, 197
    marketing research, 84, 84–85, **243,** 243–46
        primary research, 245, 245–46, 254
        television and, 245
    marketing strategies, 188–212

Marketing—*Cont.*
    marketing strategies—*Cont.*
        development of, 194–97
    merchandising, 231
    packaging, 200
    pricing, 200–205
    product life cycle, 197–200, **198**
    product mix, 199–200
    publicity, 231, 231–32
    sales-force selling, 221–26
    sales promotion, 231
    services, marketing of, 205–8
    transportation modes, 247, 247–48
Marketing High Technology (Davidow), 188
Market Overseas with U.S. Government Help (SBA), 242
Market segmentation, 194
Markup, 202
Martin, Dot, 57
Martin, Jiggs, 57
Martin Marietta, 34
MasterCard Business Card Small Business Survey, 22
MasterCard International, 44
Master-Mind, 83
Mattei, Jim, 363
Mattei Companies, 363
Mauchly, John, 13
Maumenee, Benjamin C., 160
Measuring Markets (DOC), 84
Media, for advertising, 228–30
Megginson, Leon C., 54, 241, 242, 266, 277, 281, 283, 324
Megginson, Ragan Workman, 55
Mel Farr Enterprises, 215
Menefee, Pete, 353
Merchandising, 231
Mereco Technologies, Inc., 480
Merit increases, 289
Methods, 105
Michael Levy & Associates, 299
MicroFridge, Inc., 10
Micro Support Resource Corporation, 271
Midtown Restaurants Corporation, 279
Midwest Women's Business Owners Development Joint Ventures, 47
Milbar Corporation, 405
Millard, Vince, 127
Millenson, Michael L., 237
Miller, Jim, 297
Miller Business Systems, 103
Miner, Hank, 160
Mini-Maid, 207, 208
Minnie Pearl Chicken, 123
Minorities; *see also* Asian-Americans; Blacks; Hispanics
    in business, 47–51, 117, 137–38
    business incubators and, 176
    as consumers, 232
    franchising and, 117, 132

Minorities—*Cont.*
    television targeting, 232
Minority Business Development Agency, 132
Minority Business Today, 445
Minority Vendor Profile System, 132
Minota Corporation, 15
MIS; *see* Management information system
Mission (of business), **101**
Mitchell, Charlene, 215
MIT Enterprise Forum, 83
Mitsubishi, and KFC International, 129
Mobile Press Register, 41, 50, 97, 137, 191, 196, 257, 274, 321, 339
Mom-and-pop operation, *see* Small business
Monsanto Corporation, 221
''Monthly Cash Flow Projection'' (SBA form), 389
Moody, James, 34
Moore, Ann, 32
Moore, David, 48
Moore, Michael, 32
Moore, R. Wendell, 4
Morgan, Dorothy, 167
Morgan, Henry, 72
Morgan, Roy, 167
Mortgage loan, 172
Mosley, Donald C., 241, 242, 283
Motivation (of employees), **283,** 283–87
Mulford, Ralph, 167
Muzak, 128
Mystery Bookshop, 28

Nanninga, Carol, 205
National Apprenticeship Act of 1937, 270
National Association of Women Business Owners, 47
National Council on Compensation Insurance, 293, 454
National Federation of Independent Business (NFIB), 8, 20, 33, 35, 312, 480, 482
National Labor Relations Act (NLRA, Wagner Act), 312
National Labor Relations Board (NLRB), 312, 314, 315
National Museum of American History, 199
National Retail Foundation, 461
National Safety Council, 306
National Small Business Association, 482
National Small Business United, 482
Nation's Business, 454
Nebesky, J., 138, 260
Negotiable instrument, 477
Nelson, Dave, 39
Neti Technologies, Inc., 174
Net profit, 109
Net sales to fixed assets ratio, 398–99
Net sales to working capital ratio, 398, 399–400

Networking, Asian-Americans and, 50
Net worth (owner's equity), 369, 369–70
    current liabilities to owner's equity ratio, 398, 400
    debt to owner's equity ratio, 398, 400
    fixed assets to owner's equity ratio, 398, 400
    net profit (income) to owner's equity ratio, 397, 398
New Business Opportunities, 5
Newhouse Graphics, 50
Newhouse News Agency, 196
Newsletter for Family-Owned Businesses, 5
News 2 U Store, 77
New York City Police Pension Fund, as angel capitalist, 175
New York Times, 8, 39, 73
NeXT, Inc., 51
Nichols, June, 2
Nickles, Edward, 62
Nike, 174
Notes payable, 369

Oak Beach Hotel, 81
Obernauer, Lorie, 499, 501
Obernauer, Somer, 499
Obernauer, Somer, Jr., 499, 501
Objectives (of business), **25, 101,** 101–2
    for marketing, 194–97
Objective (task) method, for advertising, 228
Occupational Safety and Health Act, 306–7
    Occupational Safety and Health Administration (OSHA), 306
O'Donnell, Timothy, 366
Office of Advocacy (SBA), 42–43
Office of Federal Contract Compliance Programs (OFCCP, of DOL), 273–74
Off-price retailers, 220
OJT (on-the-job training), 269, 269–70
Older consumers, 195–96
Older workers, 195
On the Spot Dog Grooming, 326
On-the-job training (OJT), 269, 269–70
Operating budget, 389
Operating systems, 322, 322–23
Operational planning, 99
    role of, 104–9
Operations or **production, 323**
    feedback, 395
    improvement of, 336–37
    operating budget, 389
    operations audit, 394
    performance information, 395–96
    planning and control, 352–54
    scheduling, 352
Organization chart, 303, 303–4
Organizing (a business), **300**
    delegation, 300

Organizing—*Cont.*
    informal organization, 302
    line-and-staff organization, 302
    line organization, 302
    organization chart, 303, 303–4
    span of management, 301
    specialization, 301
Osborn, Michelle, 115
Ounjian, Marylin J., 128
Our Hero Restaurant, 139
Outcry market, 174
Outputs, 322
Owner's equity (net worth), 369, 369–70
    current liabilities to owner's equity ratio, 398, 400
    debt to owner's equity ratio, 398, 400
    fixed assets to owner's equity ratio, 398, 400
    net profit (income) to owner's equity ratio, 397, 398
Ownership, forms of, 56–71
    cooperative, 68, 68–69
    corporation, 64, 64–67
    joint venture, 69
    limited-liability company, 68
    partnership, 60, 60–63
    proprietorship, 58–60, 60, 61
    trust, 68

Pacific Bell Directory, 50
Packaging, 200
Palmerio, John L., 222
Palmer, Jayne, 392
Pannell Kerr Forster, 62
Parametrix, Inc., 468
Parenting Unlimited, Inc., 366
Parson's Technology, 67
Partnership, 60, 60–63
    articles of copartnership, 63
    general partnership, 63
    limited partnership, 63
    rights of partners, 63
Partridge, Mary H., 299
Part-time and temporary workers, 263
Patchen, Charles W., 448
Patent, 476
PC Magazine, 271
PC's Limited, 3
Penetration price, 201
Penney's, 450
Peoples Drug, 193
PepsiCo, 129
Percentage of sales or profits method, for advertising, 228
Perfection Automotive Products Corp., 401
Performance
    performance appraisal, 287
    performance information, 395–96
    performance standards, 337, 387

Perreault, William D., Jr., 198
Perrin, Towers, 272, 274
Persona, Inc., 314
Personal budget, necessity of, 109–10
Personal (informal) failure (of business), **52**
Personal services, 205
Personnel Decisions, Inc., 267
Personnel Management: A Human Resources Approach (Megginson), 266, 281
Personnel Management (SBA), 259
Personnel planning, 106
Peters, Tom, 40, 278
Phillips, Bruce, 15
Physical facilities
  planning of, 331–36
  process layout, 333, 333–34
  product layout, 332, 332–34
Physical resources, 102
Pietri, Paul H., Jr., 241, 242, 283
Pinkerton®, 449
Piracy Hotline, 468
Pizza Hut, 129
Plan-a-Grams, 34
Planning, 96–115, 99
  financial planning, 109, 109–13
  operational planning, 99, 104–9
  personnel needs and, 258–67
  physical facilities, 331–36
    layouts, types of, 332–35
  production, 352–54
  role and types of, 98–99
  strategic planning, 99, 100–104
Plastic money; *see* Credit cards
Plough, Inc., 69
Policies, 105
Pollack, Andrew, 8
Polygraph, 266
Precision Tune, 129
Pre-employment integrity tests, 257
Preferred stock, 171
Preferred stockholders, 169
Price
  allowances, 202
  cost-oriented pricing, 202
  cost-plus pricing, 204
  customary price, 203
  discount, 202
  loss leader, 204
  markup, 202
  penetration price, 201
  pricing the product, 200–205
  skimming price, 200
  unit pricing, 204
Primary marketing research, 245–46
Primetime (firm), 232
Principal (in property law), **477**
Print 'n Go, 359
Processes (of operating systems), **322**
Procter & Gamble, 343

Product
  identifying a, 80–84
  packaging, 200
  pricing, 200–205
  product advertising, 226
  product layout, 332, 332–34
  product liability, 475
  product life cycle, 197–200, **198**
  product mix, 199–200
  studying market for, 84–85
Product and trademark franchising, 120
Production or **operations;** *see* **Operations** or **production**
Product/service liability insurance, 453, 482
Profit (income), **371**
  break-even point, 378
  profit planning, 364–80
  sales forecast, 373
  steps in, 372–79
Profit and loss statement (income statement), 370
Profit motive, 25
Profit sharing (as incentive pay), **291**
Progressive Grocer, 34
Promoting (employees), **262**
Property law, 476–77
Proprietorship, 58–60, 60, 61
ProServ Inc., 206
Prospecting (sales step), **223**
Prospectus (disclosure statement) (for franchising), **125**
Publicity, 231, 231–32
Purchasing, 342, 342–49
  economic order quantity, 352
  just-in-time delivery, 343
  purchase order, 348
  standing orders, 348
Pure risk, 450

QMS, Inc., 137
Quality, 354–57
  quality circles (QCs), 286, 355
Quality Croutons, Inc., 48
Quartermaine, William, 340
Quicken (software), 365
QVC Home Shopping Network, 115

Radio Shack, 291
Railroad Facts, 248
Ratios; *see* Financial ratios
RB Robot Corporation, 199
Ream's Superstore, 221
Recruitment (of employees), **264**
Reed, Mark, 363
References, of potential employees, 267–68
Regulation of small business; *see* Government

Reidel, Tod, 437
Reinhardt, Andy, 174, 308
Remington Products, Inc., 38
Remington Rand, 14
Repetitive-stress injuries (RSIs), 305–6
Research
  marketing research, 243, 243–46
  primary research, 245–46, 254
Resources for the Gifted, 87
Response Communications, 392
Retailers, 219, 219–21
Retained earnings, 369
Return on equity (ROE) ratio, **397,** 397–99
Revenue (sales income), 370
Rice, Linda Johnson, 28
Richards, Rhonda, 179
Richman, Tom, 3
Right-to-work laws, 312
Risk; *see also* Insurance
  crime prevention, 458–64
  document security, 464–65
  noninsurance methods of dealing, 457–58
  pure risk, 450
  risk assumption (self-insurance), 451
  risk avoidance, 451
  risk management, 450
  risk prevention (loss control), 451
  risk transfer, 451
  safeguarding employees, 465–66
  speculative risk, 450
Ritchie, Cheryl, 167
Ritchie, David, 167
Robichaux, Mark, 35, 185
Robotics International, 199
Rock, Arthur, 256
Rogers, Will, 404
Roper Organization, 5
Rosenberg, Joyce M., 191
Rosenblum, Stuart, 95
Ross, Gayle M., 167, 324, 382, 509
Ross Publishing Company, 382, 509
Rotary International, Four-Way Test, 486
Rousseau, Jean-Jacques, 166
RSIs (repetitive-stress injuries), 305–6
Rucker, John B., Jr. (Jack), 257
Rule of two, 225
Ryka Inc., 194

Saddler, Jean, 179
Sahlman, William A., 80
Salaminder, Inc., 102, 103, 344
Sales-force selling, 221–26
Sales forecast, 373
Sales income (revenue), 370
Sales promotion, 231
SAM computer system, 128
Sample, John W., 103, 236
Samuel, Jerry, 77

Samuel, Mona, 77
Sanders, Harlan, 116, 122
Sanitary Dry Cleaners, 190
Sanyo E&E Corporation, 10
The Savant, 260, 395, 471
SBA; *see* Small Business Administration
SBICs (small business investment companies), 173
Scarpello, Vida, 274
Scarsbrook, Phil, 345
Schering-Plough Corporation, 69
Scheumack, Thurman, 29
Schoen, John, 500
Schreier, Terry, 167
SCORE (Service Corps of Retired Executives), 18, **83**, 123, 145, 242, 315, 471, 478
S Corporation, 66–67
 taxes and, 410–11, 422
Scott, Charles E., 424
Scott, Charles R., 18
Sculley, John, 51
Sears, 450
Seattle Weekly, 286
Security; *see also* Crime prevention; Risk
 computers and, 436, 463–64
 document security, 464–63
 security dogs, 459
Selection of employees, **264**
Self-insurance (risk assumption), 451
Sellectek, 174
Selling the business, guidelines, 503
Selz, Michael, 35, 185
Service Corps of Retired Executives (SCORE), 18, **83**, 123, 145, 242, 315, 471, 478
Service industries
 growth of, 42–43
 sevices, marketing of, 205–8
ServiStar Hardware Store, 336
Shaffer, Betty, 435
Shane Musical Instruments, 81
Shapiro, Irving, 362
The Shareholders Agreements Library (software), 63
Sharp Corporation, 346
Sheets, Kenneth R., 359
Sheldon, Oliver, 470
Sheppard, Barney, 151, 160
Sherman, Stratford P., 8
Shingler-Hollis Investment Group, 132
Shoemaker, 193
Shoney's Inc., 132
Shopping centers, 329–30
 anchor stores, 329
Shopping goods, 328
Short-term securities, 172
SIGNS NOW, 279
Sikorski, Ron, 90
Silicon Valley Toxics Coalition, 308

Sinclair, Robert, 89
Sinclair Construction Company, 89
Singer company, 72
Skimming price, 200
Slayton, Donald K. (Deke), 97
Sloan, John, Jr., 20
Slovak, Julianne, 359
Small business, 9; *see also* Government; Minorities; Ownership, forms of; Women
 areas of concern, 51–52
 capital and, 15, 32–33
 contributions of, 11–15
 defined, 8–11
 development, stages in, 52
 versus entrepreneurial venture, 9–11
 failure, 15–16, **52**, 96
 Internal Revenue Service classification, 11
 location of, 324–31
 new versus existing business, 86–91, 95
 problems of, 15–16
 small business owner, 10
 starting, steps in, 79–87
 successful owners, characteristics of, 26–29
Small Business Act of 1953, 9
Small Business Administration (SBA), 4, 9, 15, 76, 166
 Checklist for Going into Business, 111
 Choosing a Retailing Location, 326
 computer access to, 179
 as financing source, 178–80
  SBA-guaranteed loans, 179
  specialized financing, 179, 243
 help for small business, 478–79
 as information source, 84, 123, 242
 Lending the SBA Way, 179
 Locating or Relocating Your Business, 327
 Market Overseas with U.S. Government Help, 242
 "Monthly Cash Flow Projection," 389
 Office of Advocacy, 42–43
 Personnel Management, 259
 on success for small businesses, 258
Small business investment companies (SBICs), 173, 180
Small Business Journal, 5
Small Business Legislative Council, 482
Smith, Alexander, 448
Smith, Barbara, 24
Smith, Ron, 480
Smithsonian Institution, 199
Snugli, Inc., 32
Social objectives, 25
Social responsibility, 484, 484–85
Social Security, 293
 Social Security/Medicare taxes, 414
Softlifting, 468

Software for
 accounting, 365
 business plan preparation, 150
 business start-up, 79
 employee benefits, determination of, 295
 incorporation, 67
 partnership formation, 63
 planning of facilities, 331
 valuation of business, 504
Software Publishers Association, 468
SolarCare, Inc., 69
Song, Dae, 50
Sonic Drive-in, 127
Southland Corporation, 220
Space Services, Inc., 97
Spain, William M., 18
Span of management, 301
Specialization, 301
Specialty goods, 328
Speculative risk, 450
Speedy Bicycle Shop, 88
Sperry Corporation, 38
Springdale Travel, Inc., 354
Standard & Poor's, 246
Standing orders, 348
Star Software Systems, 79
Starting a business
 new versus existing business, 86–91, 95
 steps in, 79–86
Statistical Abstracts of the United States, 245
Statkewicz, Michele, 57
Staubach, Roger, 24
Stockouts, 343
Straight-line depreciation, 414–15
Strategic planning, 99, 100–104
Strategies, 103, 103–4
Strickland, Kenneth, 160
Stubbs, Howard, 7
Students in Free Enterprise, 8
Subchapter S corporation; *see* S corporation
Submariner (restaurant), 90
Success (magazine), 365
Summer, Bob, 341
Summer, Kathy, 341
Sunrise Medical, Inc., 416
Superior Robotics, 199
Supervision in Action (George), 300
Supreme Plumbing and Heating Company, 277
Surety bonds, 456
Survey of Current Business, 245
Sutton, Marcel, 471
Swenson, Pamela, 190
System, 190
Systems Management American Corporation, 444–45

T. J. Maxx, 220
Target market, 194, 194–97

Taxable income, 411
  federal unemployment tax, 414
Taxes, 404–22, **406**; *see also* Internal
  Revenue Service
  corporate income taxes, 411–13
  Deficit Reduction Act of 1984, 413
  direct taxes, 406, 408–13
    selected taxes listed, 407
  Employee Retirement Income Security
    Act (ERISA), 413
  employee stock ownership plan (ESOP)
    and, 411
  employment-related taxes, 413–15
    income tax withholding, 413–14
    Social Security/Medicare, 414
  estate planning and, 417–18, 505–6
  excise tax, 409
  federal unemployment tax, 414, 414–15
  income taxes, 410–11
  indirect taxes, 406
  personal taxes for owners, 415–16
  sales tax, 409
  S corporation and, 410–11, 422
  taxable income, 411
  tax reporting period, listed, 419
  types of, 408–17
  use tax, 409
  workers' compensation, 415
Tax Guide for Small Business (IRS), 408
Taylor, Jared, 424
Teague, Joe, 321, 491
Teague, Margaret, 321
Teague Brothers Carpet and Cleaning and
  Sales, Inc., 321, 491
Teague Brothers Transfer and Storage Co.,
  Inc., 321, 491
Tebyanian, Sohrab, 184
Teipel, Henry N., 314
Telecommunications Technology, Inc., 339
Telemundo Group Inc., 232
Television, marketing research and, 245
Texas, incorporation laws, 65
Texas Long Distance, 11
Theft
  as business risk, 460–63
  employee theft, 463
  prevention of, 462–63
  shoplifting, 460–61
Thomas, J. Neal, 96
Thomas, Melinda Lou (Wendy), 226–27
Thomas, R. David, 226–27
Thomas Register of American
  Manufacturers, 344
Thompson, Renee, 57
Thomson, Bailey, 137
Tianguis (supermarkets), 49
Time management, 35–36
"Top 100 Black Businesses in America," 215
Tort, 477
Toshiba, 115

Totty, Michael, 392
Touche Ross and Company, 367
Trade credit, 177
Trade dollars, for barter, 184
Transferring (employees), **262**
Transportation modes, 247, 247–48
Trencher, Reed, 232
Trueblood, Lyle E., 324
Trust (as form of business), **68**
Try J. Advertising, 21, 230
T-Shirts Plus, 128
Tudor, Martin, 392
Tupper, Earl, 107–8
Tupperware, 107–8
Turner, Ronald, 294
Turrisi, Tom, 81

Unemployment insurance, 293, 414–15
Uniform Commercial Code (UCC),
  472–73
Unions, 312–15
  management prerogatives clause, 315
  National Labor Relations Act (NLRA,
    Wagner Act), 312, 314, 315
  National Labor Relations Board (NLRB),
    312
  right-to-work laws, 312
  union shop clause, 312
United Parcel Service (UPS), 212, 248
U.S. Chamber of Commerce, 294
U.S. Department of Commerce, 609
  Economic Bulletin Board, 480
  Franchise Opportunities Handbook, 123,
    124
  Franchising in the Economy, 118, 119,
    130
  help for small business, 479, 480
  as information source, 84, 242–43
  International Trade Administration (ITA),
    242
  International Trade Association, 122
  U.S. and Foreign Commercial Service
    Agency (USFCSA), 242
U.S. Department of Defense, *Drug-Free
  Workforce Rules,* 310
U.S. Department of Health and Human
  Services, 306
  Office of Federal Contract Compliance
    Programs (OFCCP), 273–74
U.S. Foreign Commercial Service Agency
  (USFCSA, of DOC), 242
U.S. Hispanic Chamber of Commerce, 49
U.S. Internal Revenue Service; *see* Internal
  Revenue Service
U.S. Labor Department, Bureau of
  Apprenticeship and Training, 270
U.S. News & World Report, 359
U.S. Small Business Administration; *see*
  Small Business Administration

U.S. Supreme Court
  on employment tests, 265
  on preemployment drug testing, 268
United Surgical Centers, 122
Unit pricing, 204
Unit of sales method, for advertising, 228
Univac Corporation, 13
University Entrepreneurial Association, 8
Univision, 232
Upgrading (employees), **262**
USA Today, 3, 8, 22, 31, 43, 44, 49, 115,
  117, 167, 179, 215, 245, 248, 290,
  310, 403, 465, 486
Use tax, **409**

Valentine, Herman, 444–45
Valentino, Marion, 321, 491
ValueExpress (software), 150, 504
Valuesource, 504
Valvoline Instant Oil Change Co., 129
Vancouver Stock Exchange (VSE), 174, 175
Variable expenses, 109
Vass, Vonda, 41
Venture (magazine), 221, 271, 425, 449
Venture (software), 27, 79
Venture Capital Exchange, 143
Venture capitalists, 173–74
Victoria, 81
Vietnam-era veterans, SBA loans for, 180
Villchur, Edgar, 72
Vita-Mix, 241
Volanti Ski Corporation, 228
Von Companies, 49
Von Werlhof, Sally, 102
VSE (Vancouver Stock Exchange), 174, 175

Waldorf, William, 224, 239
Walker, Blair S., 215
Walker, Don, 449
The Wall Street Journal, 2, 3, 7, 35, 49,
  103, 150, 167, 179, 184, 212, 331,
  392, 449, 489, 497, 498, 504
Wal-Mart, 203, 343
Walsh, Geoff, 115, 136
Ward, John L., 256, 499
Ward, Wendell, 218
Warranty, 475
Watson, Thomas J., Sr., 148
Watt, Isaac, 490
Weidenbaum, Murray, 480
Weiger, Ralph J., 131
Weinstein, S., 34
Well, Jenny, 77
Wendy's Old Fashioned Hamburgers, 122,
  226–27
Wesley, Dottie Teague, 321, 491
White-collar crimes, 463, 463–64
White, Jerry, 31

White, Martell, 326
White, Ronnie, 326
White Sewing Machine Company, 126
Wholesalers, **219**
Wiese, Bill, 11
Wiese, Chleo, 11
Wiese, John, 11
Wiese, Roger, 11
Wiese, Scott, 11
Wild Bill Hamburgers, 123
Williams, Al, 416
Williams, Jan, 416
Williamson, Margaret, 24
Wilson, Barbara Jean, 117
Wilson, Porterfield, 117
Wilson, Woodrow, 298

Women
    franchising and, 132
    SBA loans for, 180
    small business and, 46–47
Women's Business Ownership Act (1988),
    47
Women's Economic Development
    Corporation, 47
The Woodlands Consulting Group, 299
Wooten, James M., 385
Workers' compensation, **293**, 415, 453–54
    cost of injuries by years, 454
    premiums by years, 454
Workers' Compensation Monitor, 454
Working capital, **168**, **399**
Working Woman, 22

World Trade Center bombing, 453
Wozniak, Steve, 51
Wynton M. Blount Cultural Park, 345
Wysocki, Bernard, Jr., 2

Yao, David, 237
Yellow Pages, 229, 344
Young Women's Christian Association, 47
Your Company (magazine), 5

Zachary, G. Pascal, 331
Zero defects, **286**
Ziegenhorn, Randy, 150
Zigmond, Ric, 503